PENGUIN BOOKS

A HISTORY OF BRITISH GARDENING

As well as being a prolific writer of books and articles on gardens and garden history, Miles Hadfield was a practical gardener and keen arboriculturalist all his life, as described in *Landscape With Trees* (1967). He was awarded the Royal Forestry Society's Gold Medal and the Royal Horticultural Society's Veitch Memorial Medal. He was a founder of the Garden History Society and later its president. Miles Hadfield died in 1982.

Geoffrey and Susan Jellicoe have been in the forefront of landscape architecture and garden design for many years. They have published *The Landscape of Man* (1975), a history of world landscape art, and Susan Jellicoe collaborated with Marjorie Allen on *Town Gardens to Live In* (Penguin, 1978).

MILES HADFIELD

A History of
British Gardening

Penguin Books

Penguin Books Ltd, Harmondsworth, Middlesex, England
Viking Penguin Inc., 40 West 23rd Street, New York, New York 10010, U.S.A.
Penguin Books Australia Ltd, Ringwood, Victoria, Australia
Penguin Books Canada Ltd, 2801 John Street, Markham, Ontario, Canada L3R 1B4
Penguin Books (N.Z.) Ltd, 182–190 Wairau Road, Auckland 10, New Zealand

First published by Hutchinson and Co. 1960
Published in Penguin Books 1985

Copyright © Miles Hadfield, 1960
All rights reserved

Printed and bound in Great Britain by
Richard Clay (The Chaucer Press) Ltd,
Bungay, Suffolk
Set in Baskerville

Title page illustration from J. C. Loudon's 'The Villa Gardener'

Contents

Illustrations

Preface

Towards the end of the seventeenth century the widely travelled and cultured Sir William Temple wrote that 'the perfectest figure of a garden . . . either at home or abroad' lay in that most English of counties, Hertfordshire. Just over a hundred years later Humphry Repton could claim without fear of contradiction that landscape gardening was 'an ART that originated in England' and that 'gardening in its more confined sense of horticulture, has likewise been brought to the greatest perfection in this country'. By that time the 'English garden' and British gardeners were to be found all over Europe.

Yet in spite of our eminence in this ancient business, the reader wishing to find some general account of its history must turn to the late Lady Rockley's study, first published (when she was Miss Amherst) in 1896. This is surprising. The architecture of our country houses has, during the present century, received the most detailed attention. Why has not their setting—always in a most carefully designed garden of living trees, shrubs, and plants?

Surely, then, this aspect is due for a new survey, adding to Lady Rockley's admirable account the result of the researches of Miss Jourdain and Miss Stroud, of David Green and Laurence Whistler. And her account, too, can now be embellished by the addition of much that E. H. M. Cox has told us about the garden history of Scotland.

Though fashions in garden style have changed, that important person, formerly the 'curious gardener' and now the 'keen plantsman', has been the unswerving servant of horticulture. R. W. T. Gunther and A. Simmonds have ven us much new material to be taken into account.

And, inevitably, Lady Rockley told us little of the nineteenth and early twentieth centuries. The late Geoffrey Taylor had begun (with, alas, little encouragement) to tackle that most important period. But there remain available the contemporary accounts written by scores of generally anonymous authors in the journals of the time, which I have tried to bring into this history.

Long though this book may be, it is no more than an outline. The subject is enormous and many-branched. The great eighteenth-century Claudian landscape must not squeeze out the garden whose length of lawn is dictated by the clothes-line; both potatoes and plant-collectors who risk their lives must be apportioned their fair share of space. Orchards, trees, shrubs, flowers—even the gardener himself—must all be fitted in.

In tackling this task I have tried to bear in mind that gardeners (as all artists and craftsmen) are practical people working for a variety of reasons, but never to provide the subjects for monographs weighed down with the apparatus of scholarship. (Gardeners are indeed fortunate, for when their work is neglected, willow-herb and sow-thistle, the peace-loving elder and the watery sycamore come quickly in and obliterate all; never can even the smallest garden end in the desiccating cellar of a museum.)

It is as a gardener that I write—the erudite will observe that I possess only a modicum of conventional history. And it seems to me that the true gardener is he or she who, beyond the mundane production of food, is seeking to bring into being an elysium or a dream: the Roman scene in Kent, a bit of Tibetan alp under glass and aluminium, or the largest marrow in the show. So it is that wherever possible I have quoted from the writings of true and practical gardeners, whether they be Alexander Pope of Twickenham or Charles M'Intosh of Claremont and Dalkeith.

As this book is for general information, I have usually modernized spellings and even phraseology where this has seemed necessary to avoid obscurity.

It was my first intention to explain the origins of gold plant names that recur throughout the ages—codlin, crissane, jenneting, gillyflower, pearmain, and perdrigon come to mind. But to attempt to do so is usually valueless. In the first place, etymologists seem to be most unsure; secondly, mostly of these words have from time to time quite changed their meaning. Thus jenneting once became June-eating, and gillyflower July-flower, neither of which variations can have had the remotest connection with their originals.

I have to acknowledge much help.

First, Mr. Geoffrey Beard has always placed his wide bibliographical and other knowledge at my service; he has also made many comments on the script, which I value greatly. Miss C. S. Wilson checked and transcribed the extracts from James quoted in Miller's *Dictionary*. Mr. E. Lissimore lent me the new and complete copy of Sir Samuel Clark's Garden List that he has made. I was at a complete loss to find more than the barest facts about the late A. K. Bulley when Dr. H. R. Fletcher suggested that I should write to Mr. J. K. Hulme of the Liverpool University Botanic Garden, who kindly put me in touch with Miss Bulley—with the result that a most important patron of plant-collecting receives, I think, his due for the first time.

Miss A. Coats and Mrs. M. U. Jones have, over the years, drawn my attention to much that has been of use.

I have had the good fortune to see two important manuscripts as yet unpublished. Miss Bea Howe showed me her material relating to Mrs. Loudon, her husband and their circle, for which I am duly grateful. Mr. Peter Willis commented on my passage relating to Charles Bridgeman and let me see his extremely scholarly study of that hitherto little-known figure. I have taken many facts from it, but must be quite clear that the conclusions that I reach are entirely my own and must not burden Mr. Willis!

Then all along I have had lavish assistance in literary and editorial matters—in which he is so well experienced—from my brother John.

The following have been kind enough to reply to my enquiries, often at no little trouble to themselves: Lady Seton, Lt.-Col. Sir Michael Peto, Bart., Mr. J. K. Adams, Mr. W. O. Backhouse, Rev. J. T. Campion, Vicar of Dinton, Mr. R. E. Cooper, Dr. J. M. Cowan, C.B.E., Miss Rachel Crawshay of the National Gardens Scheme, Mrs. D. M. Owen, Mr. Clarence Elliott, Mr. H. Edland of the National Rose Society, Mr. J. W. Goodison of the Fitzwilliam Museum, Mr. A. C. Howe of the British Iris Society, Mr. R. Huntley of the National Sweet Pea Society, Mr. Rowland Jackman, Mrs. Nathaniel Lloyd, and Mr. R. H. Perry of Perry's Hardy Plant Farm.

And, of course, I am deeply indebted to those authors upon

whose laborious researches I have drawn so freely, and who are named in the Bibliographical Notes.

I am grateful to the following for permitting the use of copyright material.

The City of Birmingham Museum and Art Gallery for *The Ponte Molle* by Claude.

Cadbury Bros., Ltd., for a picture of Hidcote.

Country Life Ltd. for the use of the plan of Rousham on which the end-paper is based.

The Croome Estate Trust for *Croome Court* by Richard Wilson.

Quentin Lloyd, Esq., for a picture of Great Dixter.

Mr. Paul Mellon, for the Sieberechts painting of Bayhall.

The National Trust for items at Charlecote and Attingham.

The Royal Institute of British Architects for Smythson's plan of Wimbledon.

I am fortunate in having had the use of some of Mr. Edwin Smith's distinguished photographs of gardens. Mr. J. D. U. Ward also supplied two of subjects in which he specialized. Mr. Robert Dixon kindly lent his copy of the amusing and illuminating etching by Gillray.

Finally, I owe a particular debt to Mr. W. T. Jones, A.R.P.S., who has taken a number of difficult subjects specially for this book.

My period ends in 1939, contemporaneously with the disappearance of gardening in the grand manner. The intensely commercialized civilization that has now grown up has no use for such things. All but a handful of our most spacious gardens would have disappeared if it had not been for the action of the National Trust, which, since 1937, has been able to hold country houses and make some attempt to maintain the gardens that go with them. Further, in conjunction with the Royal Horticultural Society, from 1948 onwards the National Trust took over a limited number of properties whose importance was solely that they were gardens of exceptional merit. In the north, The National Trust for Scotland, founded in 1931, owns many fine gardens. By these means a little has been preserved and kept in a living state for the future.

These Trust gardens can, of course, be visited freely by the general public. I have therefore used them as examples when ever possible. I can only urge my readers to support these two organizations in their admirable activities.

In preparing this revised edition of the book (1979) I was helped by a number of correspondents, particularly the late Alice Coats and the scholarly John H. Harvey, to whom I am grateful for suggesting corrections and other alterations that have been incorporated.

I was happy to entrust the task of seeing the present edition through the press to Peter Hunt. Alas he died before he could complete the job, but he was responsible for engaging Susan and Geoffrey Jellicoe to write the admirable appendix which covers the last forty years. They, in their turn, would like to thank Graham Stuart Thomas for his help.

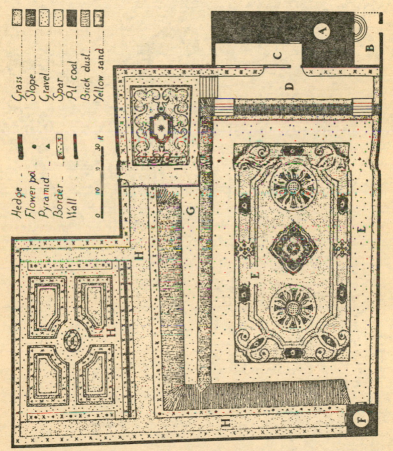

M.TALLARD'S GARDEN c.1706

A The house
B Entrance court
C Courtyard
D Terrace
E Sunk garden
F Banqueting room
G Walk on intermediate level
H The high level
I Sunk fountain garden

Hedge
Flower pot
Pyramid
Border
Wall

Grass
Slope
Gravel
Spar
Pit coal
Brick dust
Yellow sand

0   10   20   30 ft

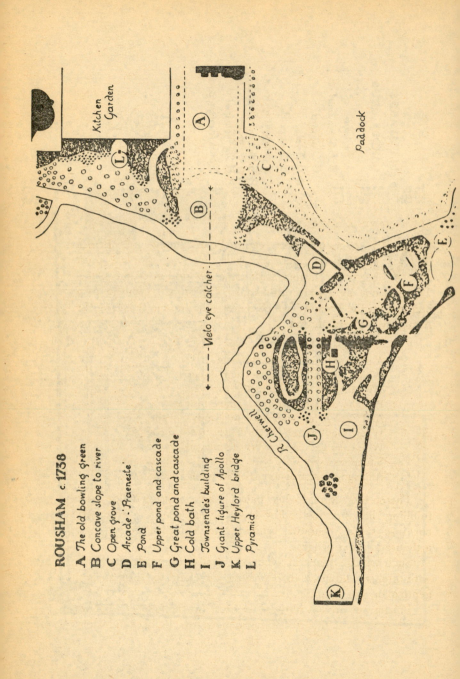

ROUSHAM c. 1738

A The old bowling green
B Concave slope to river
C Open grove
D Arcade: 'Praeneste'
E Pond
F Upper pond and cascade
G Great pond and cascade
H Cold bath
I Townsende's building
J Giant figure of Apollo
K Upper Heyford bridge
L Pyramid

Venus eye catcher

Kitchen Garden

Paddock

R. Charwell

ONE

From Eden to Utopia
To 1529

EDEN—AND A LITTLE GRASS

W E CANNOT, alas, claim Eden among our British gardens. So important is it, however, that we must begin our history with some description of the place. There is one by a sixteenth-century Englishman (who in turn had it from the French)[1] which seems suitable. He tells how the Almighty took Adam and

> . . . chose for him a happy seat
> A climate both for cold and heat,
> Which dainty Flora paveth sumptuously
> With flowery Ver's enamelled tapestry;
> Pomona pranks with fruits, whose taste excels
> And Zephyr fills with musk and amber smells;
> Where God himself (as gardener) treads the alleys,
> With trees and corn covers the hills and valleys;
> Summons sweet sleep with noise of hundred brooks,
> And sun-proof arbours makes in sundry nooks. . . .

There, too, were loving palms whose lusty females were fulfilling their marrow-boiling loves, an endless maze, rosemary cut into satyrs, centaurs, whales, and half-men horses, and a thousand other delights.

Such was the place in which the first of all gardeners, who, with ditchers and grave-diggers alone can claim to be an ancient gentleman, was set.

But for our present purpose we must (in the light of what we have learned from the fruit of that famous tree) go back in history even before the arrival of Adam—for all the gardener does is entirely controlled by geology and climate.[2]

We can begin at a time when trees and plants—some of them relatives of such modern introductions as the monkey-puzzle, sequoia, and ginkgo—flourished under conditions which were not dissimilar to those now found in Malaya; at a later stage, in the Oligocene and Miocene times, evergreen oaks were common and a tulip tree was growing here.

Moving forward to a million or so years ago, the Pliocene merged into the Pleistocene. The climate was much more like that of the present day. Many plants of earlier periods had largely died out, while representatives of the present-day European genera increased. The silver fir was a native. It was at this stage that a sweeping erasure of our wild life occurred. The ice age descended. It is a period still full of mystery; the professors tell us that the cold moved southwards in four waves, with some respite between them. It is generally held that a few patches of land in our northern and western mountains remained ice-free; some writers have suggested, too, that those parts of southern Britain and Ireland where the interesting Lusitanian flora—including such plants as the strawberry tree—with its affinities with the Mediterranean coasts, also escaped. But it can be said that, so far as most of our islands are concerned, the only plants were those of the tundras of modern northern Russia—a frigid, desert-like world of mosses and lichens.

Then, about 18000 B.C., man appears on the scene, living his Paleolithic age in a cold, dry climate, where predominant plants were the rock-gardener's dryas, dwarf birches, and willows. These had spread into Britain over the bridge of land that joined us to the Continent; as our climate improved, they came inexorably northward from those parts of Europe now unaffected by the ice.

This amelioration was not a gradual process. By about 5500 B.C. the climate was warmer and moister than it is today and consequently a number of our wild plants were to be found in more northerly situations than they are now; at this time the small-leaved lime was a comparatively common tree in our woods, with Scots pine, oak, and elm. There was birch on the hills and alder and willows in the wet places. It was at about this period that the land-bridge disappeared; no more plants could spread here from the Continent. Our native flora was fixed and by degrees reached some stability. In effect, our true native flora is, therefore, that which existed at the time of our isolation; it can be said in a general sort of way that this geographical happening alone prohibited the unaided arrival of more continental plants. Subsequent arrivals have, to all intents and purposes, been introduced by man, many consciously, others unknowingly. Undoubtedly some would have come here of their own accord if the sea had not broken through, for much of our land and its climate will support plants that have been brought here. To illustrate this (and it is an important point in our garden history) a count of the first hundred plants described in Clapham, Tutin, and Warburg's *Flora of the British Isles* shows that just over a quarter are described as introduced or doubtfully native. That some of these aliens were brought here at a very early stage is indisputable; the woad, for example, which provided the dye used by our ancestors who met Julius Caesar, is probably a native only of central and southern Europe, but it has been cultivated elsewhere since prehistoric times.

The climate has regulated the spread of plants over Britain, and at all times, particularly within the last century, its peculiarities have had a marked effect on gardening. We all know the main features—the moist, mild, and variable weather of our western and south-western districts, the cool hills of the north, and the drier, sunnier conditions of the eastern and south-eastern counties. Most remarkable are the local variations. There is, for example, only a very limited area in Ireland where the strawberry tree behaves as the native that it is; the factor upon which the natural survival of this tree depends seems to be an average January temperature of not less than 40°F. Yet our climate is such that this lovely evergreen can be grown as a *cultivated* plant over most of the British Isles.

Perhaps the most remarkable feature of our landscape and climate from the gardener's point of view is that along our western seaboard—from Cornwall* to Loch Ewe in the north of Scotland—are many districts where plants and trees from such diverse places as the Pacific coast of North America, western

* Sir Joseph Hooker, who advised gardeners on the Cornish Riviera to plant the Himalayan rhododendrons that he had collected between 1847–51, many years later was to exclaim that they flourished better than their parents in Sikkim.

China, Tibet and the Himalayas, New Zealand and Chile thrive in the moist, windy, but temperate air.

On the other hand, on the eastern side of Britain, where these will not even exist, many of the plants—particularly bulbs—cultivated so ardently over the centuries by the Dutch are happier in the drier, cooler, but sunnier climate.

As with our building, so does our geology affect not only our garden design but the choice of plants. Perhaps the most inescapable and final ruling in their selection lies between acid and base-rich soils—or, in the gardener's world, between sandy, peaty soils at one extreme and limy, chalky soils at the other. It is a remarkable fact that many of our garden plants (rhododendrons and many Japanese plants are notable examples) will not tolerate lime; yet most plants that are lime-lovers in nature will grow on quite acid soils. Because of this, all gardens, for example on that broad historic band of limestone over which the Fosse Way traverses England from Axminster to Lincoln—a territory so famous for the beauty of its stone architecture—have contents that are quite different from those, say, in the New Forest.

Climate and geology have other consequences in the British garden. First, they give us our turf 'thick yset, and soft as any velvet' which has always been our pride, and so often envied by foreigners. 'Nothing,' wrote Francis Bacon at the end of the sixteenth century, 'is more pleasant to the eye than green grass kept finely shorn';[3] at the beginning of the eighteenth century John James translated d'Argenville's advice to the countrymen of Le Nôtre: 'You can't do better than to follow this method (of cultivation) used in England, where their grass plots are so exquisite a beauty, that in France we can scarce ever hope to come up to it.'[4]

And, in the midst of the enchantments of Paris in August 1771, Horace Walpole cried: 'Methinks, I should be as glad of a little grass, as a seaman after a voyage.'[5] A few years later the German traveller von Archenholz wrote: 'The grass in England is of incomparable beauty. . . . Hence comes the taste for those beautiful grass walks which . . . are often so level, that they can play at bowls upon them as on a billiard-table.'[6]

'The velvet herbage' was, of course, among the primary constituents of that singularly English feature, the landscape garden—present, as at Hagley, even when another essential, water,* was scarcely to be seen.

In these circumstances it was only right that an Englishman should invent the first mowing-machine, and so establish the important modern industry based on the cultivation of turf for gardens, parks, and playing fields.

To the same factors of geology and climate I think may also be attributed our interest in gravel paths. From Bacon's day onward writers have made it clear that one purpose of a garden is to provide space in which the English man and woman may indulge in our national weakness of taking exercise. Unlike the gardeners of southern Europe we have to contend not with a surfeit of sun and a need for shade and cooling water, but with frequent showers and many days when there is an invigorating nip in the air. For this reason certain alleys for walking 'must be ever finely gravelled, and no grass, because of going wet'. Once again we are fortunate; much of Britain has gravel close at hand, so that Pepys was able to record that 'we have the best walks of gravel in the world, France having none, nor Italy'.[7] (He, like Bacon, regarded a prime function of the garden to be a place in which to take the air.) And, when we come to the 'landscapers' of the eighteenth century, we shall see that the gravel path played an even more important part, not only for practical but for aesthetic and symbolic reasons as well.

There are two other important geographical consequences of our island position that must ever be at the back of our minds in gardening as well as general history. The first is sometimes overlooked: it is 'the important fact that south-eastern England is very definitely a part of Europe and has never been entirely isolated from the main current of European affairs'.[8] The second is more obvious; it is that since the times of the Tudors we have been eminent as seamen and traders; the bright-eyed mariners brought home not only strange news of the albatross, but roots and seeds of plants for the curious—and the hungry.

---

* This element, in our islands flowing so frequently among contours that facilitate the construction of serpentined lakes fed by rippling brooks, ranks almost as highly as grass in the fundamentals of our garden history: see, for example, the whole long chapter 'Of Water' in Whately's *Observations on Modern Gardening* (1770).

THE ROMANS

When our ancestors began to garden for pleasure and aesthetic enjoyment even of the crudest kind is a question upon which pre-historians are silent. It is a commonplace, however, that at the time of Caesar's reconnaissance in 55 B.C. the wheeled plough had not long been introduced into south-eastern England, and civilization in the interior of Britain was still crude. During the latter part of the first century A.D., while the legionaries were subduing this country, there were active in Rome Pliny the Naturalist, his nephew Pliny the Younger, and Columella—all of whom wrote extensively on plants, gardens, and horticulture; one may therefore suggestively complete the quotation given above: 'The period of the Roman occupation is the most striking historical example of Britain's essential connection with the mainland.'

It seems generally assumed that the heterogeneous collection of races that, welded together by the power of Rome, brought us also within the confines of its civilization, introduced many plants and trees. Yet, when it comes to the proof, there is not much to show.

Charcoal from among Roman remains show us that they had the Spanish chestnut (*Castanea sativa*), which presumably they introduced for its fruit. Roman 'pignons', the edible seeds of the stonepine (*Pinus pinea*), have also been found, though it is doubtful if they ever established this rather tender tree—so typical of the classical scene.

Possibly they brought the black mulberry, *Morus nigra*, and no doubt they would be the first to make the attempt (which has been repeated intermittently ever since) to grow their most essential fruit, the vine—and to learn by hard experience that only limited and localized success could be achieved.

They certainly cultivated other fruits with greater reward: orchards seem undoubtedly to have been planted at Caerleon, and the goddess Pomona appears in a pavement at Cirencester. They would quickly learn that the apple tree* succeeds better and produces fruit of a higher quality here than in any other part of the world.

---

* The cultivated apples are derived from continental species, and it seems that our native crab, *Malus sylvestris*, with its harsh, acid fruit, played no part in their origin. The oldest apple in cultivation today is 'Pomme d'Api', possibly of Roman origin, but not recorded in England until the seventeenth century.

If it had not already arrived, presumably the Romans brought the cabbage, which 'reached its apotheosis in Rome',[9] and leek, so valued by Nero that he largely subsisted on it while training his voice. The onion, garlic, artichoke (only the globe kind, *Cynara scolymus*), cucumber, the broad bean (known to the Egyptians, but regarded rather dubiously in Rome), and asparagus were other eminent vegetables of the classical period, and must surely have been brought here, if some of them, indeed, had not arrived before the Romans.

As to the more ornamental part of gardening, we are surely entitled to assume that attempts were made to surround our largest British villas, modest though they were by the standards of Rome itself, with gardens in the Roman manner.

Of these last, we have both pictures and descriptions more or less contemporaneous with Roman invasion. Examples can be seen in the wall-paintings in the extraordinary subterranean building near Rome known as the garden house of Livia, wife of the Emperor Augustus. The scenes, painted round the walls some thirty years before the birth of Christ, are realistically treated. It is possible to identify quince, pomegranate, and arbutus among the trees; around them grew roses, periwinkles, and poppies, while upon them perch magpies, jays, orioles, and fly-catchers.[10]

The most complete descriptions are those written by Pliny the Younger in letters to his friends. They have clearly influenced many designers of much later date who looked back to the classical style for inspiration. Early in the eighteenth century antiquarians drew up and published* plans worked out from these letters;[11] it must be admitted that they are not unlike the gardens of the then contemporary scene. There is one feature, however, that is markedly different from the English garden as it is known to have been from medieval times to the eighteenth century: Pliny (and one assumes he was not unusual in this respect) loved wide and extensive views. His Laurentine Villa looked over rich meadows covered with cattle, the bay of Ostia and the villages scattered on its shore, to the distant mountains. Such sights, until the first hints of the coming of the landscape school, would have been

* Those of his Laurentine Villa and Tuscan Villa will be found reproduced in J. C. Loudon's *Encyclopaedia of Gardening*.

regarded as visually horrid in France or Britain, and shut out by walls or plantations.

It is of the smaller garden at Laurentium that Pliny writes to Gallus, describing its box tree, and rosemary hedges, its vines, the thickly planted fig and mulberry trees, and the violets. But his Tuscan garden (the Tusculan) seems more akin to our subject. Here, upon an eminence that commanded a full view of all the country around yet was approached by so insensible a rise that one did not perceive the ascent, the cool airs from the Apennine Mountains prevented the myrtle and olive from thriving.

Perhaps we may reduce these wide spaces and high mountains to the scale of the small and gentle hills of the Coln Valley around Chedworth, or the more spacious Vale of Usk around Caerleon, and fit into them an adaptation of the Tusculan.

From the portico of the house one stepped on to a terrace, embellished with figures and bounded by box hedges; thence by an easy slope, adorned by animals cut out of box, one descended to a lawn. (The Roman would find in our grass something superior to the rather mysterious plant used by Pliny described as 'soft' and 'almost liquid'.) This lawn was surrounded by a walk enclosed in topiary work. Beyond it came the *gestatio*, which seems to have been an oval space in the form of a Roman *circus*, large enough for taking exercise in vehicles, which had at its centre an ornament of box clipped into 'numberless different figures', as well as a plantation of trimmed shrubs. This *gestatio* was contained within a wall covered by box, which was cut into different levels. Outside this wall were meadows and thickets, owing their 'many beauties to nature', as all *within* does to art'.

Returning to the portico, we find that at one end is placed a 'grand dining-room' with extensive views over the neighbouring country—this is, of course, a forerunner of the outdoor banqueting hall.

Elsewhere in the garden rows of cypresses and of the oriental plane, their trunks swathed in ivy, formed shady alleys; there were walks with obelisks intermixed with fruit trees, while in the midst of 'elegant regularity' one came upon a little corner to be surprised by 'an imitation of the negligent beauties of rural nature'. Fountains, rills, vine-shaded alcoves, and refuges of 'agreeable gloominess' from the heat were all duly provided.

How much of this sun-bathed elysium was incorporated in the gardens of the little villas of Rome's cool and showery northern outpost? We had neither the cypress, nor the oriental plane (so 'doated on' by the ancients that Xerxes halted a vast army to 'admire its pulchritude');[12] nor had we the vine. Of all the plants named, ivy, box, and the violet alone would be known to any of Pliny's fellow-citizens who might have visited these shores. Box is not infrequently present among Romano-British remains and there is no doubt that this, and not yew, as is sometimes suggested, was used for their topiary work. By classical authors the yew was, as Evelyn says, considered a 'mortiferous plant'; Columella, for instance, when giving advice on the choice of land for a garden, warns against ground that will suffer yews to grow.[13]

Yet, when all is said, we really do not know much about the gardens during the four centuries of occupation. We may even conclude that they were little more than places for the cultivation of such fruiting trees and plants—particularly with medicinal virtues—as were not present in Britain and which the Romans were able to establish.

If we know little about the Anglo-Roman gardens, we know even less about the period that followed the recall of the legions. It is usually said that nearly all knowledge of horticulture must have died out, and that only those introduced plants which could naturalize themselves survived. That must be an exaggeration, for among the aristocracy and the members of the early religious organizations there were continuous comings and goings of persons between England and the Continent, where gardening was still carried on.

Yet one searches the Anglo-Saxon Chronicles and Histories, the poets, and the writings by students of the period, without gaining any horticultural information except the names of the many herbs referred to in the 'Charms' and 'Land-Remedy'; even that well-known Anglo-Saxon poem which lists the endowments of man, though it ranges from warriors through builders and jewellers to those who are quick at the dice, makes no mention of those endowed with the art of planting—or even husbandry— though the Anglo-Saxons were primarily an agricultural people.

Any modern Anglo-Saxon dictionary, however, includes names of many introduced plants. There are, too, lists of plant and tree names in the *Glossary* to *Grammatica Latino-Saxonica* of Aelfric, produced at the end of the tenth century. The words he selects are those 'most likely to be in daily use in the conversation of the monastic schools'.[14] But the names he gives often present us with problems rather than evidence of the type we want, for they include many of plants and trees that could not have then been in cultivation. His work does at least show that plants and things concerning them must have been commonly discussed by the learned people of the day.

Aelfric brings us very close to the magic year A.D. 1066, when, once again, we were drawn into the main stream of continental civilization.

THE NORMANS

The Normans, of course, had not been here long before they began to document us. Unfortunately, that confusing jumble which is commonly known as Domesday Book is of no use for our purpose, though it records some forty vineyards—which the learned have shown were in just the situations where one would expect to find them.

Domesday, however, does indicate some improvement in the state of law and order, central administration, and of other prerequisites necessary for the existence of learning and the arts, such as gardening. England, too, was soon scattered with the Norman castles, within whose gradually expanding walls it might be possible to garden without harassment.

Far more important was the great development of religious establishments—the sanctuaries of learning—that followed the Conquest. 'The Norman monasteries gave (to Britain) of their best blood for fifty years,' wrote one authority.[15] This no doubt resulted in a considerable advance in the practical knowledge and uses of plants, particularly for medicinal purposes. It is generally assumed, for example, that the monasteries introduced *Dianthus caryophyllus* and *Dianthus plumarius*, the ancestors of the pinks and carnations. The former, still 'at home on the old Norman keeps and towers such as those of Creuilly and Château Gaillard', had long been valued as flavouring for wine.[16] It is also said that the wallflower—certainly an early introduction—came at this time.

The Norman connection must also have considerably widened

the realms of our written botanical knowledge. Its origins go back
to the world of the Greeks, and particularly to Aristotle (384–322
B.C.) whose abstract theories, subtle in reasoning, concerned such
themes as why a grain of corn gave rise to a grain of corn and not
an olive. Aristotle's named successor, Theophrastus (c. 370–288
B.C.), dealt more with the description of plants, referring to some
450 of the 3,000 species now known in Greece; he was on occasion
objective, and remarked upon the difference in germination
between wheat and a bean. He wrote, too, of garden plants and
their cultivation. But for the most part the study of plants was
speculative, and, in the modern sense, quite unscientific.[17]

Aristotelian science reached northern Europe by devious
routes after the fall of Greece and Rome, and remained the un-
questioned source of knowledge throughout the medieval period.
The theories held and reiterated by the writers and disputers
within the cloisters were often quite unrelated to the simple facts
demonstrated by the gardeners without.

A striking instance of this can be seen in the writings of
Alexander Neckham. He was born at St. Albans in 1157, educated
at Paris University, and then returned to Cirencester. He wrote
of gardening in De Naturis Rerum. The plants he named have on
occasion been considered typical of a twelfth-century English
monastic garden. It is clear, however, that several of them could
never have lived in our climate, and it seems certain that this
section is derived entirely from continental literary sources.
Neckham died in 1217; Canon Raven has described his writings
as 'neither science nor art'.[18]

The evidence of progress in gardening in early medieval times
is mostly indirect and devoid of detail. One can look, for instance,
at the plans of monastic buildings and see what space was left for
gardening within the protection of their walls. These plans are
usually reconstructions. There are, however, the well-known
original plans of the monastery at Canterbury[19] dating from the
middle of the twelfth century. One of these shows the Herbarium
clearly labelled. It covers but a small area of ground, rather less
than half the space surrounded by cloisters, between the dormitory
and infirmary. There are also indications of orchards and a vineyard placed without the walls. It is at Canterbury, too, at about
the same time, that we have the first record of a mulberry tree in

England. Gervase writes that the knights who murdered Thomas Becket in 1170 'threw off their cloaks and gowns under a branching mulberry tree'.[20]

Writers who describe the more or less standardized plans of the monastic buildings of the different orders seldom include any reference to a garden or herbarium. At Durham, however, the Cathedral Priory included a garden about 100 feet by 75 feet between the Galilee and the rere dorter. In the plan of the Abbey of St. Peter, Gloucester, there is a small triangular infirmary garden lying between the infirmary itself, the infirmary chapel, and the outer wall.

Ralegh Radford while excavating Glastonbury Abbey came upon a kerbed stone path within the original twelfth-century cloisters surrounding a small area of worked earth which shows it to have been a garden.

Each member of the Carthusian order, with its grim discipline, lived a solitary life housed in a separate cell, within its small garden, enclosed by a high and windowless wall. At Mount Grace, Yorkshire, there were twenty-two of these units lying principally around the central cloister court. Each was about 1,875 square feet in area; there was also a separate sacristan's garden.[21] What sort of cultivation was carried out in the little plots within these sombre walls seems to be unrecorded. Is there, I wonder, any connection, other than nominal, between the old pink *carthusianorum* and this order? Though still in cultivation, it was recorded as early as the thirteenth century.[22]

There is an interesting reference to gardening in a building contract published by L. F. Salzman.[23] Dated about 1214, it refers to the construction of a little garden (*virgultum*) within the cloisters at St. Albans.

More conclusive evidence may be found in the records of monastic staff. For instance, at Evesham in the twelfth century, out of a total of sixty servants, three only were employed in the garden and five in the vineyard.

At a later period, during the first half of the fifteenth century, we have the published extracts from the Gardener's Account Rolls at Norwich. There is, for example, the account of Brother Bartholomew de Brettenham* from the Feast of St. Michael in

* The officer in charge of the gardens was usually described as *gardinarius* or *hortulanus*; one presumes that, as with other work such as building, the manual labour was hired and not carried out by the monks.

1419 to that of the following year. The receipts are for such items as small quantities of pot-herbs, leeks, beets, carrots, and onions, and for onions sold. Expenditure was on garlic and onion seed, for hoeing, planting, and gathering, for leather gloves, and eighteen-pence rent for 'the garden within the gate'. Thirty-two years later Brother Robert Brettenham was in charge of the garden, and again the accounts run from Michaelmas to Michaelmas. A suggestive item is 'To the cellarer, when herbs failed, 3s. 4d.'[24]

There are regular entries for such obvious requirements as boots and gloves (which seem always to have been provided for the workers); for mending the gates of the cherry orchard, for jobs of walling, and for withies. There are payments for apples, peas, and so on, and one a little more suggestive, for 'cherries for the convent'.

Other English monastic accounts are very similar—payments, usually small, for a limited range of vegetables, herbs, and fruits, and for equipment and repairs. In Scotland the details are even scantier;[25] the term 'garden' itself may mean anything from what we should now call an allotment to a small-holding. Kale was the universal vegetable.

There are early records, too, of orchards and vineyards; the apple at least would thrive here—though in Scotland the fruit was apparently of poor quality. Particularly famous were the orchards round Ely; their quality is indicated by the fact that at the Reformation they passed to the Crown, and Elizabeth I considered them worthy of presentation to her favourite, Sir Christopher Hatton.[26] Of vineyards, an eleventh-century drawing of pruning vines, done in a formalized, decorative manner, is one of the few English pictorial horticultural records that survive from medieval times. By the thirteenth century it seems possible that in the whole of the Archbishopric of Canterbury vines were only grown in the manors of Northfleet and Teynham,[27] in Kent. (In 1570 William Lambarde was to describe Teynham as 'the cherry garden and apple orchard of Kent', while Camden claimed it to be the parent of all fruit gardens in Kent—and, therefore, one may suggest, in England.)

The occurrence of medicinal and other cultivated plants on monastic sites is not unusual, and interesting if not conclusive evidence. Two instances may be quoted. When, shortly after succeeding to the Tresco Abbey estates in the Isles of Scilly in 1872, T. A. Dorrien-Smith began the cultivation of daffodils on a commercial scale, he chose for his experiments two kinds that he found growing naturalized among the Abbey ruins. Both soon became popular under the names of 'Scilly White' and 'Soleil d'Or'. Their origin is quite unexplained, though E. A. Bowles suggested that one has 'African blood in its veins'.[28] Henbane and deadly nightshade are two other plants often associated with monastic ruins, though both are rare British natives. In 1956 I was shown where these had sprung up at Buildwas Abbey in Shropshire, following excavations and consequent disturbance of the soil, though they had not grown there before in the memory of the owners.

The truth is that we know very little about monastic gardening in the British Isles; we can suspect that it was generally a second-rate version of contemporary continental gardening, and that is about all.

Nor can it be said that much evidence exists, other than bare details concerned with payments made, of the precise nature of royal or noblemen's gardens, at least before the end of the fifteenth century. There were the mazes or labyrinths, such as that made famous by Rosamund at Woodstock; inevitably, there must have been kitchen gardens, orchards, and sometimes vineyards, while 'herbers', or, as we should now call them, arbours, seemed a regular feature. The names of royal gardeners are known; they seem to have been men of some substance; but that scarcely helps us to form any real picture of the gardens.

Several old accounts are discussed in some detail by Alicia Amherst, notably those of the royal gardens at Westminster, Charing, and the Tower, during the late thirteenth century, and also that of the Earl of Lincoln in Holborn. She also quotes from those relating to fruit—apples, pears, 'great nuts', and sweet chestnuts supplied to the courts of Henry III and Edward I;* from them it is apparent that both fruit and fruit trees, especially pears, were being imported from France in considerable quantities. At this period, too, commoner vegetables such as onions and sprouts were also regularly imported.[29]

---

* As will be seen later, the Elizabethan, William Harrison, believed that gardening had reached a high standard during the reign of Edward I from which it had fallen until revived by the Tudors. There is some evidence to support this—for instance, in the records of the manor of Neyte in 1327.[30]

In Scotland there were, during the thirteenth century, royal gardens at the base of the Castle Rock in Edinburgh, and at the royal castles of Roxburgh and Jedburgh, but apparently nothing is known of their details.[31]

We can, however, gather quite a vivid picture of the medieval gardener and his tools. There is in Lincoln Cathedral a carving on a misericord of a gardener carrying an iron-shod spade (Plate I). A number of cruder and earlier carvings of Cain and Abel also exist. Though they are not, strictly speaking, gardeners, their tools, usually iron-shod spades, picks, and narrow, long-bladed draw hoes are presumably similar to those used by gardeners.

A word may be said here about medieval poetry as a source of information. There are many references to flowers and gardens in, for example, Helen Waddell's *Medieval Latin Lyrics*, but one observes that none come from British sources. When we reach the fourteenth-century translation of the *Romance of the Rose*, not infrequently quoted as a contemporary description of our medieval gardens, it is as well to recall that this is of foreign origin, and that some of the plants named are exotics (such as nutmegs, dates, figs, liquorice, and zedoary) and could never have been grown here.

It is to the illustrated versions of the *Romance of the Rose* also that those seeking pictures of the medieval garden in England usually turn, in particular to that page from a late fifteenth-century Flemish copy.* Here we have little walled and trellised gardens, connected by arched doorways. Musicians dally round a splashing fountain, lovers meet (or part) while a solitary man —one guesses him to be the gardener—walks briskly. The fact is that no pictures of English gardens at this period exist, even in the crudest form. Before Tudor times we search in vain among British sources for anything comparable with the continental work of the period. Our manuscripts, our wall-paintings,† our carving—even the realistic sculpture of the late thirteenth century, with its masterly treatment of foliage—give us no hint whatever of the existence of an art of gardening. It is suggested that what was not lost at the time of the Reformation was destroyed in Northumberland's purges under the Acts of 1549–50. But there

* There is a good reproduction in H. Avray Tipping, *English Gardens*.
† I must admit, though, that flowers shown in the early fifteenth-century wall-paintings in the chapel at Haddon Hall might be taken as formalized versions of the rose and Madonna lily.

remain, for example, many drawings and plans of medieval churches, while much relating to daily life and happenings is to be found in our old manuscripts.

Are we therefore justified in taking illustrations from continental sources—as is so often done—to fill the gap on the assumption that English gardens of the same period resembled them? It seems very doubtful. The poem written by James I of Scotland when he was imprisoned at Windsor (1413–24) has often been quoted as a description of the garden beneath his prison walls. Yet it tallies in no way with, for example, the Flemish drawing just described; there is no mention of a fountain—surely a poet's subject—or, indeed, of anything but the railed and hedged-in arbours, set deep and secret among the boughs of trees; the only plants named are hawthorn and 'the sharp green sweet juniper'.

Since much of this poem is really about the nightingale it may be apposite to remark on the love of birds—which seems to have far outweighed that of plants—displayed by our early poets. John Skelton (*c.* 1469–1529), for example, is an ornithologically minded poet, yet singularly uninterested in plants.

It seems not improbable that gardening as an art and the aesthetic appreciation of flowers scarcely existed until the late fifteenth or early sixteenth centuries. Before that, gardening was purposeful—to provide fruits, a few vegetables, herbs, and medicinal plants, a sheltered place for sitting, and, in some cases, flowers for church services* and festive occasions.

Two building contracts printed by L. F. Salzman[32] seem to indicate the small size of thirteenth-century gardens. The first, relating to Woodstock in 1249, concerns the construction of one whose extent was no more than that covered by some rooms that were to be pulled down. The second, in 1250, includes the making of a bench against the wall around the 'great garden'—which could not have been very large to be so contained.

The utilitarian aspect is also confirmed by the earliest known English treatise on gardening, the manuscript known as *The Feate of Gardening* by 'Mayster Ion Gardener', a copy made in about 1440 of a work written, it is suggested, some forty years

---

* The use of flowers, particularly roses and lilies, for 'coronets and guirlands' (as Philemon Holland translates Pliny) for ceremonial occasions goes back, of course, to ancient times: Henry VI left 38 feet of land to Eton College 'for to set in certain trees and flowers, behovable and convenient for the service of the church'.

earlier. The author's outlook is essentially practical. His treatise bears every indication that he was an authority on his subject. It is quite without those fantastic theories of plants which are to be found in other manuscripts of the same period and which are primarily medicinal works, based on ancient authors—usually Pliny at second hand.

This short document was published by Alicia Amherst,[33] who added a glossary; it gives one such a strong impression of being written by an authentic gardener that it seems worthy of closer examination than account rolls and such documents.

It is in nine parts, the first being an introduction. Next comes the planting and raising of trees, which mentions that pears were then grafted on to hawthorn (as they were for long subsequently). Then follow instructions on the grafting of trees—a good description, 'hazel-tree rind' and clay replacing the modern raffia and grafting wax. Then there are sections on vines, on the sowing of seeds (St. Valentine's Day seems to have been the time to start), on sowing and setting 'worts', on the kinds of parsley (which was highly regarded and is so often mentioned in early works), on other herbs, and finally a section describing how to plant saffron.

There are in all ninety-seven plants named, either directly for cultivation, or, as in the case of hazel and ash, for use in some garden operation. Sixty-one of them are undisputed natives; twenty-six are certainly introduced. Ten are either difficult to identify or of doubtful status; with them I include the rose, pear, and apple—which would almost certainly be foreign kinds.

The only flowers—or plants that we might today grow in the flower garden—are cowslip, daffodil, foxglove, hollyhock, honeysuckle, lavender, Madonna lily, orpine, periwinkle, hepatica, primrose, rose, and scabious.* Even so, some of these, such as hepatica, *Anemone hepatica* (*Hepatica americana*), called in the manuscript liverwort, were primarily medicinal. The only vegetables in our present-day sense are garlic, leek, lettuce, orache, onions, turnip, radish, and spinach.

Of fruits we have apples, pears, and the wild strawberry. An enthusiast for herbs might today grow borage, camomile, comfrey, fennel, mint, clary, parsley, rue, sage, southernwood, and thyme —though only a few of these are still generally grown in gardens.

* The modern English names are used here.

The remaining plants mentioned, grown for food (failing anything better) or medicinally, are today found only in the wild, or have descended to the status of weeds. Such are the adder's tongue (*Ophioglossum*), avens (*Geum urbanum*), bugle, common daisy, gladdon, herb Robert, mouse-ear hawkweed, orpine, polypody fern, and the common plantain of our lawns. The drug-producing henbane was also included, and the aromatic savory (*Satureja*), which is still cultivated as a pot herb.

The special section on 'saferowne' emphasizes the importance of *Crocus sativus* in the Middle Ages, and, indeed, long after. The stigmas, when correctly dried, provide the drug saffron, once highly valued medicinally, as well as for its scent, flavouring qualities—not to everyone's taste—and yellow dye. It was very costly; over four thousand flowers, it is said, are needed to produce one ounce. Rough weather may damage the flowers at harvest-time, which is well on in the autumn, and the plants are by no means easy to establish—they produce no fertile seed and are liable to a fungal disease.[34] It seems possible, indeed, that at least one medieval attempt was made to find a substitute. It has been pointed out[35] that the Halifax crocus (*C. nudiflorus*), which is not a native of Britain but is found naturalized in the North Midlands, Lancashire, Yorkshire (particularly around Halifax), and elsewhere, has stigmas that are very similar to saffron. It is known that many of the situations where it now grows are around rather isolated farms that once belonged to the Knights Hospitallers or Knights of St. John of Jerusalem. The inference is drawn that these orders imported the corms, which, unlike most crocuses, spread by underground runners. Proof will presumably never be forthcoming, but the suggestion makes one wonder to what extent these organizations may have introduced other plants too.

There are obvious omissions in John Gardiner's list. Of fruits, cherries, plums (the word occurs in many early place names), and medlars (Chaucer describes how they were 'bletted') are not mentioned. Cabbages and coleworts are presumably covered in the long section on worts, but peas and beans are missing. However, they may have been more of a field than a garden crop.

Yet, one supposes, the list was representative of such gardens as there were around ordinary houses in town and country until the remarkable developments that followed the coming of the

Tudors and the conclusion of that long period of strife—scarcely providing the conditions for extensive gardening—so unpleasantly named (from the gardener's point of view!) the Wars of the Roses.

ROSES AND POMEGRANATES

One would expect to find something about gardens in that repository of domestic correspondence, the Paston letters,[36] which cover the period from 1422 to 1509. But there is little enough. That gardens of some kind did exist is shown by the sad fate of Sir John Heveningham who went to church one Tuesday in 1453: he 'came home again, never merrier, and said to his wife that he would go say a little devotion in his garden . . . forthwith he felt a fainting fit in his leg . . . he was dead ere noon'. What was the garden like in which Sir John was seized so suddenly with the dread pestilence? It cannot have been anything very grand, in that crude world where tiny private armies as well as larger forces seemed continually to wreak havoc on property as well as one another.*

But, as the fifteen-hundreds roll on, we begin to gain more than hints of the great intellectual and economic transformation that was on its way. When Henry VII became king in 1485 he had as his chief aims the keeping of peace at home and abroad, the establishment of a powerful monarchy, and the accumulation of wealth. Within his kingdom, John Colet, Thomas More, and Thomas Wolsey demonstrated their passion for the new ideas and arts that were then travelling north from the Mediterranean. Abroad, Christopher Columbus, Vasco da Gama, and Sebastian Cabot entirely altered and vastly extended the European knowledge of geography, and, indeed, the physical frontiers which her travellers and traders could now reach.

These factors were to bring about conditions under which the arts and sciences were able not only to exist, but finally to thrive. In early Tudor times, however, the medieval tradition was still powerful. The great buildings of Henry VII's reign had their roots deep in an England of the past.

It is, too, in the medieval baron's castle that we find the

---

* C. G. Coulton's *Social Life in Britain from the Conquest to the Reformation* contains but one insignificant and unrevealing reference to a garden. What a contrast is, for example, F. C. Carritt's *Calendar of British Taste 1600–1800*, which from its earliest pages abounds in references to gardens!

origins of one of the few early Tudor gardens that is to some extent documented. The castle was not only the lord's home, but the base from which he conducted his private wars. It therefore included massive accommodation for his rough and noisy gang of mercenaries, carefully placed so that they were well under the control of his officers. In these circumstances, surely there could have been little space for a garden within the safety of the castle walls. This feudal system died out during the Wars of the Roses, and Henry VII was, of course, most active in preventing the revival of extreme individual power apart from the Crown. All the same, attempts were made. One of the most notable was that of Edward Stafford, 3rd Duke of Buckingham. In 1511 he began to build Thornbury Castle, described by historians as an example of 'bastard feudalism'. It lay in Gloucestershire, not far from the Severn estuary, and has been described as 'the last great baronial house in England to be built in the old castellated style, retaining something of the serious purpose of medieval fortifications, along with much of its brazen-fronted feudal pride and power'.[37] The story of Stafford is well known. At first he was a royal favourite, but the scale of his huge establishment and lavish hospitality (one feast of the Epiphany was celebrated at Thornbury by a party of 459, of whom 134 were classed as gentry), his ambitions, the royal blood in his veins—all became suspect in the eyes of Henry VIII. In 1521 he was tried and executed. On the grounds of treason, his estates were forfeited. Thornbury, still unfinished, passed to the Crown; in the same year Commissioners reported upon it. Their description, and the subsequent reconstruction of its original plan and elevations, enable us to grasp the significant differences between this and the true medieval castle, particularly as it relates to gardening.

The imposing western front, screening the large court of offices and retainers' quarters, was castle-like, designed in the old manner, arrogantly defensive. But on the south side of the inner court quadrant, along which were the private quarters of the owner, war had almost been forgotten. The architecture, with its tall and delicately finished oriel windows, made a façade as pacific as the western side was fierce. To modernize the Commissioner's report:[38] 'On the south side of the said inner ward is a proper garden, and about the same a goodly gallery conveying above and beneath from the principal lodgings both to the chapel and the parish church, the outer part of the said gallery being of stone imbattled, and the inner part of timber covered with slate.' The resulting 'proper garden' was about 40 yards both in width and average depth; the walls surrounding it had a fierce exterior aspect, but inside the two-levelled passage ways had a cloister-like effect looking on to this little garden; exactly how this was laid out can be but conjecture, that there were knots we know from a payment to a gardener for his diligence in making them. And as fountains were very soon to become widely popular in grand buildings, we can suggest that here, at last, was something resembling the pictures of continental gardens of an earlier date.

The report continues: 'On the east side of the castle (that is, of the main mass of buildings) is a large and goodly garden to walk in, closed with high walls imbattled. The conveyance thither is by the gallery, above and beneath, and by other privy ways.' Alongside this 'is a large and goodly orchard, full of newly grafted fruit trees well laden with fruit, many roses and other pleasures; and in the same orchard are many goodly alleys to walk in openly. And round about the same orchard, covered in at a good height, are other goodly alleys with resting-places covered thoroughly with whitethorn and hazel; outside these alleys, the outer part of the orchard is enclosed with sawn palings, beyond which are ditches and quickset hedges.' Then, beyond these ditches and hedges, and to the north and east of the buildings, lay the park newly taken-in by Buckingham, with 'no great plenty of wood, but many hedgerows of thorn and great elms'.

This is, perhaps, the only contemporaneous account* we are ever likely to have of a garden of the grand scale at the stage when the medieval world was disappearing. Yet the privy garden within the walls must have been a feature that was then becoming more general, for L. F. Salzman[39] gives particulars of an agreement made in 1530 to construct wooden galleries round a walled garden, with a summerhouse underneath; this was in London.

Thornbury, too, is interesting in that it is believed to have been derived to some extent from Henry VII's palace at Sheen (now Richmond, Surrey). Little seems to be known concerning the

* Drawings reconstructing the appearance of these gardens are given in H. Avray Tipping, *English Gardens*.

garden at Sheen, beyond the usual unilluminating financial accounts. There is, however, an interesting small point to be made about one Lovell, who was promoted from Greenwich to Richmond in Henry VIII's reign, with an increase in salary from £3 8s. a year to £3 a quarter. It was his duty to supply the king's table with 'damsons, grapes, filberts, peaches, apples and other fruits, and flowers, roses and other sweet waters'.[40] The same man, as 'Lovell of Richemount the King's Gardyner', forms, so far as I can find, the solitary reference to gardens or anything appertaining to them in J. H. Harvey's study of architects and those concerned with building down to the year 1550.[41] What is more, he only finds himself there as the temporary custodian of a boat mentioned in the will of a freemason and carver who died in 1536. To contrast this with a comparable biographical dictionary of architects which covers the period 1660 to 1840[42] is illuminating and salutary, for that book abounds with instances of the garden-designing activities of many of the architects that it describes. It is not, one concludes, from any lack of records that the medieval craftsman is so rarely concerned with the design or construction of gardens, but because until late Tudor times gardening was of neither sufficient magnitude nor artistic quality to warrant their employment.

At the time the venture at Thornbury failed, Stafford was, of course, one of the rivals of Cardinal Wolsey in seeking power and splendour; Wolsey it was who had the power when Stafford lost his head. From the viewpoint of the student of the arts, the significance of Wolsey's pursuit of splendour was his strong preference for and patronage of Italian artists. In the days of his glory he greatly influenced Henry VII and even more Henry VIII in matters of taste,[43] and was among the first since the Romans to attempt to bring the Mediterranean civilization across the Channel.

Wolsey's own establishment at Hampton Court was an example of magnificence in the 'modern' manner of his time:

> My buildings sumptuous, the roofs with gold and byse*
> Shone like the sun in mid-day sphere,
> Craftily entailed† as cunning could devise,

* Purple.
† Carved.

With images embossed, most lively did appear;
Expertest artificers that were both far and near,
To beautify my houses, I had them at my will:
Thus I wanted nought my pleasure to fulfil . . .

My gardens sweet, enclosed with walls strong,
Embanked with benches to sit and take my rest;
The knots so enknotted it cannot be expressed,
With arbours and alleys so pleasant and so *dulce*,
The pestilent airs with flavours to repulse. . . .[44]

In this garden, so briefly described, but apparently not unlike that at Thornbury, we read that Wolsey was accustomed to walk towards evening among the alleys so that he might say divine service with his chaplain.

To illustrate this period, one might also quote Skelton's lines:

The clouds began to clear, the mist rarified;
  In an herber* I saw, brought where I was,
There birds on the briar sang on every side
  With alleys ensanded about in compass,
  The banks enturfed with singular solas,
Enrailed with rosers, and vines engraped;
It was a new comfort of sorrowis escaped.

In the midst of a conduit, that curiously was cast
  With pipes of gold, engushing out streams;
Of crystal the clearness these waters far past,
  Enswimming with roaches, barbellis, and breams,
  Whose scales ensilvered against the sunbeams,
Englistered, that joyous it was to behold. . . .[45]

It will be noticed that the only flowers mentioned are the 'rosers'—rose-bushes.

If we are still without much detailed information about the pre-Elizabethan garden, we are at least sure of the increased use of flowers in decoration:

Christ save Henry the Eighth, our royal King,
The red rose in honour to flourish and spring!
With Catherine incomparable, our royal Queen also,
  That peerless pomegranate, Christ save her noble
    grace![46]

* herber = arbour.

37

The Tudor rose, and Catherine's pomegranate,* appear in ornament and decoration, both formally and more naturalistically treated; flowers, apparently both natural and artificial (including the fleur-de-lis), were lavishly used in the decorations at the Field of the Cloth of Gold; the sitters in portraits began to grip exquisitely painted little flowers between their stiff, long fingers (for example, the dianthus loved by Holbein).

When, in 1529, Wolsey's pageantry was summarily ended, the stage properties and scenery were taken over by his royal master, but his role was given for a short time to Sir Thomas More. More was a great humanist of the new school and in 1518 had published his *Utopia*, which I suppose today we should ingloriously describe as a planner's 'blue print' to the perfect state. Fortunately, this tiresome place is still not with us in its entirety, but More's views on gardening have been surprisingly realized in our more enlightened suburbs:

> They set great store by their gardens. In them they have vineyards, all manner of fruit, herbs and flowers, so pleasant, so well furnished, and so finely kept, that I never saw thing more fruitful nor better trimmed in any place. Their study and diligence herein cometh not only of pleasure, but also of certain strife and contention that is between street and street, concerning the trimming, husbanding and furnishing of their gardens, every man for his own part. And verily you shall not lightly find in all the city anything that is more commodious, either for the profit of the citizens, or for pleasure. And therefore it may seem that the first founder of the city minded nothing so much as he did these gardens.

More's own garden was famous in his day. In 1520 he bought land in the country village of Chelsea, close by the Thames, which would take him speedily to London. Here he built a fine house, with a farm adjoining, and laid out a garden. It was described[47] as 'a place' of marvellous beauty, full of lovely flowers and blossoming fruit trees, with a beautiful view of the Thames, and with green meadows and wooded hills on every side. It is said that the rosemary which grows to this day in many a Chelsea garden was introduced there by Sir Thomas More, who liked 'to let it run all

* The pomegranate is generally assumed to have been in cultivation here before Turner's *Names of Herbes* in 1548. Its many-seeded fruit was anciently symbolic of fertility; perhaps it was the fruit given by Paris to Venus.

over his garden walks, not only because his bees loved it, but because 'tis the herb sacred to remembrance and therefore to friendship'.

'A portion of this garden was left to the care of each of the many servants. . . . He would have no idle retainers in his service . . . they were expected to occupy their leisure with gardening, music or books.'

Further, we have in a little painting of More and his family* one of the few glimpses by a contemporary of an early sixteenth-century garden—though, having been planned by More, it was presumably in advance of its time.

It is not surrounded by those embattled walls which protected the guilty conscience of a Stafford or a Wolsey; the eye looks over a neat geometrical pattern of beds—hedged, we may assume, with rosemary—to the Thames. A wall against which lie trained fruit trees runs down one side of the garden; it ends, not in a turret, but a tall garden house. The whole design is one of simplicity; reason, one feels, underlies its planning. It is far removed from the scenes shown in medieval miniatures, nor has it any hint of Mediterranean drama or French extravagance. It was, indeed, Utopian in its simplicity and sensibilities, and, we may guess, one of the first examples of a garden in a tradition that has become typically English.

* The picture, formerly in the Sotheby collection, was reproduced in *The Illustrated London News*, 22nd October 1955.

TWO

From Utopia to Paradise
1530—1629

THE TUDOR ROSE

AFTER the death of Wolsey in 1530 Henry VIII acquired his palaces and began adding to them and laying out their gardens in a new manner—not in the traditional medieval style, but in an Anglicized version of the Italian mode that he had learned from Wolsey.

On Wolsey's death the power under the throne had passed to Cromwell, who engineered the dissolution of the monasteries. Anyone who visits our historic houses today will be made aware how many of them have their origins in the buildings put up by the *nouveaux riches* and astute courtiers of Henry's time who took over the estates of the religious houses. There was a cessation, in fact often a destruction, of ecclesiastical building, and a great accession to secular building. Something quite new came into being: the handsomely built private (and now pacific) buildings scattered all over England which became the 'seats' of noblemen and gentlemen.

This change is reflected in the records John Leland made during his 'laborious' journeys in the six years prior to 1542 as antiquary to the king. He describes many of these houses newly built or building, often with their 'orchards of great variety of fruit and fair made walks and gardens'.

In 1533 Henry himself was busy extending the gardens at Hampton Court. In that year the mount was built. Upon a foundation of over a quarter million bricks soil was piled, and planted with hawthorns. On the summit stood a many-windowed three-storeyed building, roofed with a lead cupola surmounted by a vane in the form of an heraldic lion. This 'lantern arbour' was reached by a pathway spiralling up like 'the turnings of cockle shells', bordered by heraldic beasts carved in stone.[1]

The mount was to be a feature of large gardens until late in the following century. It took various forms, but in principle seems always to have consisted of some kind of seat or arbour raised on a pile of earth above the general level of the garden to a 'pretty height', so that, having spiralled up, one might 'look abroad into the fields'[2] and over one's domain. The mount was planted with clipped shrubs, or perhaps low box hedges bordered the ascending path.*

Another feature of the Hampton Court gardens, still to be seen in contemporary pictures, was the flower-bed surrounded by rails painted green and white. Effigies of 'king's and queen's beasts'—dragons, tigers, greyhounds, bulls, harts, badgers, antelopes, griffins, leopards, rams, and yales—were set about the place mounted upon poles. Sun-dials also abounded.

In 1538 Henry began the building of his palace at Nonsuch. To secure a perfect and 'very healthful' situation, the old village and church at Cuddington, between Cheam and Ewell in the north of Surrey, were swept away. The palace lived up to its name, a fairy-tale and fantastic building with huge top-heavy octagonal towers at each end capped with bulbous cupolas. It was not finished during the lifetime of Henry, and in Mary's reign passed into the hands of the Earl of Arundel, who carried out the king's designs.

Only fragments of evidence of the precise nature of Nonsuch remain;† from them 'we see at once to what extent Elizabethan and Jacobean architecture were indebted to the palace, which in those reigns was still a cherished monument'.[4] It seems that Nonsuch, and presumably its gardens, were based on the Palace of Fontainebleau, begun a decade or so before by Francis I, after an enforced stay in Italy. Whilst there, Francis had become acutely aware of Italian architecture and art. In the gardens that he laid

---

* Leland also refers to mounts furnished with topiary work ('*opere topario*'), and a path 'writhen about in degrees like turnings of cockleshells to come to the top without pain'.[3] The remains of a large mount can still be seen at Rockingham Castle, Northamptonshire, and there is a charming one at Packwood, Warwickshire.

† It was pulled down by Charles II's Duchess of Cleveland.

out the haphazard medieval arrangement had begun to give way to a design conceived as a whole; the flower-beds were of various shapes, but planned within a main design. Terraces were built, and the garden was decorated with fountains, statues, and vases, placed not casually, but within the scheme.[5]

While the gardens of our smaller houses no doubt continued more or less on medieval lines, the grander houses undoubtedly followed the manner of Nonsuch; their inspiration for many decades was that of the Italian Renaissance brought to England after being 're-edited in France'.

We can gain an impression—no more—of these older Tudor gardens after they had matured over the best part of half a century from the descriptions written by two continental travellers. Paul Hentzner (1598) and Thomas Platter (1599) give us some idea of the original conception in the minds of those who contrived the setting of Nonsuch which, Hentzner wrote,[6] was 'so encompassed with parks full of deer, delicious gardens, groves ornamented with trellis-work, cabinets of verdure and walks so embrowned by trees, that it seems to be a place pitched upon by Pleasure herself, to dwell in along with Health'.

At Hampton Court the ornaments attracted his notice:

In the pleasure and artificial gardens are many columns and pyramids of marble, two fountains that spout water one round the other like a pyramid, upon which are perched small birds that stream water out of their bills. In the grove of Diana is a very agreeable fountain, with Actaeon turned into a stag, as he was sprinkled by the goddess and her nymphs, with inscriptions. There is besides another pyramid of marble full of concealed pipes, which spurt upon all who come within their reach.

Platter,[7] who arrived at Nonsuch when Queen Elizabeth was in residence, reports that it was so isolated from other habitations that visitors and courtiers had to camp in a meadow, from which the palace buildings were reached by a long grassy avenue, enclosed by wooden palings. He agrees that its name is suitable, 'for there is not its equal in England'. He is mostly concerned with the house, the queen, her court, and its ceremony. He adds some details not given by Hentzner. In the garden was a wood. In the densest part of it many trees had been uprooted to provide alleys and vistas, and within it was a bowling green and a tennis court, where those pastimes might be pursued to 'the delicious song of the birds in the tall trees densely planted along the sides'. He describes the maze, with hedges thick and high enough to prevent cheating, 'charming terraces', and in the pleasure gardens all kinds of imitation animals artfully set out so that one might mistake them for real ones.

There was one structure at Nonsuch which is of particular interest in the history of gardening. Standing away from the main building was the banqueting house, a substantial half-timber building with round turrets at each corner, and a lead roof. It is typical of the new fashion then prevalent of 'transplanting from the south to our uncongenial soil',[8] though there had in fact been a timber banqueting house built in the park at Kenilworth Castle for Henry V in c. 1414. Later, references to banqueting houses as being somewhat romantic places occur not infrequently in Elizabethan literature. They were part of the garden rather than the house; for example, the account books for the building of Hardwick Hall in 1596 name materials for 'the banqueting house in the garden'. Their history continues into the eighteenth century; from them, it has been suggested, were evolved the great orangeries designed by Wren and others.

Nonsuch shows the coming of Italian ideas which, influenced in varying degrees by their transmission through France, were to be the fundamentals of garden design in the grand manner until the sweeping changes brought about by the English natural school of the mid-eighteenth century.

During the late part of the reign of Henry VIII another influence began to arrive, an influence which, so far as I can find, has not been studied as systematically as it deserves. It concerns not garden design, but horticulture—the cultivation of plants. From the 1540s onwards persecution brought to England Fleming, Walloon, and French refugees in increasing numbers. Their influence on our silk and woollen industries is, of course, well known. They included a number of highly skilled gardeners, who settled particularly in East Anglia and south-east England— districts where commercial horticulture is still widely practised.*

* F. W. Jessup in *A History of Kent* points out that on the road from Sandwich to Canterbury there is a district called The Poulder, a word still used for reclaimed land in the Zuyder Zee.

Some vegetable growers were so successful that they moved closer to London, to those districts of fertile soil on either bank of the Thames which continued as nursery grounds until built upon in the nineteenth century.

In Scotland, at this stage, gardening seems to have been little developed; planting seems to have been restricted to the provision of sheltering trees and orchards.

The 1540s saw the birth of English botanical science. In 1548 was published *The names of herbs in Greek, Latin, English, Dutch and French, with the common names that herbaries and apothecaries use* (in some respects anticipated by John Bray's *Synonoma de nominibus herbarum*. Bray, physician to Edward III, died in 1381). These were 'gathered by William Turner'. The year of the publication of this book is not infrequently quoted as the date of the introduction of many foreign plants, for in it a number of them are described for the first time as being in cultivation in Britain. The author, 'the father of English botany', also wrote a book on wines.

The studies of Canon Raven[9] have brought into correct perspective the eminence of this prototype of the parson-naturalists who have played such an important part in British studies of natural history. Turner was not, however (as so many have been), a country vicar living a long life in some sequestered parish. He was a vigorous religious reformer, a protagonist of the new learning. He was born about 1508 at Morpeth, Northumberland. As a boy, he observed accurately and with a mind unprejudiced by the body of literature then current the ways of living plants and birds. This objectivity, in due course to be allied to a wide knowledge of Greek and Latin originals, was to make him the first scientific student of botany and zoology in England. It was his realization that we had no authoritative work available on the English names of plants and their application to the plants of the continental herbalists, that is the key to his botanical work.

In 1526 Turner went to Pembroke Hall in Cambridge, and in due course his outspoken religious views caused him to leave England. To his great advantage he travelled (always observing) in France, Germany, Italy, and Switzerland. He studied medicine, made perhaps the first English herbarium collection of dried specimens, and met the eminent scientists of the day.

He joined the staff of the Lord Protector, Edward Seymour,

Duke of Somerset, as physician. Somerset had been given Syon by Edward VI, and his household was a brilliant one, of advanced views. He himself was keenly interested in plants, and he laid out fine gardens.

Turner lived and had a garden at Kew. His writings of this period show that he studied plants not only at Syon and in his own garden, but in those of Dr. Richard Bartlot, a president of the Royal College of Physicians, at Blackfriars, and Lord Cobham at Gravesend. In 1551 he became Dean of Wells. On Mary's accession, for a time he retreated once more to the Continent. He died in 1568, shortly after he had completed his great *Herbal*, dedicated to his admired queen, Elizabeth I, with whom he was proud to have conversed in Latin in the days when she was a young princess.

While John Bray gave southernwood its English name in his *Synonoma* and 'pionia' or 'pianna' for paeony occurs before 1200, jasmine and winter cherry do get their first English mention by Turner. His reference to the 'velvet flower or French marigold' (*Tagetes patula*) from Mexico is interesting. He records of the pomegranate 'there are certain in my Lord's garden at Syon, but their fruit cometh never to perfection'; that *Amygdala*, in English an almond tree, is found in England only in gardens. The peach, quince, and medlar were well known, the last being common in England. He is interesting on the apricot. Some English, he writes, call the fruit an abricok, 'me think seeing that we have very few trees of this as yet it were better to call it an hasty peach tree, because it is like a peach, and it is a great while ripe before the peach trees, wherefore the fruit of the tree is called *malum precox*'. There were 'divers fig trees in England in gardens, but nowhere else'. Of vegetables, the broad bean was now grown 'in plenty enough'.

Concerning his own activities, he writes of some kind of antirrhinum, which he calls 'broad calf's snout', that he had in his garden from seeds that had come from Italy. Once again this reminds us that Britain is part of Europe. In 1545 the first botanical garden for the scientific study of plants was laid out at Padua near Venice and Turner was linking England with the fast-developing stream of botanical science in Italy, indeed Europe generally, just as Nonsuch was doing with art and architecture.

The flow of refugee immigrants was a similar influence some-what lower down the scale. Our island was rapidly and readily absorbing theory and practice, as well as material in the form of plants, from overseas.* Thus it came about that our gardens, which we like to think of as singularly British, are in fact the most cosmopolitan in the Old World.

So far, we have discussed only gardens on the grand scale and those of learned men. What of the middling gardens, the places owned for example by rich yeomen or the prospering merchants? Little enough seems recorded of them. Yet here and there we can learn something. For instance, in the 1540s Sabine Saunders married John Johnson, a merchant, of Glapthorn Manor in Northamptonshire. Before she moved there she had planned her garden, and asked her brother-in-law in London to help her. He duly visited the seedsmen and bought 'seeds for my sister's new gardens' which were sent to Glapthorn for spring sowing. Each spring after that further consignments were sent to her from the City.[10]

ELIZABETH THE GREAT

In all probability the first book on gardening in English appeared, appropriately enough, in the year of the accession of Queen Elizabeth I.[11] It is extremely rare, and was printed in black letter. The scope was fully set out on the title page:

A most brief and pleasant treatise, teaching how to dress, sow and set a garden: and what remedies may be had and used against such beasts, worms, flies; and such-like that annoy gardens, gathered out of the principallest authors, as Palladius, Columella, Varro, Dyophanes, learned Cato and many more. And now Englished by Thomas Hill, Londoner.

It includes wood-cuts of a garden of the period, and of mazes. It was successful, and later editions were published.

One may unkindly observe that this, the first gardening book published in England, was unoriginal. It was no more than a collection of old continental material translated and put together to make a 'pleasant treatise'. It was, like so many subsequent books on gardening, of a literary rather than a practical nature;

---

* Already, even at this stage, from China, whence came by devious routes the peach and mulberry.

the work of a journalist, not a man of the garden. It did, however, frankly proclaim its origins.

The significance of Hill's work is not in its contents, but in the fact that there was now a public ready to buy gardening books. And books, surely, are one of the chief glories of the first Elizabethan age; to pass on without some reference to the vision of plants and gardening seen by poets and playwrights would be to omit a large area from the background of our subject. We can find plenty of excitement in Edmund Spenser (1552–1599) (let us here break our rule of modernizing the spelling):

> Bring hither the Pincke and purple Cullambine,
>> With Gellifloures;
> Bring Coronations, and Sops-in-wine
>> Worne of Paramoures;
> Strowe me the ground with Daffodowndillies,
> And Cowslips, and Kingcups, and loved Lillies,
>> The pretie Pawnse
>> And the Chevisaunce,
> Shall match with the floure Delice.[12]

Eliza, Queen of the Shepherds, was indeed set in a prospect of flowers. Damask, red and white roses, the violet and primrose, green branches of bay, and damsons also embroider the scene with floriferous incongruity; for our purpose we can observe that nearly all are garden, not wild, plants. The learned Agnes Arber[13] considered that Spenser took his plant names and lore, at least in his *Shepherd's Calendar*, from *The New Herbal or History of Plants* published in 1578. This was 'first set forth from the Dutch or Almaigne . . . by Henry Lyte Esq.'. More precisely, it was an English version of a French translation by Clusius of the work of Rembert Dodoens (1517–1585). This work of Lyte's, which went through several editions, was another instance of the growing interest in plants.

From Spenser—with his backward look into that lovely and curious anachronistic world of chivalry—to Shakespeare is but the passage of a year or two in real time. But the difference between their worlds is great. Canon Ellacombe wrote: 'I claim Shakespeare as a lover of flowers and gardening; and this I propose to prove by showing how, in all his writings, he exhibits his strong love of flowers, a very fair, though not perhaps a very deep, love of plants.'[14] The claim is, of course, amply justified, and apposite quotations from Shakespeare perhaps too liberally adorn some books on gardening. One would, indeed, like to emphasize the extraordinary love of plants—often literary and imaginative rather than practical—of this period by quoting at some length from the minor poets, but a few lines must do to recall an elysium in the mind's eye of the Elizabethan:

> Fair is my love that feeds among the lilies,
>   The lilies growing in that pleasant garden
> Where Cupid's Mount, that well beloved hill is,
>   And where that little god himself is warden.
> See where my love sits in the beds of spices!
>   Beset all round with camphor, myrrh, and roses.
> And interlaced with curious devices
>   Which, her from all the world apart incloses.
> There, doth she tune her lute for her delight! . . .[15]

Nor can one pass on without some reference to the increasing use of accurately drawn flowers both in portraiture and decoration. The Elizabethans pose with an exquisite flower in their hand, or, as in a miniature by Nicholas Hilliard (1537–1619), among roses. The ornamentation of documents also shows this preoccupation of artists with flowers;[16] there is, for example, a grant to Sir Thomas Heneage in 1573 showing the Queen surrounded by 'exquisite flowers in pastel shades'. Strawberries, the precursor of our sweet peas, and many other kinds are easily identified.

Plasterwork also makes more use of accurately observed plant forms, and one should also mention the use of 'emblems' in books and needlework embodying flowers.[17]

Modesty about the glorious period in which he lived was not an attribute of the Elizabethan. Yet commentators agree that when William Harrison (1534–1593), Dean of Windsor, was writing of that which came within his notice he was reliable. Therefore, his general view of gardening and its development, written just about half-way through the reign of Elizabeth I, may be accepted.[18] He begins triumphantly:

If you look into our gardens* annexed to our houses, how wonder-

---

* Harrison gives a useful definition of gardens: 'all spade-dug grounds'.

fully is their beauty increased, not only with flowers . . . and . . . curious and costly workmanship, but also with rare and medicinable herbs sought up in the land within these forty years: so that, in comparison with their present, the ancient gardens were but dunghills and laystows to such as did possess them.

Of our increasing skill in horticulture, of the art of helping nature to improve colouring, to produce double flowers, and to increase size, he observes, 'our gardeners moderate her [nature's] course in things as if they were her superior'. He acknowledges the important progress made by the Dutch florists, and wishes that the great Clusius might come to England and work upon improving some of our native plants.

The improvement in orchards was comparable. They were 'never furnished with such variety as at this present . . . we have most delicate apples, plums, pears, walnuts, filberts . . . in comparison of which most of the old trees (of forty years ago) are nothing worth'. In noblemen's orchards he found apricots, almonds, peaches, figs, and the cornelian cherry (*Cornus mas*).*

Harrison's comments on vegetables are interesting. He assures us that 'I have seen by record' that kinds cultivated and esteemed in the reign of Edward I had become neglected, and fit only for hogs and the poor. Such were melons, pompions, gourds, cucumbers, radishes, skirrets, parsnips, carrots, navews, turnips, 'and all kind of salad herbs'. The Tudors had wisely revived their cultivation and use.

Of medicinal plants, he remarks that in his own little garden, in spite of his small ability, he grows nearly three hundred kinds, 'no one of them being common or usually to be had'. How many, he consequently reflects, must there not be grown in the great gardens—at Hampton Court, Nonsuch, Theobalds, and Cobham?

Harrison makes some observations on the reasons for this success. Very sensibly he remarks that 'our soil abounds with water in all places'. But the clue really lies in the Elizabethan's unending quest for the new, and his outstanding enterprise. 'Strange herbs, plants, and annual fruits are daily brought unto us from the Indies, Americas, Taprobane [Ceylon], Canary Isles, and all parts of the world', and 'I have seen capers, oranges and

* This charming tree, now grown only for its precocious little golden flowers, was formerly cultivated for its preserved and pickled fruit—'most refreshing, an excellent condiment, and do well also in tarts'.

lemons, and heard of wild olives growing here, besides other strange trees brought here from afar, whose names I know not.'

No one seems to have recorded all these marvels and arrivals as they occurred, but if we compare the number of plants described by William Turner in his *Herbal* of 1568 with those published by Gerard barely thirty years later, we realize that Harrison was not exaggerating.

TRIBUTE TO ORIANA

When mentioning the gardens at Theobalds and Cobham Harrison hints at another reason for the wonderful developments of his day. The owners of these, and the builders of the new 'prodigy houses' of Queen Elizabeth's reign, tried to surpass their fellows in producing tributes to the fabulous Oriana.

Some houses, like Holdenby and Kirby in Northamptonshire, Hardwick in Derbyshire, Theobalds in Hertfordshire, rose from the ground during her reign. Others, such as Longleat in Wiltshire, and Burghley on the Northamptonshire borders of Lincoln, were developments of earlier houses. The scale of many of these buildings was proportionate not to the households of their owners, but to that of the queen and her entourage whom they were intended to entertain. Sir Christopher Hatton built Holdenby, contemporaneously described as 'altogether even the best house that has been built in this age', for no other purpose.

The fantastic grandeur of the stone, bricks, and mortar remains in quite a number of such places for us to see. Fashion is such that under her domination the surroundings in which they were set disappeared. Unhappily, very little contemporary description of the Elizabethan gardens has survived either.

Theobalds must have been one of the most important of these Elizabethan near-palaces. The house was built by William Cecil, Lord Burleigh (1520-1598), who had been a young colleague of William Turner in the brilliant Syon household of the Lord Protector Somerset. It was for his son, Robert.

We have a brief glimpse into the garden described by Hentzner,[19] who visited it in August 1598. Leaving the gallery (in which was painted the genealogy of the kings)

one goes into the garden, encompassed with a ditch full of water, large enough to have the pleasure of going in a boat, and rowing between the shrubs; here are great variety of trees and plants; labyrinths made with a great deal of labour; a *jet d'eau*, with its basin of white marble; and columns and pyramids of wood, up and down the garden.* After seeing these, we were led by the gardener into the summer-house, in the lower part of which, built semi-circularly, are the twelve Roman emperors in white marble, and a table of touchstone; the upper part of it is set round with cisterns of lead, into which the water is conveyed through pipes, so that fish may be kept in them, and in summer time they are very convenient for bathing.

Hentzner's visit was on the day of Burleigh's funeral. Probably, therefore, the gardener who let his party into the summerhouse was not John Gerard, who a year before had achieved fame by the publication of his *Herbal*, and who was presumably attending the ceremony. Gerard was employed by Burleigh (to whom the *Herbal* is dedicated), and in his gardens must have had unsurpassed opportunities of seeing the new plants that were arriving from all parts of the world. There exists little else to show what Theobalds was like: by the time of the Parliamentary Survey made in 1650 there had been many alterations.

Holdenby, upon which Elizabeth's elegant and capable favourite Hatton spent so lavishly, was built upon the ridge† overlooking the parkland of Althorp. It was an early example of the new fashion in which great houses were built with ostentation on high land, rather than in the valley near water. One assumes that this was made possible by the improvement in hydraulic engineering, which was also demonstrated by the increasing popularity of water-works and fountains.

The long axis of the house (which, like Hardwick, was almost glass-fronted) and its gardens lay, as was then considered desirable, more or less east and west. A reconstructed plan[21] of the whole complex, which included ancillary buildings such as stables, lodges, the church, and the site of the old hall, shows that on this axis they stretched over some 675 yards.

The buildings were reached from the east by a long straight way which was called the Green. The house itself was reached through courtyards. To its south, against the walls, lay a 'rosery'

* 'There is scarce an unnatural and sumptuous impropriety at Versailles which we do not find in Hentzner's description of [Theobald's]'—Horace Walpole.

† Camden says that this now 'sweet and princely place' was raised, levelled, and formed out of a most craggy piece of ground.[20]

and terraces overlooking the old hall. On the north side of the buildings, in which was another entrance, was set another garden, and beyond it were spinneys. At the west end of the house was a big area of garden, orchard, and ponds, at the remote corners of which were set two mounts.

All that remains of Hatton's work is two giant gateways. Evelyn saw Holdenby in 1675 after its destruction in the Civil War; it was a prospect 'that shows like a Roman ruin shaded by the trees about it, one of the most pleasing sights I ever saw, of state and solemn'.[22]

Of the other Elizabethan houses that have been named, there remain but slight indications of the precise details of their original gardens. (Those now surrounding the ruins of Kirby Hall are from a later period.)

Montacute, an example of the less ambitious house of its period, still has its remarkable pavilioned courtyard as the key to the remainder, but substantial alterations have been made to the rest; much that is apparently Elizabethan is, in fact, nineteenth-century work by R. S. Balfour (Plate III).

A word should be said here about Sir Thomas Tresham (c. 1543–1605) and his remarkable buildings in Northamptonshire.[23] The uncompleted remains of his Lyveden house, the 'new bield', and his lodge at Rushton, still remain. Their design and ornamentation were informed by religious symbolism—the Rushton building being literally as three-sided as the Trinity. At Lyveden there still remain indications of the pleasaunce and terracing, the fishponds and 'water orchards' that Sir Thomas laid out. Did these, too, incorporate the same Christian conceits and symbolism?

Another garden of which we know a little was Beddington, near Croydon. The estate had belonged to the Carew family since the time of Edward III; its owner during the reign of Queen Elizabeth I was Sir Francis Carew, who had been in service under Queen Mary. In Elizabeth's reign he followed the fashion and built a grand new house, laying out the gardens and planting them with fruit trees of every kind, in the cultivation of which he took great delight, sparing no expense in importing them from foreign countries. It is generally said that here he grew the first orange trees in England. John Aubrey[24] has it that Carew imported the plants from Italy, but there was a tradition in the Raleigh family that he had the seeds from Sir Walter.[*][25] Certain it is, however, that he was one of the first cultivators of the orange in this country. Aubrey described the trees, and in 1658 John Evelyn[27] gave an account of them—it was certainly his opinion that Beddington was 'famous for the first orange garden in England'. The trees, by then overgrown, were planted in the open ground. In winter they were covered by a 'wooden tabernacle' and warmed by stoves.

The glorious climax of Carew's career as a gardener was no doubt in August 1599 when he had the supreme honour of a visit from his queen. He was able, on this late summer day, to pick for her newly ripened cherries, most popular of fruits in Elizabethan times. This feat had been achieved by keeping the tree cold by means of canvas sheets kept sprayed with water.[28]

Carew's orangery was, in 1691, still the most famous in England.[29] The garden itself, then in the hands of the Duke of Norfolk, had, however, become neglected. The original trees are said to have lasted until the bitter winter of 1739-40. Evelyn remarked that in the fertile and well-watered garden the pomegranate bore fruit—a sign of the exceptionally favourable situation.

No trace of Carew's Beddington remains, though a few parts of the rebuilding in Queen Anne's time are to be found in the heart of Croydon. The garden house, decorated with scenes showing the destruction of the Armada, commented upon by Aubrey, also disappeared long ago.

We can gain no more than a general impression of the gardens of these great Elizabethan houses. Much thought was undoubtedly given to their design; perhaps we may say, as has been said of the houses around which they lay, 'each is a prodigy, an individual romance'.

Today there is one common misconception that gives a false

---

* The actual date and method of the introduction of the orange is unknown. A clue is given in a letter written by Lord Burleigh to Paris in 1562 in which he says that he has learned from his son Thomas that Carew was there buying certain trees. 'I have already an orange tree; and if the price be not much, I pray you procure for me a lemon, a pomegranate, and a myrtle; and hope that they may be sent home with Mr. Carew's trees.'[26] This suggests that as Carew bought trees from Paris, he might well have had his oranges also from France; it is clear, too, from Burleigh's reference to his solitary tree, that the orange was still a rarity in British gardens in 1562.

view of these gardens—the belief that yew hedges and topiary abounded. There is no doubt that hedges were almost always 'quickset', which at that period meant whitethorn or privet. Box was also used, but generally for the bordering of beds, as was rosemary.

HUSBANDMAN AND HOUSEWIFE

So much for the great gardens. As a contrast, William Harrison wrote of his own garden with enthusiasm, having 'the whole area thereof little above 300 ft. of ground'. There can be no doubt that at this period the small garden was developing just as rapidly as the garden of the great house; though probably retaining something of the medieval tradition. In 1563 Dr. John Hall, surgeon, botanist, and poet, wrote of the garden as still enclosed in a manner reminiscent of Chaucer's England:

> It hedged was with honeysuckles,
> Or periclimenum;
> Well mixed with small cornus trees,
> Sweet briar and ligustrum.

> The white thorn, and the blackthorn both,
> With box, and maple fine:
> In which branched the briony,
> The ivy and wild vine.[30]

It was during the Elizabethan age that the knot garden became fashionable. According to the *Oxford Dictionary*, the word first appears in a horticultural connection at the end of the fifteenth century, when it apparently refers to something like a maze.

A knot, as it developed in Tudor times, was a small, usually rectangular bed upon which was outlined a pattern—the more intricate or 'enknotted' the better—in dwarf box, rosemary, or other suitable dwarf plant such as thrift. Sometimes the pattern took the form of objects—heraldic beasts in particular—but the designs that have come down to us are abstract and geometric; they often seem to have an affinity with the architectural decoration known as strap work, that importation from Antwerp which appealed so strongly to the Elizabethan mind (Fig. 1). One may guess, therefore, that the knot came from Italy via Holland.

Sometimes the pattern worked in living green was an end in itself, the interstices being filled with gravels or coloured mineral substances. Otherwise, the design was more open, and the spaces were filled with flowering plants.

Fig. 1. A 'variety of knots' and a maze from Lawson's *Countrie Housewife's Garden*, 1617

The Tre-foy	Oval
Flower-de-luce	Maze

We can best gain an idea of the small garden from the doggerel of Thomas Tusser (1515–*c*. 1580). Chorister, scholar, and later farmer in the valley of the River Stour on the borders of Suffolk and Essex, he published his *Hundred Good Points of Husbandry* in 1557. This was taken up by the public as a practical, down-to-earth book, whose rhymed couplets were full of wisdom and common sense. Later, the book was enlarged, becoming *Five Hundred Points of Good Husbandry*, first published in 1573, with a final edition revised by Tusser himself in 1580.

No work could belong more truly to the everyday Elizabethan world. It takes the form of a month-by-month rhymed calendar of operations and reminder that are concerned with husbandry in its widest aspects. There is much about garden work and there are also lists of those plants which one assumes from the nature of the book were generally cultivated in the Elizabethan garden.

It indicates that the orchard and fruit lay within the man's province, and that flowers, plants for the kitchen, herbs and saladings came within the housewife's there are the often-quoted lines:

> In March and in April, from morning to night,
> In sowing and setting, good housewives delight;
> To have in a garden, or other like plot,
> To trim up their house, and to furnish their pot.

Certain vegetables, such as the common peas and beans, were field crops without the garden; within it were the choicer kinds, such as rounceval peas and garden beans gathered in July on the bines.

If we take the garden year as beginning in January, the first task was to set these garden peas and beans, and to plant raspberries and roses, and all kinds of fruit trees and shrubs; in February the rounceval peas were to be sticked.

March and April were, of course, the months for planting seeds and herbs. Tusser gives a list of them—with the proviso that some should have been planted earlier. (In January he had also provided a similar list for trees and roots—mostly fruit trees and bushes.)

The March list is divided into sections, which give us an idea of the ordering and use made of the garden. First comes 'Seeds and herbs for the kitchen', with forty-three names which include several that we should now regard as weeds, but an increased number of the vegetables that we know today. Marigolds, primrose, and 'violets of all sorts' are to the present-day gardener surprisingly among the list, but they were still used in kitchens long after Tusser's day; marigolds, 'pot marigold' (*Calendula officinalis*) in particular.

Next, we have twenty-one 'Herbs and roots for sallets and sauce'. There is nothing surprising in this list, except perhaps the 'blessed thistle' (*Carduus benedictus*) and the sea-holly (*Eryngium*); violets, not surprisingly, reappear here also.

Then, nine 'Herbs and roots to boil or to butter', all of which, no doubt in greatly improved form, could be so used today; the winter-grown rounceval peas come in here. 'Strowing herbs of all sorts'—there are twenty-one of them—would still provide a good choice for the purpose of combating unpleasant smells should our hygiene revert to Elizabethan standards. Again, violets are present, but we now take the rose so seriously that few would care to throw them underfoot, as did the Elizabethans.

Nor could we disagree with the choice of the thirty-nine 'Herbs, branches and flowers for windows and pots'; most are still grown in our gardens, though bay (*Laurus nobilis*) has become uncommon. Marigolds (this time the double), roses—'of all sorts'—and violets are again included.

Seventeen 'Herbs to still in summer' (Roses, this time the red and damask, make another appearance) merely remind us that the still-room is a thing of the past. Then come twenty-five 'Necessary herbs to grow in the garden for physic, not rehearsed before'. Some we still use today, but gromwell seed and saxifrage are no longer household remedies for the stone, and mandrake has also gone out of fashion.

Interpolated among the lists is the couplet

> These buy with the penny
> Or look not for any.

They are capers, lemons, olives, oranges, rice, and samphire. In spite of William Harrison's claim, one still purchased them in shops.

Elsewhere, Tusser gives much good advice, and many side-lights on garden practice. From the couplet

> Where fish is scant, and fruit of trees,
> Supply that want with butter and cheese

we learn the importance of fruit in the diet of fast or fish days.

In September:

> Wife into the garden, and set me a plot,
> Of strawberry roots, of the best to be got:
> Such growing abroad, among thorns in the wood,
> Well chosen and picked, prove excellent good

is a reminder that until the nineteenth century the fruit of the native *Fragaria vesca* was as much favoured as the giant berries of today.*

In the same month, the lines

> The gooseberry, respis, and roses all three
> With strawberries under them trimly agree

give us an idea of the mingling of plants that now seldom occurs, though the tradition has never quite died out in the country cottage garden.

There were some twelve recorded editions of *The Five Hundred Points* during Elizabeth's reign—each including a great deal about gardening. This, surely, is a remarkable testimony to the increased interest among the ordinary people for whom Tusser wrote. Yet Hentzner in his often-quoted 'character' of the English people makes no mention of our love of plants and gardens.

A word or two will suffice for the gardens of Scotland during this period; for there seems little evidence that they developed to any extent until the seventeenth century. This has been attributed[31] to the poverty of the country, and the consequent lack of professional gardeners—a state of affairs that was eventually to be reversed in a remarkable manner.

BOTANICAL GARDENERS

We have seen that William Harrison referred in 1577 to the skill of the floriculturists of the day, and mentioned the great Clusius (1526-1609). The activities of this botanist were probably of more direct consequence to the history of gardening than those of any of his contemporaries.

To this day monographers of garden plants—particularly such florists' kinds as the tulip, crocus, and iris—often go back to the writings of Charles de L'Écluse (his name in the vernacular) for a good share of the foundations on which they build. He was born

* The accounts of Henry VIII's reign include payments for the collection of strawberry roots for the royal garden.

at Arras—then a Flemish town. His health was poor, and his early life hard, for his parents were persecuted for their religion. The versatility of his accomplishments in scholarship, particularly knowledge of ancient and modern tongues, was bewildering. His powers of apt description of plants and his pioneering botanical travels in Spain, Portugal, Austria, and Hungary make his *Rariorum Plantarum Historia* of 1601 a classical work among botanists. It is famed for its superb wood-engravings, cut from paintings made for Plantin, the publisher, by Pierre van der Borcht (1545–1608), 'the most important corpus of sixteenth-century flower paintings in existence'.[32] There was, of course, nothing comparable produced in Britain.

Beyond his work as a botanist de L'Écluse was pre-eminent in the scientific aspects of gardening, a man of international fame, known personally in many countries, including, as Harrison suggests, England. He corresponded with our gardeners, came here in 1571, and again in 1581, when he met Philip Sidney, Drake, and others of the Elizabethan galaxy.

In 1587 the enthusiasm of the Dutch for horticulture had resulted in the establishment of the Hortus Botanicus Academicus Lugduni-Batavorum; these keen gardeners early realized the importance of scientific study. The first director was de Bondt. In 1609 he was succeeded by de L'Écluse, who was responsible for the introduction and first successful cultivation of many tulips, irises, crocuses, and other bulbous plants upon which the subsequent success of the Dutch horticultural industry was largely built.[33] This industry has always been a major source of our garden plants.

The English had no one of this standing, nor that of several other continental botanists who were more or less contemporary with de L'Écluse. The best we could do was to provide patronage.

The influence of enthusiastic amateur patrons, drawn from the aristocracy and the middle classes, on the course of English botany was considerable. While zoology (and other sciences) were to remain entangled with 'morals, fables, and presages', their interest in 'medicine and horticulture gave an impetus to botany which soon led to a marked advance among English students'.[34]

Notable among them was Edward, 11th Baron Zouche of Harringworth. He succeeded to the title as a child in 1559, and was put under the guardianship of William Cecil, who has already been mentioned as one of the household at Syon and as builder of Theobalds. The boy was educated under John Whitgift at Cambridge. Later he travelled the Continent, visiting places as diverse as Hamburg, Vienna, and Verona.

He became closely concerned with the Virginia Company, and other projects in the then very New World. In 1600 he retired to Guernsey and a quiet life so that he might repair his fortunes. The reason usually given for this move, which must have been distasteful to one with an international circle of brilliant friends, gives the clue to our interest in him: it is that he had squandered his patrimony on horticulture. However, between 1605 and 1612 he was able to build Bramshill in Hampshire. The house still stands; of its original garden nothing is known.

Certain it is, however, that his garden at Hackney was famous. We have contemporary reference to the plants he brought to it from Constantinople and to his skill in successfully moving fruit trees between thirty and forty years old. Most important is his connection with Mathias de l'Obel (1538-1616), eponymous hero of the genus *Lobelia*.

De l'Obel was born at Lille. Not a great deal is known of his life. He inherited the manuscripts of the French naturalist Guillaume Rondelet (1507-1566), an authority on fishes, whose favourite pupil he was. His most famous book, written in collaboration with Pierre Pena, *Stirpium Adversaria Nova*, was published in 1570 and dedicated to Queen Elizabeth I. In 1581 he was appointed physician to William the Silent, who was murdered in 1584. Shortly after, de l'Obel settled in England, where he lived almost continuously until his death at Highgate in 1611.

When he became attached to the household of Lord Zouche is not known; he certainly travelled with him to Denmark in 1598. He was superintendent of Zouche's garden at Hackney, where he carried out much work, notably a survey of the British flora, and, through his patron's influence, was made *Botanicus Regius* in 1607. The great importance of the Hackney garden under de l'Obel's superintendence was that it was a rallying point of the growing band of Londoners interested in plants, and a link between them and the continental schools. As we shall see, de l'Obel's unpublished manuscripts were later to play an important part in the literature of gardening and botany.

De l'Obel also helped in introducing one of the most notable, and notorious, garden writers. John Gerard was gardener to Burleigh at Theobalds; he also had his own garden in London, possibly in Holborn or Fetter Lane. In 1596 was published *Catalogus arborum, fruticum ac plantarum tam indigenarum, quan exoticum, in horto Iohannis ciuis & Chirugi Londinensis nascentium.* This was, of course, a catalogue of plants growing in his own garden; it was vouched for in a preface by de l'Obel. In it are named some 1,030 plants—many for the first time. With its immense air of authority—Burleigh's name in the background, de l'Obel's in the book—it has long been accepted as the authority for the first date of cultivation for these newcomers.

In 1597 it was followed by his even more famous *Herbal*, multitudinous quotations from which have been subsequently introduced into gardening and botanical books of all kinds. For nearly four centuries Gerard has been immensely popular.

Let us speak of him with all the charity that can be mustered by a Canon of the Church of England: 'Gerard was a rogue...but like many such he was a pleasant fellow. . . . Moreover, botanically speaking he was . . . a comparatively ignorant rogue.'[35]

To begin with, it is now clear that de l'Obel developed doubts about the reliability of the *Catalogus.* As to the *Herbal*, Gerard and John Norton, a publisher, took the collected works of the great Belgian botanist Rembert Dodoens, and, with the help of Mrs. Gerard to add some snippets 'mainly for women', turned them, without acknowledging the origin of the work, into a best seller. Its wood engravings have often been described as 'quaint'. That is, indeed, true; they were a job lot bought on the Continent, in some instances attached to the wrong text.

With care and discrimination we can learn a lot from Gerard's work; that it achieved the hoped-for success with women there can be no doubt.*

There is one extremely interesting point to be noted about Gerard. His portrait in the *Herbal* of 1597 shows him holding a spray of potato in flower and with its berry; a description of the plant is given in the text, and it was also mentioned in his *Catalogus*. This figure and description of a plant whose importance was

* There is a portrait of Lady Hanmer, wife of Sir Thomas Hanmer of Bettisfield (1612–1678) (*see* p. 94), in which she holds a copy.

later to transcend the confines of the garden wall were the first to be published in Europe. Clusius, in his *Historia Plantarum* of 1601, comes a poor second, though he relates that he first saw and had the potato plant early in 1588, and that, 'since it is so fecund', it soon became quite common.

The introduction of the potato to Britain was a milestone in the history of gardening. Who introduced it, and when? The answers that have been given are numerous; those provided by Dr. Salaman will be given here, so logical do they seem.[36]

There were, it seems, two distinct introductions, the first to the mainland of Europe, and the second to Britain. The potato is a native of South America, and one would therefore look to Spain for its introduction to Europe. But at first it seemed possible to trace it only in Italy. Then, in the records of a hospital in Seville, housekeeping entries showed that potatoes, undoubtedly harvested in Spain, were purchased as early as 1573. On this assumption one concludes that the first introduction must have been of tubers gathered in South America in 1569, or perhaps a year or two earlier.

The second, and to us more interesting, introduction is that of Gerard's plants. Gerard says that he received roots 'from Virginia . . . which grow and prosper in my garden as in their native country'. This is puzzling; the potato is not a native of Virginia, nor was it cultivated there until over a century later. The only opportunity of tubers arriving from North America was in 1586, when Drake brought back the first settlers, including Thomas Harriot (1560–1621) the mathematician. Harriot introduced some Virginian plants, but these could not have included the potato.

At this stage two observations can be made. First, as we have seen, Clusius visited Drake in 1581, and if Drake had then been growing, or had even discussed, potatoes, surely the naturalist would have noted it in his description published in 1601. Second, the other traditional claimant to the honour of the introduction to England, Raleigh, never went to Virginia, and, had he done so, would not have found the potato growing there.

Without going fully into details, the conclusions reached by Dr. Salaman were that the potato was indeed introduced by Harriot on his return with the American colonists. He did not, however, bring the tubers from Virginia but obtained them *during* the voyage from Drake, who had learned of their food value and was using supplies that he had seized when raiding Cartagena, or from the stores of ships that he had captured. (It is known that Spanish ships were regularly provisioned with potatoes by 1580.)

Raleigh was Harriot's patron. There is a great deal of evidence to show that the potato was cultivated on a large scale at a very early date in Cork and Waterford. In 1587 or 1588 Raleigh went to live at Youghal, which lies almost on the border of those two counties. Though it cannot be proved beyond doubt, there are several excellent reasons for assuming that Raleigh obtained tubers either directly from Harriot, his protégé, in 1586, or shortly afterwards from Gerard, and was the first to cultivate the potato as a food plant.

There we must leave the early days of this plant in Britain, which was, beyond our island, to become no 'mere vegetable, but rather an instrument of destiny'.[37]

THE JACOBEAN GRAND MANNER

With the arrival of James I and the Stuarts documentary evidence begins to increase, and it is possible to fill out the details of gardening history with facts instead of the assumption and guesswork that had to serve for the earlier periods.

James himself is popularly famed for his energetic attempts* to encourage the production of silk in this country by planting mulberry trees in large numbers. The species on which the silkworm is fed, both in China and southern Europe, is the white mulberry (*Morus alba*) with insignificant, scarcely pink fruit—extremely rare in Britain—and not the picturesque and lusciousfruited black mulberry (*M. nigra*) of our gardens. There is no doubt that this was understood at the time. For instance, a patent granted in 1606 for the importation of mulberries stipulates that only the white mulberry should be brought in.[38]

James himself acquired Theobalds, but it is perhaps more profitable to discuss the writings and gardens of his subjects.

Francis Bacon, Baron Verulam, Viscount St. Albans (1561–1626) is now one of the great names in English history, not so much as an outstanding servant of the state, but as the possessor of one of England's finest intellects. He is also known to those who

---

* *See*, for example, *Instruction for the Increasing and Planting of Mulberry Trees*, W. Stallenge, 1609.

buy gardener's calendars studded with mottoes for the famous lines beginning 'God Almighty first planted a garden . . .'

His essay 'Of Gardens', of which this is the opening sentence, was not published until 1625. It is often quoted as a contemporary description of the late Elizabethan and Jacobean garden. Surely it is nothing of the sort; it is Bacon's vision of 'gardens . . . which are indeed prince-like . . . the contents [of which] ought well to be under thirty acres of ground'. It must be remembered that this is one of fifty-eight essays which range, with equal confidence and attention to detail, from 'Truth' to 'The Vicissitude of Things'; one cannot therefore accept that the detail is always accurate.

Considering Bacon's garden as a Jacobean elysium, let us see the elements from which it was created.

First, to have a garden planted so that there is something to enjoy in each of the twelve months. And enjoyment is used in its widest sense, covering the colours and scents of flowers, the cropping of fruits, the shiny leaves of evergreens in winter, and the fragrance of herbs crushed under foot.

The approach was to be by a green (as at Holdenby) of four acres; then came the main garden of twelve acres, and at the 'going forth' was a heath or desert of six acres. On either side were to be alleyways covering four acres each. The provision of alleys (sometimes trained over 'carpenter's work'),* and the planting of hedges to provide walks shaded in summer and sheltered in winter, is of great importance; the provision of exercise and the vigour of a *ver perpetuum* is a prerequisite of any garden.

Knot gardens filled with coloured earths, topiary work, and, particularly, pools with stagnating water are not to be permitted. A mount, banqueting houses, lively fountains, and sparkling bathing pools are, however, desirable. The heath, or 'natural wilderness', is well described, and is the prototype of all wild gardens—nature imitated and tactfully adorned. Finally, 'statues and such things, for state and magnificence' add nothing to the true pleasure of a garden.

That was Bacon's vision of a garden; 'not a model, but some general lines of it'. To what extent it resembled the great gardens of his day we shall see when we read descriptions of them by his

---

* 'Treillage', principally developed in the French garden, reached a high degree of complexity in the eighteenth century.

contemporaries. One notices that Bacon both looks back to the past—to the green at Holdenby, for instance—and surprisingly far into the future—to the school of William Robinson, with its detestation of statues and its advocacy of wild gardens singularly like Bacon's 'heath'.

.   .   .   .   .

Let us now turn to Jacobean gardens and their owners as we know them to have been.

The history of the building of Hatfield House, by Robert Cecil, Earl of Salisbury (1550–1612), can be reconstructed from the many documents that still exist. Hatfield was begun in 1607, when James I persuaded Cecil to exchange Theobalds, which, as we have seen, his father Burleigh built, for the old episcopal palace in Hertfordshire.

'If trouble was taken with the outworks, even more detailed care went into the planning of the gardens,' wrote Lawrence Stone.[39] The story he has put together from the original Hatfield papers can be summarized as follows.

The first plans were drawn up in 1609 by Mountain Jenings, the earl's gardener. He had probably been brought from Theobalds, and was later to return there in order to look after James I's silkworms and mulberry trees. Advice was also given by a merchant, Robert Bell, who had been concerned with other aspects of the building. A certain Thomas Chaundler was also called in.

For two years the planning and construction went on under Jenings, Chaundler, and John Tradescant (of whom more will be heard later), Cecil making the final decisions.

The water-works were begun in 1611, designed by Chaundler. A hydraulic engineer, Simon Sturtevant (probably Dutch), was engaged to carry them out. Before long, however, a Frenchman, Saloman de Caux, engineer to Prince Henry, was called in. De Caux proposed that the work already done should be abandoned, and a new design substituted. To this Cecil agreed. Chaundler and Sturtevant were dismissed and Jenings undertook the completion of the water-works to a new plan prepared by de Caux and Robert Lyming.*

---

* De Caux or Caus (1576–1626) is said to have been also drawing master to Prince Henry; his son or nephew, Isaac de Caux, was a contriver of gardens and grottoes; he was concerned with planning the garden at Wilton House, near Salisbury, for Philip, Earl of Pembroke (1584–1649). Robert Lyming was then a carpenter; later he was 'architect and builder' of Blickling Hall, Norfolk.

The vineyard included a collection of 30,000 French vines presented by Mme de la Boderie, wife of the French minister. John Aubrey later wrote that its beauties were such that had it been in Greece or Rome, it would have disinherited Tempe (the vale below Mount Olympus) as the poet's symbol of the perfect valley.

Trees, shrubs, and plants came from the Continent. The Queen of France herself sent 500 fruit trees. Many were collected by Cecil's agents. The most notable of these agents was Tradescant. In January 1611 he sent bills including strange and rare roses and shrubs from Leyden; cherry trees, 'flowers called anemones', mulberries, red currants, and arbor-vitae trees from Cornelius Helin at Haarlem; in Holland, too, he had many bulbs and tubers, including *Iris susiana* from John Jokkat. In Paris he bought more fruit trees, myrtles, 200 'sypris trees at one shilling the peece', gillyflowers, and obtained, apparently as a gift, many other rare shrubs from Jean Robin (1550–1629), the eminent keeper of the Jardin des Plantes. Tradescant obtained plants for other patrons besides Cecil.[40]

Gardeners were brought over from France.

In its final form, the main garden was reached from a broad terrace, edged with painted wooden rails that lay along the house, by descending a flight of steps ornamented with painted and gilded wooden lions.

It was below this terrace that the extravagantly expensive water-works were placed. These were centred upon a huge marble basin, which held a great artificial rock formed round an iron core.* On this rock stood a statue painted to represent copper.

From this centre-piece the water flowed in an artificially constructed winding stream (which, the accounts show, gave a good deal of trouble). On the bottom of this stream glistened coloured pebbles and exotic sea-shells (Tradescant had sent from Paris one case and six boxes of the latter.) Leaves, fishes, and snakes, cast in lead, lay about.

It is believed that de Caux based this design on the French gardens of the Tuileries and Saint Germain-en-Laye. Lower down the valley a dam was thrown across the stream so that an island might be formed. It was reached by a painted wooden bridge, and planted with osiers, hawthorn, and white brier-rose.

* This replaced an earlier statue of Neptune that was discarded.

Cecil, who spent so heavily on this great and deeply considered enterprise, carried out by a cosmopolitan group of artists and craftsman, scarcely lived to see its completion.

Several plans of gardens made by John Smythson, who died in 1634, still exist.* 'The platform† of my Lord of Exeter's house at Wimbledon, 1609' is a good example (Plate II). It was made when the walks in the great orchard were 'now in planting'. Once again we are concerned with the powerful Burleigh, for the manor of Wimbledon was leased by his second son, Thomas Cecil. In the family tradition he began to build this famous house in 1588. It was pulled down in the eighteenth century.

An engraving made by Winstanley in 1678‡ shows the house cresting a ridge; it stands above the courtyards, formed against the rising bank like two deep giant terraces, retained by lofty buttressed walls and reached by a complex system of stairways. The two wings project far towards this, the northern aspect, and give a dramatic effect of recession to the main body of the building, on the level of which, and almost all to the south, lie the gardens.

Smythson's plan can, to some extent, be supplemented by the detailed Parliamentary Survey made just forty years later.[41] The manor had then become no more than 'a late parcel of the possessions of Henrietta Maria, the relict and late Queen of Charles Stuart, late King of England'. (Fortunately, it was then purchased by the 'Knight of the Golden Tulip', the Cromwellian General John Lambert.) Some considerable alterations had been made, but we can now gain an idea of its levels, which are not shown on the plan.

Immediately against the east end of the house lay what by 1649 had become an orange garden. It was still 'graced with . . . two long galleries or walks adjoining to the east end of the said manor or mansion house'. In the middle part were still four knots 'fitted for the growth of choice flowers, bordered with box in the points, angles, squares, and roundlets, and handsomely turfed in the . . . little walks thereof'. At their centre was a marble fountain, standing on a pavement of small pebble stones. From the house to the fountain ran a walk 6 feet wide, of Flanders brick. The other three walks between the knots were of pebble stones, and

* They are in the library of the Royal Institute of British Architects.
† 'Platform' is here used in its old literal sense, 'in a flat form'.
‡ Reproduced in Sir J. Summerson's *Architecture in Britain*.

the remainder were gravelled. The outer walls on the north and east side were high and of brick; in 1649 the pheasantry lay without. Pales divided it from the rest of the garden proper. Though, perhaps, the detail—such as the shape of the surround to the fountain—had been modified, the general plan seems to be still that of Smythson. The garden house, presumably in the recess of the north wall, was used to winter the orange, lemon, pomegranate, and pomecitron trees that were grown in boxes.

The Great or Upper Garden lay along the south front of the house, and extended to the ten-foot-high wall of the vineyard. It was on two levels, that against the house, the lower level, being the same as that of the 'lowest rooms'. This part extended to the row of limes right across the garden which marked the higher level, which was reached by climbing ten steps. The lower level was still set out with grass plots, fountain courts, knots, plantations of fruit, and alleyways. These compartments were divided by hedges of box, hawthorn, or, in a few instances, rosemary; one fountain court was 'shadowed' by cherry trees. One pattern of knots was partly enclosed by 'very handsome' wooden rails, with spiked posts, varnished white. Other divisions were marked by stone balusters.

Against and covering most of the south side of the house grew three 'great and fair fig trees', with branches 'spreading and dilating . . . in a very large proportion, but yet in a most decent manner'. These would surely have been planted in Jacobean times.

The higher level, stretching right across the garden, took the form of a terrace marked by the row of Smythson's lime trees planted for 'shade and sweetness'. They now seemed to please the Commissioners greatly. 'Of a very high growth' in 'a uniform and regular manner', their height made them 'perspicuous to the country round about'.

The high-level garden behind this terraced alley had, however, been lately altered—a maze and wilderness had superseded the orchard. Beyond them, the vineyard remained; it was entered through a 'fair and large pair of railed gates . . . of good ornament'.

The paths were nearly all gravelled, though some were turfed, others paved, and, as we have seen, Flanders brick was also used.

It is difficult to place on Smythson's plan the numerous 'shadow or summer houses', the birdcage enclosing a fountain, or the wooden banqueting house at the east end of the long terrace.

Within the Great Garden there were 131 lime trees and sixty-eight elms. One hundred and nineteen cherry trees, which are recorded as now being of great size, give us an idea of the lavish scale of Jacobean planting. Some at least of the abundance of fruit trees—apples, plums, pears, apricots, and other sorts 'most rare and choice'—would also be known to Smythson.

There is one point upon which it is interesting to remark. Nowhere is there any reference to yews—as hedges or otherwise.

In the case of Wimbledon we have for the first time as nearly complete information as is possible of a Jacobean garden in the grand manner. With the help of other contemporary sources such as Gerard to provide us with the names of the plants likely to have been grown, we are in a position to reconstruct a garden of the past. In our mind's eye we can delight in its layout of small gardens linked one to another, the well-planned and simple use of levels, the galleried garden against one end of the house, the use of the walls for figs and other fruit, and the long lime-lined terrace overlooking all and helping to bind the units into a whole. It is a fine design, uniting architecture and gardening. Something of the architecture can still be seen, for example, at Burton Agnes Hall (Plate III).

We can also learn a good deal about other gardens of this period, when country-house visiting came into its own. A great week-ender and correspondent was John Chamberlain (1554–1628). His letters, though much concerned with the alarums, politics, and sudden deaths of his time, also contain many references to the general delight in gardening.[42]

We have from him a good description of the garden being made by Sir Henry Fanshawe (c. 1569–1616) at Ware Park in Hertfordshire; Chamberlain often stayed there. A letter he wrote on an early visit, dated 22nd April 1606, has an oddly present-day ring, with its expression of pleasure in breaking away from urban complexities. 'I heard the cuckoo presently upon my coming, but I could have no news of the nightingale almost a week after.'

Again, on 15th October of the same year, he might almost be describing a visit to the home of any present-day commuter:

Here is a new kennel of hounds setting up, and store of hawks more than partridges, and such a quoile* about gardening, that a man cannot be idle though he do but look on, nor greatly well occupied it goes slowly forward, yet here have been every day since my coming above forty men at work, for the new garden is wholly translated, new levelled, and in a manner transplanted, because most of the first trees were dead with being set too deep, and in the midst of it, instead of a knot, he [Sir Henry Fanshawe] is making a fort, in perfect proportion, with his ramparts, bulwarks, counterscarps, and all other appurtenances, so that when it is finished, it is like to prove an invincible piece of work.

What a precedent for Uncle Toby, and our contemporary builders of scale-model villages!

From his autumn visit in 1607 he took away a basket of rare plants to bestow on Sir Michael Dormer of Ascott,† and in April 1609 he wrote: 'I never knew this place sweeter . . . we have now four or five flowers from Sir Rafe Winwood that cost twelve pounds.'

In August 1613 changes were taking place. Chamberlain wrote that he was

at Ware Park, where I am as it were planted for this vacation, and where we are busied about new works, and bringing of waters into the gardens, which have succeeded so well that we have a fine fountain with a pool in the lower garden where the fort was, and a running stream (from the river) in the upper garden, between the knots and ranks of trees in the broad walk or alley, wherein we hope to have plenty of trouts fed by hand: the works with industry and cost are brought almost to perfection, and when they are well and come to the highest, I would there might be an end, for else there is no end of new inventions, for hither came yesterday Signor Fabritio . . . and as he is ignorant in nothing, so he takes upon him many new devices, and would fain be a director where there is no need of his help.

'Signor Fabritio' was Sir Henry Wotton (1568–1639), to whose new devices and ignorance in nothing (Chamberlain was peevish about him, mainly for political reasons) we shall return shortly. It was he, however, who gives us the best picture of Fanshawe and his skill as a gardener.[43] 'But though countries have more benefit of sun than we,' wrote this travelled and learned man, 'and thereby more properly tied to contemplate this delight, yet I have seen in our own, a delicate and diligent curiosity, surely without parallel among foreign nations; namely, in the garden of Sir Henry Fanshawe, at his seat in Ware Park, where I well remember, he did so precisely examine the tinctures and seasons of his flowers, that, in their setting, the inwardest of those which were to come up at the same time should always be a little darker than the outmost, and to sow them for a kind of gentle shadow, like a piece not of nature, but of art.' Here, indeed, was a subtle precedent for the planning of colour in our borders.

Chamberlain's last note on the garden at Ware was in September 1615: 'We have had a long, dry summer, and the best and fairest melons and grapes that I ever knew in England.' This was Sir Henry's last season, and fortunately a fruitful one, for shortly afterwards he died.

A view of a country seat in 1619 is given in a letter written by James Howell.[44] It is of Lord Savage's house at Long Melford, where he was staying.

. . . the park, which, for a cheerful rising ground, for groves, and browsings for the deer, for rivulets of water, may compare with any for its highness in the whole land: it is opposite to the front of the great House, whence from the gallery, one may see much of the game which they are a-hunting. Now for the gardening and costly choice flowers, for ponds, for stately large walks, green and gravelly, for orchards and choice fruits of all sorts, there are few the like in England: here you have your Bon Christian pear and Bergamot in perfection, your Muscadell grapes in full plenty, that there are some bottles of wine sent each year to the king.

In Chamberlain's letters we see 'Fabritio' as a talkative man boring the friends he visits with his news of what is thought and done on the Continent, and proffering advice on how we should do it here. That is not the impression we gain of Wotton from those who have studied his life and works.[45]

After a brilliant career at Winchester and Oxford, he went abroad to complete his education, living in France, Germany, and Spain for several years. Here he met the most learned and brilliant men of the day; he corresponded and was friendly with, for example, Clusius. Returning, he obtained political employment, but was forced to retire to Florence. Later he entered the diplomatic service, being concerned with Venice and the German states, but his frankness and wit did not appeal to James I. In 1624 he became one of Eton's most celebrated provosts.

Moving about from country to country, knowing most people of consequence in the world of wit and learning, he must have been a most important vehicle in the transmission of continental thought to England. As provost of Eton he must surely have had a formative influence of a highly cosmopolitan kind. As Cowley put it in his epitaph, he

> . . . had so many languages in store
> That only Fame shall speak of him in more.

That he brought this influence—this continual stream of European thought and practice—to bear on gardening Chamberlain has indicated. Further, one of his closest friends was Lord Zouche.* He sent seeds and plants to James I. He sent 'the sweet Cardus Fenel' ('finocchio'—*Foeniculum dulce*) to John Tradescant 'with likewise a large direction with it how to dress it'. The ideas that Wotton must have propagated as he travelled from house to house, or propounded to the parents of Etonians, are therefore of interest. Fortunately, he recorded[46] at least some of those that interest us:

Now there are ornaments also without, as gardens, fountains, groves, conservatories of rare beasts, birds and fishes. Of which ignoble kind of creatures we ought not (saith our greatest master [Aristotle] among the sons of nature) childishly to despise the contemplation; for in all things naturall, there is ever something that is admirable. . . .

First, I must note a certain contrariety between building and gardening. For as fabrics should be regular, so gardens should be irregular, or at least cast into a very wild regularity. . . . I have seen a garden (for the manner perchance incomparable) into which the first access was a high walk like a terrace, from whence might be taken a general view of the whole plot below; but rather in a delightful confusion, than any plain distinction of the pieces. From this the beholder descending many steps, was afterwards conveyed again by several mountings and vailings, to various entertainments of his scent and sight, which I shall not need to describe (for that were poetical) let me only note this, that every one of these diversities was as if he had been magically transported into a new garden.

* It has been suggested that Wotton was concerned in the design of Bramshill.

Wotton goes on to discuss fountains. They may be plain water-works, or ornate as in Michelangelo's figure of a 'sturdy woman' who wrings water out of her washing; this implies an important rule 'that all designs of this kind should be proper' —that is, one presumes, that the water should only emerge where it would naturally do so in the form that the statue takes!

He commended another kind of fountain in the form of 'a long, straight mossy walk of competent breadth, green and soft under foot' with a breast-high aqueduct on either side, down which ran a 'pretty, trickling stream' over hidden jets which 'did sprout' water 'overchangeably from side to side in the form of arches'. They were 'staggered', so that they did not meet, and he walked under a hemisphere of water 'without any drop falling on him'.

'Groves and artificial devices made under ground,' Wotton considered, were 'of great expense and little dignity.' Why not, he suggests, spend the money instead on observatories in the manner of Ticho Brahe? He delights in the Italian aviaries, covering 'great scope of ground', with bushes, trees, running waters, and sometimes a heated room attached.

From Wotton's Jacobean elysium we may turn to two brothers equally influenced by continental ideas, who achieved works rather than words. They were Henry, Lord Danvers, Earl of Danby (1573–1644), and Sir John Danvers (c. 1588–1655). Henry began life in the brilliant circle in which Sir Philip Sidney moved; he was his page. A misadventure which resulted in the death of a neighbour caused him to leave England for a while. Later, 'being minded to become a benefactor to the University of Oxford, determined to begin and finish a place whereby learning, especially the faculty of medicine, might be improved', he became the moving spirit in and largely financed the establishment of the Oxford Physic Garden.[47] This was the first botanical garden in Britain; it was opened in 1621.

The first European botanical garden as we now understand the term had been laid out at Padua in 1545. Those at Pisa, Leyden, Montpelier, Breslau, and Heidelberg had all been formed during the same century. As is usual in Britain, it required the energy of an individual to bring into being, very belatedly, an institution of national importance. Danvers, though primarily concerned with what was then the equivalent of our modern scientific interest in plants, did not divorce this from his sense of the aesthetic; the entrance gates which he commissioned (not finished till 1633) still stand to bear witness to this. And it is significant that they are the work of Nicholas Stone (1586–1647), the mason associated with Inigo Jones, who worked in the new classical manner devoid of Jacobean trimmings. In Oxford's Physic Garden, therefore, were combined a forward-looking view both of plant study and architecture; once again, both turned to Italy for their inspiration.

Sir John Danvers, who in 1622–23 built Chelsea House in a 'very modern'[48] style, is an even more definite link between the Jacobean world and the new spirit inspired by Inigo Jones. 'The garden at Chelsea,' wrote Aubrey,[49] remained a 'monument of his ingenuity. He was a great acquaintance and favourite of the Lord Chancellor Bacon, who took much delight in that elegant garden.' Yet he lived on to be one of the regicides.

Aubrey was, in his younger days, a 'relation and faithful friend' of Danvers. He describes how 'as you sit at dinner . . . you are entertained with two delightful vistas, one southward over the Thames into Surrey, the other into that curious garden . . .' in which Bacon had walked as it was being formed; now it had matured.

The garden* was not large; and was rectangular. In the centre was a large oval, surrounded by beds. 'At the four corners of the garden, about the oval, are four low pavilions of brick . . . fir and pine trees, shumacs, and the quarters all filled with some rare plant or other. The long gravel walks surrounding it were bordered with hyssop and several sorts of thyme. There were boscages of lilac and philadelphus.' Figures of the gardener and his wife, 'both accoutred to their callings', in coloured freestone, must have surprised the visitor. These, like the Physic Garden gates, were the work of Nicholas Stone, who also carved a sun-dial; for each he charged £7.

Danvers's other garden was at Lavington in Wiltshire. This also was known to Aubrey.[50] It was, he relates,

Sir John Danvers, of Chelsea, who first taught us the way of Italian gardens. He had well travelled France and Italy, and made good observations . . . he had a very fine fancy, which lay chiefly for gardens

---

* A good idea can be had of it from Kip's view of Chelsea, 1699.

and architecture. . . . The garden at Lavington is full of irregularities, both natural and artificial, that is to say, of elevations and depressions. Through the length of it there runs a fine clear trout stream; walled in with brick on each side, to hinder the earth from mouldering down. In this stream are placed several statues. At the west end is an admirable place for a grotto, where the great arch is. . . . Among several others, there is a very pleasant elevation on the south side of the garden, which steals, arising almost insensibly, that is, before one is aware, and gives you a view over the spacious corn-fields there, and so to East Lavington: where, being landed on a fine level, letteth you descend again with the like easiness: each side is flanked with laurels. It is almost impossible to describe this garden, it is so full of variety and unevenness; nay, it would be a difficult matter for a good artist to make a draft of it.

Aubrey considered that Danvers's two gardens were the first to be designed in the Italian mode; we may leave Sir John in his Chelsea garden, where 'he was wont on fine mornings in the summer to brush his beaver hat on the hyssop and thyme, which did perfume it with its natural essence and would last a morning or longer'.

One may perhaps summarize the trend of gardening in the grand manner during the Jacobean age as a move towards simplicity. The fantastic and numerous beasts and columns of Tudor days begin to disappear, fountains and summerhouses of better design remain a delight, and irregularity of ground and levels is used to advantage to give gentle views over the countryside, or back to the house across the garden. The thought given to true design (as apart from ostentation) has increased; the classical inspiration from Italy is beginning to become purer and is losing its incongruous Elizabethan and early Jacobean admixtures.

For the first time, too, there is an intimation by the travelled Wotton that at Ware Park we are beginning to excel our masters.

．　　　．　　　．　　　．　　　．

In the meantime the smaller manor houses and larger farmsteads were multiplying. Even in 1577 William Harrison had remarked that within living memory the number of chimneys to each village had increased.

Here we have a new public, wanting something more fashionable than old Tusser's doggerel. The need was met by William

Lawson's *A New Orchard and Garden*, which appeared with *The Country Housewife's Garden*, by the same hand, in 1618. Today there is no difficulty in recognizing this as a sound work by a practical man; his public took the same view, and the books, usually bound together, went through many editions, the last one appearing as late as 1683.

Lawson was proud in writing of the ways 'I have found good by 48 years (and more) experience in the North part of England'. He writes of his 'mere and sole experience'. Though admiring Pliny, Aristotle, Virgil, and the ancients he leaves 'them to their times, manner and several countries'. His whole attitude shows the new spirit, which, owing to the widespread interest in gardening, was applied to plants before other subjects: 'we must count that art the surest, that stands upon experimental rules gathered by the rule of reason (not conceit), of all other rules the surest'. Again, 'we are gardeners, not physicians'. And, as an indication of the class for which he writes: 'If you be not able, nor willing to hire a gardener, keep your profits to yourself, but then you must take all the pains.'

The orchard is still the man's concern, to the housewife belongs the responsibility for the flower and kitchen gardens. 'Not that we mean to perfect a distinction that . . . the garden for flowers should or can be without herbs for the kitchen, or the kitchen garden should be without flowers.' The division is so that garden flowers may not suffer disgrace if mingled with onions and parsnips, and, rather more practical, that those plants which must be daily dug-up for use should be kept to their own, so that 'deformity' of flower-beds is avoided. Artichokes, the globe kind (*Cynara scolymus*), were, because of the permanence of the roots, granted a 'whole plot by themselves'.* Cabbages, turnips, onions, parsnips, carrots, saffron, and skirrets also require plots on their own.

Lawson's instructions and plan for laying out a garden are not very helpful; his idea seems to be an orchard of fruit trees into which garden features such as knots, conduits, and mounts are introduced at each corner. If you are lucky enough to have a river 'with silver streams, you might sit in your mount, and angle

---

* The importance of this vegetable in early times is, to us, surprising: *The Survey of Wimbledon* records a separate 'hartichoak garden'—covering four perches (about 120 square yards) of ground.

a peckled trout, sleighty eel, or some other dainty fish'. A maze,*
a bowling alley, or (more manly and healthful) a pair of archery
butts to stretch your arms, were desirable.

A whole chapter is devoted to problems of fencing. This did,
indeed, present difficulties in an England still with much waste-
and woodland. Lawson puts his enemies in this order: goats,
sheep, hares, rabbits, cattle, and horses. (The evil neighbour is
treated separately.)

He considers that where the ground is level thorn hedges
combined with ditches or moats are best; the moat may be ex-

FIG. 2. Gardeners working in an orchard from Lawson's
A New Orchard and Garden, 1617

tended into a fish-pond ('it will afford you fish, fence and moisture to
your trees . . . and pleasure also . . . you may have swans and other
waterbirds, good for devouring of vermin, and a boat for many
good uses'.). Even today—in East Anglia, or Shakespeare's Arden,
for instance—remains of this hedge-and-moat protection are seen.

Where the ground is not level a double ditch is to be dug, the
earth thrown up in the centre and levelled to make a wide path,
whose outer bank is planted with evergreens.

Lawson also gives a good engraving of gardeners and their
tools (Fig. 2).

* To be made of fruiting shrubs and trees, 'well framed to a man's height' so as to
make 'your friend wander in gathering of berries till he cannot recover himself without
your help'.

PARKINSON AND THE *PARADISI*

In 1629 was published *Paradisi in Sole Paradisus Terrestris*. This we can amplify by its subtitle:

A choice garden of all sorts of rarest flowers, with their nature, place of birth, time of flowering, names and virtues to each plant, useful for physic or admired for beauty. To which is annexed a kitchen-garden furnished with all manner of herbs, roots, and fruits, for meat or sauce used with us. With the art of planting an orchard of all sorts of fruit bearing trees and shrubs, showing the nature of grafting, innoculating, and pruning them. Together with the right ordering, planting, and preserving of them with their select virtues : all unmentioned in former herbals. Collected by John Parkinson, Apothecary of London, and the King's Herbarist.

This book describes about one thousand plants then cultivated in Britain, nearly eight hundred of them being illustrated. The figures come from several sources and are mostly adequate and reasonably accurate, if not distinguished. The work was dedicated to the queen, Henrietta Maria.

The incredibilities of Gerard (such as the barnacle goose plant, which he claimed to have seen with his own eyes) have disappeared. Many references are made, and acknowledged, to other authors. Parkinson was a most accurate observer, with an apt turn for description. E. A. Bowles cites his straight-forward account of the two varieties of the 'Cloth of Gold' crocus, one with 'three fair and great stripes of a fair deep purple colour' on the back of 'every of three outer leaves', the other differing only in having these outer segments 'wholly of the same deep purple colour on the back of them, saving that the edges of them are yellow, which is the form of a Duke tulip, and from thence it took the name of Duke crocus'.

Or there are his precise observations on the little *Gentiana verna*: 'the roots are small, long, pale yellow strings, which shoot forth here and there divers heads of leaves, and thereby increase reasonably well, if it find a fit place and ground to grow, or else will not be nursed up, with all the care and diligence that can be used'. How many alpine enthusiasts today will endorse that!

Parkinson is far more aware of the decorative value of plants than earlier writers were. Lawson, for example, almost excuses the presence of the hollyhock in the garden with: 'The chief use, I

78

know, is ornament.' In Parkinson, on the other hand: 'The Crown Imperial for his stately beautifulness, deserveth the first place in this our garden of delight, to be entreated of before all other lilies.' Delight has replaced mere utility.

The ancient legends have largely disappeared: 'A lecture of much morality might be read upon the rose, the parts delivered by many authors, both Greek and Latin, all of which to insert in this place is not my mind.'

   .   .   .   .   .

The names of a whole circle of 'curious* gardeners' of the late sixteenth and early seventeenth centuries appears in the works of Gerard and Parkinson. Probably the most important was Tradescant the elder—in the words of Parkinson a 'painful industrious searcher and lover of all nature's varieties'—who has already been mentioned in connection with Hatfield.

John Tradescant first appears[51] in 1607, when he was married at Meopham, Kent. An East Anglian by birth, by that time he had been brought, like so many of the outstanding characters in this period, within the powerful Cecil orbit. He was then working for Burleigh's son, Robert, Earl of Salisbury, at Shorne. Soon after he was, as we have seen, travelling on behalf of his patron. After Salisbury's death in 1612 he worked for Lord Wotton at Canterbury. He became interested financially in the Virginian trade, and through this connection received North American plants, such as the spiderwort, which was later to be named *Tradescantia virginiana* by Linnaeus. In 1618 he was attached as a naturalist to a mission to Russia led by his neighbour Sir Dudley Digges—which only Tradescant could consider successful, for he returned with a load of plants and a notebook which was virtually the first flora of Russia. Two years later he was making dangerous landings on the Algerian coast as a gentleman adventurer professedly to worry pirates, but bringing back among other plants the once famous Algerian apricot, and reporting to Parkinson that the 'corn flag of Constantinople' (*Gladiolus byzantinus*) grew by the acre in Barbary.

In 1625 we find him as gardener to the Duke of Buckingham

* Used here in its old senses of ingenious, studious, taking the interest of a connoisseur.

—responsible for letters addressed to the Secretary of the Admiralty signed by the then all-powerful king's favourite urging that the commanders of His Majesty's ships should return with additions to his master's collections. In 1627 he sailed with Buckingham's fleet to Rochelle. From that unfortunate expedition he seems to have returned with the reputation of having been a successful engineer rather than a plant-collector.

A year after Buckingham's murder, in 1629, he settled down as gardener to Charles I and to form a collection of plants and curiosities in his own house and garden at Lambeth, known as the Ark.

Tradescant was the first of a long line of professional plant-collectors; we know the names of many of his introductions from the writings of his contemporaries and his list[52] of the trees, shrubs, and plants he grew in 1634; it is probable that he brought other novelties in his early days when working for Lord Salisbury.

He is known to have obtained plants from René Morin and and Jean Robin of Paris, through Sir Peter Wyche from Constantinople, and from various sources in Holland. His Lambeth garden was described in 1634 by Peter Mundy of the East India Company as 'a little garden with divers outlandish herbs and flowers, whereof some that I had not seen elsewhere but in India'.

In his later years he seems to have specialized in fruit; according to Parkinson he was famous for the varieties of plum that he collected; his list names fifty-seven kinds. In addition, his garden list names forty-nine apples, forty-nine pears, two quinces, twenty-four cherries, eight apricots, nine nectarines, and ten vines. This amply confirms Parkinson's statement that Tradescant had 'wonderfully laboured to obtain all the rarest fruit he can hear of in any place in Christendom, Turkey, yea or the whole world'.

If Tradescant was the prototype of those daring plant-collectors who worked in the nineteenth century, William Coys of Stubbers was an outstanding example of a type that has an ancient lineage, the country gentleman gardener-botanist.

His garden at North Okington was known to Gerard. In 1604 it was his skill that induced the yucca known as Adam's needle (*Yucca gloriosa*) to flower for the first time in England, though the plant had been brought here from the North American coast many years before. His garden lists of 1616 and 1617 show that apparently he had connections with America, for he was growing many plants from that continent, notably the 'choke cherry' (*Prunus virginiana*) and persimmon (*Diospyros virginiana*). He also had the sweet potato and the common potato, both then believed to be natives of Virginia. Through a certain William Boel, Coys had also a fine collection of Spanish plants; it is said that one of them, the ivy-leaved toadflax (*Cymbalaria muralis*), began its wanderings over Britain from his garden.[53]

It was from Coys that John Goodyer (1592–1664), one of our most distinguished early botanists, particularly associated with Hampshire and Oxford University, received many new plants. Goodyer himself was responsible for distributing the Jerusalem artichoke (*Helianthus tuberosus*), also a North American plant, to British gardens. In 1617 he received two small tubers from de Franqueville* one of which soon brought him a 'peck of roots' which he gave away.

Indeed, during the years between the publication of Gerard's *Herbal* and that of Parkinson's *Paradisi* we have references to many gardeners; though they remain little other than names. Among those of whom more[54] is known (in several cases their plant lists have been reprinted) one may choose a few at random. In London were Ralph Tuggy, of Westminster, 'famous for clove gilliflowers, pinks and the like'; John Millen, of Old Street, with 'the choicest fruits the Kingdom yields'; Hugh Morgan, with a garden near Coleman Street, and one Grey, apothecary, of London Wall, both of whom grew the nettle tree (*Celtis australis*) from southern Europe; and Henry Banbury of Tothill Street, Westminster, 'a famous grafter'.

In Wales was the famous garden of Sir John Salusbury (1567–1612) at Lleweni, near Denbigh. In his copy of Gerard's *Herbal* are recorded his botanical findings. He also left garden lists compiled in the years 1596, 1607, and 1608. He was a poet, as was his friend Robert Chester, who wrote for him *A Winter Garland of Summer Flowers Made in Manner of a New Year's Gift* (1598). Unfortunately, in spite of its title, the poem is of little interest to the gardener.

At Methley, in Yorkshire, Richard Shanne was planting

* There were two John de Franquevilles, father and son, who cannot be distinguished. They were London merchants trading with France and the eastern Mediterranean.

woods and orchards in 1577, and in 1615 he produced a long list of his garden plants.

There do not appear to be any comparable garden lists for Scotland. Much of that country remained outlandish, though near the big towns some fine houses were now being built. During this period the gardens of these seem to have been primarily architectural appendages, with the inclusion of banqueting houses and arbours.[55] References to garden expenses in the accounts of the Royal palaces are few and far between.[56]

Enough has now been said to demonstrate the great increase in the practice and study of gardening of all kinds that took place in the later years of the Tudors and the reign of the early Stuarts. We must return and summarize the career of the man who in our eyes outstandingly represents that period.

Parkinson was born in 1567. Early in the next century he was in London, an apothecary with a garden at Long Acre, stocked with rarities. He was appointed 'Herbarist' to James I, and after the publication of *Paradisi* was granted the title of *Botanicus Regius Primarius* by Charles I.

After de l'Obel's death in 1616 Parkinson acquired his important unpublished records and notes. A great deal of use was made of them in his *Theatrum Botanicum, The Theatre of Plants, or an Universal and Complete Herbal,* which was published in 1640. This describes nearly 3,800 plants, and is a most important and interesting work, but only indirectly concerned with gardening.

Like many who had seen the great Elizabethan–Jacobean period, Parkinson lived on to achieve success in the reign of Charles I. He died in 1650 and was buried at St. Martin-in-the-Fields. His account of his 'park in the sun' was the first great British gardening book, and we will therefore choose 1629, the year of its publication, to mark the end of one period in our history.

THREE

From the Knot to the Parterre
1630–1659

CAVALIERS AND ROUNDHEADS

Our elementary history tells us that in the year Parkinson published his *Paradisi* 'Parliament became defiant'. The period of Cavaliers and Roundheads had begun. It might seem that the social stress which ensued would interfere with the practice of gardening. But progress continued. It is probably true to say that the most outstanding gardeners and botanists were Royalists. Some retired from the English political scene either to France or Holland, where they became well acquainted with the horticultural and aesthetic developments in those countries. Others retreated to their country houses and consoled themselves in their gardens.

There were also many outstanding horticulturists who carried the label of Roundhead. Also, surprisingly, André Mollet, the French gardener employed by Queen Henrietta Maria at Wimbledon Manor from 1639 continued working here with his brother Gabriel during the Commonwealth;[1] these men were associated with the style generally considered to have come to England at the Restoration; in fact, such Restoration features as the lime avenue appear to have been present much earlier, as at Buxted (Plate IV).

Apart from the two attitudes of mind which affected in varying degrees all those who lived in the period including the reign of Charles I and Commonwealth, there is another interesting problem to consider. Inigo Jones (1572–1652)—he spanned almost the same years as Parkinson—was appointed Surveyor of the King's Works in 1615; he had, of course, already done much work for the court. It is well enough known that his importance lies in that he brought his art direct from Italy, without French trimmings. He was our first truly classical architect. Little enough of his architecture remains, but he was pre-eminent as a designer of court masques, and many of his drawings for these exist and have been published.[2] A number of them represent gardens—the elysiums seen in the mind's eye of those attending these remarkable displays, which were full of symbolism that we can scarcely comprehend today,[3] as well as mechanical devices of extreme ingenuity.

Such scenes as those showing 'the place where the souls of the ancient poets are feigned to rest' or the Indian landscape from Sir William Davenant's *Temple of Love* (1635) could not have failed to impress a garden designer. The 'lover's cabinet', an almost pagoda-like little building on a tree-covered mount, from *The Shepherd's Paradise* (1633), must have been equally inspiring to one wishing to build a new 'shade-house'.

'Spring', from *Florimene* (1635), is another garden scene. A substantial temple-like building lies at the end of an alleyway; rectangular beds enclosed within low hedges are to the front. There is also a study of a garden with a pavilion, a design of extreme simplicity, contrasting strongly with Jacobean elaboration. And must not Jones's scenes with tree-lined glades have increased the fashion for *vistas*?

Was it this Italian influence that stimulated the English passion for evergreens? A few words in Bacon and Parkinson comment on the delight of unseasonable green in winter, but the successful planting of greens on any scale does not seem to have begun until the time of Charles I. This desire for greenery was well shown on the visit in 1638 of Maria de Medici, when on a Sunday afternoon the queen strolled round the beautiful gardens of Sir John Lucas at Colchester, where the leafless walks had been prettily decorated with cut evergreens as a compliment to royalty.[4]

It was at this period that the Mediterranean cypress (*Cupressus sempervirens*) was first popularized, though it had been grown here for many years—William Turner had remarked upon it in 1548.

The influence of Inigo Jones was felt principally in the court circle. Outside it, as a number of houses still standing demonstrate, a gabled style, having affinities with the Netherlands, predominated, and there can be little doubt that the Dutch influence still largely prevailed in the gardens that surrounded them. The contemporary admiration for this type of garden is well shown by the account Sir William Brereton wrote of his journey to Holland in the summer of 1634.[5]

Visiting the garden of the Prince of Orange at The Hague, he declared it to be 'the fairest and most spacious platt that I ever saw . . . [with] the vastest walks'. The garden was rectangular, with covered walks enclosing it. In the centre was a moat, about 16 or 20 yards wide, enclosing a round island. This island was bordered with another covered walk, which surrounded a kitchen garden. At its centre was a 'poor young cypress tree'.

Brereton also visited the prince's new house with its 'mighty spacious garden plots, between one and two acres'. Between the highway and the courtyard lay a space of about 4 acres planted with sycamore trees so that 'which ever way you look they stand in order and rank'. This type of planting was to arrive in England in due course.

Elsewhere he saw and made notes on ripe oranges and lemons, an aviary of 'all manner of dainty fowl', and a remarkable garden in the shape of a square with high, trimmed hedges forming a maze. These hedges were trained on to wooden supports, and were composed of yew, box, elm, privet, juniper, thorns, dogwood, pears, apples, arbor-vitae, tamarisk, and barberry. This is reminiscent of the maze described by Lawson.

He visited the Physic Garden at Leyden, which he calls 'memorable' though 'not above half a statute acre'. Here he attended a lecture by Adolphus Vorstius. It was given in the garden. Vorstius took one bed, 4 yards by 1 yard, and, pointing with his staff, discussed each plant in turn; among those he described were lupins, hyssop, hemlock, and the mastic tree, 'though it is but like a bush'.

He also mentions that he bought some tulips from the gardener to the Prince of Orange, paying 5 guilders for 100 of the best.

As this is what Brereton tells of the country whose gardens and plants were then influencing us, it is therefore apposite to add that he found 'the ladies and gentlemen all Frenchified in French fashion'.

From his travels in the British Isles during the following year, we are again made aware of the increase in building. He describes some gardens, such as that of Sir Arthur Ingram near York Minster. It was 'a brave garden, not a third part furnished with flowers, but with little grass beds on which stood statues'. The whole was walled-in by spacious, high walls without fruit trees trained on them—which surprised him. It is interesting to note that the gardener was paid an over-all sum to keep the gardens, the orchards, the fish-ponds, and the pheasantry, Sir Arthur himself 'to be at no extra charge'. A skilled and business-like gardener could, no doubt, in such circumstances make a good living.

The mention of a pheasantry is interesting, and Brereton goes into some detail concerning the raising and management of pheasants. At this period there are several references to pheasantries, sometimes called pheasant gardens, which seem to show that they were then considered an adjunct to the garden and were under the management of the gardener.

Brereton travelled also in Ireland, but tells us little about horticulture except that in the bishop's garden, on a bare bank, was written 'in fair great letters':

O man, remember the last great day.

In Scotland, he has much to record of the rough, hard times. But from Dunbar to Edinburgh he passed very many seats of the nobles; he gives us no information about the gardens, beyond the fact that at Seaton House, though near the sea, Earl Wintour had good apple and other fruit trees, walnuts, and sycamores.

It was in 1635, too, that Lieutenant Hammond set out from Norwich to make a survey of the western counties of England.[6] Once more we have descriptions of a countryside in which fine houses abounded, as in Northamptonshire, where he passed by 'many pleasant, delicate rich situations of lords, knights, ladies and gentlemen, rendering the time not irksome to weary travellers in having such pleasing objects ever in view to beguile the same'.

Hammond gives us a contemporary picture of the then famous water-works and garden of Thomas Bushell (1594–1674) at Enstone.[7] This remarkable place stood close to the bridge where the Oxford–Birmingham road now crosses the River Glyme by Neat Enstone. He writes of the:

. . . strange and admirable rock . . . a place of itself to take up a volume, for the naturalness thereof, and the art and industry that the ingenious owner hath added thereto, makes the same unparalleled. On the side of a hill is a rock of some 11 or 12 feet, from the bottom whereof (by turning of a cock) riseth and spouts up about 9 feet high a stream which raiseth on his top a silver ball, and as the said stream riseth or falleth to any pitch or distance, so doth the ball, with playing, tossing, and keeping continually at the top of the said ascending stream: the which after it gains the top, descends not again into that current, but runs into the rock and there disperseth itself.

Elsewhere in this garden 'there is a hedge of water made streaming up, about a man's height, crossing like a plashed fence, whereby sometimes fair ladies cannot make the crossing, flashing and dashing their smooth, soft and tender thighs and knees, by a sudden enclosing of them in it'. These water-squirting jokes had long been a feature of continental gardens; in 1580 Montaigne had described how, at Augsburg, in the magnificent gardens of the Fuggers, the ladies were invited to look over a bridge at the collection of fish, when fine jets of water were unexpectedly sprayed, and 'incontinently the petticoats and legs of the fair spectators are invaded with a refreshing coolness from these tiny water-spouts'.

Above Bushell's rock was a building, 'on one side graced and set out with three neat, curious walks, 30 paces descending and ascending again, one above the other on the brow of the hill, the midst of them paved with freestone, and every descent from each to the other six freestone stairs: between every of the said walks (flanking on both sides of you) as you march to and from this fair rock and building, are pleasant fruitful plum trees, and other fruit trees. On the other side, are pleasant delightful gardens of flowers'.

Having ascended these walks to the building, one entered to find a 'fair chamber' from the roof of which descended artificial showers, under which a man might stand in the sunshine, surrounded by rainbows. Below the hill, near to the house, were 'curious pools and rare waters'.

Hammond considered the whole 'a most pleasant, sweet and delightsome place', yet 'a mad gimcrack, sure, yet hereditary to these hermitical and projectical undertakers'.

The significance of this garden is that it aroused royal interest. Charles I paid a surprise visit not long after Hammond. Then, on 23rd August 1636, he arrived in state. Bushell, disguised as a hermit, gave him a poetical welcome. By royal command the place was named after Queen Henrietta. As a memento of the occasion Bushell received from her 'an entire mummy from Egypt, a great rarity'.

Thomas Bushell was a versatile man; he speculated in minerals and soap and had a fondness for solitude and islands. At Enstone 'he did not encumber himself with his wife', and in fine weather would spend the nights walking round the garden with his servants, Jack Sydenham and Mr. Batty, 'who sang rarely'.[8]

Of the botanically minded gardeners of this period, probably the most important was the younger John Tradescant (1608-1662). At the time of his father's death in 1637 he was collecting in Virginia for their museum at Lambeth, generally known as the Ark, and its attached Physic Garden. He returned to take over his father's position as gardener to Queen Henrietta. On Charles I's execution he retired to the Ark, and there carried on his work unmolested.

In 1656 was published *Museum Tradescantianum*, a catalogue of the collection of oddities in the Ark, and the plants in the garden. That some of these came from so far afield as New England, Virginia, Barbados, Constantinople, Persia, North Africa, and China indicates the energy and skill of the Tradescants and their circle. At the time of the Restoration, John Tradescant, though once a royal gardener, was in trouble with the authorities, but the personal intervention of Charles II solved his difficulties.

On Tradescant's death (his son, a third John, predeceased him, aged nineteen, in 1652) the contents of the Ark went to Elias Ashmole, and thence to Oxford University. The garden soon deteriorated, and by 1749, when Sir William Watson, the physician and scientist, examined the site, only a few trees remained.

At Oxford the eccentric but capable Jacob Bobart[9] the elder (1599-1679) had been appointed head gardener, and his catalogue of 1648, containing about 1,600 different species and varieties, showed both his diligence in obtaining rarities and his skill as a cultivator; he too carried on undisturbed by the war.

The war interrupted John Goodyer's work for a time. He was a Royalist, and was probably at Oxford with the king. The greatest loss to gardening and botany was, however, Thomas Johnson (c. 1600–1644).[10] He was by profession a herbalist, and in April 1633 he exhibited at his shop the first banana seen in this country, which came from Bermuda. His most notable work was a corrected edition of Gerard's *Herbal* (1633), in the preparation of which he made use of the material collected by Goodyer. Johnson, an ardent Royalist and brave soldier, was killed in the defence of Basing Castle in Hampshire.

Another Royalist was Robert Morison (1620–1683),[11] a doctor and botanist, the first of a long series of eminent botanists and gardeners to come to England from Scotland. He served in the army of Charles I, went into exile in France, and returned with Charles II to be appointed, in 1669, the first Professor of Botany at Oxford University.

The reference to Morison must lead us for a moment to Scotland. Did he leave his native country because of the very low standard of medical and botanical—and hence horticultural —knowledge then maintaining? Certainly, as we shall see, Sibbald drew attention to Scotland's deficiencies in these subjects in 1661 on his return from studying abroad. Neither do Scottish garden lists, comparable with those of the Tradescants and their circle, survive from this period. One of the very few contemporary references to gardening is the account of the gardens at Coltness.[12] Here Thomas Stewart, after his marriage in 1654, settled down to enjoy a country life and in a few years to convert a small house, built for defence, into something 'modern' and more suited to the more placid times.

The garden that he formed lay to the south of the house, on a slope falling to the west, and was terraced into three cross levels by means of banks. The level ground fronting the south of the house was a flower garden; that to the east (which was higher) and that to the west (lower) were for cherry and nut gardens.

The bank above the highest level was planted with walnut and chestnut trees, while on the bank to the east of the flower garden was made a strawberry border.

Along the south of these terraces ran a high stone wall. Its sunny side was used 'for ripening and improving finer fruits'; it also formed the northern boundary of an orchard and kitchen garden, 'with broad grass walks'. The remaining three sides were protected by a thorn hedge and dry ditch, enclosing several rows of timber trees planted to form a shelter belt.

To the west of the house was a small enclosed nursery garden, and beyond it was a sparse plantation of trees. These consisted of birches on the side nearest the house, with rows of ash and sycamore along the other three sides, all enclosing a good thicket of pines.*

To the north of the house lay a grass enclosure of 4 acres† with a fish-pond in one corner for 'pikes and perches'. All these parts combined to form a rectangle of 7 or 8 acres, its longer side to the south enclosed with a strong wall and hedgerows of trees, the house being near the centre.

Of gardeners on the Parliamentary side there was Sir John Danvers, who has already been mentioned. Then there was that other regicide, Colonel John Hutchinson (1615-1664), a man of great culture who 'took great delight in perspective glasses, and for his other rarities was not so much afflicted with the antiquity as the merit of the work—he took much pleasure in improvement of grounds, in planting groves and walks, and fruit trees, in opening springs and making fish-ponds'.[13] His later career was unhappy. He was by nature far more suited to a life of improving his grounds than steering his way through politics and died a miserable death in prison. His house and gardens at Awthorpe long ago disappeared, but we have a brief picture of the 'small remains of gardens and old labyrinthine shrubbery' at the beginning of last century, in the poems of Mary Howitt.[14] There,

> . . . lithe and tall, the Rose of May‡
> Shoots upward through the ruin grey
> With scented flower, and leaf pale green,
> Such rose as it hath ever been;
> Left, like a noble deed to grace
> The memory of an ancient race!

* In Scotland sycamores (*Acer pseudoplatanus*) and Scots pines (*Pinus sylvestris*) were called planes and firs respectively.
† A Scottish acre is just over 6,150 square yards.
‡ This May-rose was probably the 'double cinnamon rose with pale leaves' of Parkinson's *Paradisi* (*R. cinnamonea plena*). It is therefore not impossible that Mrs. Howitt saw the descendants of Hutchinson's planting two centuries before.

The Parliamentarian general, Sir Thomas Fairfax (1611–1671), was, of course, also a man of culture and at Nunappleton House in Yorkshire had a fine garden; it was here that Andrew Marvell (1621–1678) came as tutor to Fairfax's daughter. One verse of the poem that he wrote on Bill-borow in, probably, 1651, after returning from the Continent, shows the horror with which mountains were then regarded. Praising the views and situation of the house and garden, he compares the gentle surrounding hills to the disadvantage of

> . . . ye mountains more unjust
> Which to abrupter greatness thrust,
> That do with your hooked-shouldered height,
> The earth deform, and heaven fright,
> For whose excrescence, ill designed,
> Nature must a new centre find. . . .[15]

It is said that the Commander-in-Chief taught the arts both of war and gardening to his fellow Yorkshireman and connection by marriage, John Lambert (1619–1684). This skilful soldier, so devoid of the rancour of many Parliamentarians, was a notable gardener* and amateur botanist;[16] it has been said that he would have been at home at the court of Charles II.

In May 1652 he acquired for £7,000 the house of Wimbledon Manor, whose gardens with their additions made by Queen Henrietta Maria have already been described. When Lambert took them over, one must assume that the unspecified 'roots' planted in the knots, which were so highly priced by the surveyors of 1649, were of exceptional quality, an assumption confirmed by the fact that the queen's gardener was Tradescant the younger. These rarities were no doubt a great attraction to Lambert.

In 1657 he refused to take the oath of allegiance to Cromwell, and retired to Wimbledon and botany; one plant that he grew there introduces us to the first distinguished English flower-painter, Alexander Marshall.† It was the Guernsey lily (*Nerine sarniensis*), and Marshall's painting (the first record of this plant in

---

* His enemies took advantage of this, and in particular his love of tulips. His portrait is shown on one of a pack of satirical playing cards inscribed 'Lambert Kt. of ye Golden Tulip'.

† Very little is known of this artist, whose fine series of paintings of tulips has been reproduced.[17]

England) is inscribed 'This flower was sent me by General Lambert August 29th from Wimbledon.'

After the Restoration it was considered safer to confine the energetic Lambert and his brilliant wife to the island of Guernsey, where he was sent in 1662. In the same year Christopher, first Baron Hatton of Kirby, an antiquary and man of learning, was made governor of the island. The Kirby gardens were never confiscated, and in the latter years of the Commonwealth they had been still further improved and choice plants added.

On Guernsey, Lambert resumed his botanizing and gardening. In the days of his triumphs he had provided Hatton with rare plants that were not then to be found in England. Now, in return, Lambert received rare irises, anemones, tulips, and other plants obtained by the governor and his family from the Continent. Lord Hatton's elder son, another Christopher, often deputized for his father as governor and was also an enthusiastic gardener; the younger son, Charles, was, as we shall see, an eminent amateur of botany and horticulture.

In 1670 Lambert was moved to St. Nicholas (Drake's) Island off Plymouth. There, one March day in 1684, he was working in his garden when visitors arrived. He hurried in to change so 'that he might wait on the company in more decent dress, and catched a cold that brought him to his death'.

At this stage it is apposite to mention, as an outstanding example of the change of attitude that was taking place towards the natural sciences, the publication in 1646 of Sir Thomas Browne's *Pseudodoxia Epidemica*. Browne, undisturbed by the war, went placidly on seeking truth about all subjects. His challenge to the ancients is well known:

> Would truth dispense, we could be content, with Plato, that knowledge were but reminiscental evocation, and new impressions but the colourishing of old stamps which stood pale in the soul before.

Observation of fact began to replace those ancient authorities whose views had for so long been accepted; magnificent names as those of Oribasus, Aetus, Trallianus, Serapion, Evax, and Marcellus disappeared, to be replaced by those of modern men—and the jargon of science.

SOME PRACTICAL MEN

We are able to gain an impression of the more practical aspects of gardening during the Commonwealth from several contemporary sources. There was, for example, Sir Ralph Verney (1613–1696).[18] His home was at Claydon in Buckinghamshire. His long life is said to have been devoted to championing lost causes, but his devotion to his estate and his enthusiasm for planting were certainly not among them.

Between 1644 and 1653 he was in exile, and from France he sent home consignments of many sorts of vegetables and salads, though his uncle, Dr. Denton, did not consider they were superior to the English kinds that he already grew.

In 1653 he returned to England. About this time other Royalist gardeners came home: for example, in this same year John Evelyn was back working on his garden at Sayes Court, Deptford.[19] One can modify the opinion expressed by Aubrey—'in the time of Charles II gardening was much improved and became common'[20]—by adding that the improvement had its origins at about the same time that Cromwell became Lord Protector.*

In the year of his return Sir Ralph was writing to France for '*Philloray vulgaire, Cardon d'Espaigne*—the best and fairest come from Tours', melons, Roman lettuce, lettuce *frize, Chou de Milan*, and *Chou frize*. 'I also desire any sorts of eatable grapes out of the best and choicest gardens; give the gardener what you think fit, a few of them will serve my turn . . . in my old garden there was wont to be good eating grapes of several sorts.'

In the years that follow he was often concerned with the welfare of his purchases from France and Holland. There are references to vines, figs, ornamental trees, Persian tulips and ranunculuses, pinks, gillyflowers, melon seeds, and pear grafts.

In October 1655 he was writing about his cousin Stafford's men, who were searching the hedgerows for elm suckers. And, of the purchase of roots of sweet brier, 'I think you told me they were about half-a-crown or three shillings a thousand, which is cheap enough, and if they are to be had at so easy a rate, I would have 2,000 gathered as soon as you please, and sent in by 500 or 1,000 a week, till the whole 2,000 were gathered. Charm them lest they send ordinary briers, for sweet briers; and let me know if I may

* The presence of the Mollets before the Restoration has already been mentioned.

have woodbines at the same rate'. His gardening activities continued far on with the reign of Charles II.

In neighbouring Bedfordshire, too, the gardens of Woburn began to receive serious attention some two or three years before the Restoration, though the major developments came later.[21]

John Evelyn (1620–1706) is also best considered as a figure of Restoration times, though Sir Thomas Hanmer (1612–1678), his senior and friendly adviser, is more surely placed in the Commonwealth period.

Hanmer was not a professional author, nor did he write, as Evelyn so obviously did, to impress the Fellows of the Royal Society with his wide knowledge; in fact his own *Garden Book*,[22] completed in 1659 (before that august body was formed), was not published until 1933. He makes it clear that he is writing of choice plants that will grow well in our climate, giving directions for their 'preservation and increase', without 'meddling with their medical qualities'. Today we can, of course, check his reliability at many points, with the result that we are impressed by his accuracy and sound practice.

Sir Thomas came from an old family that lived on the Welsh borders.[23] In his younger days he travelled on the Continent; his acquaintances were numerous, including not only Evelyn but Lambert, and later Rose, gardener to Charles II. With the war, in 1646, he retired to his house at Bettisfield in Flintshire, and to gardening.

From his writings we can gain a very clear picture of a gentleman's garden during the years of Cromwell and the early part of Charles II's reign.

Hanmer has no hesitation in remarking that gardening had lately improved, and that this was due solely to the Dutch and French, 'most diligent enquirers and collectors' (as he would himself have learned on his travels).

By 1659 the rich were no longer satisfied with grand houses approached by handsome avenues through parks, but 'their ambition and curiosity extends also to very costly establishments of their gardens, orchards and walks, and some spare no charge . . . in procuring the rarest flowers and plants . . .'. We gather that then, as often, there were many instances of more money than sense and of extravagant plantings coming to nothing owing to their owner's lack of knowledge, the 'gardeners being for the most part inexpert and dull'. The *Garden Book* itself was, perhaps, intended for publication to set things right.

It is clear from what Hanmer tells us that the cosiness, indeed 'nookiness', of earlier gardens was being replaced by spaciousness. The *vista*—limited it is true—was no longer a novelty. The borders are not now hedged about with privet, rosemary, or other such herbs which hide the view and prospect, and 'nourish hurtful worms and insects', nor are fruit trees allowed to grow so that they shadow the plants below them. All that is 'now commonly near the house is laid open and exposed to the sight of the rooms and chambers, and the knots and borders are upheld only with very low coloured boards, or stone, or tile'.*

Beyond the open space by the house, if the garden were large enough, were the *parterres*, 'as the French call them', cut out 'curiously into embroidery of flowers and shapes of arabesques, animals or birds, or *feuillages*'. The alleys between the parterres were filled with coloured gravels, sands, or dusts; the few flowers that were planted within the parterres were low-growing, so that they might not spoil the beauty of the embroidery.

At the next remove from the house were the 'compartments' and borders for flowers, which were sometimes, but not always, set among grass. Standing among these compartments were vases on pedestals. Trimmed evergreens that would endure the winter were placed at regular intervals.

If wealth and the situation of the garden permitted, there might also be labyrinths formed of hedges 5 or 6 feet high, thickets for birds intersected by gravel walks, or alleys of poplars, firs, and pines: in this part might be the fountains, cascades, and statues.

The large gardens were commonly 'a third part larger than broad, and cannot well be less than two or three hundred yards in length'. But, we learn, most gentlemen are content with a garden contained in a rectangle some 60 to 80 yards long.

These gardens taken together are referred to as the 'great garden'; within it the guests amused themselves. Sir Thomas adds that true florists have also a 'little private seminary, to keep

* The plan of the gardens laid out at Kirby Hall some thirty years later was 'determined with complete accuracy' in 1934 owing to the presence of these stone edgings.

such treasures as are not to be exposed to every one's view, and a winter house for the shelter of plants'.

Considerable remains of a garden of the type described by Hanmer can still be seen at Packwood, Warwickshire (Plate IV).

The mixture of herbs and plants and the general lack of distinction between the different parts of the garden so apparent in the writings of Lawson is fast giving way to logical separation.

The plant lists given in the *Garden Book* have descriptive and cultural notes that in many instances could scarcely be bettered today. Hanmer's prime favourite was 'the Queen of bulbous plants, whose flower is beautiful in its figure, and most rich and admirable in colour, and wonderful in variety of markings'—the tulip. He liked also anemones, 'bears ears' (auriculas), gillyflowers, primroses, and cowslips. He gives long lists of the varieties of all of these that he cultivated.

Of general hardy garden plants, however, Hanmer's friend, John Rea, gives fuller details a few years later, and we will deal with them when we reach the Restoration period.

Hanmer gives us some information on the use of the winter-house or -room (called by the French *la serre*). It must be used with judgement, lest it kills more plants than are preserved. Lack of fresh air will do as much harm as 'cold abroad'. The place should therefore be lofty, with large windows and doors on the south side alone; they are to be opened on mild days to let in the 'gentle' air, but closely shut against frosts; in very hard weather they should be covered with mats. On 'violent cold nights' the place might be warmed with a pan of coals, or a stove.

Plants wintered within the house should, in spring, for the first week or fortnight, be exposed out of doors only during the day and taken in at night. Some plants could be wintered safely in pots, plunged to the brim under a south wall, and in very hard weather covered with moss or straw, or with glasses, usually 'shaped like bells', in the less cold seasons.

The making of a hot-bed with dung—just as it is still done—is described, but Hanmer makes no reference to the use of tan-bark.

This reference to the winter-house shows the interest now being taken in tender plants, such as the 'Indian kinds' of 'Narcissi' and 'Pancratia'. At that time India was still a large and ill-defined place, and Narcissus a genus broad in its limits. For instance, under this classification was one of 'these strangers' that Hanmer had from the Barbadoes in 1656, which, being in a pot in 1656, sent up in May a great green stalk about 2 feet high without any leaf, 'on the top whereof came two flowers shaped like lilies, of a fine shining red colour, betwixt an orange and a pink'. He was clearly surprised that the leaves did not appear until September. How wide was the contemporary definition of India is also shown by Hanmer's mention of 'two other Indians', one of which was 'Narcissus japonicus rutiloflore, the Narcissus of Japan'. When one adds Japan to the East and West Indies and the mainland of India itself, one recalls another seventeenth-century authority, who wrote: 'by the name of India . . . we comprehend all that tract between India . . . on the west . . . unto China eastward'!

Many of these 'Indian narcissi' were, of course, members of the family we now know as the *Amaryllidaceae*. The wanderings of these usually bulbous plants on their way to England must have been long and tortuous. The 'narcissus of Japan', for example, is *Nerine sarniensis*, which came not from Japan, nor Guernsey (as its name suggests), but from the Cape of Good Hope.

This romantic vagueness about geography and plants must have made the possession of these exotics immensely exciting to Hanmer and his friends. He describes his method of cultivation of these 'Indians'. The bulbs were put into vessels and housed during winter. Then, in spring, they were potted up in sandy soil with which was mixed well-rotted manure ('consum'd dung') and the pots placed in a hot-bed to 'draw out' the roots. Later, the pots were set against a warm wall, to be covered with 'glasses' in the night. Hanmer's advice not to water these plants when they are dormant is sound. He rightly suggests that the reason why so many of these 'Indians' will only flower the first season after their arrival is not because 'they are so very tender that they cannot endure our winters with care over them' but because the large fleshy perennial roots that many of them carry are destroyed during their long journey to England.

We have so far said little of roses. Very few kinds were grown in Britain until the reign of Elizabeth I. Even so, Gerard in his *Herbal* named only fourteen kinds, while Parkinson in *Paradisi* adds ten more; these lists were made by experts of the day, and therefore the ordinary gardener no doubt grew fewer kinds.

Hanmer describes twenty-one kinds. He tells us that none of the single are much valued except the sweet brier (*R. eglanteria*) for its scented leaves, and the scarlet rose, yellow within and scarlet without. It is a dwarf grower, and dislikes having its red, lax shoots pruned. Budded on to a Provence or damask rose, it can then be grown against a wall. This rose (*R. foetida bicolor*) is sometimes seen in Dutch paintings. Hanmer says the fugitive flowers are borne freely.

It is possible to identify from his descriptions those belonging to what is now called the Gallica group. There is the red apothecary's rose (*R. gallica officinalis*) itself; the velvet rose, the purple rose, 'very double and scarce'; 'the purple striped with white', coming from Norwich and 'very scarce'; the marbled rose, resembling the apothecary rose but 'full speckled with an ill-faded white', and 'Rosa Mundi', or the Christmas rose (*R. gallica versicolor*), which he says was first found in Norfolk a few years before on a branch of the common gallica.*

The 'very high' pure white double with strong prickles is presumably *R. alba maxima*, the white rose of York. The white Provins, with a little centre of pale red in it, may be one of the 'Maiden's Blush' roses.

The damask rose, 'very common with us' and grown as standards, is the pink *R. damascena*; and the 'York and Lancaster' (*R. damascena versicolor*), 'a fine rose when it masks rightly', is correctly called the variegated damask. Hanmer also refers to the monthly rose—a name later given to the China rose—and this is presumably the autumn damask rose (*R. damascena bifera*). He also names a rose without thorns, and the cinnamon rose (*R. cinnamonea*).

Last of all he mentions the double yellow rose, clearly *R. haemisphaerica*. Hanmer's remark that it does not 'blow' well, the buds seeming to be eaten by worm, still holds good. He tells of one plant, however, that does flower in 'open pure air near Gogmagog hills' near Cambridge, on a light soil; he adds that he has learned by experience that it is best left to grow high and remain unpruned.

* This is quite possible, though this sport was recorded by Clusius in 1583.

A whole section of Hanmer's book is devoted to greens—which 'we esteem much' for beautifying walks and gardens since they continue green all winter, 'not casting their leaves totally at any season of the year'. He gives the admirable general rule that evergreens are best removed in September, when they will be established before the arrival of severe weather.

Pride of place is given to the cedar of Lebanon. Hanmer gives an accurate description of this species, making it clear that he is not referring to any of the other trees (usually *Cupressus* or *Juniperus*) so confusingly called cedar by earlier writers. He then remarks that 'we have of late had some few plants raised from seed, which are yet very small, so that it is rare in England, as well as in the rest of Europe'. After referring to what 'writers relate', he prophesies a great future for this, the most esteemed species of cedar in our gardens, concluding that it 'will without question prosper with us'.

This is apparently the first mention of the Lebanon cedar growing in Britain. It is now difficult to imagine our gardens without this magnificent tree with its massive tables of green.

About another evergreen Hanmer is obviously confused; he surprisingly refers to it as the scarlet oak, on account of an excrescence upon which worms feed to produce a grain from which a scarlet colour is made. That would be the Kermes oak (*Quercus coccifera*), a small and insignificant tree. But fortunately he mentions a large specimen at Whitehall of this 'fair and lovely tree'—which is undoubtedly the famous ilex or evergreen oak (*Q. ilex*) described by John Evelyn. The point to be gained, however, is that in Hanmer's time we already had 'some few' of this Mediterranean oak so closely associated with our gardens and parks.

He remarks of the cypress that it is rather tender, and that of late years it has been very much propagated from the seed that it has borne.

As we have entered on the period when the cultivation of oranges (the most distinguished of 'greens') was becoming popular, and the construction of buildings to house them during the winter was usual in every large garden that aimed to be in the mode, we may summarize Hanmer's account 'Of the Orange Tree'. One of its attractions was that it naturally grows with a 'fine round handsome head'. With great care and industry it could be brought to a height of 2 or 3 yards. At the foot of each leaf is the shape of a little heart, upon which the leaf stands, which distinguishes the orange from the lemon. 'The leaves smell well, but the flowers are deliciously and comfortably sweet.' Hanmer here remarks that though the fruit (imported) was then well known, few other than gardeners knew the tree itself. In England, he tells us, though the fruit occasionally comes to perfection, the orange is grown only for its sweet flowers and the pleasing sight and scent of the green leaves. Experience had shown that though trees were often brought from Italy or France, they were usually 'prejudiced' by the sea journey.

The best way to grow them in England was to sow the seeds in boxes in spring in fine earth, keeping them well watered. The seedlings must be shaded from the sun, and when they are big enough, taken up, with plenty of soil around them, and put in gillyflower pots of good sifted earth. In these they could remain for three or four years.

The young trees 'extremely delight' in sun and moisture when they are out of the house from the middle of April or early May to the end of October. Therefore, in summer they must stand in a sunny place and be watered plentifully. In the house they are never to get dry at the roots, but are to be watered as little as possible, and never during a frost; air must be allowed them. When too big for the pots they should be moved into wooden cases, about a yard high, narrower at the top than the bottom,* made close and jointed like wainscot, with some holes bored through the bottom. This transplanting should be done in March or April, and the cases well watered unless frosts occur. The soil is to be fresh rich mould, of fine sifted earth, 'very old consumed dung', and wood ash. Every third or fourth year the trees must be taken out, the roots 'barbed' (trimmed) and re-planted in a bigger case. Dead branches must be cut hard back, and the wounds covered with a mixture of soft red wax and turpentine mixed with resin.

Hanmer reports that there were more than twenty different kinds of orange in Italy, some sour, some very sweet, and some with a sweetness and sharpness mixed. The kinds best known in

* This is the reverse to what one usually finds today.

England* were the China orange, introduced from Portugal, to which country it had lately been taken from China, with a rind so free from bitterness that it could be eaten as well as the 'meat'; the Seville oranges, both sweet and sharp, brought from Spain, and, in Hanmer's opinion, the largest and best, and the Bermuda orange brought from the island of that name.

He mentions that the lemon (*Citrus limonia*, an Asiatic species), of which the Italians had over thirty kinds, was grown here, though we have 'very few . . . of any kind'. He also writes that the citron or pomecitron (*C. medica*, the source of candied peel and another Asian native) often fruits in this country, though the tree itself is rare and tender.

Among other 'greens' he describes laurustinus, sassafras, pyracantha, phillyrea, the strawberry tree (*Arbutus unedo*), the andrachne or strawberry bay (*A. andrachne*), molle (the pepper tree, *Schinus molle*), the coral tree (*Erythrina crista-galli*), myrtle, and oleander.

One mentions these names for two reasons. Firstly, because— as we shall see—by the end of the century among many gardeners the touchstone of success was the number and quality of 'greens' cultivated, and the manner of their winter housing. Secondly, to give an idea of the wide area from which garden plants were now drawn, ranging from Cochin-China, in the case of oranges, to Brazil in the coral tree.

Hanmer also grew much fruit; his lists and instructions are short and practical. His particular favourite among top fruit seems to have been the pear. He was deeply interested in the culture of vines, and writes at length of his own experience of viticulture in Wales.

The details of the plants set in the 'four little bordered beds in the midst of the bordered knot' in the great garden at Bettisfield in 1660 are interesting. In the first bed were seven ranks of 26 distinct kinds of tulips, colchicums, and anemones. If we regard the second as that diagonally opposite, then it contained 13 ranks each of 4 different kinds of tulip—that is, 52 kinds in all.

---

* The citrus fruits form a large complex group. The 'China orange', our sweet orange; is *Citrus sinensis*, from China or Indochina; the Seville oranges, *Citrus aurantium*, came originally from the same region; the 'Bermuda orange' is the shaddock or pummelo, *Citrus maxima*, probably from Malaysia, a parent of the grapefruit, *Citrus × paradisi*. These have many variants.

The third bed was planted with double crown imperials, six rows of iris raised from seed supplied by Rea, polyanthuses,* daffodils, and anemones. The fourth bed, diagonally opposite to the third, was planted with hyacinths, jonquils, narcissus (including Belle Semane, 'right dear'), colchicums, and black and grey fritillaries.

The actual shapes of the small beds of this period when the intricacies of the edged knot were gradually giving way to the elaborate patterns of the parterre have been recorded as they actually were in a garden of the time.[24] In 1631 the Rev. Walter Stonehouse (1597–1655) was instituted as Rector of Darfield. He was in the great tradition of botanist-parsons (and a collector of coins into the bargain). His rectory contained a 'best garden', a rectangular space of about 30 yards by 34 yards, with four beds, a fifth being in a bay, a saffron garth and an orchard. In 1640 he made careful scale plans of each, which have survived.

The old saffron garth was a walled-in strip much longer than wide; there was room on its walls for 33 trees planted 6 feet apart, and 30 apples and pears. The orchard was rectangular, and of no exceptional interest except that, like the other fruit trees, many were probably obtained from Tradescant himself. Others came from a neighbour, Sir John Reresby.

The most interesting feature of the plans is, however, the actual design of the five beds in the great garden (Fig. 3). The shapes of these may be compared with Lawson's knots of 1617 and Tallard's parterres of 1706. The plants which grew in them were listed by Stonehouse; there were no less than 866 kinds—many only of botanical interest.

Stonehouse had the tough moral fibre that seems a feature of parson-naturalists and was ejected by the Parliamentary Commissioners and imprisoned.

As the return of Charles II and his court draws near let us quote a description of a garden well known for its literary merit, though often misplaced chronologically.

In 1626 William, Lord Pembroke, bought the estate of Moor

---

* This appears to be the earliest reference to the polyanthus growing in a garden. Edward Morgan (c. 1619–c. 1677) had a garden in Westminster (perhaps that held earlier by Ralph Tuggy) and it is recorded that he grew *Primula veris polyanthos* found in Great Woolver wood, Warwickshire, and thence transferred to Westminster. This may be its origin.[25]

Park in Hertfordshire from Lucy, widow of the third Earl of Bedford. Here, between that year and 1631, he laid out a garden. In 1652 the estate was bought by Sir Richard Franklin, who was a cousin of Dorothy Osborne. After Sir William Temple married

Fig. 3. Designs of rectangular and square beds made by the Rev. W. Stonehouse at Darfield, Yorkshire, in 1640

her in 1655 the couple spent their honeymoon there. It is this garden, made in the early years of Charles I's reign, and now reaching maturity, that Temple described from memory in 1685 as 'the perfectest figure of a garden I ever saw, either at home or abroad'.[26]

Because I take the garden I have named, to have been in all kinds the most beautiful and perfect, at least in the figure and disposition, that I have ever seen, I will describe it for a model to those that meet with such a situation, and are above the regards of common expense. It lies on the side of a hill (upon which the house stands) but not very steep. The length of the house, where the best rooms, and of most use or pleasure, lies upon the breadth of the garden, the great parlour opens into the middle of a terrace gravel-walk that lies even with it, and which may be as I remember about three hundred paces long, and broad in proportion, the border set with standard laurels, and at large distances, which have the beauty of orange-trees out of flower and fruit; from the walk are three descents by many stone steps in the middle and at each end, into a very large parterre. This is divided into quarters by gravel walks, and adorned with two fountains and eight statues in the several quarters; at the end of the terrace walk are two summer-houses, and the sides of the parterre are ranged with two large cloisters, which are paved with stone, and designed for walks of shade, there being none other in the whole parterre. Over these two cloisters are two terraces covered with lead and fenced with balusters, and the passage into these airy walks is out of the two summer-houses at the end of the first terrace walk. The cloister facing the south is covered with vines, and would have been proper for an orange-house, and the other for myrtles, or other more common greens, and had, I doubt not, been cast for that purpose, if this piece of gardening had been then in as much vogue as it is now.

From the middle of this parterre is a descent by many steps flying on each side of a grotto that lies between them (covered with lead and flat) into the lower garden, which is all fruit-trees ranged about the several quarters of a wilderness which is very shady; the walks here are all green, the grotto embellished with figures of shell rock-work, fountains and water-works. If the hill had not ended with the lower garden, and the wall were not bounded by a common way that goes through the park, they might have added a third quarter of all greens; but this want is supplied by a garden on the other side of the house, which is all of that sort, very wild, shady, and adorned with rough rock-work and fountains.

Temple's recollection was illuminated by the glowing lights of youth. But his description of the plan of the garden is no doubt accurate, and it is made particularly interesting by a number of observations which indicate the changes in fashion that had taken place. Such, for example, is the reference to vine-covered cloisters, which would in 1685 have been an orangery 'if this piece of gardening had been then in as much vogue as it is now'.

One may remark, too, on the fact that Temple considered that this early Caroline design formed the ideal framework upon which to superimpose later innovations and so form an exemplary garden of the 1680s.

FOUR

France Triumphant
1660–1719

THE GREAT LE NÔTRE

ANDRÉ LE NÔTRE was born in 1613—it is said in a house within the Tuileries gardens of Paris. He was the son of a royal master-gardener, and grandson of the gardener-in-chief of the parterres of the Tuileries. He was apprenticed under his father and Claude Mollet (also the son of an eminent gardener), who was gardener-in-chief to Henry IV at Saint Germain-en-Laye, Fontainebleau, and the Tuileries. He also acquired by study the principles of architecture, painting, and design. In 1640 he was appointed designer-in-ordinary to the king's gardens; in 1657 he was made one of the three Contrôleurs Généraux du Bâtiments du Roi.

The king was, of course, Louis XIV—the 'Sun-King'—a lavish and extravagant patron of architecture and gardening over a longer period than any other monarch. Thus, while in England kings and queens came and went, and even systems of government changed, Le Nôtre worked steadily on project after project for a long lifetime. This is not the place to discuss his work. But one can say that no other gardener-designer can have had such opportunities, and none handled them with greater success. The vastness of his schemes take the breath away, while the deftness of the smallest details shows, in the hackneyed phrase, his genius.[1]

Le Nôtre took the components of the Renaissance garden and, striking out a wide and sweeping vista, arranged them with French logic on either side. His was the influence which dominated European gardening, and with which members of the

English court were in touch during their exile. Within two years of his return to England, Charles II tried to obtain his services to lay out the royal gardens. Louis XIV apparently gave him leave to come, but there seems little doubt that he never did, though it is possible that he made plans and corresponded with Charles—probably concerning Greenwich—and that Le Nôtre's suggestions were carried out by the royal gardener André Mollet.* Two English royal gardeners, John Rose (1622–1677) and a younger man, George London, both visited France; the former learned direct from Le Nôtre, and the second more probably at second hand from Rose, who conducted him round.[2]

If one examines engravings of the French gardens of the reign of Louis XIV—or the photographs of those that remain or have been restored—one is at once struck by the fact that a large proportion of their area is covered by water and wood—all laid out in geometrical patterns. In engravings of English gardens published around the end of the seventeenth century we find the same—though the water-works, being the most costly, are not on such a grand scale.

Le Nôtre and his school paid great attention to the planting of woods, through which paths were cut with mathematical accuracy, and within which were small gardens, view-points, cabinets of verdure, and other enjoyable features which we shall discuss later.

It is not entirely a coincidence that the coming of these plantations should coincide with the publication in 1664 of John Evelyn's *Sylva, or a Discourse of Forest Trees*. This, passing through several editions, remained the standard work on trees for over a century. From the Restoration until the nineteenth century the planting of trees was an integral part of garden design, and few men can have done more to initiate it than Evelyn. He was not, however, ostensibly concerned with the amenities of the countryside. His interest originated in a paper he read to the Royal Society in 1662 to answer queries propounded by the principal officers and Commissioners of the Navy who were anxious about the shortage of timber for His Majesty's ships. However, not until the Napoleonic wars was planting actively carried on for that purpose; earlier it

* Traditionally, Le Nôtre is also connected with Wrest Park, Bedfordshire, and Althorp, Northamptonshire.

was principally done for the purposes of landscape gardening and the improvement of estates (particularly in Scotland) by enlightened landowners.

Evelyn urged that trees should be planted everywhere, even when what we now call amenity value could only on the slightest pretext be linked with utility. Of walnuts, for example, 'they render most graceful avenues to our country dwellings'; of the 'perfections' of the lime 'its unparalleled beauty for walks'; the only excuse that he makes for urging the planting of the strawberry tree, 'too much neglected by us', is that Bauhin commends the charcoal for goldsmith's work. And there is his famous eulogy of the holly with its 'cheerful green rutilant berries':

Is there under Heaven a more glorious and refreshing object of the kind, than an impregnable hedge of about four hundred foot in length, nine foot high, and five in diameter; which I can show in my now ruined gardens at Sayes-Court (thanks to the Czar of Muscovy) at any time of the year, glittering with its armed and varnished leaves? The taller standards at orderly distances, blushing with their natural coral: it mocks at the rudest assaults of the weather, beasts, or hedgebreakers.

We have already remarked on the absence of any reference to the yew as a plant for hedging or topiary. Bacon and Parkinson both refer to the yew as a good evergreen for occasional planting, but that is all. The evergreen most often mentioned for these purposes was the box, which grows slowly and does not reach any great height. By Evelyn's time the quick-growing Mediterranean cypress was coming rapidly into fashion,* no doubt because it was now being raised (as he tells us) from British seed, which it produces in abundance. The criticism pointed against it was, of course, that it was 'reputed so tender, and a nice plant, that it was cultivated with the greatest care'. Evelyn disputes this; he assures us that the cypress will become 'endenizon'd' among us if we plant enough of it—he thinks the making of the experiment should be a 'wonderful incitement' to us. Yet he has to admit that our 'cruel eastern winds do sometimes mortally invade them that have been late clipped'. (In the winter of 1683-4 practically every cypress in England was killed.)[3]

On reaching his description of the yew, we realize that his

* It was now planted extensively, for example, at Wimbledon and Theobalds.

confidence in the hardiness of the cypress was not unbounded. After a description of the method of raising seedlings, he continues:

Being three years old you may transplant them, and form them into standards, knobs, walks, hedges, etc., in all of which works they succeed marvellous well, and are worth our patience for their perennial verdure and durableness. I do again name them for hedges, preferable for beauty, and a stiff defence to any plant I have ever seen, and may upon that account (without vanity) be said to have been the first to have brought them into fashion, as well for defence, as for a succedaneum for cypress, whether in hedges or pyramids, conic spires, bowls, or what other shapes, adorning the parks or larger avenues with their lofty tops thirty foot high, and braving all the efforts of the most rigid winter, which cypress cannot weather.

There is, in fact, at least one earlier reference to yews 'cut into beasts'—on a plan of Wollaton by Smythson.* But this seems to be exceptional, and Evelyn's claim that he brought our most adaptable and long-suffering evergreen into general garden use can be allowed. He was also a great promoter of the planting of the Lebanon cedar, though, we as have seen, not the first to introduce or record it.

The later editions of *Sylva* conclude with 'some encouragements and proposals for the planting and improvement of His Majesty's Forests, and other amenities for shade and ornaments'. Among them Evelyn provides a plan, 'intending this as an idea only of something which I conceive might be both convenient and graceful', of a house and its gardens. A large square space beyond the gardens is laid out geometrically, with a series of tree-lined walks which enclosed sixteen 'vacuities which are sixteen blunt triangles'. These were to be planted with timber trees, or some left for corn and meadows.

The design is entirely symmetrical about a central axis or vista; the pattern of the plan, except for certain walls, is formed by ranks of trees. To compare this with the design of Wimbledon, or other early seventeenth-century gardens, demonstrates the considerable change that Le Nôtre's influence had brought about (Fig. 4).

* In the library of the Royal Institute of British Architects.

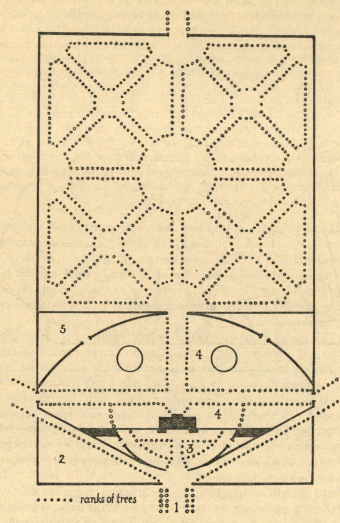

FIG. 4. John Evelyn's 'regular figure' of a garden.
1. The main avenue. 2. Pastures. 3. Courtyard.
4. Gardens, with fountains. 5. Fruit gardens and vegetables. The house, outbuildings, and walls are shown
in solid black

Most interesting is another plan, 'an instance of irregular figures, actually surveyed and disposed into walks' . . . which 'Squire Kirke'* set out in a wood of 120 acres near his house at Cookeridge in Yorkshire. There was a broad walk that passed directly through the irregularly shaped wood (which was more of the nature of a copse) on its longest axis, about 1,100 yards long. About half-way along was an oval clearing from which radiated twelve broad walks, each running to the confines of the wood.

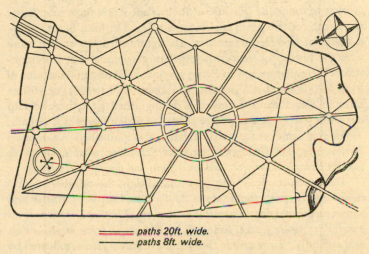

 paths 20ft. wide.
 paths 8ft. wide.

FIG. 5. Squire Kirke's irregular garden

These, like the main ride, were 20 feet wide. In between them was a secondary network of straight paths some 8 feet wide, laid out asymetrically. There were in all sixty-five intersections of paths to give view-points; the number of views within the wood to be gained from them was 306 (Fig. 5).

Evelyn was never quite converted to the rigid symmetry of the French school; he seems himself to have had a love of nature and irregularity. He wrote of Kirke's woodland garden: 'nor are such glades through coppices to be neglected, in some regards

* Thomas Kirke, F.R.S. (1650–1706). Mr. G. R. Aldersley informs me that the remains of the garden, known locally as 'Jack and his eleven brothers', still existed in the early 1930s. Moseley Wood, in which it was situated, lies to the north of Horsforth.

preferable to the woods of taller trees, obnoxious to be subverted by impetuous storms, which the humbler coppices escape, and yet let in very noble views and prospects; besides their inviting game for breed, and to shelter sonorous birds, which never are found in lofty woods, where they are exposed to hawks and owls'. Nor was his own garden at Sayes Court, Deptford, on the new French symmetrical plan.

With *Sylva* Evelyn published *Pomona: or an Appendix Concerning Fruit-Trees in Relation to Cider.* This, again, was to urge his fellow citizens to make the best use of their land; it is a most interesting work with contributions by the famed Rev. Dr. John Beale (1603–c. 1683) of Yeovil, and others. Its significance lies rather more with the history of fruit-growing than gardening, but it demonstrates increased attention being given to selecting good strains of fruit. In this the first Viscount Scudamore (1601–1671) of Holme Lacy in Herefordshire played a distinguished part; he also laid out a fine garden full of choice plants, of which traces still remain.

In the same year, 1664, Evelyn also published *Kalendarium Hortense: or, the Gardiner's Almanack, Directing what he is to do monthly throughout the year, and what fruits and flowers are in prime.*

Each month opens with its zodiacal sign, the number of days in the month, with the hours of daylight and times of sunrise and sunset on the first day. Then follow sections. Firstly, *To be done in the parterre and flower garden,* followed by *Flowers in prime or yet lasting,* and secondly, *To be done in the orchard and olitory garden,* followed by *Fruits in prime or yet lasting.* Here we may note that by 1664 'parterre' had almost superseded the word 'knot', in common use earlier in the century.

Evelyn loved high-sounding words: alas, we must accuse him of using jargon. He tells us that he writes 'not for the sake of our ordinary rustics . . . but for the more ingenious; the benefit and diversion of gentlemen, and persons of quality'. We are therefore puzzled by such terms as ablaqueation, hyemation, ichnography, and stercoration which rumble through his works.

He takes his place in our history as the father of the great movement to plant ornamental trees and woodlands in and around our gardens rather than as a horticulturist. It might have been different if he had attempted his grand design, aided by 'as many hands and subsidiaries . . . as there are distinct parts of the whole' for *The Plan of a Royal Garden*. He refers to this in the preface of *Acetaria, A Discourse of Sallets*, published in 1693—a sixty-page treatise which was to be no more than one of the forty-two chapters arranged in the three books of the *magnum opus*.

To give an idea of the adornments of Evelyn's elysium—omitting the more usual aspects of gardening—we may repeat some of the chapter headings:

Of groves, labyrinths, dedals, cabinets, cradles, closewalks, galleries, pavilions, porticos, lanterns, and other relievos, of topiary and hortulan architecture.

Of fountains, jetto's, cascades, rivulets, piscinas, canals, baths, and other natural and artificial water-works.

Of rocks, grots, cryptae, mounts, precipices, ventiducts, conservatories of ice and snow,* and other hortulan refreshments.

Of gazon-theatres, amphitheatres, artificial echoes, automata, and hydraulic music.

Of stupendous and wonderful plants.

Of the hortulan elaboratory, and of distilling and extracting waters, spirits, essences, salts, colours, resuscitation of plants, with other rare experiments, and an account of their virtues.

Of composing the *hortus hyemalis*, and making books of natural, arid plants and flowers, with several ways of preserving them in their beauty.

Of painting of flowers, flowers enamelled, silk, calicos, paper, wax, gum, pastes, horns, glass, shells, feathers, moss, pietra commessa, inlayings, embroideries, carvings, and other representations of them.

This last reminds us that Evelyn is by Vertue credited with the discovery of Grinling Gibbons (1648–1721) and of the odd fact that our first examples of realistic botanic art took the form not of drawings but exquisite wood carvings.

So we continue with the 'plan' until the final chapter, 'Corollary and conclusion'. Practically every development of the art of gardening that has since taken place—with the notable exception of collecting plants from overseas—is foreshadowed.

Though we may smile at John Evelyn as a bookman, we cannot doubt his love of gardens, and passionate wish that Britain should excel in all concerning them. He hoped that 'my executors

* This is one of the earliest references to the ice-house, a utilitarian feature later to become popular.

will gratify me in what I have desired, I wish my corpse may be interred as I have bespoke them'. This was not in chancel nor churchyard, but in his garden; and his whole body, and not the heart only as had been done with 'the elegant and accomplished Sir William Temple'.

A WORCESTERSHIRE GARDEN

Very little is known about John Rea,* who died in 1681. He described himself as 'Gentleman' and apparently spent a long life at Kinlet, which lies at the north of Wyre Forest, midway between the Severn and the massive Clee Hills.

In 1665 he published *Flora, Ceres and Pomona . . . or a complete Florilege, furnished with all requisites belonging to a florist.* It was dedicated to the Rt. Hon. Charles Lord Gerard of Gerard's Bromley (whose garden, it seems, he planned), Sir Thomas Hanmer, Bart., Lady Gerard, Lady Hanmer, and Miss Trever Hanmer ('now wife of Sir John Warwick'). Rea is several times mentioned approvingly by Hanmer, and that, added to what is obviously a well-informed and practical text, marks his book as a reliable guide to Restoration gardening and horticulture on the less grandiose scale.

In his prefatory remarks Rea states that some years ago he had found Parkinson's *Paradisi* to want the 'addition of many noble things of newer discovery, and that a multitude of those set out were by time grown stale, and for unworthiness turned out of every garden'.

Rea writes on the design of gardens in rather the same vein as Hanmer, but with more detail. He echoes his patron:

Fair houses are more frequent than fine gardens; the first effected by artificers only, the latter requiring more skill in their owner.

He goes on to remark of the simplified plans of gardens now becoming the vogue:

I have seen many gardens of the new model, in the hands of unskilful persons, with good walls, walks, and grass plots; but in the most essential adornments so deficient, that a green meadow is a more delightful object: there, nature alone, without the aid of art, spreads

* Robert Sharrock, *History of . . . Vegetables* (1672 ed.), writes of 'our great florist, Mr. Rea'.

her verdant carpets, spontaneously embroidered with many pretty plants and pleasing flowers, far more inviting than such an immured nothing. And as noble fountains, grottoes, statues, etc., are excellent ornaments and marks of magnificence; so all such dead works in gardens, ill done, are little better than blocks in the way to interrupt sight, but not at all to satisfy the understanding. A choice collection of living beauties, rare plants, flowers and fruit, are indeed the wealth, glory and delight of a garden, and the most absolute indications of the owner's ingenuity; whose skill and care is chiefly required in their choice, culture and position.

Two separate gardens, Rea instructs, should be formed within a stoutly walled rectangle, this wall to be of brick on stone foundations, and 9 feet high. The two gardens should be separated by a less substantial brick wall, or one of pales painted brick colour, with a good opening as a passage from one to the other. These, the gardens for 'delight, recreation and entertainment', should lie to the south of, and be protected by, the house—the nearer to it being the flower garden, the further away being reserved principally for fruit. The kitchen garden should be in some more remote place. If necessary, pear trees, elms, or sycamores should be planted at some little distance to abate the north and east winds.*

The wise man, Rea tells us, does not make his garden too big: the large garden is usually 'ill-furnished and ill-kept'. For a nobleman, 80 yards for the fruit and 30 yards for the flowers is adequate; for a private gentleman the figures are 40 and 20 yards.†

Consideration must be given to obtaining the right kind of gravel for the walks. Rea uses the term 'cat-brain' gravel for the best type; sandy gravel he considers the worst. Turf-laying is discussed; he describes a turfing iron such as is still used.

Instructions follow for planting trees and climbers against the walls. Pears—they are to be grafted on quince‡—are particularly favoured, as well as the double pomegranate. Between these are placed standard rose trees, each one so grafted as to supply several different colours in flower at the same time. In the borders below grow auriculas, red primroses, hepaticas, double rose

---

* To this day, ancient perry pear trees still exist in the west country planted on the exposed corners of the orchards.

† One assumes these figures are the length of the gardens—which might be either rectangular or square.

‡ The growing of dwarf pears was at this time a speciality of English gardeners.

campions, double non-such, double dame's violet, 'the best wall-flowers', double stock gillyflowers—and many other kinds.

The beds in the parterres are cut in the form of 'frets'. Sixteen designs for these are illustrated; compared with Lawson's knots or even Stonehouse's beds, they are much simpler in outline. They are planted with flowers that 'answer' each other; for example, in the corners are crown imperials, martagons, and other tall plants. In the centre there may be 'tufts' of paeonies surrounded by dwarf things like anemones, ranunculi, tulips, or irises.

The making of a rose hedge trained against lattice work is described; in front of it are stood the greens and pot plants, while at its foot are planted crocuses.

In the middle of one wall there should stand a 'handsome octangular summer house, roofed every way, and finely painted with landskips, and other conceits'. This is provided with chairs and a table. It is not only a sitting place from which to enjoy the gardens, but is for use when one is digging up (and carefully labelling) bulbs and setting them there to dry.

Without the walls there must be a nursery garden, with its hot-bed made up annually. And there must be a convenient house for keeping tools, roots, seeds, and housing tender greens. This must contain a stove or raised hearth for setting fires during frosty weather.

The tools* required are

a screen (of the kind used for sifting gravel), a fine wire riddle, two spades—a bigger and a lesser, likewise shovels, hoes of several sizes, a pruning hook, grafting knives, a saw, chisel, mallet, a small pen-knife for innoculating and layering gilliflowers, a line and rule, trowels of several sizes, two iron rakes—one longer and bigger in the head, the other smaller, with teeth thicker set—and several baskets of twigs and besoms to sweep the garden.

There is surprisingly no mention of a wheel-barrow—though this was known in the fifteenth century.

Rea then describes the evergreens and their culture, which he gives according to 'the rules observed by Mr. John Rose, the ingenious Keeper of the garden at Essex House, Strand'.

* As can be seen from a drawing made by John Evelyn,[4] in 1660, showing a very similar collection, these varied little in design from those used up to, say, 1914.

Of the greens, he considered the variegated phillyrea* the 'most beautiful of all kinds'. He remarks that the strawberry tree is 'in its greatest glory in October and November, when the berries are ripe, which mixing with the fine green leaves are a delightful object', and that the 'double blossomed wild pomegranate-tree is the rarest of all flowering trees and shrubs'.† Then, of other shrubs, thirty-one roses are described, along with five jasmines, two honeysuckles, and four clematis.

It is when we reach the bulbous plants that Rea begins to come into his element. After a number of lilies (especially 'marta-gon or mountain lilies') and thirteen different fritillaries, he tackles the tulips. This bulb was then reaching the first and highest of several peaks of popularity that it has attained in England.

On the Continent the great Dutch 'tulipomania' with its wild financial speculations had already come and, in 1637, crashed and gone. In England no such extremes were reached, though tulips were passionately admired over a longer period.‡

Rea has already given us some verses on this, beyond doubt his favourite flower:

> The tulips to delight your eyes,
> With glorious garments, rich and new,
> Like the rich glutton some are dight
> In Tyrian-purple and fine white;
> And in bright crimson others shine
> Impal'd with white and graydeline:
> The meanest here you can behold,
> Is cloth'd in scarlet, lac'd with gold.
> But then the queen of all delight
> Wears graydeline scarlet and white:
> So interwov'n and so plac'd,
> That all the others are disgrac'd
> When she appears and doth impart
> Her native beauties shaming art.

The 'queen of all delight' was Agate Hanmer, Sir Thomas's great triumph, of which he was immensely proud. In June 1655

---

* There now appears to be no record for at least a century past of a variegated form of either *Phillyrea angustifolia* or *P. latifolia* (both mentioned by Gerard).

† Both double scarlet and white are now recorded, but are exceptionally rare—at least in Britain.

‡ Addison's entertaining satire on our own tulip growers in *The Tatler* did not appear until 1710.

he had sent to General Lambert—a cavalier to a roundhead—'a very great mother root of Agate Hanmer', through John Rose; in 1671 he sent a parcel of plants to John Evelyn among which most of the tulips were 'not extraordinary', 'except Agate Hanmer and . . . some others'.

Rea describes it fully, with a tribute to Hanmer's generosity:

Agate Hanmer is a beautiful flower of three good colours, pale grideline, deep scarlet, and pure white, commonly well parted, striped, agated,* and excellently placed, abiding constant to the last, with the bottom and stamens blue. This gallant tulip hath its name from that ingenious lover of these rarities, Sir Thomas Hanmer, who first brought it into England, from whose free community myself and others partake the delight of this noble flower.

Many pages are given to the tulip, and diagrams for planting are provided. The kinds are sensibly grouped into three classes, according to the time when they flower—Praecox, Media, and Serotina.

Of the Praecox class there are thirty-one kinds, the most esteemed being the Superintendent, the tallest of the class, marked with violet, purple, and white, the bottom and stamens pale yellow. (The inside of the flower, so beautiful and now overlooked, was always taken into account.)

The second group, the Media, is much the largest. One hundred and fifty tulips are named and carefully described. Here we have the parrots—in variety, some all green; those the French call 'bizarres', and the agates. Many of the names show that most are of Dutch and—this is sometimes overlooked—of French origin. There are the Flanders Widow, and Agate Morin—after the French nurseryman—to remind us of this. Ricketts' Fine Agate sounds English enough, the product of his Hoxton nursery. The Chimney Sweeper sounds interesting, and 'the Pellican, when it comes right, is a pretty flower of good carnation colour marked thick with smaller and bigger stripes of white'. Of the Serotinas, there are only nine kinds.

There follow the other flowers in a confused order, and sometimes equally confused in their naming. By reading on we are able

---

* 'Grideline' = purple, and 'agated' = the colours disposed in parallel stripes or bands.

to gain an idea of the fine variety of flowers that were now obtainable by the gardener, and to form an opinion of the contents of a Restoration garden. We have narcissi and pseudo-narcissi (including amaryllids, the 'Indian daffodils'), hyacinths, ornithogalums, molys (*Allium* species), asphodels, paeonies, colchicums (ten kinds are described), and crocuses (twenty-two kinds, including autumn crocus). Irises have two chapters, one given to the bulbous kind and the other to the tuberous-rooted forms. Gladiolus, orchis, dog's tooth violet, and cyclamen (eleven kinds) follow. Anemones are, of course, dealt with in some detail and split into two groups, *latifolia* and *tenuifolia*; the varieties of the latter kind are numerous. The ranunculus is among the other plants discussed, and that oddity the yucca, which to this day looks strange in our gardens, is considered.

There is a great deal said about auriculas and, as always, about the details of their treatment. Rea refers to Mr. Good's purple, raised by Mr. Austen of Oxford and given to Mr. John Good of Balliol College; to 'Mistress Buggs her fine purple', raised by her in Battersea; Rickett's Sable; while 'divers other excellent flowers have been raised in Oxford by Mr. Jacob Bobart, Keeper of the public garden'.

According to the catalogue of the Oxford Botanic Gardens (1648), Bobart was a great enthusiast for the genus *Primula*, having by then collected many rare kinds of primroses (including a blue one), cowslips, and oxlips in great variety; Rea also describes some of these.

Of the other flowers, there are lychnis (several sorts), and the '*Keiri*' or '*Lucoium luteum*'*—the wallflower or winter gillyflower. *Lucoium alba*, the stock gillyflower, was only allowed in the garden when it had double flowers, the single form, however, being retained in the nursery garden to provide seed. Other kinds of gillyflower are the Queen's gillyflower, or dame's violet (*Hesperis matronalis*) and *the* gillyflower, which Rea calls *Caryophyllus hortensis*, the 'pride of summer', known to us as the carnation (*Dianthus caryophyllus*). He remarks on the difficulty of growing this in

---

* These names, with their variety of spellings, in early times denoted several very dissimilar plants. Here Rea refers to our common wallflowers, derived from *Cheiranthus cheiri*, and the stock, from *Matthiola incana*. The name comes from the Greek, *leucoion*, a white violet; it was at one time applied to the snowdrop. In its present form of *Leucojum* it is restricted to a small genus of amaryllids of which the snow flake is the best known.

gardens, as most of those raised from seed die after they have flowered. Yet he names many kinds, classified under three headings: red and white, purple and white, and scarlet and white. The clove gillyflowers were 'of the more ordinary kind'. Pinks, which he calls *Caryophyllus sylvestris,** are also mentioned.

At this point *Flora*, the first part of the work, ends. It is followed by the second book, *Ceres*, treating of summer- and harvesttime plants. Here we have herbaceous perennials such as mallows, delphiniums, scabious, the amaranth, cornflowers, lupins, and sweet peas—the old perennial kinds. Several herbs come into this section. Here, too, appears the love-apple or tomato—grown for the beauty of its fruit. And, more surprisingly, the sensitive plant (*Mimosa*), raised on a hot-bed, of which many die before they produce seeds.

So we pass on to his third book, *Pomona*. To recite many of the names of the choice fruits Rea describes would become tedious (charming though many of them sound) and of little value, so fugitive were most of them. We will be content with saying that he refers to twenty sorts of apple, including Juniting, which is ripe at the end of June. There are twenty pears; here we have (in Rea's spelling) Bon Christuns, Burgamots, and Boeure—names that are still to be found in our catalogues as Bon Chrétien, Bergamotte, and Beurré.

The poverty of kinds mentioned strongly contrasts with the profusion of varieties that were named in the next century. Rea, however, attached much importance to the quince, of which five kinds are named: the English Apple quince, 'full of burrs and branches', with its unequal fruit, harsh, often strong, and covered with white cotton; the Portugal Apple quince, large, yellow, and can be eaten raw; the Portugal Pear quince, again yellow, excellent to bake and preserve; the Barbary quince, a smaller version of the last; the Lion's quince, large, the deepest yellow, ribbed, and with a deep hollow crown; and finally the Brunswick, large and round, whiter than any of the former.

Of cherries there are twenty-four kinds—several with names that still exist. More kinds of plum are described than of any other

* Rea's names for the carnation and pink imply that the carnation was a cultivated form of what he called the *Caryophyllus*, while the pink came from the wild (*sylvestris*) and was, as it were, a poor relation. In fact, both arise from different species of *Dianthus*.

fruit. There are forty-four, including (the spelling is Rea's) Primordians, Damosines (several varieties), Prunella, Muscle plums, Perdrigons, and red and white Mirablions. Most of these names, once much used, have disappeared. Perdrigon survived into the last century, damsons remain, as does the myrobolan—if seldom grown as a fruit. The Mussel survives only as a stock.

Remarkable is the attention given to 'apricocks'. We now find them difficult to grow, and they are but rarely planted. Yet Rea, 'after passing by the common sorts', names six kinds, including the Algiers, Masculine, and Great Roman—names that were current through the next century but which have now disappeared.

The number of varieties of peach is thirty-five; one, the Newington, 'an old peach, well known, the fruit is fair, of a greenish white colour, and red on the side next the sun', was still grown in Victorian days as 'Old Newington'.

He has but one nectarine, or *Nux persica*, the Roman; this, too, was a Victorian fruit.* So we continue through almonds, nuts, vines—'more than a hundred' but nine kinds only named that are fittest for our climate—figs, sorbus (presumably the true service, *Sorbus domestica*), cornelian cherry, mespilus—the 'Neapolitan or azarollier' (the Azarole thorn, *Crataegus azarolus*)—and, rather surprisingly, three kinds of mulberry, black, white, and red.

ARCHITECT AND POET

The comparative simplicity that was coming into fashion during the Restoration period is also shown by Samuel Pepys (1632–1703) recording a conversation that he had one Sunday in July 1666 with Hugh May (1622–1684), Comptroller of the Works. May, long overshadowed by other reputations, has lately been described as in reality one of the two or three men who determined the character of English domestic architecture after the Restoration. Until 1660 he had been an exile in Holland, and while there was impressed by contemporary Dutch architecture, which has been described as 'Dutch Palladianism'.[5] This type of

---

* It may be pertinent to compare the number of varieties of these tree and stone fruits with those now in cultivation. For example, George Bunyard & Sons—then admittedly supplying a wide range—offered the following varieties in their 1938–9 catalogue: one hundred and twenty-eight apples, seventy-four pears, four quinces, thirty-seven cherries, fifty-three plums, damsons, etc., nine apricots, twenty-six peaches, fourteen nectarines, and twenty-five vines.

red-brick building, with stone facings—often having a central pediment supported not by pillars but pilasters—was to become familiar in England.

Pepys wrote[6] that he walked up and down Whitehall with that 'very ingenious man', and

among other things discussed of the present fashion of gardens to make them plain that we have the best walks of gravel in the world, France having none, nor Italy; and the green of our bowling alleys is better than any they have. So our business here being air, this is the best way, only with a little mixture of statues, or pots, which may be handsome, and so filled with another pot of such or such a flower or green, as the season of the year will bear. And then for flowers, they are best seen in a little plot by themselves: besides, their borders spoil the walks of another garden: and then for fruit, the best way is to have walls built circularly one within another, to the south, on purpose for fruit, and leave the walking garden only for that use.

From Hanmer and Rea we have now, for the first time, been able to form a detailed picture of what one might call the middling-size garden, the garden that went with the new houses, or the old ones modernized, of the increasing middle class. It has been described at some length because it was the type of garden that persisted among the unfashionable, with but little change, well on into the Georgian age. The quadrangular garden can still sometimes be traced by the remains of the walls behind an old manor or town house. It was a particularly sensible form of gardening; Rea's opening generalizations could not be bettered.

It was, too, the form of garden known to many of our most delightful, if minor, poets. It was to this period that we owe one of the few English poems of any length devoted to the garden. The author, Abraham Cowley (1618–1667), was with the court in France, and saw the beginnings of the new style; his poem was dedicated to John Evelyn.

His elysium was a place of retreat:

> O blessed shades! O gentle cool retreat
> From all th' immoderate heat
> In which the frantic world does burn and sweat;
> This does the Lion-star, ambitious rage,
> This avarice, the Dog-star's thirst assuage;

Every where else their fatal power we see,
They make and rule man's wretched destiny:
  They neither set, nor disappear,
  But tyrranize o'er all the year;
Whilst we ne'er feel their flame or influence here.
  The birds that dance from bough to bough,
  And sing above in every tree,
  Are not from fears and cares more free,
  Than we who lie, or walk below,
  And should by right be singers too.
What prince's choir of music can excel
  That which within their shade doth dwell?
  To which we nothing pay or give,
  They like all other poets live,
Without reward, or thanks for their obliging pains;
  'Tis well if they become not prey;
The whistling winds add their less artful strains,
And a grave bass the murmuring fountains play;
Nature does all this harmony bestow,
  But to our plants . . .

These are the spells that to kind sleep invite,
And nothing does within resistance make,
  Which yet we moderately take:
  Who would not choose to be awake,
While he encompass'd round with such delight,
To th'ear, the nose, the touch, the taste, and sight?
When Venus would her dear Ascanius keep
  A pris'ner in the downy bands of sleep,
She od'rous herbs and flowers beneath him spread
  As the most soft and sweetest bed;
Not her own lap would more have charm'd his head
  Who, that has reason, and his smell,
Would not 'mong roses and jasmin dwell,
  Rather than all his spirits choke,
With exhalations of dirt and smoke,
  And all th' uncleanness which does drown
In pestilential clouds a pop'lous town?[7]

It was in the prefatory essay to this poem that Cowley wrote those rather over-famous words which enshrine the wish of so many moderns: 'I never had any other desire so strong . . . as that

I might be master at last of a small house and large garden . . . and there dedicate the remainder of my life only to the culture of them, and the study of nature.' This feeling for a garden as a means of escape was to grow. Cowley gained his wish. But it seems that his Chertsey home did not prove quite the elysium of which he had dreamed.

CHARLES II AND JOHN ROSE

A good deal has been said about Charles II, and it is the due of this great patron of the arts and sciences that we should mention his activities as a gardener.

On his restoration Charles found his mother's gardener André Mollet, still working with his brother Gabriel. They became gardeners to the king, who therefore had men to hand trained in the French tradition. They were concerned with the king's first task, the alteration of St. James's Park.

From Pepy's *Diary* and Edmund Waller's poem of 1661, *On St. James's Park as Lately Improved by His Majesty*, we know that Charles wasted no time. Of the new water-works Waller wrote:

> Instead of rivers rolling by the side
> Of Eden's garden, here flows in the tide . . .*

And of the planting:

> For future shade, young trees upon the banks
> Of the new stream appear in even ranks.
> The voice of Orpheus or Amphion's hand
> In better order could not make them stand.
> May they increase as fast and spread their boughs
> As the high fame of their great owner grows!
> May he live long enough to see them all
> Dark shadows cast and as his palace tall.

Unfortunately, this last wish was not entirely fulfilled, for: 'At the first planting of the Royal garden in St. James's Park, a great number [of acacias] were planted in the walks that M. Mollet then made; but in a few years they were all cut down, by reason of the least gust of wind broke some of their branches.'[9]

Waller adds:

---

* The 'tide' flowed in a canal 2,800 ft. long and 100 ft. broad; it was 'irregularized' into its present shape by W. T. Aiton for George IV.[8]

While overhead, a flock of new-sprung fowl
Hangs in the air, and does the sun control . . .

a reference to his Majesty's delight in waterfowl; indeed, in all strange birds* and beasts. This association of St. James's with exotic creatures was nothing new; James I had his menagerie there, though it was temporarily eclipsed during the reign of William III, who apparently disliked animals.[11]

André Mollet was the author of *Le Jardin de Plaisir* published in 1651 and dedicated to Queen Christina of Sweden, whom he was then serving. It includes a number of plates,† one of which shows that Mollet understood something of Le Nôtre's principles.[12] The identity of the persons—possibly Mollet guided by Le Nôtre—who prepared the now apparently non-existent plans for the considerable alterations made by Charles remains unknown. Two facts have, however, been established: that by 1666 both Mollets were dead and that John Rose had become keeper of St. James's garden in 1661 Early on Rose had been gardener to the Duchess of Somerset at Amesbury, Wilts. Rea, after giving instructions for the tending of evergreens, adds: 'these are the rules observed by Mr. John Rose, the ingenious keeper of the garden of Essex House'.[14] The Earl of Essex had sent him to study at Versailles under Le Nôtre; presumably, too, he would know the Mollets. Yet in most of the contemporary references that we have, such as Rea's, it is his skill as a horticulturist that is praised; nowhere is he mentioned as a designer.

Hanmer[15] refers to him several times; he obviously knew him. Among the 'middle-sized bear's-ears' that flowered at Bettisfield in 1661 was 'Rose's olive . . . the colour is a very good deep olive'; he also refers to 'the King pear so called by Rose because the king liked it, but it is a French pear', and again to 'the Lombardy vine, as Rose calls it, the king's gardener', which 'bears a fair red grape which the king loves'.

Rose was an ardent viticulturist. His only publication was the *English Vineyard Vindicated* of 1666. This was, in fact, put together

---

* In 1671 Charles Hatton had from his elder brother in Guernsey three 'red billed jackdaws' and some gulls for the gardens; Baptist May, of the king's household, accepted the daws but refused the gulls. May added that the king would find strange fowl, such as more daws, a gannet or some barbelottes, a very acceptable present.[16]

† An English edition was published in 1670. It is said that few copies retain these plates, evidence that they were extracted and used as patterns.[13]

from Rose's material by John Evelyn, disguised under the pseudonym 'Philocepos'—which he gives away by referring to himself as the author of *Sylva*.

The association between the king and his gardener is probably best known through a charming painting (of which more than one version, as well as engravings, exist) that generally carries the title *Rose, the Royal Gardener, presenting to Charles II the first pine-apple grown in England*. This picture has not infrequently been reproduced; it presents a number of problems, not the least of which is that there has never been found any written account of this occasion, nor any record of pineapple cultivation in England (as we shall see later) until after the death of Charles. Another is that the house shown in the view cannot be identified; it has even been suggested that the scene is in Holland.[16] The picture is ascribed to the Dutch artist Danckaerts, who arrived in England about 1668. Rose died in 1677, so if the gardener is Rose, this presupposes that it must have been painted, and the pineapple raised, between those years.

The history of the original picture, however, appears to be this.[17] In 1780 Horace Walpole saw it in the collection of the Rev. William Pennicott, from whom he acquired it. Walpole wrote that Pennicott had it from 'London, grandson to him who was partner with Wise'. Walpole describes the picture, and it was he who was responsible for its title. Whether he had this by tradition (George London was a pupil of Rose) or whether it was based on no more than his own conclusions is not known.

Evelyn, keenly interested in greenhouses and fruit though he was, makes no reference to the event in his diary. He does, however, refer in 1661 to the king eating a Queen pineapple imported from Barbados, adding that the first in England were sent to Cromwell 'four years since'.[18]

Charles was, of course, always ready to receive presents. One instance shows how a love of gardens could overcome other feelings. Sir Ralph Verney had nothing else in common with his king, but in 1671 he received royal thanks for 'quickenberry trees'* raised at Claydon and planted at Greenwich: 'they thrive exceedingly, and I shall be very happy to see you there, that you may see how well they flourish upon a piece of as barren ground as is in England'.[19]

* Rowans.

THE RESTORATION GARDEN

The royal enthusiasm for gardening was shared by the king's subjects. 'I do believe,' wrote John Aubrey, 'I may affirm that there is now, 1691, ten times as much gardening about London as there was in 1660 . . . in the time of Charles II gardening was much improved and became common.'[20]

We have already seen that just before the Restoration serious attention was paid to the garden on the Russell estate at Woburn Abbey. William Russell (1613–1700), 5th Earl, later first Duke, of Bedford, was an early member of a family which has devoted much attention to horticulture and kindred subjects. In the year of the return of Charles he began the building of Thorney Abbey House, in Cambridgeshire. He also had, at Bedford House, a London residence. Woburn, however, had the finest garden. We are fortunate in having full and delightful records of the management of his properties. As he was not untypical of his period it will be useful to summarize the history of his gardens.[21]

To take Bedford House first. From about 1660 until 1684 the gardener in charge was Thomas Gilbank, who was paid £40 a year. He was succeeded by Thomas Todd. These men were also important as the London purchasing agents for the development of Woburn.

The garden these men controlled was simple. It lay behind the house, across which stretched a terrace. Below this a broad gravel path divided the garden, which was walled. On one side of the path were beds of geometrical shape divided by gravel paths, with stone ornaments at the points of intersection. These were no doubt planted in the manner described by Hanmer. On the other side of the dividing path was set a wilderness, an elaborate series of alleyways running maze-like between trees and shrubs. Much attention, and a good deal of expense, was devoted to its upkeep. There was a herb plot, but not enough space for a kitchen garden.

The development of the Woburn gardens took a big step forward when John Field was appointed gardener in about 1663. The gardener, or, as he was called in later times, the head gardener, was often an important member of the household. (We have seen, for instance, how Sir Arthur Ingram's gardener at York was paid an over-all sum to cover the entire management of the garden.)

Field of Woburn was an outstanding example of this friendship and trust between gardener and master, for he and his wife, an excellent sick nurse, became so beloved of the Russell family that they were almost a part of it.

At this time, too, it became not unusual for a gardener on these estates, having established his position, to engage also in business on his own account. Field was one of the original partners in the firm that eventually became renowned under the name of London and Wise.

On these big estates the gardener was probably the only member of the garden staff on the permanent pay-roll. Certainly at Woburn all the other garden labour was casual. As usual, some of it—particularly for weeding—was female.

The gardens that Field took over were of the normal type, lying on three sides of the house, with a kitchen garden beyond, two cherry orchards, and a bowling green. Soon after his arrival he was buying polyanthuses, which were then still a novelty. This gives an idea of his keenness. He seems to have been particularly interested in gillyflowers; of his order in 1671 one cannot resist mentioning a few names: Virgin of Middlesex, Virgin of England, and—no doubt to offset them—Bride of Canary. Bohemias's Crown and Grave William were others.

In that year even greater developments were begun. The extent of the orchards and kitchen garden was increased—no doubt to provide for the requirements of the now large household. Orchards and walls were planted with a far greater range of fruit —apricots, peaches, nectarines, and plums, particularly the newer kinds. The dwarf fruit trees, now so fashionable, were planted round ponds.

A list of the fruit supplied in 1674 by Captain Leonard Gurle from his Whitechapel nursery is interesting. The biggest selection was of plums. No fewer than fifteen kinds were purchased, seven of them being dwarfs. Next came the peaches in twelve varieties. There were eight kinds of pear, all described as French,* and seven cherries, two of them dwarfed. There were only three apples. Of the two nectarines one was the Elruge. Two apricots and one quince were bought.

* The spelling of French names in garden lists was often delightfully insular. Gurle's list has 'Bonchrétien' as 'Booncriton', 'Beurré' as 'Berry'.

An increasingly wide range of vegetable seeds was bought—the American scarlet (runner) bean, first grown by Tradescant as an ornamental climber, now appears—as a vegetable. Large quantities of marigold and clove gillyflowers were bought, primarily for preserving in vinegar as winter 'sallets'. Nasturtium seed was also obtained for the kitchen—the old name, Indian cress, indicates its use: 'both the flowers, tender leaves, capuchin capers (seeds) are laudably mixed with the colder plants. The buds, as also the young green seeds, being pickled or candied, are likewise used in stewings all winter'.[22] From the numerous references to the purchase of melon 'glasses', this fruit seems to have been very popular.

Celia Fiennes visited Woburn in 1697 and described the place when these new gardens had matured.[23] The house was still the old one, and did not impress her. But the park was magnificent; some of the trees in it were cut into the shape of animals. A view over the park, and of the hunting of the deer, could be had from a seat high up in a tree, to which one climbed by fifty steps from the bowling green. This green also had eight arbours 'neatly cut, with seats in them'. Miss Fiennes also admired the three large gardens. The fine gravel walks were one above another, joined by stone steps. They were full of fruit; she ate a great quantity of the thick-skinned sweet Carolina gooseberry.

On the terrace below the state rooms stood pots of oranges, lemons, myrtles, variegated phillyreas, and aloes. In winter these were moved into an orangery; it was heated by a stove obtained from George London, who himself had come down to supervise the planting of the oranges.

From the terrace one passed under an arch into a cherry orchard. In its midst was one of the marvels of the place, a stone effigy of one of the weeding women, so lifelike that it seems to have rivalled Mme Tussaud's waxworks in deceiving visitors.

The fruit trees and plants were purchased from the leading nurserymen of the day—Looker, Mordan, Gurle, and Ricketts are named—or from seedsmen such as Edward Fuller of Strand Bridge.

Some were obtained from the gardens of other nobility and gentry. That of Sir Henry Capel, later Lord Capel of Tewkesbury (who died in 1696), is mentioned. His garden was at Kew.

Evelyn[24] tells us that in 1678 Capel had the choicest fruit any-where in England, and was 'the most industrious and understand-ing of it'; he introduced several new kinds from France. In 1683 Evelyn again visited him. This time the old house was being modernized. Evelyn did not approve, but was very well satisfied with two greenhouses for oranges and myrtles, novel in that they communicated with the rooms of the house—early examples of the conservatory. Nor did Evelyn like the over-large number of 'fir' trees that Capel had planted—but he admired a cupola built between two elms at the end of a walk. On another visit he considered the myrtles and oranges 'very fine'; they were shaded in summer by a high pallisado of reeds, painted with oil.

We have a further description of Capel's garden in December 1691.[25] The garden was then as well-kept, and had as 'curious greens', as any about London. The yew hedges were in the new fashion: at regular intervals along them plants were allowed to grow tall and were 'kept in pretty shapes with tonsure'. On that winter's day the six laurustinuses, trained so that they carried large round heads, were 'very flowery'. Other objects of interest were the mastic trees (*Pistacia lentiscus*). This scarcely hardy species, well known on the isles of the Grecian Archipelago, had been introduced to Britain some thirty years before. Though no doubt the fact that the exudations or 'tears' of the sap produce the mastic of the ancients would interest the 'curious', the trees, particularly those at Kew, were held to be the finest of evergreens in England; Sir Henry had thought fit to pay £40 for them to Vesprit, the nurseryman. Other prized shrubs were four white-striped hollies. From this later account we learn more of the over-numerous firs (they were the common silver fir) to which Evelyn objected: they hedged in an enclosure to shade and protect the oranges in summer. Presumably by now the pallisado had been superseded. Another feature of the garden was the terrace. It had a bare gravel walk down the centre, with bands of turf on either side. Beyond them on the one hand was a low wall fronted with a hedge of rue, on the other dwarf trees were planted. In only one way did Capel's garden fail to excel: the ground was a 'little irregular' in an age when levelness and regularity were *de rigueur*.

This garden was not on the grand scale; it was of interest on account of its fine contents. But grandeur was achieved by Sir

Henry's brother, Arthur, Earl of Essex (1631–1683). Arthur was a man of scholarly habit, but with an excessive enthusiasm for politics which resulted in his death by suicide in the Tower.* According to Evelyn,[26] writing in 1680, he began modernizing his old house at Cassiobury near Watford, but before long found himself completely rebuilding it; this, says Evelyn, accounted for its poor situation in a hollow.

The new house was built in about 1677 by Hugh May, but the laying out of the gardens was apparently begun much earlier, presumably under Moses Cook, who in his book *The Manner of Raising, Ordering and Improving Forest Trees*, published in 1676, with a preface from Cassiobury dated 16th November 1675, refers to work he did in 1669. This book shows, too, that the plantations were well established at the time of its publication, for Cook relates that in 1675 he showed a tree to that 'ingenious artist' Hugh May. It seems, therefore, that Cook, and not May, must have been responsible for the design, which is on a vast scale, as is shown in Kip's engraving.

Evelyn visited the place in 1680, but does not tell us much. No man, he wrote, was more industrious than the earl in planting. The estate, though on 'stony, churlish and uneven' soil, was richly adorned with walks, ponds, and other rural elegances. The land about was 'singularly addicted' to woods,† though, owing to its 'coldness', not all kinds of trees would grow well. The wild cherry thrived above all; he saw avenues of it, and some trees 80 feet tall. Cook had early grasped this fact: 'I know many will say that it is not proper to rank this among forest trees; but if such did see the fine stately trees that we have growing in the woods at Cassiobury, they would then conclude it proper for . . . forests. Where they like the ground, they make a glorious show in the spring, their white blossoms showing at a distance as though they were clothed with fine white linen; their blossoms are a great relief to the industrious bees at that season.'

* He was involved in the Rye House plot; the party that went to apprehend him 'found him in his garden gathering of nut-meg peaches'.

† Another huge plantation of trees in a regular manner was made by Sir Joseph Child (1630–1699), economist and successful financial magnate, at Wanstead Abbey, which he bought in 1673. The planting, in which walnut played a prominent part along with elms, ashes, and limes, extended into Epping Forest. It was said that the ponds he made cost £5,000 and his plantations twice as much; the gardens themselves were 'but indifferent'. The house was rebuilt and the gardens somewhat altered in 1715.

Evelyn also relates that the large oval at the end of the long walk (seen in the Kip engraving) was planted with treble rows of 'Spanish fir'.* He praised Cook and his knowledge of the 'mechanics' of gardening. (Cook's knowledge of mathematics was considerable, as is shown by his book, which also gives many diagrams for the planting and laying-out of gardens.)

Soon after Evelyn visited Cassiobury, Essex became involved in political trouble. Perhaps because of this, Moses Cook in 1681 joined with George London and others to establish a nursery business. Cook is an enigmatic but probably an important figure in the history of Restoration gardening. Because of the title of his solitary publication he has been regarded as an arboriculturist. Yet the figures in his book show that he had a considerable knowledge of garden design in the French manner.† He was also, as Evelyn records, famed for his fruit-growing.

Cassiobury has virtually disappeared. Traces, however, can still be seen ‡ of another magnificent garden laid out in the 1680s. The 3rd Earl of Devonshire began the replanning of Chatsworth before his death in 1684, but it was his son, the first Duke, who signed a contract with George London in 1688 for further extensive alterations. As the history of Chatsworth has fortunately been described in great detail[27] we need not repeat it. It does, however, bring to our attention the growing mastery of the art of hydraulics. This had been demonstrated in 1677 by Dr. Plot:[28] he spent no less than seven pages describing the 'waterworks' recently invented or improved in the county of Oxford. Chatsworth in the 1690s must have been supreme in this respect, as it is today. We have Dr. Leigh's description published in 1700:

Chatsworth, like a sun in an hazy air, adds lustre to those dusky mountains, and attracts a general congress to be spectators of its wonders. . . .

The gardens, very delightful, pleasant and stately, adorn'd with exquisite water works; the first we observe is Neptune with his sea-nymphs from whence, by the turning of a cock, immediately issue forth several columns of water, which seem'd to fall upon sea-weeds:

* Evelyn's *Sylva* shows this to have been Scot's pine; the Spanish fir as we know it today is *Abies pinsapo*, not discovered until the early nineteenth century.
† We must not forget the English translation in 1670 of Mollet's *Le Jardin de Plaisir*.
‡ In a drought, the pattern of the great parterre can still be seen (and photographed) from the air.

Not far from this is another pond, where sea-horses continually roll; and near to this stands a tree, composed of copper, which exactly resembles a willow; by the turn of a cock each leaf distils continually drops of water, and lively represents a shower of rain; from this we passed by a grove of cypress, upon an ascent, and came to a cascade, at the top of which stand two sea-nymphs, with each a jar under the arm; the water falling thence upon a cascade whilst they seem to squeeze the vessels, produces a loud rumbling noise, like what we may imagine of the Egyptian or Indian cataracts. At the bottom of the cascade there is another pond, in which is an artificial rose, by turning of a cock the water ascends through it, and hangs suspended in the air in the figure of that flower. There is another pond, wherein is Mercury pointing at the gods and throwing up water; besides, there are several statues of gladiators, with the muscles of the body very lively displayed in their different postures.[29]

Another point of interest is that whereas at Cassiobury and elsewhere there were great plantations of trees, Chatsworth was surprisingly bare; this was still so in Horace Walpole's time, for he remarks upon it, and the great improvements that would ensue from the then duke's great activity as a planter.

Chatsworth and other gardens of this period were painted by Jan Sieberecht (c. 1625–1703). Born in Antwerp, he was brought to England (where he died) in about 1670 by the Duke of Buckingham. His picture of Bayhall (Plate 5), near Sevenoaks in Kent (of which virtually nothing is recorded), is representative of his precise work in the Dutch manner and of a house and garden of the time.

That the changes wrought in established gardens during the 1680s were regarded contemporaneously as considerable is, I think, suggested by Lady Winchilsea's* lines written on the decision to improve the gardens at Eastwell in Kent:

> The heavy tidings cause a gen'ral grief,
> And all combine to bring a swift relief.
> Some plead, some pray, some counsel, some dispute,
> Alas in vain where power is absolute.
> Those whom paternal awe forbid to speak
> Their sorrows in their secret whispers break,
> Sigh as they pass beneath the sentenc'd trees,
> Which seem to answer in a mournful breeze.

* Anne Finch, Countess of Winchilsea (1661–1720).

The 'heavy tidings' were of Lord Winchilsea's decision to convert 'the mount in his garden to a terrace, and other alterations and improvements in his house, park and garden'.

It is amusing to continue:

> The very clowns (hir'd by his daily pay)*
> Refuse to strike, nor will their lord obey,
> Till to his speech he adds a leading stroke,
> And by example does their rage provoke.
> Then in a moment every arm is rear'd,
> And the robb'd palace sees what most she fear'd,
> Her lofty grove, her ornamental shield,
> Turn'd to a desert and forsaken field.
> So fell Persepolis. . . .[30]

The architect of the new house, and probably the garden at Eastwell, was William Winde (*d.* 1722). A letter from him, apparently written in the 1690s, still exists: 'I do remember when I was quartered in Kent and employed altering the Earl of Winchilsea's house at Eastwell, I transplanted trees of a considerable bigness which did very well. . . .'[31]

Winde was of the same school as Hugh May. Having spent his youth in Holland, he adopted a military career and subsequently, in about 1667, devoted himself to architecture. He took considerable interest in the gardens of his houses. In 1698–9 he wrote to Lady Mary Bridgeman, for whom he was designing Castle Bromwich Hall: 'I shall tomorrow meet with Capt. Hatton, a very great vertuoso in gardening, to consult with him what plants or trees are most useful. . . .'[32]

Charles Hatton (1635–*c.* 1705) was a considerable virtuoso in subjects other than gardening—though that is what must concern us. Fortunately he was a voluminous correspondent. His letters also form a link which introduces the other virtuosi and cognoscenti of the latter part of the seventeenth century, and bring us back to the family house of Kirby in Northamptonshire. The Hatton tradition of magnificence and entertainment of royalty had been continued. Christopher III, who succeeded in 1619, though he spent most of the Civil War and Commonwealth period in exile, maintained the Kirby gardens, and at the Restoration

---

* Another example of the universal practice of employing casual labour!

they were still famous. Charles Hatton, his younger son, was sending home trees from Paris in 1660. In 1662 Christopher III was made Governor of Jersey—where General Lambert was one of his prisoners, with whose daughter Charles made a romantic marriage.

The elder son, Christopher IV (1632–1706), created Viscount Hatton of Gretton in 1683, inherited Kirby in 1670; it was to him that Charles Hatton addressed many letters. In 1685, some time after his return from Guernsey (to whose governorship he succeeded on the death of his father), Christopher IV began making the great west garden.

Since Kirby never suffered from the eighteenth- and nineteenth-century 'improvers', the officers of the Ministry of Works have, by skimming the accretions from the original stone edgings, recently unearthed the skeleton of this garden. Today it is, perhaps, the only place where, prompted by the official plan,[33] we can visualize with little difficulty a Restoration garden (Plate V).

Charles Hatton himself was for a time Lieutenant-Governor of Guernsey. His antiquarian and scientific tastes (and some valuable manuscripts) were inherited from his somewhat eccentric grandfather. He had in him, too, the same blood that flowed in the veins of the Fanshawes. For a time he served in the army—little else, except that he had a garden in London and, after the death of his first wife, married a widowed daughter of Chief Justice Scroggins, seems to be known about him other than what he tells us.

His character is revealed in a letter to his brother of 1679, in which he gives the 'very prodigious news' that the future James II had left the country; almost in the same breath he continues, 'I shall take care about the apricot trees.'

His friends called him 'the incomparable Charles', a description that has puzzled some later writers. But he was as thoughtful and wise as most of his ancestors were feckless, and one example alone will help to substantiate the epithet. In 1686 appeared *Historia Plantarum* by John Ray.* It is a landmark in the development of British natural history. It was dedicated to Hatton —and the dedication was no formality, for Ray said on more than

---

* John Ray (1627–1705) was a pioneer of science; though keenly interested in many garden plants, his work really lies outside the scope of a gardening history.[34]

one occasion that Hatton was responsible for the idea of this great undertaking ('first put him on' were the exact words).[35] Further, Hatton provided Ray with books, manuscripts, and information.

Hatton was also a friend of Dr. Robert Morison, of Oxford, who referred to him as 'a curious person, and a great lover of flowers'.[36] It was to Morison that he sent the Guernsey lily (*Nerine sarniensis*) which he found growing freely there on the island.*

Evelyn also bears testimony to him as 'the honourable and learned Charles Hatton, Esq. (to whom all our phytologists and lovers of horticulture are obliged, and myself in particular for many favours)'.[37]† Another author to praise him was Morton, the historian of Northampton,[38] as that 'ingenious gentleman' who first successfully propagated mistletoe from the seed; this was on poplars around Kirby.

It is, however, as a typical, if exceptionally gifted, amateur in gardening of the late seventeenth century that Hatton concerns us, and from his letters to his brother at Kirby we can gather the sort of horticultural talk that interested the virtuosi of the day.‡

In 1688 he told his brother that he had been at Oxford.

I have sent some seeds I procured from Mr. Bobart. Some of them are very curious plants. . . . I should advise sowing of part of each parcel of the choicest seeds now, and the rest next spring. For those plants which are annual, being sowed so late, will not I suppose come to perfection this summer, and will therefore continue all winter and flower earlier and more beautifully next year.

On 4th July 1688 he wrote announcing the forthcoming visit to Kirby of the Lord Bishop of London. This was Henry Compton (1632–1713), who became bishop in 1675. A forthright and gallant Protestant, he made at Fulham a remarkable collection of trees, particularly from North America,§ and of other exotic

---

* This was not the first introduction (*see* p. 91), but it must have been rare, for it was new to the knowledgeable Morison.

† Hatton had given Mrs. Evelyn some asparagus. The weight of each stick averaged 4 oz. Evelyn considered that this was preferable in flavour to the imported Dutch giant kind, having been raised not in a rank, manured bed (as was their practice) but in a 'more natural, sweet' soil at Battersea.

‡ Hatton was also friendly with Sir Hans Sloane, who was his doctor, and Pepys, who left him a ring in his will.

§ They were mostly destroyed or neglected by his successors; Ray had described some of them in *Historia Plantarum*, Vol. III. A number were, however, bought by two nurserymen, Furber and Gray.[39]

plants both in his stoves and gardens. Hatton writes of his 'oaks from Virginia with chestnut leaves, walnuts from thence bearing flowers', '*Larix* or larch trees', 'Breyennius his Leonorus, a most beautiful tree', and 'the quina-quina or Jesuit's bark, a bastard kind from Virginia'. But, he adds, a stove is necessary for some of them and urges his brother to ask the bishop about its construction and management.

In the same letter he records the first flowering in England of the tulip tree. It was in Lord Mordaunt's* garden; few saw it, however, for the gardener foolishly did not spread the news around.

In March 1690 he saw Elias Ashmole's† baking pear, the finest he ever saw; it was grafted on dwarfing stock;‡ a year later he reported when sending grafts of it to Kirby that some of the fruits weighed 20 ounces—at the same time he sent his brother grafts of Ashmole's famous thorn trees. In April 1690 he sent two 'lusty and strong' passion flowers in pots that he had from Chelsea, with the advice that if the gardener layers them properly 'this time twelve months you may have twenty'.

There are other letters concerning seeds being sent or obtained; and, in one: 'I am glad your Lordship likes the *Helleborus albus floreatrorabeate*. You laughed at me when I was at Kirby for liking it.'

In September 1694 comes a longer letter:

Your Lordship commends Mr. Dolben's§ walks in his garden, but, my Lord, Mr. Gylby tells me you have set up the gate you removed at the end of the middle walk in your upper garden, repaired the walls and coping, and are gravelling the walks; and he tells me he thinks you have made it the finest garden in England. I am very glad you have had such very fine weather to bring your gravel. I lately saw at Hackney a holly hedge round a garden about 10 foot high, and all so close a mouse could scarce creep through in any place. I never saw in my life so fine a hedge.

* Charles Mordaunt (1658–1735), later Earl of Peterborough and Monmouth, was himself at this time in retirement in Holland owing to his opposition to James II. His garden at Parson's Green, Fulham, and particularly its tulip tree, were famous. He was a friend of Pope.

† Elias Ashmole (1617–1692) inherited Tradescant's 'Ark' (the nucleus of the Ashmolean Museum) in 1662.

‡ The discovery that pear grafted on quince fruited early and grew slowly seems to have been an early one.

§ Probably John Dolben, Archbishop of York.

I told you of a blue hyacinth without a smell (so they called it at the King's garden, where I saw one single flower); I have since seen the whole plant. It is not a hyacinth, but a *Lilio-Narcissus*. The stem is about 4 ft. high, and at the top bears a tuft of about 40 blue flowers, in the manner of the Narcissus of Japan. It is truly a very stately, beautiful flower.

I am promised some amaranth and fine hollyoaks* seeds for your Lordship.

I hear George London has been at Burley-on-the-Hill,† and drawn a design for a very spacious garden there. Here is great talk of vast gardens at Boughton; but‡ I hear my Lord Montagu is very much concerned that the water with which he hoped to have made so fine fountains has failed to fulfill his expectation.

September 1697 saw an invitation to visit Dr. 'Udall's'§ garden at Enfield, 'and if your Lordship would be pleased to favour me with a piece of venison to present him with, it would be a very great favour, and I should not doubt to procure you, next spring, some choice plants from him'.

In 1698 he gives advice on fruit trees: 'I hear a nectarine called the Elruge very much commended. As for peaches, the Rambouillet, Violet Musk, Belle Chevreuse, Alberge, Maudlin, Sion, Newington are the most esteemed. There are white and red nutmeg peaches.'

February of the following year sees an account of the terrible storm which uprooted many trees in St. James's Park, Moorfields, and Gray's Inn Walks.

One of his last gardening letters written to Kirby was in March 1704. Having already furnished Lord Hatton with 'perry sugar' and 'manna', he now sends him seeds of the soap tree, re-

---

* From the King's garden, where the amaranths and hollyhocks were 'I believe the best ever seen in England' (September 1694).

† Daniel Finch, Earl of Nottingham, purchased the place from the Duke of Buckingham and began to build in 1694.[40]

‡ The designer was probably French; a plan exists in the Bodleian Library, Oxford. There is now little trace of the original gardens, but Montagu's successor, 'Planter John' (c. 1688–1749), left his mark on the district. About 20 of the 72 miles of avenues that he planted (mostly elm but some lime) still stride over the Northamptonshire landscape.

§ Dr. Robert Uvedale (1642–1722) became master of Enfield Grammar School; it is said that he devoted so much time to his garden that the authorities threatened to relieve him of his post. He planted the famous Enfield cedar, reputedly procured for him by one of his scholars. His garden did not 'please the eye' but he probably had the greatest collection of exotics in England (with an 'extraordinary art in managing them') which was housed in six or seven houses.[41]

cently come over from China, of which plants have been raised in England and are thriving; also some tea seeds as a curiosity, with a warning that they will not grow here. 'But,' he adds, 'the *Licer sativum* will thrive well here, and the mallows. They [the Chinese] prefer the liches before any peases, and they eat the mallows for salads. But I am inclinable to think our peas and salads exceed them in goodness.'

Hatton's pride in our kitchen garden produce of the time was justified; French visitors remarked that we excelled in it. There were, for example, the celebrated Neat House Gardens, which provided asparagus, artichokes, cauliflowers, cucumbers, and melons early in the season and of prime quality. They were restricted to the riverside district now known as Pimlico, and owed their success to the proximity of large supplies of neat's (cattle) dung from the neighbouring cattle sheds. The district has an early tradition of vegetable culture, for the situation was the same as that of the Manor of la Neyte mentioned in the fourteenth century. Hot-beds were early in use, and it seems that until the mid-eighteenth century the gardeners there were able to keep to themselves the secrets they had acquired through centuries of experience.

． ． ． ． ．

From Scotland travellers' tales of the half-century after the Restoration continue to tell of a rough and hard way of life in a countryside that was often bare and rugged. There was a series of bad harvests, and the equivalent of the smaller type of English manor house or parsonage, with its often productive and interesting garden, scarcely existed.[42]

Significant changes were, however, taking place. In 1661 Robert Sibbald (1641–1712) returned from studying medicine in Leyden and Paris. He was horrified at the ignorance of his countrymen and the poor standards maintaining in Edinburgh University compared with those he found on the Continent. Doctors were still mostly quacks, who would resort to performances on the tight-rope to attract patients when custom fell away. The serious and practical study of medicinal plants—still almost synonymous with botany—was practically non-existent. In 1670 Sibbald's initiative resulted in the purchase of a small piece of land at Holyrood for use as a botanical garden so that this state of affairs might be remedied. In 1676 the Town Council appointed James Sutherland (*c.* 1639–1719) as the 'Intendant'.*

A student of plants from his childhood days, Sutherland was a clever cultivator. In 1683 he published *Hortus Medicus Edinburgiensis*, a descriptive catalogue of some 2,000 plants that were growing in the garden.[43]

In 1683 *The Scots Gard'ner*, by John Reid, gardener to Sir George Mackenzie of Rosebaugh, was published—the first Scottish gardening book. E. H. M. Cox[44] concludes from evidence in the book that Reid, whose precepts were for the most part up-to-date and sound, had not received English training. Reid believed that the old Scottish practice of 'run-rigging' the ground should be followed in the kitchen garden. The land was formed into ridges ten or twelve feet wide, with gulleys between; the earth taken from the gulleys was used to build up the ridges. It was a wasteful form of cultivation, the gulleys being kept fallow; and its origin was in fact not concerned with agricultural technique, but with the system of communal land tenure. Cox also considers that Reid and his contemporaries were unaware of the importance of first draining wet, sour land before attempting to bring it into cultivation.

It was on the big estates that most gardening was carried out. On some, gardens rather similar to those in England were formed. But the most significant development in Scotland at this period was the planting of woodlands, shelter belts, and hedges. There was a good deal of opposition from the agricultural community, who considered corn more important than trees.

As in earlier times the alien sycamore (*Acer pseudoplatanus*) was, on account of its hardiness and ability to survive extreme exposure, a favourite. (It was only just coming into fashion in England.) At about this time, too, the planting of holly hedges—as in England—came into fashion. Joseph Sabine, who toured Scotland in 1825, described the immense holly hedges that he saw in the gardens of the big houses.[45] Many were planted in the late part of the seventeenth or the early years of the eighteenth centuries.

* Also concerned with the formation of the garden were Sir Andrew Balfour (1630–1694) and Patrick Murray, whose plants from Livingstone formed the nucleus of the collection; it is said he had over 1,000.

There is one interesting point to be made about Scots gardens of this and the succeeding period. Many of them escaped at least to some extent the 'landscaping' fashion of the late eighteenth and early nineteenth centuries; the geometrical lay-out remained and often was the basis of additions in Victorian times.

'EXOTICKS'

The second half of the seventeenth century, as will have been realized from what has already been written, saw a great increase in the number of hardy and tender plants brought into Britain. Many were brought to northern Europe by French merchants trading with Turkish Mediterranean ports. To France also came many North American plants. The most important centre for their cultivation and distribution was the Jardin des Plantes, under the care of the illustrious Jean Robin, and, after his death in 1629, of his son Vespasien (1579–1662), another famous botanical gardener.

For much of this period our relations with Holland were close; Amsterdam had the East India, Spanish, and Mediterranean trade; Flushing that with the West Indies. The magnificence of the Dutch floriculture and the variety of the exotic plants and fruits they grew is proved beyond doubt by the unsurpassed flower paintings that were produced in the second half of the seventeenth century. The suggestion that fruit was then of inferior quality is triumphantly denied by many Dutch paintings. An ardent gardener, Sir William Temple, was our Ambassador to the States-General from 1668 to 1671 and again from 1674 to 1678.

A good deal else came, largely unrecorded, direct through Englishmen, such as our 'Turkey Merchants' at Aleppo. It seems reasonable to assume that their chaplain from 1630 to 1635, the Rev. Edward Pococke (1604–1691),* who later studied in Constantinople from 1637 to 1640, obtained and raised the first plants of the cedar of Lebanon at Childrey, in Berkshire, where he became rector in 1642. It is certain that at a later date, after he had become an Oxford professor, he obtained and was responsible for the cultivation of other plants; his fig and oriental plane tree at Christ Church grow to this day.

* Not to be confused with Rev. Richard Pococke (1704–1765), a botanist and traveller.

Much must have been sent home by friends overseas. In 1663, for example, John Verney was at Aleppo and despatched a small sack of melon seeds to Claydon at his father's request, with an apology for not being able to send any choicer kinds, 'for in this country among these heathens none are known, here they are not worth 12*d*. a million'. Later he got special and more highly esteemed melon seeds 'of Mesopotamia', of a kind that grew in the river sand after the winter floods; Sir Thomas Lee of Hartwell also had some of the same kind. In January 1670 he sent a little sack of seed of a local tree unknown in England; growing as big as an elm, with leaves of 'an admirable green' and sweetly scented flowers of 'a darkish sky colour', it bore berries of no known use. Apologetically he concluded that it is 'only a delightful tree to look on'.[46]

Many new foreign plants were, of course, obtained for the Oxford and Edinburgh botanic gardens. Bishop Compton, too, received a number from the Rev. John Banister, perhaps the first of the long line of missionary botanists. He collected in Virginia, where he met his death in about 1692 in an accident while plant-hunting. Ray refers to his work in the preface to the second volume of *Historia Plantarum*. And some time in the 1690s John Road,* one of the Hampton Court gardeners, made a journey to Virginia to collect foreign plants, and was paid £234 11*s*. 9*d*.[47]

Many adventurous young men no doubt brought home seeds or plants; Charles Mordaunt, always a keen naturalist, in his early days was engaged in explorations on the Barbary coast.

In 1684 Sir Hans Sloane was able to write 'there is a vast number of East and West India seeds come over this year'.[48] In 1690 Charles Hatton went to Hampton Court with some of his 'old botanic acquaintances' to see some four hundred rare Indian plants gathered together by Herr Fagel which were new to England. They were 'very wonderful and scarcely credible'. The heated house in which they were kept was 'the best contrived in England'.[49]

During the last two decades of the seventeenth century this increased cultivation of exotic plants altered the nature of the greenhouse. Originating, as we have seen, as nothing more than a room or building to keep oranges and other tender 'greens'

* or Reed.

(hence the name) over the winter, with provision for a small stove or even an open fire to keep the keenest frosts at bay, something much more efficient and reliable was now required. Although Sir Hugh Platt (1552–c. 1611) had suggested[50] that a wall against a kitchen fire might give some 'little furtherance' to the ripening of oranges, no one seems to have done more than improve the type of stove used, presumably with a view to ensuring steady burning with the minimum escape of noxious fumes. Even by 1691, when the increase in the number of greenhouses was considerable, their management was so little understood that of the nine greenhouses (mostly remarked upon as new) described by Gibson[51] four had been built in the summer without regard to the fact that they were so placed as to be shaded from the sun in winter.

The earliest record of a greenhouse having the advantages of indirect heating seems to be when, on 7th August 1685, Evelyn went

to see Mr. Watts, keeper of the Apothecaries Garden of simples at Chelsea where there is a collection of innumerable rarieties of that sort, particularly beside many rare annuals the tree bearing the Jesuit's bark,* which had done such cures in quartans, and what was very ingenious the subterranean heat, conveyed by a stove under the conservatory, which was all vaulted with brick, so as he leaves the doors and windows open in the hardest frosts, secluding only snow, etc.[52]

The greenhouse at Hampton Court which Hatton praised in 1690 was apparently built on a similar principle. Gibson[53] says it was a long building subdivided into several rooms, all with stoves *under* them giving continued heat; he remarks that it contained none of the usual 'greens', but only tender foreign ones.

In 1691 Evelyn himself, after discussions with Sir Christopher Wren and Robert Hooke of the Royal Society, published an interesting design for a heated greenhouse. In his preliminary enquiries he had correctly concluded that continual circulation of the air by withdrawing the 'tainted', 'effete', and 'imprisoned' old air from the house and replacing it with a fresh supply from without, properly warmed, would be very beneficial. The fumes and

* Quinine.

143

dry heat of charcoal and other stoves burning within the house resulted, he rightly believed, in vitiating the 'stagnant and pent-in air'.

He placed a furnace outside the building, which drew part of its air through a duct opening in the floor of the house; the amount sucked out by the draught of the fire could be regulated by a shutter. The stale air was then replaced by 'untainted' air drawn

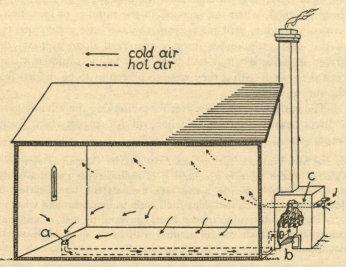

FIG. 6. John Evelyn's greenhouse. The cold air from the bottom of the house is drawn away by an underground pipe (*a*) by suction to the furnace (*b*). It is replaced by warm air drawn through the earthenware pipes (*c*) which are heated by the furnace. Note the thermometer on the wall

from outside and warmed by being passed through a series of earthenware pipes heated by the fire[54] (Fig. 6).

In 1694 Sir Dudley Cullum (1657–1720) of Hawstead in Suffolk communicated to the Royal Society's *Philosophical Transactions* details of the success of a house built and heated on Evelyn's principle.

It may, perhaps, be noted that the greenhouses at this time were quite unlike the greenhouse of today. Although Evelyn was aware of the importance of light, it was not for some years that

I. The 'Jentyl Gardener' (mid-fourteenth century). Probably this figure is that appearing in the York and Coventry Plays. It is a supporter from the misericord of the Dean's stall in Lincoln Cathedral displaying the Resurrection. He carries an iron-shod wooden spade (W. T. Jones)

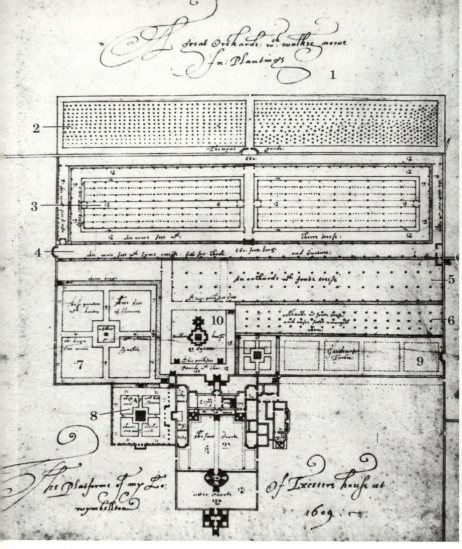

II. John Smythson's plan of Wimbledon Gardens, 1609. (1) A great orchard (outside the garden walls) 'now planting'. (2) The vineyard. (3) Two large plantations undescribed, but bounded by a hedge with cherry trees spaced along it. The outer walls at each end planted with rose trees. (4) A walk planted with 'lime trees both for shade and sweetness'. The length of these cross-walks was 660 feet. (5) An orchard with fruit trees, bounded by quickset hedges. (6) An orchard of 'fruit trees and roses set among them', bordered by hedges. (7) A garden enclosed by hedges with a pillar at the centre. (8) A garden in the angle of the outer walls, the inner boundaries of thorn hedge, centring on a pillar. The quarters laid out as knots. (9) A herb garden. (10) A banqueting house, the surround paved with stones (Royal Inst. of Brit. Architects)

IIIa. Montacute, Somerset (1588–*c*.1600). The courtyard with garden, buildings and ornaments typical of the late Elizabethan period. The gardens themselves are Victorian. A National Trust property

IIIb. Burton Agnes Hall, Yorkshire. The gatehouse (1610) viewed from the house (begun in 1601). The architect was either Robert Smythson or his son John, and the forecourt now seen would have been laid out by the architect in a manner comparable with Essex House, designed to be looked down upon

IVa. Buxted, Sussex. An early example of a lime avenue, believed to have been planted in 1630 (J. D. U. Ward)

IVb. Packwood House, Warwickshire (about 1650). Typical gateway and brick walling. The alcoves either side sheltered bee skeps. A National Trust property (W. T. Jones)

Va. Bayhall, Kent. A Restoration garden scene painted by Jan Sieberecht in about 1685 (Mr and Mrs Paul Mellon)

Vb. Kirby Hall, Northamptonshire (1685–6). Brick terrace walling ornamented with a rusticated-stone false gateway with niches, in the manner of Inigo Jones

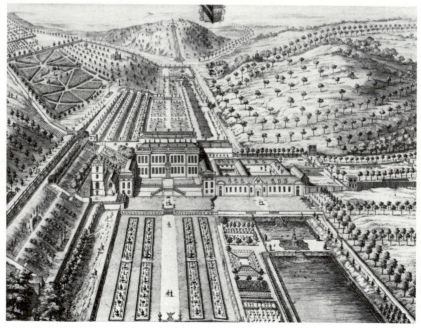

VIa. Charlecote, Warwickshire (1696). A garden in the flat valley of the Avon developed around an old house, of which the gatehouse and the avenues still survive. A National Trust property (National Trust)

VIb. Dyrham, Gloucestershire (begun 1694). An elaborate new layout and house in the hilly country of the Cotswolds. A National Trust property (Sir R. Atkyn, *Ancient and Present State of Gloucestershire*, 1712)

VIIa. Powis Castle, Montgomeryshire. A very early eighteenth-century design in the Dutch manner, yet contrasting strongly with the level landscape typical of Holland

VIIb. Powis Castle. The terraces with urns and lead figures. A National Trust property

VIII. Studley Royal, Yorkshire. The gardens laid out by John Aislabie, possibly inspired by John James, in *c.*1720–40. His son William in 1768 acquired the adjoining Fountains Abbey estate and linked its romantic scenery with his father's scheme (Edwin Smith)

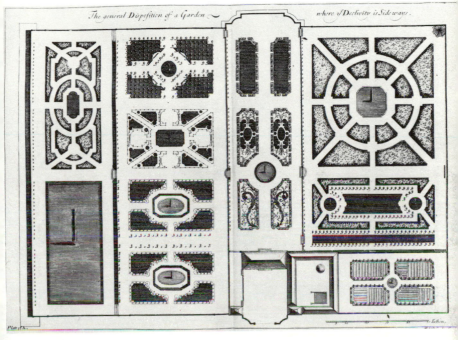

IX. A garden of twenty acres (1712). This plan includes the first known English representation of a ha-ha; it is at the top centre (J. James, *The Theory and Practice of Gardening*, 1712)

X. A Triumph of horticulture. The engraving by J. Pine (1690–1756) of a pineapple flowering. Pine later became famed for his engravings illustrating the classics (Richard Bradley, *New Improvements in Planting and Gardening*, 1726)

X Ia. The age of Le Nôtre: Melbourne Hall, Derbyshire, laid out by Sir Thomas Coke with the help of London and Wise in the first years of the eighteenth century 'to suit with Versailles'

X Ib. The age of the picturesque: *The Ponte Molle*. A Roman scene by Claude Lorrain (1600–82) (City of Birmingham Museum and Art Gallery)

XII. The butt of Addison and Pope. An early Georgian garden with clipped trees, ornate parterres, and of geometric design. But observe the ingenious and productive kitchen and fruit garden (J. Bradley, *New Improvements of Planting and Gardening*, 1726)

XIII. Stourhead, Wiltshire (*c.*1740–70). Elysium in Britain. A National Trust property (Edwin Smith)

XIV. Stourhead, Wiltshire (*c.*1740–70). The eclecticism of the English
landscape school: the classic style side by side with English cottage 'gothick'. A
National Trust property (Edwin Smith)

XV. Blenheim Palace, Oxfordshire (1764). Lancelot Brown's great success: the floating of Vanbrugh's triumphal causeway (Edwin Smith)

XVIa. A Brown landscape today. The Park, Blenheim Palace, Oxfordshire (1764–74) (Edwin Smith)

XVIb. A Brown landscape through contemporary eyes. Croome, Worcestershire, painted by Richard Wilson in 1758 (Croome Estate Trust)

the buildings took a form other than a shed with three sides of brickwork or masonry, with only the south side glazed. Nor, apparently, were the advantages of heating the house by interior flues, carrying air heated by passing through an exterior furnace, realized until well in the next century, though the extravagance and uneven heating caused by a furnace under the floor seem to have been recognized.

The large, glazed cold frame as we know it does not seem to have been much used. Something similar existed in the form of an unglazed framework which could support mats to form a protection in cold weather. This covered the hot-beds made from dung. There were also handlights, either in the shape of a miniature rectangular greenhouse glazed with numerous small panes or smaller and of polygonal shape. Bell glasses were commonly used; they were in the form of a lipped bell, with curved and not the vertical sides of the modern cloche.

Improvements were made in the eighteenth century. Fairchild's *City Gardener*, for instance, shows houses built against a wall, rather like the span greenhouse of today, but sloping down to a foot or two from the ground. In these, too, the panes were small by modern standards.

It has been said that outdoor walls were first heated by means of interior flues in 1718—but this is a matter needing further enquiry.

NURSERYMEN AND GARDENERS

The half-century following the Restoration saw a considerable development in the nurseryman's status and skill. Just after the Restoration George Ricketts of Hoxton was of high repute. In 1665 Rea described him as 'the best and most faithful florist now about London'. Hanmer often bought plants from him. In 1667, for example, he had eighteen kinds of peach at 2s. a tree, four of nectarines at 3s., ten cherries at 8d., thirty-four pears at 1s., and seventeen apples at 8d. except 'the fig apple without a core', which was 5s. At the same time he had twenty-three kinds of gillyflower at 8d. the root.[55]

In 1670 Hanmer bought from him anemones, including '2 good roots of Ricketts own Violet Imperial' for 8s., and auriculas in pots at 1s. each, except a double one that cost 4s. But by 1691 he appears to have become over successful. Gibson says that though he had a large nursery ground, he charged high prices, and as his plants were said not to do well, was losing custom.

In 1670 Hanmer bought anemones, both seed and plants, from Le Pere, a Huguenot in London. The seed varied in price very considerably, from 6*d.* to 8*s.* the ounce. The roots (of which nineteen kinds were bought) ranged from 3*d.* to 1*s.* 6*d.* each. Le Pere also supplied gillyflowers.

A prominent supplier of the finest fruit trees was Captain Leonard Gurle. Hanmer in 1661 wrote of the 'Elrug or Gurle's nectarine' as coming from 'a chance sowing of a stone and still rare'.[56] The name is, of course, an anagram, and Hanmer spells it correctly; for the sake of euphony a final 'e' was added, and as Elruge it is still to be found in catalogues as one of the hardiest and most reliable sorts. Its persistence is remarkable; very few of its contemporaries among fruit of any kind are still found in cultivation.*

Gurle, as we have seen, supplied many fruit trees for Woburn. According to Leonard Meager[57] in 1681 he had a large nursery between Spitalfields and Whitechapel and from 1677 to 1685 when he died was King's Gardener at St James's. By 1691 Pearson of Hoxton[58] was coming to the front. He had but a small nursery, specializing in flowers, of which he had a great choice. He had the best anemones in London, which he sold only to gentlemen! It is interesting to note that he was prepared to sell 3-feet-high cypress in quantities at 4*d.* each.

Darby, also of Hoxton, was an outstanding nurseryman at the end of the century; he had a little garden, but stocked 'curious greens' that other 'sale gardeners' want. He also had a '*Fritalaria Crassa*'† bearing flowers as large as a half-crown like an embroidered star; in this he excelled the great Dr. Uvedale, who, though he had the plant, could not flower it.

Darby propagated variegated hollies by budding them, while Captain Foster, of Lambeth, who had the finest striped holly in England, raised them from grafts. Darby was clearly a highly skilled propagator. He was even more successful at raising mistletoe from seed than Hatton: a large plant he grew on an apple tree was celebrated.

It was during this period that 'striped' or variegated hollies

* Only the Morello cherry, the Portugal quince, the Nottingham medlar, and the true greengage (Reine Claude) are older.
† This was a 'green'—probably *Stapelia Curtisii* (*variegata*).

and other 'greens' became popular. Besides Darby and Foster, a nurseryman named Wrench was famed for variegated hollies; he gave rewards to people spotting remarkable kinds.[59] He collected gold and silver hedge-hog holly, the saw-leaved holly, and Wrench's 'Phyllis'—a variegated kind that was still known in the nineteenth century.[60] His nursery was near to the Earl of Peterborough's garden at Parson's Green, Fulham.

Of other Hoxton nurserymen, Thomas Fairchild (1667–1729) is remembered today on account of his book *The City Gardener* (1722), already mentioned. It is the first to deal with the problems peculiar to town gardens. The most serious was the rapid increase in smoke pollution.* He might also be ranked as a pioneer of town planning, for he paid much attention to the planting of squares and public places, giving lists of the plants that were suitable.

Fairchild took part, with nineteen others, in the formation of a Society of Gardeners, which produced a *Catalogus Plantarum*. The first and only part appeared in 1731, after Fairchild's death. It is a useful work, giving much information on contemporary synonyms.

Fairchild's nursery was on the other side of 'a narrow alley to George Whitmore's at the far end of Hoxton'. Darby died, it seems, in either 1713 or 1714, and his name is not among the authors of *Catalogus Plantarum*, but the two seem to have worked together in raising and distributing the tulip tree in large quantities for the first time; they were probably responsible for bringing into cultivation other North American plants, such as the catalpa, from the introductions of Mark Catesby (1679–1749), who was in America from 1712 to 1726.

Fairchild is also of consequence because he appears to have been the first English nurseryman to experiment seriously with hybridization. It is probable that, before 1717, he placed the pollen† of sweet william on the style of a carnation. As presumably he had hoped, the offspring differed from both parents. He made other crossings, and in the Botany Department at Oxford there still exists a herbarium specimen of one, labelled 'Mr. Fairchild's Mule'.[62]

* Gibson in 1691 wrote that the 'greens' in 'my Lord of Devonshire's', at Arlington Garden excelled, but that they were smutty from the town air, and not so green and bright as those in the country.[61] The production of 'sea coal'—which caused the pollution—totalled 210,000 tons in the years 1551–60. Between 1681–90 the corresponding figure was 2,982,000 tons—a fourteen-fold increase!
† This was then generally called farina.

Several foreigners worked in England in the nursery business. One was 'Monsieur' Hermon Van Guine, gardener to Queen Catherine of Braganza, widow of Charles II, at Hammersmith. The garden was of little interest, but Van Guine, 'of great skill', raised oranges and lemons for sale by budding them.

Monsieur Antony Vesprit had supplied the famous mastic trees to Sir Henry Capel. His nursery, though small, offered the choicest selection in the country. His bay trees were admired, and his oranges and lemons—both trees and fruit—were also 'extraordinary fair'. Hatton in August 1694 remarked upon his fine aloe then in flower.

We need not mention numerous other small nurserymen and seedsmen of the period whose names are recorded, other than to remark that many of them had their nurseries either in what is now the Shoreditch district, or on the stretch of land between Brompton and Fulham.

There seems very little recorded of nurserymen outside the London area. Thus in December 1684, Lady Massingberd who lived in Lincolnshire asked her husband to buy peach and nectarine trees from Mr. Rickett's son James at the Hand in Hoxton.[63] Much was obtained from the gardeners on the big estates, who propagated material for sale, and many plants, particularly 'greens', were imported from Holland.

It is apparent that all the firms we have mentioned were on a small scale. Although gardening increased greatly in popularity— Leonard Meager's book, *The English Gardener*, a homely, sound, and for the times rather old-fashioned work, went through eleven editions between its publication in 1670 and 1710—there could at this period have been no great demand for nursery-grown plants. But this state of affairs was obviously going to change with the steadily rising prosperity of the middle classes. Perhaps with this in mind, in 1681 a new and large firm of nurserymen was founded.

Its driving force was George London (*d.* 1714), whom we have already encountered. The only account known of his early days is that given by Switzer in 1715.[64] Presumably of humble origins, he came to the notice of John Rose, the royal gardener, under whom he worked. Rose recognized his great ability and sent him to France to study. After his return he became gardener to Bishop

Compton at Fulham, with whom he continued after the nursery business was begun. His character and reliability was shown when, in 1688, he played a part in the escape of Princess Anne which the Duchess of Marlborough and Compton engineered. After the arrival of William and Mary, London became super-intendent of the royal gardens.

The other partners were Moses Cook from Hadham and Cassiobury, John Field of Woburn, and Roger Looker,* gardener to the Queen (Catherine of Braganza) at Somerset House. A site was chosen at Brompton Park covering a hundred acres of fertile soil (now buried under a clutter of museums and institutes). It was a very large area for a nurseryman of those days.

Looker died in 1685, Field in 1687, and in 1689 Cook retired. In 1687 or earlier a new partner, Henry Wise (1653–1738), had joined the firm, which from 1689 was carried on as London and Wise. Until London's death in 1714 this partnership dominated the garden scene.

London travelled and interviewed clients, proposing designs. He also went farther afield. His visit to France with Rose has been mentioned. In 1685 he was in Holland, where he met Paul Hermann (1640–1698) of Leyden, then the foremost cultivator of Cape plants.[65] He had therefore a first-hand knowledge of Dutch as well as of French gardening. He was no mean botanist, corresponding with Sir Hans Sloane. Probably he was responsible for the introduction of a number of plants. Wise superintended the business in London.

In 1691 Gibson described the big Brompton greenhouse in which the king's greens were wintered—occupying but little space compared with London and Wise's own. The back wall was of brick, the front 'all glass and wood'.[66] In 1694 the firm employed twenty men and two women. The foreman had 12s., the other men 8s., and the women 4s. a week. In 1705 it was calculated that if the stock be valued at one penny a plant, it would be worth over £40,000.[67]

THE LATER STUARTS: GREATNESS AND NOBILITY

In 1689 Dutch William and his Stuart Mary occupied the throne. Defoe[68] wrote that the king and queen had each introduced two

* Also spelt Lucre and Lookar.

customs: the queen the love of fine East India calicoes* and of furnishing houses with china ware; the king the love of gardening and of painting. 'His majesty was particularly delighted with the decoration of evergreens, as the greatest addition to the beauty of a garden, preserving the figure of the place, even in the roughest part of an inclement and tempestuous winter.' Defoe goes on to describe the king's visit to Sir Stephen Fox's garden at Chiswick, where the evergreens abounded:†

He stood, and looking round him from the head of one of the canals, 'Well,' says his majesty, 'I could dwell here five days.' Everything was so exquisitely contrived, furnished and well kept, that the king, who was allowed to be the best judge of such things then living in the world, did not so much as once say, this or that thing could have been better.

With this particular judgement, all the gentlemen of England began to fall in, and in a few years fine gardens and fine houses began to grow up in every corner. The king began with the gardens at Hampton Court and Kensington, and the gentlemen followed everywhere with such gust that the alteration is indeed wonderful through the whole kingdom; but nowhere more than in the two counties of Middlesex and Surrey, as they order on the River Thames; the beauty and expense of which are only to be wondered at, not described . . . the whole country here shines with a lustre. Take them at a remote view, the fine seats shine among the trees as jewels shine in a rich coronet; in a near sight they are mere pictures and paintings; at a distance they are all nature, near hand all art; but both in the extremest beauty.

Apart from the houses of the great and rich, the countryside was 'bespangled with villages; those villages filled with houses, and the houses surrounded with gardens, walks, vistas, avenues, representing all the beauties of building, and all the pleasures of planting'. So much for the scene around London as it developed steadily through the reigns of William and Mary, and Anne.

---

* As has already been mentioned, the East Indies trade was centred upon Amsterdam. The Dutch made contact with Japan, most secretive of countries, where gardening and horticulture were already in a state of perfection. In 1690 the German traveller Englebrecht Kaempfer (1651–1716) travelled as physician to the Dutch Embassy in that country, where he spent two years. His *History of Japan* was published in England in 1728.

† This event must have been late in the king's reign; Gibson says in 1691 that the gardens were then at 'great perfection though only five years planted'. There were hedges of myrtle, protected in winter with painted wooden cases. Fox was the principal promoter of the institution of Chelsea Hospital; he was closely concerned there, and probably at Farley, Wiltshire, with Sir Christopher Wren.

It was the same in many other places. 'As to the parks,' wrote Morton[69] in 1712, '. . . 'tis observed that there are more in Northamptonshire, than in any other county in England, and, according to Dr. Heylin, there are a greater number of parks in England than in all Europe besides.'

.   .   .   .   .

The reign of William and Mary (and, indeed, of Anne) is, as Defoe says, particularly associated with the use of greens of every kind. We have seen, however, that the fashion for them had begun at least in Hanmer's time, thirty years before the Revolution. Great Britain, like Holland, is a land where nature is niggardly in providing evergreens—though it is now difficult to visualize conditions in the seventeenth and early eighteenth centuries, when deciduous woodland was still common, with no winter greenery except occasional hollies and yews.

When London and his partners began their nursery business no doubt they intended to take away from Holland as big a slice of the trade in evergreens as they could. The arrival of the Dutch prince helped them by encouraging the fashion. In the gardens visited by Gibson in 1691 prime consideration was given in nearly every instance to the description of the kinds and condition of the 'greens', whose foliage must be 'bright'.

Another effect of the Revolution was, of course, the increased facility for obtaining rare plants, particularly from Japan and the East Indies, and—Britain and Holland now being so closely tied —of learning from the Dutch the secrets of their cultivation.

A significant figure at this stage was William Bentinck (1649–1709), a Dutch intimate of the king. He was appointed Superintendent of the Royal Gardens. Under him George London, fortunate in his loyalty to Compton and the Revolution, became Master-Gardener and Deputy Superintendent. Bentinck, created first Earl of Portland after his arrival in England, was inevitably preoccupied with affairs of state. Yet it is known that many of the choice plants growing at Hampton Court were brought from Soesdyke, Bentinck's seat in Holland.[70] Further, shortly after the declaration at Ryswick in 1697, when peace was made with Louis XIV, Bentinck took his deputy to study once again the gardens of France.[71] Bentinck retired from public life in 1700 and devoted the rest of his life to gardening and charitable works at his home, Bulstrode, in Buckinghamshire.

Another garden fashion introduced with the Revolution was the use of lead figures. John van Nost (*fl.* 1686–1729), a native of Mechelen, set up his factory in the Haymarket and, with a large school of assistants, produced much work—a great deal of which can be seen today—for ornamenting the grounds of royalty, the nobility, and gentry.[72]

At about the time Mary died and William ruled in solitary state Leonard Knyff began the topographical drawings which give a remarkable series of illustrations of the grand gardens of the period. Knyff was born at Haarlem in 1650. He was in England by 1681, practising as an artist. In 1694 he became naturalized and probably began his series of drawings. It is presumed that he made these for the purpose of gaining an entrée to the houses he depicted so that he might sell his other paintings—of still-life and animals.[73]

By 1702 he had finished sixty-nine drawings, which were engraved by Joannes Kip (1653–1722). Jointly they produced *Britannia Illustrata* (1709) and *Nouveau Théatre de la Grande Bretagne* (1724). Kip also worked on his own as artist-engraver, and his figures were used by Sir Robert Atkyns for his *Ancient and Present State of Gloucestershire* (1712) and Thomas Badeslade's *Views of . . . Seats in the County of Kent* (1720).

It may be asked whether these plates, showing grounds laid out on a scale incomprehensibly magnificent to our modern eyes, are accurate delineations. The answer is that some are; for example, it has been shown that the *View of the Seats at Chelsea* (*c.* 1699) and *Chatsworth* (*c.* 1697) are reliable. Others are not; sometimes, perhaps, it was policy to flatter the patron, at others a scheme projected or in hand was shown as completed when, following the not unusual sudden turns of fortune common in those times, the undertaking was never brought to a conclusion.

The names of William and Mary will always be associated with Hampton Court. The great fountain garden was formed by George London against Wren's new east front of the palace. It was a semi-circular parterre, with two wings parallel to the front of the building. A central avenue lined the canal, centred on the largest of the fountain basins. Two other avenues radiated at some twenty-five degrees to it, each with two smaller fountains on the same axis. There were five further fountains around and just within the periphery, and two more aligned with the wings. This semi-circle was covered with an ornate and entirely symmetrical patternwork of scroll-like beds, surrounding the circular fountain basins, among which statues were judiciously placed. At the same period a huge wilderness, designed by Wren, was planted by London and Wise. It was geometrical, based on two principal vistas intersecting as a St. Andrew's cross, and in its main parts as symmetrical as the site would permit. A fragment only of the original maze still exists.

At William's death in 1702 the annual allowance for Hampton Court gardens was £1,623, against a total of £1,845 for all the remaining gardens at Kensington, St. James's, Windsor, and elsewhere. This excluded the salaries of officials,* artisans, carpenters, and plumbers, which were lumped together (making £1,300 in all) and spread over all the gardens, as was the £200 a year paid to the Earl of Portland as superintendent. On Queen Anne's accession the 74 acres of royal gardens cost a total of £5,000 a year to run, of which something approaching half went on Hampton Court.

The detailed accounts of Hampton Court in 1696 show that its maintenance was divided into three parts, Mr. Quillinberg's, Mr. Vanstaden's, and Mr. Jasper Gemprell's respectively. Certain services—the 'grass and graves', the mole-catchers, and the rolling horse—were general to all of them.

Quillinberg and Vanstaden were paid £70 a year, Gemprell and a foreman £40. The labour force consisted of nine men each paid £14 a year, ten at £9, and ten at £7 5s. There were twenty-seven men paid £15 a year each board and wages, and ten casual men whose daily rate varied from 2s. to 1s. 6d. There were twelve women, usually paid 8d. a day. The mole-catcher had £16 a year.

It is not surprising to learn that the cost of maintaining these elaborate gardens was preponderantly that of the labour. For Hampton Court in 1696, excluding any consideration of the three senior officers' salary, which was of course spread over all the royal gardens, the total of all charges was about £1,475. Of this all materials, firing, dung, and soil accounted for less than £400.[74]

* In 1696 three officers were Jasper Hemming (£100), William Talman (£140), and George London (£200).

An essential of Dutch versions of the grand manner was that the ground be tolerably level, with an abundance of water—as at Hampton Court or, on a smaller scale, as at Charlecote by the River Avon (Plate VI). Much of England is of a very different formation, and it is interesting to see what the members of William's circle did when confronted by our typical, irregular, hilly countryside.

An example can still be seen at Powis Castle, near Welshpool, which to a considerable extent escaped an attempt to landscape the gardens. In 1696 this ancient Welsh border estate was granted to William's cousin, William Nassau-Zuylestein (1645–1709), created Earl of Rochford. For the site of his garden he was faced with a dramatic fall of a hundred or so feet from the old 'red castle' to the level ground below. Who precisely was concerned with the splendid result we can now see is not known; presumably it was conceived by Rochford himself; probably his son had a good deal to do with carrying it out; it seems certain that the work was completed by the Powis family when they were reinstated in 1722.[75]*

The slope was tackled by looking not to Holland, but to the origins of classical gardening in Italy. A series of deeply stepped terraces was formed; on one an orangery was built. These terraces were ornamented with numerous lead figures and tricked out with clipped greens. On the level below a lawn was formed, patterned with ponds and again studded with greens (Plate VII).

Another instance of the Dutch manner in hilly country was to be found in Gloucestershire, displayed by an Englishman intimately connected with the Dutch circle. William Blaythwayt (c. 1649–1717) was a brilliant linguist and a capable man of affairs; he became secretary to Sir William Temple at The Hague, and later was to serve William personally. Through marrying a Wynter he became possessed of the estate of Dyrham. This lies at the south-west end of the Cotswolds. Here, in 1694, he engaged Talman to build him a house and laid out 'beautiful gardens of great extent, with curious water-works and pleasant walks, which have distant prospects on the City of Bristol, and the forest of Kingswood'.† An engraving by Kip shows us what this English

* It is known also that William Winde (see p. 134) worked at Powis in 1697.
† As Talman was concerned, possibly George London was also consulted.

member of the Dutch circle achieved among the close-knit contours of the Cotswold scarp[76] (Plate VI).

. . . . .

On 19th May 1702 Henry Wise was instructed to 'repair to the lodge in Windsor Park, late the Earl of Portland's' and take charge. By July of the same year he had prepared a detailed estimate for managing the royal gardens for £1,600 a year, which was accepted. Henry Wise, gardener to Queen Anne throughout her reign, thus started his career as royal gardener by saving his employer £400 a year.

One of Wise's greatest achievements was, of course, the garden at Blenheim; its story—and that of its designer who refused to quarrel with the Duchess—has been fully told by David Green.[77]

On what lines did London and Wise work? Often, no doubt, they were dominated by their employers; certainly the Earl of Carlisle made, as we shall see, a startling deviation from London's plan at Castle Howard.

In 1706 they published a two-volumed work called the *Retir'd Gard'ner*, taken from the French. As an amusement it is perhaps successful; as a serious book on gardening by two of its greatest practitioners it is largely nonsense. Here and there some sound comments are interspersed by the translators, but for the most part they pass a mass of superstition. It is the sort of thing, alas, that many practical gardeners have produced—or lent their names to—for advertisement.

The book does, however, contain one most interesting garden plan. When Marshal Tallard was brought to England after Blenheim, he lived a placid life as prisoner-of-war in Nottingham. As Macky[78] says, here he made very fine gardens to the house he lived in, which, when he returned home after seven years of living 'with Nottingham ale at every meal, and good pudding and beef in his belly,' he gave to his landlord. London and Wise were concerned in the design of these gardens, very French in manner, and clearly published the plan as an example to be followed (page 13).*

We see part of the house (A) which is entered from the road

* It has been reproduced by several authorities who apparently have failed to observe that the levels as originally drawn do not make sense. I have made what seem to be obvious corrections.

by a courtyard (B), screened from the garden by a wall. The garden was entered from the house through another courtyard (C), which led on to a terrace (D). This, like the courtyard, was probably paved.

Immediately in front, and the same width as the length of the terrace—some 20 yards—was a sunk garden (E). It was four steps down, rectangular, and surrounded by sloping green banks. Set in an area of gravel was the main parterre, an exquisite design cut in a groundwork of turf. Two sunflowers consoled the Marshal in his defeat. The materials in which the embroidery was worked were the rich brown of gravel, the white glitter of spar, the jet of coal dust, the light red of brick dust, and the clean yellow of sand. The design was picked out by small, clipped pyramidal evergreens growing from the ground, or shaped greens standing in large pots. Alongside and above it was a walk on an intermediate level (G).

At the far corner was a banqueting room (F). Its north-facing opening looked up a long grass walk, bordered on either side with narrow flower borders, and lying against the wall that formed the western boundary of the property. This was part of the highest level of the garden (H), which took in an addition to the more or less rectangular main area. In this subsidiary rectangle, partly concealed by a hedge, was a simple parterre of grass and gravel, the pattern here being narrow, simple borders of flowers, again studded with pyramids and potted shrubs. This high level, where it met the banks that sloped down to the main parterre, was demarcated by a narrow flower border, with the inevitable pyramids and pots. The northern, longer slope was broken by a level on which was formed a gravelled path.

Returning to the terrace, at its northern end there was another descent, this time of six steps. Here was a little sunk garden (I), presumably surrounded by retaining walls. It consisted of a pattern in turf and gravel only, with a minute pond at its centre in which played a fountain.

It has been suggested that the gardens of the day were but clipped greens, hedges, and cut-out patterns of grass and minerals—that flowers were absent. It is true that Marshal Tallard had no fewer than thirty-three pyramids and eighty-three potted greens, but there was also some two hundred and twenty-five yards of flower border. That this was narrow did not affect its gaiety. The plants used can be guessed from Wise's list,[79] which was similar to, though not quite so varied, as those made by Hanmer and Rea.

London and Wise were experts with fruit. In 1708 Wise, most systematic of men, made a list of the fruit grown at Hampton Court, Windsor, and Blenheim. It gives the names of fourteen cherries, fourteen apricots, fifty-eight peaches and nectarines, thirty-three plums, eight figs, twenty-three vines, and twenty-nine pears. Apples, as usual, are not included. The massive walls on which some of these grew can still be seen by peeping through the grilles in the bastions that surround the acres of kitchen garden at Blenheim—all that survives of Wise's work there.

Wise retired in 1727 to Warwick Priory, which he had bought in 1709. He died a wealthy man, instructing that his funeral rites should be simple, the money that would otherwise have been spent on them to be given to the poor.

Few gardens of his period remain; in some cases the skeletons, devoid of their elaborate parterres and countless clipped greens, can still be seen. Bramham in Yorkshire is still little changed from a plan made in about 1725 by John Wood (1704–1754).[80] More often, the relics of their radiating avenues stretch in aimless majesty over the countryside.

One surely gains the truest impression of a Queen Anne garden from Melbourne in Derbyshire. Here Thomas Coke, her Vice-Chamberlain, from 1696 onwards, advised by London and Wise, formed a new garden on an old site. It was designed 'to suit Versailles'. It is said that it is now little like a French garden of the period, and not a true 'period piece'.[81] But we can still stand on the terrace looking over a toy Le Nôtre vista, or wander, in the grip of ruthlessly straight paths, through bosquets, drawn on by the sight and sound of fountains. We can finger the same works of Van Nost that Coke put in place.

Much has disappeared—lawns replace the embroidery of parterres; much become overgrown. But surely there is no greater change than when, in an old master painting, the yellowed varnish has obscured the once bright detail (Plate XI).

Of course, try how they might, Englishmen could never form even a tiny Versailles in the Derbyshire countryside; the French manner was inevitably Anglicized; our own parterre the French called *parterre à l'Anglaise,* 'the plainest and meanest of all'.

Le Nôtre himself left no records of his manner of gardening. Original plans of the French gardens that he laid out are, it seems, virtually non-existent. The theory that then inspired our English gardens would have remained unwritten if it had not been for A. J. Dezallier d'Argenville (1680–1765), a Parisian savant, naturalist, and collector. In his youth he had studied architecture under J. B. A. Leblond (1679–1719). Leblond had been a pupil of Le Nôtre; he designed the famous Peterhof gardens with their multitude of fountains.

In 1709 d'Argenville published anonymously *La Théorie et la Pratique du Jardinage.* Its importance may be judged by the fact that in Paris four more editions (including one unauthorized) were published. Three editions were also issued at The Hague, and the English translation also reached a third edition,[82] the last as lately as 1743, by which time, the historians would have it, the French school of gardening was quite outmoded.

There is a further reason for its importance in England. In 1724 appeared Philip Miller's *The Gardener and Florist's Dictionary, or a Complete System of Horticulture.* Miller, to whom we shall return later, was the greatest British gardener of the period; this small work was the prelude to the much more famous *Gardener's Dictionary* of 1731.* This dictionary was the standard authority on gardening for generations of country gentlemen; the large volume can still be seen on the shelf of many country houses. And in the early 1724 work, the 1731 version, and its 1733 edition, the instructions on 'the designing or manner of laying out a fine garden or pleasure garden' are taken straight from the English edition of d'Argenville.

The wide circulation of these precepts makes one realize their importance, and one can only conclude that they were largely followed by the unfashionable long after the sinuous lines of 'nature' had become the mode in smart quarters. Indeed, as we shall see later, gardens in the old style were still common in Jane Austen's day—to be obliterated finally by Humphry Repton and his disciples.

---

* John Ellis wrote to Linnaeus: 'Miller's dictionary is the chief book that is read by gentlemen who study the art of gardening.'[83]

There are other circumstances which make the English translation of d'Argenville important. It was done by John James
(1672–1746), for long Clerk of the Works at Greenwich. He was
a capable if not very distinguished architect.* Among his contemporaries he was distinguished for his knowledge of Latin,
French, and Italian. *The Theory and Practice of Gardening*, published in 1712 after some delay caused by the engraver of the
plates, shows also from its list of subscribers that he had a wide
connection among the influential aristocracy and gentry.

James tells us that he did not know the name of the author of
the original (it is often wrongly attributed to Leblond) but recognized his worth. The translation is accurate; its lucidity is attri-
butable to that quality in the original. Marginal notes illuminate
matters of French practice likely to puzzle the English reader.
The book is dedicated to James Johnston, who had begun building the once celebrated Orleans House at Twickenham in 1702.
(Macky, writing in 1714 of the mansions at 'Twittenham', says:
'I think that of Secretary Johnston's, for the elegance and large-
ness of his gardens, his terrace on the river, and the situation of
his house, makes much the brightest figure here.')

It would be profitable to study the names of the 236 original
subscribers and find how many were then engaged in, or about
to begin, the construction of gardens. To name a few: there were
John Aislabie, who resigned the Chancellorship in the year the
book was published—and was soon to lay out his great garden
at Studley Royal, much of which still survives (Plate VIII);
Andrew Archer, brother of Thomas, the designer of the house at
Bramham; the Duke of Beaufort, son of that Duchess who
brought fame to the gardens of Badminton; James Brydges, who
certainly had connections with James after he acquired the
Canons estate in 1713 and began his fabulous establishment
there; Thomas Bastard—presumably of the influential Dorset
family of craftsmen-architects; the Earl of Carlisle of Castle
Howard; Sir Richard Child, soon to be working on a revision of his father's garden at Wanstead;† Vice-Chamberlain

---

* On his retirement from London in 1723 he returned to his native Hampshire,
building for himself Warbrook House at Eversley, set in a garden of his own design.[86]
    † It is true that a part of this was in a manner that resulted in a reproduction of its
plan as an example of *anglo-chinois* in Le Rouge's book of 1776–87. Houghton also was
in a later manner.

Thomas Coke of Melbourne; the Earl of Haddington, developing his Tyninghame estate; Nicholas Hawksmoor, whose importance as an original architect is now established; Sir Joseph Jekyll, Miss Gertrude Jekyll's ancestor, a prodigious builder; the Earl of Pembroke, whose activities at Wilton earned him the dedication of the Society of Gardener's *Catalogue*, and the then Robert Walpole, newly released from the Tower, who, as a garden enthusiast, eventually acquired Dr. Uvedale's famous collection of plants.

So one could continue. Incongruously among the subscribers was Joseph Addison; 1712 was the year in which he published the attacks in *The Spectator* on the fashionable style of gardening, known to all readers of his essays.

The precepts for garden design taken from d'Argenville through James and published by Miller are worth quoting. They summarize the rules at the time of the climax of classical gardening, when geometric art was combined with horticultural skill to a degree never since surpassed.

The author of the *Theory and Practice of Gardening* says the true size of a handsome garden may take up thirty or forty acres, not more. And as for the disposition and distribution of this garden, he gives these general rules.

1. That there ought always to be a descent from the house to the garden, not fewer than three steps. This elevation of the building renders it more dry and wholesome, also from the head of these steps, there will be a general view or prospect of all or the greatest part of the garden.

2. In a fine garden, the first thing that should present itself to the sight is a parterre, which should be next to the house, whether in the front or on the sides, as well upon account of the opening it affords to the house, as for the beauty wherewith it constantly entertains the sight, from all the windows on that side of the house.

As for the parterres, they must be furnished with such works as will improve and set them off; and they being low and flat, do necessarily require something that is raised, as groves and palisades. But in this case you must have regard to the situation of the place, and before you plant, you ought to observe whether the prospect that way be agreeable; for the sides of the parterre should be kept entirely open, making use of quarters of grass and other flat works in order to make the best of the view; and you must take care not to shut it up with groves, unless they be planted in quincunce, or opened with low hedgerows, so as not to hinder the eye from piercing through the trees and so discovering the beauties of the prospect on every side.

If there be no vista; but on the contrary there be a mountain, hill, forest or wood, that by their being near deprive you of that pleasure, or if there be some village adjoining too near, the houses of which are no very agreeable sight, then you may edge the parterre with palisades and groves to screen those disagreeable objects from the sight.

Groves make the chief of a garden, being a great ornament to all the rest of its parts, so that there cannot be too many of them planted, if the places designed for them do not take up those of the kitchen and fruit gardens, which are very necessary for a house and should always be placed near the base-courts.

To accompany parterres, it is usual to make choice of those designs of wood-work that are the finest, as groves opened in compartments, quincunces, verdant-halls with bowling greens, arbour-work, and fountains in the middle. These small groves, being placed near the house, are so much the more agreeable in that you have no need to go far to find shade, and besides this, they communicate a coolness to the apartments which is very agreeable in hot weather.

It would also be very proper to plant some groves of evergreens that may afford the pleasure of seeing a wood always verdant in winter, when the other trees and plants are stripped of their ornaments, and to plant some squares of them to be a diversity from the other wood. It is also usual to adorn the head of a parterre with basins, water-works, and beyond it with a circular line of palisades, or wood-work cut into a goose-foot leading into the great walks and to fill the space between the basin and the palisade with small pieces of embroidery or grass-work set off with yews, cases, and flower-pots.

In gardens that have terraces either in the side or front of the house, where there is a delightful prospect so that you cannot shut up the parterre by a circular palisade, in order to continue the view you should lay several compartments of a parterre together, such as embroidery, green-plots, after the English fashion, or cut-work which ought to be divided at convenient distances by cross walks, but you must always make the parterre of embroidery next to the house because it is the richest and most magnificent. The principal walk must be in the front of the house and another large walk ought to cross it at right angles. If they be double and very wide, you may cause the walls to be pierced with grilles at the end of those, or you may make openings and ditches at the foot of them to continue the view.

If any part of the ground be naturally low and marshy and you would not be at the expense of filling it, you may in such places make bowling greens, water-works and groves, raising the alleys only to the level of those that are near them and that lead thither.

When the great lines and chief walks are laid out and the parterres and works about the sides and head of them are disposed so as it is most suitable to the ground, then the rest of the garden is to be furnished with many different designs as tall groves, close walks, quincunces, galleries and halls of verdure, green arbours, labyrinths, bowling greens and amphitheatres adorned with fountains, canals, figures, etc., which sorts of works distinguish a garden very much and do also greatly contribute to rendering it magnificent.

It must always be observed, in placing and distributing the several parts of a garden, to oppose them on to the other; as for example, a wood to a parterre or a bowling green, and not to place all the wood on one side and all the parterres on the other. Nor is a bowling green to be set against a basin, for this would be one gap against another, which is always to be avoided by setting the fall against the void and the raised works against the flat in order to cause a variety.

This diversity should always be kept not only in the general design of a garden but also in each distinct piece; as if two groves are upon the side of a parterre although their outward forms and dimensions should be equal; yet for that reason you must not repeat the same design in both but make them so as to be different within, because it would be very disagreeable to find the same design on both sides so that when one has been seen, there is nothing to invite the curiosity to see the other; so that such a garden so repeated would be no more than half a design, the greatest beauty of gardens consisting in variety.

Also the several parts of each piece ought to be diversified; if a basin be round, the walk that surrounds it ought to be octangular; and the like is to be observed as to grass plots and bowling greens which are in the midst of groves.

The same works ought never to be repeated on both sides except in open places where the eye, by comparing them together, may judge of their conformity, as in parterres, bowling greens, groves, opened in compartments and quincunces. But in such groves as are formed of palisades and tall trees, the designs and out parts ought always to be varied, but though they are to be different, yet however they ought always to have such relation and agreement one to the other in their lines and ranges as to make the openings, glades, and vistas regular and agreeable.

In the business of design, a mean and pitiful manner ought to be studiously avoided, and the aim should be always at that which is great and noble; not to make the cabinets and mazes small and basins like bowl-dishes and alleys so narrow that two persons can scarce go abreast in them. It is much better to have but two or three things pretty large, than four times the number of small ones which are but trifles.

Before the design of a garden be put in execution it ought to be considered what it will be in twenty or thirty years time when the palisades are grown up and the trees are spread. For it often happens that a design when it is first planted looks handsome and in good proportion, becomes so small and ridiculous in process of time that there is a necessity for either altering it or destroying it entirely and replanting it.

The corners and angles of every part of a garden ought to be sloped and cut hollow; this will make the cross paths more agreeable to the eye and more convenient for walking than to find points and corners advancing which looks very ill upon the ground and are very inconvenient. . . .

Gardens on a perfect level are the best, as well for the conveniency of walking as that their long alleys and glades have no risings nor fallings and are not so chargeable to maintain as the others are.

Gardens on a gentle ascent are not quite so agreeable and convenient; although the shelving be so little as not to be perceived—for it fatigues and tires a person to walk up hill or down hill without finding scarcely a resting place—these sloping grounds are also liable to be spoiled by torrents.

There is a peculiar excellency in gardens that have terraces because from the height of one terrace all the lower parts of the garden may be discovered, and from others the compartments are seen which form so many several gardens, one under another, and presents us with very agreeable views, and different scenes of things if the terraces are not too frequent and there be good lengths of level between them. These gardens also lie advantageously for water which may be repeated from one to another, but they are a great charge to keep them up, as well as that they cost a great deal to make. . . .

There are besides these many other rules relating to the proportion, conformity and place of the different parts and ornaments of gardens, of which more may be seen under other articles.

In the 1737 edition of Miller there was slight modification, with a tendency towards simplification, particularly that a level, unbroken lawn should stand next the house. In 1743, though the main principles still stand, the parterre had disappeared. It is amusing to observe that in 1909 Sir George Sitwell was still quoting d'Argenville's maxims.[85]

There are one or two other points that we may study in James, as they were not taken over by Miller. Four plates, with descriptions, afford examples of the most suitable types of garden: there is the warning that 'the designs may appear too magnificent, and too costly, to be put into execution'! But one may retrench; for example, for basins and water-works plots of grass might be substituted, 'which nevertheless may do very well'.

The gardens are surrounded by walls; iron grilles are placed in them at the termination of walks 'to extend the view, and to show the country to advantage. At present we frequently make through views, called *Ah, Ah*, which are openings in the walls, without grilles, to the very level of the walks, with a large and deep ditch at the foot of them, lined on both sides to sustain the earth, and prevent the getting over, which surprises the eye upon coming near it, and makes one cry *Ah! Ah!* from whence it takes its name'. So it was that the name, if not the use, of a feature so particularly associated with the English landscape school was first published in this country (Plate IX).

An improved method of surveying is described in which it is no longer necessary for the gardener to dig a groove to take his belly so that his eye may be at ground level! The construction of water-works—*gerbes d'eau, bouillons, goulettes, buffets, rigoles, champignons, chandeliers*, and *zic-zacs*—is described in detail.

It is interesting, too, to note that the French use of our term bowling green, *boulingrin*, though of English origin, had nothing to do with the game of bowls; it had become the term for an area of turf sloped down and sunk below the surrounding level.

The garden most likely to have been inspired by James's book, and constructed with due magnificence, was at Canons, in Middlesex.* James Brydges, eventually Duke of Chandos, Earl of Caernarvon, and Viscount Wilton, now best remembered as the eponym of Handel's anthems, did everything on a stupendous scale. J. Macky described the garden in 1722,[86] adding a few further details of the palace-like establishment:

There is a large terrace walk from whence you descend to the parterre; this parterre has a row of gilded vases on pedestals on each

---

* The name of George London has been associated with it. But he died in late 1713, after an illness of some months, and Brydges did not acquire the estate until May of that year.[87] But Brydges did carry on abortive discussions with Talman, London's colleague, concerning alterations to the original house.

side down to the great canal, and in the middle, fronting the canal, is a gladiator, gilded also, and through the whole parterre an abundance of statues, as big as the life, regularly disposed.

The canal runs a great way and indeed one would wonder to see such a vast quantity of water in a country where are neither rivers nor springs. But they tell me that the Duke has his water in pipes from the mountains of Stanmore about two miles off.

The gardens are very large and well disposed; but the greatest pleasure of all is that the divisions of the whole are only made by ballustrades of iron and not by walls; you see the whole at once, be you in what part of the garden or parterre you will.

In his large kitchen garden there are bee-hives of glass, very curious; and at the end of each of his chief avenues he has neat lodgings for eight old sergeants of the Army, whom he took out of Chelsea College who guard the whole; and go their rounds at night and call the hours as the watchmen do at London to prevent disorders, and wait upon the Duke to chapel on Sundays.

It is incredible the iron work about this noble palace, more, I must say, than I ever saw about any.

It is singular that iron balustrades replaced the usual walls. We can add some detail to Macky's account. First, we may take some glimpses at the wholesale and world-wide scale on which the materials and furnishings of the garden were acquired.[88] In 1719 grass seed ('fursee' and 'meson') was obtained not from our English turf, but from Aleppo. Henry Marsh of Hammersmith supplied one hundred and fifty evergreen oaks which were planted espalier-wise, 18 feet apart, to form an avenue; 25 feet behind them were set three rows of elms, the groundwork beneath being a sort of shrubbery. Subsequently we read of acorns imported from Leghorn, fruit trees from Jamaica, flower seeds from Aleppo, tortoises from Majorca; barrow ducks, storks, wild geese, and cherry trees from Barbados, and whistling ducks and flamingos from Antigua. There were ostriches, blue macaws, Virginia fowls and songbirds, and eagles which drank out of special stone basins.

In the May of 1721 the parterre engaged the attention of sixteen men and two women. The north and greenhouse garden employed thirteen, and there were a further six in the kitchen garden. It seems that as the season advanced further casual labour was enlisted. The turf was mown twice or three times weekly and weeded every day.

The three principal avenues were 1,303 yards, 1,000 yards, and 808 yards long. The water was brought from Stanmore in two miles of elm-trunk pipes.

The magnificence did not last long; the turf was turned to hay, the hedges grew ragged; perhaps the approaching dereliction gives more point than is generally realized to Pope's famous lines,[89] in which Brydges is manifestly Timon;* they are the antithesis of Macky's views:

> His gardens next your admiration call,
> On any side you look, behold the wall!
> No pleasing intricacies intervene,
> No artful wildness to perplex the scene;
> Grove nods at grove, each ally has a brother,
> And half the platform just reflects the other.
> The suffering eye inverted Nature sees,
> Trees cut to statues, statues thick as trees;
> With here a fountain, never to be play'd;
> And there a summer-house, that knows no shade:
> Here Amphitrite sails through myrtle bowers;
> There gladiators fight, or die in flowers;
> Unwater'd see the drooping sea-horse mourn,
> And swallows roost in Nilus' dusty corn.

And then, prophetic of what was to happen within but a few years:

> Another age shall see the golden ear
> Imbrown the slope, and nod on the parterre,
> Deep harvest bury all his pride has plann'd,
> And laughing Ceres reassume the land.

Brydges also had an estate at Shaw Hall in Berkshire. In 1733 he was paying his head gardener there, who was also a handyman, £12 a year with food and lodging. He also sold produce from the estate, such as pineapples at half a guinea a time. This fruit was now coming into cultivation, though still a high-priced luxury. Since their importation in Charles II's reign they had taken the public fancy.†

---

* When Brydges challenged Pope saying that 'the Town had made him Timon', the poet denied it. His acknowledgment to Pope of this disclaimer, written in December 1731, is a most dignified letter.[90]

† The pineapple as used architecturally has never had any symbolic meaning—at least until Sir Edwin Lutyens gave it one on the spur of the moment. It should be remembered, too, that a 'pine-apple' may also be a pine cone.

The pineapple also brings into our view two men connected both with its cultivation and with Canons. Sir Matthew Decker (1679–1749), of Dutch origin, was established as a successful merchant in London by the first years of the eighteenth century. He had 'a truly Dutch passion for gardening' and a famous garden at Richmond Green. He was a friend of Brydges, and was consulted by him about Canons. There seems little doubt that Decker, or rather his gardener Henry Telende, was the first to fruit the pineapple in Britain (Plate X). There is a painting* by Theodore Netscher of a pineapple and a memorial tablet bearing a Latin inscription. Translated, this reads:

To the perpetual memory of Matthew Decker, baronet, and Theodore Netscher, gentleman. This pineapple, deemed worthy of the Royal table, grew at Richmond at the cost of the former, and still seems to grow by the art of the latter. H. Watkins set up this inscription, A.D. 1720.

There is no earlier record of the cultivation of the pineapple in England.

We know about the method from the publications of Richard Bradley (d. 1732), sometime Professor of Botany in the University of Cambridge—but more accurately described as a pioneer of gardening journalism and author of *The History of Succulent Plants* (1717),[91] the first English book on the subject. Bradley was for a time employed by Brydges at Canons, where, in 1717, he was discharged for mismanaging funds, physic garden and hot-houses alike. He seems first to have referred to Decker's pineapples in a publication issued in August 1721.† Telende's secret was the use of a hot-bed made of tanner's bark. The brick-lined pit was rather more than 5 feet deep; it was 11 feet long and 7 ft. 6 in. wide, glass-covered. At its bottom was a foot of hot dung, upon which was laid 300 bushels of tanner's bark. Made early in February, the bed was hot in fifteen days, and would last until October.

The tan-bark hot-bed was a novelty in England, and an important one, which was shortly used by Philip Miller at the Apothecaries Garden at Chelsea to raise plants which had proved difficult. We have already mentioned this place. In 1673 the

* In the Fitzwilliam Museum.
† Incorporated later in the several editions of *New Improvements in Planting and Gardening*.

Apothecaries Company took a lease of riverside land from Charles Cheyne. The members had easy access to it by barge from the city, which lay well to the eastward so that its increasing smoke generally blew away from the garden, which in 1674 was walled in. Although John Watts (appointed in 1680) achieved some success,* in 1691 Gibson had blamed him for neglect, and the garden failed to achieve a reputation comparable with that of Oxford or Edinburgh.

Later, Sir Hans Sloane (1660–1753) bought the manor of Chelsea from Cheyne. He was able to do this thanks to a successful career as a doctor and marriage to a rich wife. Sloane was born in Ireland, and as a young man visited Jamaica. He was an ardent collector of plants—as of all natural objects.[92] In 1722 he conveyed the land on which the Apothecaries Garden stood to the Company—but under conditions ensuring that it would be efficiently managed.

The fame of the Chelsea garden followed Miller's appointment as Gardener (no doubt through Sloane's influence) in 1722. He quite eclipsed his senior, Isaac Rand, who was *Praefectus Horti Chelsiani* from 1724 to his death in 1743.[93]

Miller was of Scotch origin, though born near London. His father had come south and set up as a market gardener at Deptford. Miller himself had become a florist on his own account at St. George's Fields. In due course he combined a—literally—encyclopaedic knowledge of plants with exceptional skill as a cultivator. By 1736 his energy had brought Chelsea such a reputation outside this country that it attracted a visit from the great Linnaeus.† At times dogmatic and even quarrelsome, his forthright nature and lucid mind became so attuned to the fast-advancing ethos of science that, once convinced he was in the wrong, he would unhesitatingly reverse his opinion. So it was that he altered the classifications of the late editions of his *Dictionary* when finally convinced by Linnaeus that the old method, to which at first he held steadily, was wrong.

In Ireland during this period we have the first botanist and horticulturist of any consequence. Sir Arthur Rawdon (1660–1695) made a considerable collection of plants at Moira, Co.

---

* In 1683 he planted the once famous Lebanon cedars, apparently the first to bear cones (1732) in England, but not, as is sometimes said, the first to be grown here.

† Linnaeus also visited the Oxford Botanic Garden.

Down. He was a friend of Sloane and Sherard, and sent James Harlow (*fl.* 1660–1680) to Jamaica to obtain plants. Harlow also collected in Virginia for Watts of Chelsea.

As a contrast to these eminent persons, one may usefully examine the records of a moderate-sized garden in the Midlands. In about 1716 Sir Samuel Clarke (little is known of him) acquired the manor house of West Bromwich in South Staffordshire.* He replanted the garden and his garden lists (mostly restricted to fruit) survive.[94]

Sir Samuel's records begin in 1720. The document is headed 'This catalogue or account of fruit trees, etc. sent from London to Westbromich must be carefully preserved for future information.' The first item is a letter from Adam Holt, nurseryman, of Leytonstone, dated 15th December 1720:

I received your letter and according to your order have this day packed up all the undermentioned trees etc., and thereunto have fixed labels numbered referring unto each sort of fruit for each aspect in each of your two gardens and have writ upon each bundle or parcel what they refer to, they are all sound perfect in health, large, strong, well taken up and sure in their respective kinds.

From Adam Holt's careful listing, and from instructions given to John Thomas, the gardener, we can reconstruct the plan of the garden.

The 'parlour' or 'great garden' was on the south-east side of the house, against which fruit trees and vines were trained. Along this south-east face of the house ran a 'broad gravel walk'; there was room for five peaches and two nectarines which were interplanted with vines.

From the 'broad walk' one looked straight down the length of the garden to a wall which formed its upper end. Its garden side, facing north-west, was wisely planted with cherries and pears. To one's right was a wall, broken by a doorway into the pump court, and terminating in a summerhouse standing at the southern corner of the enclosure. With a north-east aspect, this took morello cherries, plums, and pears. The remaining wall, against which backed the barn, having a south-westerly aspect, carried the choicest pears, apricots, and greengages. Outside

* Much of the house and its original garden walls still survives; it is now in the heart of an industrial area.

these walls lay the kitchen garden. Elsewhere, in a place unspecified, were two orchards for standard trees of hardier kinds, mostly apples, but with some quinces and pears.

The first consignment to arrive from Leytonstone provided the main planting; the list gives a clue to the extent of the parlour and kitchen gardens. There are enumerated a total of thirty-three peaches and nectarines, twenty-seven pears, twenty-six cherries, twenty-three vines, twenty plums, twenty codlin apples, three mulberries and also white raspberries, red and white Dutch currants, gooseberries, filberts, and figs.

The five bundles were made up in mats, each having a hoop-stick tally 'marked No. 1: 2: 3: 4: 5 and on the mats also stands the mark with ink'. There were numbered lead labels 'to be nailed on the wall with nails through the holes made in them. It's thought four penny nails will be big enough'.

In January followed trees for the two orchards. There were fifty-four standard apples—the names (as spelt by Adam Holt) being: French Peppin, English Golden Peppin, Kentish Peppin, Holland Peppin, Jennetting, Pyles Russets, Summer Gillyflower, Summer Paremaine, Winter Paremaine, Golden Rennett, Wheeler's Russett, Non Par Elles (sic), and Bearnard's Apples for baking. There were also eight standard plums and ten standard pears. The large number of apple trees for planting out will be noticed, adding confirmation to the view that many old fruit lists were restricted to the choice fruit grown on the walls—apples, as Temple suggested, being taken for granted.

Thereafter the correspondence principally concerns replacements of trees 'which was broak', or 'were forgotten or omitted to be sent' and from time to time further additions for which 'John Thomas the gardener writes that he hath room'.

Sometimes a Mr. Grove shared in the orders, which were sent by wagon and delivered either to the Hall, at a neighbouring inn, the Cross Guns, or at the house of an acquaintance on the main road. The carriage on one consignment of 1 cwt. 21 lb. was 6s.

Sir Samuel himself sent down from London boxes of seed—of Portugal onion received both from Mr. Edward Bridges and Mr. Foster, melon and white Turkey 'cowcumber' from Mr. Elderton, and 'Cabbage seed received from Russia in the year 1722'.

Two other items of interest in 1721 were a hundred 'walnut trees 'of good sorts for the wood of them' and 'one thousand elms for the nursery'.

In 1724 a new piece of garden was taken in from a meadow and stocked, and by 1729 the garden seems to have been planted up. The lists continue, however, until 1760, when the garden was still walled and unaffected by the landscape fashion.

Nowhere is there a mention of any kind of flower; presumably John Thomas obtained those locally for his employer, but they could not have been an important feature in the garden.

From the Midlands we move to Scotland. It was now the source whence came 'the northern lads who have invaded the southern provinces'* whose ability, energy, and forthright manner (as in the case of Miller) often made them rather unpopular. There was still comparatively little employment at home for ambitious men, though the making of gardens in the fashionable manner became more frequent as the eighteenth century progressed. In 1710 Sir Robert Sibbald wrote of Balcaskie, Fife, that it was 'a very pretty new house, with all modish conveniences of planting'.[95] Thomas Hamilton, 6th Earl of Haddington (1680–1735), soon after taking up residence at Tyninghame in 1700, began improving his garden; he planted his famous holly hedges in long straight lines in 1712.[96] But even so, he wrote in 1706 of 'the dullness of this cursed country . . .' where 'drinking indeed succeeds pretty well'. In 1707 the Act of Union increased the contacts between England and Scotland. Haddington certainly introduced English ideas, as can be seen from his *Some Directions About Raising Forest Trees*,[97] written in the last years of his life, 'having been a diligent planter for upwards of thirty years, and having more thriving trees of my own raising than I believe any one man planted in his lifetime'.†

Fortunately, Haddington goes beyond his title. He tells us that he grew the cherry laurel (*Prunus laurocerasus*), the sweet bay (*Laurus nobilis*), *Phillyrea*, alaternus (*Rhamnus alaternus*), and the laurustinus (*Viburnum tinus*). But the most interesting paragraph is when he speaks 'a little of a wilderness':

* The phrase was Switzer's.
† He was friendly with Evelyn, but considered that 'he was too credulous, and regarded the age of the moon too much, and other niceties too trifling for so grave a man'.

As it is only raised for shade and ornament, and is laid out in what figure the owner pleases, there can be no rule given. They have not been long introduced into this country, and the way they were first laid out was, that they first pitched on a centre with straight views from it, terminating in as fine a prospect as could be had. Then, there were serpentine walks that run through the whole, hedged like the straight walks, and the angles planted with a variety of different trees; though now they are weary of the hedges. But people who made it their business to lay out ground for gentlemen, are, in my opinion, very unfit for it, for they are too formal and stiff; besides, they make everything so bushy, that they crowd the ground too much.

Were I to plant a wilderness, there should be nothing in it but evergreens, flowering shrubs, trees that carry a fine blossom, and a kind of willow that hath a bark of bright yellow.*

This is interesting for several reasons. It shows that Scotland was far behind England, where wildernesses—for instance, that at Hampton Court of 1689—had long been the fashion. It showed that Haddington was opposed to the clipping and shaping of trees which had been so long in vogue. And it is an early use of the word 'serpentine' in connection with paths.

An important influence on agriculture and horticulture was the marriage of Elizabeth Mordaunt, daughter of the Earl of Peterborough, to the eldest son of the Duke of Gordon in 1706. Inheriting the family energy and interest in plants and natural history, she settled with her husband in the fertile land bordering the Moray Firth. Here, again, English example led to great improvements; the estates of Gordonston and Invergordon were soon among the best in the north.[98]

We have dealt so far with gardens of consequence—aesthetic or scientific. But one of the most important developments of the period was the comparatively small garden, particularly in and around towns. There is evidence of this in the prolonged success of authors like Leonard Meager. There are, too, contemporary town plans. On them the now numerous gardens of old-established towns such as Gloucester[99] and fast-developing ones such as Birmingham[100] are shown beyond dispute.

* An early reference to the yellow-twigged form of the white willow (*Salix alba*) now known as 'vitellina'.

The distinctive position of gardener—or, as we should now call him, head gardener—has already been shown, particularly in the case of Field. At the end of this period other examples occur. In 1706 Richard Baker signed an agreement to serve the Earl of Dorset and Middlesex as gardener. He was to reserve all the fruit for his employer's use; keep all the trees and greens in good condition and duly pruned, dunged, and marled; provide all herbs and other such things for the kitchen in due season; maintain all the garden walks; preserve all flowers and plants now in the garden; keep glass frames and other equipment pertaining to the 'garden trade' in repair, and to provide for the present use of the garden fifty loads of dung.

For this he received £30 a year, with rooms and conveniences in the house for his business, all dung produced about the house, and, one suggests, not least important, the right to dispose of vegetables and herbs not needed by the kitchen.[101]

Another example of interest is the existence of a plate at Sutton Scarsdale. It commemorates the rebuilding of the house in 1724 by Lord Scarsdale, and includes among those concerned with it John Christian, 'gentleman gardener'.[102]

CHANGE IN THE WIND

We have seen the garden of the Italian Renaissance reach its ultimate form—a series of members developed and elaborated, rigidly—even mathematically—organized into a whole by Le Nôtre and his school. All this, thanks to the lavish patronage of the designers, even in England, on a vaster scale than formerly.

The pattern is unvarying. An unimpeded central vista, first over the parterres, then (the pathway dividing) over the geometrical sheet of water, next through the equally geometrically planned woods, until it finally disappears as a cleft through the remote forest. On either side are grouped, usually balanced, a variety of other delights and minor vistas. The woodland is intersected by paths, straight and triangulated; the circular goosefoot with its star-like radiation of paths is an inevitable feature.

But surely the style never sat quite so conformably on the English landscape as on those of France and Holland; nor was it quite in accord with the awkward English spirit.

Evelyn's delight in the prospect of Holdenby's ruins has

already been mentioned. In 1679, after visiting the garden of the painter Verrio (he was, Evelyn tells us, a skilful gardener) he passed on to Cliveden, that 'stupendous natural rock, wood and prospect' which William Winde was then completing for the Duke of Buckingham. He wrote:

the grots in the chalky soil are pretty, 'tis a romantic object, and the place altogether answers the most poetical description that can be made of a solitude, precipice, prospects and whatever can contribute to a thing so very like their imaginations. The house stands somewhat like Frascati as to its front, and on the platform is a circular view to the utmost verge of the horizon, which, with the serpenting of the Thames is admirably surprising. . . . The descents, gardens and avenue through the wood august and stately, but the land all about wretchedly barren, producing nothing but fern . . . as I told his Majesty that evening (asking me how I liked Cliveden) without flattery, that it did not please me yet so well as Windsor, for the prospect and the park which is without compare, there being but one only opening and that but narrow which let one to any variety, whereas that of Windsor is everywhere great and unconfined.[103]

In 1713 Windsor Forest received added aesthetic significance from Alexander Pope's great poem:

> Here hills and vales, the woodland and the plain,
> Here earth and water seem to strive again,
> Not chaos-like together crush'd and bruis'd,
> But as the world, harmoniously confus'd:
> Where order in variety we see,
> And where, tho' all things differ, all agree.
> Here waving groves a chequer'd scene display,
> And part admit, and part exclude the day;
> As some coy nymph her lover's warm address
> Nor quite indulges, nor can quite express.
> There, interspersed in lawns and opening glades,
> Thin trees arise that shun each others shades,
> Here in full light the russet plains extend;
> There wrapt in clouds the bluish hills ascend:
> Ev'n the wild heath displays her purple dyes,
> And 'midst the desert fruitful fields arise,
> That crown'd with tufted trees and springing corn,
> Like verdant isles the sable waste adorn.[104]

The English landscape was revealing its beauties to the eyes of those who lived within it; those eyes, too, were seeing not only England, but the world, as a startlingly new kind of place. Instead of Marvell's earth-deforming and heaven-affrighting mountains, we have John Dennis (who mixed with all the best persons in the literary world) writing in 1717, of the view from Leith Hill in Surrey:[105]

The sight of a mountain is to me more agreeable than that of the most pompous edifice; and meadows and natural winding streams please me before the most beautiful gardens, and the most costly canals. . . .

. . . in a late journey which I took into the Wild of Sussex, I passed over a hill which showed me a more transporting sight than ever the country had shown me before, either in England or Italy. The prospects, which in Italy pleased me most were that of Valdarno from the Apennines, that of Rome and the Mediterranean, from the mountain of Viterbo; of Rome at forty, and of the Mediterranean at fifty miles distance from it, and that of the Campagna of Rome, from Tivoli and Frescati; from which two places, you see every foot of that famous plain, even from the bottom of Tivoli and Frescati, to the very foot of the mountain of Viterbo without anything to intercept your sight. But from a hill which is passed in my late journey into Sussex, I had a prospect more extensive than any of these, and which surpassed them at once in rural charms, in pomp and in magnificence. The hill which I speak of is called Leith Hill . . . It juts itself out about two miles beyond that range of hills which terminated the North Downs to the south. When I saw from one of those hills, at about two miles distance, that side of Leith Hill which faces the Northern Downs, it appeared the beautifullest prospect to me I had ever seen. But after we had conquered the hill itself, I saw a sight that would transport a stoic, a sight that looked like enchantment and vision, but vision beatific. Beneath us, lay open to our view, all the wilds of Surrey and Sussex, and a great part of that of Kent, admirably diversified in every part of them, with woods, and fields of corn, and pastures, being everywhere adorned with stately rows of trees. . . .

About noon in a serene day, you may at thirty miles distance see the very water of the sea through a chasm in the mountains. And that which above all makes it a noble and wonderful prospect, is, that at the same time that at thirty miles distance you behold the very water of the sea; at the same time that you behold to the south the most delicious rural prospect in the world; at that very time, by a little turn of your head towards the north, you look over Box Hill, and see the country beyond it between that and London; and over the very stomacher of it, see St. Paul's, and London beneath it, and Highgate and Hampstead beyond it.

Even stranger, the Chinese world, in a fanciful form, was entering into our elysiums. There is the delightful and incongruous final scene of Purcell's *Fairy Queen* of about 1685. The directions tell us that a machine appears, from which clouds break as Phoebus enters in a chariot drawn by four horses; a symphony plays as the machine moves forward, and peacocks spread their tails. The light fades, and all goes dark. Suddenly, all is illuminated to display the transparent prospect of a Chinese garden where all—architecture, trees, plants, birds, beasts—is 'quite different to what we have in this part of the world'. Through an arch are seen other arches, with close arbours, and a row of trees to the end of the view. Over the arch is a hanging garden, which rises by several ascents, bounded on either side by pleasant bowers, various trees, and a number of strange birds. A fountain plays, six monkeys are seen, six pedestals of china-work arise, supporting large vases of porcelain in which are six China orange trees. Here is chinoiserie coming into its own.

A little earlier—in 1685—Sir William Temple published his description of Chinese gardening.[106]

What I have said of the best forms of gardening, is meant only of such as are in some sort regular; for there may be other forms wholly irregular that may, for aught I know, have more beauty than any of the others; but they must own it to some extraordinary dispositions of nature in the seat, or some great race of fancy or judgement in the contrivance, which may reduce many disagreeing parts into some figure, which shall yet, upon the whole, be very agreeable. Something of this I have seen in some places, but heard more of it from others who have lived among the Chinese; a people, whose way of thinking seems to lie as wide of ours in Europe as their country does.

Among us, the beauty of building and planting is placed chiefly in some certain proportions, symmetries or uniformities; our walks and our trees ranged so as to answer one another, and at exact distances. The Chinese scorn this way of planting, and say, a boy, that can tell a hundred, may plant walks of trees in straight lines, and over-against one another, and to what length and extent he pleases. But their greatest reach of imagination is employed in contriving figures, where the beauty shall be great, and strike the eye, but without any order or disposition of parts that shall be commonly or easily observed: and, though we have hardly any notion of this sort of beauty, yet they have a particular word to express it, and, where they find it hit their eye at first sight, they say the *sharadwadgi*** is fine, or is admirable, or any such expression of esteem. And whoever observes the work on the best India gowns, or the paintings on their best screens or porcelains, will find their beauty is all of this kind (that is) without order.

But I should hardly advise any of these attempts in the figure of gardens among us; they are adventures of too hard achievement for any common hands; and, though there may be more honour if they succeed well, yet there is more dishonour if they fail, and it is twenty to one they will; whereas, in regular figures, it is hard to make any great and remarkable faults.

As Queen Anne's reign progressed, and the domination of the school of London and Wise grew, the excessive use of small, clipped evergreens became the subject of ridicule.

In 1691 Gibson,[107] as we have seen, regarded the 'greens' as an index to the quality of the gardens that he inspected. Peter Collinson, writing of his youth in the last years of Anne's reign, wrote of the modest garden of his relatives at Peckham[108] that they were 'remarkable for fine cut greens, the fashion for those times. . . . I often went with them . . . to buy . . . clipped yews in the shapes of birds, dogs, men, ships, etc.'. Practically every kind of evergreen that would grow was subjected to this treatment, including firs and pines. And deciduous trees also were cut; the Earl of Haddington wrote of the English elm that 'in all thy hedges about London this tree grows in great plenty, and the custom there is to cut off all the side branches, close by the bole of the tree, and only leave a small head, so that in the winter they look in a manner like a very tall hedge, and in the spring are as bare as maypoles, except the small head'.

These excesses of professional gardeners laid themselves open to ridicule by the more literary-minded. In June 1712[109] came Addison's commentary on Temple, typical of the spirit informing his other garden writings and those of Steele and, with certain differences, of Alexander Pope:

---

* *Sharadwadgi*, though opinions differ, is probably not a Chinese word, but of Japanese origin, from *souro*, of which the negative participle is *soro-wa-ji*, 'not being symmetrical'. No doubt Temple heard it in Holland.

Writers who have given us an account of China, tell us the inhabitants of that country laugh at the plantations of our Europeans, which are laid out by the rule and line; because, they say, any one may place trees in equal rows and uniform figures. They choose rather to show a genius in works of this nature, and therefore always conceal the art by which they direct themselves. They have a word, it seems, in their language, by which they express the particular beauty of a plantation that strikes the imagination at first sight, without discovering what it is that has so agreeable an effect. Our British gardeners, on the contrary, instead of humouring nature, love to deviate from it as much as possible. Our trees rise in cones, globes and pyramids. We see the marks of the scissors upon every plant and bush. I do not know whether I am singular in my opinion, but, for my own part, I would rather look upon a tree in all its luxuriancy, than when it is thus cut and trimmed into a mathematical figure. . . . But as our great modellers of gardens have their magazines of plants to dispose of, it is very natural for them to . . . contrive a plan that may most turn to their own profit, in taking off their evergreens and the like movable plants, with which their shops are plentifully stocked.* (Plate XII).

In the year after this was published, George London died; within a year Henry Wise was disposing of Brompton Park Nurseries, and the great business soon went downhill.

Finally in 1715 Sir John Vanbrugh was appointed to the newly created post of Surveyor of the Gardens and Waters . . . of the Palaces of England. Wise came second to him. Though Vanbrugh was but thirteen years the junior of Wise, who outlived him by fourteen years, and though both were intimately concerned with Blenheim, there were elements in Vanbrugh belonging to the future which were missing in Wise. There was Vanbrugh's liking of the old—his attempt, for example, to save the medieval buildings of Woodstock in Blenheim's park, in which he so delighted that he made them his headquarters, and his 'real feeling for the romantic associations of the English past'.[110] Vanbrugh was the figurehead of the English baroque school. And, as Geoffrey Webb wrote,[111] baroque was essentially a pictorial style, to lead later to the cult of the picturesque.

A revolution was in the wind.

* Joseph Addison (1672–1719) was, in fact, tolerant. His phrase written in the same year, 'I think there are as many kinds of gardening as of poetry,' is often overlooked.

F I V E

The Landskip
1720–1780

POET AND PAINTER: POPE AND KENT

THE pundits—and the word inevitably, to an Englishman, must carry some of the jocularity attached to its secondary dictionary meaning—assure us that one of our few contributions to the visual arts is the landscape garden; long ago it became canonized in the world of taste as *le jardin anglais*.* It has, from the days of its creators, been written upon, in prose, verse, and jingle, to an overwhelming extent. That this is so is in part due to its literary origins; it aspired to produce visual scenes and effects that could be well described, heavily overlaid with poetic and other allusions meaningless to those who were not well read.†

Today we can see in many places the work of the Georgian landscape gardeners—perhaps now over-mature and moving towards decay. In many instances it remains unspoiled, except by time. We admire the scenes so presented almost passionately, as enshrining the spirit of England. But, alas, we are now so ill-educated that we utterly fail to apprehend their true implications for those who made them. To us, who see the great trees lying conformably on the contours, the winding lakes, and the now decaying temples, the scene can have none of the immense sig-

---

* Unfortunately, one cannot speak of the British landscape garden; only in its latest stages did our fellow islanders become concerned with it.
† William Mason[1] held that Bacon was the prophet, Milton the herald, and 'Addison, Kent, Pope, etc. [*sic*] the champions' of the true modern taste in gardening; elsewhere, he tells us, 'it is said that Mr. Kent frequently declared he caught his taste in gardening from reading the picturesque descriptions of Spenser'. It is now usual to include the Earl of Shaftesbury (1671–1713), author of the philosophical *Characteristics* (1711–23), among its progenitors.

nificance that it had for those who saw only skinny saplings, the newly turned banks of earth, the bare verges of freshly cut ornamental waters, and the shrines of new masonry (of which we quite miss the symbolism) untempered by the weather.

It must, however, be admitted that in the result these visions of poets and men of taste ultimately produced many incongruities. The new vision of nature, the genius of the place, irregularity in design, and, above all, the avoidance of straight lines and their invariable replacement by the amorphous serpentine, fully justified Temple's warning on the consequences of *sharadwadgi*; he could never have foreseen that irregularity, when it did come, would look to Italy and classical sources for its precepts, and have not only gothick* but chinoiserie inconsequently tacked on to it.†

And one cannot help reflecting that economics played an important part in the movement. The making of terraces, the structure of fine fountains and their basins, the levelling and maintenance of ornate parterres, the clipping of a multitude of greens—all cost a great deal more than a meandering natural path, a Tinian lawn, or a serpentine lake. Even so, one could spend lavishly if one was so inclined, skimming the top from a hill, or moving an entire village (as at Milton Abbas) if it spoiled the scene.

Besides economics, politics were also to some extent involved; the new fashion was essentially Whig.

It is well to realize at the outset that the landscape movement had at least two distinct phases. There is a tendency to regard it as a steady progression from Addison and Pope, through Kent to Lancelot Brown and Humphry Repton, halting on the accession of Victoria. The second stage began with what might be called the commercialized 'improvements' of Brown, as will be seen when we examine his work more closely. That it was apparent at the time is shown by Horace Walpole in 1781 (during Brown's ascendancy):

Sir William Stanhope was persuaded . . . to *improve* Pope's garden. . . . The poet had valued himself on the disposition of it, and with reason. Though containing but five acres, enclosed by three lanes, he had managed it with such art and deception, that it seemed a wood,

* It seems well to use this newly re-coined spelling to distinguish work in the mock medieval manner.
† And, in due course, the Indianesque as well!

and its boundaries were nowhere discoverable. . . . Refined taste went to work: the vocal groves were thinned, modish shrubs replaced them and light and three lanes broke in; and if the Muses wanted to tie up their garters, there is not a nook to do it without being seen.[2]

.   .   .   .   .   .

The origins of the movement, as we have seen, had long been latent. According to Loudon, even the serpentine form of pool had been described, and perhaps constructed, long before Lord Bathurst made his celebrated winding stream at Riskins, near Twickenham, or the forgotten Charles Withers joined a string of ponds to create the rather inflexible Serpentine, now the chief feature of Hyde Park and Kensington Gardens, in 1731. He tells us[3] that Bishop Wren, who died in 1667, wrote in his copy of Wotton's *Elements of Architecture*:

For disposing the current of a river to a mighty length in a little space, I invented the serpentine, a form admirably conveying the current in circles and yet contrary motions upon one and the same level, with walks and retirements between, to the advantage of all purposes, either of gardenings, plantings, or banquetings, or aery delights, and the multiplying of infinite fish in a little compass of ground, without any sense of their being restricted.

Laurence Whistler, the authority on the era of Vanbrugh and the history of Stowe and its gardens, so intimately connected with the landscape school, attributes the origin of the new manner to Charles Howard, Earl of Carlisle (1674–1738), who called in George London when laying out gardens at Castle Howard. There, in Wray Wood, 'where Mr. London designed a star, which would have spoiled the wood, but that his Lordship's superlative genius prevented it, and to the great advancement of the design, has given it that labyrinth-diverting model we now see it'. Those words were published by Stephen Switzer (*c.* 1682–1745) in 1718. A plan of Wray Wood, of about 1700, shows the beginning of the irregular walks instead of the conventional star. Switzer adds, 'it is a proverb at that place, *York* against *London*'.[4]

York against London—this time without a pun on the royal gardener—has surely a good deal of significance. We have already seen, a little out of its turn, Squire Kirke's woodland garden at

Cookridge, near Leeds. To Evelyn's eye this was in an irregular figure, though it scarcely appears to us so. And, early in the century, another 'irregular' garden, Duncombe, was formed. Is it a coincidence that William Kent—described in 1733 as 'the sole beginner of the present national taste in gardening'—was born in Yorkshire, and owed his position to the patronage of a great Yorkshire landowner, the Earl of Burlington and Cork? Switzer, too, was particularly concerned with the north country.

But we must not end our speculations on the spirit of 'irregularity' in Yorkshire without remarking that the county had some of the most magnificent gardens in the regular manner.*

The first professional exponents of the irregular school appear to have been Stephen Switzer and Charles Bridgeman who died in 1738. The former we have already met as a chronicler of the gardening history of his times; Bridgeman is a shadowy personality, though he became royal gardener.

Switzer, in spite of his name, came of English stock from East Stratton in Hampshire. He implies that he was a gentleman who, through misfortune, had turned his hand to gardening. Foreman at Brompton Park nurseries after Meager had left, he is the source of much information about George London. His great admiration of the partners was tempered only by a criticism that they attempted too much, and were therefore sometimes perfunctory in their performances. For his part, he was active in designing gardens, particularly in the north of England and, it is said (without any evidence), Scotland. He wrote several books, edited a magazine, *The Practical Husbandman and Planter*, was a good draughtsman, had a nursery garden at Millbank and a stand 'at the sign of the Flower Pot' in Westminster Hall. Besides gardening, he was an expert on—or at least wrote a book about—hydraulics and hydrostatics. He also conducted a campaign against the Scots gardeners who were coming to England in increasing numbers, and seems to have had trouble with his competitors in the nursery business.

Some idea of his outlook on garden design can be obtained from his *Ichnographia Rustica*. He explains that a little regularity may be permitted near the house, where the designer may use the bold strokes of art. But beyond that, he should pursue nature,

* Traces remain at Ledston, Scampston, and Ebberston.

and by as many twinings and windings as the villa will allow, will endeavour to diversify his views, always striving that they may be so intermixed, as not to be all discovered at once; but that there should be as much as possible, something appearing new and diverting, while the whole should correspond together by the natural error of its natural avenues and meanders. . . .

And to the end that he may know the better how to make the best use of natural advantage, he ought to make himself master of all rural scenes. And the writings of the poets on this subject will give him considerable hints, for in design the designer as well as the poet should take as much pains in forming his imagination, as a philosopher in cultivating his understanding.

Switzer's own drawings, however, show that his ideas on irregularity are hesitant; his meanders may not be laid out with rule and compasses, but they appear to have been planned on paper with a rather simplified draughtsman's 'French curve'. Avenues still stride out over the countryside, not perhaps radiating in quite so star-like a manner. Pools are still formed by simple geometry. The ornate parterre has certainly gone and is now replaced by an unbroken lawn.

He was an enthusiast for statuary. He tells in his *Nobleman, Gentleman and Gardener's Recreation* of 1715 that the nobility and gentry of that day were in great need of the 'noble decorations of statues about their country seats', and he outlined a plan for establishing a school of statuaries.

Stephen Switzer did not go very far in his partnership with nature. But his mention of the poet brings us to Charles Bridgeman, who was well acquainted with both Matthew Prior (1644–1721) and Alexander Pope (1688–1744). It was Bridgeman, according to Horace Walpole, who first introduced the ha-ha into our gardens to replace the 'unnaturalness' of walls, and who was considered by Switzer, rather unapprovingly, as attempting an 'incomprehensible vastness', with a 'fancy that could not be bounded'.

Not much is known of Bridgeman's origins. Probably before 1709 he was working for London and Wise. He duly developed a good connection with influential patrons. From our point of view, however, it is his link with the artistic rather than the scientific world of his period that seems significant. In the St.

Luke's Club he had as fellow members such men as Kent, Gibbs, Thornhill, Rysbrack, and Grinling Gibbons. He was associated with the Board of Works, Vanbrugh, and Flitcroft. Matthew Prior (who was concerned with the important gardens at Down Hall in Essex) is known to have given him a Spenser folio.

Bridgeman was a skilful surveyor and draughtsman. A number of existing garden plans are his work, or pretty confidently attributed to him. Some, such as the highly imaginative amphitheatre at Claremont, are original designs. This, as might be expected, seems to accord with the Vanbrugian vision rather than the free, 'natural' style that was to follow. Others are probably surveys of gardens that he had been commissioned to maintain or alter. There seems a possibility that he gained a reputation for simplifying and reducing the cost of maintaining the more opulent gardens.

This certainly seems the reason for his joining with Wise in 1727 to prepare a report on the management and expenses of the royal gardens since the accession of William and Mary.[5]

Significantly, there is much about the high cost of running the gardens. If it be thought, the memorandum states, 'that such expense is occasioned by their minute forms and compositions . . . and to the great collections of orange and other exotic trees, plants and flowers, that are kept at the several gardens, in very great beauty and at great expense; and to the many kinds of evergreen trees and espaliers of all sorts . . . [now] grown to extraordinary size and loftiness, and which yearly increases the labour and expense in keeping'—then the method of achieving economies is plain.

In 1727 the total net expense of the gardens under the charge of these two was £2,404 9s. 6½d. The sum paid them under contract was £2,960. That left £555 10s. 5½d. net profit. Henry Wise received £277 15s. 2¾d. and his partner Charles Bridgeman the same.

In that year Wise obtained possession of Warwick Priory, for which he had been waiting as a home for his retirement. On Lady Day, 1728, Bridgeman took over the royal gardens at a salary of £2,220 a year (based on the rate of £15 an acre).

Bridgeman, like London, was not a writer.* Nor did he, like

* In 1724 he did, however, produce *A Report on the Present State of the Great Level of the Fens called Bedford Level*. . . .

Wise, found a dynasty which retained material for biographers. His widow complained that she and her family had been left in poor circumstances, and she claimed money both for work done in the royal service and at Blenheim.*

At this stage, with Wise in retirement, and a rather limited trend towards simplification, irregularity, and economy, there is an apparent vagueness and lack of inspiration in the design of gardens in the grand manner. Switzer and Bridgeman certainly have not come down to us as powerful figures. Addison† and the literary figures behind him, ranging from Milton to the Earl of Shaftesbury, do not seem potent in practice.

Remembering the literary and, particularly, the poetic inspiration of the new movement, we should surely look for a poet-gardener to provide its initial spark of genius that was so soon to outshine the age-long illumination of Le Nôtre. It has always been held that Pope was concerned; his poems alone lay down most of the rules. But it is to his voluminous correspondence[8] that one must turn to learn that if, as is said, a writer is generally a man of action *manqué*, Pope's sphere would have been gardening. There can be no doubt that he had not only a brilliant visual imagination in which the English countryside was singularly in accord with the classical scene, but also a great keenness about the practical side of horticulture.

Pope certainly lay near the centre of the reformation from early in the eighteenth century until his death in 1744. His friends and correspondents were Allen, 1st Earl Bathurst (1684–1775), an ardent amateur of garden design and planting, both at Oakley, near Cirencester, his seat, and Riskins, his house by Twickenham; Charles Bridgeman, eventually the royal gardener; Richard Boyle, Earl of Burlington (1694–1753), whose patronage of William Kent (with whom Pope was also on very familiar terms) was a key to the future of gardening; the Earl of Peterborough, of Parson's Green, whom we have already met; Robert, 5th Lord Digby, with his

* David Green[6] shows that this claim was unjustified. The Duchess of Marlborough wrote that she had a 'kindness' for Bridgeman, 'and upon his account would agree to do anything that was tolerably reasonable'. She held his receipt for the work done.

† Addison did not acquire his own estate at Bilton, Rugby, until 1713. W. Graham's edition of *The Letters of Joseph Addison* shows little reference to gardening. In fact, Addison seems to have left the laying out of Bilton to his brother, Captain Edward Addison.[7]

ancient garden at Sherborne in Dorset, and, later, Ralph Allen (1694–1764), Henry Fielding's 'Squire Allworthy', whose brains and financial ability were creating the new Bath. Other correspondents included Philip Miller, Sir Hans Sloane, and George Lyttelton—the maker of Hagley in Worcestershire. Though Pope did not correspond with Sir Richard Temple (c. 1669–1749), later Lord Cobham, who in 1713 began those changes in his garden at Stowe which form an epitome of the garden history of his time, he knew this house well, and in 1725 made it his headquarters for a tour of Buckinghamshire.

Surely, then, this vital little cripple and unapproached poet of his day must have been as deeply concerned with the changes as anyone.

In 1718 Pope moved into a Thames-side villa at Twickenham. For the rest of his life he designed and then polished his garden to make it a work of art, and to provide an elysium and a microcosm for his old age. It was entered by a subterranean passage which he turned into a grotto

> . . . where Thames translucent wave
> Shines a broad mirror through the shadowy cave,
> When lingering drops from mineral roofs distil
> And pointed crystals break the sparkling rill. . . .[9]

In later years his interest in the minerals became more and more scientific. The Rev. William Borlase sent him rare stalactites and marbles, Sir Hans Sloane specimens from the Giant's Causeway, and the grotto became a geological museum.

But it was the garden that remained his great joy until the end of his life. In 1722 he was writing of 'the important affair' of engaging a gardener; a letter from Lord Digby a year later has a modern ring; 'How thrive your garden plants? how look the trees? how spring the brocoli and finochio? hard names to spell!' Soon Bathurst was giving him surplus lime trees from Riskins.

His practical nature is seen in a letter of 1731 to one Fortescue, giving a caution about hedge-cutting (as valid today as then). He explains that the sides must be sloped with a batter, and be left neither erect or with an overhang, as was 'the common gardener's use'.

Twice in 1732 William Kent was called in—only about a

portico, it is true, but at that time he was engaged on his revolutionary garden work at Stowe. Then there is a letter to Philip Miller about the despatch of grafts of choice pears—Chaumontell, Vingoleuse, and Epine d'Hiver.

In November 1736 Pope returned to Twickenham from a visit to the widow of his friend Peterborough at Bevis Mount, Southampton. The year before he had visited that courageous and brilliant man on his death-bed, and heard him speak of his great anxiety to be allowed life enough to finish his new garden. He wrote telling Lady Mordaunt that he was now as busy planting for himself as he had been for her; adding that his trees and shrubs 'will indeed outlive me, if they do not die in their travels from place to place, for my garden, like my life, seems to me every year to want correction and require alteration, I hope at least, for the better. But I am pleased to think my trees will afford shade to others, when I shall want them no more'.

The year 1739 brings us correspondence about a present from the Prince of Wales, offered through George Lyttelton, of small urns for the laurel circus, and two larger ones for the termination of views.

Pope, as a true horticulturist, was interested in the new art of growing pineapples. About 1724 he engaged as gardener John Searle, who stayed with him until his death and then moved on to Ralph Allen at Bath. In later correspondence he was referred to simply as 'John'. By 1739 Searle was growing pineapples. Perhaps this success followed a visit in August 1738 of Henry Scott, Lord Burlington's gardener, who was an expert in their cultivation, and who, when he set up later on his own account, was commended by Pope in 1741 to Ralph Allen as having 'a design which I think a very good one to make pine-apples cheaper in a year or two'. Nevertheless, a year later, Allen was advised not to take Scott's advice.*

Pope's anticipation of the solace that his garden would provide in old age was justified. A year before his death he wrote: 'I have lived much by myself of late . . . partly to amuse myself with little improvements in my garden and house, to which possibly (if I live) I may be soon more confined.'

* But apparently Scott succeeded. His finely engraved trade card of 1754, issued from Weybridge,[19] advertises pineapples for sale, adding that he will be cutting to the end of October.

We know the final state that Pope achieved in his own garden, for Searle left a plan of it (Fig. 7). The house lay between the Thames and the Hampton Court to London road, its lawn sweeping down to the river. The garden lay across the road. The passage-way under the road was the grotto; the house could play no part in the garden design.

The long, rectangular shape was enclosed, in an irregular manner, by plantations within which walks were devised. Some meandered, some were direct. From the orangery they radiated in the old-fashioned manner. The kitchen garden was a narrow strip outside the plantation; the vineyard and greenhouse were inside, but likewise concealed.

A large lawn, or bowling green, was approached through a grove of lime trees, geometrically aligned. The through vistas terminated in an urn, statue, or obelisk. There was no parterre; there were no clipped trees, no geometrical basins, and no hedges. Yet horticulture was practised most seriously within its confines. Pope, aided no doubt by Bridgeman the technician, and possibly by Kent, produced an original garden for all to see. It was on a small scale.

In the wider sphere we can gain an insight into his ideas from a description, with his suggested improvements, that he wrote of the garden at Sherborne, Dorset, in 1722 or 1724.* Sherborne was the seat of Pope's friend, Robert, Lord Digby. The house had been the home of Sir Walter Raleigh, and a good deal of his work remained. But what Pope saw was substantially the house and grounds formed by Digby's ancestors between 1624 and 1639—a scene formed in the time of Charles I and now matured after nearly a century. Pope is therefore also giving us a masterly picture of an early seventeenth-century garden.

On a June day he wrote that the house:

stands in a park crowned with very high woods on all the tops of the hills, which form a great amphitheatre sloping down to the house. On the garden sides the woods approach close, so that it appears there with a thick line and depth of groves on each hand, and so it shows from most parts of the park. The gardens are so irregular, that it is very hard to give an exact idea of them except but by a plan. Their beauty rises from their irregularity, for not only the several parts of the garden

* It was later totally altered by 'Capability' Brown.

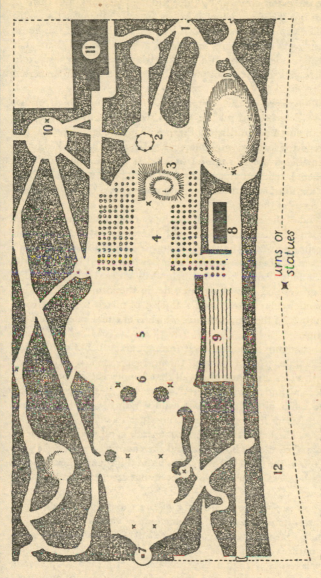

Fig. 7. Sketch plan of Pope's Garden, Twickenham, 1744. 1. The entrance from the grotto. 2. The shell temple. 3. The large mount. 4. The grove. 5. The bowling green. 6. Two small mounts. 7. Obelisk to his mother's memory. 8. The stove. 9. The vineyard. 10. The orangery. 11. The garden house. 12. The kitchen garden.

× urns or statues

itself make the better contrast by these sudden rises, falls, and turns of the ground; but the views about it are let in, and hang over the walls, in very different figures and aspects. You come first out of the house into a green walk of standard limes with a hedge behind them that makes a colonnade, thence into a little triangular wilderness, from whose centre you see the town of Sherborne in a valley, interspersed with trees.

From the corner of this you issue at once upon a high grown terrace the whole breadth of the garden, which has five more green terraces hanging one under another, without hedges, only a few pyramid yews and large round honeysuckles between them. The honeysuckles hereabouts are the largest and finest I ever saw. You'll be pleased when I tell you the quarters of the above mentioned little wilderness are filled with these and with cherry trees of the best kinds all within reach of the hand.

At the end of these terraces run two long walks under the side walls of the garden which communicate with the other terraces that front them opposite. Between, the valley is laid level and divided into two regular groves of horse-chestnuts, and a bowling green in the middle of about 180 foot. This is bounded behind by a canal, that runs quite across the groves and also along one side, in the form of a T. Behind this, is a semicircular *berceau*, and a thicket of mixed trees that completes the crown of the amphitheatre which is of equal extent with the bowling green.

Beyond that runs a natural river through green banks of turf over which rises another row of terraces, the first supported by a slope well planted with vines, as is also the wall that bounds the channel of the river. A second and third appeared above this, but they are to be turned into a line of wilderness with wild winding walks for the convenience of passing from one side to the other in shade, the heads of whose trees will lie below the uppermost terrace of all, which completes the garden and overlooks both that and the country.

Even above the wall of this, the natural ground rises, and is crowned with several venerable ruins of an old castle, with arches and broken views. . . .

When you are at the left corner of the canal and the chestnut groves in the bottom, you turn of a sudden under very old trees into the deepest shade. One walk winds you up by a hill of venerable wood overarched by nature, and of a vast height, into a circular grove, on one side of which is a close high arbour, on the other a sudden open seat that overlooks the meadows and river with a large distant prospect. Another walk under this hill walks by the riverside quite covered with high trees on both banks, overhung with ivy, where falls a natural cascade with never-ceasing murmurs. On the opposite hanging of the bank (which is a steep of 50 feet) is placed, with a very fine fancy, a rustic seat of stone, flagged and rough, with two urns in the same rude taste upon pedestals, on each side: from whence you lose your eyes upon the glimmering of the waters under the wood, and your ears in the constant dashing of the waves. In view of this, is a bridge that crosses the stream, built in the same ruinous state: the wall of the garden hanging over it, is humoured so as to appear the ruin of another arch or two above the bridge. Hence you mount the hill over the Hermit's Seat (as they call it) described before, and so to the highest terrace again.

On the left, full behind these old trees, which make this whole part inexpressibly awful and solemn, runs a little, old, low wall, beside a trench, covered with elder trees and ivies; which being crossed by another bridge, brings you to the ruins, to complete the solemnity of the scene. You first see an old tower penetrated by a large arch, and others above it through which the whole country appears in prospect, even when you are at the top of the other ruins, for they stand very high, and the ground slopes down on all sides. These venerable broken walls, some arches almost entire of 30 or 40 feet deep, some open like porticos with fragments of pillars, some circular or enclosed on three sides, but exposed at top, with steps which time has made of disjointed stones to climb to the highest points of the ruin: these, I say, might have a prodigious beauty, mixed with evergreens and parterres, from part to part, and the whole heap standing as it does on a round hill, kept smooth in green turf, which makes a bold basement to show it.

The open courts from building to building might be thrown into circles or octagons of grass or flowers, and even in the gaming rooms you have fine trees grown, that might be made a natural tapestry to the walls, and arch you overhead where time has uncovered them to the sky. Little paths of earth, or sand, might be made, up the half-tumbled walls, to guide from one view to another on the higher parts; and seats placed here and there, to enjoy those views, which are more romantic than imagination can form them. I could very much wish this were done, as well as a little temple built on a neighbouring round hill that is seen from all points of the garden and is extremely pretty. It would finish some walks, and particularly be a fine termination to the river to be seen from the entrance into that deep scene I have described by the cascade, where it would appear as in the clouds, between the tops of some very lofty trees that form an arch before it, with a great slope downward to the end of the said river.

For the sake of completeness, one must repeat Pope's lines on design, quoting from the early version called *Of Taste*, published in 1731:

> To build, to plant, whatever you intend,
> To rear the column, or the arch to bend,
> To swell the terrace, or to sink the grot,
> In all, let nature never be forgot.
> Consult the genius of the place in all,
> That tells the waters or to rise, or fall,
>
> Or helps the ambitious hill the heavens to scale,
> Or scoops in circling theatres the vale,
> Calls in the country, catches opening glades,
> Joins willing woods, and varies shades from shades,
> Now breaks, or now directs, the intending lines,
> Paints as you plant, and as you work, designs.
>
> Begin with sense, of every art the soul,
> Parts answering parts, shall slide into a whole,
> Spontaneous beauties all around advance,
> Start, even from difficulty, strike, from chance;
> Nature shall join you; time shall make it grow
> A work to wonder at—perhaps a Stowe.
>
> Without it, proud Versailles! thy glory falls,
> And Nero's terraces desert their walls:
> The vast parterres a thousand hands shall make,
> Lo! Bridgeman comes, and floats them with a lake;
> Or cut wide views through mountains to the plain,
> You'll wish your hill, and sheltered seat, again.

In later versions poor Bridgeman is replaced by Lord Cobham. We should look, too, at Pope's activities as a gardener outside his own walls. Best known is his connection with Bathurst at Cirencester: 'I look upon myself as the magician appropriated to . . . that enchanted forest,' he wrote; in 1732 Bathurst, when inviting him down, says there is enough work to employ him for a week and the consumption of quires of paper 'in draughts'. Bathurst used to send him plans for consideration.

With Bridgeman and Bathurst he was in 1724 engaged in designing Mrs. Howard's (the Countess of Suffolk's) garden at Marble Hill. Bridgeman submitted the plans to Pope. In the same year Bridgeman wrote that he was anxious to discuss matters of 'great moment' with Pope, and a little later Pope when sending his regrets that he is unable to visit the Earl of Oxford at Wimpole, Cambridgeshire, adds: 'I am heartily disappointed, as so is another man of the virtuoso class as well as I; (and in my notions, of the higher kind of class, since gardening is more antique and nearer God's own work than poetry) I mean Bridgeman.'

There seems little doubt, too, that Pope and Bridgeman were concerned in the planning of Oxford's garden at Down Hall, Essex.* In Pope's own garden a turfed 'Bridgemannick' theatre was made by a gang of Bridgeman's men who were working for the Prince of Wales during 1726.

At present Bridgeman as a personality lives more in Pope's correspondence than elsewhere, and one cannot help feeling that Pope's friendship and help, and his great sensibility combined with a practical interest in gardening, must have helped Bridgeman, the consummate surveyor and well-trained gardener, to move towards those wider horizons of which his colleague Switzer was so suspicious.

Of Pope's friendship with and influence on William Kent (1684–1748) there is no doubt; his correspondence makes that quite clear. Besides, we have Horace Walpole's statement,[11] which also gives us a delightful glimpse of Pope's garden:

Mr. Pope undoubtedly contributed to form Kent's taste. The design of the Prince of Wales's garden at Carlton House was evidently borrowed from the poet's at Twickenham. There was little affected modesty in the latter, when he said, of all his works he was most proud of his garden. And yet it was a singular effort of art and taste to impress so much variety and scenery on a spot of five acres. The passing through the gloom from the grotto to the opening day, the retiring and again assembling shades, the dusky groves, the larger lawn and the solemnity of the termination of the cypresses that led up to his mother's tomb, are managed with exquisite judgement; and though Lord Peterborough assisted him to form his quincunx and to rank his vines, those were not the most pleasing ingredients of his little perspective.

Variety of scenery, the planned lights and shades, the literary and emotional overtones of the conventional cypress-shaded obelisk—all are new things in the gardener's world. Yet in the

* After Prior's death.

works and thoughts of Pope there is still something missing. Pope had not been to Italy; never in his correspondence does he mention the paintings of Poussin or Claude.* We must change our course a little once again, and steer into a sea whose currents flow somewhat incongruously.

. . . . .

Richard Boyle, 3rd Earl of Burlington, and 4th Earl of Cork (1694–1753), was born to great estates—particularly in Yorkshire—which descended to him at the age of nine. He made the Grand Tour of Europe, now become fashionable to the extent of being inevitable, and was early interested in architecture. In due course he became convinced that the key to perfection lay in the theories and works of Andrea Palladio (1508–1580), who was born at Vicenza and studied at Rome. Palladio was deeply interested in classical literature and art, and was influenced by *De Architectura* of Vitruvius, the Roman architect and engineer who lived at the time of the Emperor Augustus. Palladio's classic work, *I quattro libri dell' architettura*, was published in 1570. The rules of architecture that he set down—and they were very precise ones, founded on classical practice—had, for a variety of reasons, a singular attraction for English architects from the time of Inigo Jones.†

To Burlington and his school—politically Whig—Palladio was the master and Jones his local prophet. Burlington's munificent patronage and personal skill as an architect brought about, of course, our Palladian school of architecture. The porticoed villa (designed in accordance with strict rules) contrived to give coolness in the hot Italian sun, was set down here, there and everywhere in our breezy and freely watered landscape.

In 1719 Burlington brought William Kent back with him from Italy, installed him at Burlington House, and until Kent's death was his patron and, no doubt, something of a master. Kent, as has already been remarked, was a Yorkshireman. Frank, pushing, later affecting—of all things in a north-countryman—an Italianate manner, he was of a friendly disposition and well received in all

---

* My confidence is grounded on George Sherburn's index to his edition of Pope's letters.
† Hints of Palladianism did, of course, exist in British architecture before Burlington's full-blooded advocacy.

circles. Born at Bridlington into a family of no account, he was trained as a sign painter, but later made his way to Rome where he was patronized by the English gentry—the virtuosi and men of 'taste' (a word now coming into fashion)—as a painter; indeed, he was claimed to be a second Raphael. In 1716 he met Burlington.

One could claim rather crudely that Pope was a gardener of genius *manqué* and Kent was a painter without it who turned to architecture and decoration, and whose pictorial sensibilities were devoted to garden design. His purpose can, perhaps oversimply, be stated: to re-create around Burlington's (or his own) buildings

> Whate'er Lorrain light-touched with softening hue
> Or savage Rosa dashed, or learned Poussin drew. . . .[12]

The pictures of Claude Gelée, of Lorraine (1600–1682), were greatly admired by Englishmen. The wide, idyllic landscape, bathed in a blue sky that radiates light, the ruins and temples so excellently placed, and the little figures enacting some classic legend are too well known to need further description (Plate XI). Gaspar Poussin (1613–1675), protégé of the great Nicolas Poussin (1594–1665), was also a notable painter of the Roman Campagna, and imbued with the classical and allegorical feelings of Nicolas. These, it may be recalled, were French painters who preferred Rome to the court of Louis XIV.

Salvator Rosa (1615–1673) was of the Neapolitan school; Evelyn, no doubt, would have used the word 'romantic' of his work: it is spectacular, with hermits and similar properties scattered about the wild scene: 'rock pil'd on rock, they Alpine heights retire'.*

Like all great artists, these men worked to a formula:

> Three marked divisions we shall always find:
> Not more, where Claude extends the prospect wide. . . .[13]

Kent's achievement can still not be better expressed than in Horace Walpole's famous words: 'He leaped the fence, and saw

---

* Franceso Albani (1578–1660), the 'Anacreon of painting' of the Bologna school, was also favoured—as were, indeed other lesser-known artists working in a similar manner. The popular writings of Jonathan Richardson (1665–1749) on art and connoisseurship should also be noted.

that all nature was a garden.'[14] But we must qualify it. First, in practice, he threw down the walls, and substituted the ha-ha; the landscape and beauties were brought (if required) almost up to the windows of the house; cows, sheep, and deer played their part in the scene—but the ha-ha kept them from peeping through the glass. The scene he attempted was not the English scene, but compiled from the works of the painters we have enumerated. Temples, obelisks, urns, and other symbolic objects were provided to furnish the picture in the true Roman manner; gothick and features of chinoiserie were shortly added to give even fuller value.

Once again Rome was the inspiration of English gardens, now in a rather odd way, for no longer was it the Italian garden, subtly designed in architectural magnificence, but the countryside and its antique corroding ruins. The cold, rigid logic of Palladian architecture stood in a lax and artificially wrought scene. The stage management was still French, no longer that of the now condemned Le Nôtre, master of the art of gardening, but Claude and Poussin, mere painters.

Nor, of course, was Kent a gardener. Was the result gardening? Its very circumstances give his work a charming incongruity and slightly comical quality—he once planted dead trees to give an effect. One thing is certain; it introduced to the English gardener, and to the world, a new attitude of mind that, with variations, still predominates.

Kent inevitably did comparatively little garden designing, for he was employed on other activities. At Chiswick (for Burlington himself), at Claremont, at Stowe (where he continued what Vanbrugh, Gibbs, and Bridgeman had begun) he was, too, working over other men's foundations. Possibly his most personal work was for General Dormer at Rousham in Oxfordshire between 1720 and 1725. Here Bridgeman had, it seems, already been called in, but Kent almost entirely obliterated his work. The garden can still be seen—its lines almost identical with a contemporary plan (page 14).

Rousham is, in every way, sensationally different not only from a design by Wise but from a contemporary plan such as that made in 1738 by Bridgeman for Eastbury. The garden lies to the north-east of the house, which stands on the level, adjoining a shallow escarpment beside the little River Cherwell. Its shape is dominated by the river, which makes two highly 'irregular' acute bends in the course of a few hundred yards. The garden does not extend across the river, but where the land has gently risen beyond it an artificial ruin stands as a point of focus.

The garden front of the house looks out on to a level lawn, which ends in a rough, concave slope down to the river, wooded on either side; within the trees to the left, on unevenly sloping ground, lie the delights of the place. There is the glade dedicated to Venus—with its small ponds and cascades and an ice-cold bath, now deeply shaded by yews, whose overflow runs speedily in a narrow, serpentining rill. Near the extremity of the garden one stands beneath a statue and looks back down a straight tree-lined alley to a scooped-out lawn surmounted by an arcade; this end of the garden gives a view in the other direction of the ancient Heyford bridge. Other buildings are strategically placed; it has been pointed out that these must not be regarded as follies—they were designed as memorials, or symbols.

One realizes on studying Rousham that Kent revolutionized the whole conception of garden design. Perhaps Pope was the spark that set his genius aflame. That genius was, alas, extinguished at a comparatively early age—'high feeding and an inactive life' bringing on a fatal illness.[15]

It seems that other gardeners, more or less contemporaneously with Kent, worked somewhat in his manner. One such, named Wright, was highly commended in George Mason's *Essay on Design in Gardening* (1795).

ELYSIUM AND ARCADY

The origins and aims of the new school were to be partly forgotten, often commercialized, sometimes elaborated; but they long remained—in part still do—the key not only to much of subsequent designs of gardens, large and small, but to the appearance of such of our countryside as retains its park-like quality.

This quality was, indeed, largely acquired during the later eighteenth and early nineteenth centuries. The rising class of industrialists, merchants, and new rich from India and North America sought political power, pleasure, and gentility through the building or acquiring of country houses. Soon, in spite of the vulgar taint of trade, they were in a position equal to—and often financially sounder than—the inheritors of the old parks and country seats. The machinery for obtaining their lands was, of course, often the use of the Enclosure Acts. At that time industry and country houses not infrequently stood side by side.

The English countryside became *un paysage humanisé*, with its own distinctive quality, remarked upon and not infrequently praised by foreign travellers. Archenholtz wrote 'the whole country is adorned with parks remarkable for their situation or picturesque views: almost at every step we meet with alleys of fruit trees, leading to elegant villages'.[16]

Road books, such as Tunnicliff's *Survey*,[17] or Russel and Price's *England Displayed*,[18] carefully describe the gentlemen's seats that are passed; they are now numerous, even in the remote counties.

Another feature that distinguished our great houses from those on the Continent became apparent during the middle of the century. This was the Englishman's love of solitude, of placing his house in the centre of a park, well away from his fellows, or in an elevated position so that he might enjoy the view and the air, and at the same time be observed only from an unembarrassing distance. Ralph Dutton quotes[19] the French Duchess de Dino, staying at Woburn at the beginning of the nineteenth century, on this peculiarity (which had become so marked in the eighteenth):

The English detest being seen and will gladly forego any prospect beyond their own limited boundaries. . . . One cannot hope to have the pleasure of seeing passers-by on the highway, travellers, labourers working in the fields, or the glimpse of a village and the adjacent landscape. Green lawns and flower-beds with superb trees which obscure all view, that is what the English like, and what one finds everywhere here.

It was all very different from the French château.*

Horace Walpole never fails to comment derogatorily on a house standing low. Of Drayton, a building he admired, he wrote: 'it stands in as ugly a hole as Boughton: well! that is not its beauty'; of Berkeley Castle: 'the situation is not elevated nor beautiful'.[20] Again and again one finds the new Georgian mansion built on a hill, the old house by the river being pulled down for its materials. The antiquarian and traveller, the Hon. John

* Her own home, Valençay, is set so that it may be seen from the highway; an English country house displays little of itself to the road but its massive gates.

Byng,[21] was often to record his dislike of these 'new' naked houses in the classical style set on the top of draughty hills, to be stared at—from a safe distance. Economic historians have seized on their existence to conclude that landowners had now gained control of all water supplies.

It is a mistake to assume that all these houses had truly Kentian landscapes; the more conservative would consult Miller's *Dictionary*, with its instructions based on James, or the more fashionable Batty Langley (1696–1751), whose *New Principles of Gardening* was issued in 1728 and was still popular in the late 1750s.* Langley laid down a numbered series of rules for garden design, but, apart from the fact that he decries topiary work and cut parterres, encourages the use of meandering paths and discourages 'many absurdities' of the past, the chief constituents of 'a beautiful rural garden' remain much as before. He names avenues, groves, wildernesses, plain parterres, coppiced quarters, 'green openings like meadows' (something a little fresher here), mounts, terraces, basins, canals, fountains, cascades, aviaries, menageries, cabinets, statues, obelisks, kitchen gardens, bowling greens, dials, amphitheatres—all the stock-in-trade of Le Nôtre.

After Kent, the most important contribution to the new style was made by Philip Southcote, who in 1735 bought Woburn Farm, of some 150 acres, in the Thames Valley between Chertsey and Weybridge. Here, with 'a sense of the propriety' of the 'improvements' now possible in such a place, 'joined to a taste for the more simple delights of the country', Southcote devised his *ferme ornée*.†

Thirty-five acres were 'adorned to the highest degree' by planting trees, and shrubs, and the making of flower borders; the rest remained as farm, though with clumps of trees added. The whole was contained within an ornamental walk: 'this walk is properly garden: all within it is farm'. Great variety of scene was encompassed around the path, which was conducted in a waving line. Groups of shrubs merged with the native hedgerow, 'enriched with woodbine, jessamine, and every odoriferous plant whose tendrils will entwine with the thicket'. It passed through clumps of firs, thickets of deciduous shrubs, or as a contrast merely,

---

* At this period Shenstone still refers to the existence of 'parterre gardening'.

† Mason wrote that: 'Mr. Southcote was . . . the inventor of the *ferme ornée*, for it may be presumed that nothing more than the term is of French extraction.'

through the rich verdure of cut grass. A ruined chapel was to be seen; a neat gothick building formed an embellishment; little seats, alcoves, and bridges continually occurred. Everywhere, the ancient pursuit of farming was the theme to be developed; the dairy, a haystack ('generally an agreeable circumstance in any position'), pasture, and tillage—all played their part. But each was brought up to a standard adequate for a retreat that was a mansion; the master himself, by his surroundings, had to be 'sufficiently distinguished from his tenants'.[22]

Southcote was devising something rather different from the Kentian scene. A dictionary will, I think, define it. Kent strove to create an Elysium: a classical paradise seen through the eyes of a Claude. Southcote's ambition was an Arcady: the ideal countryside. The Roman gods themselves dwelt within the first; mortal Strephons and Uranias, Phillidas and Corydons, slip in and out of the second.

The ideals of Southcote and his school were closer to those expressed in 1740 by Dr. Warton, in his poem significantly called *The Enthusiast, or, the Lover of Nature*:

> Rich in her weeping country's spoils Versailles
> May boast a thousand fountains that can cast
> The tortur'd waters to the distant heav'ns;
> Yet let me choose some pine-topt precipice
> Abrupt and shaggy, whence a foamy stream,
> Like Arno roars. . . .

And, delightfully:

> Low, lonely cottages and ruin'd tops
> Of gothic battlements appear.

Later:

> Can Kent design like Nature? Mark where Thames'
> Plenty and pleasure pour through Lincoln's meads,*
> Can the great artist, though with taste supreme
> Endow'd, one beauty to this Eden add?
> Though he, by rules unfetter'd, boldly scorns
> Formality and Method, round and square
> Disdaining, plans irregularly great.

* Esher Place, near to Claremont, where 'Kent and nature vie for Pelham's love'.

Even Kent is not quite approved, and

> What are the lays of artful Addison,
> Coldly correct, to Shakespeare's warblings wild?

If Southcote was largely the originator of this kind of gardening, William Shenstone (1714–1763) was, to use a word he would
have abhorred, its publicist. Well into the nineteenth century the
precepts of his Leasowes were followed and his name remembered
by many to whom Southcote was unknown.

Shenstone was a sensitive if minor poet of the pastoral school.
He was a gentle individualist who disapproved of the Grand
Tour, and was something of a solitary. As such, he invited attention to himself. His garden, perhaps because it was situated
near to Birmingham and the famous establishment at Hagley—
both then fashionable novelties—and alongside an important
thoroughfare, was visited by everyone of consequence from
Horace Walpole to Samuel Johnson, as well as 'the Sunday
starers' from the neighbourhood.

The Leasowes was a small farm, lying on and below the
westward-facing escarpment of the plateau upon which Birmingham and the industrial midlands stand. Farther west, the
country breaks up into the multiple little hills and valleys of
Worcestershire. He inherited the place and a small income from
his mother, and took up residence in 1743. He had previously
done something in the way of planting while his tenant was in
occupation, and also—traditionally—at Mickleton Manor, on
the edge of the Cotswolds.* Here he frequently stayed with his
friends the Graves. Through this scholarly family he learned
something of Woburn Farm.

Almost at once Shenstone began the work of creating the
perfect 'landskip' with which he was busy for the rest of his life.[23]
There are many more descriptions of The Leasowes than of
Woburn. As early as 1758 the Rev. Dr. Alexander Carlyle wrote
that it was already needless 'to describe' the grounds, adding, 'the
want of water was obvious, but the ornaments and mottoes, and
names of the groves, were appropriate'. When about to pass on
from The Leasowes to Admiral Smith's at Hagley, Carlyle learned
that the poet was travelling the same way.

* He is supposed to have planted an avenue between Mickleton and Kiftsgate.

We asked Mr. Shenstone to ride with us. His appearance surprised me, for he was a large, heavy, fat man, dressed in white clothes and silver lace, with his grey hair tied behind and much powdered; which, added to his shyness and reserve, were not at first prepossessing. His reserve and melancholy (for I could not call it pride) abated as we rode along, and by the time we left him at the Admiral's, he became good company.[24]

The best description of the garden is that written by Shenstone's publisher, Richard Dodsley;[25] it shows the place in its final state. The house stood on a lawn, protected by a shrubbery and a ha-ha. From it a path twisted and turned across and around, up and down, the hilly estate. Those who followed it were invited to rest on, ponder, or to admire the prospect from no less than thirty-nine seats. The first was within a root-house, wherein a verse of welcome concluded with the admonitory lines:

> And tread with awe these favour'd bowers,
> Nor wound the shrubs, nor bruise the flowers;
> So may your path with sweets abound!
> So may your couch with rest be crown'd!
> But harm betide the wayward swain,
> Who dares our hallow'd haunts profane.

Other seats take the form of 'common benches' (set as hints to spectators to halt lest some contrived view should escape their notice); 'natural bowers'; a lofty gothick seat; a seat in a temple of Pan, an octagonal and also a pyramidal seat. Each carried an appropriate motto. The views included Halesowen Church (in two aspects of light); a real ruined priory (again, glimpsed differently from several situations); a cataract ('we find the stream is not a Niagara'), and glass-house some four miles away ('not ill-resembling a distant pyramid'). At one stage, passing along a dark umbrageous walk, one entered a high natural terrace, 'whence the eye is thrown over all the scenes we have seen before . . . all beheld from a declivity that approaches as near a precipice as is agreeable': at a prodigious distance, the mountains of Wales 'finish the scene agreeably'.

Urns, obelisks, trophies, all engraved with memorial verses to a host of friends, stand by the pathway; piping Pans and other appropriate figures terminate the glades. Shenstone was, indeed, fortunate in the surroundings among which he made his Arcadia, with a 'back scene' of hills 'diversified with wood, scenes of cultivation, and enclosures'.

Shenstone wrote his own *Unconnected Thoughts on Gardening*. The title well describes them; today they merit the closest attention of designers. On the strength of this essay Shenstone is, because he speaks so highly of Edmund Burke's *Inquiry Into the Origin of our Ideas on the Sublime and Beautiful*, sometimes held to have obtained inspiration from that source. But Burke's book was not issued until 1756, by which time not only The Leasowes but a number of similar gardens had already been created; no doubt Burke crystallized a certain current of thought which had been working through Shenstone's as well as other minds.*

A few quotations from the *Unconnected Thoughts* are necessary:

Gardening may be divided into three species—kitchen-gardening —parterre-gardening—and landskip, or picturesque-gardening: which latter is the subject intended in the following pages. It consists in pleasing the imagination by scenes of grandeur, beauty, or variety. Convenience merely has no share here; any farther than as it please the imagination. . . .

I have used the word landskip-gardeners; because in pursuance of our present taste in gardening, every good painter of landskip appears to me the most proper designer. The misfortune of it, is, that these painters are apt to regard the execution of their work, much more than the choice of subject. . . .

What an advantage must some Italian seats derive from the circumstances of being situated on ground mentioned in the classics! And, even in England, wherever a park or garden happens to have been the scene of any event in history, one would surely avail one's self of that circumstance, to make it more interesting to the imagination. Mottoes should allude to it, columns, etc. record it; verses moralize upon it; and curiosity receive its share of pleasure. . . .

A large, branching, aged oak, is perhaps the most venerable of all inanimate objects. . . .

Apparent art, in its proper province, is always as important as apparent nature. They contrast agreeably; but their provinces ever should be kept distinct. . . .

* The same may be said of Hogarth's serpentine 'line of beauty and grace' enunciated in 1753.³⁶ For a time Hogarth worked under Kent, his senior by thirteen years.

This phase is so important in our garden history that it is well to take a look at some of its rather more intimate and practical details. In 1739, or even earlier, Shenstone met Lady Luxborough (1699–1756), and from that year on they corresponded and met regularly. She was the devoted half-sister of the famous Lord Bolingbroke. High-spirited, rather frail, and extremely intelligent, she had been banished by her husband, for alleged infidelities, to his derelict estate at Barrels. This lay on the south of the same escarpment as The Leasowes, 16 miles away. Instead of abandoning herself to despair, she became friendly with the local aristocracy—the Archers, the Plymouths, and the Hertfords and in so doing no doubt indirectly widening the sphere of Shenstone's influence—as well as that of the rural poets William Somerville and Richard Jago. She also set about improving her dilapidated house, and making a garden:

> The prospect is a very near one, being surrounded by hills, but is diversified and pretty enough, and I have made a garden which I am filling with all the flowering shrubs I can get. I have also made an aviary, and filled it with a variety of singing birds, and am now making a fountain in the middle of it, and a grotto to sit and hear them sing in, contiguous to it.[27]

Gardening does not enter into her letters to Shenstone[28] until 1748. Henceforth he is kept informed of all that goes on, and is often asked for advice, which is not always taken. Shenstone, in turn, sometimes sought her approval.

In 1748 (as a true gardener she describes its exceptionally early season) she was at work altering her garden to the modern style. Urns rather than fountains engage her attention; she observes that some kinds are better for a church than a grove. Then:

> I am now busy in planting the lane that joins the coppice, and have chosen trees according to my years. The abele is what I plant; which in four years time will produce a multitude of setts, and grow to be a good shade.

Shortly follows the problem of her hermitage. Shenstone believed that it should become part of the shrubbery. But how? 'Might I not plant that straight walk, which is now gravelled, full of shrubs, and not let it lead to the hermitage, but return in a serpentine manner on one of my crooked sand walks?' One must remember that Lady Luxborough was tackling problems that were quite revolutionary. A little while later Shenstone is thanked for a drawing giving the solution.

In May of 1749 the alterations continued. She was ungravelling the lime walk and laying mould on it, the 'seven plots in the shape of Lord Mayor's custards' were made into one large one, with a 12 ft. 6 in. instead of a 5 ft. wide gravel walk around it; slopes were made gentler and the upper garden was also ungravelled and sown with grass to form a bowling green. By June it was 'tolerably green', but the problem now was 'to keep off beasts of all kinds; those in human shape chiefly'. Shenstone replies that he is also suffering from damage by trespassers and the pilfering of flowers and shrubs (which, we have seen, he countered with admonitory verses). Lady Luxborough, more practical, erected a fence, to be concealed by shrubs. 'The Ha! Ha! is digging,' she writes. At the same time she tells Shenstone that she is keeping Langley's book 'till you come to pick out some serpentine walks. I wish his ideas had been more confined, or my territories less so'.

From this and other references it is clear that Shenstone's practical text-books, which he lent to Lady Luxborough, were Batty Langley, and Isaac Ware's collection of Inigo Jones's drawings. Langley was, it seems, considered a little inelegant; he suggested that statues of Minerva and Pallas should embellish the garden; Lady Luxborough would have neither (she jokes), nor Flora, nor Pan in her wood: 'nor have I a drop of water to admit of so much as one Naiad'.

Shenstone's man 'trusty Tom' is often mentioned; he sometimes stays to help—and advise—on such tasks as the construction of a root-house. Her garden was kept in 'very nice order, by the indefatigable care of my Scotch gardener'.

For several months during 1749 the design, execution, placing, and composing of lines for an urn to the memory of William Somerville are discussed. Shenstone had submitted half a dozen designs, but just after Christmas she wrote: 'Now for the inexhaustible topic of the urn . . .' and asked for just one more design. In February 1750 it was in place—and to be seen from the shrubbery, terrace, bowling green, long walk, and the end of the kitchen garden.

She tells of days spent in the woods, 'or to be less poetical, I have stood from eleven to five each day, in the lower part of my long walk, planting and displanting, opening views, etc.'. She was a keen practical horticulturist. In 1751:

My brother Bolingbroke . . . has sent me the most exquisite sorts of melon seeds, and lettuce. Mr. Hall has got me seeds of the greatest curiosity of a flower which the world produces, if I can but raise it. The merchant showed him one pod only, which is as big as a pine-apple, and perfumes a room even now it is not in flower. He has also got a water-engine* made of lignum vitae, which will water my garden with much ease. . . . The snowdrop, to which Mr. Whistler pays so genteel a compliment, I have also had given me, as double as a yellow rose.† My gardener designs to raise some Spanish broom from seed; and you may command what you please of it.

From 1753 onwards she was frequently unwell, but still often in her garden, and made a 'not uninterested' enquiry after Shenstone's friends, the Graves, for 'I confess I wish for the pretty polyanthus root . . . which Mrs. Graves kindly offered me'.

But we must leave Lady Luxborough and mention other gardens in which the new style was being evolved. Probably the most important were Painshill, Stourhead, and Hagley. Painshill

is situated on the utmost verge of a moor, which rises above a fertile plain, watered by the Mole. Large valleys descending in different directions towards the river break the brow into separate eminences; and the gardens are extended along the edge, in a semi-circular form, between the winding river which describes their outward boundary, and the park which fills up the cavity of the crescent: the moor lies behind the place, and sometimes appears too conspicuously: but the views on the other sides into the cultivated country are agreeable: they are terminated by hills at a competent distance.[31]

* Water-engines, or simply 'engines', were much used. They consisted of a wheeled water-tank in which stood a pump that would squirt the water over the plants through an adjustable jet.

> † The snow-drop first but peeps to light
> And fearful shows its head;
> Their modest merit shines more bright
> By self-distrust misled.
> —*Anthony Whistler* (1732–1754).[39]

The absence of literary reference to the snowdrop before the eighteenth century is puzzling. At about this time in Scotland they are described as 'very common: there are double and single ones'.[30] The comparison with the difficult and now rare *Rosa hemispherica* (*see* p. 98) is interesting.

Here, at about the same time* as Southcote was making his 'ornamental farm', the Hon. Charles Hamilton was forming an 'ornamental park'. A 30-acre lake was made, fed from the river by a machine worked by a horse, much later to be replaced by a water-wheel, and large sums of money were spent on the erection of ornamental buildings and the planting of trees and shrubs, many of which were new and rare. Hamilton's aim seems to have been not only to form 'out of a most cursed hill' an idealized landscape after the manner of painters but, by availing himself on a scale then unprecedented of the exotic trees and shrubs which were now becoming available, to create something that had hitherto not been attempted. In 1838 Loudon wrote:[32]

Among the trees remaining are some remarkably fine silver cedars, pinasters and other pines, American oaks, cork trees and ilexes, a tupelo tree, tulip trees, deciduous cypresses, Lombardy and other poplars, etc. Here some of the first rhododendrons and azaleas† introduced into England by Mr. Thoburn, who was gardener to Mr. Hamilton, and who afterwards became an eminent nurseryman at Old Brompton.

Hamilton seems to have been his own designer; he is known to have advised on the planting of Bowood and probably other estates.‡ He 'not only indulged the public with a sight of his improvements . . . but allowed strangers the use of low chairs, drawn by small horses, which were provided at the inns at Cobham, to go over the ground'.[33] These visitors would remark on such features as the Gothic tent, 'in point of lightness, few buildings exceed this temple', or the bridge, which turns out to be the 'covering of a most beautiful grotto . . . immediately under it is a large incrustation of fossils, and spar everywhere hanging like icicles has a most pleasing effect. On each side of the water is a small path, parted from the stream by marine fossils. Nothing can have a more elegant effect than the ceiling of this grotto (in which is stuck, with great taste, a profusion of spar) hanging over the water, as if of a kindred, but congealed nature'.[34]

Hamilton, like Thomas Bushell, had a taste for hermits. One

---

* The exact date is not known, but in 1748 Horace Walpole wrote of the 'really fine place' that Hamilton had made.
† The first azaleas and rhododendrons in our gardens were American species.
‡ It is interesting to note that Painshill had its parterre and orangery, set within a secreted space 'where the exotic plants are, during the summer, intermixed with common shrubs, and a constant succession of flowers'.

he employed, however, soon departed—either on account of his damp hermitage or of an over-fondness of beer. There seems no documentation of this point.

As the youngest son of the Earl of Abercorn, Hamilton was not wealthy, and in 1775, greatly impoverished, he was forced to sell Painshill. Moving to Bath, he lived to the age of eighty-three, gardening to the end.

Probably a little later than Painshill in its inception was Stourhead. Here again a bleak spot was tamed to make a landscape. Henry Hoare the younger (1705–1785), who inherited the fine house in an early Palladian manner built by his father, planted in 1741 a bare valley, such as those still seen on the neighbouring Salisbury Plain, with beech and fir trees (he made great use of the cherry laurel as an undershrub) and linked a series of fish-ponds to form a serpentine lake. Here, even more than at Painshill, we can now see the finished result: the Temple of the Sun, the rustic cottage, the Temple of Flora, the grotto, the rustic convent, and Alfred's tower. Some of the buildings and the sculpture they contain are of very high quality. Horace Walpole concluded his description, written in 1762 (the garden was not finished until about 1772): 'the lake is full of swans, and large tame carp, and the whole composes one of the most picturesque scenes in the World'[35] (Plates XIII and XIV).

Yet the existence of Stourhead in its present form was a matter of much discussion. There are in its library two plans, both apparently by the same hand. One is in a geometrical manner, looking back to Bridgeman. The other is as it is today. One would like to know much more about the origins of this garden.

The other exemplar of the new school was Hagley. Here, on still another type of site, among the gentle hills of Worcestershire, backed by the more inspiring Clents—already a park of great natural beauty—George Lyttelton (1709–1773), saddened by the death of his first wife, sought distraction in gardening. Shenstone's Leasowes was but a few miles away, and as secretary to Frederick, Prince of Wales, Lyttelton would have known Hamilton, who was also on his staff. (This, incidentally, would have brought both into touch with William Kent, who, after the prince leased Kew House, laid out the grounds.) In 1747 Lyttelton began by building, from Sanderson Miller's designs, the now famous 'ruined

castle'. Until his death he continued to build and plant. In time
he rebuilt the hall to suit the new surroundings.

Lyttelton was helped, in addition to Miller, by John Pitt and
James Stuart, whose Doric Temple of Theseus (1758), built on
a hill commanding a fine view, marks the introduction of the
Greek manner into England. He was no doubt also greatly influenced by Pope, for evidence of their friendship abounds.[36] Hagley
has little water, a failing noted by contemporaries. With the
exception of the castle, its conceits are restrained. The sweeps of
trees now contain nothing more exotic than red-stemmed pines
and flat-topped cedars; it is very near to cultivated nature.

These few gardens—there were others almost contemporaneous
—may be taken as setting the style for the years to come; Painshill
in particular, with its employment of exotics and appreciative use
of their wide range of colour and form, seems to be a predecessor
of the twentieth-century manner. The Leasowes, too, had a lasting
influence. One may say that it particularly appealed to the
expanding middle section of society. There was, for instance,
Mrs. Thrale, who, on a September day in 1774, sitting by the
boathouse while Mr. Thrale and Mr. Johnson went to look
more closely at the waterfall, wrote:

> To Shenstone in his grot retired
>   My truest praise I'll pay;
> And view with just contempt inspired
>   The glitter of the gay.
>
> From Kedleston's offensive glare
>   From Chatsworth's proud cascade,
> From artful Hagley I repair
>   To thine and nature's shade.
>
> When Rubens thus too fiercely burns,
>   When Lucan glows with rage
> The soul to softer Guido turns
>   And Virgil's pastoral page.[37]

As late as the 1820s, when James Luckock, a Birmingham
jeweller, moved to Edgbaston and built a villa, it was upon his
recollection of The Leasowes, seen half a century before, that he
modelled his little garden, erecting a sarcophagus of imitation

marble inscribed: 'To the creative genius and amiable qualities of Shenstone.'[38]

As the century proceeds it is well to emphasize once more the connection of gardening with politics and particularly 'English liberty—that liberty of which the new gardens themselves were a sort of symbol'.[39] The sense of justification felt by those who supported the new movement is well shown in an odd sonnet by one of its chief propagandists, the Rev. William Mason. He lived on into the turbulent times after the French Revolution, and it seems clear that the serpentine path was to him a symbolic safety valve which had allowed us to let off steam, while the compressing geometry and regularity of the French avenues and bosquets had held down the pressure till France exploded:

> Smooth, simple path! whose undulating line
>> With sidelong tufts of flow'ry fragrance crown'd,
>> 'Plain in its neatness' spans my garden ground;
> What, though two acres thy brief course confine.
> Yet sun and shade, and hill and dale are thine,
>> And use with beauty here more surely found,
>> Than where, to spread the picturesque around,
> Cast ruts and quarry holes their charms combine!
>> Here, as thou lead'st my step through lawn or
>> grove,
> Liberal though limited, restrain'd though free,
>> Fearless of dew, or dirt, or dust, I rove,
> And own those comforts, all deriv'd from thee!
>> Take then, smooth path, this tribute of my love,
> Thou emblem pure of legal liberty![40]

CAPABILITIES AND SUBLIMITIES

In 1751 Horace Walpole visited Warwick. 'The castle,' he reported, 'is enchanting; the view pleased me more than I can express . . . it is well laid out by one Brown, who has set up on a few ideas of Kent and Mr. Southcote. One sees what the prevalence of taste does; little Brooke, who would have chuckled to have been born in an age of clipt-hedges and cockle-shell avenues, has submitted to let his garden and park be natural'.[41] Walpole so accurately assessed 'one Brown' that the reader will see why the greatest landscaper of all (at least in quantity) has until now not been mentioned.

Warwick Castle grounds had been altered by Brown some ten years previously, while he was gardener at Stowe. In the year that Walpole wrote, he had moved to London and set up on his own as garden designer.

Lancelot Brown (1715–1783) was born of a family in modest circumstances at Kirkharle, Northumberland. He died at Wilderness House, near Hampton Court, now Sheriff of Huntingdon, something more than mere gardener to George III, friend of the great Chatham—and on occasion trusted political mediator between him and the garden-loving Bute—and men of calibre ranging from the Earl of Coventry to Garrick. In the meantime he had swept away old gardens, even whole villages, and created vast new scenes to replace them on an unprecedented scale. Miss Stroud, in her monumental study of Brown,[42] describes in some detail about a hundred and fifty estates for which he was certainly entirely responsible—by no means all with which he was in some way connected.* In addition, Brown's manner was widely copied by professional and amateur imitators alike.

The principal events in his career are these. After a good education at Cambo School, he was taken on as a gardener by Sir William Loraine on his estate by Kirkharle. There he was grounded in the practice of gardening—in which Kent and the other amateurs were deficient. In 1739 the ambitious youth moved southward, to Wotton, whose owner was Sir Richard Grenville, brother-in-law to Lord Cobham whose estate at Stowe lay only fourteen miles away to the north. No doubt through this connection he moved after a year to Stowe—at first only in the kitchen garden. His outstanding ability, charm, and integrity were soon noticed. He duly became head gardener and, with Cobham's assent, from time to time worked on other gardens, one of the first being Warwick Castle. It was, of course, from Stowe that Brown picked up the 'few ideas from Kent'. While there he also married. Cobham died in 1749, and in 1751 Brown moved to London to become 'Capability' Brown—the landscape designer who saw capabilities for improvement in every garden; even his youngest son, educated at Eton, inherited the nickname 'Capey'.

Brown early took to architecture, designing several houses,

---

* As a comparison, it seems unlikely that Bridgeman was concerned, even including minor alterations, with more than a third of this number.

and many small buildings to set in his gardens. His work, in the fashionable Palladian style of Burlington, was sound but undistinguished. Later, he took into partnership the son of his neighbour, a builder. With this young man, the distinguished Henry Holland (1704–1806), a powerful combination came into being which was firmly cemented when he married Brown's daughter. Both Holland and Brown were favoured by the Whig circle* and the then Prince of Wales. This fact prevented his appointment as royal gardener—in spite of attempts to gain the post—until 1761, after the accession of George III. Little enough interrupted Brown's successful career other than asthma, and an inconsequential attack upon him by Sir William Chambers in 1772.

Brown worked to a formula: avenues, parterres, terrace, basins, and canals—everything partaking of the old art and geometry—were obliterated. Nature—in Shenstone's definition of the beautiful rather than sublime species, for Brown's curves and serpentines were smooth and suave—was everywhere. The flower, fruit, and kitchen gardens were banished to a walled enclosure discreetly placed out of sight. If the canals and fountains were destroyed, water was still *l'âme du jardin*, but now

> Some sedgy flat, where the late ripened sheaves
> Stand brown with unblest mildew, 'tis the bed
> On which an ample lake in crystal peace
> Might sleep majestic. . . .[43]

Brown was essentially a practical man, with an eye for a certain type of landscape. After riding round an estate for a few hours, he would have visualized not only how his standardized landscape could be imposed upon the existing scene, but how it could be done at the least expense. He could see just where the extensive length of ha-ha should run, gauge the precise spot where a trickling stream might be dammed to form an 'ample lake', or slightly modified to create a sparkling cascade. The placing of the trees—the clumps derived from Kent, the outer, screening band from Southcote—were all conceived in practical as well as in (rather limited) aesthetic terms. The levellings and smoothings of sharp banks, the winding path, the placing of ornamental buildings, even occasionally the retention of some bit of an old avenue

---

* This was no doubt due to Brown's early association with Cobham.

or other outmoded feature, all were worked out almost to a rule. Horace Walpole said of him that 'such was the effect of his genius that he will least be remembered; so closely did he copy nature that his works will be mistaken for it'. This showed fine prescience when one considers that his plantings, which we now so often take for the natural scene, were then no more than saplings; the margins of his lakes still hard, as yet unsoftened by rushes and flags; his serpentine walks bright new gravel, and as yet unshaded.

Brown is criticized for the destruction that he wrought before he created: for the avenues felled and the handiwork of his predecessors that he obliterated. That is true enough, but economics have, unfortunately, proved him right. The wooded glades have provided timber to pay death duties; his designs, so dependent on the ha-ha, which

> divides,
> Yet seems not to divide the shaven lawn,
> And parts it from the pasture; for if there
> Sheep feed, or dappled deer, their wandering teeth,
> Will, smoothly as the scythe, the herbage shave,
> And leave a kindred verdure . . .[44]

have, beyond the 'lawn's brief limit', provided grazing on which 'the fleecy foragers will gladly browse' and valuable pasturage for cattle sheltered from wind and sun by the Kentian clumps.

Brown's most dramatic design was the damming of the River Glyme at Blenheim, so that Vanbrugh's triumphant viaduct now spans not a trivial rivulet but a fine sheet of water whose source and termination seem to be remote, so cleverly are they concealed (Plates XV and XVI). His most remarkable achievement was the conversion of a useless piece of ground at Croome d'Abitot, marshy and wet from the junction of the rivers Severn and Avon, into the Earl of Coventry's famous seat. Here Brown obliged with the design of the house, Croome Court, in addition. It is reputed that all this cost the earl £400,000; he said that the place was entirely Brown's creation, on 'originally as hopeless a spot as any in the island' (Plate XVI).

Brown's method was quite different from that followed by London and Wise. He worked more or less on the modern system of subcontracting, supervising the work, and checking the costs. He had no nursery, and all his trees and plants were bought from the trade. His care and honesty in ensuring that clients were always charged fairly for work done are much in evidence.

In talent he abounded, but of the true genius of a Kent or Hamilton, or the sensibility of a Shenstone, he had none:

> Virtues were his, which art's best powers transcend:
> Come, ye superior train! who these revere,
> And weep the Christian, husband, father, friend![45]

was the appropriate conclusion of the epitaph that the Rev. William Mason composed for his tomb at Fenstanton.* G. W. Johnson[46] in 1829 summed up his work and standing acutely: 'By his opponents he has been too much decried, as by his followers he has been too lavishly extolled . . . smoothness of gradient and lack of originality were in general his faults.'

We must not forget that though he destroyed much, he created many of those arboreous landscapes that we now take for granted. At Fisherwick, in Staffordshire, he planted over a hundred thousand trees, mostly oaks and pines. He and his patrons planted courageously for future generations—their eyes saw but saplings where in their dreams grew gnarled monsters. We, who have seen their visions fulfilled, have only too often failed to justify their faith.

Among the planters, Thomas Sandby (1721–1798) should also be mentioned. He held the post of Deputy Ranger of Windsor Great Park from 1746 to his death. He planted extensively, advised by his younger brother Paul (1725–1809), who has some claim to be the first English artist to paint individual trees as portraits; both were masters of the picturesque. In the 1750s they formed Virginia Water, which, with the help of a disastrous flood in 1768, became the largest sheet of artificial and ornamental water in Britain.

A number of other men worked in the manner of Brown, some being trained by him. John Haverfield, John Spyers (Brown's draughtsman), Richard Woods, Webb, and William Emes (or Eames)† are all known to have been concerned with important

---

* At his home there, Brown retained the old-fashioned garden, without improvement.

† Emes, of Derby, was responsible for Hawkstone, Shropshire, and Belton, Lincolnshire, among numerous other seats.

gardens. Little is as yet recorded of their lives, and to detail their work here would be premature.

In passing to the latter part of the eighteenth century it may be well to examine a little more closely the contemporary attitude of mind of the patron and connoisseur. Arthur Young[47] in 1768 visited Duncombe in Yorkshire. He wrote: 'Mr. Duncombe's ornamental grounds . . . cannot be viewed without yielding a most exquisite enjoyment.' A few paragraphs, with their salient sentences italicized, will indicate the objects that appealed to, and the emotions that they aroused in, men of taste. But first one should add that today the place is famed for its avenues, and sweeping terraces, with their due temples, curling round the escarpment above the valley of the River Rye, with Rievaulx below; it is a palimpsest of the more advanced garden styles from about 1720 onwards, overlaid by the free style of planting made by the Thomas Duncombe who succeeded in 1746.

Moving along the gently curving promenade towards a Tuscan colonnaded temple, one looks down upon a valley, forming a noble amphitheatre below hanging woods, which

fringe the very shore of a beautiful river . . . which forms, almost in the centre [of the view], a considerable cascade. *Nothing can be more truly beautiful than the bird's-eye assemblage of objects*, which are seen from hence. The valley is intersected by hedges, which form enclosures of grass; the meanders of the river are bold and well broken by scattered trees; the cascade almost overhung with the pendent wood; the Tuscan temple crowning a bank of wood, *form together a distinct landscape, in which every object is such as the warmest fancy would wish for, or the correctest taste approve.*

The view is beheld *with a moving variation* as you walk along the terrace to the Tuscan temple, with fresh objects breaking upon the eye as you advance. That building being situated at what one may call a promontory of high land, projecting into a winding valley, and planted, the views from it are doubled; another terrace then appearing, the temple commands such *various scenes of the sublime and beautiful as to form a theatre worthy of the magnificent pencil of nature.*

From this point the woods on the opposite side are now seen 'in a *much greater bending extent* than from the former point of view'.

Then, 'in front, between the hills, an extensive woody valley opens *beautifully variegated*. An old tower, Helmsley church, and the town scattered with clumps of trees, are seen in the midst of it at those *points of taste which make one almost think them the effects of design*'. Even a swelling hill, 'scattered with fern and rubbish', fits into the scheme as an effect different from the others. All is of the greatest beauty—except that the earlier garden's yew hedges 'clipped in the exactest line of form are in circumstances which act in a very different style from the wonders beneath, where the bold touches of nature's pencil, are graces snatched beyond the reach of art, and rather dissonant from such regular works'.

The art of gardening in the grand manner had certainly changed vastly in half a century. In 1770 Thomas Whately, an accepted arbiter of taste, found approval[48] for the following places, which he described (in addition, of course, to Woburn, Painshill, and Hagley—Stourhead he surprisingly omits): Moor Park in Hertfordshire, on account of its fine lawns; Ilam in Staffs for the introduction of a large hill into the scene; Claremont and Esher for their groves; Blenheim, and Brown's early place, Wotton, for their lakes; Enfield Chase in Middlesex for the perfection and setting of its temple; Caversham, near Reading, for its concealment of the house during the mile-long approach; and Stowe, simply as a garden 'occupying the whole enclosure'. Piercefield, by Monmouth, came into a peculiar category, that of a 'riding', which appropriates a whole countryside—including a village—to ornament the surroundings of a mansion.

As to nature itself, the rocks at Middleton near Chatsworth, and the scenes of rock and river at Matlock, Dovedale, and Symonds Yat, were highly approved. Tintern Abbey was a model upon which 'fictitious ruins should be formed'.

·   ·   ·   ·   ·

In Scotland the building of country houses and the making of gardens increased following an improvement in trade dating from the 1730s. But the new style did not make the same appeal there as it did in England; the 'sublime' in the form of the natural wildness and barrenness of much of their own mountain scenery was, perhaps, a little too real. Agriculture improved, and the planting of woodlands increased. But when that popularizer of the picturesque, the Rev. William Gilpin (1724–1807), Vicar of Boldre in the New Forest (whose natural beauties he extolled), toured Scotland in 1776, he was horrified by the walls, canals, and other now old-fashioned features that still deformed what he considered the native beauty of the countryside.

Some gardens were laid out in the new manner, though, as in the earlier stages of Scottish garden history, little is known of their designers.[49] Hopetoun House is an exception. Here, where trees had already been planted, a certain P. Godfrey made new gardens for the old house, which had been extensively modernized by William Adam. He made a wide lawn, with a pool in the centre, cut irregular vistas through the surrounding woods, planted to hide the Firth of Forth (not considered beautiful), and made use of the old seventeenth-century buildings as a decorative feature.[50] Yet Scotland produced in Henry Home, Lord Kames (1696–1782), an eminent judge, one of the soundest writers on the new style, who was also an ardent gardener on his own estate at Blair Drummond. In his *Elements of Criticism* of 1762 there is much more sense than is found in many English writers. 'The most perfect idea of a garden,' he wrote, is 'to inspire all the different emotions that can be raised by gardening.' He believed in regularity near the house, gradually merging into the irregular and picturesque at a distance.

Pictures and literary associations inspired the landscape garden, which came into being at the same time as British landscape painting developed into a serious form of art. The pictures by George Lambert (1700–1765) of Westcombe House and Chiswick 'are the first portraits of a country house which are not of purely topographical interest but show an eye for picturesque arrangements and involve an awareness of landscape gardening. . . . In a sense, the greatest English landscapes are not the work of Lambert, or Wilson or Gainsborough but the gardens of Rousham . . . and Stourhead'.[51] Richard Wilson (1713–1782) is, of course, the master of the garden landscape; his pictures of Croome (Plate XVI), Wilton, Woburn, and other estates 'lie with classic grace on his canvases, basking in a mellow sunlight that never ventures past an August noon'.[52]

That is the season when our Elysian landscapes glowed as they should: at high summer. 'To see one's urns, obelisks, and water-falls laid open; the nakedness of our beloved mistresses, the naiads and the dryads, exposed by that ruffian winter to universal obser-vation, is a severity scarcely to be supported by the help of blazing hearths, cheerful companions, and a bottle of the most grateful burgundy,' was one of Shenstone's *Disconnected Thoughts*.

We should now refer rather more explicitly to the influence of the new English style on the Continent. Le Rouge's *Détails de Nouveaux Jardins à la mode* of 1776–87 gave plans of English gardens. Even before this, Horace Walpole had, in 1771, written from Paris: 'English gardening gains ground here prodigiously—not much at a time, indeed—I have literally seen one that is exactly like a tailor's paper of patterns. . . . They have translated Mr. Whately's book, and the Lord knows what barbarism is going to be laid at our door. This new *Anglomanie* will literally be *mad English*.'[53]

There was a demand for British gardeners in France. One of them from Scotland, Thomas Blaikie (1758–1838), has left an account of his experiences. In 1776 he entered the service of the Comte de Lauragais, survived the Revolution, and died in Paris.[54]

The vogue spread even further. James Meader, who made a reputation for himself as gardener at Syon, was at the Russian court between 1779 and 1787. There, also, English and Scottish gardeners were in great demand owing to their enthusiasm and skill, particularly as fruit-growers. But, he adds: 'the nobles who have been in England are so much enraptured with the English pleasure gardens that they are cried up here. This has set them all gardening mad. Any of the nobility will give £100 per annum for an English gardener'.[55]

The sublime often conceals the ridiculous within its shadow; the gods may go a-begging and Strephon have a chipped nose. But, happily, the comic spirit rules in England: what might be a Teutonic disaster with us becomes nothing worse than a charming joke. The back door of our elysium must now also be visited to ob-serve some of its oddities.

GOTHICK AND CHINOISERIE

Gothick has been native to Britain since, when its original was scarcely dead, Spenser revived it in a literary manner in paying tribute to Elizabeth I. Kent, as we have seen, was an admirer of Spenser (he painted a series of not very good pictures illustrating *The Fairy Queen*). But there were other odd influences. Robert Morris, an architectural theorist, in 1734 published a series of *Lectures on Architecture*. He was an early advocate of the new manner: 'our modern way of planning gardens is far preferable to what was used 20 years ago, where, in large parterres, you might see man, birds and dogs cut in trees'. He himself was responsible for 'designs for fly-traps, bee palaces, and emmet houses, in the Muscovite and Arabian architecture, all adapted to the latitude and genius of England'!

Chinoiserie, however, was the most exotic of influences. In 1753 Walpole describes the Chinese buildings at Wroxton; in 1750 a reference was made to the 'barbarous gout' of the Chinese which was becoming fashionable. About that time appeared W. and J. Halfpenny's *Rural Architecture in the Chinese Taste*—a series of concoctions probably based on French designs. More serious were our connections with the Chinese missions of the French members of the Society of Jesus. But these brave men learned comparatively little.

Père Nicholas d'Incarville (1706–1757), who between 1740 and 1756 spent most of his time in Pekin, was probably the first trained botanist to work in China. There is a letter from him dated 15th November 1751 to Cromwell Mortimer, which was read before the Royal Society. 'We are much confin'd,' he begins, and 'we have not even the liberty of going where we please by ourselves to see things; nor can we, with prudence, believe the reports of the Chinese. . . .'[56] It is not therefore surprising that the European version of Chinese work usually degenerated into delightful nonsense. But d'Incarville managed to send seeds of plants to Paris and London along the caravan routes to St. Petersburg. The tree of heaven (*Ailanthus altissima*) was one of his introductions; he sent the seeds to the Royal Society, which were raised by Philip Miller at Chelsea, and Philip Webb* on his estate at Busbridge near Haslemere.

In 1752 was published *A Particular Account of the Emperor of China's Gardens Near Pekin*. This was a translation from the French

---

* He is better known as a Treasury Solicitor at the time of Wilkes's trial—the corrupt 'cow of Haslemere', called by Walpole 'dirty wretch' and 'sorry knave'. But he was an eminent and successful amateur arboriculturist.

by 'Sir Harry Beaumont'. The author was another Jesuit, Jean-Denis Attiret (1702–1768), who spent much of his life in China, sending home the *Account* in 1749. 'Beaumont' was, of course, the Rev. Joseph Spence (1699–1768), a minor writer who was interested in gardening; he had, alas, the misfortune to be drowned in his own ornamental canal.

Sir William Chambers (1726–1796) had visited China as a supercargo before he set up as an architect. In 1757 he brought out *Designs of Chinese Buildings*. In the following years he designed some buildings at Kew, including the famous pagoda. But he was, of course, to become pre-eminent as an architect in the classical manner—his one return to the Chinese style being *A Dissertation on Oriental Gardening* published in 1772. It is a somewhat imaginative pamphlet so far as facts are concerned, and was an attack on 'Capability' Brown, rather thinly veiled:*

Their gardeners are not only botanists, but also painters and philosophers, having a thorough knowledge of the human mind, and the arts by which its strongest feelings are excited.... In China, gardening is a distinct profession, requiring an extensive study; to the perfection of which few arrive. The gardeners then, far from being either ignorant or illiterate, are men of high abilities, who join to good natural parts, most ornaments that study, travelling, and long experience can supply them with: it is in consideration of these accomplishments only that they are permitted to exercise their profession, for with the Chinese the taste of ornamental gardening is an object of legislative attention, it being supposed to have an influence upon the general culture, and consequently upon the beauty of the whole country. They observe, that mistakes committed in this art, are too important to be tolerated, being much exposed to view, and in a great measure irreparable; as it often requires the space of a century, to redress the blunders of an hour.

Brown's protagonist, Mason, promptly replied with a poem, of which this is a specimen:

> ... at our magic call,
> Monkeys shall climb our trees, and lizards crawl;
> Huge dogs of Tibet bark in yonder grove,
> Here parrots prate, there cats make cruel love,

---

* Dallaway relates that this resulted from Robert Clive's preference for Brown over Chambers at Claremont.[57]

In some fair island will we turn to grass
(With the Queen's leave) her elephant and ass.
Giants from Africa shall guard the glades,
Where hiss our snakes, where sport our Tartar
    maids. . . .

The *Dissertation* was, if not exactly truly oriental, an extremely interesting pamphlet, full of suggestions; it has been said that it foreshadows the ideas of Miss Gertrude Jekyll. Voltaire was certainly impressed with it. In France a number of British gardens were considered to be in a style called *anglo-chinois*; plans of several, made by La Rocque in the 1730s, were published by Le Rouge.

The modern manner, particularly if embellished by chinoiserie, was often associated with *nouveaux riches*. As early as 1753 Francis Coventry, writing in *The World*, asks whether a modern gardener would consent to enter heaven if any path there is not serpentine. He considers the 'vast multitude of grotesque little villas' rising, with their labyrinths and meanders, 'fatal proofs of the degeneracy of the national taste'. He tells of Squire Mushroom, the present worthy possessor of Block Hill, who was born in a dirty little village in Hertfordshire. Making a fortune, he set up as a man of taste and pleasure. He bought an old farm, which immediately shot up into gothick spires and battlements, and was covered with stucco; Venetian windows appeared on its façade. The triumph of his genius was seen in the disposition of the gardens, containing everything within 2 acres. There was a yellow serpentine river, stagnating through a beautiful valley nearly 20 yards long. Over it, a bridge in the Chinese manner; on it, a little ship with streamers flying. In the grove, 'perplexed with errors and crooked walks', there was a root-house; here one was expected to pause and pass encomiums on the estate. Then on to a clumsy, gilded building, consecrated to Venus, because here the squire 'riots in vulgar love with a couple of orange wenches'.

And there is Robert Lloyd's poem of 1757, *The Cit's Country Box*, describing the transformation:

Now bricklay'rs, carpenters and joiners,
With Chinese artists and designers
Produce their schemes of alteration
To work this wond'rous reformation.

The useful dome, which secret stood
Embosom'd in the yew-tree's wood,
The trav'ler with amazement sees
A temple, Gothic or Chinese,
With many a bell, and tawdry rag on
And crested with a sprawling dragon;
A wooden arch is bent astride
A ditch of water, four feet wide,
With angles, curves and zig-zag lines
From Halfpenny's exact designs.
In front, a level lawn is seen,
Without a shrub upon the green,
Where taste would want its first great law
But for the skulking, sly ha-ha,
By whose miraculous assistance
You gain a prospect two fields distance.

In Garrick and Colman's *Clandestine Marriage*, 1766, there is
the newly enriched Mr. Sterling: 'The chief pleasure of a country
house is to make improvements. . . . I spare no expense.' And:

Sterling: How d'ye like these close walks, my Lord?
Lord Ogleby: A most excellent serpentine! It forms a perfect maze, and
winds like a true lover's knot.
Sterling: Ay, here's none of your straight lines here—but all taste—
zigzag—crinkum-crankum—in and out—right and left—to and again
—twisting and turning like a worm, my lord.

Surely it cannot be said, as is often done, that the new style
raised no opposition.

.   .   .   .   .

A word should be said about the London pleasure-gardens.
Both Finch's Grotto Gardens at Southwark and the Grotto in
Rosoman Street were products of the 1760s. They had lofty trees,
and grottos in which cascades played over artificial rock-work.
At Rosoman Street was an enchanted fountain, and a water-mill,
invented by the proprietor, which when set to work represented fire-
works, and formed a beautiful rainbow. A variety of gold and silver
fish which 'afford pleasing ideas to every spectator' were on sale.[58]
Jonathan Tyers, who made a fortune out of the pleasure
gardens at Vauxhall, bought the estate of Denbies, near Dorking.

Here he laid out one of the most fantastic gardens ever made. The house itself overlooked a beautiful and fertile vale, but in the grounds there was a labyrinth of walks which, when correctly followed, were a proper emblem of human life, and its awful conclusion. Finishing the journey, 'we are conducted through an iron gate which leads to the Valley of the Shadow of Death'. Instead of a portico, two coffins stood erect, capped by human skulls with inscriptions to the different sexes. That to the male (the skull was that of a noted highwayman) indicated that men are altogether vanity; while the female (of a famous courtesan) denigrated all female accomplishments, proclaimed that favour is deceitful and beauty in vain.

'The spectacle which offers itself upon descent into this gloomy vale is quite awful. . . . One alcove contains an unbeliever dying in the greatest distress and agony.' The whole was 'drawn up by a masterly hand'—apparently that of Francis Hayman, R.A. (1708–1776).[59] It is not surprising that in old age 'the master builder of delight' used to slip away from his country seat and look in at Vauxhall.

As Temple foresaw, beauty without order and regularity had taken some surprising forms within half a century of his death.

QUAKERS AND PEERS

Much emphasis has in recent years been placed on the literary, architectural, aesthetic, and even moral values of the style of gardening that evolved through the period we are now considering. Earlier writers, however, passing quickly over the moods of nature and the picturesque, considered it rather a period of rapid advance in horticulture, both in its practical and botanical aspects.

And so, in fact, it was. The period saw the beginnings of the systematic collection and introduction of plants from eastern North America, an accession from the Cape, a slow stream of the often strange plants cultivated in Chinese gardens coming direct from China (instead of making their way slowly by a gradually extended range of cultivation via the legendary 'Persia'), and Captain Cook's epoch-making voyage to the Australian continent. It also saw the establishment of Kew Gardens as a place of horticultural and botanical importance.

There was a remarkable increase of interest in the cultivation of exotic plants, and the rise of a number of fine botanical draughtsmen—a craft in which we were formerly deficient—to record their beauties.

Of the many persons and events that might be used to illustrate this period, it seems well to take a group of Quakers, not only because they will supply particularly distinguished and representative examples, but because their lives are well documented.[60] Their connections outside the Quaker circle also introduce us to some other prominent gardeners.

The first, certainly in time and probably in importance, was Peter Collinson (1694–1768).[61] Born in London, he became a haberdasher and linen-draper in Gracechurch Street, his firm having business with the North American colonies and the West Indies. Apart from an early visit to the Netherlands, he never travelled abroad. Collinson recalled that he first received a liking for gardens as a boy when visiting relatives at Peckham, then a village in Surrey; at the age of sixty-eight he declared that the plants in his garden furnished his greatest pleasure.

It was adjoining his small house at Peckham that he made his first garden; Peter Kalm (1715–1779), the Swedish traveller and naturalist, wrote that it was a beautiful place, full of all kinds of the rarest plants, especially those from America. In 1749 Collinson moved to Ridgeway House, Mill Hill. Here he made a singularly rich collection of plants, including trees that survived long after the place became part of Mill Hill School.

Collinson's name, as Kalm remarked, is particularly concerned with plants from North America. His interest in them was aroused by Mark Catesby, who had returned to England in 1726. Collinson helped to finance the publication of Catesby's work. But he was more actively connected with the American John Bartram (1699–1777).[62] Bartram, also a Quaker, came of Derbyshire stock. He was largely self-educated—an amateur doctor who became more and more devoted to botany, and by occupation a farmer. In 1728 he bought a house,* with 5 acres of land sloping down to the Schuylkill River, then a few miles outside Philadelphia. Here he made the first botanical garden in America. In about 1730 he obtained an introduction to Collinson, to whom from then on he regularly sent collections of plants.

* This he largely rebuilt; it still stands.[63]

He also sent specimens to be named; these were passed on to Linnaeus. In return Collinson forwarded supplies of general goods, books, and other things difficult to obtain in the colony. In 1739, for example, he sent Russian rhubarb, together with instructions for making rhubarb pie.

At first Bartram was financed by Collinson and his friend Lord Petre; payment was at the rate of 5 guineas for each box he despatched. From 1740 the dukes of Richmond, Norfolk, and Bedford joined with them. Each year Bartram was thereby enabled to make regular plant-hunting trips and scientific surveys.

One interesting plant sent to Britain by Bartram was the choice and rather tender shrub *Franklinia altamaha*, since 1790 extinct as a wild plant. Though not introduced until after Collinson's death, its name commemorates Benjamin Franklin, whose scientific works Collinson was largely instrumental in introducing to British society; the specific epithet refers to the river on whose banks it was found.

In 1765 Collinson and his influential friends obtained for Bartram the post of Botanizer Royal for America, with a salary of £50 a year and a commission to explore. Bartram's son William (1739–1823) was his principal assistant and also a talented artist whose drawings were commissioned by English patrons.

One of the gardens praised by Collinson was that of Archibald Campbell, 3rd Duke of Argyll (1682–1761), at Whitton, near Hounslow. Loudon[64] says it was begun in about 1720, when Campbell was still Earl of Islay. Not only did he obtain new plants, and particularly trees, from every source, but he raised great numbers himself. He seems to have supplied them freely to his friends. Lyttelton of Hagley is one instance.[65] His oranges and other citrus fruit, the finest in England, were grown against an unheated wall protected by glass lights. At Argyll's death many choice things were moved to the garden of the Dowager Princess of Wales at Kew House, and in 1765 more trees were sold; the catalogue contained no fewer than three hundred and forty-two items.

Another of Collinson's early friends was Admiral Sir Charles Wager (1666–1743). He was a keen plant-collector; and gave his name to Wager's maple,* and in 1726 Collinson records that he

---

* The name, however, fell into disuse and was replaced by silver maple. It is *Acer saccharinum* (*dasycarpum*). Wager introduced it from North America in 1725.

brought a consignment of plants from 'Gibraltar Hill'. Also intimate with Collinson was Robert James, 8th Baron Petre (1713–1743), joint financer of Bartram. In the last three years of his short life Petre raised and planted in his park 40,000 trees. This was at Thorndon Hall, in Essex, to which he moved from Ingatestone. As an instance of the skill then possessed by gardeners, Collinson relates that twenty-four elms about 60 feet high and 2 feet in diameter were carried from Ingatestone on to Thorndon to extend an existing avenue. In 1762 he described them as indistinguishable from the original trees.

Petre does not seem to have been touched by the new fashion of irregularity of design. In 1728 he planted lines of elms leading to an esplanade; at either end of this was raised a great mount, crowned by a cedar and four larches, with its banks covered with other larches and evergreens.

Collinson wrote to Linnaeus[66] that Petre's untimely death was 'the greatest loss that botany or gardening ever felt in this island; he spared no pains or expense to procure seeds and plants from all parts of the world, and then was as ambitious to preserve them'. His stoves were such as 'the world never saw, and may never see again'. The collection of trees, shrubs, and evergreens in his nurseries at this time numbered 219,925, mostly exotic. All were sold by auction. Many went to Woburn and Goodwood.[67]

Collinson was also concerned with Goodwood and its planting owner, Charles Lennox, Duke of Richmond (1735–1806),* for whom he acted as agent in obtaining the famous cedars. A Mr. John Clarke, butcher, of Barnes, 'conceived an opinion that he could raise cedars of Lebanon from cones of the great tree at Hendon Place' and succeeded so perfectly that within a few years he was supplying the nurserymen and many noblemen. He went on to raise magnolias and other exotics with equal success. On 8th June 1761 Collinson paid him £79 6s. for 1,000 five-year-old cedars that the duke had planted during the previous March and April.

Apart from American plants from Bartram, Collinson received others from many parts of the world. He records the receipt of seed from St. Petersburg and through that city also came seeds from the Jesuits in China by 'the Caravan'; in 1746 he received

* The fact that he was a great grandson of Charles II is, perhaps, not insignificant.

from his friend Mr. Brewer of Nuremburg 'the first double Spanish broom that was in England . . . it cost there a golden ducat; and, being planted in a pot all nicely wickered over, came from thence down the river Elbe to Hamburgh, from whence it was brought by the first ship to London. I inarched it on the single-flowered broom, and gave it to Gray* and Gordon, gardeners, and from them all have been supplied'.

In 1756 he flowered a Siberian lily, received from a Mr. Demidoff, proprietor of Siberian iron mines: 'the nearest of black to any flower I know'. One of his most interesting introductions had been much earlier, in 1731, when he received from Providence Island in the Bahamas *Bletia verecunda*, so far as can be ascertained the first exotic orchid to be flowered in Britain.[68]

Two other of Collinson's incidental notes are now interesting. In October 1765 he saw, at Mrs. Gaskry's at Parson's Green in Fulham, not only an excellent crop of apricots, peaches, and nectarines, but a fine crop of ripe pomegranates; Collinson's comment that this was most remarkable certainly applies today not only in Fulham but elsewhere in England. And the following December he regrets the death of a Mr. Bennet: 'very curious and industrious in procuring seeds and plants from abroad'. His extensive greenhouses originally lay behind Shadwell water-works, but the effect of one of the new 'fire-engines' to raise the water was so deleterious that he had to move to Whitechapel.

Collinson's correspondence was prodigious. That with John Custis, of Williamsburg, has been collected[69] and gives a remarkable insight into the horticultural-botanical world of the day.

During this period there were no doubt many other undocumented introductions, often through relatives and friends in service overseas. For example, George Lyttelton's brother was Governor of South Carolina and sent plants to Hagley;[70] the Earl of Coventry is believed to have introduced plants direct from China, notably koelreuteria and the winter-sweet (*Chimonanthus fragrans*). Many trees and shrubs planted at Arbury in the 1750s came direct from South Carolina.[71]

A member of a Yorkshire Quaker family, rather younger than

* Christopher Gray, who died about 1764 at a considerable age, founded the Fulham nursery. He was one of those who had bought Bishop Compton's rarest plants from his successor, Bishop Robinson, who took no interest in them, and allowed the gardener to sell what he liked. Gordon is discussed later.

Collinson but almost equalling him in importance, was Dr. John Fothergill (1712–1780),[72] from Wensleydale. Coming to London, he established a lucrative medical practice in Lombard Street. From 1762 onwards he formed a botanical garden at Upton House, East Ham. This soon became recognized as the finest in England, with plants from all over the world. His greenhouse, made 'at an expense rarely undertaken', was described by Sir Joseph Banks as the amplest in this or in any country. Entered directly from his house, it was 260 feet long. He also made a considerable 'wilderness', where exotics likely to be hardy were naturalized. Banks considered that no garden in Europe had so many scarce and valuable plants. Fothergill also had a garden at Lea Hall, his summer residence, in Cheshire, which he began in 1765. It seems that he shares with Collinson the honour of being one of the earliest cultivators of exotic orchids, having imported and flowered *Phaius grandifolius* from China in 1778.[73]

Fothergill is memorable as one of the earliest cultivators of alpine plants, and possibly the first to commission a collector to go plant-hunting in the Swiss mountains. This he did jointly with another physician, William Pitcairn (1711–1791). They engaged Thomas Blaikie, who had been Fothergill's gardener, and who has already been mentioned as an exponent of the English style of gardening in France.

In April 1775, having agreed 'to undertake a journey to the alps in Switzerland in search of rare and curious plants the production of that country', Blaikie set sail for Boulogne. The following November he sent home some four hundred and forty packets of plants, specimens, seeds, and cuttings. As Loudon observed,[74] Fothergill and Pitcairn took the credit for these without mentioning Blaikie's name. Fortunately, Blaikie kept a diary of his journey.[75] It shows his enthusiasm for alpine plants, and gives a lively account of all that he saw—and of his adventures and mishaps. It is the earliest, and still one of the most delightful, of the many narratives written by alpine-plant hunters.

Another distinguished amateur was John Ellis (*c.* 1710–1776). Born in Ireland, he became a London merchant, living opposite Christopher Gray's nursery in King's Road. Like Collinson, he was a considerable correspondent. Though primarily a botanist, he was an early student of the practical problems of plant introduction. His conclusions were published in *Directions for bringing over seeds and plants from the East Indies and other distant countries in a state of vegetation* (1770). The difficulties at that time were extreme; living plants had often to be brought slowly through temperatures of extreme variations. Many seeds—such as acorns—soon lose their viability and Ellis devised a system of enclosing them in wax.

Ellis was helped through his connections as Agent for West Florida (1764) and Dominica (1770). He published works on coffee (1774) and the mangosteen (1775), and was an early student of coral and its formation. One of his principal correspondents, with whom he exchanged seeds and plants, was Dr. Alexander Garden (*c.* 1730–1791), a graduate of Edinburgh University, who practised medicine at Charleston, Carolina, for some thirty years. His botanizing and plant-collecting were eventually much interfered with by the American Revolution; finally, unable to conform with the new government, he returned to England. His name is commemorated in *Gardenia*; he sent one plant of *G. florida* from which, out of four cuttings, James Gordon made £500 in less than three years.[76]

Of the scientific gardens, Chelsea, under Philip Miller (still another Quaker), had, thanks to his international correspondence, 'excelled all gardens in Europe for excellence and variety'.[77] In 1771 Miller died, having been succeeded in 1770 by another Scot, William Forsyth (1737–1804), from Old Meldrum, Aberdeenshire, then gardener to the Duke of Northumberland. Chelsea never again attained the supremacy it had under Miller, but Forsyth's period in charge gives it one further claim to fame. In 1774 he began building possibly the earliest rock garden in England. His material consisted of forty tons of old stone from the Tower of London, flints and chalk, and lava brought from Iceland by Sir Joseph Banks.[78]

The decline of Chelsea was offset by the development of Kew Gardens as a home of scientific horticulture. The famed gardens of Kew House have already been mentioned when, in the seventeenth century, their owner was Lord Capel. He had no children and on his death the place was inherited by Lady Elizabeth Capel; Kew, however, still retained its 'curious' connections, for she married a Mr. Molyneux, who set up a telescope in the grounds and was concerned in astronomical discoveries. In 1730 Kew House was leased by Frederick Prince of Wales, the much-disliked son of George II, but who, as we have seen, was well acquainted with such gardening enthusiasts as Pope, Hamilton, and Lyttelton. He employed Kent to remodel the grounds. Just before his early death in 1751 he had met John Stuart,* 3rd Earl of Bute (1713–1792), who was appointed to his staff. Stuart had spent nine years of his life farming and studying botany on the island of Bute, and was not only a notable amateur botanist but achieved distinction as an influential and discriminating patron of the arts and sciences. His daughter-in-law shared his interests, and in 1789 introduced the first dahlia from Spain.†

On Frederick's death Bute became adviser to his widow, the Dowager Princess Augusta. Her enthusiasm and his discernment and ability soon brought the garden international fame. Under Bute's general direction William Aiton (1731–1793) was appointed gardener and, in 1757, also at Bute's suggestion, William Chambers was engaged to design ornamental buildings‡ (Plate XVII) and, in 1761, one of the largest stoves yet constructed. In 1762 the best trees from Argyll's Whitton collection were acquired. By that time George III was on the throne, and actively supported the Princess, his mother, in her activities. Within a walled area of some 9 acres was formed the first really extensive botanic garden in England.[80]

It is here interesting to remark in view of Chambers's subsequent attack on Brown that Kew, apart from a few other ornamental buildings, was his only connection with garden design. Bute a few years later employed Robert Adam to design the magnificent new house that he built at Luton Hoo in Bedfordshire (where he formed his own botanical garden) and Lancelot Brown to 'improve' his garden at Highcliffe in Hampshire.

It was Brown, too, who, in the next phase, constructed what is now the rhododendron dell—the excavation being by a company of the Staffordshire Militia in 1773. By now George III had purchased Kew House, and united it with the adjoining Richmond Lodge. This followed the death of his mother in 1772. Kew now became a royal garden, the personal property of succeeding sovereigns until 1840.

* His name is commemorated in the lovely shrubs called *Stewartia*, which, owing to the rules of plant-naming, perpetuates a stupid mis-spelling. Collinson called him 'a very good critic in botany'.[79]
† It did not, however, survive.
‡ The orangery, the Roman arch, and the pagoda are his best-known surviving works there; the orangery is now a museum.

When Bute ceased his association with the gardens Sir Joseph Banks (1743–1820),[81] 'the aristocrat of the philosophers', became virtual director in his stead. His father, of Revesby, in Lincolnshire, had died in 1761, and left him an ample fortune. He devoted his life and vigorous personality to the promotion and study of natural history. At the age of thirty-five he was elected president of the Royal Society; in 1766–7 he had been to Newfoundland, in 1768–71 he travelled, with Daniel Carl Solander (1736–1782), as naturalist with Captain Cook on the famous voyage round the world in *Endeavour*.* In the year of the princess's death he had made that trip to Iceland, again in the company of Solander, which provided the lava for Forsyth's rockery.

Under royal patronage and vigorous leadership, with Aiton as its skilful and learned gardener, Kew progressed and prospered. In 1768 'Sir' John Hill† (1716–1775) published a catalogue of the collection, which has been reckoned to include 3,389 species.[82] In 1789 William Aiton, helped by a number of botanists, published a more accurate and critical list, *Hortus Kewensis*, which named 5,535 species in cultivation. Even before Miller's retirement botanists had begun to send seeds and plants to Kew rather than Chelsea, for as Miller became crotchety in old age, Aiton became the more enterprising cultivator.

In 1772 Kew sent the first of a long line of its collectors overseas. He was Francis Masson (1741–1805).[84] Born in Aberdeen, he became an under gardener at Kew. He was selected by Banks to collect and study plants at the Cape, chosen, no doubt, not only because he was a personable man and capable gardener, but since he could both describe plants in clear and lively prose, and make good figures of them on the spot.‡ His first visit was made in 1772. In 1775 he opened a correspondence with Linnaeus, whom he informs that

---

* Cook and his party, having observed the transit of Venus, sailed to Australia and New Zealand, and were the first to make a scientific study of the Continent. For this reason Banks is particularly associated with it; *Banksia* (Australian honeysuckle), a genus restricted to Australia, commemorates the connection. Sydney Parkinson (d. 1771) was attached to the expedition as artist; a woollen-draper, he had earlier been engaged by Banks to draw plants at Kew.

† An odd and unreliable, yet in some ways clever, character. His claim to knighthood was based on an order received from the King of Sweden. Ellis[83] told Linnaeus that he achieved his unmerited position through Bute's patronage.

‡ He wrote of this work: 'The figures were drawn in their native climate, and although they have little to boast in point of art, they possibly exhibit the natural appearance of the plants they represent better than figures made from subjects growing in exotic houses do.'

I have been employed some years past, by the King of Great Britain, in collecting of plants for the Royal gardens at Kew. My researches have been chiefly at the Cape of Good Hope, where I had the fortune to meet with the ingenious Dr. Thunberg, with whom I made two successful journeys into the interior parts of the country. My labours have been crowned with success, having added upwards of 400 new species to his Majesty's collection of living plants.[85]

The Cape was, of course, a Dutch settlement, and that plant-loving race had, since the seventeenth century, maintained botanic gardens there.[86] Masson's South African friends who helped him were a Dutch soldier, Colonel Gordon (1741–1795), who was a keen botanist and able draughtsman, and more important, as he told Linnaeus, Carl Pehr Thunberg (1743–1828), a Swedish doctor, botanist, and traveller, who is often described as the 'father' of South African botany.

Masson visited the Canaries. In Madeira he noted that 'all the rare plants grow either on the high cliffs near the sea, or in horrible deep chasms, that run towards the middle of the island'. He went, too, to Spain, Portugal, New York, and Montreal. We owe to him the first South African heaths, at one time so popular, the *Senecio* species from which the florist's cineraria has been evolved, and many choice hardy and half-hardy plants such as *Centaurium scilloides* and *Ixia viridiflora*.

One other botanic garden was founded during this period. In 1762 Richard Walker, the Vice-Master of Trinity College, Cambridge, presented some 5 acres of land in the centre of the city to the university for a garden. It was laid out by the Professor of Botany, Thomas Martyn* (*c.* 1735–1825), with the help of Philip Miller, whose son Charles (1739–1817) was curator from 1762 to 1770.[87]

.   .   .   .   .

From these early developments on the grand scale, in which science was still so happily combined with art, let us turn for a moment to the ordinary gardener. Once more we may obtain our evidence from a parson, the Rev. Gilbert White (1720–1793).[88] He is, of course, well enough known for his writings on the natural

* Martyn revised Miller's *Dictionary* for the important edition published in 1803–7. After Charles Miller left to go to the East Indies, Martyn for some years acted also as unpaid curator.

history of his parish at Selborne in Hampshire, but much less frequently mentioned as the author of the garden diary that he kept from 1751 to 1771. This gives us an insight into the routine work of a small garden. To make comparisons with the routine of the present-day amateur is illuminating. As an instance, the jobs recorded in sequence through one 1st January were:

> Sowing two rows of early Spanish beans.
> Earthing up of celery.
> Planting 250 loaf cabbages.
> Planting 5 bulbs of crown imperial.
> Setting 14 cuttings of the large white Dutch currant.
> New staking the espaliers.

White did most of the work with his own hands. But, of course, this was far from being so with most of the eminent gardeners that we have described; a reference to many of them in a biographical dictionary shows that they lived very active lives, usually as politicians; often their connection with horticulture or botany is not even mentioned. It is to their gardeners that much of the credit must be assigned, and to them we must now refer.

GARDENERS AND NURSERYMEN

Little enough is known of most of these men, unless they became nurserymen and florists. There was, for instance, Daniel Croft or Craft, who signed, as head gardener to the Duke of Argyll, the catalogue of the trees at Whitton sold in 1765.[89] Then there was John Morrison, who, on his death at Stratford, Essex, in March 1781, was described as 'an ingenious botanist and principal gardener to Dr. John Fothergill'.[90] What prodigious skill these men must have had, to raise and succeed with plants from remote parts of the world with which they were quite unacquainted! The employer of the first was engaged actively in public life, and the employer of the second conducted one of the largest medical practices of the day. The responsibilities of such as these two were set out in 1773:[91]

> The person who acts as gardener to noblemen or gentlemen must take care to make himself well acquainted with cultivation of fruits, flowers, vegetables, and in general everything growing in gardens either for pleasure or use.

He was advised to

take every opportunity of entertaining those who come to visit your master, with a particular description of every thing in the garden, and have always some places ready for them to rest themselves on, while passing from one part to another.

Although the gardener was not housed with the main body of the domestic staff he must have been readily available as a guide. Ordinarily he had a cottage on the estate; sometimes he had an office in the main house as well.

In spite of Switzer's diatribe against 'the lads from the north', nothing shows more the improving standard of education and horticulture in Scotland than the steady flow of its sons southward to obtain on their merits responsible positions as head gardeners. A good instance is given in the memoirs written by Dr. Alexander Carlyle, Minister of Inveresk, of his visit to England in 1758.[92] His account shows also how, at that time, such a traveller expected as a right the privilege of being shown over the seats of the aristocracy and gentry. On this occasion Dr. Carlyle had just viewed the park, house, and chapel at Bulstrode, now one of the seats of the descendant of William III's gardening favourite, the Earl of Portland. On coming to the garden

It was here that we discovered the truth of what I had often heard, that most of the head gardeners of English noblemen were Scotch for on observing to this man that his pease seemed late on the 4th. of May, not being then fully in bloom, and that I was certain that there were sundry places which I knew in Scotland where they were further advanced, he answered that he was bred in a place that I perhaps did not know answered this description. This was Newhaills, in my own parish of Inveresk. This man, whose name I have forgot, if it was not Robertson, was not only gardener but land-steward, and had the charge of the whole park and of the estate around it;—such advantage was there in having been taught writing, arithmetic, and the mensuration of land, the rudiments of which were taught in many of the schools in Scotland. This man gave us a note to the gardener at Blenheim, who, he told us, was our countryman, and would furnish us with notes to the head gardeners all the way down.

Of one at least of the famous Lord Petre's gardeners we know a certain amount. James Gordon*—his name suggests an origin in Scotland—had, at his death in 1780, become respected as the most learned and skilful of nurserymen. 'Bred under Petre and Dr. Sherard',† before 1748 he had set up as a nurseryman at Mile End, with a seed shop in Fenchurch Street. In 1758 John Ellis described him to Linnaeus:[93]

He has more knowledge in vegetation than all the gardeners and writers on gardening in England put together, but he is too modest to publish anything. If you send him anything rare, he will make you a proper return.

In 1764 Collinson[94] described him as one of the modern nurserymen who had raised new things from all parts of the world 'with a sagacity peculiar to himself'. Collinson helped him with both seeds and plants. He was of an experimental turn of mind, and succeeded in showing that certain plants considered tender would grow out of doors. His memorial stands in many old specimens of the maidenhair tree (*Ginkgo biloba*) now growing in this country. He was responsible for introducing this prehistoric Chinese tree, probably from the Continent, in about 1754, and for some years layers from his specimen were the main source of supply.[95]

Next to Gordon, and according to Collinson 'not far behind him', came James Lee (1715–1795). He was born at Selkirk. About 1732, carrying his sword, he walked south—his journey being broken by an attack of small-pox at Lichfield. He took service at Syon, and later under the Duke of Argyll at Whitton. In about 1745 he joined with Lewis Kennedy in partnership at The Vineyard, Hammersmith. Kennedy seems to have been an older man, who in 1731 was gardener to Lord Wilmington, in 1739 to Spencer Compton, and was later with Lord Burlington at Chiswick.

The Vineyard (now under Olympia) was, during the previous century, still producing Burgundy wine; within its sheltering

* Not to be confused with James Gordon of Fountainbridge, Edinburgh whose nursery was flourishing 1758–1774, and who published a pocket dictionary of gardening.

† Dr. James Sherard (1666–1737) had a botanic garden at Eltham. He was younger brother of William Sherard (1659–1728) who was consul at Smyrna 1703–15 and collected many plants from Greece and Asia Minor which James grew. William founded the Sherardian professorship of botany at Oxford; the first professor, J. J. Dillenius (1687–1747), both compiled and illustrated *Hortus Elthamensis* (1732.)

walls stood a thatched house, the upper part used for dwelling and the sale of wine, the lower being cellarage.

Lee seems to have been the dominating partner in the business. In 1760 he published (not without some outside, and acknowledged, help) a successful *Introduction to Botany*. It was also a general introduction to the British of the new Linnaean system, and went through five editions. He was joined in business by his son, another James, while his daughter Ann was a talented botanical artist.[96] Lee was a man of good sense, with a wide knowledge of natural history, and a manner which secured patronage from the nobility. He employed collectors and agents overseas. He formed an important connection with France, partly through Thomas Blaikie, who frequently visited him when in England, bringing both new plants and orders.[97]

In 1774 Kennedy and Lee issued an important catalogue of their plants; at this time they were responsible for introducing *Buddleia globosa* from Peru.

In the provinces other gardeners on large estates were becoming nurserymen. In 1718 Thomas Ball, F.R.S., began his extensive planting at Mamhead, in South Devon, which he seems to have done in a rather experimental manner, being probably the first to plant the evergreen oak (*Quercus ilex*) on a large scale. He employed William Lucombe, who, in 1720, set up as a nurseryman at St. Thomas, Exeter, and in about 1763 raised the hybrid Lucombe oak, which he successfully propagated and sold in great quantities. Lucombe was joined by his son in business. He in turn was joined by his great nephew, Robert T. Pince—a family business that as late as the 1880s was still famous for its cinerarias and fuchsias. Full of years, the original Lucombe cut down one of the hybrid oak trees he had raised to provide his coffin; outliving his own expectations, he eventually used the timber otherwise. A few years later he cut down another tree for the same purpose, which it duly fulfilled when he died at the age of 98.[98]

In Scotland several nurseries of future consequence came into being. Robert Dickson of Hassendeanburn founded a business in 1729, in which he was followed by at least five generations of his descendants;[99] it specialized in trees, which were more and more extensively planted as the century progressed. The Duke of

Argyll was as active in this respect, but on a larger scale, as he had been at Whitton.

To quote Collinson[100] again, during the 1760s 'as the taste [for gardening] increased, so nursery gardens flourished'. One described by Collinson as having one of the most extensive nurseries in London in the first half of the eighteenth century was Robert Furber. He was at Kensington, and, with Gray, had bought many plants from Bishop Compton's garden. In 1730 he gained the distinction of being the first English nurseryman to issue a lavishly illustrated catalogue. True, it was not called anything so vulgar, but *Twelve Months of Flowers*. Nor were prices mentioned. The twelve plates, one showing the flowers for each month, were hand-coloured engravings by F. Fletcher after the Flemish artist Pieter Casteels.[101] Furber died in 1756, aged 82.

This brings us to the subject of flower-paintings. We have mentioned some of the artists who, as was now becoming customary, were taken on voyages of exploration. There were a number more engaged on figuring the collections of the 'curious' and 'virtuosi'. For instance Collinson's collection was delineated by William King of Totteridge. By far the most distinguished was Georg Dionysius Ehret (1708–1770),[102] who introduced to Britain standards of skill and artistry hitherto unknown. He was born of humble stock at Heidelberg and was put to work as a gardener's apprentice. Later, through his stepfather, one Kesselbach, he entered the gardens of the Elector of Heidelberg. There he attracted the attention of the Margrave of Baden, who took him into his service. For him, Ehret painted flowers in his spare time. This apparent favouritism made his fellow workers jealous, and Ehret resigned. The next years were difficult, and he passed from employer to employer—gardening, botanizing, and drawing. Eventually he came to England and made the acquaintance of Sir Hans Sloane and Philip Miller—then back to Holland, where he met and impressed the great Linnaeus—and finally to England again in 1736. Here he lived the rest of his life, marrying Miller's sister-in-law.

Ehret became a popular figure in London, teaching botanical drawing to numerous fashionable persons, including (as he proudly recounted) duchesses and countesses. He illustrated very skilfully with engravings half a dozen or so botanical works, but it is his superb paintings on vellum that rank him as one of the finest of all botanical artists. As a purely scientific artist, immensely skilled in drawing sections and details, he was paramount, and his teaching and example greatly raised the general standard of work in this country.

Symptomatic of this fashionable enthusiasm for exotic plants* was Mrs. Delany (1700–1788), the 'highest bred woman in the world', an ardent amateur of natural history in many branches, but specially famous for her cut-out paper mosaics of flowers, which she did not begin until she was seventy-two years old.

> . . . Delany forms her mimic bowers
> Her paper foliage, and her silken flowers;
> Her virgin train the tender scissors ply
> Vein the green leaf, the purple petal dye:
> Round wiry stems the flaxen tendril bends,
> Moss creeps below, and waxen fruit impends.
> Cold Winter views amid his realms of snow
> Delany's vegetable statues blow;
> Smooths his stern brow, delays his hoary wing,
> And eyes with wonder all the blooms of spring.

So wrote Dr. Erasmus Darwin (1731–1802) in his *Loves of the Plants*; adding a note that she had 'finished nine hundred and seventy accurate and elegant representations of different vegetables with parts of their flowers, fructifications, &c.'.

Mrs. Delany obtained papers of every hue from many sources, including China. It is said that her mosaics were sufficiently accurate to enable Sir Joseph Banks to name the plants without making a mistake. Darwin mentioned also a Mrs. North who was forming a similar *hortus siccus* with 'such elegant taste and scientific accuracy, that it cannot fail to become a work of inestimable value'.

Darwin's own poem *The Botanic Garden* (of which the *Loves of the Plants* is a part†), was highly successful—again an indication of the tastes of the period.

By the middle of the century the London 'kitchen gardeners' —or, as we should call them, market gardeners—had become highly skilled. No doubt the secrets of the Neat House men had spread to other of the fertile Thames-side districts such as West-

---

* They were, of course, kept well away from the 'landscape'.
† It was published separately and previously to the whole work in 1789.

minster, Fulham, and Chelsea. One assumes that what was being done around London occurred to some extent elsewhere.

August saw the sowing of cauliflowers on an old hot-bed. In October these were planted out in rows, six under a cloche. Lettuce and spinach were sown between the rows. In March some of the cauliflowers were put out from the cloches to give a succession. When cloches were emptied of cauliflowers, cucumbers (sown on a hot-bed in spring) were put under them. In July either endive or more cauliflowers to mature for Michaelmas were planted between the rows.

Peas were sown in October, moved into glass-covered pits in November, and harvested in spring; the pits were then used for melons. Asparagus, mustard, cress, and radishes were also grown. Cauliflowers were the most important crop, and were exported to the Continent. An early cauliflower fetched from 2s. to 3s. In addition to his 'colly-flowers' a kitchen gardener tried to raise five other crops in a year on the same ground.[103]

We can gain some idea of the kinds, and relative popularity, of fruits in cultivation from Clarke's lists (p. 169). Over the period 1720–60 are named forty-five different kinds of pear, twenty-eight of plum, twenty-three of apple, fifteen of peaches, fourteen of cherries, twelve of grapes, seven of apricots, five of nectarines, and three of figs. This, one may assume, represents the usual range for a gentleman's garden and orchard of middling size. These figures may be compared with those of the fruits offered for sale by the Rev. William Hanbury (1725–1778)[104] in September 1760, 'all reared on the most barren soil':

> Peaches, rich and curious, near 50 sorts
> Of nectarines, near 20 sorts
> Of apricots, 12 sorts
> Of pears, more than 60 sorts
> Of apples, near 50 sorts
> Of vines, near 40 sorts
> Of figs, near 10 sorts
> Of gooseberries, near 30 sorts . . .

with the addition of currants, quinces, medlars, and nuts. Hanbury is an interesting and reliable author; he raised these fruit trees while incumbent at Church Langton in south Leicestershire.

The mention of that county in the year 1760 may take us for a moment from the south to the north, to Dishley Grange, near Loughborough. There, Robert Bakewell (1725-1795) was already famous for his pioneering work in breeding stock on scientific lines to achieve an ideal type. Thomas Knight, who was to be the first to work along similar lines with fruit and plants, was then but a year old.

.   .   .   .   .

A word should be said about the technique of gardening during this period. There do not seem to have been any fundamental changes or improvements, but numerous minor refinements and an increase in skill due to wider experience. And we must no doubt thank the keen and intelligent immigrants from Scotland for a good deal of this. Contemporary engravings show that some development took place in the construction of glass-houses; larger panes came into general use. They were now warmed by passing the products of combustion through brick flues; steam or hot-water heating were still some time off.

SIX

From Picturesque to Gardenesque
1781–1840

MISS AUSTEN'S MR. REPTON

I T MAY be recalled that one evening Mr. Rushworth, of
Sotherton Court, was dining at Mansfield Park,* in the
county of Northampton, after a visit to his friend, Smith of
Compton, in the neighbouring shire:

'I wish you could see Compton,' said he; 'it is the most complete
thing! I never saw a place so altered in my life. The approach, *now*,
is one of the finest things in the country: you see the house in the most
surprising manner. I declare, when I got back to Sotherton yesterday,
it looked like a prison, quite a dismal old prison.'

'Oh, for shame!' cried Mrs. Norris. 'A prison indeed? Sotherton
Court is the noblest old place in the world.'

'It wants improvement, ma'am, beyond anything. I never saw
a place that wanted so much improvement in my life; and it is so
forlorn that I do not know what can be done with it . . . I must try to
do something with it, but I do not know what. I hope I shall have
some good friend to help me.'

'Your best friend upon such an occasion,' said Miss Bertram
calmly, 'could be Mr. Repton, I imagine.'

'That is what I was thinking of. As he has done so well by Smith,
I think I had better have him at once. His terms are five guineas
a day.'†

'Well, and if they were *ten*,' cried Mrs. Norris, 'I am sure *you* need

---

* It is often said, on what authority I do not know, that Miss Austen had in mind
Harleston Park as the model for the home of Sir Thomas Bertram. Harleston was, in
fact, improved by Repton; it lies not far from Holdenby and Althorp.

† This reference to Repton's fees while he was still active is rather surprising in
one so discreet as Miss Austen.

not regard it. The expense need not be an impediment. If I were you, I should not think of the expense. I would have everything done in the best style, and made as nice as possible. . . .'

'I never saw a place so altered in my life': Rushworth's phrase could be applied to many gardens of Britain (indeed, to other aspects of our countryside also) during the period we are now discussing—the last years of the eighteenth and the beginning of the nineteenth centuries. It was during that period—as *Mansfield Park*, begun in 1811 and published in 1814, shows clearly enough—that the great rage for improvement, begun by Lancelot Brown with a hundred or two noblemen's seats, flared up under the fanning of Brown's successor Repton (and a host of imitators who could learn their lessons from his publications). It affected country residences almost by the thousand, from the larger Comptons and Sothertons down to the house at Allington, in the ha-ha of which, as Trollope* tells us, Bernard Dale proposed unsuccessfully to his cousin Bell.[1]

It was, indeed, the period when every house of any pretensions had its walls (except those protecting the kitchen garden) swept away, and a ha-ha substituted. No one, so far as I know, has studied their relative costs; nor is it easy to find figures for the building of walls. In 1783 Dr. Johnson told Boswell: 'We compute, in England, a park wall at a thousand pounds a mile.'[2] In 1795 a ha-ha at Moseley Hall, Warwickshire, '8 yards wide at top, 1 ft. flat bottom, 8 ft. 9 ins. deep, turf to be plotted on the bank', was charged at 7s. 11d. a yard, or at the rate of about £696 a mile.[3] Today we can find many old ha-has much less than 8 feet deep and they must have been correspondingly cheaper.

Not only was there this vast change in garden design: David Douglas made his first introductions from western North America of plants and trees which were to be of almost equal significance in changing not only our gardens but our woodlands; the modern system of heating greenhouses was evolved; the most influential horticultural society in the world was brought into being; regular horticultural journalism first emerged, and the mechanical grass mower was invented. And the middle-class gardened as it expanded (Plate XVIII).

---

* Fiction, perhaps, gives us better pictures of many gardens than facts.

Surely, then, the period we are now about to discuss was, and remains, most significant in the history of the garden.

．　　　　．　　　　．　　　　．　　　　．

Humphry Repton (1752–1818)[4] was born at Bury St. Edmunds, his father holding a lucrative position as Collector of Taxes. He was educated at Bury and Norwich grammar schools. It was his family's intention that he should become one of the then prosperous Norwich merchants trading with Holland. To this end, as a youngster, he went to live there. On his return at the age of sixteen he was something of a dandy and well equipped with the more refined and fashionable social graces, notably drawing.

He married young—and happily—and duly engaged in various enterprises which were unsuccessful. He returned to Susted, near Aylsham in Norfolk, and spent five years studying the beauties of nature, gardening, botany, entomology, and other gentlemanly sciences; he made drawings of many of the old country seats in the neighbourhood. He was helped in this work by a school-fellow, James Edward Smith (1759–1828), later to be knighted, one of the most outstanding botanists of the day.* He had access, also, to the fine library of his learned neighbour at Felbrigg, William Windham[5] (1750–1810), who introduced him to Sir Joseph Banks.

In 1783 Windham was appointed Chief Secretary to the Lord Lieutenant in Ireland, and took Repton as his confidential secretary. Within a month the secretary was carrying the responsibilities of his chief, Windham resigning the post without warning. Repton seems thoroughly to have enjoyed the experience, which lasted for several weeks.

Back home, he settled at Hare Street, near Romford in Essex, took to gardening again, helped to finance a business which failed, and so lost much of his money. Now with a large and growing family, and no training in any profession, he spent a worrying period. Waking in the middle of one night, he decided there and then that his mixture of qualifications was such as fitted him to be 'Capability' Brown's successor. The next morning he began writing to all his numerous influential acquaintances to tell them

---

* He wrote the text, anonymously, to James Sowerby's *English Botany*, whose thirty-six volumes, published from 1790 to 1814, form the basis of all later British floras.

that he had set up as a landscape gardener. That was in 1788. His success was immediate; young Lancelot Brown, M.P., honoured him by granting access to his father's papers.

Repton, it is clear, had an education and intelligence superior to that of any of his predecessors. He was a man of wide reading, something of a mathematician, who could demonstrate his theories of design with geometrical diagrams, while his botanical writings appeared in the *Transactions* of the learned Linnean Society.* He published his theories, and engaged in literary argument in their defence.

Repton, like Brown, was concerned with architecture. It was still often necessary to 'improve' a mansion to suit it to the 'improved' setting. Repton had no training in architecture. Probably through his Herefordshire client, the Hon. Edward Foley, M.P., of Stoke Edith, he met John Nash (1752–1835). Nash had earlier made, financially, a false start as a London architect, and had retired to Wales, where he had soon built up a local practice extending into the border counties. In about 1795 Nash joined Repton in partnership, and provided the necessary architectural adjuncts.[6] 'In doing so he adopted a style intended to be *in itself* picturesque.'[7] Briefly, one may say the Brownian picture-like landscape lay *around* a house—usually of classic form—while in the Reptonian-Nash conception the house itself was part of this Claudian scene. To requote Rushworth on Compton, altering Miss Austen's use of italics: 'The approach, now, is one of the finest things in the country: *you see the house* in the most surprising manner.' The house and the incidental buildings were, in Nash's hands, as irregular, even fantastic, as the landscape itself.

Repton, it will be seen, soon moved away from Brown. Eventually there was as distinct a difference between his work and Brown's as between that of Brown and the Pope-Kent school. Yet Nature, Claude & Co. were the inspiration of all. It must, I think, be added that while Pope's added requirement of Sense is often absent from the work of Kent and Brown, it returns in the case of Repton: he is quite clear, for instance, that planning a garden is quite a different matter from producing a picture—that

* Though primarily a scientific organization, this body, particularly in its early days, had at times been closely concerned with certain aspects of horticulture. It was founded in 1788 following the purchase of Linnaeus's library and herbarium from Sweden, cleverly engineered by Sir J. E. Smith and Sir Joseph Banks.

is, a painter is a very different person from a gardener—which was by no means the view of all gentlemen of taste. Late in his career,[8] in 1806, he affirmed his creed:

The perfection of landscape gardening consists in the four following requisites: *First*, it must display the natural beauties, and hide the natural defects of every situation. *Secondly*, it should give the appearance of extent and freedom, by carefully disguising or hiding the boundary. *Thirdly*, it must studiously conceal every interference of art, however expensive, by which the natural scenery is improved; making the whole appear the production of nature only; and *fourthly*, all objects of mere convenience or comfort, if incapable of being made ornamental, or of becoming proper parts of the general scenery, must be removed or concealed. This latter article, I confess, has occasionally misled modern improvers into the absurdity of not only banishing the *appearance*, but the *reality* of all comfort and convenience to a distance; frequently exemplified in a bad choice of a spot for the kitchen garden

He adds: 'Congruity of style, uniformity of character, and harmony of parts with the whole, are different modes of expressing *unity*, without which no composition can be perfect.' He returns to this unity again and again: 'one of the greatest errors in modern gardening has been that of placing a large house, not only on a naked lawn, but in the centre of it . . . so that the park might surround it in all directions'. The result, he points out, is that the gardens, the pheasantry, the dairy farm, etc., 'become so many detached establishments' banished at an inconvenient distance.

Repton reintroduced the terrace as enriching the foreground, and serving as a basement for the house to stand upon; the avenue was no longer forbidden: 'the eye of taste or experience hates compulsion and turns away in disgust from any artificial means of attracting; for this reason an avenue is most pleasing which . . . climbs up a hill, passing over the summit, leaves the fancy to conceive its termination'. He also reintroduced flower-beds and small specialized flower gardens (for, say, roses or American plants) near to the house.

But the most important development propounded by Repton was 'the proper distinction between *Painting* and *Gardening*'—the differences between a scene in nature and on canvas. The principle may be summarized thus: first, the spot from whence the view is taken is in a fixed state to the painter; but the gardener surveys his scenery while in motion; secondly, the field of vision in nature is much greater than in a picture; thirdly, the light which a painter brings to a picture is fixed as he wishes it at a certain time of day —in nature it varies from hour to hour.

Later, he destroys by practical reasoning the theory of the three distances in the perfect landscape. The first, the detailed foreground, is, for the gardener, that part of the scene which it is within his power to improve; the second, the middle distance, is that which is not (always) in his power to prevent being injured, and the third—the horizon—which is not within anyone's power to alter. Thus, though Repton started from the Claudian or Brownian standpoint, he progressed logically far beyond it; he was himself more concerned in trying to achieve the *beautiful* than the *picturesque* with which he has wrongly come to be associated.

Much of this statement and restatement of his views was produced in answer to attacks, from different angles, on the Brownian manner made by two Herefordshire squires, Sir Uvedale Price (1747–1829)* of Foxley, and Richard Payne Knight (1750–1824) of Downton Castle. These culminated in Knight's *An Analytical Enquiry into the Principles of Taste* in 1805, in which Repton considered that his own developments onwards from Brown, and his own publications, had been ignored.

Payne Knight, it has been suggested, was the influence behind Nash's picturesque architecture; he was certainly first in the field with the new irregular type of mock castellated building that shortly came into fashion. His own Downton Castle, standing in the romantic valley of the Teme near the spot where it cuts through from Herefordshire into Shropshire, was begun in 1774. The interior was (incongruously) in the classical style, and housed a superb collection of works of art. His own contribution to garden design, apart from his more philosophical *Enquiry*, is to be found in *The Landscape—A Didactic Poem*, addressed to Uvedale Price in 1794. Two quotations will epitomize, even define, the idea of the picturesque in gardening:

> The bright acacia, and the vivid plane,
> The rich laburnum with its golden chain;
> And all the variegated flow'ring race,
> That deck the garden, and the shrubb'ry grace,

* Author of *An Essay on the Picturesque* (1794) and translator of Pausanias

Should near to buildings, or to water grow,
Where bright reflections beam with equal glow,
And blending vivid tints with vivid light,
The whole in brilliant harmony write:
E'en the bright flow'ret's tints will dim appear,
When limpid waters foam and glitter near,
And o'er their curling crystals sparkling play
The clear reflection of meridian day;
From buildings, too, strong refluent lights are thrown,
When the sun downward shines upon the stone;
Or on the windows darts its evening rays,
And makes the glass with fire responsive blaze.

But better are these gaudy scenes display'd
From the high terrace or rich balustrade;
'Midst sculptur'd founts and vases, that diffuse,
In shapes fantastic, their concordant hues;
Than on the swelling slopes of waving ground,
That now the solitary house surround.

Curse on the shrubbery's insipid scenes!
Of tawdry fringe encircling vapid greens;
Where incongruities so well unite,
That nothing can by accident be right;
Thickets that neither shade nor shelter yield;
Yet from the cooling breeze the senses shield:
Prim gravel walks, through which we winding go,
In endless serpentines that nothing show;
Till tir'd, I ask, *Why this eternal round?*
And the pert gard'ner says, '*Tis pleasure ground*.
This pleasure ground! astonish'd, I exclaim,
To me Moorfields as well deserve the name:
Nay, better; for in busy scenes at least
Some odd varieties the eye may feast,
Something more entertaining still be seen,
Than red-hot gravel, fring'd with tawdry green.

O! waft me hence, to some neglected vale;
Where, shelter'd, I may court the western gale:
And 'midst the gloom which native thickets shed,
Hide from the noontide beams my aching head.

and:

Though the old system against nature stood,
At least in this, 'twas negatively good:—

> Inclos'd by walls, and terraces, and mounds,
> Its mischiefs were confin'd to narrow bounds;
> Just round the house, in formal angles trac'd,
> It mov'd responsive to the builder's taste;
> Walls answer'd walls, and alleys, long and thin,
> Mimick'd the endless passages within.
>   But kings of yew, and goddesses of lead,
> Could never far their baneful influence spread;
> Coop'd in the garden's safe and barrow bounds,
> They never dar'd invade the open grounds. . . .

In 1829 G. W. Johnson summarized the arguments in this wordy battle of styles:

After studying the writings of the general partizans I have been able to draw but one conclusion, which is, that the principles of Knight and Price are correct if impartially considered and have been acted upon by the general consent of modern designers; nor can there be greater proof of this position than that in his maturer practice, Repton acted upon them himself. They differed in no one point of importance, that I have been able to discover, as to what constitute beautiful points in a landscape. . . .*

Today, when time has added the rough and colourful textures and that hint of decay which Price and Knight missed from the Brownian scene, the difference is still further minimized.

The influence of Repton was great and lasting. His theories were, for instance, perpetuated after his death by J. C. Loudon. In 1806 he himself calculated that over a million and a half impressions of his explanatory sketches and views were in circulation; 3,000 of these were in manuscript in private possession, many no doubt as part of the 'Red Books' that he prepared when called in for advice. Each 'Red Book' included a survey and a reasoned argument explaining the suggested changes. A careful drawing of the place in its present state was given, and folding flaps were provided, which superimposed upon it, showed the client the appearance after 'improvement' (Plate XIX). He was a consultant; apparently his clients carried out the work themselves to his designs.

Repton classified architecture broadly into two parts, the

* A wittier summary is to be found in T. L. Peacock's *Headlong Hall* (1815); all three contestants were, in fact, friends.

classic and the gothic; each belonged to its own world, and must be surrounded by its own appropriate scenery. His sensitivity to the form and quality of different species of tree and the type of architecture with which they blended was acute. He hoped also to bring in a third style of architecture, the Indian; this followed the publication of the illustrated works by the Daniells and others. Beyond Brighton Pavilion, Sezincote in Gloucestershire, and the Regency fashion for verandahs, not very much came from this enthusiasm.

There appears to be no true record of the gardens designed by Repton; the existence of a 'Red Book' (of which many still exist) does not necessarily mean that the work was carried out to his instructions. He himself recalled being shown gardens which he was alleged to have improved, but about which he knew nothing. Many imitators of his style made use of his descriptive publications.[9]

Charming and genuine examples can still be seen at Luscombe in Devon[10] and Sheringham Hall, Norfolk.[11] his connections with East Anglia resulted in several 'improvements' in a district which had remained old-fashioned. An early commission for the Duke of Portland at Welbeck helped to give him standing. Other of his works include Ashridge, Attingham, Cobham Park, Garnons, Gayhurst, Holkham, Tyringham, and Warley Abbey—the last now a public park.

Though strictly outside our province, the enormous scale of tree-planting in Scotland during this period should be mentioned. Many ornamental trees were planted, and in a good deal of the general afforestation considerable efforts were made to obtain picturesque effects. The Dukes of Atholl were the most lavish; between 1740 and 1830 three of them planted 14,096,719 larches —enough to cover over 10,000 acres. The greatest of them all was John, the 4th Duke, who succeeded to the estates in 1774 and held them until his death in 1830. At Dunkeld he had the services of Alexander Nasmyth (1758–1840) as designer.

Nasmyth, a most interesting man and the founder of a distinguished and clever family,[12] began his career as an Edinburgh portrait painter. His politics were rather advanced, and he began in consequence to lose his fashionable connection. So he took to landscape painting, and eventually to landscape designing. His style was formed on Price and Knight, rather than on Repton, and some of his earliest work seems to have been in 1807–13 for Sir James Hall, F.R.S. (1761–1832), the eminent geologist, chemist, and student of gothic architecture, at Dunglass, Haddingtonshire. Nasmyth recalled an amusing episode when he was working for the Duke of Atholl at Dunkeld. A bare and inaccessible crag, the Craigybarns, was just the place to be capped by a plantation of trees, but no one could reach it. One day Nasmyth, noticing two old cannons, had them charged with canisters of tree seeds which were then shot into place. The seeds duly germinated.

This remarkable but now forgotten man takes a place in history as a pioneer of town planning; as will be seen later, he also achieved some reputation as a rock-garden designer.

One should remark, too, on Sir Walter Scott (1771–1832). It is well known that the lavish scale of his garden-making and tree-planting at Abbotsford was one cause of his financial troubles. But he was both thoughtful and influential in these enterprises. He fortunately recorded his opinions, when, in 1828, he reviewed for *The Quarterly Review*, anonymously, *The Planter's Guide* by Sir Henry Steuart. This was primarily concerned with tree-planting and the activities of the Highland Society.* It gave Scott, however, an opportunity to write a brilliant essay on the history and art of gardening. He stood closer to Uvedale Price and Payne Knight than to Repton, but was quite clear that some of the theories of the former two carried to their logical conclusion were, to say the least, silly. He regretted the wholesale destruction of the work of the London and Wise period, arguing that they should have been modified to suit modern taste rather than suffered what he calls the 'spade, matlocks, and pickaxes' activities of Brown's school. Again, he delighted in old-fashioned water-works as such —needing no specious arguments to defend them against their 'unnaturalness'. He was quite definite about one fundamental: 'Nothing is more completely the child of art than a garden.'

    .   .   .   .   .

The number of architects, other professionals, and amateurs devoting their energies to garden 'improvements' was now considerable. The works of Repton, Knight, and Price were available.

* Steuart, his book, and the Society were strongly criticized by J. C. Loudon, the foremost arboriculturist of the day.

Publications of the 'pattern-book' type became numerous. One such instance was *Ferme Ornée or Rural Improvements*, 'a series of domestic and ornamental designs suited to parks, plantations, rides, walks, rivers, farms, etc. . . . calculated for landscape and picturesque effects'. The edition of 1803* contains engravings in 'aqua-tinta' of fences and gates, ha-has, lodges, a fishing bridge, a wood-pile house, American cottages, dog kennels, stables, cow- or ox-houses in every conceivable style of architecture. The author was John Plaw (*c.* 1745–1820) of Southampton, and it appears that some of his designs were put into effect.

A much more important, but now forgotten, figure was John Buonarotti Papworth (1775–1847).[13] He possessed a renaissance-like versatility and ability; one cannot help feeling that his assumption of the name Buonarotti, added to the simple John given him by his parents, had some justification. He took this name, it seems, in connection with a triumphal painting conceived as a tribute to Wellington's victory at Waterloo. The Royal Academy did not hang it.

He was architect to the King of Württemberg, to whom he introduced the English style; he laid out the Montpellier estate at Cheltenham (the pump-room was his design); he prepared plans for a Utopia on the Ohio River—which its speculative projector failed to bring to fruition; he designed many elegant shop-fronts, a steam pleasure-boat, chandeliers, armchairs, decanters, and lustres—and a garish, indestructible form of tile. We must, however, ignore these activities and recite the names of some of the gardens in which he was concerned as designer or furnisher of ornamental buildings. He was active with J. W. Hiort (1772–1861)† in the alterations and garden buildings at Claremont when the unfortunate Princess Charlotte and her husband acquired the estate. He designed bridges (1818–22) for the Earl of Shrewsbury's great phantasmagoria (which included Stonehenge, the monument of Lysicrates, a Chinese temple and fountain, and goodness knows what else) at Alton Towers in the hills of north-east Staffordshire.‡ He is known to have worked at White Knights, Kew Priory, How

* The publisher, J. Taylor, includes a list of several comparable books designed for the amateur's use.

† The actual designs were Papworth's; Hiort was engaged in 1816 in a supervisory capacity.

‡ The whole was lavishly planted with exotic trees, shrubs, and plants; its remains now form a playground for the Potteries.

Hatch (Brentwood), Monney Hill House (Rickmansworth), Clapton House, Holly Lodge (Highgate), Harefield Grove, Turret House (South Lambeth), Twickenham Park, and Bedding Rectory (Surrey). He was concerned with laying out estates at Blackheath, Dulwich, Clapham Common, Winchmore Hill, and Chorley Wood—the originating centres of London's suburbia. What remains of these today? That one who worked on so great a scale should now be disregarded is surprising.

He is, however, commemorated by the exquisite coloured lithographs that he made for Ackermann's *Repository*. A number of these, appropriate to our subject, were brought together in his *Rural Residences . . . designs for cottages, decorated cottages, small villas and other ornamental buildings . . . interspersed with some observations on landscape gardening* (1818).

His style might be called 'picturesque-classical'. An instance of his outlook is the design for 'an ice house calculated for an embellishment to the grounds of a nobleman' (Plate XIX). Ice-houses had, by the nineteenth century, become a necessary adjunct to every sizable mansion. Well-like, usually with an earth-covered, domed top for insulation, and placed handily by lake or river, they were used both for the storage of ice and as refrigerators. Their operation and maintenance since Evelyn's time had always fallen within the purview of the head gardener.[*] The design was usually functional; but Papworth thought otherwise. 'Besides the luxuries which the various uses of ice afford, the building to preserve it may be made usefully ornamental.'

Papworth's drawings of garden seats designed as embellishments to the lawn or shrubbery are most elegant; they provide the subject for some of his observations. He tells us that when the designs of gardens had depended on geometric skill

vases and groups of figures, in fantastical shapes, were occasionally introduced for 'eye-traps', as they were called, and continued to promote the encouragement of our lead mines, if not of true taste,[†] until the simple, yet varied beauties of rural nature obtained their well-merited imitation. The business of the landscape gardener was now to disencumber the ground of such objects, and to give strong effect to particular points of view composed of different scenery. . . . Rustic seats,

---

[*] At least one old English ice-house, at Rufford Abbey, was still used in the 1930s.
[†] Shenstone, however, approved of lead figures.

bowers, root-houses and other such small buildings now decorate our gardens, when something more in character with the scene, and more analagous to classic art, might be used.

The two designs illustrated both make use of cast-iron. The first, situated overlooking a marine view, is of light ironwork with a roof of copper sheeting. The second, more suited to parkland, is marquee-like. The ornamental fabric covering is stretched upon ironwork supports.

Another of these forgotten designers of whom we should like to know more is Thomas Trubshaw (1802–1842). Coming from a Staffordshire family, which, like its neighbours the Wyatts, produced a number of architects, he seems to have done some interesting work in his short life. A gothick-baronial style house near Lichfield called Manley Hall, with its grounds, was described at some length by Loudon.[14] And what was his 'architectural flower garden' at Heath House, Tean?

THE MAGAZINES ARRIVE

One of the landmarks of gardening history was the publication of the first periodical devoted to scientific horticulture. In 1787 appeared the first issue of *The Botanical Magazine, or, Flower Garden Displayed, in which the most ornamental foreign plants, cultivated in the open ground, the greenhouse and the stove, are accurately represented in their natural colours.* The editor was William Curtis (1746–1799), whose publication was issued from the Botanic Garden, Lambeth Marsh. The price was 1s. per copy. The first plate was an exquisite figure of *Iris persica*; that of the Moss Rose (Plate XX) is another lovely example.

There is not much to be said of Curtis personally.[15] His unspectacular life was devoted to the study of plants, and also of insects, particularly in conjunction with plants. He was born at Alton, in Hampshire, became an apothecary and in 1772 a demonstrator at the Chelsea Physic Garden. In 1777 he produced the first part of the magnificent *Flora Londinensis*, an illustrated description of the wild flowers growing in and around London. He lost money on this, for those prepared to pay for works on local floras were few in number. It was otherwise with those exotic plants that were cultivated by the rich and fashionable. As an instance of the money such persons were prepared to spend one may cite the sale at auction in 1781 of the late Dr. Fothergill's specimen of *Arbutus andrachne*, a relative of the strawberry tree, for £53 11s.[16] Although first grown here by Dr. Sherard at Eltham in 1724, this plant of Fothergill's had, in 1765, been the first to flower.

Curtis realized that money was not to be made by the pursuit of native botany, but in what one may call botanical horticulture. *The Botanical Magazine* was, as he foresaw, successful; the name was, and still is, rather misleading. He edited the journal until his last illness. His gravestone in St. Mary's, Battersea, recalls that

> While living herbals shall spring profusely wild
> Or garden cherish all that's sweet and gay;
> So long thy works shall praise, dear nature's child,
> So long thy memory suffer no decay.

The Botanical Magazine still bears out this prophecy.

Curtis's success was partly due to those who helped to finance him, particularly the Earl of Bute and a Quaker, Dr. John Coakeley Lettsom (1744–1815). Even more did it lie in the skill of his artists. In the early days the chief of these was Sydenham Teast Edwards (*c.* 1769–1819), the son of a Welsh schoolmaster. Some copies that he had made from the plates in *Flora Londinensis* came to Curtis's notice, and he arranged for the youth to be brought to London and trained. Henceforth the two worked together on intimate terms; of the first 1,721 plates, Edwards probably made all but about seventy-five.[17]

The success of this periodical soon brought rivals. In 1797 was begun *The Botanist's Repository*, with plates by Henry C. Andrews (1794–1830). This ran for ten volumes, and was restricted to describing newly introduced or rare plants. Andrews also produced beautiful works on heathers and geraniums. Little is known of him. He was apparently a comparatively uneducated man, with scant knowledge of botany—the descriptive part of his books was by other hands. He married the daughter of John Kennedy, partner of the enterprising Lee. We may suspect, therefore, that the firm had some interest in his *Repository*.

Sydenham Edwards, following a disagreement with Curtis's successors, left *The Botanical Magazine*, and in 1815 James Ridgway launched *The Botanical Register*, consisting of coloured figures of exotic plants cultivated in British gardens, to which Edwards transferred his activities. This continued until 1847.

Now we must transfer our attention from this elegant and expensive type of publication to the first periodical designed for gardeners of all kinds and every standing. *The Gardener's Magazine and Register of Rural and Domestic Improvement* first appeared in 1826. Its 'conductor' was J. C. Loudon. The publishers were Longman, Rees, Orme, Brown, and Green. The purposes of the new journal were set out at very considerable length in the first issue; in the preface to the first completed volume the 'conductor' rather more briefly wrote:

We had two grave objects in view: to disseminate new and important information on all topics connected with horticulture, and to raise the intellect and the character of those engaged in this art.

Throughout its career the social aspects of gardening, and the need to encourage the working gardener to 'improve' himself, and for his employer to pay him a proper wage, is continually stressed. The practical man, feeling diffident about his skill as a writer, is invited to 'fix on a subject, and begin it at once, and write straight on to the end, regardless of anything but the correctness of his statements. This done once or twice, a good style will come of itself'. The resulting magazine, the size of today's 'pocket' periodicals, illustrated by small wood engravings, was balanced and representative. Loudon was a man of good sense, sound taste, and wide knowledge, and only published contributions that were good in their respective kinds.

Something should be said about that enterprising journalist, William Cobbett (1762–1835). His stay in America made him an advocate of the use of American plants in this country, notably the tulip tree and the false acacia. His advocacy of, and dealings in, the false acacia under its American name of locust were most profitable. He bought large quantities from nurserymen who listed it as *Robinia* (under which name the public did not recognize it) and resold them at a good profit. He was the author of *The American Gardener* (1821) and *The English Gardener* (1838).

MR. AND MRS. LOUDON

John Claudius Loudon (1783–1843), the founder and 'conductor' of *The Gardener's Magazine*, was also responsible for *An Encyclopaedia* *of Gardening*, first appearing in 1822, and *Arboretum et Fruticetum Britannicum*,* which, in eight volumes published in 1838, described and illustrated the trees and shrubs, native and introduced, cultivated in the British Isles, with a vast amount of information as to their history and other attributes. Beyond our scope are his works on agriculture, *The Magazine of Natural History* (founded in 1829) and *The Architectural Magazine* (begun in 1833).† All were distinguished and influential undertakings, displaying an advanced sense of social conscience, and an idealism delightfully tinctured with realism—if somewhat humourless.

It would not be difficult to justify the claim that Loudon‡ remains the outstanding figure in the age when modern gardening originated—that is, when the scientific outlook was first seriously and universally considered—and yet the elegance of the eighteenth century lingered on. In 1829 the scholarly George Johnson wrote of him:[18]

Whoever wishes for a complete view of English gardening as at present practiced, will find no works better calculated for his satisfaction than those of Mr. Loudon. Being a landscape gardener by profession, he might be excused if in his publications on that branch of our art, the abilities of a master were chiefly apparent; that in such he is correct, that he possesses taste to discriminate the beauties, and to reproduce the incongruities of his predecessors; that he has taste to select, and ability to execute; is saying all that can be said of any landscape gardener who may succeed to Kent, Mason, Whatley, Knight, Price and Repton. It may be said without any reservation of Mr. Loudon.

Years later, in 1872, another tribute came from a rather surprising source. When William Robinson published *The Garden*,

* This great work, the like of which has never been attempted since, would alone assure an international fame for Loudon. Its production, with the help of several first-rate assistants and innumerable correspondents, was carried out as a skilfully organized campaign. Yet every part of it, from the great sweep of its conception down to the smallest detail, displays the depth of Loudon's personality, vigilance, 'acceptable simplicity of writing', and blessed common sense.

† An early contributor to both was the very youthful John Ruskin; 'your son is the greatest natural genius that ever it has been my fortune to become acquainted with', Loudon wrote to his father in 1838.

‡ Surprisingly, no one has yet attempted a thorough survey of the work of this awe-inspiring monument of industry, and the many facets of his work, and influence; perhaps it is impossible, for no one without some practical knowledge of the several subjects that Loudon mastered could succeed. But one must be thankful for Geoffrey Taylor's admirable short study.[19]

a paper which reorientated the course of British gardening, it was inscribed 'To the memory of John Claudius Loudon . . . the first volume . . . is dedicated by its founder', and the frontispiece was an engraving of his sensitive, determined head.

Loudon, the son of a farmer, was born at Cambuslang, Lanark, in 1783. From his earliest days he studied in every spare moment, learning French and Italian as a youth, and becoming an accomplished draughtsman. He was apprenticed to the Edinburgh branch of Robert Dickson, of Hassandeanburn—a nursery firm founded in 1725. At twenty he came to London, and soon made his mark with the Banksian circle. His health broke down (it never fully recovered) and during convalescence at Pinner he was so struck by the inefficiency of English farming that he took Tew Park, Oxfordshire, and set up a practical school to teach the Scottish methods of husbandry. By 1812 he had become so prosperous that he sold the place, and, in the wake of the Napoleonic wars, travelled in northern Europe. He returned home to find that his investments had failed. He embarked upon his *Encyclopaedia*, travelling in southern Europe during the course of its completion.

At the age of forty-seven he married Jane Webb (1807–1858), then aged twenty-three. He met her following his review of her fantastic and witty novel, *The Mummy*, describing England of the twentieth century, which he believed to be written by a man. From this marriage in 1830, even past John's death in 1843, and until Jane's in 1858, we are always dealing with Mr. and Mrs. Loudon as a single entity. They lived at 3 Porchester Terrace, Bayswater, a house that Loudon designed, with a remarkable garden. Through financial difficulties and crippling ill health they worked and travelled together. After his fatal collapse—while at work—in her arms, she reissued, revised, and republished his writings; she wrote, too, on botany, gardening, and natural history, securing her own little niche in fame, and some credit as a pioneer of woman's freedom.

We cannot better epitomize gardening as it was on the eve of the changes that brought about Victorian fecundity than by reference to *The Suburban Gardener and Villa Companion*, published in 1838. From descriptions of existing gardens which Loudon considered exemplary we get a good picture of gardening at that time. Its title (combined with repeated references to science) show that it also has a forward look, directed to the class that was gradually assuming power.*

The expanded title makes this last point even more clearly: '*the whole adapted for grounds of one perch to fifty acres in extent and intended for the instruction of those who know little of gardening and rural affairs, and more particularly for the use of ladies*'. Here we have two still unsolved problems almost unconsciously expressed—the new dichotomy of British life into 'town' and 'country', and the entry of women into activities for which they are so often temperamentally and physiologically ill-designed.

Loudon's theories on garden design, as on architecture, were eclectic, with a strong bias towards the later work of Repton. His logical and unbiassed views may be quoted; they summarize, too, the aims of the different schools of the past:

There are two principal styles of laying out grounds in Great Britain, viz. the geometric (or architectural) and natural. The latter is what, on the continent, is emphatically called English gardening; to which epithet a vague general idea is attached, of grounds and plantations formed in flowing lines, in imitation of nature; as contradistinguished from ground formed into regular slopes and levels, or plantations in straight lines, or included in plots, bounded by lines always decidedly artificial, and it may be divided into three kinds: the picturesque, the gardenesque and the rustic.

By picturesque gardening is to be understood the production, in country residences, of that kind of scenery which, from its strongly-marked features, is considered as particularly suitable for being represented by painting.

By the gardenesque style is to be understood the production of that kind of scenery which is best calculated to display the individual beauty of trees, shrubs and plants in a state of nature; the smoothness and greenness of lawns; and the smooth surfaces, curved directions, dryness and firmness of gravel walks; in short, it is calculated for displaying the art of the gardener.

The rustic style has reference to what is commonly found accompanying the rudest description of labourer's cottages in this country. The object of this style, or rather manner, is also to produce such facsimile imitations of common nature, as to deceive the spectator into an idea that they are real or fortuitous.

* It is amusing to recall that *The Gardener's Magazine* indexed descriptions of gardens under two classifications: *Seats*—the country homes of the aristocracy, and *Residences*—those of the rest.

Loudon accepts all these styles as valid in their correct contexts: parterres, grottoes, fountains, plantations, terraces, rustic arches, architectural ornaments—all are indexed and described. And, of course, we have all the practical details of planting, of greenhouse management; poultry and bees, ice-houses; even the position and construction of clothes-line posts are discussed.

It is interesting to note the social graduation of the gardens he describes. He begins with 'fourth-rate gardens . . . of houses in a connected row or street; the gardens of double detached houses, that is, of houses built in pairs, and forming part of a row; and the gardens of houses which are detached on every side, but which still form part of a row, or line of houses'. Finally come 'first-rate suburban gardens which have a park and a farmery' which 'can scarcely be less than from 50 to 100 acres'.* This frank avowal of social status based on houses and acreage is now difficult to comprehend; it was, indeed, as widely accepted as the bearing of arms. Repton, for instance, is now accused of obsequiousness because of his intentional reflections on the wealth or high birth of his patrons in the designs he submitted to them, and for commenting on them in his 'Red Books'. But surely this display of high breeding or worldly success is today widely acceptable, only its methods and media have changed.

For the Loudonian period we may take as a representative first-class middling-sized garden Drayton Green, Middlesex, the home of Mrs. Lawrence (c. 1803–1855) (Plate XXI). Born Miss Senior, of Broughton House, near Aylesbury, in 1828 she married William Lawrence, an able and prosperous surgeon (who, incidentally, did much to improve Loudon's health), and went to live at Drayton. Here she lived until 1840, when she moved to a larger estate, Ealing Park. There, one evening, she was visited by the Queen and Prince Albert, to see her night-flowering cacti.

Mrs. Lawrence was a woman of great ability and a brilliantly successful gardener. She was herself responsible for the design and planting of the Drayton garden, and all its ancillaries. By 1838 she had received from the Horticultural Society fifty-three awards, including the prized Knightian medal.† She was one of the few

---

* In the 1850 edition of *The Suburban Gardener* (the title changed to *The Villa Gardener*) these ratings disappear.
† Struck to commemorate T. A. Knight's twenty-five years as President.

women to be honoured by the dedication of a volume of *The Botanical Magazine* (1842).

As evidence of her skill, in April 1838 she lent Loudon the manuscript catalogue of her collection. It named 3,266 different species, varieties, and garden forms of trees, shrubs, and plants surviving in cultivation after the losses following the severe weather of January in that year. Among them were 500 roses, 200 varieties of heartsease, 140 florist's pelargoniums, and 227 orchids. There were, however, only 140 classed as alpines.

The defect of the 'Lawrencian villa' was its lack of repose: 'the brilliancy of the flowers, the immense number of statues and vases, and the sparkling waters of the various cascades, produced an effect perfectly dazzling'. This failing, indeed, makes the garden typical of the period, when elegance and some restraint, still advocated by Loudon, were beginning to fall away before the 'perfectly dazzling', triumphantly sponsored by that young Proteus later to become Sir Joseph Paxton.

Entering the garden from the drawing-room, facing east, we cross a small lawn to a path. From it, turning our head to the right, we see the large foliated vase, its base covered by a plant of tree ivy. Proceeding onwards, we are able to look back at the house. It is surrounded by plantations of rhododendrons, azaleas, and choice evergreen shrubs, enlivened by baskets of pyramid roses and pelargoniums.

Observing the various ornaments, specimen trees, and shrubs planted on the big lawn about us, we cross to the north-east corner, where we again strike the path, and look, through a rustic arch and over a vase, into the paddock grazed by Alderney cows. Westward, in the opposite direction, is the Italian walk, margined by statuary on the south side, and terminated by a span-roof greenhouse. As we walk beside the statues towards it, on the right lies a bed of choice herbaceous plants, interspersed with standard roses; the wall behind is planted with choice fruit, 'climbing roses and other climbing or twining shrubs of fragrance or beauty'. To our left, we catch an effective glimpse through a rustic archway of the lawn; then, on our right, a fountain is passed. Reaching the greenhouse, we find beside it a French parterre garden.

Back on the corner of the lawn, we find ourselves surrounded by a variety of objects; looking to the north-west is rockwork, to the south the 'pollard vista'. Proceeding again towards the centre of the lawn, we should notice the fountain with its basin full of water-lilies, and a Napoleon willow (*Salix babylonica*) by its side; from its side we can see the obverse of the arch already passed by in the Italian walk. It is of rustic work, crowned by Cupid; on either side fountains play.

To enter into a detailed description of the greenhouses, forcing-pits (there was one specially reserved for Cape heaths), and so on is not necessary. The dung-pit for the elaborate stabling makes us envious today, while a rubbish-pit and rot-heap were there to provide what we now call compost. The elaborate but thoughtfully designed kitchen and reserve garden lay across the road, near to the gardener's house.

Loudon considered the design was fundamentally in the picturesque manner, with single plants, such as standard roses and some of the choice shrubs, treated in the gardenesque style.

He himself did not practice as a garden designer to any great extent, though he should always be remembered for the change he brought about in public parks, particularly Kensington Gardens. Leigh Hunt wrote of the latter:

The late public-spirited Mr. Loudon, who had a main hand in bringing about the recent improvements, both here and elsewhere, got the old wall in Bayswater Road exchanged for an iron railing, which gives the wayfarer a pleasant scene of shrubs and green leaves as he goes along, instead of dusty old brickwork.[20]

Mrs. Loudon lived on far into the Victorian age, maintaining the Bayswater garden, but with some simplification in design to save labour. She re-edited many of her husband's works. She wrote delightful books enthusiastically urging ladies of the Victorian middle-classes to engage in horticulture,* country pleasures, and natural history. The precision and common sense of her husband (who was throughout her inspiration) were well-maintained; she possessed in addition a charm that he lacked.

OPERATIVE MANUFACTURERS AND DUKES

During the period we are now discussing horrifying social changes were taking place in Britain. The enlightened early pioneers of

* This liberation and reintroduction of women into horticulture raises the question —to which I cannot find an answer—as to when the earlier practice of the flower and herb gardens being particularly the woman's sphere died out. Perhaps it never did among old-fashioned country families.

cast iron and steam power came and went and were replaced by crude and harsh industrialists. The final, most vigorous, stages of the enclosure of the countryside were often the means of extending the work of the landscapers and 'improvers', but they altered, sometimes for the worse, the economic structure of the countryside. More terrible, the satanic mills and the increased population that they bred were occupying and soiling more and more of England's green and pleasant land. Successful manufacturers now moved far away from the dirt and squalor of their manufacturies into more genial surroundings, to become country gentlemen; *le paysage humanisé* disappeared as the smoking chimneys arose and spread their fumes upon ever-widening acres.

It will have been observed that the fashionable taste in plants had, by the late eighteenth century, completely changed. The exotics of *The Botanical Magazine*, and particularly plants from North America, had eclipsed the favourites of Hanmer and Rea—or at least so it seemed. But while this was so among the fashionable it was not true of the industrial population. It was in Britain's sooty towns that the old florists' flowers—tulip, auricula, carnation, pink, anemone, ranunculus, hyacinth, and polyanthus*— were largely brought to new standards of perfection. Their cultivation became a 'mystery' that provided the artisan with an absorbing interest and jewel-like colour in his hard life among drab surroundings. As was the case among colliers and iron-workers with their bull-terriers and whippets, during hard times men would themselves go without necessities so that their hobbies should not suffer. As an anonymous writer of the period wrote:

The auricula is to be found in the highest perfection in the gardens of the manufacturing class, who bestow much time and attention on this and a few other flowers, as the tulip and pink. A fine stage of these plants is scarcely ever to be seen in the gardens of the nobility and gentry, who depend upon the exertions of hired servants, and cannot therefore compete in these nicer operations of gardening with those who tend their flowers themselves, and watch over their progress with paternal solicitude.[21]

There were several eminent writers on florists' flowers. James Maddock, a Quaker from Warrington who had a nursery at

* These eight flowers were those defined as florists' flowers in the rules of florists' societies.

Walworth, published his *Florist's Directory* in 1792; Thomas Hogg, a schoolmaster and later florist, of Paddington Green, issued in 1812 the first of several editions of his *A Concise and Practical Treatise on the Growth and Culture of the Carnation, Pink, Auricula, Polyanthus, Ranunculus, Tulip, Hyacinth, Rose and Other Flowers*—though the carnations, pinks, tulips, and auriculas received the lion's share of attention. In 1816 Isaac Emmerton, nurseryman, of Barnet, published *A Plain and Practical Treatise on the Culture and Management of the Auricula*. All these authors were highly successful growers—it has been suggested that some of the cultural methods they advocated were designed to ensure their continued supremacy!

The critical standards applied by the florist, and the state of perfection in which the flowers must be displayed, were forbidding. A Mr. Kendall, florist, of Stoke Newington, wrote of him: 'he loves nature . . . but not in deshabillé; for him she must be clad in all her charms. He takes the wild beauty from its rustic homes, sees hidden charms beneath the rustic guise, makes it his fondling . . .'[22]

The tulip, once prime favourite, declined somewhat in rank. Yet it was still fetching good prices, and had many followers. For example, in 1790, Luke Pope (1740–1825), a victualler, acquired some land at Gib Heath, but a few hundred yards from the famous Soho manufactory of Boulton and Watt (built in 1762), whose products were then revolutionizing the world. Here he founded a nurseryman's business. His own interest was in tulips, for which he was locally famous. On his death-bed he declared he had spent £3,000 on them; for some kinds he paid as much as £50 each. In 1832 his collection was still being maintained by his son John, with specimens valued at £20. In that year Loudon described them as making a fine show in the first and second weeks of May.[23]

The tulip grower replanted his bulbs every year into fresh ground; he hooped them over so that in very wet or frosty weather they could be covered with mats, yet availed himself of every opportunity to give them air. When the east winds of spring blew, or hail threatened, again they should be protected—but never must they become drawn by undue shading. At flowering times

an erection ought to be raised over them, and covered with stout Scotch sheeting, reaching to the ground, to be drawn up and let down with pulleys; by doing this you may keep them in high condition for three weeks, during which time you will have full opportunity of gratifying your friends with a view, for the true enjoyment of every pleasure is to share it with them.

Hogg describes only three classes of tulips—rose-coloured, bibloemen, and bizarres; other authorities classified them as early (a few kinds only); perroquets, or those flowering in the middle period; the doubles; and the late-flowering sorts, of which several hundred named varieties were available, and which included the bibloemens and bizarres. Variegated (broken) kinds were particularly admired.

Because of their high prices, tulips were never so popular among working-men florists as carnations or pinks. One is tempted to quote their delightful and odd names: Bigg's Defiance, Brady's Braw, Stourbridge Regulator, Bond's Agenora, Cope's Suwarrow, Davey's King David, Hine's British Farmer, Wild's Cottage Girl, and at one period everybody's Duke of Wellington, Waterloo, and Lord Nelson—for the raiser's name was part of the title.

The criteria for double carnations set by the florists of the 1820s are given by Loudon.[24] The stems must be stout and straight, between 30 and 45 inches; the flowers surmounting them at least 3 inches in diameter, with many well-formed and shapely petals, which should appear neither overcrowded nor thin. The petals should be regularly disposed, equally imbricated, so that 'their respective and united beauties may captivate the eye at the same instant'. The whole corolla should be nearly hemispherical. The calyx should be shapely, and hold the blossom tightly in a close, circular body.

The colours composing the petals should be quite distinct, disposed in long, regular stripes—each stripe broad at its edge and tapering to a fine point at its base; they should be laid on a clean white ground, which must be quite unspotted, and form about one half of the petal.

Regularity of form and marking, and richness of colouring, were the prerequisites of perfection.* The most prized kinds were bizarres, with at least two colours laid on the white ground; in a scarlet bizarre the scarlet stripes were predominant, pink

---

* By 1863, according to George Glenny's *The Properties of Flowers and Plants*, the standards had become somewhat less strict; a diameter of 2½ inches was acceptable.

bizarre when pink abounded, and so on. Unusual combinations were highly valued. Flakes were those with but one colour laid on the white. Picotees* were quite distinct; the ground was usually yellow, or sometimes white, and the other colouring applied in spots; the margin of the petal was serrated.

The cultivation of carnations, from the sowing of the seed, piping (taking cuttings) or layering, to the moment when the flower opened, shaded by a little paper cap, was an undertaking of the greatest complexity.

The florists' pink is particularly associated with the 'operative manufacturers of Paisley', which, according to the Rev. William Ferrier of that place,[25] was in a considerable degree due to an effect of the peculiar manufacturing habits of the people, who were unrivalled for the execution of the most delicate ornamental muslins, and their continual ingenuity in providing new and pleasing elegancies to diversify these fabrics. Their Florists' Club, Ferrier adds, was notable for its peacefulness and sobriety. The weekly meetings always dismissed at ten in the evening.

Between 1785 and 1790 some of these workers obtained seeds of pinks from London. Most of the seedlings were quite ordinary, but a few showed a pattern of lacing. These caused excitement, and seeds from them were saved and sown; further pinks were for some years obtained from London, and again the laced forms were segregated and propagated from seed. This careful selection resulted in a widely increased range of laced pinks of superior form, and by the early nineteenth century Paisley pinks were being exported to the rest of the country.

Of the other florists' flowers, the double ranunculus (derived from *R. asiaticus*) was, according to Hogg, a 'flower very generally but at the same time very unsuccessfully cultivated'. But when seen at its prime 'yellow globular blossoms present themselves in all shades, from the pale straw to the golden crocus; red of all tints—pink, rose and flame colour; purple and crimson of every dye; black, brown, olive and violet of every hue. Besides these, there are yellow spotted flowers, brown spotted and white spotted, red and purple streaked, red and white striped, red and yellow striped, besides mottled and bridled in countless varieties'. Maddock grew upwards of 800 kinds.

* The name comes from the French *picoté*, marked, dotted.

As with the anemones (the poppy anemone and the star anemone), the single and semi-double forms were nearly as high in the florists' estimation as the double kinds. But of the hyacinths, the least widely grown of the florists' flowers, the double yellow, white, red and blue far exceeded the singles in estimation, value, and number; many were grown in glasses.

Of the many tints and shades of the polyanthus, the most admired were a bright red or scarlet, a very dark crimson, and chocolate with brimstone or lemon-coloured eyes and edging of the same colour.

From polyanthus we move easily to that other, and supreme, primula—the auricula. No florists' flower—indeed, no flower—can have had so faithful a following in Britain for so long a period—even if the band of the devoted has never formed a multitude; for it must receive devoted personal attention from its skilled owner.

From the days of Hanmer the great tradition passed through Rea to his son-in-law Samuel Gilbert (who died in about 1692), and whose *Florist's Vade-Mecum* reached its third edition in 1703. Then we have James Fitton, of Middleton, Lancashire (the home of the weavers), a famous grower and raiser of show varieties who lived to the age of eighty-six; in 1831 his son aged eighty still cherished his father's collection.[26] There was, too, James Douglas with his *The Distinguishing of a Fine Auricula* in 1757. In the year 1769 one James Barnes issued an invitation to florists and gardeners to a show of auriculas and polyanthuses at his home in Lichfield. From then on, there are many records of auricula shows being held at inns.[27]

The florists' auricula—the 'show' auricula of today—reached its acme of perfection in the early and middle nineteenth century. The stronghold of the cult has long been the north-west (it has been associated with the Huguenot weavers)—in Cheshire, parts of Scotland, and Lancashire, particularly (as we have seen) the district around Middleton. Hogg devoted a whole section to the Lancashire system of cultivation. As the standards of the Utopian auricula have remained practically unchanged, and can be found in several modern publications, it is not necessary to repeat them.

It may be of interest to remark that many of the successful growers were men of such singular character that their contemporaries thought it worth while to record something of their lives.

Such a one was George Lightbody,[28] who achieved a European reputation for florists' flowers, and particularly his auriculas. Born in 1795, he entered naval service as a boy, serving in the defence of Cadiz and in the Mediterranean. He was on active service throughout the American War: he

was twice a prisoner in the hands of Brother Jonathan, on the second occasion making his escape out of Portland. He was at that time a well-known character among the Americans. Our hero was selected for carrying secret despatches . . . had he fallen into the hands of the enemy, his fate would have been that of Dr. André. . . . The medal which he wears on his breast was bestowed for capturing a French vessel in the Mediterranean.

From these adventures he retired in 1817 to lead the life of a florist at Falkirk, his birthplace—a place long renowned for its floristry. He began with auriculas in 1822, buying Pope's Champion for a guinea, Leigh's Colonel Taylor for £3 15s., and Booth's Freedom for 30s. From these, and others, he raised the seedlings which made him famous. Towards the end of his life he said he considered himself well rewarded if he got one good plant from a thousand seedlings. No man was more honourable in his dealings; he was kind-hearted and courteous, and among his closest friends were his brother florists who were in rivalry with him.*

As the century progressed not only these specialized florists' societies increased in number, but horticultural societies in general. *The Gardener's Magazine* devoted much attention to their encouragement, from the smallest village organization to bodies such as the Birmingham Society for the Advancement of Floricultural Knowledge, whose aims were embodied in an announcement in which platitude followed platitude. In 1838 nearly 200 received mention, not excepting the gooseberry-growers. In that year the champion berry seems to have been produced at the Clayton (Lancashire) Gooseberry Show; it weighed 28 dwt. 16 gr. and was of the prize-winning strain appropriately named 'Loudon'.

.   .   .   .   .

* One of them, Richard Headly, in 1857 raised a grey-edged auricula which he named George Lightbody in his honour; it is still grown, and today 'it would be rash to try to name its superior'.[29]

While these numerous little organizations were being formed, so that fellow enthusiasts might meet, display the result of their works, boast, gossip, quarrel—and involve themselves in all those other enjoyable activities of civilized communities—something much bigger was on foot. On 29th June 1801 John Wedgwood wrote to William Forsyth, now gardener to George III at Kensington, a letter which began: 'I have been turning my attention to the formation of a Horticultural Society . . .' With it he enclosed a draft plan, under nine heads, designed to this end. He asked Forsyth to show it to Sir Joseph Banks, to see if it would obtain his backing—for Banks was now a powerful and influential figure in the world of scientific affairs. Banks approved 'very much of the idea'. On Wednesday, 7th March 1804 the proposal was discussed further by seven men at Hatchard's bookshop in Piccadilly. They met for 'the purpose of instituting a society for the improvement of horticulture'.[30]

These seven men formed a diverse body of persons, representative of different social groups, yet all united in their ardent pursuit of horticulture.

John Wedgwood (1766–1844),[31] the youngest, was the son of Josiah Wedgwood, the potter from Stoke-on-Trent. He had studied at Edinburgh University, travelled abroad, and then studied art under Flaxman. He had entered the family firm, soon left it, and taken to banking. His hobby was gardening, and Forsyth had been to visit and advise on his garden at Bristol. His social background was that brilliant group in Staffordshire with which his father was associated, the Lunar Society. He was a part of that extraordinary circle of intermarrying families which included the Darwins, and he seems to have possessed his share of its scientific powers allied with a strange foresight and an active sensibility.

A contrast to this man of imagination—for the conception of the society was his idea—and unease (he moved house and garden several times) was the Rt. Hon. Charles Greville (1749–1809),[32] second son of the Earl of Warwick. He was the holder of state appointments, personal friend of the king, and the successful developer on behalf of his uncle, Sir William Hamilton, of the estate around Milford in South Wales. Among the virtuosi he was known as an authority on precious stones and minerals, of which he had an exceptionally fine collection. He was a connoisseur and collector of engravings, sculpture, coins, women—and plants. His garden and conservatory at the little house on the edge of Paddington Green provided a number of rarities for the plates of *The Botanical Magazine*.

Sir Joseph Banks, by now sometimes teased in the popular Press on account of his dominating position in the growing world of science, we have already met. Two royal gardeners were present; the elder, William Forsyth,[33] we have also already encountered. After leaving Chelsea he had been in charge at St. James's and Kensington for twenty years. Apart from the genus *Forsythia*, his name is remembered as the inventor of a 'plaister' to restore injured trees to health. For revealing the secret of this useless composition, he obtained a grant of £1,500 from the Government. The falseness of his claims was proved by Knight, one of the original, and among the greatest, Fellows of the Society. As Forsyth died in the July following the Hatchard meeting, an embarrassing situation was presumably avoided.

The other gardener was William Townsend Aiton (1768–1843), son of William Aiton of Kew, who had succeeded his father in 1793. The royal family held him in high favour, and he is remembered as the lavish propagator and distributor of *Lilium tigrinum*, following its introduction in 1804,[34] and for his devotion to Kew when, after Banks's death and the accession of George IV, favour and interest were withdrawn from that royal establishment. He laid out the gardens at the Brighton Royal Pavilion.

Also at Hatchard's were two botanists. Richard Anthony Salisbury (1761–1829),[35] born at Leeds, was a man of peculiar and difficult character, but from his early years a botanist of extreme determination and patience, as well as having exceptional skill as a gardener. His first garden was at Chapel Allerton, where he lived until 1797, when he bought Collinson's house at Mill Hill—finding, however, that many of Collinson's plants had disappeared. For a time he acted as secretary of the Society, and was most active in its development. James Dickson (*c.* 1738–1822)[36] came from Peebleshire as a very young man, and for a time worked with Jeffries, the proprietor of Brompton Park nursery. He was an enthusiastic collector of the British flora, particularly mosses. In 1772 he opened his own seedsman's and nursery business at

Covent Garden. Banks was an early customer, and, finding him knowledgeable, no doubt helped him in building up a good connection. In due course Dickson became vice-president of the Society. He also contributed to its proceedings, specializing in little-known vegetables.

The first meeting stood adjourned. At the second, a friend of Wedgwood, John Hawkins (c. 1758–1841), was present, and it was agreed that he should be included as a Founder, with which went the right to recommend Fellows.[37] Hawkins was a wealthy Cornishman, who settled at Bignor Park, Sussex, which he rebuilt to house a collection of works of art. He had travelled with John Sibthorp (1758–1796) (whose sister he married) when he was collecting the material for his monumental *Flora Graeca* (1806–1840).*

So it was that the Horticultural Society of London† came into being. The then Lord Chamberlain, the 3rd Earl of Dartmouth (1755–1810), who had a fine garden at Sandwell Hall, Staffordshire, became the first president.‡

At a meeting in April 1805 a paper was read entitled *Introductory remarks relative to the objects which the Horticultural Society has in view*. It was prepared at the request of the Committee by Thomas Andrew Knight (1759–1838), the first of many that he offered to it displaying a mind of great lucidity combined with superb powers of observation and an imagination fertile in experiment. The document began by pointing out that by now societies for the advancement of most of the sciences and arts had been formed:

'horticulture alone appears to have been neglected, and left to the common gardener, who generally pursues the dull routine of his predecessor; and if he deviates from it, rarely possesses a sufficient share of science and information to enable him to deviate with success'.

* The drawings for this were made by Ferdinand Bauer (1760–1826), who later was botanical artist on Matthew Flinders's voyage of exploration to Australia. His brother Francis (1758–1840) was in 1790 appointed by Banks as artist at Kew, where he remained till his death. Both were born in Vienna and made England their home; they are among the finest botanical artists of all time; this fact reflects the high standards of both art and exotic botany then maintaining in this country.
† The Caledonian Horticultural Society was founded in 1809, the Horticultural Society of Ireland in 1830.
‡ The first woman Fellow, the Countess of Radnor, was elected in 1830, it having been agreed that there was nothing in the charter or byelaws disqualifying women.[38]

Two needs were particularly emphasized: the importance of careful selection of good forms of plants, and attention to the design and construction of greenhouses, which had been neglected.

Knight stands out as one of the most significant figures in the history of British horticulture.[39] He was the younger brother of Richard Payne Knight. Both were born at Wormsley Grange, Herefordshire, and that is about all their distinguished careers had in common.* Their father had inherited great wealth and much property in the northern part of the county, originally derived from the mines and ironworks around Madeley in Shropshire.

Payne Knight, as we have seen, was collector, connoisseur, and at Downton able to build and design his gardens on the grand scale to conform with his own theories. He travelled widely on the Continent. His house in Whitehall was a meeting-place for the learned and cultured. In 1814 he became Keeper of the British Museum.

Thomas Andrew, apart from his schooldays and a period at Balliol College, Oxford (when he seems to have spent most of his time wandering about—by no means aimlessly—with a gun under his arm and a dog at his heels), and regular but infrequent visits to London, spent his whole life in the north of Herefordshire. On his marriage in 1791 he moved to Elton Hall, lying under High Vinnals—the scene of the adventures in Milton's *Comus*—and in this quiet and fertile place, with a farm, a greenhouse built to his own design, and a walled garden likewise, he settled down to a lifetime spent in the pursuit of the scientific (and practical) study of agriculture and horticulture, which he had begun in 1786 with his experiments in grafting apple trees.

In 1795, through Payne, he met Sir Joseph Banks, who at once realized his great ability, corresponded with him freely, and encouraged him not only in his work but also to publish his findings.

In 1808 Payne gave up Downton, and Thomas Andrew moved in, to manage also the estate of 10,000 acres. It has been

* Knight blood (and money) also flowed in John Knight and his son, Sir Frederic, famed for their reclamation of much of Exmoor,[40] and Thomas Johnes (1748–1816), who combined aesthetic, scientific, and social attributes in the improvement of his desolate and uncivilized estate at Hafod, where he made a fine garden.

well said that his interest and intellect were equally devoted to such matters as the social problems of his time, the welfare of his workers, and the cultivation of Persian melons. Today he is recalled as a pioneer of genetics who failed to find the principles later disclosed by Mendel. But whereas Mendel and most other theoretical geneticists have little to show except publications, Knight's practical work added considerably to the improvement of plants and stock.

There seems to have been some odd, mysterious, and often tragic genius that haunted those with Knight blood. Johnes's heroic endeavours at Hafod were ended by fire, financial failure, and the death of his beloved daughter (a talented botanist and gardener greatly admired by Sir James Smith). Richard Payne is believed to have ended his own life; and Thomas Andrew's last years were saddened by the death of his son in a gun accident. From our point of view the great mystery is the disappearance of all his personal papers, which must have included the voluminous records of his scientific work, leaving only his contributions to learned journals, a book or two, and letters to Banks.

The titles of some of his published papers (which can be read today with interest, if only to observe, in the light of our present knowledge, the energy* and clear sense of direction with which he pursued his experiments and the acuity of his observations and conclusions) will give us some idea of the grandeur of their range.

Thus we have, on the physiological side, studies of the ascent of sap in trees, the formation of branches on trees, the supposed influence of pollen on the colours of seed coats of plants, the comparative influence of male and female parents on their progeny and that most important subject, the effects of different kinds of stock on the growth of scions.

These papers, like all else he wrote, were supported by observation and experiment, and it will be seen that he had already seized on topics that were later found to be of first importance.

Of his more horticultural titles one may show their diversity by mentioning those on the means of producing new and early

---

* In *A Treatise on the Culture of the Apple and Pear* (3rd edition, 1809) he writes of 20,000 apple-tree seedlings that he has raised experimentally.

fruits, on the construction of peach-houses, the prevention of mildew, and on the practical cultivation of such differing plants as the Guernsey lily, celery, walnut, and strawberry. He was, so far as I am aware, the first Englishman publicly to point out (in 1817) the advantages of heating greenhouses by the circulation of hot water rather than by heated air or steam.

He realized that a grafted tree was not a new entity but a mechanically produced continuation of an old one, and that the only way that improvement could be sought was from seed produced by hybridization, followed by careful selection. To this end he worked purposefully, and, with the (now lost) records of his activities, crossing different varieties. He was the first systematic plant breeder, as we now understand the term, and he worked on and produced improved kinds of apple, pear, cherry, nectarine, damson, potatoes, peas, and cabbage.

Knight's influence through his twenty-seven years of presidency of the Horticultural Society was profound. His work has been dealt with at some length because it indicates the new conception of horticulture as a practical science. (The financial failure of *The Temple of Flora*, issued by Dr. Robert John Thornton (c. 1768–1837), with its magnificent if fantastic plates, issued between 1797 and 1807, is surely also symbolic of the changed outlook. The text was pseudo-scientific, and it really belonged to an earlier age.)

In 1807 the various communications submitted to the Society were collected and published. In the first volume of *Transactions*, forty-one papers were included. Fifteen were contributed by Knight, Banks coming next with seven. The magnificence and good taste of these early volumes have never subsequently been excelled. Many of the beautiful coloured engravings, principally of fruit, were by William Hooker (1779–1832)—inventor of the green colour that bears his name. Other excellent artists were also employed (Plates XXII and XXIII).

In 1809 The Horticultural Society of London was granted its Charter.

Largely due to the energy of Joseph Sabine (1770–1837), a barrister and tax-inspector who was secretary* from 1816 to 1830, the Society began in 1818 an experimental garden,

* Until 1892 the secretaryship was an honorary post.

a mere 1½ acres at Kensington. In 1822 it was moved to a site of some 33 acres at Chiswick. At first Fellows brought interesting plants to the meetings at the Society's rooms, and, later, competitions were held there. These proved so popular that in 1833, at Lindley's suggestion, larger shows under canvas were held at Chiswick. A band was engaged, and refreshments were provided. So began the modern flower show.[41]

There are many other amateur gardeners belonging to this period who deserve mention. Most must be passed over, but the Hon. and Rev. William Herbert (1778–1847), son of the 1st Earl of Caernarvon, cannot be ignored. He was a brilliant classical scholar, and talented linguist, translating German, Danish, and Portuguese poems. His own epic, *Attila, or the Triumph of Christianity* (in twelve books), was published in 1838. He was also a talented naturalist. His ability as a draughtsman was such that after Sydenham Edwards had left *The Botanical Magazine* he drew a number of figures for that periodical; he also illustrated his own books. In 1814 he became Rector of Spofforth, in Yorkshire, where he remained until appointed Dean of Manchester in 1840.

He was, with Knight, one of the early scientific experimenters in hybridization. It is as a skilful cultivator and student of bulbous plants, rather than as a poet, that he is now remembered. He travelled to collect specimens himself in eastern Europe. His two great works are *Amaryllidaceae* of 1837, and his *History of the Species of Crocus*, which, almost finished a few days before his death, remains 'a masterly work and the foundation of all later classifications of the genus'.[42]

One would like also to have adequate space to discuss that interesting trio, Sir Abraham Hume (1749–1838), his wife Amelia (1751–1809), who was a pupil of Sir J. E. Smith (he dedicated his *Spiceligium* to her), and their gardener James Mean —of Wormleybury in Hertfordshire, early cultivators of Chinese plants, especially tree paeonies. The name lingers on in 'Hume's Blush' tea-scented China rose, a variety now extinct, but an important ancestor of the tea rose; and in *Humea elegans*, or 'Amaranth Feathers'.

John Russell, 6th Duke of Bedford (1766–1839), brought Woburn into the forefront once again, sponsoring such notable publications as James Ford's *Pinetum Woburnense* (1839). The comparatively short incursion of another duke into gardening in the grandest manner calls for mention. The Marquis of Blandford, George Spencer-Churchill (later 5th Duke of Marlborough), resided from 1800 on the estate of White Knights, Reading.[43] The place had already a reputation as a *ferme ornée*. Almost at once he began to collect plants of every description, building numerous hot-houses and exotic aquariums. He filled the large walled garden with hardy herbaceous plants, all planted in compartments sunk 18 inches below the surrounding turf so that the spectator might have a more commanding view of them from above. The choicest trees and shrubs were obtained. Soon his lavish schemes demanded more space, and several acres of wood were taken in. There, 'mixed with the oaks, hazels and beeches of the aboriginal wood' were planted, in lavish numbers, all the known species of magnolia, red and snake-barked maples, horse-chestnuts and buckeyes, strawberry trees, walnuts, American Judas trees, koelreuterias, gleditsias, stewartias—indeed, trees and shrubs in unending variety; elsewhere, azaleas and rhododendrons were planted to form huge banks of flowers. In the open parkland was formed a collection of all the thorns then known, and other specimen trees.

At that time many of the American trees and shrubs were still most expensive. But the Marquis never considered price; nor was he content with one specimen of a rarity. Lee, of the Hammersmith Nursery, told Loudon that he had sold him several plants of the same species when they were at twenty or even thirty guineas each and that in 1804 his account exceeded £15,000.

One of the sights was the magnolia wall, 145 feet long and 24 feet high, on which grew twenty-two plants of *Magnolia grandiflora* purchased in 1800 at 5 guineas each. There were also fountains, long arcades, covered seats, and rustic houses designed by J. B. Papworth.

It is not surprising that by 1816 the Marquis was in debt. White Knights was mortgaged for £85,000. Fortunately in 1817 he succeeded to the dukedom; though in 1838 Loudon wrote: 'he has still, however, the same taste for plants, and indulges it, as far as his limited resources will permit, in the pleasure-grounds of Blenheim, where His Grace at present resides'.

When circumstances forced him to move from a house into a

palace, he took with him Mr. Jones, who had been his gardener since operations were begun at White Knights. Mr. Jones was apparently still in charge at Blenheim when the duke died.

We have said enough about the great men of this period. A word or two must be spared for the almost anonymous working journeyman. *The Gardener's Magazine* of 1826 shows what he looked like—standing beside a fine specimen of *Yucca gloriosa* (Fig. 8). With a good employer his conditions were no doubt satisfactory—though Loudon frequently draws attention to his precarious position. In 1826 Loudon printed a letter from Archibald McNaughton:[44]

. . . I have been upwards of fifty years in the line. . . . I left Edinburgh in the year 1777, and, after working some time in Mr. Christopher Gray's nursery, I got a very good place with a Mr. Rolls, a great stockbroker, whose affairs went wrong after I had been six years with him, and I was obliged to quit. After going down to Scotland to see my friends, I came up again and got a place from Mr. Hare, then a seedsman in St. James's Street, to go to Mrs. Wilson at Putney, where I remained till her daughter married, when her husband having an aversion to Scotch servants, I was obliged to leave. Soon after this a fellow workman and myself attempted to set up a small nursery at Epsom . . . but after struggling hard for little more than two years, we were obliged to give up, after losing all we have saved, and almost £50, which my partner had borrowed from his aunt at Kinross, and which preyed so upon his mind, that I verily believe it was the cause of his death, which happened about a year afterwards at Windsor. . . .

Not liking to go into servitude again, I began jobbing on my own account, and a poor business I have found it ever since. When I first began, the highest wages I could get were 3s. a day, and obliged to find my own tools. I had a good deal of employment at first, partly from the circumstances of being a Scotchman. . . . My wife also took up a greengrocers shop about this time, and we did very well till we lost our only daughter, which obliged us to take in a maid-servant, who let in some fellows into the house one Sunday afternoon when we were at chapel, and took away all my savings, most of my wifes clothes, and concealed the bedding in an outhouse, to be taken away no doubt at night. . . . After doing nothing for some time, I began the jobbing again at Paddington, and my wife took in washing; but she falling ill, we removed to Hackney, on account of the air, where I have been ever since, being just able to gain a livelihood, by laying out the gardens for the new buildings going on in the neighbourhood. . . .

Fig. 8. Summer gardening costume of a journeyman gardener in the neighbourhood of London.
The hat is of straw, the jacket and trousers of
cotton. *The Gardener's Magazine*, 1826

During this period another significant change was taking place
in the gardener's world: modern education was entering into it.
Reviewing the events of 1836, Loudon wrote:[45]

The most remarkable circumstance which had occurred during the
past year was the decision of the Horticultural Society of London to
admit no young men into the garden as journeymen who had not some
school education, and to recommend no one from their gardens for

277

situations as head gardeners who had not been regularly examined in scientific knowledge and received a certificate stating their degree of proficiency.

The gardener's world was changing fast.

VOYAGES OF DISCOVERY

Of the many explorations made during the last years of the eighteenth and the early years of the nineteenth centuries none exceeded in its botanical, horticultural, and arboricultural consequences that of Captain George Vancouver (c. 1758–1798), which he described in his own record as *A Voyage of Discovery to the North Pacific Ocean and Round the World*. This great journey began in 1791 and included visits to the Cape, Australia, New Zealand, and Tahiti. Important as were the surveys and discoveries made there, from our point of view they were secondary to his sighting of the coast of California on 18th April 1792. Much of the rest of his voyage was spent in exploring and charting this then almost unexplored coast; indeed, little was then known of the whole of the North American continent west of the Rockies. Its significance for us is that much of its climate sufficiently resembles that of the British Isles to enable us to cultivate a high proportion of its rich vegetation, particularly trees, out of doors.

Vancouver eventually reached Britain in September 1795, after visiting a number of places on the western coast of South America. He took with him as surgeon Archibald Menzies (1754–1842), a very capable naturalist and botanist, and it is to him that we principally owe our first knowledge of the flora of the Californian coast.* Menzies made a considerable collection of herbarium material.

Little else was known of the flora of this area beyond a small collection of specimens made on the celebrated Lewis and Clark transcontinental journey, which the American botanist Frederick Pursh (1774–1820) had received and described in 1806.

One of the aims of the Horticultural Society was the introduction of plants from overseas: their first collectors in the early 1820s visited the ports of China, the West Indies, the Cape, and

---

* Menzies himself introduced little other than the monkey-puzzle tree (*Araucaria araucana*) from Chile. He obtained some seeds (the story that he had them as dessert and put them in his pocket is most improbable) which he sowed on board, and gave the resulting plants to Sir Joseph Banks.

the Zambezi, without any marked success. James Macrae (*d.* 1830)* was more effective on a journey to Brazil, Chile, the Galapagos Islands, and Peru, lasting from 1824 to 1826, whence he sent stove plants and a further supply of monkey-puzzle seeds.[46] But none of these early collectors was comparable with David Douglas (1799–1834),[47] whose fame rests on his journeys, requiring great courage and skill, to collect in those areas of California—and, indeed, well inland beyond them—whose treasures had been described by Menzies.

He was born at Scone, near Perth. While no more than a child he was apprenticed as a gardener to Lord Mansfield. In 1818 he went to work for Sir Robert Preston, of Valleyfield on the Forth. Here the foreman realized that young Douglas had an intelligence and enthusiasm for plants and natural history out of the ordinary, and he was allowed to make use of Sir Robert's excellent library. In 1820 he applied for work at the Botanic Garden at Glasgow University, where Dr. W. J. Hooker had just begun his distinguished period as professor. Hooker liked him, and took him on some of the journeys to the Western Highlands and Islands when collecting material for *Flora Scotica*.

In 1823 Douglas was recommended by Hooker and Stewart Murray, then Curator of the Glasgow garden, to Joseph Sabine, secretary of the Horticultural Society, as an explorer to collect seeds and herbarium material of new plants suitable for cultivation.† In the same year he made his first journey to the eastern United States. There he was largely concerned with horticulture, and visited many gardens. He also studied and wrote a paper on the oaks of eastern North America; one suspects this may have been influenced by the shortage of our own oak following the Napoleonic Wars.

The series of journeys that were to bring him fame began the following year when, on 26th July 1824, he sailed from Gravesend for the North Pacific coast, which he reached eight months and fourteen days later. He had carefully studied the records of Vancouver, Menzies, Lewis and Clarke, and Pursh before sailing. The surgeon on his ship was the adventurous naturalist, Dr. John

---

* He seems to have spent his life working in tropical gardens.

† It was originally intended that Douglas should go to China, but conditions there were too disturbed.[48] Sabine's brother, General Sir Edward (1788–1883), the eminent geographer, taught Douglas surveying.

Scouler (1804–1871), later to become professor of botany, zoology, and geology to the Royal Dublin Society.

From then until his tragic end on 13th July 1834 when, in Hawaii, he fell into a trap and was crushed to death by the wild bull that it had ensnared, Douglas devoted his life to exploration. To describe the adventures and extreme hardships of this adventurous young botanist, ornithologist, and, in his later trips, surveyor, is beyond our scope. He was temperamental and, though lionized on his visits to London, was inclined to be quarrelsome when the urgency of travel and exploration did not keep him occupied. He remained devoted to his early patrons, such as Hooker and Sabine, and when the latter was in 1830 forced to resign* from the secretaryship of the Horticultural Society, Douglas also severed his connection with that body.

Lately, in this country, the work of Douglas as a collector has been decried on account of the number of plants that he failed to observe or collect in what was virgin territory of immense botanical wealth. Against this, his work as explorer and surveyor is now held in considerable esteem in the United States, and one must recall that that most eminent American botanist, C. S. Sargent (1842–1927), wrote: 'No other collector has ever reaped such a harvest in America, or associated his name with so many plants.' It would, indeed, be difficult to find a garden in which one of the following of his introductions is not grown: *Acer circinatum, Mahonia aquifolium, Camassia esculenta, Clarkia elegans, Garrya elliptica, Limnanthes douglasii, Mimulus moschatus, Nemophila insignis, Symphoricarpus racemosus*, and that universal favourite, *Ribes sanguineum*.

'The great beauty of Californian vegetation,' Douglas wrote, 'is a species of taxodium [this was the old name for the redwood, *Sequoia sempervirens*] which gives the mountains a most peculiar, I was almost going to say awful, appearance, something which plainly tells us that we are not in Europe.'

Douglas by his Californian introductions not only gave us many plants loved and grown in every garden, but by means of the conifers that he brought (and those that he discovered only, leaving for succeeding collectors) he transformed the garden scene, and much of our landscape. In the course of a few decades

---

* Owing to embezzlement of funds by his assistant.

Douglas's own introductions—the Douglas fir, Monterey pine, Sitka spruce, *Abies grandis*, *A. nobilis*, and the western red cedar (*Thuja plicata*) and Lawson's cypress, introduced subsequently— completely altered our winter scene by adding the solidity of evergreens to the host of deciduous aliens—sycamore, walnut, horse-chestnut, sweet chestnut, robinia, laburnum, larch—which already thrived throughout our gardens and plantations.* How the gardeners of Restoration days would have applauded and welcomed his many additions to their much-prized 'greens'—and hardy ones at that!

In his day Douglas was the outstanding collector, though many other men were working. Practically nothing is known about most of them, generally the agents and collectors for wealthy gardeners. There were, too, introductions by members of government missions, such as that of Lord Macartney's Embassy to China in 1792–3.

Then enterprising sea captains brought plants. Organized use of those trading with China was made by John Reeves (1774–1856).[49] Born at West Ham and educated at Christ's Hospital, he entered a firm of tea-brokers. His aptitude was such that in 1808 he was appointed an inspector of tea in England for the East India Company; in 1812 he was sent as an inspector to China, where he remained, with but two holidays in England, until his retirement in 1831. He lived, and had an important garden, at Macao; apparently he had some influence on Chinese horticulture of the day, presumably because he introduced Western plants and methods. During the tea season he moved to Canton.

In 1815 a Committee was established by the Horticultural Society to acquire drawings of fruit and plants. Among the first paintings commissioned were those to be obtained through Reeves and made by Chinese artists of Chinese plants.† They are principally of cultivated forms of paeonies, chrysanthemums, camellias, and azaleas[51]—very different from the wild plants with

---

* Their economic importance in our forestry is even greater.

† Reeves was described as 'a correspondent and very active member of the Society'. (In 1819 there were sixty-four foreign and corresponding members resident outside the United Kindgom, 'scattered from China to Brazil and from St. Petersburg to New South Wales'.[50]) The artists worked, often in Reeves's house, under his supervision. The figures are therefore accurately drawn. Many are now in the British Museum and Lindley Library.

which Douglas was concerned. But it was the successful introduction of these that gave Reeves his fame. On obtaining specimens, he first established them thoroughly in pots, which in due course were carefully packed for the journey. Most important, he gained the goodwill of the ships' captains, who took great care to bring the plants home in safety—it was no doubt a rewarding sideline. In 1818 he sent his first consignment to the Horticultural Society. After having been housed temporarily at Chelsea the plants were set out in the new Chiswick gardens.

Another important collector was Karl Theodor Hartweg (1812-1871). For once in a way we have an exception to the usual story of the hard-working Scot coming to Kew or Chiswick as a young gardener and making good. Hartweg was a German, employed by the Horticultural Society as a clerk. In 1836 he was sent off to Mexico, Guatemala, and then to the equatorial Andes. He was away for six years and ten months, mostly spent in difficult and dangerous country. He was singularly careful and industrious, sending home large collections of orchids, cacti, and the Mexican pines. Except for a few of his orchids* and his tender pines, which can be grown only in the milder regions, none of his introductions, interesting as they were, have become common in British gardens.[52]

COMMERCIAL AND BOTANIC GARDENS

With the growth of population the need for vegetables, salads, and fruit increased. London, with the biggest market, had the greatest needs. Supplies came from Kent, by water, though a great deal was grown much closer at hand.

By now the nurseryman's trade in plants, shrubs, and trees had become an important one; here again a number of provincial firms of some size developed, but the centre of this remained in and around London. We have Middleton's description of the 1790s:[53]

From Kensington, through Hammersmith, Chiswick, Brentford, Isleworth and Twickenham, the land on both sides of the road, for seven miles in length, or a distance of ten miles from market, may be denominated the great fruit garden, north of the Thames,† for the

* Perhaps *Odontoglossum crispum* is the best known.
† There were also considerable gardens on the Surrey side, for about the same distance.

supply of London. In this manner, much of the ground in these parishes is cultivated. The pleasure-grounds and villas of some of the nobility, and wealthy commoners, comprise most of the remainder of this district.

The ground was stocked with apples, pears, cherries, plums, and walnuts; among them were grown raspberries, currants, strawberries, 'and all such herbs and shrubs as will sustain the drip of trees'.

Some of the gardens had walls, and these, according to their aspect, were planted with nectarines, peaches, apricots, and other fruit. Greenhouses and frame lights were little used for the production of crops. Instead, during autumn, banks about 3 feet high, sloping at about 45 degrees to the sun, were raised. On the slope endive was sown in September, and near the bottom, from October to Christmas, peas were sown.

A great asset to these Thames-side districts was the high water-table; an abundance of water was always to hand. There were numerous shallow wells from which the water was drawn by dipping a bucket hanging from a low balance-like arm, mounted and swivelling on a post at its centre, with a counter-poise weight at the other end.

In Essex there were many nursery gardens on the outskirts of London, and at Chelmsford and Colchester. The latter, with Purfleet, provided early peas. Around Ilford, Barking, and Plaistow immense quantities of early potatoes were grown for the London market. From Essex the London seedsmen obtained more seeds than from any other county; they were grown principally in the low land of the Thames estuary, around Coggeshall and Colchester, and in the Isle of Mersea. From the Marquis of Buckingham's woods at Gosfield Hall, Braintree, were procured 'most sorts of fir-tree seeds' that were sown in England.

Kent, of course, produced fruit—principally cherries and filberts, but all other kinds, from strawberries to walnuts. Vegetables were grown along the Thames estuary and, particularly in the Isle of Thanet, nurserymen's seeds were also produced. Here, as in Essex, even less glass was used than in the London district. Kent abounded in small farms and cottages, which were maintained in a higher state of cultivation and tidiness than in any other English county.[54]

Intensive gardening of a similar type was carried on elsewhere in or near towns; there is a description of the profitable cultivation of strawberries on a large scale near the big towns of Scotland in 1826;[55] they were grown along with gooseberries, currants, and raspberries.

It was during this period that the strawberry we know today —or something very near to it—came into existence. The strawberry of Tudor and Elizabethan times which, as we read in Tusser and other authors, was collected from the woods, was no more than the native wild strawberry, *Fragaria vesca*. The story of its improvement is this.[56] At an early stage the Hautbois strawberry, *F. moschata* (*elatior*), a little larger and with a musky flavour, was introduced from the Continent. In 1642 Jean Robin recorded the arrival of *F. virginiana* from eastern North America; this was still not much larger but of better flavour; its offspring were known as 'scarlets'.

The next development was the discovery in Chile by the Frenchman, Frézier, of a much larger, but whitish-fruited, species, *F. chiloensis*. This was established in cultivation around the Brest district in 1712. The introduction consisted of pistillate plants only, but, grown side by side with the older, pollen-bearing kinds, it produced fruit.

In 1762 a hybrid seedling from this, with *F. virginiana* as the pollen parent, arose at Cherbourg; it became known as the pine or ananas strawberry (*F.* × *ananassa*). This was still a poor thing by modern standards.

In 1806 Michael Keens, a nurseryman of Isleworth, raised many strawberries from seeds of the large white Chile. The fruit of the seedlings was mostly white, and with but little flavour, but there was one exception. This had red fruits so large (up to 1⅝ in. across) and of such beautiful appearance that the Horticultural Society ordered that an engraving of it be published.[57] The flavour, however, was 'not exccellent'. Keens continued raising seedlings from this, which he called 'Imperial', and on 3rd July exhibited to the Society his 'Keens' Seedling'. This was a sensational triumph, the first modern strawberry. The fine-coloured red fruit, held well above the ground, was nearly 2 in. in diameter, and the flavour now approached that of the earlier pine[58] (Plate XXII).

Middleton also tells us that

at Chelsea, Brompton, Kensington, Hackney, Dalston, Bow, and Mile End much ground is occupied by nurserymen, who spare no expense in collecting the choicest sort, and the greatest variety, of fruit trees, and ornamental shrubs and flowers, from every quarter of the globe, and which they cultivate in a high degree of perfection; the latter to a very great extent, and to an almost endless variety. . . .

Many of them are annually exported to Ireland, Spain, Portugal, Italy, Russia, and until lately, France; but there are still greater quantities sold for use in this country.

Several of these nurseries had long been in existence, carried on by descendants of the original owners, or by successors (London and Wise's Brompton Park establishment existed until 1835, though reduced to 30 acres, and in the occupation of Gray and Son). One of the most influential nurseries was that of Loddiges at Hackney. It had been founded by a German, John Busch, about the middle of the eighteenth century, but in 1771 he left England to enter the employ of the Empress Catherine of Russia. His successor was a Dutchman, Conrad Loddiges (1743–1826), who soon made a name for himself among the knowledgeable. In due course the firm became Conrad Loddiges & Sons. It received many American plants from John Bartram's son, William (1739–1823). The firm, continuing the tradition of earlier eighteenth-century nurserymen—some, such as Furber, and Fairchild's Society of Gardeners, have already been mentioned—published works partly as an advertisement. Loddiges's took the form of a periodical, *The Botanical Cabinet*, which was first issued in 1817 and concluded, after twenty volumes had been issued, with a complete index, in 1833. The page was small, and the numerous neat, coloured figures were produced by Conrad's son George (1784–1846) and George Cooke (1781–1834).* The text, while not without interest, is more appropriate to the *Cabinet* type of publication than to a botanical study.

In the pages of *The Botanical Cabinet* are to be found figures of many of the early orchids cultivated in Britain, for the Loddiges were among the first nurserymen to grow them on a commercial scale. This they began to do in about 1821; their *Orchideae in the Collection of C. Loddiges & Sons* of 1839 was one of the earliest

* The Loddiges and Cooke families intermarried; it seems probable that they, and other nurserymen in the district, were members of one of the nonconformist sects then flourishing in Hackney.[59]

orchid lists issued in this country.* George Loddiges was responsible for devising a satisfactory method of heating the greenhouses by steam.

The firm also became pre-eminent for their collection of trees and shrubs, obtained from all parts of the world. In 1818 they had above 1,200 species and varieties, exclusive of roses, azaleas, and willows. They were arranged alphabetically on the right-hand side of a walk forming a scroll like an Ionic volute, covering an area of 7 acres. *Zizyphus* came near the centre, which consisted of a sort of eye formed of several concentric beds, devoted to peat-loving plants. The collection of roses exceeded 1,500 sorts; that of willows was extensive, while the firm was also famed for its yuccas. The nursery was surrounded by walls on which was trained a collection of half-hardy trees and shrubs.† Loddiges put their stock of orchids up to auction in 1856, and shortly after ceased business.

The nursery of Richard Williams at Turnham Green should be mentioned. In 1817 the Horticultural Society's *Transactions* first described and illustrated in colour‡ his new pear, 'Williams' Bon Chrétien' (Plate XXIII). It had been raised by a schoolmaster at Aldermaston in Berkshire about 1770. By the end of the century it had emigrated to an estate in Massachusetts which in 1817 passed to Enoch Bartlett, who was unaware of its origin—hence its well-known synonym, 'Bartlett' pear.[60]

In the late 1820s Loudon considered Lee and Kennedy's Vineyard Nursery at Hammersmith was now 'unquestionably the first nursery in Britain, or rather in the world'.[61] James Lee had a number of triumphs, including the introduction of the fuchsia into commerce.§ One delightful account records that he saw a fuchsia plant in the window of a small house at Wapping. He went

* The collection and cultivation of tropical orchids first became popular in the latter part of the period now under review. John Lindley (1799–1865) was an early writer on the subject, beginning with his notes to Francis Bauer's *Illustrations of Orchidaceous Plants* (1830). Lindley, the son of a nurseryman at Catton in Norfolk, and a protégé of Banks, was Professor of Botany at University College, London (1829–60), and makes so many subsequent appearances in these pages that further biographical notes are unnecessary.

† J. C. Loudon, in giving this description in *Arboretum et Fruticetum Britannicum*, adds that many of the figures in that work were made from material supplied by Loddiges. At this period the collection of species and varieties of willow was fashionable.

‡ The plate is one of William Hooker's best.

§ The species involved was in all the early accounts described as *F. coccinea*—which is, in fact, very rare, and no doubt some commoner kind was concerned—presumably *F. magellanica*.

in and, after some bargaining, obtained it—a present from her sailor husband which the owner wished to keep—for eight guineas and two plants if he succeeded in increasing it. He raised about 300 cuttings, which brought the fashionable to his nursery, and made him a profit of £300. This story was first recorded by Shepherd, the curator of the Liverpool Botanic Garden, curiously enough in *The Lincoln Herald* of 4th November 1831.

Loudon,[62] however, gives a much more prosaic version. He tells us that the fuchsia was first introduced into Kew Gardens in 1788 by a Captain Firth. Soon afterwards Lee obtained a plant of it (there is no indication of the source), and found it could be multiplied with great ease. He produced many hundreds, which, by only showing two or three at a time, he sold for a guinea apiece.

Lee also supplied Archibald Menzies with a large stock of seeds considered suitable for the South Sea Isles on Vancouver's voyage of 1791–5.

In 1795 Lee died, Kennedy having predeceased him. The business was carried on by their sons, James Lee, junior, and John Kennedy (1759–1842), until 1817, when Lee acquired the whole business; by that time he had nurseries in other parts of the county on the land best suited to their particular purposes. He also had four sons, whom he intended to bring up to the business each in four departments: the seed business, the counting-house, greenhouse exotics and fruit trees, and fruit trees with hardy plants. This plan failed, however, for he died in 1824 when his son John was the only one old enough to be in the business of which he took charge.

Among their collectors was one engaged at the Cape of Good Hope for eight years in partnership with the Empress Josephine* to collect Cape heaths. Among their other interesting customers at this time were Thomas Jefferson (1743–1826), the architect-gardener President of the United States,† and, of course, the Marquis of Blandford at White Knights.

In the West Country, the firm of Lucombe & Pince, of

---

* Josephine Bonaparte (1763–1814) acquired Malmaison in 1798 where 'she amused herself in light studies in botany', spending vast sums on forming a collection of choice plants in a garden laid out by Berthoud in the English manner, assisted by a Mr. Hudson. Eminent botanists described the flowers and Pierre-Joseph Redouté (1759–1840) painted them.

† Visiting Britain in 1786, he considered English architecture unsatisfactory, but praised our gardens. He visited all those described by Whatley.[63]

St. Thomas, Exeter, was prominent. The original William Lucombe had been succeeded by his son, who in turn had been joined by old William's grandson, Robert Pince. A most energetic man, he corresponded with Loudon and other eminent horticulturists. The firm specialized in fuchsias, raising *Fuchsia exoniensis*, cinerarias, and other greenhouse plants and continued as a family business until the end of the nineteenth century.

Rather later, another dynasty of nurserymen was founded at Exeter, one that was far to excel the fame of Lucombe, and to become known throughout the world. John Veitch (1752–1839) travelled south from Jedburgh, and settled in the West Country as a landscape gardener; there are records of work he did in Somerset and Devon in about 1792.[64] He was engaged to carry out work for Sir Thomas Acland, at Killerton* near Broadclyst, and stayed on as land-steward. In 1808 he founded the Killerton Nursery at Budlake nearby; this it seems was then rather a remote spot and in 1832 he moved to land at Mount Radford. With him in partnership was his son, James (1772–1863). Clearly the business prospered, for the Royal Academy of 1839 displayed the designs made by one S. A. Grieg for a villa for James in the 'Old English style'.[65]

His son, another James (1815–1869), who did not long survive his father, was always known as James 'the younger'. At about the age of eighteen he went to London for two years, working under Chandler and Son at Vauxhall, and also studying the new fashion of orchid-growing with William Rollison† at Tooting. He returned to Exeter full of new ideas, and with a fine selection of orchids—the origin of the Veitchian collection which, in the later nineteenth and early twentieth centuries, brought international fame to the firm.

In 1838 the firm became James Veitch and Son, when James the younger became partner with his father. At this time he was a prime mover in developing the dahlia, now beginning to assume its glory, and the Exeter Dahlia Shows became noted. During this period also two young Cornish brothers, William and Thomas Lobb, were receiving their training with the firm. After occupying private posts, they returned later as collectors who brought even greater renown to the firm.

* A National Trust property.
† Famed also for his Cape heaths, and as the first Englishman to flower the Nankeen lily (*Lilium testaceum*) in 1842 which he had imported from the Continent.

But these events belong to the next part of the story, and we must make mention of two important, but less successful, ventures.

Chandler and Son (formerly Chandler and Buckingham), under whom Veitch studied, were joined by Loudon with Loddiges as first among the raisers of camellias;* during the season, a visit to their ground at Vauxhall was a fashionable jaunt. The son, Alfred (1804–1896), is today particularly remembered as the portrayer of that flower (as well as of Veitch's orchids) though he lived on to see it fall quite out of favour. In 1825 came *Camellia Brittanica*, with text by E. B. Buckingham, illustrating plants raised following crosses made in 1819. *Illustrations and Descriptions of . . . Camelliae* (1830–7) had forty-four plates and a text by William Beattie Booth (*c.* 1804–1874). Booth was a most able and intelligent gardener. A Scot, he was at Chiswick from 1824 to 1830, and then head gardener to Sir Charles Lemon at Carclew in Cornwall.† He left in 1858 to become assistant-secretary to the Horticultural Society.

Two interesting catalogues have been reprinted. One of about 1790 was published by 'John Fraser, Nursery and Seedsman, Sloane Square, Chelsea', and the other, of 1796, carries in addition to that address 'John and James Fraser, Planters, Charleston, South Carolina'.[66] John Fraser (1750–1811) arrived in London from Inverness-shire, when he was about twenty years old. He married and set up in hosiery and drapery at Paradise Row, Chelsea. At the neighbouring Physic Garden he became interested in plants, and determined to visit America. This he was able to do in 1780, when he sailed to Newfoundland—it is said thanks to the help of Sir J. E. Smith and William Aiton. He returned the same year. He made further visits to America in 1784, 1790, 1791, and 1795, latterly, as we have seen, with his son, and establishing some sort of headquarters in Charleston. In 1796 he visited Russia, with success, selling a collection of plants to the Empress Catherine. He returned there in 1797 and 1798, obtaining a commission to collect in America for Czar Paul. On his return, Czar Alexander now being on the throne, he suffered one of those strokes of bad luck which, according to contemporaries, dogged him, for the new Czar refused to acknowledge the appointment.

* They were also general nurserymen, with chrysanthemums and hollies as specialities.

† *See* p. 357.

Between 1806 and 1810 he was again in America, finally suffering a severe accident. He returned to die at Sloane Square.

Fraser's most important contribution to gardening was the introduction of *Rhododendron catawbiense*, a native of the mountains of the south-eastern United States. This plant, 'perhaps the most valuable evergreen shrub for ornament ever introduced', will stand 60 degrees of frost, and became an important element, particularly in the hands of the Waterer family,* in the series of hardy hybrid rhododendrons which now decorate our gardens and parks. Fraser did not collect it until 1809, so he never knew of its success.

Loudon considered that the catalogue of roses issued by Rivers and Son in 1836 represented the finest collection in the country.[67] The firm was founded by John Rivers at Sawbridgeworth, Hertfordshire, in 1725. Thomas Rivers (1798–1877), a descendant, from his youth specialized in roses. He was a cultured man, devoted to his plants, enterprising, and an unremitting worker. As this was a great period in the development of the rose, it is interesting to see what was offered in 1836.

The price for dwarfs ranged from 1s. to 3s. 6d. each, for standards 7s. 6d. to 10s. 6d. The roses were grouped as follows; Rivers's comments on each group are added:

Moss roses, 24 sorts. Some only suited to those who consider *all* moss roses beautiful. The newest and darkest crimson is Rouge du Luxembourg, a good grower. Most like a cool soil; what we should now call a heavy surface mulch is prescribed for the autumn.

Provence, or cabbage roses, 25 sorts. A distinct, excessively fragrant group, the large flowers on their slender stalks droop to give the bushes a pendulous and elegant appearance.

Perpetual, or autumnal roses, 50 sorts. 'The most desirable of all sections'; even more fragrant from September to November than in June. The soil cannot be too rich, and if the shoots are shortened to half their length in June, and the plants watered with manure water through July and August, they will bloom luxuriantly in autumn.

Hybrid China roses, 89 sorts. These include 'the most beautiful roses known'; George IV, raised from seed by T. Rivers, junr.,

* Of Knaphill Nursery, Woking. Michael Waterer was one of the first nurserymen (in 1832) to make effective use of the brilliant scarlet but tender Himalayan *Rhododendron arboreum* (introduced in 1817) by crossing it with the hardy *R. caucasicum*.

ranking among the best. All are robust, will grow in poor soils, and make the best standards.

Varieties of Rosa alba, 25 sorts. With glaucous foliage, and flowers, from white to peculiarly vivid rose-colour, of the most delicate hues imaginable.

Damask roses, 19 sorts. The original damask, very fragrant and thorny, 'still found in old gardens', makes a good stock for tender kinds, as it does not sucker.

Rosa gallica, or French roses, 99 sorts. Of trim and neat appearance, with erect growth, and well suited to small gardens, but too lumpish and stiff for standards. This section cannot be surpassed for brilliancy and diversity of colour; 'the spotted, striped and marbled roses in it are very novel and beautiful'.

Climbing roses, 53 sorts. The four sections are Ayrshire, Sempervirens, Multiflora, and Boursault; much is written about these, and those that cannot be so classified, such as *R. banksiae*. Mr. Rivers urges the use of the more vigorous kinds of *R. sempervirens* as an undergrowth in wildernesses* near the pleasure-ground.

Rosa indica, or China roses,† 70 sorts. 'From six to eight months in the year, form bright ornaments to our gardens', the robust forms making beautiful standards; all are hardy, some of the most brilliant colours, others white; some of the large doubles having a peculiar delicate blush.

Rosa indica odorata, or tea-scented China roses, 51 sorts. These are the China roses having a strong scent of tea; tender, they require the warm dewy nights of August and September to bring the flowers, fleeting in the hot sunshine of earlier months, to perfection.

Miniature, or dwarf, China roses, from Rosa lawranceana, 16 sorts. Some are known as 'fairy roses', their minute and vivid flowers having an excellent effect on rockwork; they, too, reach their perfection in the cool, autumnal months.

Noisette roses, 66 sorts. From 'a happy intermixture of the

---

* He himself trained Ayrshire roses over a steep bank by his house.

† According to Loudon[68] the first China rose was introduced, as *R. semperflorens*, in 1789 by Gilbert Slater, of Low Layton, Essex, 'a gentleman to whose memory a genus has not been devoted, though he was the means of introducing several of our finest plants'. This was one of the four 'stud' roses from which the 'China' group was raised.[69] Gilbert Slater (*d.* 1794) and his brother John, of Leytonstone and the India House, engaged James Main (*c.* 1775–1846) to visit China, in 1793–4, 'to get the double camellia'.[70] Main was later associated with Loudon's *Gardener's Magazine*.

China rose with the old musk'.* Very hardy, excellent as standards, some having as many as 60 to 80 flowers in one corymb.

L'Île de Bourbon roses, 38 sorts. 'A most beautiful section, scarcely known in this country . . . quite hardy, and bloom in greater perfection late in autumn than any other perpetual rose.'

Musk roses, 10 sorts, *Macartney roses and Rosa microphylla*, 10 sorts.†

Sweet briar, 17 sorts, Scotch roses, 27 sorts, and a number of unclassified kinds conclude the list.

This alone is evidence of the great increase in variety, as well as enthusiasm for the cultivation, of the rose during the late eighteenth and early nineteenth centuries, also shown by the considerable increase in literature on the subject at this period. It remains to be added that shortly after the publication of Rivers's lists, in 1837, Laffay, a rose-breeder of Auteuil, introduced the Hybrid Perpetual 'Princesse Hélène', the first of a race that was soon triumphant.

The mention of *Rosa lawranceana*‡ brings in the name of James Colvill, nurseryman and florist, of the King's Road Nursery, Chelsea. He raised this rose in 1805, and was also concerned in the early history of the China roses.[72] Colvill had a remarkable collection of plants, many of which were the subjects of plates and descriptions by Robert Sweet (1782–1835), who was employed by him and his son James from 1819 to 1831. Sweet's most important works include *The Geraniaceae* (1818–30), *Flora Australiaca* (1827–8), and *The Cistiniae* (1825–30). But, among his other publications, *The British Flower Garden*, with 712 coloured plates, published posthumously in 1838, deserves the epithet 'a treasure'. Sweet led an industrious but troubled life. In 1824 he was charged, apparently quite unjustly (for he was acquitted), with larceny of plants. On leaving Colvill, he set up as nurseryman on his own account, but in 1831 his mind gave way.[73]

Other important nurseries existed far from London. In Edin-

---

* The 'intermixture' was made by John Champneys, a wealthy rice planter of Charleston, U.S.A., in about 1802. Philippe Noisette, nurseryman, of Charleston, raised seedlings of this hybrid which he sent to his brother, Louis-Claude (1772–1849) in Paris, who was a distinguished and progressive horticulturist and agriculturist. Their father had been gardener to Louis XVIII at Brunoy.

† The origins of these groups have been well described by C. C. Hurst and Ann P. Wylie.[71]

‡ In honour of Miss Mary Lawrance (*fl.* 1790–1831; becoming Mrs. Kearse in 1830), teacher, but not very skilful exponent, of botanical drawing. Her *Collection of Roses from Nature* (1796–9), consisting of ninety hand-coloured etchings, are of some consequence to the historian of the rose. She also executed a series of passion-flowers.

burgh, Peter Lawson (*d.* 1820) founded the firm long known as Peter Lawson and Son, in 1770.

Firms were thriving near the villadom of the prospering new industrial areas. In 1831, for example, Loudon described[74] the nurseries of John Pope and Sons, Handsworth, a few miles outside Birmingham, as having the best collection of herbaceous plants apart from the Epsom Nursery,* including 'above a hundred species of rare articles'. We have already met the founder of the firm, Luke, growing tulips near Boulton and Watt's factory. His son John—who visited America to collect plants—had acquired additional ground† placed strategically beside Telford's London–Holyhead road some 4 miles past Birmingham, and opposite the seat of the first president of the Horticultural Society, the Earl of Dartmouth. His son, Alexander Pope (*d. c.* 1853), was now the enterprising member of the firm, contributing to the gardening press. Alexander's brother, Luke Linnaeus, an excellent self-taught botanical draughtsman, made drawings of all the more rare plants in the nursery as they came into flower.‡

One of Alexander's most interesting experiments was the cultivation in the open of plants then considered tender. In 1837, somewhat triumphantly, he published a list[76] of those which were thriving in the cold Staffordshire air; then, at the end of that year, came the great frost lasting far into 1838, and with scientific candour he recorded his losses:[77] *Banksia australis*, *Acacia dealbata* (which had reached 10 feet), *Pittosporum tobira*, *Eriobotrya japonica*, a hakea, and all kinds of cistus. Badly damaged, but reviving, were *Magnolia grandiflora*, a leptospermum, a greatly admired plant—but not layers (presumably snow-covered)—of *Rhododendron arboreum*, and small plants of *Arbutus unedo*—but not mature shrubs. Triumphant survivors were camellias and *Deutzia scabra*, which, it is rather surprising to learn, was considered tender. The firm also did much laying out of gardens—including the planting of the new urban cemeteries, and, it is believed, much work at Alton Towers.

    ·   ·   ·

* The Epsom Nursery was notable for raising the first English seedlings of *Mahonia aquifolium*. Introduced in 1823, and then described as 'perhaps the handsomest hardy evergreen we yet possess', plants for some years fetched 10 guineas each.[78]

  † Now occupied by West Bromwich Albion Football Club.

  ‡ In 1831 there were four quarto volumes; do they still exist? The firm supplied material of rare plants for plates in the works of Benjamin Maund and Mrs. Loudon.

The increase in the kinds of cultivated fruit of all sorts and a great number of synonyms caused a great deal of confusion. Apart from the Horticultural Society, several other persons deserve credit for their attempts to reduce the chaos. Nothing seems to be known of Leonard Phillipps, junr., other than what can be read in his catalogue. This was clearly popular, as a number of editions exist. The first appeared in 1812, and tells us that the author had collected on about 6 acres of ground by the Portsmouth Road, just beyond Vauxhall turnpike, as many varieties as he could find. These were named, and those interested were invited to come and study for themselves the characteristics of each kind. However, the existing synonymity soon defeated him, and he made a heroic decision: all existing names were abandoned and each tree given a new name, which was that of some notable person (thus the three quinces he lists become 'Peter Dionis', 'Sir William Davenant', and 'James Ferrand'). These new names were first published in his 1814 catalogue.

Phillipps's system was, of course, not generally followed, but he must have been held in high esteem, for he was awarded a gold medal by the Society of Arts, and from his catalogue it seems that he was responsible for putting some of T. A. Knight's new varieties into commerce.

John Lindley also came on the scene with three volumes of *The Pomological Magazine* (1828–30). One of the most expert pomologists was Hugh Ronalds (1759–1833), nurseryman and seedsman, of Brentford. In 1831 he summed up his life's experience of apples in *Pyrus Malus Brentfordiensis*, which was illustrated by forty-two coloured plates by his daughter Elizabeth, displaying no fewer than 179 different kinds. It is interesting to compare this greatly increased number with the earlier lists that have been quoted.

From nurserymen we must turn to those other repositories of professional horticulture, botanic gardens. Kew had maintained its great reputation until the death of George III and Banks, both in 1820. After that, as has already been mentioned, the establishment had been officially cold-shouldered.

Those who worked, mostly behind the scenes, to effect improvement, did not achieve success in arresting the steady decline.[78] But this was to follow shortly, as will be seen in our next section.

In Scotland, however, things were happier. In 1789, under the direction of the Regius Keeper, Dr. John Hope (1725–1786), the Edinburgh Botanic Garden was moved to Haddington Place, and laid out in a form related to the Linnaean system. The greenhouses on the new site were of considerable size, and a notable feature of the garden.

With the increased introduction of plants further space became necessary, and in 1823 the collection was moved to its present situation. The hero of this occasion was the then curator, William McNab (1780–1848), who had returned north from Kew, and was extremely successful in transferring trees, shrubs, and plants with little loss.[79]*

In 1790, with a grant from the Irish Parliament to the Dublin Society, the Irish National Botanic Garden was formed at Glasnevin on 16 acres of ground. The first curator was John Underwood (*fl.* 1780–1834), who had been recommended by William Curtis. In 1834 the energy of Ninian Nevin (1799–1879), his successor, brought further improvements. He had previously come from Scotland to the gardens at Phoenix Park, which in a decade he made famous. But the fame of Glasnevin is linked with the Moore family, David Moore (1807–1879) succeeding Nevin in 1838, and not relinquishing his post until forty years later, when he was succeeded by his son. David became one of the most notable botanist-gardeners in Europe.[80] He had been foreman at Trinity College, Dublin, from 1829 to 1834, and then Botanist to the Ordnance Survey of Ireland.

Elsewhere, with the increasing fashion for education, public-spirited bodies raised funds to establish botanic gardens. Owing to the energies of that remarkable and versatile man, William Roscoe (1753–1831), patron and practitioner of the arts and sciences, the Liverpool Botanic Garden was formed in 1803. His own *Monandrian Plants*, illustrated by lithographs, appeared between 1824 and 1828; Sir J. E. Smith founded the genus *Roscoea* in his honour. The first curator was John Shepherd (*c.* 1764–1836), a knowledgeable and respected man.

In Cambridge, the central situation of the Botanic Garden having now become unsuitable, 40 acres of land to the south of

---

* Researches made by R. E. Cooper (curator 1934) show that McNab designed the garden on the principle of a Constable landscape.

the city were acquired in 1831, and, under the Professor of Botany, the Rev. John Henslow (1796–1861), a new garden was rather slowly constructed.[81]

Other provincial gardens came into being. In 1829 the Birmingham Botanical and Horticultural Society was formed and began operations under the presidency of the 4th Earl of Dartmouth. J. C. Loudon prepared plans in 1831 (owing to shortage of money, they were not completely executed) and David Cameron (c. 1787–1848) was appointed superintendent. Loudon was also concerned with designing the Arboretum at Derby in 1840; this was a gift from Joseph Strutt (1765–1844), the wealthy son of an inventive-minded spinner.

Other similar botanic gardens concerned largely with horticulture, founded by societies and private subscriptions, but brought into being primarily owing to the enthusiasm of a single individual, were formed at Cork (1809), Hull (1812), and Bury St. Edmunds (1819);[82] there were no doubt others.

At Glasgow University, William Jackson Hooker, its Professor of Botany from 1820 to 1840, was making the small botanic garden a place of considerable consequence, and a stepping-stone by which he later moved to a position of the highest eminence in scientific horticulture.[83]

THE ROCKERY

We have seen how William Forsyth raised a rockery in the Chelsea Physic Garden. This was, one assumes, principally of scientific interest. It is difficult to say when the aesthetic and even spiritual attributes of rockwork and mountain plants were developed. There were specialists in rockwork and grotto-making in Le Nôtre's day; Pope's enthusiasm for his grotto had a mingling of the aesthetic and the scientific, but it was scarcely the same kind of emotion that elevates the alpine enthusiast of today.

Feelings akin to this were coming into being in the late eighteenth century. William Beckford (1760–1844), for example, wrote of the Cintra Mountains in 1787:

Amidst the crevices of the mouldering walls, and particularly in the vault of a cistern . . . I noticed some capillaries and polypodiums of infinite delicacy; and on a little flat space before the convent a numerous tribe of pinks, gentians and other alpine plants, fanned and invigorated by the pure mountain air. These refreshing breezes, impregnated with the perfume of innumerable aromatic herbs and flowers, seemed to infuse new life into my veins, and, with it, an almost irresistable impulse to fall down and worship in this vast temple of nature the source and cause of existence.[84]

In 1795 he began his 'ornamental building which should have the appearance of a convent, be partly in ruins, and yet contain some habitable apartments', which became the huge gothick extravaganza that was Fonthill. It is not surprising to learn that, as part of his extensive garden and planting,* he made a considerable alpine garden in a quarry.

As the nineteenth century progressed, the rockery was more seriously considered. In 1831 *The Gardener's Magazine*[85] carried *An Essay on Rockwork in Garden Scenery* by 'R.T.P.':†

The use of rockwork in gardens may either be as a distinct feature; as a situation for cultivating plants; as a screen for concealing objects; or for two, or more, or all of these purposes combined. As the expense of collecting large stones is considerable, rockworks, in general, are made on too small a scale, and more resemble heaps of stones, with the interstices filled with weeds, than the protrusion from the soil of a portion of real rock, decorated with ornamental plants. In a grand place, every thing ought to be on a grand scale; and few objects produce a more striking effect than immense masses of stone, piled together in such a way as at once to give a particular character of rocky mass, and to form a proper nidus for valuable plants.

The grand difficulty in rockwork is to form and maintain a particular character or style in the disposition of the masses; and the only way to conquer this difficulty is to observe the manner in which masses of rock are disposed in nature, or rather in such natural scenes as are admired by men of taste, and especially painters. And here the study of geology will assist both the painter and gardener.

Then follows a description of a typical rockery: 'a goodly assemblage of large stones, and perhaps old roots and trunks of trees, lying loosely together on a mound of earth'—no one having thought to have placed them as they were in nature. Those who have not the confidence to tackle the construction of a rockery

* His gardeners, Milne and Vincent, were clearly men of intelligence and learning; the former corresponded with Sir J. E. Smith.[85]
† Possibly R. T. Pince, a regular contributor, of Lucombe and Pince, Exeter.

on natural lines are advised to take 'the advice of a landscape-painter who has been accustomed to rocky countries. Of all men that we know, the fittest for this purpose is, or was some twenty years ago, Mr. Nasmyth of Edinburgh'.*

A note is added by 'J.D.' for 'the Conductor' of the magazine which gives us a rather more precise description of the typical rockeries of the period. 'J.D.' adds: 'The hillock of flints and fused bricks, usual in gardens, correspond so ill to the terms "rock", "rock-work", and "rockery", that a new term would not be amiss for them.' He mentions that Benjamin Maund† had suggested 'lapideum' as a new term for such features, adding that in Staffordshire and Cheshire they were called 'stoneries'. He also tells us that the rockery in Liverpool Botanic Gardens was said to be an assemblage of foreign rocks used as ballast for ships, obtained by 'sea-faring gentlemen' devoted to the welfare of that garden, and that the rockery at Syon House was composed of large blocks of granite.

We are fortunate in having contemporary descriptions and illustrations of two very different rock gardens built purposively and on a considerable scale. The first looks to our eyes somewhat fantastic.[87] It was at Hoole House, on the level ground some two miles from Chester on the road to Liverpool (Plate XXIV). The rockwork was designed to make a striking contrast to a large, smooth lawn studded with regular round beds. The artist who designed this (and from the patience, time, and thought she brought to the work she deserved that title) was Lady Broughton.

The design was a small model of the mountains of Savoy with the valley of Chamonix. It took some six or eight years to complete; rain washed away the soil, frosts swelled the stones and the rockwork collapsed. It was built on a base of local red sandstone, with other materials collected chiefly from Wales. But by 1838 it was covered by creeping and alpine plants‡—all except that part representing La Mer de Glace, made from grey limestone, quartz, and spar, with broken fragments of white

---

* Alexander Nasmyth (*see* p. 249).

† Of Bromsgrove, Worcestershire (1790–1864), joint editor with the Rev. J. S. Henslow of *The Botanist*, a journal 'consisting of highly finished representations of tender and hardy ornamental plants', which was issued in 1837–46, and author of *The Botanic Garden*, 1850–1.

‡ They were enumerated; and were much as one would expect to find in a good rock garden today—apart, of course, from subsequent introductions.

marble to represent snow. The height and extent of this remarkable achievement are, in the terms of modern rockeries, staggering. It surrounded three sides of the lawn, with an outer perimeter of over 150 yards.

Hoole may seem reprehensible to the modern alpine gardener. But he would approve of another made at about the same time; though it is true that when Loudon described it in 1839 he remarked that it was 'totally different from anything else of the kind in England'.[88] It was the principal feature of the gardens at Redleaf, near Penshurst, the seat of William Wells who, in his day, had some repute as an amateur artist and patron of the arts; Wells himself designed the place. The scenery in which this was set was fortunate in being naturally much like a Brown landscape, with appropriate clumps of trees. The rockery was, in fact, a large lawn set in the heart of the garden, just below a natural ridge that obscured it from the house. On excavation, this ridge was found to be caused by rock just under the surface. Mr. Wells took his cue from this, exposing and turning it in a rocky bank, and elsewhere on the lawn making beds and placing rocks to simulate further outcrops of the same material. The construction of these showed an understanding of the formation of artificial rockwork that would do credit to the modern alpine enthusiast. In the more rocky part the beds were linked by a winding stone path.

Mr. Wells planted many choice conifers and hardy shrubs in the open lawn-like parts, and in the beds and rockwork a large variety of plants, a number of which, however, would not meet with the approval of the modern purist—though they must have made a very gay display, not inappropriate to the setting (Plate XXIV).

THE MECHANICAL ARTS

The prodigious advance during the late eighteenth and early nineteenth centuries in the techniques of utilizing iron had, of course, a revolutionary effect on horticultural practice. First, one would suggest, came its application to structural work—affecting alike the building of greenhouses and the provision of cast-iron 'arched frames for bestriding walks', and other similar devices on which to train fruit and climbers; cast-iron garden seats, often of most intricate design, became popular (Plate XXV).

In 1805 one of Knight's remarks 'relative to the objectives the Horticultural Society have in view' pointed out that the construction of forcing houses had been neglected. A number of new designs were soon forthcoming and communicated to the Society; some were more ingenious than practical. Commercial production of greenhouses was stimulated. Birmingham firms manufacturing metallic and copper sashes were eager to make use of these improvements. Richards and Jones, 'patent metallic hot house manufacturers', were early in the field; Thomas Clark,* formerly of Jones and Clark, Lionel Street, was soon leading it. His first orders, with working drawings, taken in 1818, still exist. An engraving published in 1830 of a conservatory he built at The Grange, Hampshire, gives an idea of the developments that had taken place. Clark supplied hot-houses to many of the great gardens of the day—eventually to the queen at Osborne and Frogmore.[89]

A number of the new designs were based on a more scientific methods of trapping the sun. But the systems of artificial heating remained fundamentally unaltered. Heat was provided by fermentation beds, or by passing the products of combustion through a flue.

Loudon as late as 1826 observed[90] that 'the most general mode of heating hot-houses is by fires and smoke flues'. He does briefly mention the use of high-pressure steam. Some of these systems had been described in the Horticultural Society's *Transactions*, but they do not seem to have progressed much beyond the experimental stage. George Loddiges at Hackney had evolved a system that worked, and a firm named Bailey also supplied steam-heating. The disadvantages at that time of steam under pressure need not be enumerated; Thomas Knight, in 1817, commenting upon a paper describing a method of heating by blowing it both through flues and out into the house, pointed out that the circulation of hot water would overcome them.[91]

In 1826 William Whale read a paper to the Horticultural Society[92] describing a circulating hot-water system first used by his employer, Anthony Bacon, on his estate at Aberaman, Glamorgan, in 1822. He added that at about the same time W.

* Henry Hope later joined Clark; the firm in due course became Henry Hope & Sons Ltd. The horticultural business was given up.

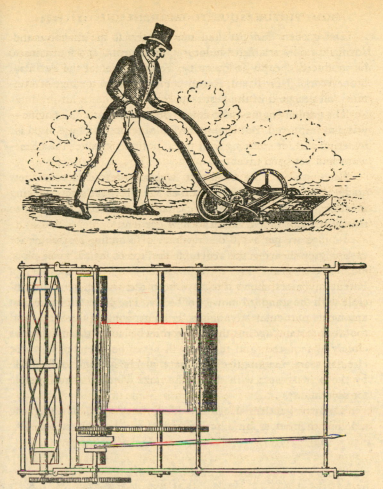

FIG. 9. Budding's mowing machine illustrated in *The Gardener's Magazine*, 1832

Atkinson had independently devised a similar method.* This was the principle soon to become universal. Atkinson seems at first to have been primarily responsible for further developments. By the late 1830s several makes of boiler were being advertised.

* According to Charles Hood's *A Practical Treatise on Warming Buildings by Water* (1837), domestic hot-water heating had been used in France prior to the Revolution. Matthew Boulton, who died in 1809, had it in his home at Soho.

The garden designer had new materials at his command. Artificial stones enabled 'sculpture', ornaments, and fountains to be produced cheaply in quantity; Felix Austin, of the Artificial Stone Works, New Road, Regent's Park, offered a range of fountains, all designed in the best taste.[93]

The garden engine—also convertible for use as a fire-engine—was also improved. But it remained a laborious machine, used for watering and for spraying fruit trees; nothing stronger than lime-wash had yet been invented.

Each issue of *The Gardener's Magazine* described some new 'gadget', but nothing so important as Mr. Ferrabee's new mowing machine, first mentioned quite casually in 1831 in a reference to the Surrey Zoological Society's new gardens.

In 1832 we get a full description* of 'Budding's machine for cropping or shearing the vegetable surface of lawns, grass plots, etc.'. The diagram (Fig. 9), reproduced from the Repository of Patent Inventors, shows it to have been identical in general principle with the standard mowers of today. The patentee wrote that among its particular advantages 'grass growing in the shade and too weak to stand against the scythe, may be cut by this machine as closely as required; and the eye will never be offended by those circular sears, inequalities, and bare places so commonly made by the best mowers with the scythe, and which continue visible for several days . . .'

'Country gentlemen,' it is added, 'may find, in using the machine themselves, an amusing, useful and healthy exercise.'[94]

---

* Written in September 1831, its appearance was delayed, and other quite trivial inventions given precedence. The design was based on that of a machine used to cut the pile on certain cloths.

SEVEN

The Glorious Victorians
1841–1882

THE SUCCESS OF JOSEPH PAXTON

THE year 1841 saw the first publication of *The Gardener's Chronicle*. It was described as 'a stamped newspaper of rural economy and general news', though in the 'first place a weekly record of everything that bears upon horticulture or garden botany'. The horticultural part was edited by Professor Lindley, but the presiding genius in this undertaking—the first weekly gardening newspaper—was Joseph Paxton, his fellow-founder being Bradley, the publisher of *Punch*.

In this important journal we have the first of the modern weekly gardening papers. As advertising now began to play a considerable part in their success, we may consider the advertisements in this first issue.

Lucombe, Pince & Co., of Exeter, offered a splendid new and most hardy rose, *R. devoniensis*, with camellia-like flowers, of which they had the whole stock. H. Youell, of Woolwich, advertised orchids; Salter and Wheeler, of the Victoria Nursery, Bath, a new *Ipomoea*. Then there were announcements of galvanic plant protectors for dahlias, a patent portable fire-engine (which could, of course, also be used for spraying), Cottam's patent boiler, and the New Zealand Company offering allotments of land for the settlement of New Zealand.

One of the principal articles was, appropriately, on the British oaks.

Another weekly, on a more modest scale—as its title implies—was *The Cottage Gardener*, founded and edited by George William

Johnson (1802–1886), which first appeared in 1848. Johnson was a barrister. In 1829 he had published *A History of Gardening in England*, the first book devoted entirely to the subject, and in 1847 *The Cottage Gardener's Dictionary*, which he edited. This, a much handier volume than Loudon's massive work, went through several editions, the epithet 'cottage' shortly being dropped.

The Gardener's Chronicle has outlived its rivals; its solid qualities have persisted when other periodicals, illuminated only by the genius of their founders, have run their span. *The Gardener's Magazine* lasted till 1843, having already suffered from two of Paxton's earlier ventures, *The Horticultural Register*, which first appeared in 1831, and *Paxton's Magazine of Botany*, begun in 1834. This last had, as a bait, rather poor colour plates. The title was misleading, for it was essentially a popular horticultural journal in which 'the author has studiously made everything as plain and intelligible as possible'.*

The career of Paxton, thanks to his eminence in public affairs and a masterly life by his grand-daughter,[1] is well known. Born of humble parents in 1801, after a youth of hardship, during which he educated himself, he obtained work at the Horticultural Society's gardens at Chiswick, becoming foreman of the Arboretum in 1824. The gardens were leased from William George Spencer Cavendish, 6th Duke of Devonshire (1790–1858). The Duke had his own private doorway into them from Chiswick House. In passing through he became acquainted with the stocky young foreman (whose ambitions then centred on emigration to America). In 1826 the Duke found himself, on the eve of a visit to Russia, without a head gardener at his great Chatsworth estate. The post was offered, more or less on the spur of the moment, to young Paxton, at 25*s.* a week—with a cottage. Only twelve years later he was asked to be head gardener at Windsor Castle at £1,000 a year, but he was faithful to the Duke. That was a measure of his success, and an indication of his character.

The Chatsworth gardens were in a bad state; lately the dukes, fabulously wealthy though they were, had lacked the interest of their predecessors who had made them. The 6th Duke had enthusiasm neither for gardening nor plants. Paxton changed all

* Yet it should be remarked that Paxton himself was no inconsiderable botanist.

that.* The gardens soon became celebrated, particularly for their greenhouses.

Loudon visited Chatsworth in April 1831. He was critical. He began his subsequent description of the great house and its gardens[2] ominously. 'Chatsworth has always appeared to us an unsatisfactory place . . .', and after pointing out possible improvements, concluded, 'we protest against the same edging to flower-beds as are adopted in common shrubberies, but we shall defer further objections and suggestions till we have leisure thoroughly to explain them'.

Paxton, he observes, was 'not at home', had he been, possibly the account would have been of a rather different tone. However, Loudon adds, 'all the neighbouring gardeners agree in stating that he has improved the garden department at Chatsworth, and we are happy in adding our testimony to this effect'.

Later, Loudon came to know Paxton and succumbed to his charm, ability, and enthusiasm. The two became most friendly, and when Loudon died Paxton was one of those who helped his widow.

Paxton, as he gradually inspired the Duke with a passion for horticulture, at the same time became his Admirable Crichton. He travelled the Continent with him as a sort of personal attaché. One December night he turned Chatsworth into a flowering garden of lights for the Queen and her consort. He laid out anew the ducal village of Edensor on model lines, the architect being John Robertson. Then he became a great man in his own right: Member of Parliament, director of railways, designer of the famed glass hall for the 1851 Exhibition, and the engineer of its transference to Sydenham (where he now lived) as the Crystal Palace.

In 1858 Sir Joseph (he was knighted in 1851) organized with unapproachable efficiency the magnificent funeral rites of his master, severed his connections with Chatsworth, and, supremely successful, gradually lost interest in life. In May 1865, just thirty-nine years after he had made his first entrance to Chatsworth by climbing over the wall (he arrived there at half past four in the morning), he made his last public appear-

---

* The Duke became President of the Horticultural Society in 1839. He held the post until 1857. In 1834 a volume of *The Botanical Magazine* was dedicated to him.

ance. It was at a flower show, in a wheeled chair. Soon after, he died. So ended the triumphant career of a man of almost infinite capabilities, blessed with charm and integrity, blessed in his wife and family life, yet, it is said, finally a somewhat unhappy man.

We must consider him briefly as a gardener only. At Chatsworth he made one of the famous gardens of Europe. Those as wealthy as the Duke strove to outdo him, but generally failed. Chatsworth had the most magnificent of all conservatories. Paxton designed it. Work began in 1836. It was 277 feet long and 123 feet wide. Its 75,000 square feet of glass covered exactly 1 acre. The ridge of the roof was 67 feet off the ground (a coach and horses could drive through the building). Rockwork concealed a stairway up which visitors could climb to gaze on the exotic display below. Construction, heating, ventilation, drainage, were all ingeniously designed and highly efficient. (It was pulled down in 1920.)

Again it was at Chatsworth that, on 2nd November 1849, at about 2 p.m., the water-lily *Victoria amazonica*,* with leaves so big that they could carry a child, opened its flowers under cultivation for the first time. The success was sensational; nothing like it had been known before—and the triumph was Paxton's.[3] He built a new house there specially so that it might cover the big expanse of water required; from its design he evolved the biggest glasshouse ever—the one that housed the 1851 Exhibition.

Success, it is true, did not follow the Duke's adventures in plant introduction. Paxton selected an intelligent young gardener from Chatsworth, John Gibson, and in 1835 sent him to India, where botany then centred on Dr. Nathaniel Wallich† (1786–1854) and the Calcutta Botanical Garden. Gibson arrived there when one of its greatest treasures, *Amherstia nobilis*, a sacred tree of the Burmah teak forests, was opening its geranium-red flowers for the first time in cultivation. The Duke and Paxton instructed Gibson to obtain this rarity, and after two years he returned with two specimens, one of which was dead. The survivor was installed

---

* This plant was long known as *Victoria regia*, after the Queen (who graciously accepted a flower and leaf handed to her by Paxton). A good deal of credit is due to Sir W. J. Hooker of Kew, who obtained the seed and raised the seedling that went to Chatsworth.

† A Danish surgeon; he was superintendent of the garden from 1815 to 1841.

in the Painted Room at Devonshire House—Paxton arrived one morning to find the Duke breakfasting beside it—so that all the cognoscenti of the gardening world might see it. Afterwards Paxton himself carried the tree to Chatsworth, where it grew, but failed to flower. (The honour went to Mrs. Lawrence, now of Ealing Park, but not till twelve years later.) Gibson also brought home many orchids, and in turn enriched the Calcutta Garden with a choice collection of rarities from Chatsworth.

The Duke's other plant-collecting venture ended in tragedy. He joined in a syndicate that sent two other young Chatsworth gardeners, Peter Banks and Robert Wallace, to work over the ground covered by Douglas where, it was realized, much more remained to be done. The expedition was planned by Paxton with his usual care. The two reached Canada, and the expedition promised well. In 1839 it ended abruptly, when they were drowned in a boating accident on the Columbia River. But these were among the few setbacks in a triumphant—and also domestically happy—career.

We must surely ask what were Paxton's failings. For, as time passes, his reputation as gardener and botanist recedes, while that of Loudon, whom he so soon outshone and eclipsed, advances. Is it that there is something seriously lacking from a doctrine whose aim is ever 'bigger and better', with ever-increasing efficiency, which Paxton so warmly espoused?

Is there no significance in the fact that in 1851, the Great Exhibition year, the year of Paxton's biggest glass-house on record, and of his knighthood, Loudon's 'greatest natural genius ever' published the first volume of *The Stones of Venice*?

This slogan, 'bigger and better', with not much else (certainly little aesthetic sensibility) is indeed the key to the period that we are now considering. Most that occurred—and much of it was valuable—was little more than a thoughtless aggrandizement of the achievements of the late eighteenth and early nineteenth centuries. When Mrs. Lawrence moved from her villa to Ealing Park there was no change other than an increase in the profusion of ornament, a magnification of the 'effect perfectly dazzling', the successful cultivation and flowering of more and more difficult exotic subjects.

Similarly, the mechanization of horticulture developed

rapidly, the rate of collection and introduction of plants from overseas increased, as did the raising of new kinds of fruits and plants.

ARCHITECTURAL AND GARDENESQUE

Charles M'Intosh (1794–1864) published his two-volume encyclopaedic *The Book of the Garden* in 1853. He had been gardener at Claremont and later at Dalkeith; he had great practical knowledge and wrote with authority on what was then meeting with approval in the best circles.

He analyses and divides the different styles of gardening much more closely than Loudon, but it is clear that his preference is, at least around large houses, for 'the modern good taste of architectural gardening'. In practice, too, it seems clear from his book that the most popular style was the gardenesque, 'a mixed style' in which 'common as well as exotic trees, shrubs and plants are introduced with architecture, sculpture, etc.' (Plate XXVI).

The most typical, and probably the most thoughtful, garden designer of this period was William Andrews Nesfield (1793–1881). He was the son of the rector of Brancepeth, Durham, and had an engineer's training at Woolwich. An obituary notice refers to him as 'Lieutenant' Nesfield, and relates that he fought at San Sebastian in the 95th Regiment, when he can only have been twenty, and afterwards in the battles of the Pyrenees; he was also in Canada—at the siege of Fort Erie and the defence of Chippewa.

In 1816 he retired on half pay and devoted himself to painting; he was friendly with Turner and other 'moderns' of the period. His specialities were waterfalls and seascapes. Some of these were painted on the Continent, but more usually he worked in Wales or northern Britain. Ruskin urged the reader of *Modern Painters* to stand by his 'Fall of Schaffhausen' for half an hour, observing it acutely: you will—he remarks—then find that there is something more in nature than has been given by Ruisdael; at the moment no modern artist may come to mind, but 'you will remember, or ought to remember, Nesfield' for his 'management of the changeful veil of spray or mist', the justness of his curves and contours—and, indeed, much else.

In 1840 we have an illustrated description of his house and

garden at Fortis Green, Muswell Hill.[4] It was one of two villas designed by Anthony Salvin (1799–1881), who had married Nesfield's sister. The houses, though somewhat Italianiate, were quite plain, of convenient layout, and bore no resemblance to Salvin's towering piles in the medieval manner. Nesfield was responsible for the layout of the gardens of both these adjoining villas. This was done in a complementary manner: where ground was planted thickly in one villa it was planted thinly in the other, and vice versa, so that each garden (of 1¼ acres) aided the other in creating a general effect. The gardens ended in a field, divided into two by a wire fence at right angles to the central axis, and so giving, with its trees, a sense of spaciousness. Over the fields were seen the woods of the Earl of Mansfield's grounds at Kenwood,* and Highgate Church. The design made the best of this prospect; Nesfield's garden looked over a fairly simple parterre towards it, with bands of trees and shrubs serpentining on either side. The Italianate air of the house and its surroundings, treated geometrically, gradually merged into the country-like view. In the field Nesfield kept sheep rather than cows, as requiring less looking after (his family was small, and the district abounded in dairy farms), and also because they enhanced the view. Compared with the Lawrencian villa, Nesfield's design was refined and practically without architectural ornament; nor could the effect have been dazzling.

Within a few years Nesfield had achieved some standing as a garden designer. In 1845 the pleasure-grounds at Kew—that part of the estate outside the then Botanic Garden, and still used for sport—was placed under Sir William Hooker, Director of the gardens. Wooded and covered with rough scrub, it was proposed to form there a national arboretum. Nesfield was called in and made the original plan, which he developed during the next few years. When the position of the Palm House (completed in 1848) was decided it was made the central pivot; he opened the great Syon vista towards it in 1851 and was responsible, too, for the Broad Walk and the Pagoda vista.[6]

In its broad lines Nesfield's plan has been developed and remains unaltered to this day, a tribute to his ability and fore-

* Loudon considered Kenwood 'beyond all question, the finest country residence in the suburbs of London, in point of natural beauty of the ground and wood, and in point also of the main features of art'.[8]

sight. Yet the design he was commissioned to make for the immediate vicinity of the Palm House, a design in geometric manner, long since disappeared, has been not unjustly described as puerile.

He contributed something in the same manner to the Horticultural Society's gardens at Kensington. These, covering 22½ acres, stood near the site of the present Albert Hall, on land which must have been part of London and Wise's Brompton Park Nursery. The somewhat complex story of their origin—they were part of a scheme to house works of art from the 1851 Exhibition— need not be discussed here; they were begun in 1858 and opened on 5th June 1861* by the Prince Consort, who described them as 'an attempt at least to reunite the science and art of gardening to the sister arts of architecture, sculpture and painting' (Plate XXVI).

'The modern good taste of architectural gardening' upon which M'Intosh had remarked was here displayed unrelievedly. The garden was surrounded by arcades: the Lateran arcade, 'Byzantian in tone', by Captain Fowke; the Milanese arcade, the style borrowed from Milanese brickwork, by Mr. Sidney Smirke, R.A.; an arcade after the Villa Albani at Rome, also by Smirke— and so on. Statuary and ornaments abounded and 'there are a good many (some think too many) examples of coloured gravel and ribbon beds in the garden'.

These, it seems, were Nesfield's contribution to the design. The most notable were four beds composed of gravels and box, without other plants, representing the rose, thistle, shamrock, and leek. The design was worked in colours:

White: Derbyshire spa.
Purple: Blue John, or purple fleur spar.
Pale blue: Welsh slate.
Red: Pounded red brick.
Yellow: Pounded yellow brick.

Some of these materials were mixed to provide intermediate shades, and other colours, less liberally distributed, were formed by fragments of coloured glass.

Many other plots and coloured walks were made from these coloured materials—which, it was said, relieved the bareness of

* The Queen, owing to a bereavement, was unable to perform the ceremony, which took place a month after a new charter which decreed that the Society should henceforth bear the prefix 'Royal'.

the lack of flowers in winter and combined with them in summer. The best were ribbon patterns as seen executed in marble on the floors of some Italian churches. Nesfield's most complicated design, edged by artificial stone, was around the Great Basin. In the first year this was planted with the scarlet pelargonium, 'Crystal Palace', margined with purple *Verbena violacea*; next year this was repeated, with an additional band of the tropaeolum 'Crystal Palace Orange'; a year later a silver-leaved pelargonium replaced the tropaeolum. Elsewhere, calceolarias, verbenas of various colours, and lobelias abounded, together with small beds of holly and skimmia surrounded by golden yew.[7]

Nesfield also worked at Drayton, Northamptonshire, and Stoke Edith, where he restored parts of the gardens to the state in which they had been prior to landscaping. At Grimston, Lord Londesborough's seat near Tadcaster, in Yorkshire, he designed an Italianate Emperor's Walk, lined with busts of the Caesars, which received the qualified approval of Miss Jekyll. Trentham, Arundel Castle, and Alnwick are among his other works.

Today perhaps his most magnificent design, dramatic in decay, is to be seen at Witley Court. Here, in the undulating Worcestershire countryside that lies below Woodbury Hill, topped by its ancient earthworks, the Foleys had their park of 700 acres. The house, around a Jacobean core, had been Italianized by John Nash in the early nineteenth century. A little later the place was bought by William Ward, 1st Earl of Dudley (1817–1885). It is said that he spent a quarter of a million in aggrandizing what he had acquired. Even so, the garden which Nesfield designed within massive walls was never quite finished. It was in the Italian manner, and in the 1860s the *Illustrated London News* was able to claim that here was an instance of the revival of art in England.

The garden was arranged around two great fountains, one in the south court, the other to the east front. The grand fountain was in the south front; it is interesting to observe it through contemporary eyes.[8] The subject was Perseus striking at the dragon to rescue Andromeda; though not treated in accordance with Ovid, no objection could be raised against it, since the Old Masters had taken similar liberties! The figures were carved from Portland stone by James Forsyth to Nesfield's drawings. It was one of the largest groups of statuary in Europe; weighing 20 tons, its greatest width was 18 feet, and it rose 24 feet high from the waterline. A 40-h.p. steam-engine threw the main jet 120 feet high (Plate XXV).

The spray formed 'dissolving views of shifting rainbows, and with the rush, dash, splash and light feathery spray of the many rising and falling streams or jets one seems riveted to the spot, as by the spell of all the water-nymphs' enchantments. The flowers even seem to lose their brilliance . . .'. One recalls Ruskin.

The cost was over £20,000.

Nesfield died at 3 York Terrace, Regent's Park. For the last ten years of his life his practice had been carried on by his son, Markham Nesfield, who was killed in an accident not long after his father's death. His other son, William Eden, gained some fame as an architect.

An account of this period would be incomplete without a mention of Sir Charles Barry, R.A. (1795–1860).[9] He is, of course, best known as the architect of our rather odd, if magnificent, Houses of Parliament. His garden design was invariably in a quite different manner, the style of his true-love—that of Italy. He was a scholarly man and had travelled widely. A number of gardens that he designed still exist, though transmogrified in a manner of which he would surely disapprove.

One example is to be found at Trentham, at that time the Duke of Sutherland's seat, on the edge of the Potteries, whose inhabitants now visit the park in multitudes. Here, assisted by suggestions from Nesfield, he succeeded in making a great deal of a site that Loudon had described as most difficult owing to its flatness.

The principle on which he worked was logical and simple. It was, by means of a succession of gardens of regular design, formed by terraces and balustrades, to link architecturally the base of the house with the garden and thence, of course, the landscape.

Few of the gardens he designed were, his son tells us, 'so much after his own heart as Shrubland'. The park lies, with a south-western aspect, above the shallow valley of the River Gipping near Ipswich. It is an ancient place, once the home of Elizabeth's Chancellor, Nicholas Bacon; giant chestnuts and oaks still give the place the requisite picturesque look.

The house stands on an escarpment some 70 feet high. In the last century its possessor was a very wealthy landowner, Sir William Middleton. In about 1848 Barry was commissioned to aggrandize the house and work on the gardens soon followed. The result was one of great yet depressingly mechanical architectural grandeur; it covered some 65 acres of made ground, and was maintained by forty gardeners.[10]

A wide terrace stretched in front of the house, reaching to the edge of the escarpment. The descent from it was entered through a temple-like building and is made down a giant stairway after the manner of the Villa D'Este; at a low level it parted on either side of a circular, fountain-centred area. Beyond this a vista continued towards a loggia at the remote edge of the park. At different levels during the descent further vistas into the park lie to left and right.

The great terrace gardens were treated in the manner of a parterre. They took the form of beds in the shape of scrolls and other intricate patterns edged with box and designs in coloured sands and bricks. The beds were filled with plants, restricted to a few of the brighter colours. Nowhere in England was this kind of thing done so well; in the 1850s the pelargonium, 'Shrubland Pet', was celebrated.

The feature of this garden was its architectural form and the geometrical patterning of its beds. No creepers were allowed to soften the hard, mechanical Victorian masonry of the house or the walls and balustrades of the terraces; nor were the lax and graceful growth or the soft colourings of the many herbaceous plants that we now grow permitted to disturb the precision and garish colours of the bedding-out.[11]

As the century progressed the precedents of Italy fell out of favour as the gothick revival manner became more and more fashionable—particularly for urban residences of middling size. As early as 1834 H. Noel Humphreys* wrote that the revival in the gothick manner during recent years had resulted 'in a degree of excellence . . . even in its higher attributes', and 'has innocu-

* H. Noel Humphreys (1810–1879), author and artist, illustrated his own and others works on subjects such as coins, aquaria, butterflies, and art. He wrote for Loudon's magazines on garden design and architecture, to reappear as an old man in William Robinson's *The Garden*, which heralded the reaction against Victorian geometry and bedding-out. He also illustrated Mrs. Loudon's books.

lated the British architectural world with a mania' for erecting new buildings in that style.[11]

There was, of course, no documented gothick style of gardening which could be imitated and placed around the spiky, befinialled villas that were arising so numerously, not only in the new suburbs, but as country residences for the rich in the remoter parts of Britain. The gardens that resulted were, therefore, rather in the Nesfield-Barry manner around the house, extending beyond in a gardenesque or picturesque manner. In the former part, unimaginatively designed geometrical beds were seasonably planted, first with spring bulbs and then with half-hardy bedding-out plants. Beyond these, one rule was to avoid the use of straight lines; the edges of the borders surrounding the lawns were reminiscent of the French curves used by draughtsmen. Gravel paths —often unduly narrow—wound in and out to reach their objectives (if any) by the most circuitous route. The trees which formed the permanent feature of such gardens were distinctive. A whole range of new kinds of conifers came into use. The 'retinosporas' from Japan were found to be very easily propagated. Holly in variety was immensely popular. Whereas Miller in 1737 described thirty-three kinds, Thomas Moore in the 1870s named something like three times that number.[12] There was now a profusion of gold, silver, and other variegated evergreens, in addition to hollies. The blotched forms of *Aucuba japonica*, the first of which was introduced in 1783, were found to be extremely tolerant of town air and were propagated and planted in abundance.

It was an age, too, which delighted in weeping trees. The weeping ash (first recorded in the mid-eighteenth century) and wyche elm (probably not cultivated until the early nineteenth century) were, as can be seen today, much used. Their arbour-like form, particularly when young, was much to the Victorian taste.

On large estates the rows of frames, the hot-houses, peach-houses, vineries, and walled fruit and kitchen gardens were on an unexcelled scale. Frogmore well illustrates this (Plate XXVII).

Multitudinous gardens were made on these lines. In particular, the style was favoured—with the addition of cast-iron fountains, bandstands, benches, and warnings to keep off the grass—in the public parks which were now beginning to be an essential part of the fast-growing urban scene. Unlike London, many of the provincial cities were without parks. To munificent and public-spirited citizens, mostly of this period, who wished to move from the growing urbanism, and perhaps take advantage of the enhanced value of their estates, we owe some open spaces which are now of inestimable value.

Usually they were ornamental grounds surrounding family mansions that were retained in their original form and presented to the local authority for the use of the public—the remaining parts of the estate being profitably developed. As time went on the more enterprising local authorities themselves acquired further land and spaces for recreation. Consequently there came into existence a new and specialized form of gardening. Generally conservative in style, designed to appeal to the masses with ostentatious display, and liberally financed, municipal gardening has inevitably been subject to a good deal of criticism.

It should be remembered, however, that many Victorian gardens, and, indeed, public parks, were within a permanent setting of a Brown or Repton landscape. The artistic merit of these was never questioned, and they were allowed to mature unharmed.

THE LEARNED INSTITUTIONS

There can be no doubt that one of the most important horticultural and botanical events of the early Victorian period was the appointment of W. J. Hooker in 1841 as the first Director of the Royal Botanic Gardens, Kew—at a salary of £300 per annum with an allowance for the rent of a house.

Since the declining days of George IV, W. T. Aiton had, as we have seen, carried on in depressing circumstances. It became known that the Lord Steward wished to turn the whole into a royal demesne, which the surrounding estate already was. He proposed turning over the greenhouses to the cultivation of hot-house fruit and offered the rare collection of plants to the Horticultural Society and the Royal Botanic Society's garden in Regent's Park. The offers were refused.

In 1838 a committee was formed of John Lindley (chairman), Paxton, and a Mr. Wilson, gardener to the Earl of Surrey. Their report urged that Kew should become an Empire botanical

garden, controlled by an independent board. In the meantime
John, 6th Duke of Bedford, had been working hard behind the
scenes and using his great influence to have the place made a
national garden; he died in 1839 before success had been achieved.
In March 1840, however, the Earl of Aberdeen raised the matter
in Parliament, and on the first day of April 1840 it was announced
that the gardens, pleasure-grounds, deer park, existing botanical
garden, and arboretum were to be transferred to the Commissioners of Woods and Forests (though the Chief Commissioner,
Lord Duncannon, was opposed to spending any money on them).
In less than a year Hooker was appointed. He had charge of about
11 acres. In 1844 another 47 acres were added for the formation
of a pinetum, and in 1845 further land was placed under Hooker's
charge.[13]

Born in Norwich of a Devonshire family (his father had there
a collection of succulent plants, 'a favourite pursuit of his fellow-
citizens') William Jackson Hooker (1785-1865) had been recognized when a youth as a capable botanist, entomologist, and ornithologist. He was also a talented draughtsman. He became
friendly with that great Norfolk figure, Dawson Turner (1775-
1858), and helped him in his study of mosses; in 1815 he married
his daughter. He moved in the wide and cultured world of Sir
Joseph Banks, who recognized his ability. In his early days he
botanized in the highlands of Scotland—an adventurous proceeding at that time, for among other mishaps he was once arrested
as a spy. In 1809 he visited Iceland, where he was involved in a
revolution and a last-minute rescue from a burning ship. He later
made important botanical journeys into south-west England and
the Isles of Scilly. Finally, after a period as a brewer at Hales-
worth—the business failing to compete successfully with his other
interests—he settled down as Professor of Botany at Glasgow in
1820, and made a reputation there. He was now editor of *The
Botanical Magazine* and known to be a keen and successful scientific horticulturist; further, he wished to be near London. In
1840 he resigned from Glasgow, with an eye to succeeding Aiton.
Bedford and other influential persons knew him and considered
his qualifications to be well fitted for the directorship of a national
garden.

Here, indeed, was a man rich in knowledge and experience

and well suited to form an Empire institution. Almost at once he opened the gardens to the public. In 1843 the first of the Kew collectors since the days of Banks set out.* In that year, too, Queen Victoria and the Prince Consort gave their blessing to the new conception when they made an official visit. As we have already seen, in the 1850s, with Nesfield's help, he laid down a general plan on which the gardens were to be developed, centred on the new palm-house, and obtained more land for a pinetum. The collections of plants, particularly hardy herbaceous kinds, were rapidly enlarged. In 1863 he obtained government backing for the series of floras of our colonial possessions. He was knighted, and in August 1865 he died, active in the interests of Kew until a few days before his death.[14]

He was succeeded by his son Joseph Dalton Hooker (1817–1911), who also in due course received a deserved knighthood. The younger Hooker had his father's talents, and had been connected with the gardens since his 1847 commission to collect in the Himalaya. In 1872 his firmness and tact triumphed over a political controversy engineered by a certain Ayrton, which ended by establishing once and for all the independent position of the Director of the Royal Botanic Gardens. From that post he resigned in 1885.[14]

Another important development—not primarily horticultural —of the first importance was due to Sir John Bennet Lawes (1814–1900). He inherited the lordship of the manor of Rothamsted in 1834. An interest in chemistry caused him to experiment with drug-producing plants; gradually the importance of the chemical aspects of botany, particularly of soil nutrients, became his principal interest. He developed the manufacture and use of bone meal and other chemicals, and in 1843 began the valuable long-term practical experiments at Rothamsted which continue to this day.

At Oxford there were no significant developments. William Baxter (1787–1871), primarily an authority on our native plants, was curator from 1831 to 1851, as was his son William Hart Baxter (c. 1816–1890), curator from 1854.[15] This latter was associated with the writings of J. C. Loudon, and probably more so, at a later stage, with those of Mrs. Loudon.

At Cambridge the gardens on the new site, which had been

* Mention of their work is made on p. 328.

under development since 1831, were formally opened in 1846. Botany, under Henslow, was now receiving more serious attention than it was at Oxford. In 1867 a rock garden was built—at the time considered the most remarkable in England; 1879 saw the appointment of R. I. Lynch as curator. He was to hold the post for forty years and was a successful scientific gardener, whose work, however, belongs to a later period.[16]

The Chelsea Physic Garden was undergoing a series of ups and downs—preparatory to the final decline of its one-time international reputation. The curatorship of William Anderson (1766–1846), which began in 1814 (previous to which he had been 'botanic gardener' to a wealthy silk merchant, James Vere), ended with his death. Anderson, a Scot, was a competent man, and much respected, but of very conservative outlook, and not amenable to the improvements suggested by the Director, John Lindley, who had been appointed in 1835. He was succeeded by Robert Fortune on his return from China. Fortune collaborated in Lindley's reorganizations.[17] Within two years, however, Fortune was released so that he might return to the Orient for the East India Company, and Thomas Moore (1821–1887) was appointed curator in 1848. From this time onwards the reputation of the Chelsea garden declined to a very modest standing. Moore himself was, however, a man of some consequence. From 1844 to 1847 he had worked in the gardens at Regent's Park. He had there attracted the attention of Lindley, whose influence no doubt secured for him the curatorship at Chelsea. He engaged in journalism and was editor of *The Gardener's Magazine*, 1850–1, and co-editor with Lindley of *The Gardener's Chronicle* from 1866 to 1882. In that paper during 1874 he described and classified the many forms and varieties of holly in cultivation. With Lindley he also edited the popular and excellent *Treasury of Botany* (1866). He published books also on wild flowers and ferns, and revised the later editions of Thompson's *Gardener's Assistant*, referred to subsequently.

The Horticultural Society suffered a period of ups and downs. In the 1840s all went reasonably well. The Chiswick garden—and its shows—paid. In 1846 a small *Journal* had replaced the costly *Transactions*. Then two wet summers, 1853 and 1854, caused a fall in the income, and the finances of the Society became unsound. The garden was costing far too much, although the Duke of Devonshire reduced the rent. The publication of the *Journal* ceased in 1855. It was resolved to close the gardens and sell its plants, but this was never done. In 1858 John Lindley, assistant secretary for thirty-six years, became secretary, to face a period of extreme difficulty. That year, too, the Duke of Devonshire, who was more than a nominal president, died; he was succeeded by the Prince Consort.

During the following year, 1859, the premises in Regent Street were sold and replaced by a single room with a lobby in St. Martin's Place. More serious, the library and some 1,500 original commissioned drawings—a collection of immense value—were sold for £994. James Veitch the younger was one of the influential Fellows who considered that the Society should be wound up. At that stage the bankers would no longer advance money. Then Lindley and some others provided the necessary funds. Further, they were responsible for an approach to the Commissioners for the 1851 Exhibition with a suggestion that the Society might have a site for shows on the ground occupied by the Exhibition. This plan received Royal support; the result was the opening in 1861 of the Kensington garden which has already been described. On 8th May of that year a new charter was sealed, and the Royal Horticultural Society was born; success returned, but at some cost to its horticultural activities. Much was due to the enthusiasm of the Prince Consort, but the ever-faithful Lindley and his friends deserve the real credit. The triumph was short-lived, however. The true gardeners gradually drifted away; the other aspects of the Kensington garden brought sightseers only. The Commissioners took a big share of the revenue, and the Society was again in low water. The Chiswick garden was reduced in size. Finally, in 1882, the Commissioners ended the Society's lease.

There followed another phase of eclipse; the reason for it was that the Society had become involved in objects other than 'the improvement of horticulture'—brass bands, a skating rink, tennis courts, and so on.[18]

The outstanding figure of this period was, of course, John Lindley, who resigned from the secretaryship, his health failing, in 1863. A contemporary of his, however, calls for mention.

Robert Thompson (1799–1869) was the son of a small farmer at Echt, Aberdeen. After a beginning spent in private gardens, he joined the staff at Chiswick in 1824, where he remained until his retirement in 1868—through all the ups and downs of that garden. In the 1830s he helped Loudon with a revised classification of fruit for a new edition of *The Encyclopaedia of Gardening*, and soon became recognized as one of the greatest pomologists of the day.* In 1859 he published *The Gardener's Assistant*, which deservedly went through several editions as the soundest treatise on practical gardening of the mid-Victorian period. He was a modest man, most careful and systematic in his work, much liked, and undoubtedly a considerable influence for good in the Victorian horticultural world.

In Scotland James McNab (1810–1878) succeeded his father as curator of the Royal Botanic Garden, Edinburgh, in 1849, and continued to his death in that position. He was a vigorous personality and an enthusiastic and scientific gardener. In 1834 he had visited the United States and Canada; it was an account of the plants that he saw there that caused a *cri de cœur* from Loudon: 'Were all botanists, who like Mr. McNab, are at once scientific observers and practical cultivators, to exercise their commonsense as he does in this instance. . . .'[20] He became gardener to the Caledonian Horticultural Society, which was eventually added to the Botanic Garden. It was he who in 1860 built the forerunner of the now famous rock garden. It was made to utilize the stones of an old wall and contained 5,442 compartments for plants, was studded with monkey-puzzle trees and spanned by geometrically patterned rustic-work bridges.[21]

During the period 1845 to 1879 the Regius Keeper was Professor John Hutton Balfour (1808–1884).† A man of academic attainments, he was largely concerned in the formation in 1850 of the Oregon Association 'of gentlemen interested in the promotion of arboriculture and horticulture of Scotland', who, impressed by the reports of the conifers in western North America, combined to finance a collecting expedition. The man chosen was John Jeffrey, born at Clunie, Perthshire, in 1826. He was in 1849 employed at the Botanic Garden, where his botanical and

* E. A. Bunyard described him 'as our greatest British pomologist'.[19]
† Author of a once well-known *Manual of Botany* (1848) and *The Flora of Edinburgh* (1863).

general abilities caught the eye of Balfour. In 1850 he left for the Pacific coast; in 1851 seeds and specimens arrived, and a number of interesting introductions of trees and plants achieved. By degrees his activities slackened, and contact with him was eventually lost. He is believed to have been in San Francisco in January 1854, but after that disappeared without a trace—an unexplained mystery of plant collecting.[22]

In Ireland, Glasnevin prospered under David Moore, whose reputation both as an authority on the Irish flora and as one of the most skilful scientific gardeners of the day was respected throughout the world. In 1878 he retired and was succeeded by his son Frederick.

Something should be said about the activities of Frederick William Burbidge (1847–1905). Born at Wymeswold, Leicestershire, he became a gardener at Kew. During 1877–8 he travelled for Veitch in Borneo. Here he was remarkably successful in collecting and introducing orchids and ferns, a number of which were his own discoveries. His most spectacular achievement was the successful introduction of the giant pitcher plant of Kina Balu, *Nepenthes rajah*, which, though quite well known, had eluded previous collectors. It proved to be equally difficult to grow. In 1879 he became curator of the Botanical Gardens of Trinity College, Dublin, and in 1894 keeper of the College Park.

Burbidge wrote a number of books, and from 1873 to 1877 worked for *The Garden*. He was a passable draughtsman, and in 1873 published *The Art of Botanical Drawing*. *Gardens of the Sun* (1880) was an admirable account of his Borneo journey, including much about the people and natural history of the places he visited. He was interested in the improvement of plants—his *Cultivated Plants* (1877) dealt with that matter—and was an enthusiast for the chrysanthemum, about which he also wrote.

Perhaps we cannot do better than end by returning to Glasnevin and repeating an anecdote of 1879 that was published many years after by Sir (as he had then become) Frederick Moore; it will show something of the furious enthusiasm and wide culture of gardeners of that day, and at least introduce the names of three of them who merit a much less fleeting mention.

In that year young Moore, recently appointed curator, was descended upon by three voluble and excitable men. They were

Edward Woodall (1843–1937) with gardens at Scarborough and La Selva, Nice; John Bennett-Poë, of Nenagh, Tipperary, the eponym of a beautiful, but now forgotten, little daffodil; and W. E. Gumbleton (1830–1911), sportsman, art collector, and a learned botanical gardener famed for his garden at Belgrove with specialized collections of different genera. All were quarrelling as they arrived, but the presence of the new curator made things worse, for each insisted that he should be taken to see his own speciality, which was different from that of the others. Gumbleton, in addition, repeatedly corrected Moore's pronunciation of Latin names, and furiously beat the flags on the ground with his umbrella to emphasize each point (he was, incidentally, unable to roll his 'r's'). The climax came when Gumbleton denounced as a 'tush plant' a valuable new arrival, and smashed it with his now flailing umbrella.

It is scarcely necessary to add that the quartet soon became the closest and happiest of friends.[23]

PLANT-COLLECTORS

Probably the most permanent contribution that the early Victorian period made towards gardening was the introduction of new plants. The western part of North America, opened up by Douglas, was systematically explored and exploited, with a long-lasting effect on British woodlands and ornamental gardening. China and Japan were also visited by collectors, who brought back many fine plants that are now commonplace in Britain.

The first for consideration must be the Cornish brothers Lobb, William (1809–1863) and Thomas (1817–1894).[24] They were sons of an estate carpenter, who neglected his craft owing to a deeper interest in wild life, trapping, and hunting, and eventually became a gamekeeper. Both youths entered private service, then worked for a time with Veitch, re-entered private service, and finally returned to Veitch as plant-collectors. Both were energetic, capable, and excellent judges of what to bring home.

William was the first to go overseas. In 1840 he sailed for Brazil, thence to Chile. Many of his plants were therefore tender, but his great triumph was the collection of a large quantity of seeds of the monkey-puzzle tree (*Araucaria araucana*). This tree had been introduced by Menzies, and some seed had also been brought by James Macrae,* but it remained very scarce: its unusual qualities had great appeal to lovers of plants, and the price remained very high. Thanks to Lobb, Veitch were able to announce in May 1843 that they had raised many thousands from seed, which they could offer in quantity at a very low price (for plants 4 in. to 6 in. high it was £10 per 100 or 30s. a dozen). This alone was a great triumph for the firm.

In 1845 William Lobb went back to Chile, and introduced *Berberis darwinii, Desfontainea spinosa*, and *Escallonia macrantha*, all duly marketed by Veitch with great success, and many others, some on the tender side, which have become fairly well known. Returning to England in 1848, Lobb spent some time working on the flora of Cornwall. In 1849 he went to California. Here again he sent home in quantity seeds of many trees and plants that had been introduced in small numbers by David Douglas. In addition, he himself introduced the silviculturally important giant thuja, or western red cedar (*Thuja plicata*), and in 1853 he brought home specimens and much seed of the wellingtonia (*Sequoiadendron giganteum*), which was as sensational a popular success as had been the monkey puzzle.

Lobb returned to California in 1854, where he died in 1863, having worked for Veitch until 1857. He introduced, or reintroduced on a commercial scale, many other plants, notably *Sinningia speciosa*, from which the many fine garden 'gloxinias' have been evolved.

The fame of Thomas Lobb has not spread so wide, for he collected principally orchids and tender plants. In 1843 he went to Java, where he obtained some fine orchids, and later he visited north-east India, Lower Burma, Malay, and Borneo, whence he brought a number of greenhouse rhododendrons. He also made a considerable collection of botanical specimens.

From 1860 onwards Veitch engaged other collectors, by no means all of them British, to travel in many parts of the world. The work of some seventeen during this period (until 1880) is described in *Hortus Veitchii*. To give an idea of the type of plants in favour, one may record that they worked in Australia, Central and South America (including Colombia, Costa Rica, Brazil, and Juan Fernandez), the Malay Archipelago (Java and Borneo),

* *See* p. 279.

South Sea Islands, Madagascar, Burma, and South and West Africa. It will be guessed that orchids were their main objectives.

One of these collectors was Richard Pearce, who was born at Stoke Devonport, and worked in the nursery of Pontey at Plymouth.* In about 1858 he joined Veitch, and in 1859 he went to Chile, Peru, and Bolivia, the first of his trips to South America, which continued until 1866. The results of his labours were re-introductions of some fine shrubs brought earlier by Lobb, and, on his first trip, the introduction of *Eucryphia glutinosa* from Chile. On his expedition of 1865 he collected species of *Hippeastrum*, which played an important part in the parentage of modern hybrids, and of *Begonia*, from which are descended tuberous-rooted kinds now grown in gardens. He also did well with orchids, and in 1867 transferred his services to another orchid specialist, William Bull, of Chelsea. Soon after his arrival at Panama in that year he contracted a tropical disease and died, a comparatively young man, in 1868.

Of greater consequence was John Gould Veitch (1839–1870), eldest son of James Veitch the younger. Few countries had for long remained more inaccessible to outsiders than Japan. The Dutch East Indies Company traded in a restricted way through some of the ports. They had a foothold on the small island of Deshima, in the bay of Nagasaki. From this base Engelbert Kaempfer (1651–1715) and C. P. Thunberg† had made limited reconnaissances and collected some plants—mostly by proxy. The Bavarian, Philipp von Siebold (1796–1866), appointed physician-naturalist to the Company, had, at considerable risk and because of his ability as an eye specialist (the Japanese suffering greatly from eye troubles), been much more successful. He collected a great number of plants, many of which got into the hands of the Ghent nurserymen, and so into commerce. With J. G. Zuccarini, he published *Flora Japonica* (1835–42), illustrated by Japanese artists.

In 1858, however, more ports were opened to foreigners. In 1860 Veitch was attached to the staff of the British Envoy, Sir Rutherford Alcock. He was highly successful in collecting plants of great importance and subsequent popularity. To him we owe the commercially valuable Japanese larch (*Larix leptolepis*), the

---

* Not to be confused with William Pontey of Huddersfield, the arboriculturist.
† Thunberg had published *Icones Plantarum Japonicarum* (1794–1805).

range of conifers so popular in later Victorian and Edwardian times and long known as 'retinosporas' (*Chamaecyparis obtusa, Ch. pisifera,* and their garden forms), the extremely popular creeper known generally as Virginia creeper* (*Parthenocissus tricuspidata*), *Primula japonica,* and the 'golden-rayed lily' (*Lilium auratum*).

Veitch travelled on to China and the Philippine Islands, and in 1864 went to Australia and the Pacific. He was responsible for introducing other good plants, notably irises, maples, and hardy bamboos. In 1867 he fell ill, and died at the early age of thirty-two.[25]

.   .   .   .   .

We must now go back again to John Reeves, whom we last met when Inspector of Tea at Canton. In 1831 he retired from that post, and on his return to England he became active in the affairs of the Horticultural Society. In 1842 the Treaty of Nanking opened up to the British a number of ports in China, to which country access had previously been very restricted. Reeves and other members of the Society, particularly the vice-secretary, John Lindley, realized that greatly increased opportunities for the introduction of Chinese plants now existed. The Treaty was signed in August: in December Lindley's request that official help should be given to a collector appointed by the Society was met with the reply that the time was not yet opportune. All the same, on 26th February of the following year its agent Robert Fortune set sail for China on board the *Emu.*

Reeves had now become the leading member of the Chinese committee of the Society, and considered that he and his friends in Hong Kong and Canton would be more knowledgeable and helpful than newly appointed government officials, whose arrival, it was officially suggested, the proposed collector should await.

Robert Fortune (1812–1880) was born at Kelloe, Berwickshire. Apprenticed and first employed in private gardens, he entered the Royal Botanic Garden, Edinburgh, in 1839. After two and a half years William McNab was able to recommend him as superintendent of the hot-houses at Chiswick. He had only held

---

* It is still widely known as *Ampelopsis veitchii,* under which name it received a First Class Certificate when exhibited before the Royal Horticultural Society in 1868. Veitch first advertised it as 'a miniature-foliaged Virginian Creeper'. It has supplanted the true Virginian creeper in British gardens.

that post a few months when he applied for, and was appointed to, the position of collector in China.

Fortune was overloaded with instructions; the list of plants and objects—some little more than legendary—for which he was to seek show how little was yet known about China. One over-riding instruction should be quoted: 'In all cases you will bear in mind that hardy plants are of the first importance to the Society, and that the value of the plants diminishes as the heat required to cultivate them is increased. Aquatics, orchidaceae, or plants producing very handsome flowers are the only exceptions to this rule.' Apart from ornamental plants he was to seek for certain peaches, the plants that furnished tea and rice-paper, and oranges.[6]

The transportation of living plants has, of course, always been the plant-collector's greatest problem. Fortune was the first to use the new Wardian case on a considerable scale. Nathaniel Bagshaw Ward (1791-1868) was a doctor practising—as his father before him—in the East End of London, and living in Welcome Square, near London Docks. In spite of discouraging surroundings, he was a keen naturalist, visiting the country as often as possible. From one expedition he returned with a chrysalis, which he wanted to hatch, and so buried it in some earth over which was placed a glass jar. In due course he observed that seeds were germinating within, and that they were of plants which would not normally grow in the desiccated air of an East End room. He therefore transferred his attention to studying the growth of plants under practically air-tight conditions in glass containers. Shortly, he evolved what was known as the Wardian case, soon to be a popular novelty, in which ferns and other moisture-loving plants thrived amidst the gas and coal fumes of Victorian drawing-rooms. An account of his experiments was communicated to the *Companion to the Botanical Magazine* in 1836; in 1839 he described his methods in *The Gardener's Magazine*, and in 1842 he published his important booklet *On the Growth of Plants in Closely Glazed Cases*.

Here, at last, was a method of protecting living plants on long journeys from the often fatal effects of sea air and changing temperatures.* Ward himself and others had already experi-

---

* The Wardian case made possible the introduction of the tea plant to India, of quinine-producing plants from the New World to the Old, and of the banana to countries outside China. This invention by the modest and virtually unrewarded doctor thus changed the economy of much of the world.

mented with travelling cases, but it was left to the Horticultural Society and Fortune to try them out on a considerable scale:

You will take out three cases of live plants for the purpose, 1st of making presents to those who may be useful to you, and, 2nd, of watching the effect upon the plants of the various circumstances to which they may be exposed during the voyage—the facts relating to this will form part of your report.[27]

Not the least important feature of Fortune's travels was that he published admirable accounts of them. He was a calm and accurate observer of everything in Chinese life; he wrote as one of the first modern Englishmen to travel freely in the almost fabulous land of Cathay. His first visit lasted from 1843 to 1846. He had an adventurous time, escaping with his life on several occasions. His base was Hong Kong, and he did not penetrate far inland. Many of his introductions were of plants cultivated in Chinese gardens; he got on well with the people whom, however, he rather despised as having too high an opinion of themselves and their works. The cost of this expedition was just over £1,800.[28]

After his return he became for a while curator of the Chelsea Physic Gardens. Then, from 1848 to 1851, and again from 1853 to 1856, he was engaged in obtaining tea plants and a knowledge of the cultivation of tea for the East India Company. As had been the case with the silk industry, tea production and all to do with it was a closely guarded secret. Fortune, at great hazard, passed himself off as a Chinese. With the aid of the Wardian case, he was able to collect plants and was instrumental in founding the tea industry in India.

From 1860 to 1862 he visited the Orient again, this time including Japan in his tour. This visit was probably a private speculation; though it seems that Standish, the Bagshot nurseryman, was interested. There was some little rivalry in the relative claims of J. G. Veitch and Fortune as to the priority of some of their Japanese introductions.

All these journeys yielded plants of great garden value which are found today in most gardens. Fortune introduced the Japanese anemone, *Jasminum nudiflorum*, *Weigela florida* (*rosea*), *Dicentra spectabilis*, *Forsythia viridissima*, *Prunus triloba*, *Primula japonica*, *Cryptomeria japonica*, rhododendrons, azaleas, tree paeonies, the parent of the pom-pom chrysanthemums, the double form of *Deutzia scabra*, and the umbrella tree, *Sciadopitys verticillata*. His last journey brought a collection of Japanese chrysanthemums.[29] His activities seem to have been reasonably well rewarded, for he was able to spend the last eighteen years of his life comfortably in retirement at Kensington.

Another group of collectors were those sent out by the Royal Botanic Gardens, Kew, between 1842 and about 1863, by which time commercially sponsored collectors were adequately covering the field. Many of these were primarily concerned with plants of economic value to the Empire, or of botanic importance in connection with the national floras under preparation. Under the guidance of the director, W. J. Hooker, Kew collectors, often attached to Admiralty or other official expeditions, visited New Grenada, California, Oregon, Japan, Formosa, Korea, the Cameroons, Gabon River, Fernando Po, the Niger, Zambesi, East Africa, Madagascar, the Himalayas, Canada, British Columbia, Arctic America, the Fiji Islands, the Torres Straits, the Pacific Islands, Ecuador, and the Azores.[30] From our point of view the most important was the director's son, Joseph Dalton Hooker (1817–1911), on account of his Himalayan journey of 1847–51.[31]* This adventurous trip—he was at one time imprisoned—resulted in the introduction of many new rhododendrons, which were described in his *Rhododendrons of Sikkim-Himalaya* (1849). This has fine plates lithographed from Hooker's drawings by W. H. Fitch.

These rhododendrons, many of them scarcely hardy except in our mildest districts, gave a new impetus to the cult of this genus. Hooker realized that many would thrive in western coastal areas, from Cornwall to the north of Scotland, and they were extensively planted. They also resulted in a renewal of hybridization,† many of the offspring being reasonably hardy. It is no exaggeration to say that Hooker was one of the principal originators of British rhododendronomania, which has given a

* He travelled and collected elsewhere: in New Zealand and the Antarctic, Morocco and the Great Atlas.

† The blood of *R. griffithianum*, for example, which Hooker introduced in 1849, flows in no less than 128 hybrids named in the *Rhododendron Stud Book* (1952). Eventually, crossed with Fortune's introduction of 1859, *R. fortunei*, by Sir Edmund Loder, it produced the magnificent range of 'Loderi' hybrids, the first of which flowered in 1907.[32]

distinct quality and feeling quite singular to British gardens on acid soils, and played an important part in the movement for 'natural' gardens in later periods.

PROFESSIONALS AND THEIR PLANTS

It was within our present period that the science of genetics, quite unnoticed by the scientific world until 1900, came into being. Between 1856 and 1874 John (Gregor) Mendel (1822–1884), working in his little garden at the monastery of St. Thomas in Brunn, made those discoveries of laws of inheritance with which his name is now associated.

There are two morals to be drawn from this complete, if perhaps accidental, neglect of Mendel's work. First, he was only one of a number of scientists who were at this period deeply interested in hybridizing and breeding new strains not only of plants but animals. Second, without any knowledge of the basic laws involved, nurserymen and some amateurs were being markedly successful in producing improved forms of fruit, vegetables, and flowers.

The rivalries between firms and the mystery and secrecy of raising and marketing novelties have been described. It can be read between the lines of nurserymen's announcements. We can use the advertisements, mostly from *The Gardener's Chronicle*, as clues upon which to build some account of the nurserymen and the plants they raised or traded in, and the change of fashion, during the period.

One of the most interesting personalities was John Standish (1814–1875). Standish was born in Yorkshire, but came south with his father, who was gardener at Bowood. It was in that famous garden that the boy learned his gardening. He then moved to the Duchess of Gloucester at Bagshot Park, to become foreman under her well-known gardener, Mr. Toward. We next find him, somewhere around 1840, as a nurseryman on his own at Bagshot, offering some successful fuchsias and calceolarias of his own raising. By 1848 he had been joined in partnership by Charles Noble. In that year the Bagshot Nursery was offering seedlings of *Cryptomeria japonica*, quoting Fortune's description of the tree, which he had introduced in 1844 ostensibly for the Horticultural Society. This connection between Fortune and Standish persists (*Lonicera standishii*, introduced in 1845, is another example) until, when the partnership was dissolved, Standish alone was offering a whole range of Fortune's Japanese plants. In 1858, for instance, he was advertising the largest stock of the winter-flowering *Mahonia japonica* ('hardy as the holly') in the trade. The partnership also offered Douglas's plants. (Presumably, after he had become an independent collector.) Whatever may have been the circumstances, Standish and Noble were undoubtedly instrumental in bringing into general cultivation a most important series of new introductions.

In 1852 they offered their manual *Practical Hints on Ornamental Plants and Planting*, which included treatises on the cultivation of American and the new Sikkim rhododendrons. There is no doubt about the origin of the latter, for J. D. Hooker lived close to the nursery, and they had seeds from him in 1849[33] and were among the earliest to use them for hybridizing.* They brought the seedlings prematurely to flower by grafting them as scions on to old plants in a greenhouse. In this way they flowered *R. thomsonii*, a new addition to the brilliant reds, in 1857.

In January of that year appeared two announcements, the first by Charles Noble stating that he was establishing a nursery on his own near Sunningdale railway station, and the second by John Standish, that he would in future carry on alone the nursery that he had earlier established. He points out that it is about 2 miles from Sunningdale station, and furthermore, that he has engaged a landscape gardener as consultant. Standish was the outstanding cultivator and breeder of the pair. In 1860 each separately offered 'Lord Palmerston' and 'Cynthia'—one and the same thing, resulting from *R. thomsonii* pollen. In 1865 Standish offered 'Ascot Brilliant', having, in 1862, moved to Ascot, a bigger nursery. On his death the Rev. S. Reynolds Hole, writing in *The Garden*, spoke movingly of his rich, rugged, and generous Yorkshire character.

Noble's career is relatively uninteresting. He raised the first white hybrid clematis, × *jackmani*,[35] but not, apparently, much else. He retired from the business in 1896. Subsequently the Sunningdale Nursery, under successive owners, has had a most interesting career.

* It may be remarked that *R. nobleanum*, a cross between *R. caucasicum* and *R. arboreum* raised by Michael Waterer at Knap Hill in 1835, was so named because Noble admired it.[34]

Among the old firms, Lucombe & Pince remained prominent. They specialized in bedding-out and greenhouse plants. In
1842 they achieved a great success with their hybrid fuchsia ×
exoniensis, described as 'very superb', and to this day grown,
though now called *F. × corallina*.

We may here diverge for a moment to discuss the rise of the
fuchsia for, in 1842 also, Thomas Cripps, nurseryman of Tunbridge Wells, introduced the famous little 'Venus Victrix', the
first fuchsia with white sepals; it was raised by Mr. Gulliver,
gardener to the Rev. G. Marriott of Horsemonden. The price was
one guinea a plant. Even the less-sensational new varieties fetched
good prices: in 1847 Edward Titley of Bath 'offered to the world'
his new 'Jenny Lind' at 10s. 6d. The first double was brought out
by a celebrated raiser, W. H. Storey of Newton Abbot, in 1850,
and in 1872 Thomas Milner sent out his tricolor 'Sunray', probably raised from an early Belgian variegated form.[36]

As to Lucombe & Pince, one suspects that their neighbours,
the energetic Veitch family, were already troubling them. As a
pendant to their 1858 advertisements was a prominent *nota bene*
pointing out that the Exeter Nursery* founded in 1720, was
contiguous to the St. Thomas station of the South Devon rail, and
at an easy distance from the ancient city of Exeter. When Pince
died a Dr. Woodman, his nephew, became the principal; for some
time the name had been Lucombe, Pince & Co., and their catalogue contained as a feature an illustration of part of their Italian
garden. The firm still existed at the end of our period, the nursery
shaded by fine old Lucombe oaks, and famous for its 'Wonder of
the West' strain of cinerarias, calceolarias, and an extensive rockery. Soon, however, it disappeared. Pince's Road is today a
reminder of it.

It was during the 1850s that the announcements of Sutton &
Sons of Reading began to take a prominent place in the advertisement columns, though it was principally seeds for farmers, and in
particular grass, that they then offered. The firm was founded by
John Sutton (1777–1863) in 1806 as an agricultural business, but
it was Martin Hope Sutton (1815–1901) whose enterprise was
now bringing success and widening the firm's activities. The

* In 1855 *The Cottage Gardener* had described Veitch's Mount Radford Nursery as
'better known by the name of "the Exeter Nursery"'.

success was the reward for supplying pure seeds unadulterated with inferior kinds, and of good breeding.[37]

In 1855 William Thompson (1823–1903) of Ipswich issued his first seed catalogue. Originally a scientist who studied photography, he became interested in raising seeds, which he exchanged with his friends. This developed into the seedsmen's business later known as Thompson & Morgan. Thompson, by means of seeds, introduced a number of new plants. In the 1870s he was concerned with the origin of the long-spurred aquilegias.

In the 1850s, too, the name of George Jackman, of the Woking Nurseries, becomes prominent in the advertisement columns. At first general nursery stock was offered, but later the firm's advertisements stressed clematis, for which, of course, it became famous. The business was begun in 1810 by William Jackman (1763–1840). It was carried on by his sons, George and Henry, until 1832, when the partnership was dissolved and George carried on alone. George Jackman (1801–1869) was the raiser of the most celebrated of all hybrid clematis, *C.* × *jackmani* (a cross between *C. lanuginosa* and *C. viticella*)* which received its first award when exhibited to the Royal Horticultural Society in 1863. The firm, as George Jackman & Son, prospered, and by 1871 was advertising that their nursery covered 180 acres.

Several nurserymen, as we have seen, produced books, or offered sets of coloured plates of the plants they sold. In the 1850s and 1860s E. G. Henderson & Son produced *The Illustrated Bouquet*. This is interesting in that it deals with hardy plants— many similar early books were, of course, concerned with tender exotics. Henderson's seem to have specialized in seeds of German origin. Their Wellington Nursery, St. John's Wood, was on the site of Lord's Cricket Ground.[39]

Everywhere, particularly around the new suburban districts of the large industrial areas, small nurserymen's firms came into being. A few developed and became of national importance. Others, as streets and factories sprawled their way over the countryside, were forced to move. Many kept their now urban premises as shops, or acquired shops in the centres of towns, and took their nurseries away. Typical was the still important Midland

* At the time, French hybridizers insisted that it was a true species and not a successful hybrid. The first recorded clematis hybrid was raised by Henderson in 1835.[38]

firm of Pope. As the Black Country spread they moved in about 1867 to the neighbouring village of King's Norton in Worcestershire, selling their produce in the Birmingham Market Hall.

In York the family business of Backhouse became prominent. James Backhouse (1794–1869) was born at Darlington, a member of the Society of Friends. He was an able botanist, and as a youth explored Teesdale. In 1816 he entered the nursery business with his elder brother Thomas. They acquired 'The Friars Gardens', a nursery long in the hands of the Telford family—which had gone into the textile industry. In 1831 James set off on a missionary journey to the Australian continent and Mauritius and southern Africa. He combined botanical exploration and plant collecting with his spiritual duties. Thomas received from him parcels of the seeds of trees and shrubs of 'Mount Wellington and other elevated and exposed situations in Van Diemen's Land to test their hardiness in England'. Later, James visited Norway, and thence penetrated into the Arctic Circle. His son, also James (1825–1890), at an early age joined his father in botanical explorations in the remote parts of the British Isles (they worked as one; their respective shares are usually indistinguishable) and built up the business. They constructed a number of large rock gardens in a 'natural' manner. The nurseries moved to Fishergate, and later to a site between Holgate and Acomb. The firm remained outstanding until well into the present century.[40]

In Yorkshire, too, were William Jackson & Co. of Bedale, who in the early 1840s raised the well-known early flowering red rhododendron 'Jacksonii'. During this period the nurseries of Fisher & Co.* of Handsworth, near Sheffield, raised and incorporated the name of their nurseries in the early flowering hardy rhododendrons 'Handsworth White' and 'Handsworth Scarlet', the green-barked and very spiny holly 'Handsworthensis', and the variegated holly 'Handsworth New Silver'—all shrubs typical of the Victorian age.

There were several prominent nurserymen in Scotland, with reputations extending beyond its borders. The descendants of Robert Dickson, who founded the Hassendeanburn Nursery in 1729, split up and formed other businesses. From the late

---

* Later, Fisher, Son & Sibray; their Handsworth nursery was, of course, quite distinct from the Handsworth, Staffordshire, nursery of Pope & Son referred to earlier.

eighteenth century Dicksons & Co., of Edinburgh, have been one of the most prominent general nurserymen in the British Isles.

Peter Lawson & Son prospered greatly under Charles L. Lawson (1794–1873), who had taken charge on the death of his father. He was interested in agriculture and forestry, having introduced Italian rye grass in 1833 and the Austrian pine (*Pinus nigra*) in 1835. In 1854 he received the first consignment of Lawson's cypress (*Chamaecyparis lawsoniana*) collected by William Murray* from the valley of the Sacramento River in California; this, in its many varieties, is now the most popular of garden conifers. The firm had premises both in Edinburgh and in London, by Southwark Bridge.

Lawson lived at Borthwick Hall, Midlothian, which he planted with forest trees, and he was a Lord Provost of Edinburgh. He was also concerned in breaking down 'the Mark Lane monopoly'—a seedsmen's ring. In the end, however, he was overcome by commercial misfortune.

In the 1840s and 1850s many new plants were offered at comparatively cheap prices by Youell & Co. of the Royal Nurseries, Great Yarmouth, 'Florists to Her Majesty the Queen Dowager' (Queen Adelaide, who died in 1849). It seems probable that they imported nursery stock from the Continent—their address suggests Holland—as they were offering certain plants in quantity such as the monkey-puzzle and deodar before they were generally available from British sources. They also supplied numerous greenhouse and bedding plants; pompom and Japanese chrysanthemums were early featured in their lists.

A great many new plants were, of course, raised on the Continent. Such names as Baumann, Carrière, Lemoine, van Geert, van Houtte, and Vilmorin became prominent; they are still well commemorated in the names of plants they raised, but to discuss them here is outside our scope.†

It was from the Continent that most of the new roses came; their names alone show how many were raised in France. It was

---

* Brother of the secretary of the Oregon Association; he was at that time also trying to find John Jeffrey (p. 321).

† Holland was famed for bulbs; Belgium azaleas, palms, bay-trees, and camellias; France for roses, lilacs, syringas, and hydrangeas. British raisers also sent plants and seeds to continental growers for propagation on a large scale, retaining their own stock for improvement.[41]

a French breeder, Guillot, who brought about an important development when in 1867 he introduced 'La France', the forerunner of the Hybrid Tea roses—crosses between Hybrid Perpetual and Tea roses. Hardier than Tea roses, with a long, continuous flowering season, in colour generally ranging from deep red through pink to white, the new rose gradually became the most popular in gardens.[42]

The favour in which the rose was now held was marked by the formation of the National Rose Society in 1876. The moving spirit in this—and its secretary for the next twenty-five years—was the Rev. Henry Honywood D'Ombrain (1818–1905). He was of Huguenot stock that came to England at the time of the massacre of St. Bartholomew. For some time he lived in Ireland, where his father was Inspector-General of the Coastguard, and in 1838 he was instrumental in forming the Natural History Society of Dublin. From 1860 to 1876 he was editor of *The Floral Magazine*, a periodical devoted to florists' flowers, with coloured plates by Fitch and others. For many years he was vicar of Westwell, near Ashford in Kent. D'Ombrain, also in 1876, founded the Horticultural Club, which still exists.[43]

In Britain the Paul family was particularly associated with roses. A. Paul & Son were founded in 1806 at Cheshunt, and by the 1850s were prominent advertisers of roses. In 1848 William Paul (1823–1905) issued *The Rose Garden*. Its many editions and supplements prove that it was a popular success, and it now provides an important source-book for the historian of the rose. In 1860 William parted company with his brother George (1841–1921), who continued with the old business at Cheshunt. William formed the firm of William Paul & Son, of Paul's Nursery,* Waltham Cross—making it very clear to his customers that he alone carried on the genuine Paul traditions. George, however, was a successful hybridizer, particularly of shrubs, notably weigelas, and cannas and amaryllis.

Other nurserymen, now almost entirely forgotten, with their specialist plants of the period, can be no more than named. There were John Bell, of Bracondale, Norwich, noted for pansies; William Miller, of Providence Nursery, Ramsgate, specialist in pelargoniums and fuchsias; John Miller of Bristol, with his hot-

* The name still exists as an area within the present Epping Forest.

house plants; and W. Maule & Son, of Bristol, offering new conifers, and, it is said, bringing failure upon themselves by speculating on a great public demand, which never materialized, for *Cydonia maulei* (*Chaenomeles japonica*), which they introduced from Japan in 1869.

The firm of Lee continued to prosper, though their international supremacy noticed by Loudon had long ago been lost to Veitch. John was in due course joined by his brother Charles as J. & C. Lee. In the middle of the century they had nurseries at Ealing, Isleworth, Hounslow, and Feltham, in addition to Hammersmith; by degrees these were surrendered to the builders. John Lee retired in 1876, leaving the business in the hands of Charles and his son William. In 1881 Charles died, and John returned once more into harness. By now he was the doyen of nurserymen, with an encyclopaedic knowledge of plants and the nursery trade.

A number of flowers that are now immensely popular were only just coming into their own during this period. The sweet pea did not enter upon its triumphant progress until later. Daffodils and other bulbous plants such as lilies were only just beginning their career as florists' flowers. Their success was in a considerable part due to the endeavours of Peter Barr (1825–1909). Born in Scotland, an enthusiastic amateur botanist and horticulturist, he made collections of every species that he could acquire of those plants that interested him, notably hellebores, lilies, and daffodils. He travelled abroad collecting plants in the wild, and acquired others wherever he could. He worked as a nurseryman—at one time in Worcester—with varying success, and in 1862 founded, with a partner, the firm of Barr & Sugden,* of King Street, Covent Garden. They were general nurserymen, but specialized in bulbs, and particularly daffodils. Three men besides Barr are associated with the early developments of the daffodil. They were Edward Leeds (1802–1877), botanist and nurseryman of Pendleton, who raised the 'Leedsii' varieties, and William Backhouse (1807–1869),† a banker, of Wolsingham, Durham. Barr was in touch with both, and when Backhouse gave up his plants, owing to ill-health, Barr acquired them and they became known as the

---

* The firm in due course became Barr & Sons.
† He was not related to James Backhouse of Darlington.

'Barrii' daffodils. The third pioneer was F. W. Burbidge* of Dublin, whose *The Narcissus: Its History and Culture* of 1875 was one of the first important studies of the new cult of the daffodil. The band of the faithful included, of course, several others, and increased notably towards the end of the century. The pattern set by perhaps the earliest enthusiast, Dean Herbert, was followed: several of the most successful raisers were clergymen.

It remains to be added that Barr himself published *Ye Narcissus or Daffodyl Flowre* in 1884—in spite of its affected title an important book. Barr remained active and enthusiastic, with a passion for thoroughness, to within a few days of his death.

The rise of the gladiolus from obscurity also begins in this period. James Kelway (1815–1899) was a young working gardener who was attracted by the scarlet and yellow South African *Gladiolus psittacinus* and saw within it possibilities of improvement. In 1850 he began business on his own at Langport, Somerset, and in 1861 he distributed the first of the modern florists' gladioli.

Throughout this period conifers were extremely popular. Variegated, coloured, and weeping sports appeared in the rapidly increasing seed beds of nurserymen and gardeners, to be seized upon and propagated and advertised. There was now a rich variety of form and colouring with which to provide foliage in winter. This aspect was emphasized by the title *The British Winter Garden: A Practical Treatise on Evergreens*, published in 1852. The author was William Barron (1800–1891), gardener to the Earl of Harrington at Elvaston Castle, Derbyshire. The beautiful *Cephalotaxus drupacea pedunculata* had at first been called 'Lord Harrington's Yew in compliment to the Earl, who has formed a superb collection of the finest conifers at Elvaston, where they are planted in rich profusion and with so much taste and judgement as to produce the most surprising effect'.[44] Barron was celebrated for his skill in moving big trees, using a machine of his own invention. He later set up as a nurseryman with his son, at Borrowash and Nottingham, specializing in landscape gardening and, of course, tree removal.†

One of the most enterprising firms of this period was Knight

* *See* p. 321.
† In 1880 he successfully moved the ancient yew at Buckland Church, near Dover, a feat at least equal to Lord Petre's transplantings at Thorndon Hall.

& Perry. In about 1800* Joseph Knight (*c.* 1781–1855) founded his Exotic Nursery in King's Road, Chelsea. He had been gardener to George Hibbert (1757–1837), a wealthy man who had sent his own collectors to the Cape and Jamaica. Knight eventually acquired the plants from his botanic garden, which was in Clapham. Pineapples and fuchsias seem to have been among the early specialities of the Exotic Nursery. Knight is also known to have had plants from William Baxter (*d. c.* 1836), who collected in South Australia in 1823. Conifers soon took a prominent place in his collection, and in *The Gardener's Magazine* of 1839 there are several references to Knight's rare specimens. In 1840 he published a *Catalogue of Coniferae*, which included 140 species and varieties. He was later joined in the business by Thomas A. Perry. In 1850 appeared *A Synopsis of Coniferous Plants Grown in Great Britain and Sold by Knight and Perry*, an excellent booklet botanically and from a practical point of view, and with laudable care displayed in its nomenclature. It is prefaced by an engraving of the King's Road premises—with the two-horsed carriage of one of their rich patrons drawn up by the awning over the footpath—and concludes with details of the firm's other activities.

As these give a good idea of the setting-out and stock of an important nursery of the mid-nineteenth century they may be summarized. Pride of place among the departments was given to the collection of hardy ornamental trees and shrubs, many of which had been acquired by annual personal visits to the Continent and elsewhere, and now including 'many beautiful and rare kinds, not readily to be met with'. Second in importance were the 'beautiful and now fashionable' American plants, particularly their own hybrid scarlet rhododendrons (a little Asiatic infusion here!)† and the finest kinds of the new azaleas raised in Belgium.‡

The large nursery at Battersea, with its extensive walling, ensured a first-rate supply of fruit trees, on which fibrous root systems were specially induced, and all of which were labelled in accordance with the Horticultural Society's *Catalogue*. Although herbaceous and alpine plants 'have been much and undeservedly

* 1809 is the date usually given, but their catalogue implies that 1800 was the year Knight set up in business.
† In April 1841 'admittance gratis' was advertised to see *R. arboreum*, 20 feet high, in flower.
‡ A. van Geert (1818–1886), the distinguished Belgian nurseryman, received his training with Knight & Perry.[45]

neglected', an interesting collection had been retained (a revival, of course, was on the way). Fifth in the list came hot-house plants, the collection of Indian azaleas and camellias being more than ordinarily rich.

The culinary, agricultural, and flower-seeds department always received 'marked attention'. From Belgium, France, Germany, Italy, Spain, and the United States were annually imported such seeds as ripen better there than in England. As for bulbs, a 'competent person' had been specially despatched to the Dutch States during the blooming season for the selection for acquisition of only the finest roots of each kind.

Then, among the miscellanea, a few exceptionally well-trained 'beautifully formed' standard sweet bays in tubs imported from the Continent—as a substitute for orange trees; modern implements; Archangel mats received from Russia every autumn; home-made mushroom spawn, and, as garden embellishments, the excellent vases manufactured by Mr. Falcke. Trained gardeners could also be supplied.

There is a further significance in the full description of this business. Presumably because of the ageing of Knight, it was bought, and the King's Road establishment leased, by Veitch of Exeter in 1853, and subsequently developed sensationally. Within a few years it had become the most important nursery in Great Britain and was internationally famous. James Veitch the second moved to London to take charge, and until 1863 the Exeter and Chelsea establishments were united. In that year, on the death of James Veitch the elder, the firm divided into two, under the brothers—Robert Veitch & Son* at Exeter, and James Veitch & Sons† of the Royal Exotic Nursery at Chelsea. The latter firm also developed nurseries at Coombe Wood in Surrey, Feltham, and Langley.

We have already seen something of the work of the early

* Robert Toswill Veitch (1823–1885) and his son Peter C. M. Veitch (1850–1929). From 1867 the latter worked at Chelsea and in foreign nurseries. In 1875 he went plant-collecting for the Chelsea firm in Fiji and Australia, and later in New Zealand, New Guinea, and Borneo—where he worked with Burbidge. Twice he lost his collections through shipwreck. He returned in 1878, remaining with the Chelsea firm until 1880 when he returned to Exeter, eventually succeeding his father. In spite of misadventures, he brought back many new plants, and made a successful introduction of the difficult *Ranunculus lyallii*. The Exeter firm still exists as a family concern.

† The sons were John Gould (*see* p. 324), Harry James (1840–1924), knighted in 1912, who took charge when James died in 1869, and Arthur (1844–1880), who died from typhoid.

Veitchian collectors, particularly those concerned with orchids and greenhouse plants. One, however, is particularly connected with the Chelsea business at the end of our present period: a man who, though by no means unsuccessful, might easily have fore-stalled the great collectors of the early twentieth century. Collectors in China, as we have seen, seldom worked far away from the coast. But the travels of French Jesuit missionaries in the central and western districts were drawing attention to the rich flora far inland up the headwaters of the great rivers. The firm of Veitch were the first to grasp the significance of this, and in 1877 sent Charles Maries (*c.* 1851–1902) to collect in Japan and China; he was told while in China to concentrate on the valley of the Yangtze. In the spring of 1879 he reached the Ichang Gorges but, dissuaded partly by his inability to come to terms with the Chinese, and by a disbelief in the possibility of finding more valu-able plants, he turned back. Had he but known, he was on the threshold of a land whose flora was to alter the face of the twen-tieth-century garden. As it was, his Chinese collections included *Primula obconica*, and the Chinese witch-hazel (*Hamamelis mollis*). From Japan he brought *Enkianthus campanulatus* and *Styrax obassia*, as well as some notable conifers.

Was this lack of determination that Maries showed because he was born not with the background of Scotland's mountains, against which so many of the early plant-collectors were bred, but in the gentle Avon Vale at Hampton Lucy? Here, at the Free Grammar School, he had learned his botany under the Rev. George Henslow.* Soon after his return from the East he went to India, working for the Maharajahs of Durbhungah and then Gwalior. He was superintendent of the Gwalior State Gardens when he died—in the same year that E. H. Wilson returned from reaping the first of many fine harvests from beyond the point where Maries turned back.

The Veitches employed some of the greatest plant hybridizers of the day. One of them, John Dominy (1816–1891), has a par-ticular claim to fame as the raiser of the first man-made hybrid orchid. Dominy was born in Devonshire, and moved from a

---

* The Rev. George Henslow (1835–1925) was son of Professor Henslow of Cam-bridge. At this time he was headmaster of Hampton Lucy School. He became a popular lecturer and writer on gardening, and Honorary Professor of Botany to the Royal Horticultural Society.

private garden to Lucombe & Pince. After a very short stay with them he joined Veitch, where his skill as a cultivator was soon noticed. He made friends with a clever amateur botanist, a surgeon, John Harris. Harris explained the manner in which orchid flowers were fertilized, and suggested hybridization. In 1854 Dominy crossed *Calanthe masuca* with *C. furcata*. In 1856 this flowered and was named *C.* × *dominii*, the first of many thousands of hybrid orchids, but otherwise long ago forgotten. Dominy was successful also with fuchsias and nepenthes, moving from Exeter to Chelsea in 1864.[46]

Veitch employed several other hybridizers. John Seden will be mentioned later, but during this period, about 1869, he raised the first hybrid tuberous begonia. He raised the first winter-flowering hybrid begonia in 1882.

James Veitch & Sons dealt in every kind of plant and seed; their advertisements eclipsed those of all their competitors. Their workers, with whom they were satisfied—and none stayed long who were not first rate—were often recommended and placed in the best positions in the private gardening world. The firm by tradition had a scientific outlook. Their travellers were always instructed so far as they were able to collect any information and specimens of all kinds of natural objects likely to be of value to learned institutions.

.   .   .   .   .

Here one should mention the increasing use of flowers and plants for the decoration of rooms—not so much flowers in vases of water (a fashion that was scarcely yet creeping in), but hot-house plants piled up on tables, embedded in moss, and liberally garnished with maidenhair fern. Glorified and highly elaborated forms of the Wardian case, usually enclosing ferns and sometimes including an aquarium, were also an object of admiration. It was the period, too, when much attention was first paid to plants with strongly coloured leaves of remarkable form. This was exemplified by the publication of Shirley Hibberd's *New and Rare Beautiful-leaved Plants*. The preface, written at Stoke Newington and dated 1869, tells us that

The increased attention paid to beautiful-leaved plants constitutes a distinct phase in the history of horticulture. It is but recently that the beauty of leaves has been fully recognized, and the passion that has arisen for collecting and cultivating fine foliaged plants is one of the newest, but it is not at all likely to be transient. We do now and then hear that ferns are less cared for than formerly, and perhaps we shall soon be told that begonias, caladiums, palms, cycads, and yuccas have had their day. . . . Nevertheless, we do not anticipate that a single plant figured in this work will be less interesting fifty years hence than now, for our purpose has been to select without regard to fashion, but with an eye to intrinsic beauty only. . . .

The type of plant that Hibberd particularly admired was the blotchy leaved *Abutilon striatum thompsonii*. He recalls that it was at first grown in the stove, where it was a poor, skinny thing; then in a greenhouse, when it was better, but is at its best when 'of later years it has been adopted freely by Mr. Gibson in his masterly system of embellishing the parterre with sub-tropical plants at Battersea Park'.

Instructions are given for designing and planting such a sub-tropical garden, but Hibberd's interest ranged over a wide field, from such hardy plants as variegated *Acer negundo* and the forms of *Acer palmatum*, and *Saxifraga fortunei* to stove plants as, for example, species of *Bertolonia*.

James Shirley Hibberd (1825–1890) was a prolific writer, a successful editor, and a leader of what one might call the urban and suburban world of horticulture. Devotion to the cause of the Centenary Exhibition of the Chrysanthemum Society and the Chrysanthemum Conference, with consequent overwork, contributed to his death. The son of a sailor who had served under Nelson, he was born in Stepney while it was still a pleasant place. After a period in the bookselling and bookbinding business he turned to journalism. On marrying he moved to Pentonville, and with his wife began to study experimentally the problems of urban horticulture. Then he moved to Stoke Newington, where he had a considerable collection of hollies and ivies grown in pots; he also maintained experimental plots elsewhere. Building, however, drove him from his 'little nest' there to Muswell Hill. In 1858 he became editor of a new periodical, *The Floral World*, which achieved a circulation hitherto unreached by any gardening paper; he continued with it until 1875. From 1861 until his death he edited a revived *Gardener's Magazine*. He produced many sound, practical articles, and books such as *Profitable Gardening*—an excellent and several times reprinted study of vegetable- and fruit-growing—*The Amateur's Rose Book*, and *The Amateur's Greenhouse*. More original and singular to the period were his books on foliage plants, already mentioned, and on ferns and ivies.

The Fern Garden—'how to make, keep and enjoy it, or fern culture made easy', with many illustrations, including coloured lithographs—was first published in 1869 and within a decade had reached its eighth edition. *The Ivy*, a 'monograph, its history, use and characteristics', 1872, is a remarkable book, describing and illustrating many different kinds. Possibly, however, Hibberd's own favourite would be his *Brambles and Bay Leaves: Essays on the Homely and Beautiful* of 1855.

·　　　　·　　　　·　　　　·

The working gardener's lot during this period was by no means always an easy one. During the 1840s, of course, times were difficult; gardeners were often underpaid. Loudon was always emphasizing the need for adequate pay; George Glenny (1794–1874)* wrote among his 'golden rules' that 'gardeners should be paid well. It is cheaper in the end to make a man easy in his mind; he does his work better when he is not pinched in his circumstances'.

The head gardener on an estate was, as before, often in a secure position. One recalls the independence, even truculence, combined with devotion, of Hopkins in Trollope's *The Small House at Allington*. But what does one make of an announcement such as appeared in *The Gardener's Chronicle* of 4th September 1852?

A few friends to the family of Mr. James Carton, once gardener at Syon House, and now wholly destitute, having formed a small purse, in order that he may emigrate with his family to Australia, solicit some further aid. . . .

Donations were to be sent to John Edwards, Esquire,† of Hollo-

---

* A journalist and amateur gardener who, from his youth onwards, was a consistent prize-winner at flower shows, usually for florists' flowers.
† Founder-Secretary of the National Floricultural Society, established at 21 Regent Street in 1851 to further the cultivation of florists' flowers.

way. Advertisements such as this were by no means unusual; sometimes they took the form of a list of acknowledgements to the donors. It was to deal with such cases that in 1839 the *Benevolent Institution for the Relief of Aged and Indigent Gardeners and Their Widows* was formed. Paxton, needless to say, was prominent in bringing it into existence.

A gardener recalling the seventies and eighties of the century has described the conditions of work.[47] A ten-hour day was almost universal, and in many gardens a sixty-hour week was common, with unpaid Sunday duty. Holidays were usually confined to three feast days in a year. Sometimes half a day was as a great favour conceded to visit a flower show, but the time was usually made up.

Pay varied. A head gardener had from 20s. to 23s. weekly, with a house, coal, and vegetables in addition. Foremen got about 18s. with a bothy, coal, and light; journeymen 16s. with the same perquisites. Apprentices generally lived at home and were paid 8s. weekly the first and 10s. the second year. It is not surprising that a successful gardener often set up on his own as a nurseryman.

THE FRUIT AND VEGETABLE GARDEN

Our present period was particularly rich in the development of new fruit, specially apples—a fruit that in the past, perhaps, had been taken rather as a matter of course. Though several originated before 1841 they had remained relatively unknown beyond their own locality until after that date, by which time prominent nurserymen had discovered, propagated, and introduced them to a wider public. It is significant that those named below—whose fame remains undimmed—were raised by amateurs entirely without the knowledge of genetics that we now possess. Some were working seriously to produce better fruit, others were just lucky.

The first in point of time seems to have been 'Bramley's Seedling'. It was raised in the garden of a cottage in Church Street, Southwell, from a pip sown by a Miss Brailsford. The seedling probably first fruited between 1819 and 1823. Much later the cottage with its tree passed into the hands of a Mr. Bramley from whom Henry Merryweather, of the old Southwell firm of nurserymen, obtained grafts in about 1856. The tree did not achieve more than local fame until 1876, in which year Merryweather apparently first exhibited the fruit in London. Mr. Bramley, whose name is probably now borne by more British apple trees than any other variety, was no more than a cipher in its production.[48]

Not much later was the arrival of our other most famous apple, 'Cox's Orange Pippin'. Richard Cox (c. 1776–1845) was a successful brewer, reputedly in Bermondsey, who retired in about 1820 to the village of Colnbrook, near Slough. Here he devoted his time to raising apples. It has been shown that Cox was a methodical man, and it is probable that he went about his task systematically. Yet neither the parentage nor the date of raising 'Cox's Orange Pippin', or his other success, 'Cox's Pomona', is recorded. There seems no doubt that in 1836 he supplied scions of both to a local firm of nurserymen, E. Small & Son, who sent out the plant four years later. Even so, it remained practically unknown until Charles Turner (1818–1885) of the Royal Nurseries, Slough, a prominent and successful florist and nurseryman with a flair for 'spotting' first-class plants,* took the apple up in about 1850. When it received a prize for the first time at the Horticultural Society's Grand Fruit Exhibition of 1857 it was still a novelty, but this award started it upon a career of fame that has not yet ended.[49]

In about 1864 a Bath nurseryman, Cooling, put 'Beauty of Bath' on the market; it had originated at Bailbrook, a village to the north of the town.[50] In 1868 a Leicester nurseryman, John Harrison, received from the Royal Horticultural Society a First Class Certificate for a new kitchen apple, 'Annie Elizabeth'. This had been raised in what is now Avenue Road, Leicester, by Samuel Greatorex (1804–1871), who seems to have been a solicitor's clerk. It was named after his daughter Annie Elizabeth, who died as an infant in 1866.[51]

Also in this period the gay colours of 'Worcester Pearmain' first appeared on the scene. In 1874 it received a First Class Certificate when exhibited by Richard Smith, nurseryman, of Worcester.† It is said to have been raised by a Mr. Hale, of Swan

* Including the pink, 'Mrs. Sinkins', first exhibited in 1880.
† At this date, according to his catalogue, Smith had 50 acres of fruit trees, 50 acres of conifers and evergreens, 12 acres of rose trees, as well as space given over to other plants; there were 32 miles of walks and 2½ acres of glass. This gives some indication of the development of provincial nurseries.

Pool, Worcester.[52] In all these instances astute nurserymen profited from the enterprise of others; several firms, however, worked methodically over a long period at the improvement of all kinds of fruit.

Some of these should be mentioned. Thomas Rivers of Saw-bridgeworth has already been named in connection with roses. While visiting France to study them he became interested in, and shortly an authority on, the growing of pyramid fruit trees. Subsequently he acquired plants of practically all the continental varieties of fruit—and, after trial, was, it is said, able to destroy most of them as worthless! In his endeavours to protect fruit from its many enemies he developed the system of growing trees in pots in a greenhouse, and his pioneering of the orchard house, as it was called, was a feature of the 1850s. At his death he had raised and fruited some 1,500 peach trees, all under glass, of which but a handful proved worth naming; several of these are still found in catalogues.[53] Thomas Rivers was followed by his son, Thomas Francis Rivers (1831–1899), who continued to work most successfully with stone fruit, and by others of his line.*

Thomas Laxton (1830–1890) was born at Tinwell, near Stamford. He was a follower of Thomas Andrew Knight in believing that vegetatively reproduced plants degenerated. Though he worked commercially, all his work had a strong scientific bias. He published his own study of peas in 1872, before that of Mendel was generally known, and carried out breeding experiments for Charles Darwin. Thomas Laxton made great improvements in peas, strawberries, and zonal pelargoniums. His work was carried on by his sons as Laxton Brothers at Bedford; later their attention was turned to apples, pears, and plums.[54]

This period saw the rise of another enterprising firm that did much to improve fruit. George Bunyard (1841–1919) was bred to a typical family nurseryman's business begun in 1796 at Maidstone. In 1869, not without a good deal of quiet planning, he launched out on a national scale at Allington. In 1871 he introduced 'Gascoyne's Scarlet', raised by a Mr. Gascoyne of Sittingbourne, and in 1885 'Lady Sudeley', raised by a Mr. Jacobs at Petworth—a good start.

The leading pomologist of the period was Robert Hogg (1818–

* The family and firm happily still continue.

1897). Born in Berwickshire, he worked with Peter Lawson & Son at Edinburgh. Coming south, he joined Ronalds, of *Pyrus Malus Brentfordiensis* fame. After a spell studying the French nursery trade, he went in 1845 to the Brompton Park Nursery, now rapidly declining. In 1854 he took part in founding the British Pomological Society, which had Paxton as its first president. In 1860 was issued the book that made his name, *The Fruit Manual*. Its fifth and final edition appeared in 1884. Hogg was also concerned with Johnson in the conduct of *The Cottage Gardener*, whose title in 1861 became *The Journal of Horticulture*. On Johnson's death in 1886 he became the proprietor.

One of those whom Hogg consulted in connection with vines and pears was Richard Dodderidge Blackmore (1825–1900), the author of the novel *Lorna Doone* (1869). Blackmore was, for most of his life, an unbusinesslike but skilful and knowledgeable fruit-grower in the mornings who wrote in the afternoons to recover (so he used to say) the £250 a year that he lost on his gardening—principally the cultivation of pears and vines. He was for some time on the Royal Horticultural Society's Fruit Committee, and wrote a paper on pests of the vine. Ill-health had in 1860 caused him to give up his career as a barrister and to divide his life between literature and market gardening, with 11 acres of land at Gomer House, Teddington. The first result of this arrangement was, appropriately, a translation of the *Georgics* of Virgil—surely the only one by an author who had the necessary practical qualifications.

For our purpose, quite the most interesting of his novels was *Kit and Kitty*, published in 1890. The background is a most detailed picture at first hand of a Thames Valley fruit farm in the 1860s; the book is, indeed, a source of much information on country life of that period. The central figure is the owner, crusty old Uncle Corney, a composite picture of a typical market gardener of the day, and Blackmore himself: bearded, wearing a baggy coat with its capacious pockets 'wherein he carried a hammer, a stick of string, a twist of bast, a spectacle-case full of wall nails, a peach knife, a little copper wire, and a few other things to suit the season'.

The *deus ex machina* of the story is the exceptionally wet summer of 1860 and the bitter winter and spring that followed it—all well enough documented by the papers of the day.* The villain of the story is helped by that villain of all gardens, a late May frost. Uncle Corney proposes to introduce the new continental method of smoking his orchards to keep it at bay. Knowing that until it is proved his men will think it a foolish whim, he arranges that Kit, the hero, alone shall help him. The absence of spraying with washes forms a striking contrast with the present day; sometimes

FIG. 10. Dean & Co.'s galvanized garden engine advertised in *The Gardener's Chronicle*, 1860

'the engine' (Fig. 10) is used to squirt the trees with clean water. Picking remains unchanged: 'the scent becomes cloying and even irksome, and the beauty of the form and the colour too, and the sleek gloss of each fine sample, lose all their delight in the crowd of their coming'.

The fruits by which Uncle Corney set great store were 'Grosse Mignonne' and 'Galande' ('Bellegarde') peaches, 'Keswick' and 'Cat's Head' codlins, 'Quarantene' ('Quarrenden') apple, the 'Williams', 'Glou Morceau' and 'Beurre Rance' pears, 'the jet-

---

* The weather was a repetition of 1836–7—as we have seen, another devastating period in the history of gardening.

black shoulder of "Hamburgh" and the amber-coloured triplet of "White Muscat"' grapes, and two strawberries, 'President' and 'Dr. Hogg'.

Marketing was rough and ready; dishonesty of every kind was common, and, Uncle Corney considered, foreign competition was unfair.

THE MARCH OF PROGRESS

The pages of *The Gardener's Magazine* in the 1830s bore evidence that the age of mechanical invention—and the production of innumerable 'gadgets', many of them (as today) ingenious but useless—was at hand. A good many of these ingenious devices had come to stay, and were being adopted.

It is therefore interesting to follow the advertisement pages of *The Gardener's Chronicle* over its early years. In 1850 more than one firm was offering wire netting; the price was (and for some years remained at) 1d. per square foot plain and 2d. galvanized. Vulcanized rubber hosepipe was available. In 1852 the hand-powered 'engine' still provided most of the water for irrigation and such washing or spraying—with plain water or lime-wash. Richard Read, of 35 Regent Circus, Piccadilly, was now a prominent advertiser of an improved engine that would provide anything 'from a POWERFUL STREAM to a gentle shower or dew fall'. From the use of capitals it was clearly the power that was most required. He also offered a new hand syringe with an adaptable nozzle that made it possible to spray the undersides of leaves.

Burgess & Key, of London, advertised gutta-percha tubing, which, after two years' trial at Woburn, was being laid down to replace lead piping. The flexibility and mobility of these hose-pipes was just being appreciated; the wood-cut shows a length in use, held by the hand, the pressure provided by an elevated water-butt: this presumably illustrates the activities of Mr. J. Farrah, gardener at Holderness House, Hull, who wrote a testimonial describing his method of using four of the standard 100-ft. lengths joined together.

In this year, too, James Lyne Hancock, of Goswell Mews, London, sole licensee of patent vulcanized indiarubber hosepipe, included in his advertisement, as a great novelty, a hose reel for winding-up and wheeling it away.

The greenhouse was developing fast, yet it remained a complex and usually individually designed architectural structure. In 1852, for example, an ornate 'Gothic ridge and furrow conservatory' was offered by J. W. Thomson, landscape gardener, hot-house designer and builder, of Hammersmith, 'architect at Her Majesty's Royal Gardens at Windsor, Kew, and other places'. It was available heated by hot-water or 'common flues'; there is other evidence to show that the old dry flues were still generally used for another decade or more. There were even more magnificent edifices such as the circular conservatory at Dalkeith (Plate XXVIII). On 14th January 1860 we find an advertisement headed sensationally (for the period) 'Hot-houses for the Million'. In it Samuel Hereman begged to inform the public that he had been appointed sole manufacturer and agent of the new portable and economical hot-houses invented by Sir Joseph Paxton, M.P. The accompanying figure shows that they were simple, triangulated span greenhouses of the kind that were soon to become general (Plate XXVIII).

At this period commercial remedies for pests are not very prominent. Tobacco in various forms was still the panacea. In 1851 there appears to have been a mobile machine in use for fumigating with tobacco smoke. The required pressure and draught were developed by a pump driven by a chain from the axle.[55] By 1861, however, the advertisement columns have more to offer. Mr. J. Neal refers to 'upwards of 70 testimonials received from gentlemen personally unknown to him' praising the efficacy of his Patent Aphis Pastils. One, from the distinguished nurseryman William Paul of Cheshunt, is printed: half a packet, at the cost of a shilling, works as well as half a pound of tobacco. The advertisement is accompanied by an alarming woodcut of magnified aphides. Even more horrifying is an enlargement of a red spider, which can be destroyed by a winter wash of Gishurst compound,* sold wholesale by Price's Patent Candle Co. Ltd.

Then there is a cut of two cockroaches that have seized a large ball of Chase's Beetle Poison (also efficacious against rats and mice); one has already paid for his rashness. Those who have permitted their names to be used as substantiating the claims of this poison are most interesting. They are the Rev. Edward

* A mixture of flowers of sulphur and soap.

Sidney, of Cornard Parva Rectory, near Sudbury; James Veitch, Junr., Esq., of the Royal Exotic Nursery, Chelsea; Lucombe, Pince & Co. of Exeter; E. G. Henderson & Son, Wellington Nursery, St. John's Wood; C. Loddiges, Esq., of Hackney; and George Eyles of the Royal Horticultural Society's Gardens at Chiswick.

On 3rd April 1858 it was announced that 7,000 of Ferrabee's mowers had now been sent out. In 1860 Green's of Leeds were advertising a machine that not only mowed, but rolled and collected its own grass. Shanks's new mowing machine sold by Brown of London also had a grass 'delivery'—the cast-iron framing of this was delightfully ornate.

Yet the fundamental tools of gardening, spade and fork, hoe and rake, did not change.

INDIVIDUALISTS

So much for the fashionable and popular types of garden common during this period. But, of course, the Victorians included a high proportion of men—and women—of high intelligence and refreshing enterprise and individuality. Of the many who might be named only a few can now be described.

From our point of view one of the most singular was James Bateman (1811–1897) who was, indeed, already quite well known in horticultural circles when the Queen came to the throne. He was born at Redivals, near Bury in Lancashire, but as little more than a youth we find him gardening at his father's home, Knypersley Hall, which stands on the bleak edge where the north of Staffordshire joins Cheshire—horticulturally a discouraging district, but where young Bateman was the first in England to fruit the tropical carambola.*

As an undergraduate of Magdalen College, Oxford, he was already nurturing (a little in advance of his time) a deep passion for orchids. He had seen a coloured figure of *Renanthera coccinea*† and to his delight had found a plant in the Oxford nursery of Fairbairn, who had at one time worked for Sir Joseph Banks. He spent so long examining, and eventually acquiring, the orchid (and, one may guess, discussing plants generally with so experienced a

---

* *Averrhoa carambola*, a small tree cultivated in tropical Asia for its golden, acid fruit (it is a member of the Oxalis family) from time immemorial.

† It had flowered for the first time in England at Chatsworth in 1827.

gardener) that he overstayed his leave of absence and in consequence was forced to write out half the Book of Psalms.

His interest in, and knowledge of, orchids soon gained him the friendship of John Lindley—in spite of his habit and behaviour of a dandy, a class Lindley detested. Bateman's hobby was liberally encouraged by his father, with whose assistance he was able in 1833 to engage a man named Colley to collect orchids in Demerara and Berbice. Colley's collection was a poor one. Lindley rather inappropriately honoured both patron and collector in naming *Batemania colleyi*; it has dull purplish-brown flowers, of undistinguished form, and an unpleasant odour.

In 1834 Bateman met George Ure Skinner (1804–1867), a Leeds merchant who dealt with, and travelled in, Guatemala. Skinner was also an able botanist, and through his connections obtained many good orchids, so that within a decade the Knypersley orchid houses contained one of the finest collections in England. It was from this collection that the specimens came for the plates of *The Orchidaceae of Mexico and Guatemala*, written and issued by Bateman in parts between 1837 and 1841. He described it both as his '*mega biblion*' and the librarian's nightmare. No botanical book has appeared before or since with plates of such size—they are double-crown. They were made from the drawings of two talented lady artists, Mrs. Withers, 'Floral painter to Queen Adelaide', and Miss Drake of Turnham Green. Little seems to be known of either beyond their work. Bateman was one of the earliest Englishmen to use lithography* for their reproduction, which was in this case superbly carried out. In his later publications he employed one of its greatest exponents, Walter Hood Fitch (1817–1892).†

One has only to read Bateman's text to realize that he was a man of wide sympathies and knowledge, and incapable of the pompousness so often, if wrongly, associated with the Victorian era (George Cruickshank provided small vignettes for the '*mega biblion*').

* The first important English work illustrated by this process was *Britannia Delineata* of 1822; from the 1860s onwards lithography as an art went into an eclipse, with the exception of technical work such as botanical illustration. Its worst form was the chromolithograph—an artistic triumph, however, compared with the modern colour photograph.

† Fitch was apprenticed to a firm of calico printers in Glasgow; W. J. Hooker discovered his talents when Professor of Botany there, repaid his indentures, and brought him to Kew Gardens in 1841. Nearly 10,000 of his drawings are recorded. As Hooker said, he had a remarkable power 'of seizing the natural character of plants'.

In 1838 Bateman married Maria Warburton, sister of Peter Warburton, the Australian explorer. It was her knowledge and enthusiasm (so he claimed) that encouraged him to widen his activities to include hardy plants. In about 1842 he acquired a farmhouse, with its surrounding swampy and hilly ground, near to Knypersley, on the bleak Biddulph moorland. By 1856 Biddulph Grange, as it was now called, had a garden which required seven successive articles in *The Gardener's Chronicle* to describe adequately its layout and varied contents. Contemporary plans and a series of photographs published in 1905,[56] when it had matured, show how untypical of the period it was (Plate XXIX).

The place inevitably recalls, if only indirectly, the Sir William Chambers' 'Chinese' gardener and garden of 1772, and one suspects that Bateman, with his wide knowledge, had *A Dissertation on Oriental Gardening* to some extent in mind.* In its variety of parts, each in a different style—some eclectic, some original, yet skilfully integrated to form a whole—Bateman's plan looks forward to such twentieth-century gardens as Hidcote.

The one advantage of the situation was a diversity of surfaces and aspects, which enabled Bateman, who must have had an uncanny knowledge of the wants of plants, to grow an immense number of different kinds, some of which one would suspect impossible in north Staffordshire. The site also gave him great scope in making the design, for which he and Mrs. Bateman were alone responsible, except for sketches for the buildings made by C. W. Cooke, R.A., of The Ferns, Kensington. As the greenhouses and other utilitarian parts remained at Knypersley the Grange gardens could be purely ornamental.

The Grange was approached by an avenue of old limes which were almost parallel with the main road. Just before the house was reached a stepped amphitheatre was disclosed; it was the 'rainbow garden', and planted with massed rhododendrons and azaleas.† Besides the house itself was a conservatory for rhododendrons: Bateman had first tried the Bhutan and Sikkim species out of doors, but they were overcome by the strong Staffordshire air.

* Bateman, cultured and learned, was much nearer to Chambers's oriental gardener than 'Capability'!

† This was a precursor of the now fashionable 'bowl plantings' of similar plants.

Against the southern face of the house were terraces, parterres, and a rose garden; all were simple in design. At one end was 'Mrs. Bateman's garden', which adjoined her boudoir. Descending from this, one found on the left the long and narrow dahlia walk. This was between yew walls, with buttresses of yew. Ahead, through another parterre, was a pool of most irregular outline with an island, surrounded by the rhododendron ground. The main path then wound round, passing an ancient ash turned into an arbour, and, driving through a tunnel cut in the elevated rockwork, entered the pinetum and arboretum. Deodars and wellingtonias, many other conifers, thorns, and oaks of numerous species bordered the path, paved with stones from the Appian Way. This pinetum walk ended in a mountain of evergreens, behind which lay, on the one side, a pond furnished with a rich variety of rushes and ferns, on the other an archway in the manner of a Cheshire half-timbered cottage, through which one entered a long, gloomy corridor and emerged into the Egyptian court. This, with some ornaments in the Egyptian style, gained its effect from the bastion-like masses of clipped yew. Emerging from Egypt, one returned to the parterres near the house by way of the decorative cherry orchard.

To the south-east lay a long, straight walk passing through another arboretum scattered with thorns, maples, and liquidambars to the wellingtonia avenue, in which, to be precise, the wellingtonias were interplanted with deodars.

But the most delightful parts lay within the area enclosed by the pinetum walk and the dahlia walk. Here were the sheltered bowling green, bordered by delicate Mexican pines, and the quoit ground. But most exciting was the Chinese ground. Secluded and irregularly circumscribed by high rocks planted with yews, banks of evergreens, massed weeping trees, and the ruined wall of China itself (with a watch-tower) are the Chinese waters (over which projected the temple), a joss house, a gigantic frog, a red gravel dragon parterre, and moutans in an irregular bed. Here, too, was the grotto, a pitch-dark subterranean passage, and the ferneries in which grew practically every fern native of the British Isles; the 'stumpery'—old, fantastically gnarled oak stumps crowned with golden yews and planted with anemones and other woodland plants; nooks full of *Cardocrinum giganteum*; rare alpine plants on tufa; banks planted with the winter-flowering mahonias; a bog-garden; and a large group of funkias and other foliage plants.

The whole of this garden seems to have been conceived with a singularly un-Victorian *panache*, and with a great deal of wit and learning.*

The cold air, however, was too much not only for the Sikkim rhododendrons but also for Mrs. Bateman, and in the 1860s the family left for Worthing. There Bateman had a small rock garden in which he cultivated rare alpine plants with great success, and concerned himself with the activities of the Church of England and the Royal Horticultural Society. He was an exceedingly popular speaker on theology, botany, and horticulture.

Another unconventional gardener was Alfred Smee (1818–1877), the eminent surgeon and authority on the eye. He was a man of titanic energy and brilliant intellect. His garden was in the horticulturally famous parish of Beddington, at Wallington Bridge. In 1872 he published *My Garden: Its Plan and Culture*. In this we are shown a garden quite unlike those made in the manner of a Paxton or Nesfield. The book is full of learning and observation—and of a great delight in the wonders of gardening. It begins with the geology and history of the site, and continues to describe the birds, animals, and insects of the garden, as well as its plants. That there are 1,250 engravings and plates gives an idea of the range of Smee's interests. Nothing, surely, could be more remote from Victorian geometry and carpet-bedding than this:

Under a large willow is arranged a bower for shade from the midday sun, where nightingales, sedge-warblers, and wrens delight to dwell, and the babbling brook runs every hour of the day, and all the year round, making music of its own to soothe the nervous system after the excitement of an overgrown city. The lower branches of the willow tree are turned down, and over them are trained roses, honeysuckle, and clematis, to cover the bower.

> *Quite overcanopied with lush woodbine,*
> *With sweet musk-roses and with eglantine.*

It is not possible for the writer to describe the fern glen by words, nor is it possible for the artist to delineate it with his pencil . . . visitors

* The place is now a hospital, but thanks to the enthusiasm of Mr. John Lambert much of the garden remains.

have observed that it was a spot to be pictured by a fanciful imagination in their dreams, but not actually to exist in the reality of nature. . . .

The brook falls into the backwater below the overfall, and trout delight to visit it, and when disturbed to rush back to a place of shelter under the overfall. They may be watched for hours selecting their food as it passes by. The stones of the brooks are covered with insects, diatomes, and fresh water limpets. It truly may be said that:

> *He makes sweet music with the enamelled stones,*
> *Giving a gentle kiss to every sedge*
> *He overtaketh in his pilgrimage,*
> *And so by many winding nooks he strays*
> *With willing sport to the wild ocean.*

The land, as well as the water of my fern glen, is well furnished. As we enter it we see gigantic osmundas rearing their stiff and majestic forms; enormous lady ferns gracefully showing their flowering feathery forms, with the noble broad ferns expanding their curved fronds to view. Every stump glistens with the gold-spored common polypody, and near every stone the triangular oak fern shows its fronds. Turning round, another view discloses alpine polypody, marsh fern, beech fern, and oak fern. *Cystopteris* grows luxuriantly. The beautiful *Adiantum trichomanes* and *A. nigrum* are healthy, but to the observant eye only do the Woodsias, the filmy ferns, and the Killarney fern appear.

In one part I have attempted a mossery, and literally:

> *Here are cool mosses deep,*
> *And through the moss the ivies creep,*
> *And in the stream the long-leaved flowers weep,*
> *And from the craggy ledge the poppy hangs in sleep.*

The grass of Parnassus abundantly lends its aid to decorate so lovely a spot, mosses of many kinds appear, and the Northern cloudberry and *Rubus arcticus* grace the scene with their presence. American adiantums flourish, and a little tiny pond shows frog-bit, the water soldier, and other aquatic plants. On emerging from the glen we have to traverse little tiny mountains, such as children might make as toys, but then they are lit up with Alpine snapdragons, the lovely gentians, primulas, and other Alpine plants, with sempervivums at the apices of the stones and many terrestrial orchids at their base. Here the 'lily of the field' expands its beautiful flowers in autumn with such effect that 'Solomon in all his glory was not arrayed like one of these'. A cranberry plantation is arranged on the slopes towards the stream, so that the mind is led from this weak horticultural sham to the real glorious natural scenery of Zermatt and the high Alps, where such plants delight to grow.

We pass from the glen, and wonder how in so small a place and short a time our minds could have been bewildered by so many objects beautiful and curious to the eye, and by so many sounds pleasing to the ear.

Here, surely, there is some consultation with the genius of the place, so often absent from the work of Nesfield, Paxton, and Barry. It should be added that Smee also grew, and enjoyed in full measure, the old florists' flowers.

       .   .   .   .

It was during the present period that the possibilities of growing half-hardy plants in the western coastal regions of the British Isles, and also obtaining horticultural produce at an early date, were first properly appreciated.

Borlase in 1758 and Polwhele in 1816 had remarked on the tender plants that could be grown in Cornwall with little or no protection. William Rashleigh (1777–1855) of Menabilly, an authority on seaweeds, had a noted collection of exotic plants, including Australian natives, as early as 1820.

In 1841 W. B. Booth, then head gardener to Sir Charles Lemon at Carclew, reported regularly in *The Gardener's Chronicle* on the weather and its effects on New Zealand plants in that garden. At Tremough, the estate of Henry Shilson, the Himalayan rhododendrons raised from seed collected by J. D. Hooker during his journey of 1847–51 were, it seems, first grown in quantity; it is said that many Cornish gardens were supplied with the scarlet *Rhododendron arboreum* and other tender species by him.

Cornwall, however, was not the only scene of these experiments. Among the individualists of the south-west we should include Augustus Smith (1804–1872) of Berkhampstead, who in 1834, as lessee, became Lord Proprietor of the Isles of Scilly. He was a ruthless but beneficent and far-sighted dictator, and a keen botanist and gardener. The bare and poverty-stricken islands, with their mild but gale-stricken climate, began to prosper. Around the ruins of Tresco Abbey he planted trees for shelter, and built there a low, stone house to withstand the winds. Here he gradually evolved a terraced garden, and made the first plantings of the garden full of rare plants from warm climates, which today is one of the botanical gardeners' paradises. More particularly did he collect—and in many cases naturalize—trees, shrubs, and plants from the Cape, the Australian continent, and parts of South America. The history of Tresco Abbey garden is well recorded.[57] As early as May 1850 Smith was writing of his ixias, sparaxis, and mesembryanthemums—and that he was already eating new potatoes of fine size. Soon after, veronicas, acacias, fuchsias, pelargoniums, cinerarias, aloes, and a multitude of other plants requiring greenhouse treatment in most of Britain, were thriving out of doors, most skilfully placed and planted by this remarkable man, who was learning to master his one enemy, the wind.

Augustus Smith pioneered the commercial production of early potatoes. It was his successor, in 1872, a nephew, Thomas Algernon Dorrien Smith, who (as has already been related) found old daffodils growing around the abbey and, starting with them, within a few years developed the most profitable daffodil-growing industry. In 1886, on 30th March, there was held the first of the Isles of Scilly flower shows;* Smith exhibited 160 varieties of narcissus which were either being profitably cultivated or on trial. It was he, too, who found an answer to the gales. Sailing one day after a storm that had devastated his woodlands, he noticed one tree that still stood firm and undamaged. He took a bearing on it so that he might identify the species, which was the Monterey pine, *Pinus radiata*. This was not surprising, as the tree, discovered and introduced by Douglas to England in 1833, grows only on a small area of hilly land by the side of the sea in Monterey County where it withstands the force of the salt-laden Pacific gales. It has since been used as a windbreak in many coastal areas of Britain where severe frost is absent, for it is not entirely hardy.

At about the time the great gardens of Cornwall and the south-west were being planted with tender Californian, Himalayan, Cape, and Australasian plants, it was realized that the west coast of Scotland, far up into the north, provided rather similar conditions; that is, absence of severe frost, a good (some-

---

* The first of the Cornish March flower shows at Truro did not take place until 1897.

times too good) rainfall, and over-abundant storms and tempests. One of the first to grasp this was Osgood Hanbury Mackenzie (1842–1922) who in 1862 bought Inverewe,* an exposed, bare, rocky, and windswept site on Loch Ewe in Wester Ross. There was but one tree, or rather shrub, on the estate—a dwarf willow. In the crevices of rocky soil Mackenzie began to plant those trees and shrubs which he believed would withstand the storms (sometimes having to import earth). Here the native strain of Scots pine and the Corsican pine (another island tree) proved so successful that after fifteen years he began planting many other species, now of choicer and tenderer kinds, such as eucalyptus. The shelter achieved, rhododendrons, hydrangeas, tricuspidarias, dicksonias, and numerous other rare trees, shrubs, and plants were added and in the moist, frost-free air grew with abandon on the hitherto bare shore.[58]

Moving over to the very different climate of south-eastern Scotland, the garden and writings of Miss Francis Jane Hope of Wardie Lodge, Edinburgh, should be mentioned. Dying as an old lady in 1881, her writings in the gardening Press showed her to be far in advance of her times. She was one of the first to break away from the rigid conventions of flower decoration, and her delight in such then unfashionable plants as the hellebores, and of kale for its winter beauty, are refreshingly original.[59]

* A property of the National Trust for Scotland.

EIGHT

Nature Returns as Science Advances

1883–1939

THE ROBINSONIAN WORLD

OUR last phase—and it is a long one—begins in glory, illuminated by the possible wonders of science, and ends with man appearing to have an hitherto unbelievable control over his plants and their pests and even their environments. As we advance the scene inevitably becomes more blurred, until we lose the focus almost entirely, and can pick out no more than a few of the brightest and darkest spots.

In the year 1883 was published William Robinson's *The English Flower Garden*, treating of 'the design and arrangement shown by existing samples of gardens in Great Britain and Ireland followed by a description of the best plants for the open-air garden and their culture'. The 'existing gardens' exemplify the triumph of the 'natural' style of gardening evolved by Robinson and his school, which is in general the style that has been maintained—perhaps only under the force of economic circumstances—ever since.

The origins of the Robinsonian manner go back much further than his own time. There are broad hints of them in Biddulph Grange and Wallington Bridge. It would probably be true to say, though it never seems to have been so stated, that Robinson's aim was to obliterate the Paxtonian era and to pick up the threads again that Loudon let fall when he died in his wife's arms. Surely it is significant that it was to Loudon that the first volume of Robinson's earlier important achievement, the weekly journal *The Garden*, was dedicated?

The few facts—and they are extraordinary—that we seem

likely ever to know of Robinson's early life have been related by Geoffrey Taylor.[1] He was born of humble Protestant parents in Ireland in 1838. By the age of twenty-one he was foreman in the gardens of the Rev. Sir Hunt Henry Johnson-Walsh, Bart., of Ballykilcavan, Stradbally, which position he had gained after entering them as a boy. He was in charge of a considerable range of glass-houses. In the famous severe winter of 1861 for some unexplained reason this bright foreman drew the fires from the houses, opened all the windows, and by the next morning was in Dublin. There he called on David Moore at Glasnevin—who rather surprisingly recommended him for employment under Robert Marnock* in the Royal Botanic Society's gardens in Regent's Park. Within two years he was in charge of the herbaceous section of the garden. He was also responsible for a small collection of English wild flowers. Collecting plants for this he came to know English wild flowers and the English countryside, with its cottage gardens, intimately. Indeed, it would be no exaggeration to say that he came to love them passionately. From his observations he gradually conceived a vision of a garden contrived as a part of the natural scene but embellished by the choice and delightful representatives of the flora of other temperate parts of the world—from China to South America.

In his early London days Robinson must have devoted much time to his education. He was elected a member of the Linnean Society through Marnock, and learned to write the excellent and at times very forceful prose that made him nearly the equal of a Loudon. He also learned French so that he might go as a representative of Veitch and *The Times* to the Paris Exhibition of 1867. So it was that at the age of twenty-nine he left the Botanic Society's garden and was henceforward a successful man, of increasing influence. Visits to France and an alpine walking tour followed, with the consequent *Alpine Flowers for English Gardens* (1870), to all intents and purposes the first British book on the subject. In that year Robinson visited, and delighted in, the United States of America, and also produced *The Wild Garden*, which was from time to time revised; in a late edition he

* Robert Marnock (1800–1889) belonged to the Loudon circle; he was Curator of the Royal Botanic Society's Garden until 1869. During the 1840s he was in partnership as Marnock & Manley, nurserymen. He laid out a great many residences in the picturesque manner.

described 'the idea of the wild garden is placing plants of other countries, as hardy as our hardiest wild flowers, in places where they will flourish without further care or cost'. The title of his illustrations make this clearer: 'Double Chinese paeonies in grass at Crowsley Park', 'Tiger lilies in the wild garden at Great Tew', 'Large white clematis on a yew tree at Great Tew',* 'A Liane in the North — Aristolochia and Deciduous Cypress', 'A beautiful accident—a colony of *Myrrhis odorata*'—and so on.

In these early years Robinson was working up his campaign against bedding-out, 'pastry-work gardening', the subjection of gardeners to 'decorative artists', and everything to do with the Crystal Palace. Generally, except in small matters such as plant names and the imagined sins of the authorities at Kew, he was not intolerant. An opponent of terraces and 'railway embankment' gardening, he saw the rightness and beauty of steep, falling terraced ground at Powis Castle; scornful of fantastic topiary, he delighted in the neatly cut yews of a Cotswold garden. His watchword was Pope's: *Good Sense*.

In 1871 he used his savings to launch *The Garden: An Illustrated Weekly Journal of Horticulture In All Its Branches*. This was never a great financial success, but with frequent colour plates it attracted contributions from a number of highly talented amateurs belonging to the new school.† In 1879 he began *Gardening* (later, *Gardening Illustrated*), written for the new suburbans. It was an admirable paper, and very successful.

Robinson was first and foremost a writer—a writer of great imagination, knowledge, skill, and experience. He was also a keen practical gardener, not beyond cultivating those plants he affected to despise. His ideas of wild gardening were opportune. He came at a period when the host of hardy, self-reliant shrubs and plants from Western China were on their way; new gardens for a wealthy suburbia were being made in southern home counties—perfect homes for rhododendrons, magnolias, and so much that was now being introduced. And he arrived just prior to a period when labour costs were to rise and finally extinguish all possibilities of large gardens in the old manner. Nature was most helpful.

* Robinson delighted that Great Tew, with its associations with Loudon, should be early in the field with a wild garden.
† Many of them, it must be admitted, found him a rather trying person.

The Robinsonian tradition of gardening around the house is so well known that it need scarcely be described: wide, sweeping lawns, shapely beds filled with roses, shrubs, or hardy plants, and flowery creepers covering the walls. Always at the back of his mind was the image of a traditional English cottage garden.

One of his successes was the conversion of Shrubland Park in the 1880s to his style. He never, of course, triumphed finally over his enemies, but his success was, and remains, pretty substantial.

The Garden was a paper covering all aspects of gardening— including greenhouse plants and orchids!—except the 'pastry-cake' and 'fountain-monger's' work. It had, however, particular requirements of its contributors. The first essential was a true interest in plants and skill in handling them. The second was a standard of good taste, and usually education.

It is profitless to ask how the Robinsonian garden would have developed if in about 1875 he had not met Miss Gertrude Jekyll (1843–1932).[2] Miss Jekyll belonged to that class of society which had, for generations,* well earned the title gentlefolk. Never wealthy and overpowering, never disappearing into obscurity, the Jekylls had a long tradition in which was embodied intelligence and culture. Brought up in a household where music and to some extent the other arts and sciences (particularly if they involved skilful handicraft) were encouraged, during a childhood spell of by no means unhappy loneliness, Gertrude Jekyll came to know flowers and trees and their qualities with an intimacy that was surprising, as she did the old Surrey craftsmen about her home.

In due time Miss Jekyll decided to become a professional artist, and travelled widely; she knew Ruskin, and in addition to painting became proficient in several crafts—notably that of gilding, which she learned in Italy. Throughout this period her interest in plants never left her. Shortly after meeting Robinson, with whose views, of course, she sympathetically agreed, she laid out a new garden in the then wilds of Surrey for her widowed mother. This work, and the articles that she was now writing for Robinson, brought her a wider reputation. In the 1880s she began to design gardens—the first, it is said, for a factory lad in

* The most eminent of the family, Sir Joseph (1662–1738), a keen amateur of architecture who was concerned with the erection or restoration of thirty-nine houses, was a subscriber to James's book.

Rochdale who wanted his plot to include as many varieties of plants as could be contained within its confines.

The style of gardening in which she excelled was well suited to the heathy woodlands of Surrey, with their oaks and birches, and the adjoining counties that she understood so well. Woodland and water, treated 'naturally' in the Robinsonian manner, were the principal element in their composition. Her own particular contribution to the garden was her artist's sense of colour and planting for colour effect. And we should not underrate the critical faculties used in the selection of the best from the overabundance of plants now available; her standards were high, her choice often subtle and quite unswayed by the fashions of the wealthy.

There were, of course, other and earlier influences that brought about the Surrey school, but, not being writers, their names are not so well known. One of the most important was George Fergusson Wilson (1822–1902). A man of great versatility whose occupation in reference books is given delightfully and unusually as 'inventor', he was, in fact, a successful Russian merchant, who in 1842 was jointly responsible for a patent that enabled 'malodorous' fats to be used for candle-making—the profitable Price's Patent Candle Company was the outcome. Settling at Heatherbank, Weybridge, he devoted his experimental and inventive powers to gardening. His own account relates that, impressed by the success of his sister with an orchard house built on the Rivers system in about 1855, he made one himself. Before long, although he had to do the pruning by candlelight, he was triumphant at shows. Old Mr. Rivers said it was because the wasps could read the moral of· the old Spanish proverbs which Wilson had rather incongruously placed on the beams of his building.

His next venture was with lilies. Disregarding the advice of the experts, he bought cheaply large quantities of Japanese bulbs offered at an auction as 'damaged by sea-water'. These he planted in cut-down wine-casks, which were put in the orchard house. Several new and rare kinds shortly appeared and flowered among the profusion of lily blooms that resulted. The ingenious Wilson was shortly acknowledged by the experts as the most successful cultivator and exhibitor of lilies in the country.

In 1878 he bought cheaply an estate then known as Oakwood at Wisley, near Ripley in Surrey. Here was agriculturally poor land, with ancient, undisturbed woods on a deep, acid, vegetable soil. Wilson saw this as an ideal habitat for his lilies, for irises, rhododendrons, and other plants. Here he made pools, and planted lavishly. Once again he succeeded; pictorially it was also a delight. When someone told him that it was a fascinating place but no garden, 'I think of it,' he said, 'as a place where plants from all over the world grow wild.'[3] The influence of Wilson on garden history is profounder than is generally realized, for his Oakwood estate formed the nucleus of the present Royal Horticultural Society's Wisley Gardens.*

Robinson and his disciples were vociferous; the virtues of the natural style of gardening were not only propounded in his own publications but elsewhere, for the Robinsonian school did not lack journalists of a high calibre, several of them avoiding the extreme, and even nonsensical, whims that marred their master's work.†

In 1892, however, a strong challenge was issued by Reginald Blomfield, in *The Formal Garden in England*. On the title page he described himself as Master of Arts, Fellow of the Society of Antiquaries, and Architect.‡ Today this book is notable for two reasons—first, perhaps, for the perfect little drawings and reconstructions made by F. Inigo Thomas. The other is the surprising one that it brought the term 'formal', relating to gardens,§ into the general vocabulary for the first time.

Blomfield's book attempted to separate garden design from horticulture—the design to be by an architect, based on some traditional pattern, the horticulturist being very much an 'also ran'. It is a fallacious argument, for so often the examples that he cites were designed by men who were gardeners first and architects secondarily. Nor had he (as we now see) adequate knowledge or understanding to conduct the historical enquiry with which so

---

* Wilson was closely connected with the Society, of which he was at one time Treasurer.

† One of the most stupid of these was his intolerance of any systematic international method of plant nomenclature; he was anxious that every plant should be invested with an English name. He had also fanatical dislikes of the authorities at Kew and—not quite so unreasonably—of the half-tone process of reproducing illustrations.

‡ Sir Reginald Blomfield (1856–1942), also author of *A History of Renaissance Architecture in England*.

§ Joseph Warton in 1740 talks of 'formality and method'. Horace Walpole uses the word very rarely; subsequently, it seems to have died out until Blomfield revived it.

much of the book is concerned. His general thesis, however, that there was plenty of good in the geometrically designed gardens of the past was salutary; particularly was this so when applied to those areas of limestone country in which stone for buildings and walls was still the common material, and where the flora the ground would sustain was very different from that which was at its best on the acid soil of the Surrey school.

Though Blomfield is the best known of Robinson's opponents, there were other far more thoughtful exponents of formalism. One was John Dando Sedding (1838–1891), whose *Garden-craft Old and New* was published in the year of his early death. Sedding was by training an architect, a member of the Art Workers' Guild, and emotionally an artist—his work was admired by so fine a judge as W. R. Lethaby. He had a considerable understanding of plants and gardens—was appreciative of much that Robinson wrote—and his modest thoughtfulness is pleasing and still worth consideration, as a contrast to the Robinson-Blomfield dogmatism.

Harold Ainsworth Peto (1854–1933) was another distinguished formalist.* He was a practising architect who was early attracted by old Italian gardens and made them the model of his work. A certain simplicity underlies the fundamentally architectural form of his gardens, normally in the classical style. He delighted in colonnades formed of rather simple, often Ionic, pillars. His gardens were understandingly embellished with well chosen trees, shrubs, and plants and ornamented with statuary and other architectural features. At Easton Lodge, Essex, he successfully reverted to the long out-moded construction of *treillage*. He designed a number of gardens on the Riviera. In England examples of his work can be seen at Wayford Manor in Somerset, and in Ireland his garden designed for Mr. Bryce on Garinish Island in the Bay of Glengariff has now been acquired by the Commissioners of Public Works.

His own delightful garden at Iford Manor, near Bradford-on-Avon, is, however, clearly the most representative example of his work. In 1899 he purchased the small stone manor house lying below woods in the steep valley of the little River Frome and

* His art was esteemed by Miss Jekyll and was well represented in her book *Garden Ornament*.

around it evolved a garden of terraces, courtyards, and colonnades, the whole most skilfully merged into its natural surroundings. In it he placed—most aptly—a collection of architectural ornaments, ranging from an eighteenth-century garden house to Greek, Roman, and medieval French sculptures.

Then there was Sir George Sitwell (1860–1943), whose deep —indeed, passionate—study of garden design and 'of the nature of beauty' made principally among the old Italian gardens is recorded in *An Essay on the Making of Gardens* (1909) and displayed at Renishaw in Derbyshire. We have his son's recollections of the man himself in action, striding round his garden with measuring-stick and binoculars, ever seeking to embody in material form his visions of light and shade; or, erecting Piranesi-like contraptions from whose altitude he might—shaded from the sun by an umbrella, telescope in hand—plot more accurately some projected, but seldom effected, series of water-works in the grand manner.[4]

Yet, by a paradox, the true revival of what we may now call formal gardening was brought about through the Robinsonians. Not far from the Jekylls lived the Lutyens family. Edwin Landseer Lutyens (1869–1944), becoming an architect by rather unorthodox means, had very much in common with Gertrude Jekyll, including a deep understanding of traditional craftsmanship and materials—an understanding of the cause and effect that produced a given work, not (as was so common) a knowledge of the finished work only that was achieved by mechanical imitation.

In 1896 Miss Jekyll built her own house, Munstead Wood, and Lutyens was the designer. This partnership was a fruitful one, and Munstead Wood is probably of greater significance in the history of gardening than Stowe or any other of our British precedents. The purely architectural—or geometrical—surrounding of a house as conceived by Lutyens, and embellished by Miss Jeykll, merges into a garden in which she not infrequently takes the greater share.

In his wider schemes Lutyens brought an extraordinary and refreshing virility to the design of fountains and canals, stairways and terraces; the play of fine materials and surfaces one against another and a delight in solid geometry were something that had scarcely existed in garden architecture for generations. Yet

Lutyens always glanced backwards and in some degree revived or echoed the past: Miss Jekyll's own work looked to the future for, in spite of her devotion to the principle of the cottage garden, she was employing new materials and new colours in a new manner well suited to the modest gardenerless gardens that economics were forcing upon the British Isles.* Her style was also welcomed and adopted in the United States of America, though not on the Continent.

Also associated with this movement of moderate formalism round a house in the traditional manner built of traditional materials—or preferably an old house itself—was Nathaniel Lloyd (1867–1933). He was, indeed, a most scholarly student of English buildings and their materials, but the gardener recalls his understanding and practical knowledge of hedges and topiary, well displayed in his *Garden Craftsmanship in Yew and Box* (1925). His theories are well exemplified in his own Sussex home, Great Dixter (Plate XXX).

Two women writers also no doubt swayed a wide public towards naturalism.

Juliana Horatia Ewing (1841–1885), daughter of the novelist Mrs. Gatty, opposed all that Paxton represented. She wrote for children, and *Mary's Meadow*, begun as a serial in 1883 in *Aunt Judy's Magazine*, influenced more than one rising generation.

Mrs. C. M. Earle (1836–1925) was Maria Theresa Villiers, and a much more sophisticated writer. After the death of her husband she published *Pot-Pourri from a Surrey Garden* (1896) and *More Pot-Pourri from a Surrey Garden* (1899). Both of these admirable books were widely read.

We must return from the subtleties of Miss Jekyll and Lloyd to William Robinson. It seems that he had invested the profits from his gardening journalism very successfully in London property, and in 1884 he bought Gravetye Manor, near East Grinstead in Sussex, an old stone manor house. For the rest of his life he was continually improving its 200 acres of ground and restoring the fabric to its pristine condition—including a return to wood fires (which didn't burn) from coal (another dislike). Old Robert Marnock planned the garden for him—a return to

---

* In *Home and Garden* (1900), her most revealing book, devoted largely to Munstead Wood, she refers to it as little more than a cottage; by today's standards it is a moderate-sized house.

XVII. 'Botanicks' and chinoiserie. Sir William Chamber's pagoda, of about 1761, in the Royal Botanic Gardens, Kew

DELICIOUS WEATHER.

XVIII. The rise of the middle-class gardener (1808). *Delicious Weather*, an etching by James Gillray. Note the Lombardy poplars – introduced about 1750 – already a feature of the suburban scene, the collection of somewhat imaginative pot-plants, the ingenious garden seat, and the introduction of humour into gardening

XIXa. Attingham, Shropshire (1798). The 'Red Book', so called from the red morocco in which it was bound, showing Repton's proposals for improvement. The shadow indicates the folding flap which superimposes the existing scene upon the new design. A National Trust property (National Trust)

XIXb. An ice-house for the grounds of a nobleman (1818). A typical example of the work of J. B. Papworth

XX. The moss rose. A hand-coloured engraving of a flower popular in the late eighteenth century and typical of the period in every way (*The Botanical Magazine*, Vol. I)

XXI. Views in the 'Lawrencian villa' at Drayton Green, *c.*1838. (1) The French parterre. (2) Rustic arch and cupid, 'where a tent is often pitched'. (3) A vase and rustic arch terminating a vista through to the paddock. (4) The pollard vista, seen from the lawn. (5) Looking back to the house from the lawn. (6) The Italian walk (J. C. Loudon, *The Villa Gardener*)

XXII. The first modern strawberry (1826). 'Keen's Seedling', from the drawing by John Robertson (*Transactions of the Horticultural Society*, Vol. V)

Williams' Bon Chretien

XXIII. Williams' Bon Chrétien Pear. William Hooker's coloured figure illustrating the original description of this fruit communicated on 3rd December 1816. It will be noticed that the blemishes, such as would today make a pear unmarketable, are carefully delineated (*Transactions of the Horticultural Society*, Vol. II)

XXIVa. Hoole House, Cheshire (1838). Lady Broughton's rock garden, seen from the centre of the flower garden (J. C. Loudon, *The Villa Gardener*)

XXIVb. Redleaf, Surrey (1839). The rocky lawn, showing the descent of the rock walk to the rocky hollow designed by William Wells (*Gardener's Magazine*, Vol. XVIII)

XXVa. Victoriana (i). An early cast-iron garden bench

XXVb. Victoriana (ii). The giant Perseus fountain at Witley Court, Worcestershire, by T. R. Smith (1858) (W. T. Jones)

XXVIa. Royal Horticultural Society's Gardens, Kensington (1861). The Victorian revival of the architectural and geometric design (A. Murray, *Book of the Royal Horticultural Society*)

XXVIb. Nuthill House and garden (1853). Victorian geometric design merging into the gardenesque and thence into the landscape (C. M'Intosh, *Book of the Garden*)

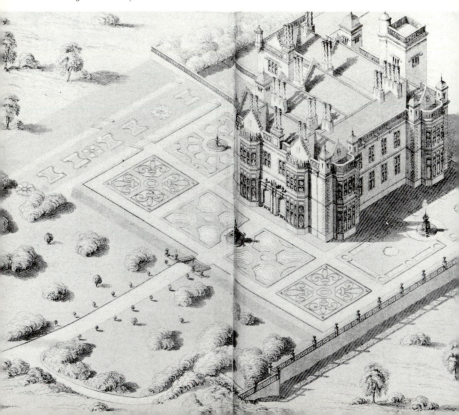

XXVIIa. Decimus Burton's Palm House, Kew (1844–8). A landmark in the development of glass-house construction and in the formation of the Royal Botanic Gardens

XXVIIb. Hidcote Manor, Gloucestershire (1903–39). The end of the main vista, the ground falling sharply away beyond the gate. A National Trust property (Cadbury Bros. Ltd)

HOTHOUSES FOR THE MILLION.

SAMUEL HEREMAN

BEGS TO INFORM THE PUBLIC THAT HE HAS BEEN APPOINTED SOLE AGENT FOR THE MANUFACTURE AND SALE OF

THE NEW PORTABLE AND ECONOMICAL HOTHOUSES,

INVENTED AND PATENTED BY

SIR JOSEPH PAXTON, M.P.

These Buildings are of unparalleled cheapness, and being composed of simple parts can be enlarged, removed, or adapted to any Horticultural purpose by ordinary labourers.

They are calculated for gardens of the highest order, or gentlemen's gardens generally, for market gardens where they may be made to cover any extent of surface, and also for suburban, villa, and cottage gardens.

XXVIIIa. Glass-houses for the million. Paxton's design advertised in *The Gardeners Chronicle and Agricultural Gazette*, January 1860 (*Gardeners Chronicle*, 1860)

XXVIIIb. Glass-houses for the aristocracy (1853). The famous circular conservatory at Dalkeith, Edinburgh (C. M'Intosh, *Book of the Garden*)

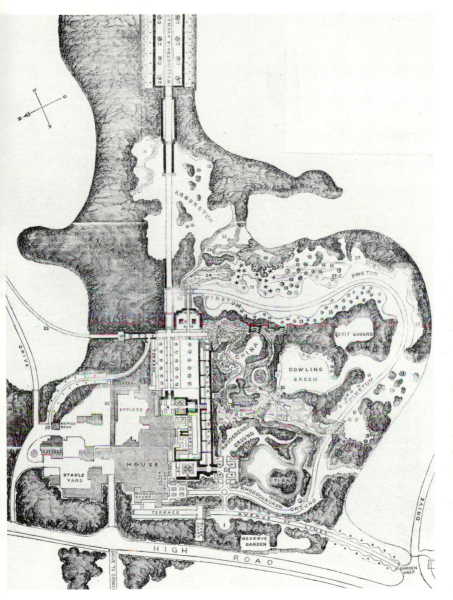

XXIX. Biddulph Grange, Staffordshire (1862). The plan of Mr and Mrs James Bateman's garden (*Gardeners Chronicle*, 1862)

XXX. Great Dixter, Northiam, Sussex. An example of the revival of the small manor-house garden in a formal style. The wall designed by Sir Edwin Lutyens in 1911, the actual sunk garden the work of Nathaniel Lloyd in 1921 (Quentin Lloyd)

XXXIa. Westonbirt, Gloucestershire. Early twentieth-century use of trees and shrubs in an imaginative manner (J. D. U. Ward)

XXXIb. Sheffield Park, Sussex. An early twentieth-century landscape dramatically altering an undistinguished Lancelot Brown design. A National Trust property

XXXIIa. A Chelsea garden. This is shown in Figure II

XXXIIb. A Hampstead garden. A romantic town garden, rich in foliage

Loudon—and another great friend, Alfred Parsons,* advised him on the restoration of the building.

The respective elysiums of Robinson and Miss Jekyll set the pattern of the best in British gardening for many decades. Robinson was typical of one trend in that he acquired a derelict house—Gravetye had at one time become no more than a lodging for harvest labourers—restored it, and developed the existing gardens and grounds around it in what he considered a suitable manner, though certainly not in the same style or period as the house. Miss Jekyll and her kind started from scratch, building a new house, but adapted from the traditional native style, and laying out the ground around it in a manner that was peculiar to the late nineteenth century and onwards.

Robinson's attempts at making his own home and garden were not nearly so successful as Miss Jekyll's. Far from leaving nature alone, he moved many tons of earth to make a landscaped entrance. Great numbers of trees were felled, and in other places cedars, Corsican pines, willows, and almonds were planted *en masse*; for one who talked so freely of 'nature' his extravagant attempt to transplant large bushes of gold and silver hollies is surprising (it was a failure). The establishment of large colonies of chionodoxas, dogs-tooth violets, aconites, and daffodils (of the last, 100,000 were planted in 1897) was by no means always successful. His strenuous efforts to naturalize the hardier herbaceous plants in his hedgerows and woods seem to have failed completely.

Ironically enough his greatest successes seem to have been with florists' flowers—tea roses, outdoor carnations, and violas in the more formal beds, and hybrid water-lilies in his ponds. His own records (not the sumptuously produced *Gravetye Manor* (1911) based on them) show his severe limitations as well as his successes.[5]

Robinson's attempts at farming ended in failure; this alone tempts one to compare him with J. C. Loudon, whose career was launched by his success in agriculture. Nor, it seems, in spite of his wealth and acres, was he so successful a cultivator of garden

---

* Alfred Parsons (1847–1920) was a talented landscape painter; he illustrated Robinson's *The Wild Garden*—his manner touched a little by the more popular style of Corot. His paintings for Ellen Willmott's *The Genus Rosa* are delicate and of high standing botanically. Unfortunately, his work when published always suffered from the use of poor methods of reproduction.

plants as the Loudons, with their 2,000 species thriving in Bayswater. Nor did he leave any enduring monument such as the *Arboretum*. Gravetye itself, on his death, when times had changed, proved an unsalable property.

Robinson was one of the great figures in garden history, but as time passes it seems a little difficult to explain precisely why. As I have said, it is profitless to discuss what form later stages of flower gardening would have taken if Miss Jekyll had not called at his office. In 1899 Robinson retired from the editorial chair of *The Garden* and, jointly with E. T. Cook, she succeeded him. She herself retired in 1902, leaving Cook in charge. The paper ceased in 1927.

A word should be said about the last of the Robinsonian publications, the costly and extravagantly produced *Flora and Sylva*, which lasted for only three years, from 1903 to 1905. There is much of it that is interesting, but neither its contents nor its lavish production achieved the high quality at which Robinson aimed.

This was particularly so with the many colour plates, mostly by Henry George Moon (1857–1905).* This painter was long associated with Robinson. Competent and facile, his pleasant work is entirely without any quality of liveliness combined with botanical understanding, those two prerequisites of such colour plates. His work, and the kind of flowers that he painted, have, however, already acquired a rather undistinguished tone recalling their period. It can be said in mitigation that his painting was gayer than the figures of the reliable and industrious G. Worthington Smith (1835–1917), who from 1875 to 1910 provided a regular flow of drawings for *The Gardener's Chronicle*, of monotonous accuracy combined with a peculiar feeling of staleness that was no doubt increased by the now debased mechanics of wood engraving. We must face a fact that Robinson would not: the halftone reproduction of a photograph was fast replacing the work of the botanical artist, who became an unessential luxury.

The Gardener's Chronicle was, in this period, in some ways unduly shadowed by the dominating Robinsonian journalism. Needless to say, it continued as an important periodical, invaluable to

* The popular tulip 'Mrs. Moon' was named after his wife, a daughter of H. F. C. Sander, the orchid-grower.

the working and scientific gardener, even if it did still present its readers with chromolithographed plans of carpet-bedding long after Robinson believed he had killed that fashion. It was directed principally by a remarkable and learned man, Dr. Maxwell Tylden Masters (1833–1907). He became senior editor, with Thomas Moore as his fellow, in 1865, and from Moore's death in 1887 to a few weeks before his own in 1907 he was responsible for the highly reliable standard of the paper. Masters was the son of a Canterbury nurseryman noted both for his hybridization of passion-flowers and the foundation of the Canterbury museum. The son was ambitious, and wished to follow a more intellectual career. He qualified as a Doctor of Medicine at Edinburgh. Botanically, he was an authority—and published important works on—teratology (the study of plant abnormalities), the large and chiefly tropical passion-flower family (an interest presumably inherited from his father) and, of much consequence to the horticulturists of the day, a leading expert on conifers. He took a very active part in the working of many gardening organizations, particularly the Royal Horticultural Society, which perpetuated his memory in the important Masters Memorial Lectures.

On 3rd May 1884 first appeared the weekly paper *Amateur Gardening*. This was directed to the steadily increasing class of owner-gardeners who employed little or no labour. Shirley Hibberd was its first editor, but success did not come until 1887 when he was succeeded by Thomas W. Sanders (1855–1926). Born at Martley in Worcestershire, Sanders was first a builder and then a working gardener. After employment in several large gardens, including a period at Versailles, he entered upon horticultural journalism. His success was great. Not only did he cause *Amateur Gardening* to flourish, but his name still lives on in *Sanders' Encyclopaedia of Gardening* and other sound, practical, and popular books. He was followed on his death by Albert James Macself (1869–1952), who moved into journalism from the nursery trade.

One other periodical, originally associated with the Jekyll-Lutyens school, should be mentioned. In January 1897 the first issue of *Country Life* appeared. Ever since, it has given much attention to gardening in its aesthetic, practical, and historical aspects. Week by week some notable house or building has been described and well illustrated, as often as not with its surrounding garden. The first of this long and honoured series of articles was devoted to the moated Warwickshire house of Baddesley Clinton. A little later the contributions of H. Avray Tipping (1855–1933), who combined a practical knowledge of gardening and garden-design with considerable historical and architectural learning, introduced a new element into the study of old gardens. Sir Lawrence Weaver (1876–1930) was also a contributor, and collaborator with Miss Jekyll.

HARDY PLANTS—AND CLERGYMEN

As we have seen, each volume of *The Garden*—there were two in a year—carried a dedication to a well-known gardener of the past or present. Those written by Robinson reveal his own tastes and throw light on the subject from other than the angle of an obituary. The year 1883, which opens our period, honoured a gardener who had lived on from another era, for the Rev. Henry T. Ellacombe was born in 1790, though he lived until 1885. Yet he was entirely in tune with the best in Robinson's theories. He was a man of wide education, for he was trained, and showed great promise, as an engineer. He decided, however, that the Church was his vocation. It is in connection with the parish of Bitton that the name of Ellacombe will always be associated, though Henry was vicar only from 1835 to 1850. But in that year he was succeeded by his son, who had already been his curate for two years, and as a gardener followed devotedly in his father's footsteps.

Henry T. Ellacombe, Robinson could not help boasting, wrote only for *The Garden*; thanks to him, Bitton, with its collection of hardy plants, trees, and shrubs (notably a collection of rose species) 'remained unchanged through all the caprices of fashion' and was quite untouched by the bedding-out craze. Here again we have an instance of Robinson's desire to return and take up the threads from Loudon.

Henry Nicholson Ellacombe, the son (1822–1916), was at Bitton for sixty-eight years. The vicarage garden lying in a warm and sheltered spot between Bath and Bristol, on a limy soil, had within half an acre probably a greater variety of plants than had ever been grown under similar conditions elsewhere. Ellacombe did not claim to be a botanist, yet he was a valued correspondent of Kew. Twenty plates in *The Botanical Magazine* were drawn from his plants. His taste was catholic. His love for a common plant such as the snowdrop and all connected with it was, if anything, more deeply felt than his interest in the other, often extremely rare, species and varieties which he so skilfully cultivated. The associations of a plant often meant as much to him as the plant itself; the many subjects upon which he wrote learnedly and gracefully included the flowers, plants, and plant lore to be found in the works of Chaucer, Gower, Shakespeare, and Milton. He would write with equal insight on his garden under snow, or the wild flowers that he saw on a foreign holiday—or even a subject so recondite as plant names from animals. His two small books of essays—*In a Gloucestershire Garden* (1895) and *In My Vicarage Garden and Elsewhere* (1902)—were early examples in style and manner of a handful of similar books by other authors which are among the best things in gardening literature.* He was, too, a man of most liberal mind—he did much for education in his district, and, aided only by his parishioners, restored Bitton church—and liberal nature: 'if generosity in the giving of fine plants be the test of a good gardener, then Henry Nicholson Ellacombe was a prince among them'.

Another parson particularly concerned with Robinson, again a man coming from the Loudonian era, was the Rev. Samuel Reynolds Hole (1819–1904). He was born at Caunton Manor, near Newark. There he was curate, vicar, and squire. After being Canon of Lincoln he became Dean of Rochester in 1887. In all these places his garden and his encouragement of gardening were famous. His enthusiasm was great, 'alike in the palace or the bothy, the same genial smile, the same ready wit were manifest'. This cheerfulness and vigour had much to do with bringing the National Rose Society into being—and is exuded by his many writings. Though he was closely concerned with *The Garden*, and wrote much for it on many subjects, it was as the author of *A Book About Roses* (1869), which went through many editions, that he was best known. This book appealed even to the non-expert

---

* Predecessors were Forbes Watson, *Flowers and Gardens: Notes on Plant Beauty by a Medical Man* (1872); Henry A. Bright, *A Year in a Lancashire Garden* (1879). Successors were Rose Kingsley, *Eversley Garden and Others* (1907); Sir Herbert Maxwell, *Flowers: A Garden Notebook* (1923); Sir Arthur Hort, *The Unconventional Garden* (1928) and *Garden Variety* (1935); and 'Jason Hill' (Dr. F. A. Hampton), *The Curious Gardener* (1932) and *The Contemplative Gardener* (1940).

and well exemplified the views he expressed when an 'octogeranium' (he seems to have invented this word): 'I welcome the sentimental, the poetical in our works upon gardens . . . I even venture to plead for a few glimpses of humour.' Unlike many subsequent authors, Dean Hole combined these with a profound knowledge.

In 1904 also the rose world lost another 'genial cleric', the Rev. R. A. Foster-Melliar, of Sproughton Rectory, near Ipswich. *The Book of the Rose*, first issued in 1894, became another standard work.

In 1908 came *Roses, Their History, Development and Cultivation* by the Rev. J. H. Pemberton (*d.* 1926), another influential book. Pemberton was one of the few parsons who bred roses with success. He worked with *Rosa moschatus*: 'Danae', 'Penelope', 'Thisbe', and 'Moonlight' are still to be found scenting some gardens, if not those of the multitude.

The modern successful kinds of roses were, in fact, all raised by continental professionals. The Pernet (or Pernetiana) roses were patiently bred by the French raiser Pernet-Ducher of Lyons, who worked from 1883 to produce deep yellow roses, the first of which was distributed in 1900—its colour was subsequently incorporated in the Hybrid Teas. The modern Poly-pompon (Polyantha or Floribunda) roses were also bred in Lyons, following the work of Jean Sisley, whose 'Mignonette' (1881) is their chief ancestor. The third popular modern group made a sensational appearance in 1924, raised by Svend Poulsen in Denmark.[6]

Roses bring one of the most remarkable of the many famous women gardeners into our story, Miss Ellen Ann Willmott (1860-1934).

Ambitious, proud and beautiful, it is still not possible to write so as to do justice to her complex personality. She was a woman of wealth and of many gardens, by turns munificent and mean. Her skill as a cultivator—and something of her vanity—is witnessed by the great number of plants that have been named after her. She was a capricious and implacable enemy, and a loyal friend.[7]

The friends included that deeply contrasted personality and figure, Miss Jekyll, and men such as Canon Ellacombe; her enemies those who saw her as climbing the ladder of fame through the art of gardening, and failing to acknowledge those who had helped her up the rungs.

At one time she had gardens on the Continent—in Savoie, on the Mediterranean coast—and at Warley Place, Essex. It was the last that was famed for its horticultural and botanical excellencies. She was skilled with a camera, and her fine photographs record the loveliness of the place, notably her masterly grouping and naturalizing of bulbs. After her death—by which time she had become financially affected by the aftermath of the First World War—practically all trace of it was obliterated. Her memorial must therefore be *The Genus Rosa*, issued in parts between 1910 and 1914, with every species she describes illustrated in colour by Alfred Parsons.* This work shows both her knowledge as a botanist and the wide background of her general culture.

No brief historical discussion of the rose and rosarians should end without some reference to the crude commercialization that has overtaken the flower. 'Bigger and Brighter' are too often the contemporary criteria. Nor should we fail to mention that small band of gardeners who continued to see beauty in the roses of past centuries and were not unmoved by their histories and associations. A great debt is owed to Edward Ashdown Bunyard (1878–1939), the son of George Bunyard, who sought out and collected a multitude of old kinds, and classified and discussed them with affection, wit, and learning in *Old Garden Roses* (1936).

Parsons were closely concerned both with the breeding and the furtherance of the daffodil. After the early successes of Backhouse and Leeds, the enthusiasm and the commercial acumen of Peter Barr was largely instrumental in gathering together those interested in this plant at the first Daffodil Conference in 1884. In that year, too, W. Baylor Hartland (1836–1931),† a nurseryman of Ardcairn, Cork, issued the first catalogue devoted solely to narcissi under the title *A Little Book of Daffodils*. His classification was original; he had, for example, the large-crowned or coffee-cup section, and the tea-saucer section. The most expensive in his list was 'Sir Watkin' at 3s. 6d.

In the meantime, about 1880, the Rev. George Herbert

---

* The reproduction by chromolithography unfortunately takes most of the life out of Parsons's drawings.

† He was also concerned with a revival of the tulip, issuing in 1896 *The Original Little Book of Irish-grown Tulips*.

Engleheart (1851-1936),* then vicar of Chute Forest in Wilt-shire, had begun his experiments which transformed the daffodil. By 1898 he had six bulbs of his seedling 'Will Scarlett', which he exhibited at the Birmingham Show.† John Pope (1848-1918), nurseryman of King's Norton, great-grandson of the Luke Pope who boasted that he had spent £3,000 on tulips, bought three of them for £100. 'This was the first instance of so large a sum being paid for a daffodil, but proved so successful a speculation that others were encouraged to try their luck or judgement.'[8] Engle-heart retained the other three for breeding. In 1910, when there were many successful breeders obtaining high prices, another eminent gardening parson, famed for his bulbs and apples, the Rev. Joseph Jacob of Whitewell Rectory, wrote: 'it must be re-membered that their successes have been obtained from flowers that Engleheart gave them to work upon'.[9]

To name the countless breeders who have subsequently suc-ceeded would be impossible, but we must again mention the Backhouse family, of Wolsingham. The son of William Backhouse was Robert Ormston (1854-1940), who came south to Sutton Court, Hereford.‡ He and his wife, Sarah Elizabeth (1857-1921), hybridized daffodils, lilies, and colchicums. At the London Daffodil Show of 1920 a small group of Mrs. Backhouse's daffodils 'created quite a sensation'. But the climax was reached by her husband, who in 1923 was able to show the first pink-cupped, white-perianthed daffodil, which he named 'Mrs. R. O. Back-house'.

Mrs. Backhouse is also remembered by her series of lilies, crosses between forms of the Martagon lily and Lilium hansonii, upon which she started to work in 1890. The cult of the lily was, of course, an old one, though only a few different kinds were grown. During the 1870s many new species were being suc-cessfully cultivated, following the example of G. F. Wilson, who wrote of his experiences freely in the Press. Rather later came Henry John Elwes (1846-1922), squire of Colesborne in the

* Engleheart was a good general gardener and wrote on the cultivation of veget-ables. He was descended from Dean Herbert; as Herbert's work encouraged Leeds and Backhouse to begin breeding, his influence on the daffodil was, indeed, potent.
† The first British daffodil show was held at the Botanical Gardens, Birmingham, in April 1893.
‡ The third generation, W. O. Backhouse, still at Sutton Court, carries on the family tradition.

Gloucestershire Cotswolds (where he was born and died), with his *Monograph of the Genus Lilium** in 1880. This work was on the same grand scale as its author, with forty-eight magnificent coloured lithographs by Fitch.

Elwes began life as a soldier, and achieved an enviable reputation as a big-game hunter, ornithologist, lepidopterist, botanist and gardener, and forester. He travelled the world pursuing these interests: Turkey, Asia Minor, Russia, Siberia, China, Japan, and North America were visited—some more than once. Of even greater consequence than his study of lilies was his study of trees, though this, as it does not include shrubs and deals largely with timber trees, is only on the borderline of our history. With him worked Augustine Henry. The first volume of their joint publication, *The Trees of Great Britain and Ireland*, appeared in 1906; the seventh and final volume in 1913. As to his skill as gardener and botanist, ninety-eight *Botanical Magazine* plates from plants he grew at Colesborne bear witness. Nearly all he had cultivated himself. The first to appear, in 1874, was *Galanthus elwesii*, the delightful snowdrop that braves an English January. It well commemorates a man whose figure and attitude were so often described as 'burly', but who was yet so sensitive to the finer shades of natural beauty.

Neither clergy nor dons seem to have entered to the same extent into the history of the sweet pea. Henry Eckford (1823–1905) was born at Liberton near Edinburgh, and had the traditional Scottish training in private gardens. In 1847 he came south to Hugh Low of Clapton on the recommendation of James McNab. In 1854 he became head gardener to the Earl of Radnor at Coleshill, and there made a reputation as a raiser of new verbenas, pelargoniums, and dahlias. His successes resulted in an invitation in 1870 to work for Dr. Sankey, of Sandywell, Gloucester, an enthusiastic raiser of new florists' flowers. Here Eckford began his slow and painstaking work on improving the sweet pea—at that stage biologically difficult, with the consequence that there were only a handful of varieties available. In 1882 he introduced his first, 'Bronze Prince', through Bull of Chelsea.

In 1900 a Bi-Centenary Sweet Pea Exhibition was held to

* Supplements have been added subsequently.

celebrate the raising of the first plants of *Lathyrus odoratus* by Dr. Uvedale from seed sent him in 1699 by the Sicilian monk Cupani. Of the 264 varieties shown, 115 were raised by Eckford: his name was now 'as music to the ear of all who love flowers'.[10]

In 1901 the 'sweet pea world lost its head' when 'Countess Spencer' was exhibited. Silas Cole, gardener to Earl Spencer at Althorp, had been crossing Eckford's plants and one shell-pink seedling arose with wavy edges to its standard and wings. Robert Sydenham of Birmingham bought all five seeds that it produced and sent them to California to be grown for seed. Unfortunately the seedlings varied greatly, and the wavy edges were often missing. But the waviness had appeared elsewhere. A chance seedling in the nursery of W. J. Unwin at Histon, Cambridgeshire, possessed it in a lesser degree. 'Gladys Unwin', as it was called, was inferior in all ways to 'Countess Spencer'—but her progeny came with true wavy edge and from them was raised the modern sweet pea.[11]

In 1888 Eckford left Sankey and set up on his own account as nurseryman at Wem, Shropshire.

Dons and parsons were concerned in the first steps of the rise of the old simple flags* to the present glories of the bearded irises. Sir Michael Foster (1836–1907) was an eminent Professor of Physiology at Cambridge and Secretary of the Royal Society—which career brought him his knighthood. It was on the difficult soil of Cambridge that he grew some 200 species of iris obtained from all over the world, 'huddled in a little garden' at Shelford. Foster's notebooks still exist, covering his studies from 1878 to 1902. He was the first to publish descriptions of a number of species, some of which, such as *Iris bucharica*, are now not uncommon as garden plants.[12] Lucid drawings accompanied and amplified his notes.

Between 1880 and 1890 he acquired those Eastern species, notably *Iris cypriana*, *I. trojana*, *I. amas*, and *I. kashmiriana*, which are the basic plants involved in the modern bearded iris. Besides forming his collection, Foster made, between about 1878 and 1901, anything up to 100 crosses a year, recording the results with minute care.

---

* The first collection of named tall bearded irises was offered for sale by the French firm Lemon in 1840; later successful continental raisers were Cayeux and Vilmorin.[13]

The information he acquired was made available to a number of people, particularly William Rickatson Dykes (1877–1925), who produced an important monograph, *The Genus Iris*, in 1913. Dykes, who was educated at Oxford and the Sorbonne, became a master at Charterhouse, and the fine plates for his monograph were painted by a colleague there, Frank Harold Round (1877–1958). Dykes also wrote extensively on other subjects, and translated Louis Lorette's celebrated book on fruit-tree pruning (1925). His work was ended by his death in a motor accident. In 1920 he had been appointed Secretary of the Royal Horticultural Society, succeeding Wilks.

It was, however, George Yeld (1845–1938) who first successfully used Foster's new Eastern species in England to inaugurate the modern bearded iris of complex origins, probably in 1896 or 1897.* His 'Sir Michael' and 'Lord of June' were long famous.

Yeld was a remarkable character. From Hereford Cathedral School he went as a scholar to Brasenose College, winning the Newdigate Prize in 1866. On taking his degree he became a master at St. Peter's, York, where he stayed for no less than fifty-two years. It has been said that this remote northerly situation delayed recognition of his work as a breeder of irises and his other favourites, day-lilies (*Hemerocallis*). He was a traveller and mountaineer in Wales, Skye, the Alps, and the Caucasus. On his retirement he moved south to Gerrards Cross. He was first president of the Iris Society,† founded in 1924.[14] From 1907 onwards many fine varieties that he raised became available. Foster's own hybrids, apparently a little later in origin, came on the market after his death, between 1909 and 1913; several of his plants are direct ancestors of the later (particularly American) kinds.

One cannot describe the systematic and highly scientific development of iris breeding that followed except to remark that the sensational 'Dominion', put on the market in 1917 by Bliss‡ at the then astounding price of 7 guineas, was a chance seedling which appeared among a whole series of undistinguished plants—unobserved by the raiser himself but picked out by his little niece!

---

* Vilmorin in France did the same more or less concurrently.
† Since 1952 the British Iris Society.
‡ Arthur John Bliss (1860–1931) was a surveyor and mining engineer, who on retirement spent some thirty years at Tavistock devoted to breeding narcissi, gladioli, and irises on scientific lines.[15]

Dykes himself eventually transferred his allegiance from species to breeding, and produced some good kinds, particularly those with yellow flowers: in this he was helped by his wife,* who admitted that some of the best had come from chance self-set pods.

The dianthus in its various forms has continued to receive great devotion and attention during our present period. We read of William Robinson forming in 1886 a large collection of hardy border carnations at Gravetye. These he had from France, and by 1887 he had planted out 2,000 of them.

The florists' greenhouse carnations were developed internationally, while the hardy perpetual-flowering border was introduced in 1913. In 1910 Montagu Allwood (1880–1958) of Wivelsfield, Sussex, began his attempts to cross the perpetual-flowering carnation with the old hardy white, fringed pink, *Dianthus plumarius*. After nine years he established the very hardy and successful 'Allwoodii' range of pinks, which he continued to develop.[16]

The modern herbaceous paeony, as can be seen from many of its names, has its origins on the Continent. But the Kelway family had a hand in it too, and raised many good kinds. James Kelway the second (1871–1952) was particularly associated with these; he was grandson of the original James. Kelways, too, were the first to develop the small 'Primulinus' gladiolus hybrids. They first received *G. primulinus* in 1904 from the Victoria Falls of the Zambezi,[17] when William, son of the first James (who died aged ninety-four in 1933), was proprietor of the firm.

The delphinium, latterly with a good deal of help from the United States of America (as with the bearded iris), owes much of its improvement to the firm of Blackmore & Langdon of Bath, founded in 1900.

But of all the flowers that have been completely transformed in the first part of the twentieth century the most remarkable, next to the bearded iris, is the Michaelmas daisy. William Robinson had an abiding passion for the starworts, as he called them, and at Gravetye collected and grew in great numbers all the kinds he could get—mostly species—in all, about a dozen

* Mrs. Dykes, 'a handsome and gifted lady', continued her husband's work most successfully at Bobbingcourt, Woking, where Dykes moved when he left Charterhouse. She illustrated with coloured drawings his studies of tulips. In 1933 she was killed in a railway accident returning from Chelsea Show.

kinds with a few varieties. Few of them would today earn their space in a garden. As a young man Ernest Ballard (1870–1952), working in a garden lying under the Malvern Hills, tackled the genus. In 1907 his 'Beauty of Colwall' received a high award at a Royal Horticultural Society show. Thenceforward, until his death, a whole new range of variations on the theme of *Aster* was evolved, hardy and reliable, bringing an enriched colour scheme of lilacs, pinks, crimsons, purples, and white. None of his seedlings departed incongruously from the innate nature of the plant. Together with a few other raisers he has altered the aspect of the garden in autumn.

A nurseryman—one we must take as representative of a class—who left his imprint on the British garden was Amos Perry (1871–1953). He was the son of another Amos Perry,* a partner in the Tottenham nursery firm of Ware. Here he was apprenticed, and later took charge of the bulb department. In 1899 he began on his own at Winchmore Hill, to be joined by his father, and specialized in hardy plants. He travelled extensively, visiting gardens in Britain and on the Continent to find better forms of well-known plants, or little-known plants which his skilled eye realized would be valued additions to the garden flora. By 1930 he had already gained something near a hundred high awards from the Royal Horticultural Society for plants which he had introduced or bred. Between 1900 and the early 1930s he raised some of the finest of the bearded irises, as well as a number of remarkable hybrids between Californian and Chinese *sibirica* species (he grew many iris species, and was concerned with the marketing of Sir Michael Foster's irises). He was also responsible for the introduction of improved forms of *Iris sibirica*. His name is also closely linked with the improvement, by hybridization or introduction of new forms, of the oriental poppy, bergamot, lilies, trillium, and latterly day-lilies (*Hemerocallis*). He and his firm specialized in water gardens of every conceivable kind and size, from lakes to bowls in the room, and aquaria. The manual he issued in the 1930s, *Water, Bog and Moisture Loving Plants*, remains the best compact book on the subject. He was described as a little man of such energy and enthusiasm that on retirement from business he continued his plant-breeding.[18]

* Amos Perry the younger named plants in his father's, not his own, honour!

We must return to parsons. Canon Horace Rollo Meyer (1868–1953), with his faithful gardener Izzard (who was with him for half a century), raised a whole series of distinguished daffodils and bearded irises, noted for their quality of refinement and feeling of style, which received the highest awards. Meyer also deserves mention as the founder of the Gardens Guild movement. He came down from Cambridge at the same time as his great friend Noël Buxton. Both went to London, Meyer to take Orders and Buxton to join his family brewery. Meyer was shocked at the gloom and slum-like conditions around the brewery, which was in South London. He succeeded in persuading his friend to provide window-boxes. From this grew the London Gardens Guild which, in 1927, developed into the National Gardens Guild. Lord Noël Buxton (as he now was) became first president.

As a contrast to these men of versatility (Ernest Ballard, for example, was responsible for several distinguished hybrids other than Michaelmas daisies—*Dianthus* and *Hepatica* are both linked with his name) the devotion to the lupin of George Russell (1857–1951) should be mentioned. A Yorkshire working gardener, he began experimenting with lupins in 1911, apparently sowing seeds of many species and kinds. Following his own system of selection he had by the 1920s achieved astonishing results. Not till June 1937 did the new strain come before the public when his flowers provided a sensational display at a Royal Horticultural Society's show. Baker's Nurseries, of Wolverhampton, had in 1935 secured both his plants and his services. Grown in masses on their trial ground at Boningale alongside the Holyhead Road, the Russell lupins attracted thousands of visitors when in bloom.[19]

Our last great modern gardener must be Edward Augustus Bowles (1865–1954). He might well have been a parson, but was prevented by family circumstances from entering (as he deeply wished) into Holy Orders. Once again we have the traditional English gentleman of culture and intelligence, this time fortified by a Huguenot ancestry, resulting in a singular and simple moral sense. We have, too, the typical old family house and grounds—Myddleton House, Enfield—with its ageing trees, quarry turned into pond, and frontage to the New River which, completed by

Sir Hugh Myddleton in the first years of the seventeenth century, brought water to London.

Bowles's father was, in fact, the last Governor of the New River Company, and on his Board was Canon Ellacombe—who inevitably tried and soon succeeded in interesting the son in gardening. After family bereavements had made it necessary that Bowles should stay at home rather than enter the Church, he devoted himself to social work, painting, and natural history, particularly entomology. But in the end it was by his garden, horticultural writing, painting, and his long and prominent association with the Royal Horticultural Society (he was first elected to its Council in 1908), that he became known. He converted the rather gloomy Victorian Myddleton House garden into something quite different. By 1895, only five years after he had taken charge, it was receiving favourable notice both on account of its layout and the choice plants it contained. Many he himself brought from the Continent and North Africa, where he travelled widely —not infrequently to avoid hay fever—and with such companions as Reginald Farrer.

During the sombre years 1914 and 1915 appeared his first three books, *My Garden in Spring, My Garden in Summer,* and *My Garden in Winter.* His aim, briefly, was to show how much pleasure could be had from a garden planted with immense diversity, so that on each day of the year there was to be observed something of interest. Years later he wrote that within his overcrowded 5 acres he had experimented with most plants which appear in lists marked 'new' or 'rare', losing many but never giving up until he had tried each of them three times in different positions. He was deeply anxious to transmit his enjoyment to any 'who love a plant for its own sake'; and, one may add, for its associations— botanical, literary, historical, or even comic. Surely no other trilogy of gardening books combine so much practical sense, wide learning, and relevant anecdote.

One may gather where his interests lay. First, perhaps, in the rock garden that he made—conventional by no standards—and over which his ashes were in the end scattered. Next came his crocuses; then daffodils, hardy cyclamen, anemones, snowdrops, and his iris beds by the New River. He had a love of curious and monstrous forms of plants, his 'lunatic asylum' in which grew the oak-leaved laburnum, a hazel with branches like cork-screws, the green-flowered strawberry ('a botanical dodo'), the rose plantain, and many other oddities.

All his qualities, including his ability as a botanical draughts-man, were brought to the *Handbook of Crocus and Colchicum* (1924) and *Handbook of Narcissus* (1934). The book on the crocus is of singular excellence, the only successor to George Maw's *Monograph of the Genus Crocus* (1886).*

Bowles also wrote on his other favourites, and whatever he produced was as useful to the beginner as to the learned botanist. In his later years his eyesight steadily failed, but he was the fortunate possessor of an acute sense of smell (he wrote on fragrance in the garden) and of touch. Nearly ninety years of life wore out his body, but not his mind: he presided over Royal Horticultural Committees until a few weeks before his death. His garden passed to the University of London. Presumably the passer-by will for long be able to see the giant 'blueburnum' (a wistaria) which covers his boundary wall.

Bowles was a link between the lively figures of the late Victorian age and the world that followed what he called 'Hitler's war'. Great abilities which might have brought him fame in a more prominent sphere were devoted to gardening. Of a scientific turn of mind, he yet used a horse-drawn brougham until 1929. For long, in both winter and summer, he wore an old straw hat. We can aptly close this section with a glimpse of him, past his eightieth year, wading about the pond in a bathing dress to supervise the thinning of his water-lilies.[20]

. . . . .

Little enough has been said about the greenhouse during this later period. That is because the years of the late nineteenth and early twentieth centuries were so largely devoted to the development of hardy plants. Correspondingly, and particularly after the war of 1914–18, economic circumstances discouraged interest in the stove-heated greenhouse and conservatory. Against this the small, cheap, and practically unheated greenhouse became popular—particularly with the working man with his devotion to

---

* George Maw (1832–1912), of Benthall Hall, Broseley, Shropshire, was, until his health broke down in little more than middle age, a man of uncanny brilliance. The plates he made for his crocus book are exquisite—yet he was a successful industrialist. He was a traveller and plant-collector, and distinguished as both chemist and geologist.

the chrysanthemum, so extensively developed by a number of nurserymen.

The tender cyclamen and begonias, too, received a good deal of favour. Cyclamen, coleus, and the winter-flowering azaleas were raised in steadily increasing quantities for the florists' trade in pot plants; but, except in a few public parks and botanical gardens, the grand conservatories and greenhouses of the Paxtonian era decayed and at last collapsed.

FRUIT AND VEGETABLES: SCIENCE DEFEATS ART

William Robinson had nothing new to say about either the orchard or kitchen garden. In the 1870s he revised Loudon's *The Culture and Management of the Kitchen, Fruit and Forcing Garden*. Later, as a good Francophil, he edited an English version of Messieurs Vilmorin-Andrieux's work which he called *The Vegetable Garden*. This is not without significance, for in these matters there was no such revolution as had occurred in the late nineteenth-century flower garden. Little change occurred until the twentieth century was in full swing.

Our period begins with the introduction of another haphazard seedling apple that soon became, and remains, a favourite, 'Newton Wonder' was raised by a Mr. Taylor of Kings Newton, near Melbourne in Derbyshire, and marketed by Pearson & Co., nurserymen, of Lowdham, in about 1887.[21] It ends with a number of government research stations, a few firms of nurserymen working scientifically to raise new kinds of fruit and vegetables, and engaged in developing techniques for their cultivation. At the same time research is carried out by vast companies into an ever-changing series of chemicals to combat pests. But for a time all went quietly.

Mechanical improvements such as the knapsack sprayer were introduced from France in 1891.[22] The sons of Thomas Laxton, who died in 1890, followed on with a carefully organized breeding programme of apples, pears, and plums. Within a decade they had bred something like 10,000 of these crosses, of which a number became successful. The family firm of Rivers continues to this day.

Mention should be made of Charles Ross (1825–1917), perhaps the last of the great individualist fruit breeders in the line of Thomas Knight. He was born at Dalmeny, Midlothian, and after the usual thorough training came south. In 1860 he was head gardener at Welford Park, in Berkshire. Here until 1908, when he retired, he remained undisturbed as one occupier succeeded another, and worked on at his experiments in his own private quarters, which only the favoured were permitted to enter. He raised a number of apples, the most successful being 'Charles Ross', exhibited at the Royal Horticultural Society in 1899. Realizing that this was the best he had done, it was first named after his hero, 'Thomas Andrew Knight'—but he was asked to alter it. The parents were 'Cox's Orange Pippin' and 'Peasgood's Nonsuch'.

There is no doubt that the disappearance of horse-drawn transport after 1914 completely revolutionized fruit- and vegetable-growing. No longer, particularly in urban and suburban areas, was there an abundant source of dung available for every gentleman's and many a tradesman's garden. The radical nature of this change can be seen by reference to the account of a typical market garden, of 44 acres, close to Barking, Essex, in 1879.[23] William John Gay worked in 'the most approved manner', with every inch of his ground cultivated. He had no particular rotation, but aimed to take two crops yearly off all his land. In early spring, after the winter brassicae had gone, he raised onions, carrots, parsnips, spinach, peas, and potatoes. At the end of May, following cabbages, more potatoes, scarlet runner and French beans, blue peas, beet, marrows, cucumbers, and lettuce came along. He also grew common and lemon thyme, sage, marjoram, mint, and parsley. His land was worked by four horses and a pony, which also hauled his produce to market, returning with manure from stables and cowsheds. Thirty tons of this was put on every acre of land, more if possible. In addition, he used the few artificial manures then obtainable equally lavishly: horse-hoof parings, from 3 to 4 cwt. an acre; horn shavings, 8 to 10 cwt.; bone dust, 10 cwt.; guano, 5 cwt.; and nitrate of soda from 2 to 4 cwt. to the acre.

At the same time John Lancaster, of Stratford, was succeeding not with a variety of crops, but by specializing in celery. He was one of the first men to realize the value of irrigation, and drove the flow of water with a steam-engine. Robert Bakewell at Dishley had to some extent applied irrigation to farmland, yet even so it was not until well on in the present century that the practice was introduced to any extent, notably by F. A. Secrett, on his extensive gardens at Milford near Godalming in the late 1930s.

It was not until the present century that such matters as the siting of orchards and nurseries, manuring of plants of all kinds, and the pruning of fruit trees were scientifically studied in an adequate manner.

Fruit-growing was revolutionized by the studies of Sir Ronald Hatton at East Malling Station on the effects of apple stocks on the growth of scions. Carried out in the years immediately before and during the 1914–18 war, Hatton published the remarkable results in 1918 and 1919. The consequent standardization of stocks which behave in a known way, and produce eventual bushes and trees of well-defined types, has since been applied to other fruits.

The developments in spraying were equally revolutionary. Until about 1920 dormant eggs of insects had been rather ineffectively destroyed by caustic soda. In 1921 the first tar-oil wash was used—in the Wisbech area—with results that amazed all growers. And in the 1920s lime-sulphur washes were introduced to attack fungal diseases, which had formerly been treated with a preparation based on copper which, as they adversely affected a number of important kinds, were restricted in their use.[24]

The study of growth-producing substances, and selective weedkillers, and of new ranges of insect-killing substances of increasingly lethal power, was making progress in the 1930s, but did not come into general use until after our period ended.

These sometimes horrifying marvels of science (so many of them placed in little packages for the use of Mr. Everyman) were even before 1939 bringing a new series of problems. Not the least was the need to provide that organic material in which the tons of Mr. Gay's manures were so rich, and which is quite absent from chemical fertilizers. This problem was overcome towards the end of our period by the production of chemical agents that would accelerate the rotting-down of soft garden refuse, and even such comparatively enduring materials as straw.

The scientific approach in conjunction with economic circumstances has also resulted in a standardization, with lack of variety, of fruit, vegetables, and even flowers.

This brings us inevitably again to Edward Ashdown Bunyard, of the Allington firm. With an inherited practical knowledge of pomology and vegetable culture, he combined the qualities of historian and man of taste. During the early twentieth century he led the field in the history and description of fruit. The two volumes of his *Handbook of Hardy Fruits*, the first (1920) including apples and pears, the second stone and bush fruits, and nuts (1925), carried on the tradition of our great pomologists. Perhaps more important was his insistence that quality was more important than mass-produced quantity. His little book, *The Anatomy of Dessert* (1933) or his *Epicure's Companion* (1937), as well as his collection of a rich variety of vegetables, led to a healthy new fashion, particularly among those who garden on a small scale. His work brings us to a paradox: scientific breeding has yet to surpass 'Cox's Orange' ('The elements so mixed in him that nature might stand up and say, "This is indeed an apple" ') or the even older 'Orleans Reinette'. Overcome, one suspects, by the then black prospects for civilization, Bunyard died tragically in the year our history ends.

'HORTUS VEITCHII': ORCHIDS AND CIGARS

The nurserymen's world was dominated from the beginning of our period until within a year or two of the outbreak of the 1914-18 war by the firm of James Veitch & Sons Ltd. of King's Road, Chelsea. Here they still had a big nursery, almost entirely of glass-houses in which orchids were grown and raised, as well as such other fashionable greenhouse plants as amaryllis, nepenthes, anthuriums, codiaeums, gloxinias, and ixoras. For long, in spite of Robinson, they did a big trade in the choicer bedding-out plants. At Chelsea, too, was their Decorative Plant department, which provided the lavish floral displays at society functions —not, be it remarked, mere flowers in water!

At Coombe Wood in Surrey was their tree and shrub nursery. This was receiving a wealth of hitherto uncultivated and sometimes difficult subjects. While the names of their collectors are rightly remembered, those of Maule and particularly his successor George Harrow (1858-1940), whose skill first grew and then increased them, is generally forgotten. There was another nursery at Feltham, and a celebrated fruit-house at Langley, where they raised a number of new kinds. They also successfully marketed a number of varieties produced by other raisers.

From 1869, when James Veitch the second died, Harry James dominated the firm; his powerful personality, commercial acumen, and imagination brought a new standard to the nursery trade. The firm through its collectors contributed much information to scientific institutions—including a good deal on subjects other than botany. By 1906 it had supplied material for no fewer than 422 plates for *The Botanical Magazine*.[25]

The success of their hybridizers was also remarkable. John Seden (1840–1921) has already been mentioned as Dominy's successor. Born at Dedham in Essex, he was working as a private gardener in London when he got to know a prominent orchid grower, Dr. Butler, whose gardener was Robert Bullen, later curator of the Glasgow Botanic Garden. In 1860 Bullen went to Chelsea as Veitch's orchid grower, and in 1861 Seden, on his recommendation, was also engaged. After a few months at Chelsea he moved to Exeter to work under Dominy. In 1864 he returned to London with Dominy and took charge of the Chelsea orchids. In 1867, being a man very much after Veitch's own heart, he went to him as private gardener at Stanley House, Chelsea. In 1889, needing a change to outdoor work, he went to Langley to hybridize fruit. In 1905 he retired from the firm, and thereafter lived comfortably owing to the generosity of his employer.

That is an outline of his uneventful life. His work is another matter. He produced 490 hybrid plants which Veitch, strictest of judges, considered worthy of bringing before the public. Besides orchids, we owe to him the foundation of the hybrid strains of gloxinia and tuberous begonia, the early hybrid veronicas, escallonias, hemerocallis, and several once successful roses. He also produced a distinguished range of strawberries, some apples (including crabs) that are still grown, a blackberry × raspberry cross, new raspberries, and greengages. Seden, it must be recalled, was but the master-hand among a band of other skilful hybridizers all succeeding at a time when scientific genetics was unknown.

The other outstanding achievement of the firm of Veitch was the promotion of E. H. Wilson's first journey to Western China.

The purpose was 'to obtain seeds of species likely to prove hardy in Great Britain, and living representatives of certain plants only known to exist in the herbaria of various European countries'. How this was successfully achieved in his two journeys of 1899–1902 and 1903–5 must be dealt with elsewhere. Later, in 1909–12, William Purdom collected jointly for the firm and Harvard University.

But soon the house of Veitch was to go into the shadows. Sir Henry James Veitch (one of the few horticulturists to be knighted) had, since the death of his brother Arthur from typhoid in 1880, been the only one of the 'Sons' left in the firm. He was succeeded by John Gould's son, James Hubert (1868–1907), who compiled the *Hortus Veitchii* of 1906 and for a time conducted the vast business ably. Unhappily he had not the necessary mental stamina, and became eccentric. Sir Harry returned for a while, but he was now an ageing man. There was no one else to carry on. The nurseries and the stock of Veitch were sold, but not the name; Sir Harry would not agree that this should pass to any person who might not honour the great family tradition. Kew Gardens acquired some of the rare trees and shrubs at the sale of Coombe Wood—just before war broke out in 1914.[26]

The name of Veitch takes us back to the great days of the orchid, and we may turn to a recollection of the 1880s which, though little more than a list of names, brings back something of the rich excitement and cosmopolitanism of those days.[27]

Baron Schröder (1824–1910), we read, had the finest collection of the rarest orchids in the kingdom at The Dell, Egham.

The Cheapside sale-rooms of Protheroe & Morris,* on the days that orchids were offered, filled with wealthy private and trade growers. There would be seen Sir Trevor Lawrence, Lord Rendlesham, Lady Alice Rothschild, His Grace the Duke of Marlborough, De Barri Crawshay, Mr. Buchanan (of Scotch whisky fame), and the Rev. Kineleside of Tunbridge Wells, dressed to the nines, smoking a fine Havana cigar, and looking more like a city magnate than a clergyman.

* This firm of auctioneers, who for many decades disposed of plants, particularly the surplus stocks of nurserymen, deserve, but cannot here receive, more lengthy discussion.

Henry Frederick Conrad Sander (1847–1920)* was one of the great commercial specialists.

He would not be denied in securing importations of any new or rare species. Wherever the plants were likely to be found, thence he would send a collector. Some months afterwards there would be held a sale which would bring not only the English growers, but cultivators from Paris, Brussels, Ghent and other continental centres. All were eager to buy the dried specimens in the hope that, when they flowered, something would appear of outstanding merit, either a new natural hybrid or a new type of the species.

Once again, gambling on plants was in fashion.

The firm of Sander has been responsible for several important orchid publications, including periodic complete lists of hybrids.

There were other outstanding orchid firms. William Bull, Rollinson's foreman, set up on his own in King's Road. He was followed by his son, another William, who died in 1913. Each year they had had a grand exhibition to which the fashionable were invited, usually opened by some notability. A strikingly gay awning protected the visitors as they walked from their carriages over the footpath. Hugh Low & Co. of Clapton was also well known. A son of the founder, Sir Hugh Low (1824–1905), became celebrated both as an administrator in the Colonial service and as an authority on orchids and tropical vegetation.

As the century progressed, and particularly after the war of 1914–18, most of the great collections were disposed of when their owners died. Against this, the number of smaller growers increased, as did the commercial production of orchid blooms for decoration—an important line in floristry.

.   .   .   .   .

The end of the great firm of Lee coincided with the last years of the nineteenth century. John Lee, who was born in 1806, had retired in 1876, leaving the business in the charge of his younger brother Charles, whose son William came into the business.

---

* Born in Bremen, he came to England in 1867 with little other than determination to become a nurseryman. While learning the seed trade with James Carter & Son, Forest Hill, he met the explorer and plant-collector Benedict Roezl (c. 1824–1885). Moving to St. Albans, Sander began a small seed business on his own. Before long, however, he arranged for Roezl to send him orchids. These were so successfully marketed that both made a great deal of money. Sander then developed his business on an international scale; at one time he had twenty-three collectors working for him. The business was continued by his sons.

Charles, however, died prematurely, and John returned; the business continued until his death in 1899. By then nearly all the firm's early grounds had turned to bricks and mortar. Hammersmith and Ealing had quite gone; some of the American oaks sent over by their early American collectors still stood at Isleworth, but the main business of popular florists' flowers and general nursery stock was finally concentrated at Feltham. John Lee's knowledge of plants, and of horticulture over the greater part of a century, was understandingly encyclopaedic; would that he had inherited some of his grandfather's literary ability!

Another influential firm of florists and nurserymen ended with the death of Arthur Turner in 1921. He had succeeded his father Charles as proprietor of the Royal Nurseries, Slough. The firm had continued its interest in apple trees ever since the days of 'Cox's Orange Pippin', and is still remembered by the apple 'Arthur Turner', which the Slough Nurseries first exhibited at the Royal Horticultural Society in 1912. Also, a Turner Memorial Prize for fruit-growing was established in 1885 to commemorate Charles Turner. Both father and son played a considerable part in the domestic affairs of the horticultural trade.

Any further attempt to discuss individual or even representative nurserymen from the late nineteenth century onwards is impossible. The difficulty of the task can be shown by a random example. William Robinson's *Garden Annual* of 1909 included over 4,800 names in its directory of nurserymen, seedsmen, and florists in the United Kingdom. All, one assumes, were of some consequence to justify their inclusion.

SCIENCE ADORNED AND NAKED

As in our last period the most important event in the organization of scientific horticulture was the revival of Kew Gardens after a period of decline, so this period opens with the Royal Horticultural Society almost defunct, and then, within a few years, not only reviving, but set on a course of success which has never altered.

The Society's gardens in Kensington eventually failed to attract the right kind of visitor. (The Trollopian will recall that when Lily Dale went to London, the gardens were classed with Mme Tussaud's as among the 'sights' she saw.)[28] In 1882 the lease of the gardens was terminated; and but for the Queen's interest, the Society might have been evicted from its premises. The assets covered only some three-quarters of its liabilities.

In 1885, when the outlook seemed hopeless, Sir Trevor Lawrence, Bart. (1831–1913),* became President.[29] He was the son of the famous Mrs. Lawrence of Drayton Green and Ealing Park; from her he inherited a devotion to gardens and plants. At Burford, Dorking, he had a notable collection of orchids, and many other fine plants. He had, too, fine collections of Japanese lacqueur and Chinese and Japanese porcelain. From his father he inherited both a baronetcy and an interest in medicine (his early life was spent with the Indian Medical Service in the Himalayan regions; subsequently, he devoted his energies to hospital administration). But what concerns us is his determination to revive the Society and insistence on the principle that its first objective was 'the improvement of horticulture' rather than the provision of skating rinks, tennis courts, and brass bands.

Sir Trevor, unlike many of his predecessors, was an active President. In 1888 several members resigned from the Council when it was decided to move from Kensington, take cheaper rooms in Victoria Street for offices, and hold fortnightly shows in the Scottish Drill Hall at Buckingham Gate. A novelty was a two-day spring show, held in the Temple Gardens, the precursor of the world-famous shows at Chelsea, to which the Society moved after the Temple shows ended in 1911 owing to inadequate space for the exhibits.

New and energetic members—such as Harry Veitch—joined the Council. And the Rev. William Wilks (1843–1923) became its secretary. Wilks, with an able President and Council behind him, can claim most of the credit for the revival of the Society. At his death it was said of him that he not only aspired and inspired, but also worked: at the end of his first twenty-five years as secretary the number of Fellows had risen from 1,100 to 13,500; the cash in the bank exceeded £67,000.

Again, we have an example of the stature and ability of an English parish priest. Wilks had gardening in his bones—his father and grandfather before him were enthusiasts—and he himself had been elected a Fellow of the Society in 1866, the year

* Sir William and Lady Lawrence, Sir Trevor's son and daughter-in-law, carried on the tradition of Burford; both were eminent and learned gardeners.

he had become a curate at Croydon. In 1879 he was vicar of nearby Shirley,* where he remained until 1912. In 1894 he was struck suddenly dumb with cancer of the larynx, from which he largely recovered. But the strain of preaching had, by 1910, become so considerable that he bought 7 acres of land near Croydon so that he might build a house and garden for his retirement. The Wilderness, as he called it, was very much his own work. Every detail of the house he designed himself, and the garden—with its woodland—he described as a 'cultivated common'. The small house had a little lawn, with some specimen shrubs, and there was an orchard† in which fruit trees were mixed with flowers. Elsewhere grass paths wound in and out, beside them being naturalized trees, shrubs, plants, and bulbs. Here he was photographed—an old-fashioned wheel-barrow by his side, holding a muddy spade, and wearing that insignia of the gardener, a large, battered hat.

As the Society prospered, it was felt new premises, including an exhibition hall, were needed; the building, at Vincent Square, was opened in 1904, the Society's centenary year. Baron Schröder, of orchid fame, played a great part in its establishment.

Meanwhile, the now entirely urban Chiswick gardens had become unsuitable. In 1903 Sir Thomas Hanbury (1822–1907),‡ after the death of G. F. Wilson, offered to buy Wisley estate and give it in trust for the Society. This, too, was opened in 1904.

In 1866 the Society acquired Professor Lindley's fine library for £600. This has been continually increased by purchase and benefactions until it is the best horticultural library at least in Europe; over the years it has been possible to buy back some of the contents of the original library, including some of the Chinese drawings obtained by Reeves.[30]

In July 1899 the Society held an international Hybridization Conference. It was attended both by practical plant breeders and

---

* The Shirley poppies, a strain selected and bred by Wilks (and subsequently further improved) from the common field poppy, *Papaver rhoeas*, takes its name from this connection.

† He was a keen fruit grower; the excellent cooking apple 'Rev. W. Wilks' (raised by Veitch) commemorates him.

‡ Hanbury was a member of a Quaker family of Shanghai merchants. Horticulture and botany were his hobbies, and at La Mortola, near Ventimiglia, he formed a garden famous for its collection of plants (still further developed by his son, Cecil, and his daughter-in-law). He was a generous benefactor to both British and Italian botanical organizations.

scientists. In the preceding years the Society's Scientific Committee, urged on by Wilks and Maxwell Masters, had been co-operating with scientists such as William Bateson who had been studying hybridization scientifically and by means of statistics. The Conference was the first ever held to consider the problems of plant breeding, and its consequences went far beyond the rather limited agenda. Wilks followed up its success energetically, and arranged for Bateson to speak on heredity to the Society on 8th May 1900. In the train on his way to attend the meeting Bateson read for the first time an hitherto unknown paper sent to him by Hugo de Vries (1848–1935), the eminent Dutch botanist and scientist. The paper was Mendel's, in which he stated his now famous laws, which had remained buried since first published in 1865. Bateson immediately saw its significance, and the Fellows present on that evening were the first body in England to learn of Mendel's work. Wilks also grasped its importance, and arranged for Mendel's document to be translated into English and published in 1901.[31]

In 1906 the Society organized the third International Conference on Hybridization, at which the term 'genetics' was born from Bateson's fertile brain.[32]*

An important development was the opening at Wisley in 1907 of a laboratory, and the appointment of Frederick James Chittenden (1873–1950) as its director and also head of the School of Horticulture, and in 1908 as editor of the *Journal*. Chittenden was born at West Ham, but spent his early life at Leyton and studied botany in the neighbouring Epping Forest. In due course he qualified as a teacher and lecturer. In 1902 he was elected a member of the Society's Scientific Committee. The subsequent years proved him to be among the singular figures of the Society. His pioneer work on the self-sterility of fruit trees and the destruction of eel-worm in bulbs were notable among his scientific work. His influence on the training of horticultural students was important, and the number of ordinary gardeners who benefited from his profound practical and scientific know-

* Other Fellows who played an important part in the pioneering of genetics were C. C. Hurst (1870–1947), long a member of the Scientific Committee, responsible for the *Orchid Stud Book* and genetical research into the origins of the garden rose; E. A. Bunyard, and George Nicholson. Masters also 'featured' the Conference in *The Gardener's Chronicle*.

ledge so generously and courteously put at their disposal must be almost uncountable.

In 1919 he became director of Wisley* at a time when new land had been acquired, and he now showed himself a talented garden designer. He arranged the planting of much of the Chinese material now coming to maturity, made the lake from a gravel pit, and was largely responsible for the heath garden. In 1931 he moved from Wisley to become keeper of the Lindley Library, editor of the Society's publications, and technical adviser; these posts he relinquished in 1939 to become editor of the Society's new *Dictionary of Gardening*—under most difficult conditions, and a task uncompleted at his death.[33]

Education of gardeners was put on a formal basis by the establishment of a National Diploma of Horticulture in 1913, the first examinations being held the following year. Important, too, have been the Society's publications—both specialized and popular. Among them is Curtis's *Botanical Magazine*, of which, thanks to the initiative of H. J. Elwes, the copyright was secured in 1922.

The hybridization conferences have been mentioned. The reports of some other conferences have become valuable reference books. Notable were those on Conifers (1891 and 1931); Primula (1928); Rock Gardens and Rock Plants (1936); and Ornamental Flowering Trees and Shrubs (1938). In spite of wars, the *Journal* has maintained its unbroken run.

Honours and awards to gardeners and plants alike, trials of fruit, vegetables, and decorative plants—too many to be recorded —have been instituted.

Mention should be made of the specialized committees and groups, some of them formed jointly with other bodies, which set national (and sometimes international) standards. For some, the Society publishes year-books. In 1939, besides the important Scientific Committee, the subjects so specially covered were fruit and vegetables, general florists' flowers and plants, orchids, daffodils and tulips, border carnations and picotees, perpetual-flowering carnations, dahlias, delphiniums, early flowering chrysanthemums, irises, rhododendrons, rock gardens, sweet peas, and lilies. These subjects give a good clue to the fashions of the 1930s.

* S. T. Wright, superintendent at Chiswick, was in charge of the move and the Wisley garden during its early days. Sir Frederick Keeble was director from 1914 to 1919. Chittenden was succeeded by R. L. Harrow.

The steady growth of the Society has been a singular feature of this last phase in gardening. In 1928 a new hall was opened —one of the earliest buildings in the functional manner of architecture. By 1939 the number of Fellows was over 36,500. From 1931 Lord Aberconway (1879–1953), formerly the Hon. Henry Duncan Mclaren, proved himself to be an exceptionally able President.

The Royal Botanic Gardens at Kew during the same period saw some increase in the adornment of its scientific activities, and several members of its staff are consequential figures in garden history.

Hooker was succeeded as director in 1885 by Sir William Turner Thistleton-Dyer (1843–1928), who for a decade had been his assistant, and since 1877 his son-in-law. Thistleton-Dyer remained until 1905, to be followed in turn by Sir David Prain (1905–22) and Sir A. W. Hill (1922–41).

Thistleton-Dyer ranks with the two Hookers as one of the formative genii of the gardens that we now know. It was he who made the place of far greater interest to the gardener, as distinct from botanist, by introducing a wide selection of hardy herbaceous plants and bulbs and displaying them in a manner well designed to show their garden uses, and, indeed, greatly to enhance the beauties and interest of Kew in the eyes of the general visitor, whom he was particularly anxious to attract.

He was in many ways a contrast to the second Hooker, who was pre-eminently a botanical and scientific traveller. Thistleton-Dyer began as a medical student, transferred his attention to mathematics, and finally obtained a distinguished degree in natural science. He never travelled, yet was acknowledged as a profound authority on Empire botany. He was particularly concerned, too, with the trees and shrubs. The Arboretum had received over the years, by way of gift and exchange, innumerable specimens whose identity was uncertain. Many now flowered, and he was responsible for naming them; much thinning and reorganization became due, and in this he displayed taste and skill. In 1894–6 he issued the first *Hand-list of Trees and Shrubs* (excluding conifers) grown in the Arboretum. It stated that some 3,000 species and distinct varieties were under cultivation. In 1902 a revision was issued. It now enumerated about 4,500 kinds; comment is unnecessary.

Harriet Hooker (1854-1945), who became his wife—her portrait charmingly graces Vol. 131 of *The Botanical Magazine*, which is dedicated to her—must also claim a place in her own right in this history. She inherited her father's talents and love of plants. Shortly after her marriage a crisis developed in the affairs of *The Botanical Magazine*: no artist was forthcoming. She stepped into the breach, and, sometimes in the most difficult circumstances, provided a number of plates. Two plants she drew have since become widely known: *Magnolia stellata* (1878) and *Primula rosea* (1879). The last was described in Hooker's accompanying text as the humblest of plants, which had proved one of the greatest attractions of the spring shows in that year. She was a keen gardener, latterly in Devonshire, to the end of her long life.

Three men are particularly associated with Thistleton-Dyer's administration, and have played an important part in horticulture; all rose to be curators* of the Gardens.

George Nicholson (1847-1908) was born in Ripon. His horticultural training included spells with the French nurserymen La Mouit, of Paris, and with Low of the Clapton Nursery. In 1873 he joined the staff at Kew, and his principal work there was in the formation and development of the Arboretum; it seems to have been generally accepted that, as a result, he knew more about the cultivated hardy trees and shrubs than any man in Europe. Elwes and Henry were deeply indebted to him; in particular, his knowledge of oaks and maples was outstanding. But this was by no means his only accomplishment; he was, for example, the first to make a serious study of both the flora and fauna within the Gardens. The ardours of his plant-hunting expeditions in the Swiss mountains were believed to have caused the illness that resulted in his early retirement from Kew in 1901 (he had been curator since 1886). He was very successfully self-taught in many subjects, including French and German. He was extremely musical, and, it is said, in middle life tried to master the piano; in this alone was his failure complete.

Nicholson's ability was shown in, and his fame rests upon, *The Illustrated Dictionary of Gardening: A Practical and Scientific Encyclopaedia*, which he edited in a masterly manner. The five volumes (including a Century supplement) were spread over the

* The curator is in charge of all the living plants in the gardens.

years 1885–1900. With their precise illustrations they long held the field unchallenged. The description of the sub-title, 'practical and scientific', was well borne out by the balanced treatment of its contents.

Nicholson was succeeded as curator by another man who left his mark on the gardening world. William Watson (1858–1925) was another north-countryman; he was born at Liverpool, and had his early training in local nurseries. He came to Kew in 1879, and was made foreman of the propagating department. In 1886 he became assistant curator under Nicholson. One likes to think of this trio, Thistleton-Dyer, Nicholson, and Watson, working together on the Gardens—and particularly among the trees and shrubs—to give them so much of their present beauty and general interest. Watson was particularly interested in rhododendrons and azaleas; his book on them, published in 1911, was apparently the first to be devoted entirely to these shrubs. As a contrast, he was an authority on and built up the Kew collections of cacti, succulent plants, and palms.

When Watson retired in 1922, the curatorship returned to Yorkshire. William Jackson Bean (1864–1947) might be added as a late addition to bring the Kew trio up to a quartet, for he joined the Gardens as a student in 1883 and so came under the influence of Thistleton-Dyer, and, like the others, was early associated with trees and shrubs, being appointed foreman of the Arboretum in 1892. In 1900 he became assistant curator. In 1929 he retired from the staff, by now indisputedly the greatest authority on the cultivation of trees and shrubs in the British Isles. Like Nicholson, Bean was fortunate in arriving on the scene at a stage when their study and uses were becoming popular. In addition he was able to observe the flood of twentieth-century arrivals from China and elsewhere reaching maturity—which was denied to Nicholson. Bean travelled examining arboreta in several parts of the world; in addition to an encyclopaedic knowledge, he had the power of assessing the garden value of a plant, and a great ability in expressing himself lucidly when writing. This was shown in his two-volumed *Trees and Shrubs Hardy in the British Isles* (1914). Later, a supplementary volume including the newer arrivals was added. This valuable work appeared at a most opportune moment, and was a powerful influence on twentieth-century practice.

Flowering trees and shrubs, permanent and lovely subjects for a garden, often giving second seasons of beauty in autumn leaf-colour or fruit, and not infrequently (unlike herbaceous plants) a delight in mid-winter, provided at least in part an answer to the economic and labour difficulties that emerged after the war of 1914–18.

The Royal Botanic Garden, Edinburgh, during this period will always be associated with the names of Sir Isaac Bayley Balfour (1853–1922), whose reign as keeper extended from 1888 to 1922, and Sir William Wright Smith (1875–1957),* his successor (and deputy from 1911). A continuity of policy therefore occurred, and it would not be an exaggeration to say that it had throughout as its principal aspect the botanical elucidation and experimental cultivation of the newly discovered flora of western China and its surrounding countries, notably rhododendrons, but also particularly alpine plants, such as primulas and gentians.

Balfour was the son of J. H. Balfour, already mentioned. He qualified as a doctor, travelled and held various positions before taking office at Edinburgh. He became, it was said, the most efficient all-round botanist in the British Isles. His energies transformed the garden at Edinburgh; the alterations were made with admirable taste. In 1908 he began the reconstruction of the Victorian rock garden on natural lines—made not from old walls, but with stone brought from Callander. The site was particularly suited to alpine plants, and thanks also to skilled cultivators it soon became the foremost rock garden in the British Isles. Rather later, a woodland garden was added.

Balfour realized the importance of an interested general public, and arranged for Sunday opening.

Wright Smith continued from the point at which Balfour left off. His own particular speciality was the genus *Primula*, but he, too, was a man of wide knowledge and experience. British horticulture owes much to these two men and their staffs.[34]

At Glasnevin was Frederick Moore (1857–1949). He was knighted in 1911, the year before he retired, having reigned, internationally famous, since 1878. Here progress was inevitably on different lines from that at Kew and Edinburgh. It was controlled

---

* Balfour had persuaded him to join his staff in 1902, but in 1907 he went for four years to the Calcutta Botanic Garden.

by a soil rich in lime. Sir Frederick, like his wife, was himself a keen and highly skilled gardener. He had much to do with advising on the planning and planting of such famed Irish gardens as Mount Usher and Rowallane.[35]

The old Oxford garden was not prominent during this period. Cambridge is notable on account of three men. Richard Irwin Lynch (1850–1924), curator from 1879 to 1919, was a Cornishman who was trained at Kew. He was a clever hybridizer, taking a part in the first Hybridization Conference, and raising the first modern hybrid gerberas, as well as cinerarias and other plants. His proximity to Sir Michael Foster had no doubt something to do with his interest in irises, and his *Book of the Iris* (1904) was one of the first in Britain on this plant. He was succeeded by F. G. Preston, well known as a writer on the (for the most part) unusual plants that he grew, and on greenhouse practice. In 1921 the post of Scientific Director was instituted, and Humphrey Gilbert-Carter was appointed.[36] His brand of science fortunately has a singularly practical ring about it—as shown in his little book *British Trees and Shrubs* (1936), perhaps a misleading title as it deals with all kinds commonly planted in Britain. He also made a valiant attempt to elucidate botanical names for the inexpert.

All these institutions, though primarily scientific, are deeply concerned also with appearance, even aesthetics; science, in varying degrees, is treated decoratively by displaying its wonders so that they appeal alike to the mind and eye.

The twentieth century brought into being more and more establishments that were entirely scientific and practical; no attempt was made to adorn them. Such, indeed, was Rothamsted. After Rothamsted came the John Innes Horticultural Institution, founded in 1909. John Innes, of an old and distinguished Scots family, had made a considerable fortune by dealing in land in and around London. He acquired the Manor House at Merton, in Surrey, farmed on a big scale, and planted the roads on his estate with a fine selection of trees. On his death in 1904 he left his estate and fortune for 'the study of the growth of trees and for the improvement of horticulture by experiment and research'.

These vague objectives were resolved by appointing William Bateson (1861–1926), whom we have already met, as director. He had been appointed to a Chair of Biology specially created for him at Cambridge in 1908, but at Merton he saw the possibility of carrying out genetical experiments in his own way on a grand scale. Much else, of course, evolved from this work.

On Bateson's death, Sir Alfred Daniel Hall (1864–1942)* was appointed; he remained until 1939. It was during his tenure of office that the name of John Innes became known to the world of gardeners in general. In 1933 a crop of *Primula sinensis* failed owing to root rot. The use of sterilized soil not only failed to cure this, but brought other troubles. Why? Investigation found the answer, and by 1936 a series of standardized sterilized composts had been evolved, including components which overcame the ill-effects of sterilization. The 'J.I.' formulae for potting and seed composts have been of immense value in every form of horticulture.[38]

The fruit research station at East Malling, at first an offshoot of Wye College, was established in 1912 on 22 acres. Researches into root stocks, and their subsequent classification and standardization, enquiries into methods of pruning, and many other investigations proved so valuable and practical in their application that by 1939 East Malling had become an independent organization on its own, covering 360 acres.[39]

And in due course other scientific centres came into being, even more specialized, and rather beyond our scope.

FROM THE EAVES OF THE WORLD—AND ELSEWHERE

Maries's and E. H. Wilson's first visits to central and western China have been briefly mentioned where credit places them— under the annals of the firm of Veitch. Wilson and his successors now fall to be discussed at greater length.

It may be well to summarize the events that led to the realization that the long, inaccessible, and inhospitable mountainous area which is covered roughly by the north of Burma, the Chinese provinces of Szechwan and Yunnan, and the eastern border of Tibet, contained a flora of great richness, with an abundance of highly decorative species, many of which—like the

---

* Sir Daniel, best known as an agriculturist, was an enthusiastic amateur gardener from his boyhood days in Rochdale, Lancashire, where he was a member of the Rochdale Gooseberry Club, and an exhibitor of florists' flowers. He was head of the Wye Agricultural College, Kent, from 1894 to 1902, and was one of the first to interest fruit and hop growers in scientific methods. He had a passionate belief in the complete supremacy of English apples, and a profound knowledge of tulips, resulting in *The Genus Tulipa* (1940). In retirement, under difficult war-time conditions, he undertook to edit the Royal Horticultural Society's *Journal*.[37]

flora of the Pacific coast of America—could be cultivated in the open in much of Europe (specially the southern and western coasts of the British Isles), in many parts of the U.S.A., New Zealand, and elsewhere.

Two botanists (of identical age), Maximowicz and Hance, stand out as particularly concerned with the new era. They never met, but corresponded freely, and each represents one of the two traditional approaches to the heart of China: from Russia overland, and from western Europe over the sea and through the ports.

Carl Johan Maximowicz (1827–1891) was Russian. He was a pupil of Alexander von Bunge (1803–1890), a German traveller and botanist who had been directly associated with Chinese botany since his attachment to a Russian Ecclesiastical Mission at Peking in 1830. Maximowicz was appointed in 1851 curator of the Herbarium of the Botanic Gardens, Petersburg; from 1869 to his death he was Chief Botanist. In the meantime he had made some important journeys to the Far East, going well off the beaten track. Though scarcely a plant-collector, he did introduce some important plants by seed to the Petersburg gardens, where they were raised and distributed.* It was, however, his descriptions and elucidations of the Far Eastern flora that were of the greatest importance. He arranged for vast quantities of material to come to him, which in due course he classified, described, and published.

Henry Fletcher Hance (1827–1886) was an Englishman who went to China at the age of seventeen; in China he died, having spent forty-three years there. Hance himself collected little but induced a large band of helpers to collect specimens for him, all of which were duly described and distributed to herbaria.

In 1860, the conclusion of a war waged by Britain and France resulted in the setting up of the Imperial Maritime Customs under Sir Robert Hart, the easing of travel restrictions, and greater freedom for missionaries. And it was to a handful of these Jesuit missionaries that we principally owe the botanical exploration of the still outlandish and dangerous areas.

Jean Pierre Armand David (1826–1900), the first and greatest, had a mystical passion for all natural history; his journey of

* Important botanical discoveries were made by other Russian travellers to the Orient, notably N. M. Prezwalski (1839–1888), who reached the district of Kansu later described by Farrer in *The Rainbow Bridge*. He died on his fourth unsuccessful attempt to reach Lhasa. Sosnovski and Potanin should also be named.

1868–70 was the first scientific study of the alps bordering Tibet; it was an 'eye-opener' and of supreme importance to zoologists and botanists.

Jean Marie Delavay (1834–1895) first collected for Hance, but was persuaded to send his specimens to France, where they were dealt with in an inadequate manner (he prepared some 200,000 in all, each collected and dried by his own hands, and with field notes appended; he was a supreme artist in this work). Delavay lived in one place in north-west Yunnan for ten years, and his intimate study of a small district was of great interest. Incomplete recovery from bubonic plague and the loss of his right arm did not deter him. He introduced a number of plants to cultivation, which were mostly killed by unsuitable treatment in Paris. Delavay alone of the missionaries seems to have had any real interest in the garden value of his plants.*

Paul Guillaume Farges (1844–1912) collected only from 1892 to 1903, but his 4,000 species include some now well-known garden plants. He worked in north-eastern Szechwan. Jean André Soulié (1858–1905) was able to pass himself off as a native traveller on the Chinese–Tibetan border; from that district he collected some 7,000 specimens in ten years. Though loved and popular among the Chinese he was shot after torture by Tibetan monks.

The davidia, *Buddleia davidi*, *Incarvillea delavayi*, *Rosa fargesi* and *Rhododendron souliei* are but a few names that commemorate these men, who, with taxonomists such as Maximowicz and Hance, and a number of minor figures, opened the eyes of the West to the newly discovered Aladdin's cave. They themselves sent little home in a living state, and it was left principally to a handful of British collectors to follow in their footsteps, with the necessary organization and paraphernalia required for the collection of seeds and living plants.[40]

To some extent this early British monopoly was due to chance. Augustine Henry (1857–1930)[41] was born in Londonderry, and after a brilliant career at Belfast University turned to medicine. He qualified at Edinburgh, but found that he disliked a doctor's

---

* The Jardin des Plantes at Paris was generally unsuccessful in raising the seeds sent them, but better results were had by Maurice de Vilmorin (1849–1918). The botanist principally concerned in describing the specimens sent by the missionaries was Adrien Franchet (1834–1900).

practice. Learning that the Chinese Maritime Customs were needing a well-educated man with some knowledge of medicine, Henry applied for the post. In 1881 he went to Shanghai and a year later moved to Ichang, by the gorges of the Yangtze River. It seems that it was a lack of any occupation after his working day was over that caused him to study and collect local plants, which, though knowing next to nothing of botany, appeared to him profuse in their variety and abundance. Unable to find other than their local names, Henry in 1886 sent off a box of specimens to Kew—as a bashful novice. Unlike the French authorities, who had done little to encourage the missionaries, the people at Kew were extremely interested, gave him all the help they could, and urged him to send more.

So began Henry's important contribution to the botany of western China; doubly important, because his work in due course came to the notice of men like Harry Veitch and A. K. Bulley, who sent out collectors to bring home alive what Kew and Edinburgh had received as dried specimens. By the time he retired from China in 1900 Henry had sent some 158,000 dried specimens. Hundreds of his plants were new to science, and many were of great beauty; some are now common in our gardens.

During his leaves Henry travelled about. Later he held posts in remote districts elsewhere. He studied other aspects of Chinese natural history, learned Chinese, and became an expert on certain local dialects. He trained native collectors, some to a high degree of skill, to bring him specimens. It was one of these men who brought in the famous *Actinotinus sinensis*, a puzzling plant of a genus unknown to botanists, which in due course was carefully described by the Kew authorities. It was later found to be a viburnum flower grafted with Chinese skill on to a spray of horse-chestnut.

On his retirement, Henry began another distinguished career as a pioneer of scientific forestry and an authority on trees; his share with Elwes in *The Trees of Great Britain and Ireland* has been noted. From 1913 to 1926 he was Professor of Forestry at Dublin. He was one of the first to study the genetics of trees, and his pioneer work on their hybridization would alone be adequate to secure him a reputation.

It was one of Henry's specimens that brought about Wilson's first journey, initiating a new era in plant-collecting. The keeper of the Kew Herbarium, after examining Henry's *Davidia involucrata* in 1891, had written that it alone was almost worthy of a special expedition to bring it into Western gardens. As a consequence, on 27th March 1899 Harry Veitch signed a contract with Wilson to proceed to China, with seeds of davidia as his main objective.

Ernest Henry Wilson (1876–1930) was then a young man who had never been overseas. He was born at Chipping Camden, and was apprenticed to Hewitts, nurserymen, of Solihull, Warwickshire. Thence he moved to the Birmingham Botanical Gardens at Edgbaston, studying botany at a technical school. In 1897 he went to Kew, intending to become a teacher of botany, but when Veitch enquired of Thistleton-Dyer, then director, if he had a man likely to prove a successful collector, Wilson was suggested.

After six months at the Coombe Wood Nursery Wilson set out, in April 1899, to meet Henry, then at Szemao in the south-west corner of Yunnan, near the border of Burma, and learn from him the whereabouts of davidia. *En route* he called upon Professor Sargent* at Boston to learn from that already experienced authority modern methods of packing, and such matters. Then, via the American continent, Hong Kong, and Tonking he reached China proper, where he crossed the province of Yunnan to find Henry.

Wilson himself has told the story of this dreadful journey. In French Indo-China he was held for weeks in the fever-haunted town of Laokai, suspect as a spy, whilst Europeans around him died like flies from fever. On his journey up the Red River, with an opium addict as boatman, his boat was nearly wrecked on the rocks; the natives were hostile and murders of Europeans not infrequent. At last he reached Henry, who described the situation of the only davidia known to him. He had last seen it twelve years before. Wilson set out, and after surviving further dangers reached his goal. The tree had lately been cut down and was now part of a house.

In despair he went back to Ichang, and began collecting plants from the gorges prior to setting out on a thousand-mile

* Charles Sprague Sargent (1842–1927) was concerned with the foundation of the Arnold Arboretum of Harvard University at Jamaica Plain, near Boston, in 1872. Here was formed one of the most representative collections of hardy woody plants in the world; its policy of generosity has singularly benefited British gardens. Sargent travelled extensively in North America and also in Japan, studying and bringing into cultivation principally ligneous plants, on which he was pre-eminent as an authority.

journey to search for the davidias originally discovered by Père David. Then, to his surprised joy, he found a dozen trees, quite near his quarters, from which in due course he sent seed to Coombe Wood.*

During this period, it will be recalled, the Boxer Rising was at its height, yet Wilson collected extensively. His first trip (1899–1902) yielded 976 species in the form of seed, 1,610 herbarium specimens, and many cases of bulbs, rhizomes, and roots of living plants. He went again to China for Veitch in 1903, returning the next year. By now he was experienced, and planned his journey beforehand, down to the smallest detail; yet a number of disasters occurred which he triumphantly overcame. He next took up a post on the staff of the Imperial Institute, but his friend Sargent knew his worth, and he was in China in 1907–9 and 1910–11 collecting for Harvard. In this last expedition he found *Lilium regale* and was collecting its bulbs by the hundred when he was caught in a landslide which smashed his leg.

In 1914, now permanently employed by the Arnold Arboretum, Wilson visited Japan. There he studied the Japanese cherries and, near Tokyo, first saw the Kurume azaleas which he later did so much to popularize. In 1917 he made a further expedition to islands in the Japanese seas, to Korea and Formosa, and to Japan again, where he visited the town of Kurume itself, the home of Sakamoto (*fl.* 1815), who originated the azaleas. In 1919 he was appointed assistant director of the Arnold Arboretum, and on Sargent's death, in 1927, its keeper. In 1930 he and his wife† were killed in a motor accident.

Wilson's early introductions to England were unlucky; there had not been sufficient time to flower and then propagate and distribute them before the decline of the firm of Veitch began, and a number were lost. Americans, however, valued his work highly, and in turn he introduced to them something of the accumulated skill and traditions of British gardening.[42]

The enterprise shown by Veitch was not emulated by any other nurseryman. The fact that for several more decades Britain held the field in Chinese plant collection seems due solely to the initiative of Arthur Kilpin Bulley (1861–1942). He was the

* He later learned that Maurice de Vilmorin had already raised a few trees at Les Barres from seed sent by Farges, but Wilson's was the main introduction.

† Mrs. Wilson is recalled in *Rosa helenae* and their daughter in *Arundinaria murielae*.

thirteenth of the fourteen children (all of whom grew up and married) of Samuel Bulley, a Liverpool cotton-broker. He was born at New Brighton, and went into the family business, after education at Marlborough—a school which seems to have bred a good proportion of naturalists. When young he joined a rambling club led by Charles Brown, an enthusiastic field botanist. Through him, Bulley acquired an extensive knowledge of the wild flowers of Wirral. He was concerned, both as an authority and as a financial supporter, with the Liverpool Naturalists Club.

Gardening was his hobby. Though he had several business interests, which were generally most successful financially, at one time, when business was not good, he used part of his garden as a commercial nursery. The result was so profitable that he founded Bees Ltd., nurserymen and seedsmen.

Early in the century the garden that he made at Mickwell Brow, Ness, Neston, had become celebrated. It stands above Kingsley's 'sands of Dee' at the base of the peninsula, and looks on to the mountainous coast of Wales across the river.* Bulley, who was an ardent Fabian, gave the public access to it. The recruitment in 1912 of J. Hope, head herbaceous foreman at the Royal Botanic Garden, Edinburgh, as his gardener, formed (it is said by those who knew them) an ideal combination.

Bulley was interested in the acclimatization of foreign plants. At first he obtained them from foreign missions. But, helpful though they were, the results were not satisfactory. He asked Professor Isaac Bayley Balfour to recommend a man adequately qualified to travel and collect personally for him in western China. George Forrest was chosen, and in 1904 set out. In 1911, again through Balfour, he engaged F. Kingdon Ward, and in 1914 R. E. Cooper. Forrest and Kingdon Ward of course spent the rest of their lives as collectors, and Cooper's shorter career as such revived interest in a little-known but important district.

Bulley was later concerned as a shareholder in many other jointly financed expeditions in many parts of the world, and in 1926 he sent a collector to Asia Minor in search of the bulbous plants that abound there. Bulley was, without doubt, the first of the great twentieth-century patrons of plant-collecting; he led the

* In 1948 the house and garden were endowed and given by Miss A. L. Bulley (A. K. Bulley's daughter) to Liverpool University, as a Botanic Garden. One condition was that part should always be open to the public.

way that others followed.[43] One of his collectors describes him at his prime: 'a cotton-broker who preferred to spend British winters in less austere climes . . . tall, imperial bearded, blue eyes . . . own brand of humour (asked for tablespoonfuls of seed from one *Meconopsis discigera*!)'.

George Forrest (1873–1932) had the traditional background of a plant-collector, with some notable exceptions. Birth at Falkirk and education at Kilmarnock Academy were typical enough, and a career begun in a chemist's shop, training as a pharmacist, gave him some knowledge of botany; he became sufficiently interested in plants to make a herbarium of those growing locally. He also learned the elements of medicine and first aid which were to be so useful to him as a traveller.

Next, he broke away from all this, and lived an out-door life in Australia and South Africa. But there was no future for him overseas, and he returned, toughened and fit, to Edinburgh. Here he reverted to the usual pattern—employment at the Royal Botanic Garden, but only as an insignificant member of the herbarium staff, in the hopes that something better would turn up. The work he undertook was, however, to prove invaluable. He was engaged on examining and arranging thousands of specimens of plants from all over the world—under the most knowledgeable Regius Keeper. He kept fit by walking the six miles to and from his home and fishing and shooting.

When he was selected to go to China, his first visit, lasting from 1904 to 1907, was to Yunnan. This district was to be the centre for his eight expeditions, though from it he moved into Burma, Tibet, and Szechwan. This first journey was his most adventurous. The Tibetans were at that time fighting and slaughtering the Chinese on their borders, with foreigners included among the enemy. Forrest was one of a dozen survivors out of a party of eighty from a French mission which was attacked. Of Forrest's own team of seventeen, only one was left alive. He himself escaped after a desperate solitary journey, at first pursued by armed bands and man-hunting dogs, and finally over high mountains, his foot pierced through by a bamboo spike upon which he trod.

Undeterred by this, within a few months he was again making his way towards the Tibetan borders, this time up the Salween

Valley with the British consul at Teng-yueh, G. L. Litton. This journey was purely exploratory, undertaken outside the plant-hunting season. Both Forrest and Litton became seriously ill; with Forrest the illness recurred on subsequent occasions; Litton died from blackwater fever shortly after their return.

Forrest soon came to understand the natives of these wild places, and gained their confidence (particularly as a doctor). He trained a number of native collectors to a high degree of efficiency. They would work to his instructions loyally and enthusiastically. Thus, at seed time, or during illness, his men could carry on here, there, and everywhere in his absence. He was a skilful organizer, and, with a great knowledge of the work of his predecessors, a most methodical searcher. As a botanist, he sent from Yunnan some 30,000 specimens—of a particularly high standard—probably the finest collection that will ever be made of that rich flora.

His organized methods resulted in plant introductions on a much larger scale than ever before. In general, however, many of his best plants are, because of the localities in which he worked, not hardy except in the milder parts of Britain.

In his subsequent expeditions* Forrest received generous financial support from the exclusive Rhododendron Society,† formed in 1915 of some twenty-five members. To them, with their passion for breeding hybrids to 'aristocratic' standards from the Chinese species—stud book and all—may be attributed the 'rhododendronomania' that prevailed during the first half of the twentieth century. Forrest was responsible for the discovery of 309 reputed new species in the genus, and of those he introduced at least sixty received Royal Horticultural Society awards.[44]‡

Forrest had a natural predilection for the genus, but he was particularly (and financially) encouraged by John Charles Williams (1861–1939), a prominent member of the Rhododendron Society. Williams was born at Caerhays Castle, in Cornwall, which had been purchased by his grandfather in 1854; there, and

---

* Forrest's expeditions were as follows: 1904–7, 1910–11, 1917–19, 1921–3, 1924–5, and 1930–2.
† It held the first Rhododendron Show in 1926.
‡ *R. griersonianum* (which he found in 1917) is probably the best known. With the related *R. auriculatum* it is one of the most distinctive of all rhododendrons, and has been used extensively as a parent in hybridization (the 1952 *Stud Book* lists 131 of its offspring). The name honours C. S. Grierson, of the Chinese Maritime Customs at Teng-yueh, Forrest's friend and helper.

at Werrington, near Launceston, he spent his life: it was the Caerhays garden that he made famous.

Once again we have an 'English gentleman' of the finest tradition: devoted to public service, an ardent worker for education, a keen general naturalist and sportsman, of generous disposition, and an individual character (though a public figure he rode in an old Ford car).

From 1895 to 1934 he kept a record of his plantings at Caerhays. He was catholic in his likings—whether plants were common, such as winter jasmine, or extremely rare, as some of his magnolias —was immaterial as long as they were in his eyes beautiful. He is, however, particularly associated with magnolias (the Caerhays collection is probably unique), camellias, daffodils (he began to breed them in 1893 and one of his closest friends was the Rev. G. H. Engleheart), and, above all, rhododendrons. All these, of course, thrive in the moist and mild air of Cornwall, given protection from wind.

He began growing rhododendrons in about 1885, and was early a successful hybridizer of species; he was one of the first to realize the importance of Wilson's travels, and in 1903 bought twenty-five of Veitch's earliest 'Chinamen'.* He took a leading part in forming the Rhododendron Society. But it is as friend, correspondent, and financer of Forrest—and, of course, as a raiser of his introductions—that he plays an important part in the history of the twentieth-century rhododendronomania. An idea of the scale upon which he grew this genus was given in 1917, when he had in cultivation 267 species and their natural varieties.[45]

What if the fashion for Chinese rhododendrons passes? Then Forrest and Williams jointly will surely be remembered by another shrub. One of Forrest's most important introductions was *Camellia saluenensis*, collected from the volcanic mountain sides near Teng-yueh. This first flowered at Caerhays, and Williams crossed it with unnamed forms of *Camellia japonica*. The result was the hardy hybrid *Camellia × williamsii*, of which there are several named variants in cultivation. This shrub was described by Lord Aberconway when President of the Royal Horticultural Society as one of the best that had ever been introduced to our gardens.[46]

* Wilson's *Rhododendron williamsianum* (introduced in 1908) is named in his honour. Many Wilson plants went to Caerhays; *Rosa moyesii*, for example, first flowered there.

On a March day in 1939 J. C. Williams took his usual after-breakfast walk through his garden to a favourite seat overlooking the sea, where he died. Seven years previously, on 5th January 1932, George Forrest, having a few weeks before ended his last expedition ('I have made a rather glorious and satisfactory finish to all my past years of labour,' he wrote) had gone shooting. He called to his Chinese servant as he fell, and in a moment was dead.

In order of arrival, the next collector in China was William Purdom (1880-1921), of Heversham, Northumberland. He came south to work for Veitch at Coombe Wood, whence he passed on to the staff of Kew Gardens. In December 1908 he left, and 1909 saw him in Kansu, collecting jointly for Veitch and the Arnold Arboretum. This first expedition lasted until 1912. Purdom's work was less sensational—or perhaps received less publicity—than that of his contemporaries. For instance, in 1910 he introduced *Viburnum fragrans* into cultivation, but it did not become well known until Reginald Farrer subsequently wrote of, and reintroduced, it.

It is, indeed, as the man who introduced Farrer to the Chinese mountains that Purdom's name is generally mentioned. Purdom had great ability in getting on with the Chinese and Tibetans (at the time of his early death in Peking he was Inspector of Forests employed by the Chinese government), and no doubt from him Farrer learned his own understanding of the natives.*

Farrer's real place in our history belongs to the rock garden and its twentieth-century development; under that heading, therefore, will be found some biographical notes. As a plant-collector in the Orient, he arrived with Purdom in 1914 and began work in the hills south of Lanchow, the capital of Kansu. They returned in 1915 to find Britain at war. Their introductions, or successful reintroductions, included *Viburnum fragrans*, *Buddleia alternifolia*, *Meconopsis quintuplinervia*, *Gentiana farreri*, *Rosa farreri* (the threepenny-bit rose), lilies, and primulas. There was almost a refreshing absence of rhododendrons. The journey also resulted in Farrer's *On The Eaves of the World* (1917) and *The Rainbow Bridge* (1921). To a stay-at-home the impression given in these books of the Chinese–Tibetan borders, their people, mountains,

---

* Farrer himself became a Buddhist—but whether with true conviction or not seems a little doubtful.

and flora—and the exuberant personality of Farrer—remains unsurpassed. For the geographer, Farrer's idiosyncrasies in transliterating names makes the journey difficult to follow, but at least one botanical authority on the district, Sir William Wright Smith, has spoken of the importance of his books.

The war over, Farrer set out again. His need to find unworked country that was accessible (Hupeh, Szechwan, and Nepal, all fancied, were ruled out on account of political unrest) restricted his area to Upper Burma. The country chosen, with a monsoon climate, has a rich flora, but little of it will grow in Britain, even in Cornish gardens. In 1919, now with E. H. M. Cox,* Farrer arrived at Hpimaw. From March to November the two covered the neighbouring mountains, where the hardier plants grew. Botanically, the exploration was valuable, but only a few rhododendrons and a juniper, *J. recurva coxii*—a beautiful and hardy tree—are all that came back for the benefit of our gardens.

In the winter Cox came home. Farrer moved on alone into even more remote country. It was difficult to work, and the wet, sunless climate proved intolerable. Farrer collected a valuable set of herbarium specimens and his hut was surrounded by innumerable paper trays on which were laid his harvest of seed capsules in the hope that they would dry 'in that land of everlasting rain and mist', when he died on 17th October 1920. His ardent spirit was stronger than his body. His specimens came home, but not his seeds.[47]

Purdom is so closely linked with Farrer and Cox that they have been considered together. This has put our chronology out of order, and we must return to A. K. Bulley and the year 1911. Once again he had asked Balfour to recommend a plant-collector, and the choice was Francis Kingdon Ward (1885–1958).

Ward was the son of H. Marshall Ward (1854–1905), Professor of Botany at Cambridge from 1895. He was born in Manchester, educated at St. Paul's School and Christ's College, Cambridge. In 1909–10 he had travelled across Asia with the Bedford expedition of the Natural History Museum. For Bulley, he spent the years 1911–13 in Szechwan and Yunnan. The rest of his life, with the exception of war periods, was spent almost

* Euan Hillhouse Methven Cox (*b.* 1893), of Glendoick, Perth, later wrote on several aspects of gardening. He published *Wild Gardening* (1929), founded *New Flora and Silva* (*see* p. 430), and is the historian of Scots gardening (*see Bibliography*).

continuously in the field as a plant-collector* and geographer. He travelled simply, living on the land, and did not employ plant-collectors. Fortunately for the general reader he has left a series of books describing his journeys, beginning with *The Land of the Blue Poppy* (1913), while accounts of the botanical aspects of his journeys were published in *The Gardener's Chronicle*. All were illustrated by his own excellent photographs. His name (apart from his geographical discoveries and botanical studies) will always be associated with rhododendrons, lilies, meconopsis, gentians, and primulas, though he brought much else. Probably the best known of his discoveries and introductions is *Primula florindae* (named in honour of his first wife), collected in 1925 in Tibet—a fine giant cowslip that will maintain itself unaided in many parts of Britain. His collection of the blue poppy, *Meconopsis betonicifolia baileyi*, in the same year, also brought us an immensely popular flower.

Again we must return to Bulley. The district lying on the southern side, and at the eastern end, of the Himalayas had long been neglected. William Griffith (1810-1845),† one-time superintendent of Calcutta Botanic Gardens, had collected in the 'forbidden' state of Bhutan in 1837-8, but, with adjoining Sikkim, the country had subsequently been virtually unworked.‡

Bulley engaged Roland Edgar Cooper (*b.* 1890) to travel in those parts. Cooper was born at Kingston-on-Thames. He lost his parents when four, and was brought up by a relative, who married William Wright Smith. When the latter went to India in 1907 Cooper went with him, and until 1910 studied both botany and horticulture at the Calcutta and Darjeeling botanic gardens. Then followed a spell at Edinburgh until 1913, when Bulley appointed Cooper as his personal collector. In that year Sikkim was visited, without any very notable results, and in 1914 and

---

* His subsequent journeys (prior to 1939) were as follows: 1919 N.E. Upper Burma; 1921 N.E. Yunnan, Yunnan–Schezwan borders; 1922 Yunnan–Schezwan–Tibet and N.E. Burma; 1924–5 Tibet and Bhutan; 1926 Burma and Assam; 1927–8 Assam and Mishmi Hills; 1931 N.E. Upper Burma and Tibetan frontier; 1933 Assam and Upper Burma; 1935 Tibet, Assam–Himalaya frontiers; 1937 N.E. Upper Burma and Tibet; and 1938 Assam–Himalaya.

Of his many books, perhaps *The Riddle of the Tsangpo Gorges* (1926) is most interesting to the general reader.

† His name is commemorated in the Bhutan pine, *P. griffithii* (also called *P. excelsa*), and *Rhododendron griffithianum*.

‡ These states have none of the old trunk routes passing through them—they lie, so to speak, sandwiched in between, and therefore isolated from, the rest of the world.

1915 Bhutan. In the first year *Viburnum grandiflorum* was introduced; in the latter the isolated peaks in the south of the state yielded a number of plants. *Rhododendron rhabdotum*, though tender, has received high praise. An interesting discovery was *Lobelia nubigena*, the sole recorded locality in Europe or Asia of a species related to the giant lobelias of the Mountains of the Moon in Central Africa. Considerable work was done on primulas also. One shrub deserves particular mention. Cooper slipped from a narrow and dangerous pathway. His fall into the depths below was fortuitously stopped by a bush. It turned out to be a new species, later named *Buddleia cooperi*; it was *not* introduced!

After a further expedition in 1916 to the difficult country of Kulu and Lahaul in the western Himalayas, followed by war service, came botanical appointments in Burma. Then in 1930 Cooper comes back into our history, first as assistant curator, and then, from 1934 (until his retirement in 1950), as curator of the Royal Botanic Garden, Edinburgh. The period was, of course, an important one, with many new rhododendrons, primulas, and other alpine plants either coming to maturity or arriving for addition to the collection. Cooper has as his other interest anthropology.

Bhutan and the area northwards into Tibet has subsequently, from 1933 onwards, yielded much of interest during a number of expeditions made by Frank Ludlow and Major George Sheriff.

So much for those who, within half a century, first learned about, and then revolutionized our gardens with, the trees, shrubs, and plants of those mountainous areas which roughly cover the headwaters of Yangtze-kiang, the Irrawaddy, and the Brahmaputra. To our gardens they have brought, first of all, rhododendrons. Next, a great many other hardy shrubs, some of which are now common, among which are camellias, hamamelis, berberis, viburnums, cotoneasters, and roses. Then there are the lilies, gentians, primulas, and a hundred and one alpine and herbaceous plants. Many trees were introduced, of which a number of species of *Prunus*, *Sorbus*, and *Acer* are now becoming well known, most withstanding the lime which rhododendrons resent.

Yet we must remember that plant-collecting went on in many other parts of the world. In the Southern Hemisphere there were several expeditions. Probably the best known are those undertaken by H. F. Comber (*b.* 1897). He was brought up in the fine garden of Nymans (the home of the Messel family)* with its rich collection of plants, where his father was head gardener. As a boy he collected local wild plants, and in 1914 (unable to serve in the forces) became gardener to H. J. Elwes at Colesborne. A spell at the Royal Botanic Garden, Edinburgh, followed. Financed by a syndicate, in which the Hon. H. D. Mclaren of Bodnant was prominent, he spent the years 1925-7 in the Andes of Chile and the Argentine, hoping to obtain hardy forms of South American plants from the higher altitudes. This expedition produced much of interest, but little that was hardy except in our mildest districts. *Fabiana violacea* and some berberis, however, went into more general cultivation. In 1929-30 Comber collected in Tasmania for a syndicate formed by Lionel de Rothschild (1882-1942).[49]†

As the twentieth century progressed many amateurs and some enterprising nurserymen joined the ranks of the collectors in increasing numbers. The mountainous parts of Europe were visited by these doctors, lawyers, and other professional men on holiday. Besides the alps of Switzerland and the Pyrenees, the mountains of the Balkans were arduously searched. Asia Minor and North Africa were visited. For the most part their trophies were for the growers of alpine plants. To name these would be impossible. Many of the plants they introduced, often of great beauty or interest, never found their way into the general currency of gardening.

As an outstanding example of this type of collector one may take a nurseryman, Clarence Elliott, who, in addition to running his business, has wandered far and wide in search of plants whose prerequisite was that they should be good in the garden. Born in 1881, son of that Elliott who founded the eminent firm of photographers 'by royal appointment', Elliott and Fry, he began gardening during childhood at Hadley Green in Hertfordshire. Then, when he was a schoolboy at Giggleswick, came solitary plant-hunting expeditions—out of bounds to Malham Cove for Jacob's Ladder or perhaps to the lily-of-the-valley woods. Training with the Rivers firm at Sawbridgeworth followed, and, of more lasting influence, in the alpine nursery, with its long tradition, of Backhouse at York. Then a sudden change, and off to South Africa for three years' farming. Finally, after further English

* Acquired by the National Trust under the will of Lt.-Col. L. C. R. Messel in 1954. The hybrid *Eucryphia* × *nymansay* originated there.[48]
† Of Exbury, Hampshire, a noted hybridizer of rhododendrons and azaleas.[50]

wandering, came the establishment in 1907 of the Six Hills Nursery at Stevenage in Hertfordshire—a return to mountain plants, and to plant-collecting in a more serious manner.

The first expedition, on a cycle, was to Corsica in 1908. *Helleborus corsicus, Morisia monanthos (hypogaea)*, and *Thymus herba barona*, the seed-cake thyme, all came back to Six Hills as novelties, and were soon in many other catalogues. In 1909 the Falkland Islands were searched, again alone; the year after, the European Alps with Reginald Farrer. Many trips followed to the mountains of Europe—or even to the forgotten, remote gardens and nurseries of England and Scotland. These journeys, almost like week-end trips compared with the planned campaigns of a Wilson or Forrest, yet gave us delightful plants, ranging from the dwarf London Pride (*Saxifraga primuloides* Elliot's variety), of wide and deserved popularity, to campanulas, oxalis, aquilegias, and many others now to be found in most self-respecting rock gardens.

Rather more extensive journeys were made in 1927 and again in 1928 to Chile and the Andes with Dr. Balfour Gourlay, who collected botanical specimens for Kew and Edinburgh. The first saw the introduction of *Leucocoryne ixiodes*, the 'Glory of the Sun', and the odd *Calceolaria darwinii*, so often attempted, but except in Scotland not usually with great success, by the ardent alpine gardener. The second trip gave us the fantastic *Puya alpestris*, 'my most beautiful and important introduction . . . that beats anything else I ever discovered'. Unfortunately, it does not seem to have taken kindly to us. In 1932 followed a collecting and lecturing tour in western North America.

.   .   .   .   .

THE TWENTIETH-CENTURY GARDEN

It is interesting to isolate those features peculiar to the development of our gardens in the first half of the twentieth century— which, of course, had become apparent before our closing year of 1939. (The rapid progress of scientific methods and mechanization was nothing new, but merely an alarming accleration.)

First and foremost comes the development of the old-fashioned patch of fernery and rockwork into the almost universal rock garden, a development in some instances raised almost to the status of mysticism as the 'alpine garden'.

The cult had developed steadily during the last part of the nineteenth century. There was William Robinson's encouragement. The York firm of Backhouse had built some fine and massive rockeries whose structure was informed by the principles of geology. The vogue for mountaineering brought with it the study of plants in high places: for example, a book such as E. Newell Arber's *Plant Life in Alpine Switzerland* (1910) had found its way on to the bookshelves of many gardeners.

The making of the rock garden at Kew was a landmark. Pressure had for some time been brought to bear on the authorities to improve their collection of alpine plants; but nothing was done. However, in 1882, George Curling Joad, an amateur botanist, left to the Gardens his collection of 2,630 alpine plants. A grant was then forthcoming, and the present rock garden was begun. On that riverside site a miniature valley was scooped out, and with Somerset limestone a Pyrenean glen was formed. Unfortunately, funds ran out and the glen had to be concluded with unearthed ruins, stumps, and similar material.

In 1887 an unheated glass-house was constructed in which to grow those high alpines which could not tolerate the damp and fog of a London winter.[51]

Another important event was the construction of a rock garden begun in 1893 at St. John's College, Oxford. This was something quite new in the university. It was built, with his own hands, by the Rev. Henry Jardine Bidder (1847-1923), in an unusual and rather odd style, by no means 'natural', yet its influence on the fashion for the cultivation of alpine plants—or, one should say, plants fitted to grow on a rockery—was considerable. Bidder, when a young Fellow of St. John's, had persuaded the officials to appoint him *custos sylvarum*. He was an exceptionally clever gardener, and was later helped by such capable exponents of the art as Reginald Farrer and Miss Willmott, who in their turn no doubt learned much about plants from him. He was a man of singular and forthright character—alarming unless one was a knowledgeable fellow enthusiast—deserving a high rank among the band of parson-gardeners, but in a very different category from Dean Hole![52]

And one should mention the celebrated rockery at Friar Park, near Henley. This was made by Sir Frank Crisp, Bart. (1843–1919), a solicitor whose specialization in company law proved most lucrative. He was clearly a man of great capability and intelligence; botany, microscopy, and horticulture were his hobbies. He was treasurer of the Linnean Society, and his posthumously published collection of some 600 reproductions of pictures of medieval gardens is remarkable.* But it was as the constructor of Friar Park, a garden on which no expense was spared, that Crisp was best known—and which some, but by no means all, of the knowledgeable mocked. The place contained every form of garden, and was full of 'conceits and surprises', but none achieved such fame as the rock garden, climbing up to a scale model of the Matterhorn. It was thus described in 1909:[53]

The mountain top appears clothed in snow, the effect being obtained by the use of some alabaster. Appropriate plants are disposed at suitable spots, and the visitor can imagine himself to be in the midst of the Alps. Some idea of the extent of the rockery may be obtained from the fact that 7,000 tons of stone (from near Leeds) have been used in its construction, whilst it is furnished with 4,000 distinct plants.

There can be little doubt, however, that all these early influences were united in the forceful, bizarre person of Reginald Farrer (1880–1920). Although we have earlier seen him as a plant-collector, his memorial really lies among the stones cunningly placed in a 'natural' manner on their flat sides, and in the alpine houses of his countless followers.

His geographical background is surely important and relevant to his career. It was Ingleborough, among the great limestone 'scars', wild yew woods, and singularly rich hill flora; a place where the climate is mild and moist, like 'Fanny Price in its stupid, gentle dullness', up to the New Year—and then, 'in the cyclones of snow and ice, begins the spring'. It was here that, from childhood onwards, he gardened and later had a nursery; here were his home-made glens, gorges, moraines, precipices, and bog-gardens—some in what he called the 'old garden' with a soil too

---

* *Medieval Gardens*, arranged by C. C. Paterson (1924).

meagre, even for alpine plants, others in his 'new garden', where in rich soil they thrived.

Equally influential was his family background. The Farrers had long been in Yorkshire. His father was High Sheriff, an occasional writer, and traditionally Liberal in politics. Here was the gentleman's ancestry that, alternatively with humble birth in Scotland, seems to have given us most of our great gardeners. In the case of Farrer there was, however, a marked distinction. He had a cleft palate, and, presumably for that reason, went to no public school. Following family tradition, he did, however, go up to Balliol College, Oxford.[54]

The consequences of this were that he was not shaped to a mould, retained an uninhibited enthusiasm, and both a manner and a pen unbridled by the good form of the day. He was slightly macrocephalous, moustachioed, noisy—his voice was penetrating, marred by his disability; he could be ostentatious and sometimes ill-mannered (though with a flair for getting on with the natives of a country, particularly in the Orient). His writing was by the standards of today verbose—but glittered with the richness of the whole English vocabulary, and rang with the rhythms of old English prose: one cannot resist repeating:

Dead bones in their grave lie Mary and Elizabeth, Queens; and dead dust of death is all they did; but the flowers they grew in their gardens still continue giving comfort and delight perpetually, down through the continuing generations, to whom the people of the past are mere phantasmal fictions in books, diaphanous, desiccated as dried flowers themselves. . . .

And who, having at last achieved a sombre-flowered spike on an oncocyclus iris, will fail to remember that passage on 'the more fractious Irids of the East'?

Words only, it is true: but we see him in his last years, among the remote hills, stocky in figure, in shorts, wearing an old topee, tie-less and collarless, stockings hanging round his ankles—a man whose indomitable enthusiasm for plants drove on a body classed as unfit for soldiering to a lonely death in the mountains, defeated in the end by exhaustion, rain, and mist.[55] There is a short answer to Farrer's critics—those who say that he over-wrote, that his journeys were imprecisely recorded, that he was but a minor botanist, that he was in the lower ranks as a plant-collector, and that as a gardener he was not really successful. It is simply that, like the Georgians before him, Farrer was seeking an elysium; the Georgians would risk and lose their fortunes: Farrer his life.

His intentions as an alpine gardener are quite clear. In his first book on the subject, *My Rock Garden*, published in 1907, he wrote: 'It is, in effect, an imitation of nature, and, to be successful, must aim at reproducing with fidelity some particular feature of nature—whichever you may choose.' It was to be situated away from the garden proper. In his well-known phrases the old 'almond-pudding schemes' and 'the style of the Dog's Grave' were derided. Elsewhere he wrote that 'ill-furnished acres of Portland cement blocks, sham stalactites . . . burrs, clinkers, odds and ends of Norman arches, conglomerated bricks . . . must be refused . . . granite, flint, porphyry, syenite, or calliard is only to be used as a resource of despair'. His rules of construction—few large stones, lying on their broadest face, firmly set, deeply buried —have become fundamental laws. Probably he did not evolve them entirely on his own—but they are directly opposed to the work of Bidder, who is sometimes said to have been Farrer's model. He admits a debt to Kew and Warley. Possibly, his debt to Japan (also admitted) is overlooked.

Farrer wrote much, and influentially, for the horticultural Press. His reputation stands, however, firmly based on the two stout volumes of *The English Rock Garden*. Written in 1913, war prevented its appearance until 1919. Before the end of our period it was reprinted five times* without, so far as I know, any noticeable alterations.

If any other instance is needed of the power of Farrer it can be seen in the formation of the Alpine Garden Society in 1929 to encourage the cultivation of alpine plants. It is an organization of the highest standing, with a *Quarterly Bulletin* that is a model of what such publications should be; the continual references in it to Farrer and the Farrer ideals is again evidence of his singular influence.

The early influence of Japan on Farrer has been mentioned; he lived in Tokyo during 1903, and in *The Garden of Asia* (1904)

* And has been subsequently.

described his delight in the country and its gardens. At that time the cult of the Japanese in Britain was of some importance; it was impermanent, and never produced here anything comparable with chinoiserie. Occasionally one may still see a bronze crane, or some other Japanese architectural property, lying neglected in an overgrown rockery, and that is all that remains. John Gould Veitch had much to do with the origins of the fashion in the 1860s; by 1885 *The Mikado* was laughing at it. A. B. Freeman-Mitford (1837-1916), later first Baron Redesdale, had some effect on it. After some time spent in Japan with the Foreign Service he published *Tales of Old Japan* (1871), and at Batsford Park, in the Cotswolds, the influence was shown in his enthusiasm for bamboos; his study of them, *The Bamboo Garden*, was published in 1896.

In 1889 appeared *The Theory of Japanese Flower Arrangements* by an English architect, Josiah Conder, later revised and issued as *The Floral Art of Japan* with illustrations by Japanese artists. This was a serious study and much admired. In 1908 there came another understanding book, *The Flowers and Gardens of Japan*, described by Florence du Cane and illustrated from paintings made by Ella du Cane.

The seriousness with which this Japanese fashion was sometimes taken has been delightfully described. In 1907 the traveller Miss Ella Christie, knowing Japanese gardens at first hand, began to make one at her home, Cowden, at the foot of the Ochills in eastern Scotland. The site was a swampy field. A woman artist, Taki Honda, came from a school of garden design in Japan to supervise. A ditch was turned into a lake; the rules of Japanese art, based (as so often) on that variable quantity nature, were followed. Thus, no mountain stone was used near the water. Everywhere there was symbolism. The trees and shrubs were pruned and shaped to the rules; they were particularly required to play their part when naked in winter. A stone lantern was brought from Kyoto and duly washed with rice-water to revive the moss. Miss Christie herself raised Korean pines from seed that she had collected; they were planted on a simulated Fujiyama, carrying a red-lacquered Shinto shrine, properly roofed with the true Japanese cedar (*Cryptomeria japonica*). Weeping willows, spiraeas, azaleas, and primulas were planted; later, the new plants from China were permitted a place.

In 1925 a Japanese gardener named Matsuo became himself a part of the garden; his life in Scotland, until a decade or so later when he died from eating the rich food of London, cannot, unhappily, be part of this history.[56]

.   .   .   .

From Japan we move naturally to that fashion peculiar to the twentieth century: the decorative use of cut flowers in water. Some mention has been made of the use of banks of orchids or mounds of other exotic hot-house flowers that alone were sufficiently choice to grace the tables of the refined. The old tightly bunched and complex posy, too, or the rather newer buttonhole, still remained generally in fashion until the late nineteenth century—even though Mrs. Loudon had attracted some attention by decorating her rooms with cut flowers in vases.

'It was left to Queen Alexandra, when Princess of Wales, to sweep all this away. With bated breath, Sir Maurice Holzmann, told us that the Princess had large vases of "common" beech-boughs in the drawing-room of Marlborough House.' So wrote Sir William Lawrence.[57]

I think that R. P. Brotherston's *The Book of Cut Flowers*, published in 1906, was the first book to deal entirely with flower arrangement in the new manner, though something had been said of it by Miss Frances Jane Hope in her *Notes and Thoughts on Gardens and Woodlands*, as early as the 1870s, by Miss Jekyll, and by Mrs. C. W. Earle in her *Pot-Pourri from a Surrey Garden*. Brotherston's book is prefaced with a plate showing a 'free arrangement of spring wild flowers', which, with its single container, and radiating gentle lines, would today still be regarded as meritorious—as, indeed, would be many more of the designs he shows; Conder's Japanese influence is freely admitted.

The book, it may be added, in addition to its sensitive feeling for the subject, is most sensible and practical; its author, a burly looking man, died in 1923—the year he retired after half a century in the gardens of the Earl of Haddington at Tyninghame.

As the century proceeded the fashion for cut flowers in a room became obligatory, and its commercial aspects were astutely—and by no means always tastefully—exploited.

.   .   .

Before examining the trend of garden design during the first part of the twentieth century—that is, as exemplified by actual gardens begun after 1900 that were reaching maturity by the year our period closes—it may be well to mention two books.

The first is well-called *Twentieth Century Gardening* by Charles Eley, first published in 1923. This is a realistic book, written in a time of financial depression, and is concerned primarily with a garden of trees and shrubs, their selection from the immense variety now available, and their uses—the establishment, in other words, of a *permanent* garden.* The design of this type of garden may be said to resemble the development of its near contemporary, the symphonic poem in music; it moves ceaselessly on, logically in a form that is loosely knit compared with the regularity of the older symphony proper with its repetitions. The framework is formed by trees in their abundance of form and colour, which, rather than stone or brick, or geometrical ground plan, form the architectural setting. Shrubs, bulbs, and even long-lived herbaceous plants provide the decorative and textural elaboration.

The second is Christopher Tunnard's *Gardens in the Modern Landscape*, which, published in 1938, comes just within our period, and should receive some attention. It is, however, in the same category as Blomfield's book, and, as such, surely fails to comprehend the true nature of gardening. It, too, delves into the past without much understanding, while it misses the present and points to a future that does not arrive. It is, however, to be commended for the attention of the horticultural student.

It is rather difficult to single out for description gardens in the grand manner particularly associated both in time of construction and ideals with the first part of the twentieth century. If domination of all else except the lie of the ground is to be by trees and shrubs, purposefully arranged to make use of their form, texture, and colour throughout the seasons (autumn and winter are then nearly equally valued as spring and summer)—and this surely is a distinguishing feature of our present century—then Westonbirt must take a high place. Lying on the limestone of the south-western

* Enterprising nurserymen by this time were specializing in, and propagating, good forms of trees and shrubs, many of them still rare. The Hillier family, whose business at Winchester was founded in 1864, became prominent in this sphere. So did W. J. Marchant, of Keeper's Hill Nursery, Stapehill, Wimborne, who offered a rich and carefully chosen selection.

Cotswolds, on level ground, it yet has a freak patch of greensand on which rhododendrons can be grown.

The estate had belonged to the Holford family since the seventeenth century. In 1863 a transformation scene took place on a scale comparable with the days of Lancelot Brown. The old house was pulled down, as were a farm, cottages, and the village—which was moved. By 1871 a grand mansion, designed by Lewis Vulliamy in the 'Jacobethan' style, had arisen. In front of it were raised terraces and an Italian garden; beyond them were serpentine walks, and a lake. The whole was then planted with trees and shrubs—here massed, there grouped, and elsewhere single. Nowhere was there any regularity. Form was played against form, colour contrasted against colour. In 1951 there were no fewer than 179 species and variants included in the hundreds of trees and shrubs planted around the house and within its garden alone.[58]

The originator of this imaginative undertaking was Robert Staynor Holford (1808–1892); he, too, developed the arboretum (already begun in 1829) outside the garden proper. His son, Sir George Lindsay Holford (1860–1926), carried on the planting in the arboretum and surrounding grounds (Plate XXXI). Within a few years he had available the introductions from western China. These he acquired and planted on the grand scale. He was highly selective, choosing the best forms, and, like his father, placing the trees and shrubs so that they were seen to their best advantage. He was, perhaps, the first to show how these new introductions, particularly maples, white beams, rowans, the Chinese form of the Katsura tree (*Cercidiphyllum*), and other trees and shrubs, could be used to give the garden a final season of brilliant colour in the autumn; indeed, people crowd to see the blaze at Westonbirt in mid-October.[59]

On a vaster scale is Bodnant in the Conway Valley, looking westward over the river, over the hills and on to the peaks north of Snowdon; a prospect of grandeur, brought within the garden scene. Here again there was the advantage of early planting; for from 1875 Henry Pochin began to plant choice conifers. Then at the beginning of the present century his daughter, and principally his grandson, later Lord Aberconway, began to make a terraced garden on the side of the valley. Even so, fine as these terraces are, it is the magnolias, camellias, azaleas, eucryphias, embothriums and, above all, rhododendrons in the surrounding grounds that give this garden its importance. Beneath them grow such plants as primulas and gentians.[60]

There can be no doubt that Bodnant is the most magnificent twentieth-century garden in Britain; it can compete almost on level terms with the ranges of Snowdonia.

Yet—are the scarlets of the rhododendrons a little inclined to clash with the opening leaves of the Welsh oaks, and is the Cotswold pin mill moved bodily from those neat limestone hills a little uncomfortable in the shaggy mountain landscape? If one thinks so, then one can turn to Sheffield Park in Sussex (Plate XXXI). Here is no dramatic landscape. The garden has its origins in a calm, Brownian landscape; as its feature, a series of moderately sized lakes. The house, in the gothick manner, plays no important part in the scene.

Sheffield Park was acquired on the death of the then Earl of Sheffield in 1909 by Arthur Gilstrap Soames (1854-1934). It was he who seized upon the lakes, whose shores already carried some fine trees, including a group of the cluster pine (*Pinus pinaster*) said to have been planted in 1800 by Banks, and made of them the great vistas in the garden. There are two down the main axis of the garden, linked by a cascade, extending for some 400 yards; at their end, crossing them as the stroke of a giant 'T', are the other two lakes. Their margins are richly planted with a great variety of trees and shrubs. So we have, instead of Robinsonian glades, or the old formal canals, irregular, long, wide, and watery views, over whose floor spread countless water-lilies.

The surrounding grounds are intersected with paths forming glades among trees and shrubs, fastidiously chosen and most skilfully placed. Nowhere else in England, perhaps, can one see such masterly use of this material so sensitively matched to its surroundings. When seen in its spring glory, the conifers discreetly used to give solidity, and a foil to the tracery of the newly leafing trees—all, with the shrubs, rising from a sheet of bluebells—one is also continually observing the skill that will make the garden flame again in autumn.

Other twentieth-century gardens from all over our islands deserve description. There is, however, one that surely exceeds them all in brilliance of conception and execution. Hidcote

Bartrim Manor garden, seen, say, in the summer of 1939, when every small touch of its maker showed and added brilliance to the minutest detail of its decoration, this was surely the 'perfectest figure' of a twentieth-century garden (Plate XXXII). When his hand had gone, the broad outlines of the masterly plan, the maturing trees, shrubs, and hedges, were alone adequate to give it supreme distinction—and oddly enough, to provide practical suggestions for the smallest suburban garden.

It was begun in about 1903 by Lawrence Johnston. The site was on the level immediately above the northerly escarpment of the Cotswolds; there, up a by-lane that ended abruptly, stood a good old stone manor house, with a cluster of thatched cottages close at hand. By the manor was a cedar; a little way off, some large beeches showing their typical delight in the situation.

One would have said that the spot was cold, and that apart from the fine view over the heart of England a few moments' walk from the house, the place had no exceptional possibilities as a garden site. Today, so apparently intricate is the plan that it is not easy to grasp its underlying simplicity. The house, its out-buildings, entrance court, nursery garden, orchard, and large lawn among the great beeches, stand as a group on their own; they are hedged in, almost pushed aside—there are no wide vistas seen from the windows. All is sheltered, and the many walls and angles harbour tender plants—for here, high up, though the winter winds blow cold, the dangerous airs of a treacherous spring frost do not lie, but flow down into the vale.

When Major Johnston came he found that from the cedar below the house a broad band of ground rises gently until it reaches the crest of the escarpment; there the land falls away, first gradually, then sharply. Running parallel with this band, and also originating not far from the cedar, is a small descending and ever-widening stream-filled valley.

The master-plan was this. The rising land was levelled and ascended from time to time by flights of steps; it was enclosed by a variety of hedges, and formed into a series of geometrically designed gardens, each with its own delights, such as gazebos or pleached limes. All are symmetrically placed on an axis with a clear vista through, ending in the piers of a fine gateway.

The valley was turned into a wild garden; a path winds above the stream, which is shadowed by rare trees, its banks planted with shrubs, lilies, primulas, and other naturalized plants. This little valley diverges somewhat from the main axis of the vista, and it is in this broadening space that we see the true genius of design, for it is packed with a number of little hedged compartments into which one descends, each different and each a place of enchantment, to make one's exit into the valley.

One broad-grassed vista, closed by high hornbeam hedges, goes, as it were to unite both parts, at right angles to the main axis; at its end one sees, through iron grilles, nothing but the sky. It is the sky, too, that is seen as one mounts up the main walk from the cedar—slowly, because of continued diversions as one passes. When one at last goes through the terminating gateway into a grove of ilexes, there is suddenly disclosed that view to which I have referred: no less than the Vale of Avon, leading into that stretch of land in which lies the heart of Shakespeare's poetry. Closer at hand, one may remark, at Mickleton, just below us to the right, was the home of the Graves family, where Shenstone first learned of the 'landskip'.

To describe the plants, shrubs, and trees would be tedious; Major Johnston travelled widely, and their variety and quality are enchanting. Here the ancient worlds of China and the Mediterranean* lie side by side, as do, equally happily, those once bitter enemies, nature and formality. It is pleasant to see them so; indeed it is a moving experience—in the company of an old Cotswold manor, in the heart of England.

So much for twentieth-century gardens designed in, or approaching towards, the grand manner. Yet the real feature of the century was the growth of a huge suburbia of small houses. They are of but one general type—the small total number of rooms varying little—and an almost invariably rectangular patch of garden covering but a few square yards. A new kind of gardener appeared; coming from the town, without inherited knowledge, many were truly enthusiastic, others merely trying to emulate, or perhaps excel, their identically minded neighbours on either side. The result was a new class of 'week-enders', for the most part of a standardized outlook brought about by their commercial ex-

---

* Major Johnston died in 1957 at his other, and equally famous, garden, Serre de la Madone in the south of France.

ploitation by chain stores and some nurserymen. It was a class ministered to by the popular Press and the radio.

Possibly the greatest influence for good horticulture was the choice by the British Broadcasting Corporation of Cecil H. Middleton (1887–1945) as a speaker. He was a Northamptonshire man, trained at Kew, and had held horticultural posts under both the Government and Surrey County Council. In 1934, at the suggestion of Col. F. R. Durham, Secretary of the Royal Horticultural Society, he was engaged to give a series of talks, 'In Your Garden', on Sunday afternoons. He was immensely successful, and was listened to alike by practical gardeners and those who only dreamed of gardening.

The increase in planning of large estates of small houses, and the building of somewhat larger houses by persons who were prepared to engage a designer to lay out their small realm, led to a considerable increase in the number of landscape and garden designers—many of dubious ability and taste. With this in view there was formed in 1929 the Institute of Landscape Architects, whose objects were 'the advancement of the art of landscape architecture: the theory and practice of garden, landscape, and civic design; the promotion of research and education therein; and the creation and maintenance of a high standard of professional qualification'.

As in the past, however, the talented and experienced amateur, devoting a lifetime to one garden, almost invariably produced something nearer perfection than the professional who was called in to provide a design, carried it out, and then departed.

Unhappily, during this period little imagination—though much expensive and first-rate cultivation—was to be seen in our public parks. Mention should be made of one of the exceptions that invariably go to prove the rule. Thomas Hay (1874–1953), after private work in Scotland, came south to Greenwich Park. His imaginative and unconventional planting received their acknowledgement when, in 1924, he was placed in charge of the Central Royal Parks. He retired in 1940. Something of his quality is to be seen in his *Plants for the Connoisseur* (1938).

Of gardening, as of other journalism there was a spate. Most of it was popular, repetitive, and reasonably sound. *The Garden* ceased to appear in 1927, but *Gardening Illustrated* continued to cater for the gardener still largely unimpressed by the popular demands of the masses. More important was the publication in October 1928 of the first number of *New Flora and Silva*, founded and at first edited by E. H. M. Cox, designed to be of interest to 'all gardeners who are anxious to cultivate more than the standard varieties of garden plants . . . without casting aspersions at tried favourites or belittling the ordinary gardener'.

Nor should one omit to mention Arthur Tysilo Johnson (1873–1956). After some experience as schoolmaster and market gardener he began writing about the garden he made at Tyn-y-groes near Conway. Bulkeley Mill, as it was called, was a combination of rock garden and woodland garden in the Robinsonian manner, though later a fine collection of old roses was added. Johnson had a wide first-hand knowledge of plants—mostly species—and their cultivation. He was also a talented photographer, his pictures showing his plants as they grew. He was gardening correspondent to several periodicals and a regular contributor to the horticultural Press. Three of his books belong to our period: *A Garden in Wales* (1927), *A Woodland Garden* (1937), and *The Garden Today* (1938).

The increasing use of motor transport made the age-old custom of garden-visiting much easier. Advantage of this was taken in 1927 to start a National Gardens Scheme. Six hundred gardens were opened to the public, the admission fees going to a fund providing a memorial to Queen Alexandra. The following year the Scheme was handed over to the Queen's Institute of District Nursing. A similar scheme exists for Scotland. In 1932 was first published an illustrated and annotated list of the gardens so opened, the first of a series that forms an interesting brief survey of the gardens of the period.

The war of 1939–45 inevitably halted ornamental gardening. Food production had priority and the need for this was a spur to scientific research which progressed and still progresses rapidly. With the return of peace, even improved mechanization failed to make large gardens practicable. The rapid increase in the number of small houses, however, has brought into being a large new class of often highly intelligent and enthusiastic plantsmen. The future of gardening in Britain is largely in their hands.

APPENDIX

1939–1978

by Geoffrey and Susan Jellicoe

The sociological movements that affected gardening and landscape throughout the thirties gained immense impetus from the Second World War. In 1945, when the mood of the country was dominated by hopes for a better Britain, the collective or public landscape was one of the answers to the national conscience. From then onwards, gardening has been divided into two separate cultures, the domestic and the collective, expanding on a scale never previously reached by any country.

The rise of the specialist in modern society is now inevitable. In England, gardens in recent years have (with a few notable exceptions) always been the province of the gifted layman. While this has retarded professionalism in landscape more than in architecture or town planning, the apparent brake on progress may prove to have been invaluable. The professional is technically more proficient, gaining in mystique thereby, but owing to his formal education he may be imaginatively constrained by an aesthetic fashionable at the time. His approach is primarily intellectual, whereas the layman is intuitive and often exploding with ideas that he is technically unable to express. It is to feed these intuitions and turn them into reality that a wide range of gardening media has come into being, planned almost entirely for the layman.

THE DOMESTIC GARDEN
The levelling of incomes and rising cost of labour has meant that the great private garden can no longer be maintained in its

431

previous style and that maintenance is a more serious consideration than capital costs. The middle-income garden, with its one gardener, has given way to labour-saving, self-help gardens based on new techniques, often reduced in size by the sale of part of the plot for building. In contrast to these negative developments there has emerged a vast new public no longer content with a garden of pseudo rockery and crazy paving; a public which realizes that a garden is a necessary escape into nature and away from the mechanical world. A desire for knowledge has led to a huge increase in gardening books, journals, television programmes; in gardening societies; and in visits to gardens open to the public, both historic and modern. These last are more fully discussed in Miles Hadfield's *Landscape With Trees* (1967). In the build-up of a background to knowledge, perhaps the most important contribution was the Royal Horticultural Society's *Dictionary of Gardening* (four volumes, 1956–69). It was quickly followed by Roy Hay and Patrick Synge's *Dictionary of Garden Plants in Colour* (1970) and by John Murray's commissioning a major revision of W. J. Bean's *Trees and Shrubs Hardy in the British Isles*, four volumes 1973–1979/80, under the chief editor D. L. Clarke. Of the many books on special subjects, Graham Stuart Thomas's *Old Shrub Roses* (1955) stands out; his advocacy led to a revival of interest in old fashioned species, previously neglected but now a popular feature in most gardens. Books on history range from the particularised *Genius of the Place* by John Dixon Hunt and Peter Willis (1975) to *The Landscape of Man* (1975), a history of world landscape art by the present writers. One of the most intriguing books of the period is undoubtedly Jay Appleton's *The Experience of Landscape* (1975), which tentatively puts forward a theory of primitive instincts, of 'prospect' and 'refuge' that was certainly not considered in Edmund Burke's *The Origins of the Sublime and the Beautiful*. 1970 saw the publication of two outstanding books on broader themes—Brenda Colvin's completely revised *Land and Landscape* and Nan Fairbrother's *New Lives, New Landscapes*.

Gardening journalism was given a new dimension by such writers as Victoria Sackville-West, Edward Hyams and Margery Fish, who broadened their subject far beyond the particular. The number of journals increased, but there were also changes of ownership: the old established *Gardeners' Chronicle*, orientated towards the private gardener, was taken over by the *Horticultural Trade Journal* in 1969 and became the *Gardeners' Chronicle and Horticultural Trade Journal*, largely devoted to horticulture and amenity.

Looming over all other sources of knowledge is television, a medium that brings into millions of homes scenes that would otherwise remain unknown. The most popular have probably been *Gardeners' World*, presented by Percy Thrower and others, and the historical series by Dr. W. G. Hoskins on *Landscapes of England*, drawing attention to a countryside that is almost wholly man-made. Visible only through colour television and magnification, the hitherto unknown insect life that exists within any suburban garden was revealed in *Mr. Beesley's Secret Garden*, a film comparable in kind to the introvert nature of a Japanese garden.

Growing interest in the history of garden design and anxiety for the future of historic gardens and parks led in 1965 to the formation of the Garden History Society, with H. F. Clark as first President, followed in 1971 by Miles Hadfield and in 1977 by Professor W. T. Stearn. The Society produces a scholarly journal, organises historical research, arranges visits not only in England but abroad, and attacks any attempt to tamper with or destroy an acknowledged masterpiece. It played an active part in supporting the Town and Country Amenities Act, 1974, which includes provisions extending the powers of the Secretary of State for the Environment to make grants, through the Historic Buildings Council, for the upkeep of gardens and other land of outstanding historic interest even where no building of historic interest is involved. This is the first direct reference to historic gardens in British legislation and has been followed up by a grant of £16,935 to the Swiss Garden, Old Warden Park, Bedfordshire in 1977.

Public interest in historic gardens has gathered momentum partly because of the increase in the number of gardens now open (which number more than 2,000, modern as well as historic, including arboreta and botanically orientated gardens like the Savill Gardens, Windsor) and partly due to increased mobility in a motorized age. Led by the National Trust, these gardens provide a standard of excellence in design and maintenance that enables the gardening public to appreciate values of which they might otherwise have been unaware—quality in design has little to do with size; the smallest garden can draw inspiration from the greatest. Unlike most other arts, however, a garden depends continuously on the personal love and supervision of its owner, especially when plants are as important as architectural form. However excellently such masterpieces as Sissinghurst or Hidcote are maintained, experience has shown that a collectively owned garden inevitably loses some of the impetus that inspired the original.

Aesthetic design may change, may fail to advance, or even go backwards; technique can only advance. In the present technological age the garden designer must be perpetually on guard against technique becoming the end and not the means. He must use it only to advance creative ideas which could not otherwise have been realized. The advances and variations can be divided into the biological and the mechanical, and in the domestic field are almost entirely directed towards self-help. Containerization, for instance, means that plants in flower can be moved at any time of year and transplanted complete with roots, in a sense analogous to the old system of bedding out for immediate effect. There are growing-bags for very small gardens with little soil, such as roof gardens; foliar feeding, which fertilises the leaves and not the roots; grass seeds that grow slowly and others than can tolerate shade; pelleted seeds that can be set where they are to grow, thus speeding up the growing process and cutting out time-consuming operations; hard surfaces that can be weed-proof. Planting must be easy to maintain: the splendid but labour-intensive herbaceous border, for instance, has given way to mixed shrubs, perennials and ground cover.

The range of plants continually widens. Some attractive new roses have come from breeders in the United States, in Britain (McGredy, Wheatcroft and many others), from Kordes in Germany and Meilland in France. The latter's Hybrid Tea 'Peace' (1947), pale yellow with pink edges, was easily the most widely planted in the immediate post-war years. Colour in roses is subject to fashion changes, as in any other sphere. The 1950's saw several new mauve or purple introductions; two of the best were 'Lavender Lassie' (1958) and 'Magenta' (1954). A new style in roses with parti-coloured petals was set by 'Masquerade' (1949) and 'Cavalcade' (1950)—more useful for mass planting than as individual specimens in a mixed border. Even more difficult to accommodate, from a design point of view, are roses like 'Super Star', (1960), whose brilliant orange-red tones, derived from the pigment pelargonidin, make them uneasy bed-fellows for the blue-based reds and pinks of most other roses. Most floribundas will fit anywhere and with their long flowering period are a boon to park superintendents and private gardeners alike; 'Iceberg' and 'Queen Elizabeth' are among the favourites.

Except for the non-flowering *Stachys lanata* 'Silver Carpet', designed to be used as ground cover, the general tendency with perennials seems to have been towards producing varieties with longer flowering periods (particularly among the smaller species) and sturdier plants that need less staking; some of the new irises, for example, have appreciably shorter stems. Not all changes in habit are for the better, however. Foxglove hybrids with flowers all round the stem are stiffly upright and have lost the graceful swooping curves that characterize the plant in the wild.

Advances in the breeding of annuals include the F1 and F2 (F for filial) hybrids, the result of a process known as heterosis—the crossing of two separate strains of the same species to increase vigour and health, exemplified by the rust-resistant Antirrhinum. Mist propagation (the ensuring of an even climate and constant vaporised moisture under glass), scientific storage of seeds and specialization in the large nurseries have all increased mass production. The nutrient film technique, which recirculates to the roots of rows of plants water that contains all those elements required for plant growth, is still in its infancy but may ultimately revolutionize nursery techniques in some departments. With labour in short supply, such mechanical aids are essential if the demand for plants is to be met; the use of ground cover plants to suppress weeds must, by itself, have placed the industry under strain.

Unfortunately, in the pursuit of novelty some old favourites have disappeared from the catalogues of the larger nurseries and must be sought in small nurseries and private gardens. This is causing concern among horticulturalists and plans are afoot for tracking down and registering the whereabouts of little known varieties of plants and vegetables. With a similar end in view, the

International Dendrological Society is compiling a tree survey.

Garden equipment has developed even more dramatically. The mechanically powered tool has displaced the hand tool in nearly every field. Automatic irrigation, once confined to elaborate gardens in hot countries, is now economically possible in this country. The ubiquitous electric pump can circulate water for a fountain in the smallest garden, whose basin may be delicately made of fibreglass or kept watertight by polythene or PVC. Garden centres for the sale of both equipment and plants have mushroomed, inevitably influencing public taste and demand, if only by directing them away from herbaceous perennials, which cannot be so successfully containerized as shrubs. As with all mass-produced goods, the personally owned nursery is regrettably beginning to give way to the larger impersonal company.

The word 'ecology' was scarcely known before the war. Now it is recognized as a science by which the human race exists as a part only of a sequence of nature. Disturb a sequence that has taken millions of years to evolve and a chain reaction takes place that is endless. Since the War, both fertilization and pest control have been vigorously developed in laboratories, but success or failure is only determined after trial and error, and there may be unexpected and unwelcome side effects which are not immediately apparent. The most striking instance was DDT (dichloro-diphenyl-trichloro-ethane), an insecticide which at first promised to be a boon to gardeners and farmers, but was withdrawn from general use in Britain in 1968 because of its potential cumulative effect on the environment. On fertilizers, too, there are divided opinions; valuable work is being done by the Henry Doubleday Research Association, an international body of gardeners and farmers without chemicals, founded in 1954 by Lawrence D. Hills, its Director-Secretary.

Ecology and maintenance are closely allied, for a balanced ecology means that nature requires less grooming. This is creating a trend in garden design itself. Form and tone are beginning to take precedence over colour, especially among professional designers and flower arrangers who, under the inspiration of Constance Spry, are particularly interested in foliage, most of all when variegated. The landscape architect Brenda Colvin illustrates this trend in describing her own garden at Filkins in Gloucestershire:

The planting is intended to give continuous calm enjoyment at all seasons, rather than to dazzle the eye in the height of summer. The ground is well covered with low plants chosen for beauty of foliage; many are evergreen and there are masses of spring bulbs. In and over the ground cover plants are many flowering shrubs, roses, viburnums, hydrangeas, tree peonies, etc., to provide flower all through the year.

I have tried to get a feeling of quiet space in this small area, enclosed as it is by grey stone walls and farm buildings. I try, too, to engender a sense of anticipation and interest by the progression from one interesting plant group to the next in a rhythm, giving definite contrasts without loss of unity. But it is difficult to reconcile simplicity with one's enthusiasm for plants in so small a garden, and I probably let the plants jostle one another too much.

Another development in the pursuit of form rather than colour is the use of grass as a design material in its own right. The patterned lawn, using grasses of different tones and textures, was initiated by the Brazilian designer Burle Marx as a chessboard and was later carried a stage further in Denmark, on more fluid lines. The method is to conceal a thin hardwood or non-corroding metal strip about six inches deep immediately below the surface, which separates the grasses without impeding the mower. In England the contrasts are more often between close-mown and long grass; thanks to powered motors with variable cuts, a curving path may easily be delineated in a flowered meadow of the same species.

Apart from these internal influences, English garden philosophy is not quite so insular as in the previous two and a half centuries, and is at least aware of movements in design which are taking place in other countries that have not the same inhibiting traditions. The foremost designer in the world aesthetically is generally considered by professionals to be Dr. Roberto Burle Marx of Brazil, whose work was exhibited at the Institute of Contemporary Arts in London in 1955. Burle Marx began as painter and horticulturalist, and sees gardens through the eyes of a modern painter, much as they were seen by earlier designers through the work of Claude and Poussin. Influenced by William Robinson, he works with local plants from the Brazilian forests but uses them as texture, much as a painter uses pigment. The gardens have a sense of movement, with sweeping curves that seem to emphasize their ephemeral life when seen against the mountains among which they are usually set.

Very different, and more directly influential on the English garden, has been the work of Thomas Church of California, one of many U.S. experimentalists. Church is best known for his creation of perhaps the first biologically shaped swimming pool at Sonoma, California, a shape that has since been blindly copied throughout Europe without appreciation of its relation to the terrain. In the small formal garden Church was a pioneer in abstract angularity and the aesthetic use of both hard and soft materials. C. Th. Sørensen of Denmark and Willi Neukom of Switzerland are only two among a number of European garden architects whose work has stimulated professional designers to an awareness of ecology as a scientific basis for aesthetics.

For purposes of analysis, gardens in Britain fall into four groups: the town garden, the suburban or country garden, the very exceptional and often very large garden and the new garden inserted into an historic setting.

THE SMALL TOWN GARDEN

The small town garden in idea dates back to ancient China, has similar rules and has remained virtually constant throughout the ages. The Chinese laid down that the garden must have privacy and be such that its owner could commune with nature and converse with his friends. Here for a short time man can escape and return to the rhythms of nature for which his perceptive faculties were originally fashioned. Such a garden is fundamental to a modern democratic society; it occupies so little space that it has been calculated that the entire population of the British Isles could be housed in this way within a circle with a radius of thirty-five miles from Charing Cross.

There are already tens of thousands of such gardens in London alone and it is possible to detect within them the two trends in design that run through English garden history: the classical and the romantic. The classical accepts the garden as an extension of the interior of the house. Such a garden is basically geometrical, sometimes with nature clipped, but more often in the present age allowed to grow free. Within such an area, which might be no more than a sunny brick-walled back yard of less than fifteen hundred square feet, can be places of varied use—a paved terrace for sitting out and meals out of doors, play space for children, pots and formal beds for flowers and shrubs, divided by trellis covered in the climbing roses that do so well in London.

The formal or classical garden is concerned with the finite: that is to say that the limiting boundaries are apparent, as they are in the house. The informal or romantic garden is concerned with the infinite, where the boundaries are subdued or eliminated and the imagination is encouraged to roam at will beyond the confines of the site. This is an especially English concept and not only inspired Bridgeman and Kent to 'leap the fence and see that all nature was a garden', but led such later writers as Uvedale Price to establish Picturesque principles for parks and gardens which may equally apply to the small gardens of the present day. Philosophically, the romantic garden is not so much an extension of the house as an incursion of nature into the site. This is the ancient Chinese concept of a town garden and is symbolic, not a copy, of nature. Today the design is an art form that symbolizes what the western mind conceives to be the most beautiful in nature, varying in its contents from one individual to another.

The Picturesque of the eighteenth century was so called because the art belonged to an élite and (it was said at the time) could only be appreciated by those who had studied paintings such as those of Claude. Their analysis was that the eye enjoyed stimulus and irritation, not the unrelenting straight line. But it was left to a post-Darwin nineteenth-century writer, Grant Allen, in *Physiological Aesthetics* (1877) to record the scientific view that all our sense perceptions are based on those of man the forest dweller, and that our organs were virtually complete before we left the forest to become hunters on the savannah. The owner of a small garden in a dense urban area has in fact only to lie on his back on a summer's day, and look upwards through foliage to the sky, to realise that he is able to reach back to his origins.

The geometrical garden may need the advice of a professional, but the romantic may not. Preferably it is the intuitive design of the owner, briefed by other gardens, books and journals, to supply the technique. Reflecting as they should an individual ethos and taste, no two gardens will ever be alike. The basic design can be simple, nature supplying the intricacies and mystery. If the sides cannot be concealed by planting (and there is nothing more effective than a brick wall used as a base), the end certainly can, giving the impression of infinite length from the windows of the house, even though the rear silhouette of buildings opposite may trouble the illusion. Before 1939, local authority housing consisted mainly in semi-detached dwellings with broad frontages and short gardens, leaving gaps between buildings which created draughts harmful to people and plants and left space for a garden that was bounded by post and rail fencing without privacy from neighbours or protection from wind. Today, partly thanks to the continuous efforts of the Town & Country Planning Association (a descendant of the garden city movement) the garden is recognized as essential to the good life, whether passive or active. However it is used, its universal therapeutic value is incalculable, and its privacy is not unneighbourly, for the adjoining shrubs and trees become part of the scene. Indeed, it is the careful blending of private gardens and free-flowing communal landscape that constitutes one of the chief attractions of the Span housing estates designed by Eric Lyons and Ivor Cunningham in various London suburbs. Their landscape approach has set new standards for housing everywhere.

Quite apart from the fact that the small owner-designed garden is generally more varied and original, there is little economic inducement to a professional designer to make such gardens part of his practice; exhibitions gallantly encouraged by the Royal Horticultural Society in the design tent at Chelsea Flower Shows have proved this to be so. The outstanding geometrical designer is John Brookes, author, among other works, of *Room Outside* (1969) and *The Small Garden* (1977), and one of the small band of designers who are interested in the domestic garden as a modern art form. The plan of a garden in Chelsea (fig. 11) is typical of his mathematical division of space based on a unit of size. Unity with the interior of the house is a primary consideration, the paving of the terrace being carried a few feet into the living room. A secondary paved area round an existing horse chestnut is linked to the main terrace by a wide paved path. A cloistered effect connecting the two terraces is given by horizontal beams on metal supports of the same dimensions as the living room window frame. A small pool with fountains runs across the end of the terrace, the line of

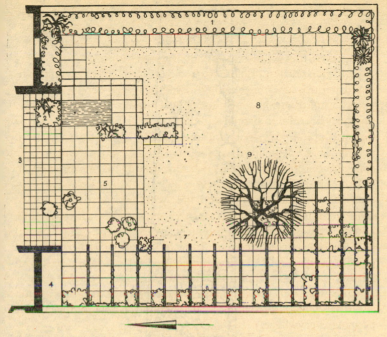

FIG. 11.

Key to plan
1. Shrubs
2. Indoor plants
3. Sitting room
4. Garden store
5. Raised terrace
6. Pots
7. Pergola
8. White gravel
9. Chestnut

which is carried on inside by a thick container for house plants. The central space is covered with white gravel chippings which draw light down into the garden and reflect artificial light from the house at night. The only complex planting is against the one sunny wall. (See photograph opposite p. 321.)

Although the garden in Wimbledon by Timothy Cochrane shown in fig. 12 is above average size for a town garden, it illustrates in principle the power of illusion to bring the country to town. The view from the house is paramount, since it is there all the year round whereas in our climate the garden itself is only

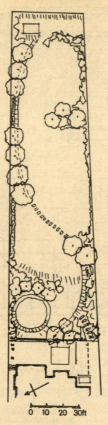

0   10   20   30ft

FIG. 12.

used for comparatively short periods. From indoors, it is much as a picture on the wall, and like a landscape painting it is designed with foreground, middle and far distance. The boundaries have been ingeniously concealed and spaces created by tree planting like receding scenery in a theatre. The far distance, seen through intricacies which confuse the eye but stimulate the imagination to wander further afield, might be infinite; the scene, unlike a painting, is in constant movement of colour and form, never quite repeating and almost imperceptible.

442

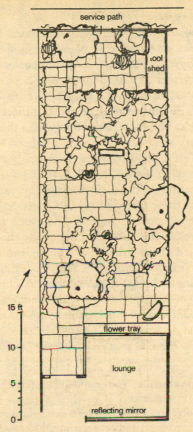

service path

tool
shed

15 ft

flower tray

10

lounge

5

reflecting mirror

0

FIG. 13.

The small paved garden in Islington seen in fig. 13 is an ingenious amalgamation of the two ideas, where the house has been projected into woodland scenery of unknown extent. The space is eighteen feet by forty-three, or about eight hundred square feet, and the plan allows not only for a picture to be seen from within, but for variety of views in sitting out: each of the two seats presents an original viewpoint. To increase the impression of space, the garden seems to flow into the living room, to be reflected in a mirror on the opposite wall.

THE COUNTRY GARDEN

The average new country garden is conditioned as to size and complexity almost solely by cost of maintenance. Many such gardens are run by a part-time gardener or pensioner, the owners usually taking a practical part themselves. There is probably no one more conservative than the English garden lover when it comes to design; in general designs are traditional, adapted to modern conditions. The middle-income garden that began in the nineteenth century with Loudon's villa gardens, simulating the aristocratic park on a small scale, evolved slowly into the widely differing gardens of Robinson, Jekyll, Lutyens and Blomfield at the turn of the century. Although present-day gardeners in the main look back to these historic figures, Gertrude Jekyll is probably the only one to remain significant. Through sheer necessity as well as an increase in plants, planting as the chief content of a garden is still based on her principles. Among leading professionals, Russell Page (mainly working in France, and the recipient in 1978 of the National Medal of Landscape Architecture of the French Academy of Architecture—a rare honour for a foreigner) has developed Jekyll's ideas to bring them into the modern world. With a splendid style personal to himself, he sees gardens with a new vision. In his *The Education of a Gardener* (1962) he writes of composition:

Tensions of a certain kind play a large and unsuspected part in composition. As with the interrelations of patches of colour in painting, so between the solid objects in a garden certain tensions or vibrations are established around an object and between one object and another across the intervening air. This is not, I think, true of sculpture, which often represents an object where the tensions are contained, but between the branches, the twigs and the foliage of a tree the air in which they all exist seems to respond and become impregnated by a subtle interplay of forces.

and of execution:

I try first to look at my planting as an exercise in monochrome—to see form only and, for the moment, let the colour ride. For any given situation I endeavour to decide where I need dark, where light, where flower and foliage should glitter and where they should be matt and quiet in tone.

Almost always I find that it is quite impossible to think out even this first, colourless stage with only the usual run of herbaceous plants in mind. I will have to use foliage as part of my picture. So I add a new range to my plant repertoire: plants whose flowering is secondary to their form and texture. Funkias, now called hostas, come at once to my mind, and bergenias, eulalias and ferns—these and many others for their lustre and distinction of form. In another category are all the grey-leaved plants: artemisias, stachys, pinks, catmints, rue, certain salvias, *Elymus arenarius* and *Festuca glauca*.

Lanning Roper, an American who has practised in this country for many years and who has been honoured by an American Garden Club award, recognises two approaches to planting and that 'there is room for both'. As early as 1957 he wrote, in *Successful Town Gardening*, of the first approach:

Plants are selected because of the wealth of colour they will provide and a succession is worked out so that the beds and borders are always gay. Plants with handsome foliage are not included as a foil. No space is wasted, as the exponent of colour gardening would say, on different textures and forms of leaves or on any plant not sufficiently floriferous. We have all seen the results, been cheered by their gaiety and astounded at the skill with which so many flowers have been produced simultaneously, a little like the dazzling gardens at Chelsea.

But he emphasizes the difficulties of maintaining this colour in the country garden, suggesting frames for growing on plants such as 'wallflowers, Canterbury bells, foxgloves, Michaelmas daisies and chrysanthemums, which thus can be held in reserve until needed'. Of the second approach to planting, which he describes as restful and more architectural, he writes:

The garden is planted so that there are always pleasing foliage contrasts in texture and colour, but with emphasis on the form. Plants like bergenia, epimedium, iris, artemisia, sage, hosta, myrtle, sedum, lavender and rosemary are included as much for their foliage as for their flowers. Walls are carefully covered with well-grown shrubs and climbers like figs and vines, again very often selected for their fine leaves. Into this framework goes a carefully made selection of flowering plants. A few clumps of tulips can be as effective as a hundred making a solid bed.

THE INDIVIDUALIST'S GARDEN

Although Britain is no longer supreme in design, there are always a few gifted laymen who will stake out a claim for individuality, if not eccentricity. These are pioneers in the exploration of landscape ideas, who are not afraid to put their ideas into practice and to a limited extent still have the means to do so. In the nineteenth century a layman, Edward Hussey, quarrying for stone between the old castle at Scotney and the new one, fashioned a Picturesque scene that is unique and original to himself. In mid-century, James Bateman created at Biddulph Grange the first comprehensive design of a garden that can truly be described as eclectic (p. 353). History will be grateful that similar experimentalists exist at the present unfruitful time. Among the many who have stood firm against collectivism are Sir Gordon Russell, first Director of the Council of Design, at Kingcombe in the Cotswolds; Sir Frederick Gibberd at The House, Marsh Lane, within the orbit of Harlow New Town, which he designed; and Mr Michael and Lady Anne Tree at Shute House near Shaftesbury, who inherited the Chatsworth tradition of fundamental eclectic research and experiment.

Kingcombe, on the slopes of a hill overlooking Chipping Campden, was begun in 1922 and before the Second World War developed as a charming orthodox stone house with garden terraces extending along the contours. Later the mood changed; the house doubled in size and a curved canal with a fantastic retaining wall decorated with the bottoms of wine bottles set in concrete, was added below the terrace. The yew-enclosed herbaceous garden was transformed into a long open air gallery of informal flower furnishings with many places for sitting. A circular stone tower was built at the house end of the canal 'for the grandchildren'. At a lower level, a long embanked grass terrace united the composition as a whole. The carvings and much of the stonework have been done by the owner, as has the planting. This astonishing garden in some respects recalls the eccentricity and beauty of Antoni Gaudi's work at Barcelona, fitting harmoniously into a Cotswold landscape that also embraces Hidcote.

In contrast to this stone garden, The House, Marsh Lane, is on low-lying clay leading down to a woodland bog garden and stream. The house was acquired in 1956 for the potential of the site rather than its bungalow charm. The present romantic garden has been created over the years by an owner who was awarded the rare Gold Medal of the Royal Town Planning Institute in 1978. It is therefore all the more gratifying that the garden should be highly individual and irrational, at first appearing to be a sequence of scenes and surprises set among foliage, rather than a comprehensive, rational whole. The scenes are enriched with modern sculpture, each piece giving meaning to its environment. Being chiefly abstract, the sculpture is dateless, and as if to emphasize this timelessness of modern art, two Corinthian columns from Coutts' Bank in the Strand have been re-erected in a glade. Nothing is easier than for a 'folly' to become a 'silly'; it is to the credit of the owner-designer that he has so convincingly re-assembled and composed these classical objects and their attendant vases, moulding them into a modern landscape composition which without them might seem incomplete.

The site at Shute House is remarkable for the constant flow of spring water from its highest point. On a nineteenth-century landscape of lakes, rhododendrons and forest trees a garden has been devised which, in its sequence of events, is eclectic in to-day's sense rather than that of Biddulph Grange. The composition that unifies the whole is intricate and not easily apprehended. The essence of the garden is water: its sound and sight permeate everywhere. A long rill has been designed with the first four water chutes so adjusted in detail that together (in theory at least) they form a harmonious chord of treble, alto, tenor and bass. Elsewhere are cascades falling over stones personally selected from adjoining quarries; a long canal that terminates in twin grottoes, each of which is the headwater of a river; a hexagonal ivy-clad temple of modern non-corroding metal; a water garden based on three symbolic stones; a green bedroom with four-poster bed, dressing table and armchair executed in box; three baroque statues brought from the owners' previous home, Mereworth Castle; and over all a luxury of planting only possible on such a watered south-facing and protected site.

THE CONSERVATION GARDEN

With Britain's rich and varied inheritance, it is not surprising that much new gardening is an extension of, or insertion into, what already exists. This may involve historic gardens first created at any time during the past five hundred years, at their most vulnerable when taken over by a new owner with a layman's well-meaning dual desire to preserve and bring up to date. At present there are few professionals who are qualified either to reconstruct old gardens as art historians or to create new designs that would fit into an old setting. The issues are more complex than in a new design for a new site, for there exists an ethos of place which, in its extra dimension of time, is a formidable challenge to the personal views of the new owner and his consultant, if he has one. There are examples throughout the country where sheer love of gardening has destroyed historic ethos, but there are others where twentieth-century thought and inclinations have added to what already exists. Three examples, taken from different periods, are: St. Paul's Walden Bury, Hertfordshire; Sheringham Hall, Norfolk; Horsted Place, Sussex.

St. Paul's Walden Bury is probably the best surviving example in England of formal garden planning under the influence of Le Nôtre. Avenues radiating from the house and bisecting the woods are strictly geometrical. The *charmilles* in their entirety and some of the features in the woodland interstices were restored before the war by Sir David Bowes-Lyon, President of the Royal Horticultural Society 1953–61, who later began to introduce romantic rhododendron and azalea planting in the woods. Inspired by animal tracks from clearings in the Himalayan forests, his son Simon has further developed the woodlands with sensitivity and restraint. There is no conflict between the two schools of thought of classicism and romanticism, for nowhere do the two impinge upon one another. Elsewhere, where the original structure of the avenues had been broken in the nineteenth century, restoration is in progress. At the same time, Victorian romanticism is being retained by weaving it visually into the geometry.

Sheringham Hall on the Norfolk coast is one of the few great landscapes of the English Landscape School to survive almost complete. Laid out by Humphry Repton for Abbot Upcher, its site is unusual in that it has a north aspect, towards the sea. In his description, which is included in Loudon's publication of 1840, Repton wrote: 'It may be a bold assertion, to pronounce that Sherringham possesses more natural beauty and local advantage, than any place I have ever seen.' The Upchers have always conserved these beauties and when the present owner, Thomas Upcher, developed the gardens over the past forty years, he not only designed the planting with skill and understanding but (historically more important) placed his new gardens between the Repton-designed house and the fine walled kitchen garden which at that time was traditionally placed out of sight. The resulting composition, partly of specimen trees and shrubs in groups lying along the contours and partly within existing woodlands, seems to enhance rather than conflict with the original Repton park.

Horsted Place, near Uckfield, Sussex, was built in the mid-nineteenth century, a fine example of Victorian romanticism which (like the Houses of Parliament) was based on a classically symmetrical plan, countered by a tower and astonishing silhouette of chimneys. When the property was acquired by the present owners some ten years ago, there was little garden. Under the inspiration of Lady Rupert Nevill, who herself was responsible for the planting, the new garden that materialized so compounded two dates and styles of design that the resulting mixture seems Victorian. Rose-filled baskets based on those designed by Repton for Brighton Pavilion seem to be floating irresponsibly on green rivers of grass, to disappear among woodlands. The feeling of the garden is that a stately Regency movement has mingled with the accelerated modern movement of Burle Marx.

THE COLLECTIVE LANDSCAPE

Unlike the domestic garden with its long history and processes of evolution, the modern collective landscape has a short past, the first publicly owned park having been laid out at about the time of Queen Victoria's accession to the throne. The first vision of a collective landscape greater than the public park came with the garden city movement initiated by Ebenezer Howard at the turn of the century, and by the endeavours of a few socially minded industrialists. By 1939 these movements were still in embryo, but two of the garden cities had been built, giving encouragement to the much more comprehensive and majestic concept that good landscape was in the national interest. Led by Government and backed by industry, who quickly also recognized that good landscape was good business, the country immediately after the war embarked on an ambitious programme of renovating old landscapes and creating new ones. The Scott Report of 1942 emphasized the need for professional skill in all works concerning the countryside. The first of the post-war new towns, Stevenage, inaugurated a sequence of town planning/landscape architecture projects that was unique in the world—one where the early concept (rising out of the philosophy of the garden city movement) was not of a park within a town, but of a town within a park. The towns were enriched by planting ranging from the popular but tough rugosa roses to forest trees that could, since the Clean Air Act of 1968, survive in the now unpolluted atmosphere of most towns. In the latest new town, Milton Keynes, the park and open space system makes provision for all kinds of open air activities such as fishing and also for wild life habitats.

Parallel with these creative ideas was concern for the hideous industrial scars of the past. The West Midland Planning Group, financed by Cadbury Brothers, initiated in 1948 a plan to turn the Black Country into green, an objective that has largely been reached.

At this time the need for professional skill in landscape became of first importance. The few practising landscape architects with long domestic experience, such as Brenda Colvin and Geoffrey Jellicoe, had to adapt themselves overnight to the collective landscape. Sylvia Crowe (later to be created Dame) emerged without such experience but with a natural gift for the collective ecological landscape. Apart from the urban parks, which were the acknowledged province of the park superintendent, the most important pioneer landscapes were probably those of the Roads Beautifying Association. Like other bodies founded by far-sighted laymen, it was later professionalised, but it illustrates how much post-war design owed to the fertile soil of domestic experience.

Encouraged by Government, the Institute of Landscape Architects (incorporated in the Landscape Institute in 1978) expanded from what had virtually been a small garden designers' society to one that now has many hundreds of qualified or student members; nearly all are employed on collective landscapes, either public, semi-public or commercial. The first lectureships in landscape design, initiated by the chemical and cement industries, were founded in 1948 at London and Durham Universities respectively, with Peter Youngman and Brian Hackett (later made professors) as the first lecturers. In 1948 the first post-war international conference of landscape architects was held in London under the auspices of the Institute, followed immediately, at Jesus College, Cambridge, by the founding of the now flourishing International Federation of Landscape Architects. The technically well-equipped British landscape architect of today is now employed widely in the emerging countries throughout the world.

Proportionately to the costs involved, the part played by gardening itself in the collective landscape is comparatively small. As an art, it is still young, with a potentially great future. Unlike planting for privately owned estates, where the future is unknown and the efforts of one generation may not necessarily benefit the next, the public landscape is transmitted to posterity greatly enhanced. Thus the community profits by its long term investment, while the private individual may not.

In response to demand, landscape techniques have multiplied. Massive machinery can manipulate the land to change the scenery in one day where hard manual labour would have taken weeks. There is gigantic mechanical equipment for all purposes, from forestry planting to hydro-seeding along the embankments of motorways. Mature or semi-mature trees can be moved on the instant, the roots being pinned and the stays made invisible. In the hands of technicians and planners this power can be, in the same measure, magically creative or destructive. As already described, however, a more hazardous advance is being made in biological technology, whose effects cannot always be seen immediately.

The first objective of a national landscape policy in an over-industrialized country such as Britain is to make it seemly; the second, following closely, is to make it beautiful. Seemliness entails restoring waste areas and organizing landscapes from new wastes; screening the unpleasant with trees and shrubs and preventing new unscreenable eyesores; properly planning for quarries and mines and domesticating the environment of factories; fitting new roads *into* a landscape rather than *on* it; and generally combating what is unsound and an affront to human dignity. In short, to create some degree of order out of landscape chaos.

The second objective, to make the countryside beautiful, has opened up an inspiring new range of gardening design that extends from such a grand concept as the Lea Valley Country Park to a totally artificial landscape over an underground garage in a city square; or, more spectacularly, to a sky garden on a

451

commercial roof. The vast increase in relatively small, mostly suburban roads has introduced a whole new series of problems fundamental to garden design. What is the philosophy motivating this apparently new art? Has it any relation to the past other than its immediate gardening associations?

The present separation of ideas between domestic and collective seems to be repeating the old conflict between Uvedale Price and Capability Brown, which in turn clearly grew from the conflict arising from the dual personality of the original *Homo erectus*—first arborealist and later hunter. Eighteenth-century Picturesque with the intricacy and ethos of diversity of forest scenery is the root of the domestic garden. A Brown park, on the other hand, based on the open savannah and sense of infinity, is majestic and universal in its sequence of land forms. It is ordered and architectural in its feeling of form. It is without literary or romantic content, and being apprehended only through the eye is not tactile. It is at the same time professional and somewhat inhuman—a foil to a Palladian mansion with its universal mathematical proportions. Equally, it is a foil to a modern building in the international style, as was shown by Walter Gropius in a theoretic design for a block of luxury flats to replace the palace at Blenheim but not the park. In its noble sweeps, its groups of trees and water leading to infinity, therefore, it appears to be the ideal corollary of mass-produced building, the site providing variations where the architecture cannot. But the awesome repetitive scale of the modern structures of recent years is no longer a social or prestigious objective: 'small is beautiful' has, we hope, come to stay. Tall communal flats are now regarded as anti-social. Already the gigantic hospitals that are the consequence of the functional age are being designed with landscapes on a human scale, where patients can be in contact with plants; therapy unconsciously practised by every gardener is thus practised professionally. The plant helps the patient to restore his confidence and therefore his zest for life. Perhaps more than any other the hospital landscape pin-points the present-day conflict between bigness and smallness, mass production and personal sensitivity.

LANDSCAPE PLANNING
The problem quite simply is one of relationship and proper plan-

ning. The potential scope and range of collective gardening can be polarized between a small public park—for example the Water Gardens at Hemel Hempstead New Town, and a motorway planted under the distinguished supervision of the Advisory Committee on the Landscape of Trunk Roads of the Department of the Environment.

The Hemel Hempstead Water Gardens were laid out in 1955 in a narrow strip of the Gade valley, between the town centre (begun 1948) and a major road, with massive off-street car parking. The river was canalised into a formal but romantic shape, with a lake, cascades, gardens and access bridges. Existing trees were retained and islanded where necessary. The town side is open, with a wide grass verge; the further side is densely planted to a few yards' width. A lovers' walk meanders through this woodland scene. Between the path and the canal are water-loving plants like *Salix elaeagnos*, *Stephanandra incisa*, *Rheum palmatum* and astilbes. On the dry side of the path, mounded earth from the canal excavations is densely planted with evergreen shrubs and ground cover, with occasional flashes of colour. The path is only about ten feet from the car park, but the illusion of a peaceful woodland walk is complete.

In contrast to the static Water Gardens, a motorway is a phenomenon that has no precedent in gardening history. The speed of a car being more than four times that of a horse and carriage, the standard proportions of spatial landscape cannot apply. When a road fits a contour, the curves are as agreeable as in a Brown park and there is the same sense of infinity, inhumanity and lack of tactile values; beyond that, there is little resemblance, for a new time dimension is involved. The technical requirements of motorway planting are exacting: trees must be small-leaved and disposed for uninterrupted vision on curves; the problem of salting has not yet been solved; planting for anti-dazzle on the central strip takes too long to mature; and light flicker mars many of the charming pre-war roads planted by W. J. Bean. Techniques are new and subject to trial and error. Nevertheless, it may well prove that the motor landscape will be the greatest contribution of the present century to the history of gardening.

At present, collective landscape design, dominated by increasingly proficient professionalism, is controlled by what the eye sees. Visual landscape evaluation is a professional's way of legalizing aesthetics, the invisible being unacceptable in law and generally incomprehensible to a committee. Yet history shows that romantic garden art is one in which the imagination plays a large part: each individual mind, *if properly stimulated*, can create its own exciting world. Similarly, the modern collective mind has common memories in the subconscious to which it could respond. The design that is shared between the designer and the onlooker or recipient is many times richer than one confined to the former alone. This concept of a shared landscape was first recognized by that true classicist, Sir Joshua Reynolds, when he eulogized the founder-painter of the picturesque, Thomas Gainsborough, in his Fourteenth Discourse. He somewhat reluctantly concedes that Gainsborough's incompleteness or inexactitude of drawing allows the imagination of the observer to 'supply the rest . . . more satisfactorily to himself than the artist . . . could possibly have done.'

The same is true of gardens.

BIBLIOGRAPHICAL NOTES

The first comprehensive British history of gardening was that published by G. W. Johnson in 1829, *A History of English Gardening : Chronological, biographical, literary and critical*. It remains an important source. In the absence of further, more exhaustive, research, much that it includes must be accepted.

In 1822 J. C. Loudon's *Encyclopaedia of Gardening* contained much historical matter; its greatest value, however, lies in the information that it gives of more or less contemporary history known first-hand to Loudon. I have made use of the editions of 1827 and also that published in 1878, edited by Mrs. Loudon, which is virtually identical with the 1850 edition.

Of great importance is the miscellaneous historical information, and the bibliographical references, embedded in the four text volumes of J. C. Loudon's *Arboretum et Fruticetum Britannicum* (1838), mostly unindexed.

In 1896 came the Hon. Alicia Amherst's *A History of Gardening in England*. This is particularly valuable for the author's researches into medieval gardening, and because she had access to the Hatfield House archives. Later editions were issued. (On her marriage she became the Hon. Mrs. Evelyn Cecil, later Lady Rockley.) Her study forms the starting point for any subsequent attempts at garden history, and I am greatly indebted to it.

In 1925 H. Avray Tipping published his lavishly illustrated *English Gardens* with a useful historical introduction.

Mention should also be made of John Steegman's *The Artist and the Country House* with notes by Miss Dorothy Stroud.

For Scotland, we have Elizabeth S. Haldane's *Scots Gardens in Olden Times 1200–1800* of 1934 and E. H. M. Cox's important and well-documented *History of Gardening in Scotland* published in 1935. To this last also I owe much.

There is one important anthology of garden literature, A. Forbes Sieveking's *The Praise of Gardens* (1899). To this, with its scholarly notes and historical epilogue, I am under great obligation.

For biographical matter there is, of course, the so-often unacknowledged *Dictionary of National Biography*—used with caution. Frequent use has been made of *A Biographical Index of Deceased British and Irish Botanists* by J. Britten and G. S. Boulger, of *Curtis's Magazine Dedications 1827–1927* by E. Nelmes and W. Cuthbertson, and *A Biographical Dictionary of English Architects 1660–1840* by H. M. Colvin. These are, of course, readily accessible standard works. For the reader's sake, I have not overloaded the text with repeated acknowledgements of the invaluable help that I have obtained from them.

For the architectural background I have had Sir John Summerson's *Architecture in Britain 1530 to 1830* constantly at hand. I have also regularly relied on Miss Alice Coats's *Flowers and Their Histories* and Wilfrid Blunt's *The Art of Botanical Illustration*.

The bibliographical references in Chapters Seven and Eight have provided me with a problem: if every acknowledgement of the almost innumerable minor references to contemporary horticultural journals had been cited the resultant list would be unwieldy. For that reason I have given as many dates as possible, and the reader who is not helped by my bibliography need do no more than search the periodical literature for that year.

REFERENCES

Below are given, keyed to index numbers shown in the text, the principal sources to which reference is made.

They are arranged chapter by chapter.

Sources already adequately described in the text are excluded, as are the names of books mentioned only in passing. (Both these will be found in the index.)

At the end of each section are listed some publications relevant to it, but not otherwise referred to.

Chapter One: to 1529

1   J. SYLVESTER.   *The Divine Weeks of Du Bartas.*
2   A. C. SEWARD.   *Fossil Plants*,   vols. i and iv.
    J. R. MATTHEWS.   *Origin and Distribution of the British Flora.*
    H. GODWIN.   *History of the British Flora.*
3   F. BACON.   *Of Gardens.*
4   J. JAMES.   *Theory and Practice of Gardening.*
5   H. WALPOLE.   *Letters* (edited Mrs. Toynbee).

6   W. VON ARCHENHOLZ.   *A Picture of England.*

7   S. PEPYS.   *Diary,* 1666.

8   E. W. GILBERT in *Historical Geography of England Before 1800.*
     (C. H. Darby, editor.)

9   E. A. BUNYARD.   *The Epicure's Companion.*

10   M. GABRIEL.   *Livia's Garden Room.*

11   C. S. PLINY.   *Letters* (edited W. M. L. Hutchinson).

12   J. EVELYN.   *Sylva.*

13   L. J. M. COLUMELLA.   *On Trees.*

14   P. H. BLAIR.   *Introduction to Anglo-Saxon England.*

15   D. KNOWLES.   *The Religious Orders in England.*

16   C. O. MORETON.   *Old Carnations and Pinks.*

17   A. ARBER.   *Herbals, Their Origin and Evolution.*

18   C. E. RAVEN.   *English Naturalists from Neckham to Ray.*

19   REV. R. WILLIS.   *Archaeologia Cantiana,* vii.

20   GERVASE.   *Translations of the Church Historians of England,* v.

21   R. L. PALMER.   *English Monasteries in the Middle Ages.*

22   C. O. MORETON.   *Old Carnations and Pinks.*

23   L. F. SALZMAN.   *Building in England Down to 1540.*

24   *Royal Commission, Historical Manuscripts,* i. (1870).

25   E. H. M. COX.   *History of Gardening in Scotland.*

26   F. WORMALD.   *English Drawings of the 10th and 11th Century.*

27   D. SUTCLIFFE.   *Archaeologia Cantiana,* xlvi.

28   J. W. HUNKIN.   *Journal, Royal Horticultural Society,* lxxii.
     E. A. BOWLES.   *A Handbook of Narcissus.*

29   N. S. B. GRAS.   *The Early English Customs System.*

30   C. T. GATTY.   *Mary Davies and the Manor of Ebury.*

31   E. H. M. COX.   *A History of Gardening in Scotland.*

32   L. F. SALZMAN.   *Building in England Down to 1540.*

33   A. AMHERST.   *Archaeologia,* liv.

34   E. A. BOWLES.   *Handbook of Crocus and Colchicum.*

35   W. B. CRUMP, W. A. SLEDGE and G. A. NELSON.   *Naturalist,* 1950.

36   *Paston Letters 1422–1509* (edited J. Gairdner).
     H. S. BENNETT.   *The Pastons and Their England.*

37   W. D. SIMPSON.   *Antiquaries Journal,* xxvi.

38   J. GAGE.   *Archaeologia,* xxv.

39   L. F. SALZMAN.   *Building in England Down to 1540.*

40   A. AMHERST.   *History of Gardening in England.*

41   J. H. HARVEY.   *English Medieval Architects.*

42   H. M. COLVIN.   *A Biographical Dictionary of English Architects.*

43   E. AUERBACH.   *Tudor Artists.*

44   G. CAVENDISH.   *Life of Cardinal Wolsey.*

45 J. SKELTON. *The Garland of Laurel.*
46 J. SKELTON. *Speak Parrot.*
47 E. M. G. ROUTH. *Sir Thomas More and His Friends.*

General
W. E. MATTHEWS. *Mazes and Labyrinths.*

Chapter Two: 1530—1629

1 E. LAW. *The History of Hampton Court Palace.*
  M. SANDS. *The Gardens of Hampton Court.*
2 F. BACON. *Of Gardens.*
3 L. TOULMIN SMITH. *The Itinerary of John Leland.*
4 A. W. CLAPHAM and W. H. GODFREY. *Some Famous Buildings and Their Story.*
  J. SUMMERSON. *Architecture in Britain 1530–1830.*
5 D. MCDOUGALL. *Two Royal Domains of France.*
6 P. HENTZNER. *Travels in England in the Reign of Elizabeth.*
7 C. WILLIAMS. *Thomas Platter's Travels in England.*
8 A. W. CLAPHAM and W. H. GODFREY. *Some Famous Buildings and Their Story.*
9 C. E. RAVEN. *English Naturalists From Neckham to Ray.*
10 B. WINCHESTER. *Tudor Family Portrait.*
11 B. HENREY. *Journal of Society for Bibliography of Natural History,* ii.
12 E. SPENSER. *A Ditty.*
13 A. ARBER. *Herbals, Their Origin and Evolution.*
14 H. N. ELLACOMBE. *The Plant Lore and Garden Craft of Shakespeare.*
15 B. GRIFFIN. *Fidessa.* sonnet xxxvii.
16 E. AUERBACH. *Tudor Artists.*
17 R. FREEMAN. *English Emblem Books.*
18 W. HARRISON. *Description of England.*
19 P. HENTZNER. *Travels in England in the Reign of Elizabeth.*
20 W. CAMDEN. *Brittania.*
21 J. A. GOTCH. *The Old Halls and Manor Houses of Northamptonshire.*
22 J. EVELYN. *Diary* (edited E. S. de Beer).
23 J. A. GOTCH. *The Buildings of Sir Thomas Tresham.*
24 J. AUBREY. *Natural History . . . of Surrey.*
25 REV. O. MANNING and W. BRAY. *History . . . of Surrey.*
26 A. AMHERST. *History of Gardening in England.*
27 J. EVELYN. *Diary* (edited E. S. de Beer).

BIBLIOGRAPHICAL NOTES

28   SIR HUGH PLATT. *The Garden of Eden.*

29   REV. DR. HAMILTON. *Archaeologia,* xii.

30   W. ROBERTS. *The Gardener's Chronicle,* 1924.

31   E. H. M. COX. *History of Gardening in Scotland.*

32   W. BLUNT. *The Art of Botanical Illustration.*

33   J. C. T. UPHOF in *The Contribution of Holland to the Sciences.*

34, 35   C. E. RAVEN. *English Naturalists from Neckham to Ray.*

36   R. N. SALAMAN. *Journal of the Royal Horticultural Society,* lxii.

37   E. A. BUNYARD. *The Gardener's Companion* (edited Miles Hadfield).

38   A. AMHERST. *History of Gardening in England.*

39   L. STONE. *Archaeological Journal,* cxii.

40   A. AMHERST. *History of Gardening in England.*

41   J. CALEY. *Archaeologia,* x.

42   N. E. MCCLURE (editor). *The Letters of John Chamberlain.*

43   SIR H. WOTTON. *Elements of Architecture.*

44   *The Familiar Letters of James Howell* (edited J. Jacobs).

45   I. WALTON. *Lives.*
      L. P. SMITH. *The Life and Letters of Sir Henry Wotton.*

46   SIR H. WOTTON. *Elements of Architecture.*

47   R. W. T. GUNTHER. *Oxford Gardens.*

48   A. W. CLAPHAM and W. GODFREY. *Some Famous Buildings and Their Story.*

49   O. L. DICK. *Aubrey's Brief Lives.*

50   J. AUBREY. *Natural History of Wiltshire.*

51   D. GARDINER. *Journal Royal Horticultural Society,* liii.

52, 53, 54   R. T. GUNTHER. *Early British Botanists and their Gardens.*

55   E. H. M. COX. *History of Gardening in Scotland.*

56   H. M. PATON. *Accounts of the Masters of Works for the Building and Repairing of Royal Palaces and Castles* (Scotland).

General

J. LEES-MILNE. *Tudor Renaissance.*

F. MORYSON. *Itinerary.*

C. J. S. THOMPSON. *The Mystery and Art of the Apothecary.*

Chapter Three: 1630—1659

1   D. GREEN. *Gardener to Queen Anne.*

2   P. SIMPSON and C. F. BELL. *Designs by Inigo Jones,* Walpole Society, xii.
      A. NICOL. *Stuart Masques and the Renaissance Stage.*

3 P. PALME. *Triumph of Peace.*

4 D. GRANT. *Margaret the First.*

5 SIR W. BRERETON. *Travels in Holland . . . England, Scotland and Ireland* (edited E. Hawkins).

6 *A Relation of a Short Survey of the Western Counties,* Camden Miscellany, xii.

7 R. PLOT. *Natural History of Oxfordshire.*

8 J. W. GOUGH. *The Superlative Prodigall.*

9 R. W. T. GUNTHER. *Oxford Gardens.*

10 H. W. KEW and H. E. POWELL. *Thomas Johnson, Botanist and Royalist.*

11 S. H. VINES and G. C. DRUCE. *An Account of the Morisonian Herbarium.*

12 *Maitland Club Publications,* lviii.

13 L. HUTCHINSON. *Memoirs of the Life of Colonel Hutchinson.*

14 M. HOWITT. *Birds and Flowers.*

15 A. MARVELL. *Upon the Hill at Bill-borow.*

16 W. H. DAWSON. *Cromwell's Understudy: The Life and Times of General John Lambert.*

    C. E. L. PHILLIPS. *Cromwell's Captains.*

17 W. BLUNT. *The Art of Botanical Illustration* and *Tulipomania.*

18 F. VERNEY. *Memoirs of the Verney Family.*

19 W. G. HISCOCK. *John Evelyn and His Family Circle.*

20 J. AUBREY. *Natural History of Wiltshire.*

21 G. SCOTT THOMSON. *Life in A Noble Household.*

22 I. ELSTOB (editor). *The Garden Book of Sir Thomas Hanmer.*

23 JOHN LORD HANMER. *Memorials of the Family and Parish of Hanmer.*

24 R. W. T. GUNTHER. *The Gardener's Chronicle, 1921.*

25 R. W. T. GUNTHER. *British Botanists and Their Gardens.*

26 SIR W. TEMPLE. *Upon the Gardens of Epicurus.*

    SIR L. WEAVER. *Country Life,* xxxi.

General

F. CARRIT. *Calendar of British Taste, 1600–1800.*

W. VAN DIJK. "Some Plant Introductions in the Seventeenth Century", *Journal Royal Horticultural Society,* lxxi.

J. EVELYN. *Directions for the Gardener at Sayes Court.*

LORD LECONFIELD. *Petworth Manor in the Seventeenth Century.*

H. V. S. and M. S. OGDEN. *English Taste in Landscape in the Seventeenth Century.*

Chapter Four: 1660—1719

1   D. MCDOUGALL.   *Two Royal Domains of France.*
2   D. GREEN.   *Gardener to Queen Anne.*
3   J. RAY.   *Historia Plantarum.*
4   W. G. HISCOCK.   *John Evelyn and His Family Circle.*
5   J. SUMMERSON.   *Architecture in Britain 1530–1830.*
6   S. PEPYS.   *Diary,* 1666.
7   A. COWLEY.   *The Garden.*
8   A. AMHERST.   *London Parks and Gardens.*
9   J. LONDON and H. WISE.   *The Retir'd Gardener.*
10   *Correspondence of the Family of Hatton* (edited E. M. Thompson).
        Camden Society N.S., xxii, xxiii.
11   A. AMHERST.   *London Parks and Gardens.*
12   D. GREEN.   *Gardener to Queen Anne.*
13   W. ROBERTS.   *The Gardener's Chronicle,* 1924.
14   J. REA.   *Flora, Ceres & Pomona.*
15   I. ELSTOB (editor).   *The Garden Book of Sir Thomas Hanmer.*
16   LORD HARLECH.   *Country Life,* ciii.
17   F. J. B. WATSON.   *Ibid.,* ciii.
18   J. EVELYN.   *Diary* (edited E. S. de Beer).
19   F. VERNEY.   *Memoirs of the Verney Family.*
20   J. AUBREY.   *Natural History of Wiltshire.*
21   G. SCOTT THOMSON.   *Life in a Noble Household* and *Family Back-
        ground.*
22   J. EVELYN.   *Acetaria.*
23   C. MORRIS (editor).   *The Journeys of Celia Fiennes.*
24   J. EVELYN.   *Diary* (edited E. S. de Beer).
25   REV. DR. HAMILTON.   *Archaeologia,* xii.
26   J. EVELYN.   *Diary* (edited E. S. de Beer).
27   F. THOMPSON.   *A History of Chatsworth.*
28   R. PLOT.   *Natural History of Oxfordshire.*
29   DR. C. LEIGH.   *Natural History of Lancashire, etc.*
30   LADY WINCHILSEA.   *Upon My Lord Winchilsea's Converting the
        Mount in His Garden to a Terrace.*
31, 32   G. W. BEARD.   *Country Life,* cxi.
33   G. H. CHETTLE.   *Kirby Hall, Northamptonshire.*
34   C. E. RAVEN.   *John Ray.*
35   R. W. T. GUNTHER.   *Further Correspondence of John Ray.*
36   R. MORISON.   *Plantarum Historia Universalis Oxoniensis.*
37   J. EVELYN.   *Acetaria.*

38   J. MORTON. *Natural History of Northamptonshire.*

39   A. B. LAMBERT. *Transactions Linnean Society*, x.

40   C. HUSSEY. *Country Life*, liii.

41   REV. DR. HAMILTON. *Archaeologia*, xii.

42   E. H. M. COX. *A History of Gardening in Scotland.*

43   J. MCQ. COWAN. *Journal Royal Horticultural Society*, lxv.
      E. H. M. COX. *A History of Gardening in Scotland.*

44   E. H. M. COX. *Ibid.*

45   J. SABINE. *Transactions Horticultural Society*, London, vii.

46   F. VERNEY. *Memoirs of the Verney Family.*

47   PIPE ROLLS. *Wren Society*, iv.

48   C. E. RAVEN. *John Ray.*

49   *Correspondence of the Family of Hatton* (edited E. M. Thompson).
      Camden Society N.S., xxii, xxiii.

50   SIR H. PLATT. *The Garden of Eden.*

51   REV. DR. HAMILTON. *Archaeologia*, xii.

52   J. EVELYN. *Diary* (edited E. S. de Beer).

53   REV. DR. HAMILTON. *Archaeologia*, xii.

54   J. EVELYN. *Kalendarium Hortense.*

55   J. REA. *Flora, Ceres & Pomona.*

56   I. ELSTOB (editor). *The Garden Book of Sir Thomas Hanmer.*

57   L. MEAGER. *The New Art of Gardening.*

58   REV. DR. HAMILTON. *Archaeologia*, xii.

59   A. B. LAMBERT. *Transactions Linnaean Society*, x.

60   J. C. LOUDON. *Arboretum et Fruticetum Britannicum.*

61   REV. DR. HAMILTON. *Archaeologia*, xii.

62   C. O. MORETON. *Old Carnations and Pinks.*

63   MS. in Lincoln Archives Office.

64   S. SWITZER. *The Nobleman, Gentleman and Gardener's Recreation.*

65   J. BRITTEN. *Journal Linnean Society (Botany)*, xlv, and *The Sloane Herbarium* (edited J. E. Dandy).

66   REV. DR. HAMILTON. *Archaeologia*, xii.

67   J. BOWACK. *Antiquities of Middlesex.*

68   D. DEFOE. *A Tour Through England and Wales.*

69   J. MORTON. *Natural History of Northamptonshire.*

70   J. C. LOUDON. *Arboretum et Fruticetum Britannicum.*

71   D. GREEN. *Gardener to Queen Anne.*

72   R. GUNNIS. *Dictionary of British Sculpture.*

73   H. HONOUR. *Burlington Magazine*, 1954.

74   F. J. CHITTENDEN. *Journal Royal Horticultural Society*, lxiv.
      D. GREEN. *Gardener to Queen Anne.*

75   C. HUSSEY. *Country Life*, lxxix.

76 SIR R. ATKYNS. *Ancient and Present State of Gloucestershire.*

77 D. GREEN. *Gardener to Queen Anne.*

78 J. MACKY. *A Journey Through England.*

79 D. GREEN. *Gardener to Queen Anne.*

80 *King's Maps,* British Museum. (*See also* A. Oswald, *Country Life,* cxxiv).

81 LORD JOHN KERR. *Melbourne Hall.*

    D. GREEN. *Gardener to Queen Anne.*

82 M. CARDEW. *Journal Royal Horticultural Society,* lxxiv.

83 SIR J. E. SMITH. *Selections of the Correspondence of Linnaeus.*

84 C. HUSSEY. *Country Life,* lxxxv.

85 SIR G. SITWELL. *On the Making of Gardens.*

86 J. MACKY. *A Journey Through England.*

87, 88 C. H. C. and M. I. BAKER. *The Life of . . . James Brydges.*

89 A. POPE. *Moral Essays.*

90 *Correspondence of Alexander Pope* (edited G. Sherburn).

91 W. ROBERTS. *Journal Royal Horticultural Society,* lxiv.

    V. HIGGINS. *Ibid,* lxv.

92 E. ST. J. BROOKS. *Sir Hans Sloane.*

93 F. D. DREWETT. *Romance of the Apothecaries Garden at Chelsea.*

    G. W. ROBINSON. *Journal Royal Horticultural Society,* lxv.

94 MS. in All Saint's Church, West Bromwich.

95 SIR H. MAXWELL. *Scottish Gardens.*

96 J. SABINE. *Transactions Horticultural Society,* London, vii.

97 M. L. ANDERSON (editor). *Forest Trees.*

98 E. H. M. COX. *A History of Gardening in Scotland.*

99 SIR R. ATKYNS. *Ancient and Present State of Gloucestershire.*

100 W. WESTLEY. *Plan of Birmingham Surveyed in 1731.*

101 HON. V. SACKVILLE-WEST. *Knole and The Sackvilles.*

102 M. JOURDAIN. *Country Life,* xlv.

103 J. EVELYN. *Diary* (edited E. S. de Beer).

104 A. POPE. *Windsor Forest.*

105 J. DENNIS. *Original Letters.*

106 SIR W. TEMPLE. *Upon the Gardens of Epicurus.*

107 REV. DR. HAMILTON. *Archaeologia,* xii.

108 A. B. LAMBERT. *Transactions Linnean Society,* x.

109 J. ADDISON. *The Spectator,* 1712.

110 L. WHISTLER. *The Imagination of Vanbrugh.*

111 G. WEBB. *Proceedings of British Academy,* 1947.

General

F. C. CARRITT. *Calendar of British Taste 1600–1800.*

M. C. KARSTEN. *The Old Company's Garden at the Cape.*

H. V. S. and M. S. OGDEN. *English Taste in Landscape in the Seventeenth Century.*

Chapter Five: 1720—1780

1   W. MASON. *The English Garden: A Poem.*

2   H. WALPOLE. *Letters* (edited Mrs. Toynbee).

3   J. C. LOUDON. *The Gardener's Magazine,* III.

4   L. WHISTLER. *The Imagination of Vanbrugh and His Fellow Artists.*

5   D. GREEN. *Gardener to Queen Anne.*

6   D. GREEN. *Gardener to Queen Anne.*

7   A. F. SIEVEKING. *The Praise of Gardens.*

8   G. SHERBURN (editor). *The Correspondence of Alexander Pope.*

9   A. POPE. *On His Grotto at Twickenham.*

10 J. S. GARDNER. *Country Life,* ciii.

11 H. WALPOLE. *On Modern Gardening.*

12 J. THOMSON. *The Castle of Indolence.*

13 R. P. KNIGHT. *The Landscape.*

14 H. WALPOLE. *On Modern Gardening.*

15 M. JOURDAIN. *The Work of William Kent.*

16 W. VON ARCHENHOLZ. *A Picture of England.*

17 W. TUNNICLIFF. *A Topographical Survey.*

18 A SOCIETY OF GENTLEMEN. *England Displayed* (revised by P. Russell and O. Price).

19 R. DUTTON. *The Chateaux of France.*

20 H. WALPOLE. *Letters* (edited Mrs. Toynbee).

21 HON. J. BYNG. *Torrington Diaries* (edited C. B. Andrews).

22 T WHATLEY. *Observations on Modern Gardening.*

23 M. WILLIAMS. *William Shenstone: A Chapter in 18th Century Taste.*
    A. R. HUMPHREYS. *William Shenstone: An 18th Century Portrait.*

24 REV. DR. A. CARLYLE. *Autobiography.*

25 W. SHENSTONE. *Works in Prose and Verse.*

26 WM. HOGARTH. *The Analysis of Beauty* (edited J. Burke).

27 B. M. EDGE. *Lady Luxborough* (in manuscript).
    W. COOPER. *Henley-in-Arden* (in manuscript).

28 *Letters Written by the Late Rt. Hon. Lady Luxborough to William Shenstone,* 1775.

29 A. WHISTLER. *Flowers.*

30 J. REID. *The Scots Gardener* (1766 edition).

31 T. WHATLEY. *Observations on Modern Gardening.*

32 J. C. LOUDON. *Arboretum et Fruticetum Britannicum.*

33 J. C. LOUDON. *Ibid.*

34 A SOCIETY OF GENTLEMEN. *England Displayed* (revised by P. Russell and O. Price).

35 P. TOYNBEE (editor). *Horace Walpole's Journals of Visits to Country Seats,* Walpole Society, xvi.

36 G. W. BEARD. *Hagley Hall.*

37 A. M. BROADLEY (editor). *Mrs. Thrale's Tour in Wales with Dr. Johnson.*

38 J. LUCKOCK. *The Gardener's Album* (edited M. Hadfield).

39 L. WHISTLER. *The Imagination of Vanbrugh and His Fellow Artists.*

40 *The Works of William Mason,* 1811.

41 H. WALPOLE. *Letters* (edited Mrs. Toynbee).

42 D. STROUD. *Capability Brown.*

43 W. MASON. *The English Garden: A Poem.*

44 W. MASON. *Ibid.*

45 W. MASON. *Works.*

46 G. W. JOHNSON. *A History of English Gardening.*

47 A. YOUNG. *A Six Months' Tour Through The North of England.*

48 T. WHATLEY. *Observations on Modern Gardening.*

49 W. GILPIN. *Observations on Picturesque Beauty, particularly the Highlands of Scotland.*

50 J. FLEMING. *Country Life,* cxix.

51 E. WATERHOUSE. *Painting in Britain 1530–1790.*

52 G. W. BEARD. *The Saturday Book, 17* (J. Hadfield, editor).

53 H. WALPOLE. *Letters* (edited Mrs. Toynbee).

54 T. BLAIKIE. *Diary of a Scottish Gardener* (edited F. Birrell).

55 E. H. M. COX. *The New Flora and Silva,* xi.

56 ROYAL SOCIETY. *Philosophical Transactions,* xlviii.

57 REV. J. DALLAWAY. *Supplementary Anecdotes on Gardening in England.*

58 W. WROTH. *The London Pleasure Gardens of the 18th Century.*

59 *The Scots Magazine,* xxix.

60 A. RAISTRICK. *Quakers in Science and Industry.*

61 N. G. BRETT-JAMES. *Life of Peter Collinson.*
A. B. LAMBERT. *Transactions Linnean Society,* x.

62 A. RAISTRICK. *Quakers in Science and Industry.*
J. HERBST. *New Green World.*

63 D. T. POVEY. *Country Life,* cxix.

64 J. C. LOUDON. *Arboretum et Fruticetum Britannicum.*

65 G. W. BEARD. *Hagley Hall.*

66   SIR J. E. SMITH. *Selections of the Correspondence of Linnaeus and Other Naturalists.*

67   A. B. LAMBERT. *Transactions Linnean Society*, x.

68   C. H. CURTIS. *Orchids : Their Description and Cultivation.*

69   E. G. SWEM. *Brothers of the Spade.*

70   G. W. BEARD. *Hagley Hall.*

71   Newdigate Papers in Warwick Archives Office.

72   R. H. FOX. *Dr. John Fothergill and His Friends.*

73   C. H. CURTIS. *Orchids : Their Description and Cultivation.*

74   J. C. LOUDON. *Encyclopaedia of Gardening*, 1827.

75   T. BLAIKIE. *Diary of a Scottish Gardener* (edited F. Birrell).

76   SIR J. E. SMITH. *Selections of the Correspondence of Linnaeus and Other Naturalists.*

77   A. B. LAMBERT. *Transactions Linnean Society*, x.

78   G. W. ROBINSON. *Journal Royal Horticultural Society*, lxv.

79   SIR J. E. SMITH. *Selections of the Correspondence of Linnaeus and Other Naturalists.*

80   W. J. BEAN. *The Royal Botanic Gardens, Kew.*

81   H. C. CAMERON. *Sir Joseph Banks : Aristocrat of the Philosophers.*

82   Royal Botanic Gardens, Kew. *Hand-List of Trees and Shrubs.*

83   SIR J. E. SMITH. *Selections of the Correspondence of Linnaeus and Other Naturalists.*

84   J. BRITTEN. *Journal of Botany*, xxii.
        J. BRITTEN. *Journal Linnaean Society (Botany)*, xlv.

85   SIR J. E. SMITH. *Selections of the Correspondence of Linnaeus and Other Naturalists.*

86   M. C. KARSTEN. *The Old Company's Gardens at the Cape.*

87   F. G. PRESTON. *Journal Royal Horticultural Society*, lxv.
        J. S. L. GILMOUR. *Ibid*, lxxx.

88   REV. G. WHITE. *Garden Kalendar.*

89   J. SMITH. *The Gardener's Chronicle*, 1944.

90   A. HEASEL. *The Servant's Book of Knowledge.*

91   W. ROBERTS. *The Gardener's Chronicle*, 1917.

92   REV. DR. A. CARLYLE. *Autobiography.*

93   SIR J. E. SMITH. *Selections of the Correspondence of Linnaeus and Other Naturalists.*

94   A. B. LAMBERT. *Transactions Linnean Society*, x.

95   J. C. LOUDON. *Arboretum et Fruticetum Britannicum.*

96   *Journal of Botany*, liii.

97   T. BLAIKIE. *Diary of a Scottish Gardener* (edited F. Birrell).

98   J. C. LOUDON. *Arboretum et Fruticetum Britannicum.*

99   E. H. M. COX. *A History of Gardening in Scotland.*

100   A. B. LAMBERT.   *Transactions Linnean Society*, x.
101   W. BLUNT.   *The Art of Botanical Illustration.*
102   W. BLUNT.   *Ibid.*
103   R. WESTON.   *Tracts on Practical Agriculture* (1773 edition).
104   REV. W. HANBURY.   *An Essay on Planting.*

General

B. S. ALLEN.   *Tides in English Taste.*
F. CARRITT.   *Calendar of British Taste 1600–1800.*
I. W. U. CHASE.   *Horace Walpole, Gardenist.*
H. F. CLARK.   *The English Landscape Garden,* and in *England and The Mediterranean Tradition.*
J. J. HECHT   *The Domestic Servant Class in 18th Century England.*
C. HUSSEY.   *The Picturesque : Studies in a Point of View.*
E. W. MANWARING.   *Italian Landscape in 18th Century England.*
S. H. MONK.   *The Sublime.*
O. SIREN.   *China and the Gardens of Europe of the 18th Century.**
J. STEEGMAN.   *The Rule of Taste from George I to George IV.*

Chapter Six: 1781—1840

1   A. TROLLOPE.   *The Small House at Allington.*
2   J. BOSWELL.   *Life of Johnson.*
3   MS. Birmingham Reference Library.
4   J. C. LOUDON.   *The Landscape Gardening of the Late Humphry Repton.*
5   R. W. KETTON-CREMER.   *The Early Life and Diaries of William Windham.*
6   J. SUMMERSON.   *John Nash : Architect to King George IV.*
7   J. SUMMERSON.   *Architecture in Britain 1530–1830.*
8   H. REPTON.   *An Enquiry Into the Changes of Taste in Landscape Gardening.*
9   H. REPTON.   *Sketches and Hints on Landscape Gardening* (1794), *Observations on the Theory and Practice of Landscape Gardening* (1803), and *On the Introduction of Indian Architecture and Gardening* (1808).
10   C. HUSSEY.   *Country Life*, cxix.
11   C. HUSSEY.   *Ibid.*, cxxi.
12   JAMES NASMYTH.   *An Autobiography* (edited S. Smiles).
13   W. PAPWORTH.   *John B. Papworth.*

* This has an exceptionally good series of illustrations of British gardens, notably the drawings and plans made by F. M. Piper in the late 1770s.

14   J. C. LOUDON. *The Gardener's Magazine*, xv.

15   J. E. LOUSLEY. *Journal Royal Horticultural Society*, lxxi.

16   SIR J. E. SMITH. *Selections of the Correspondence of Linnaeus and Other Naturalists.*

17   W. BLUNT. *The Art of Botanical Illustration.*

18   G. W. JOHNSON. *A History of English Gardening.*

19   G. TAYLOR. *Some Nineteenth Century Gardeners.*

20   L. HUNT. *The Old Court Suburb.*

21   ANON. *Flora Domestica, or the Portable Flower Garden.*

22   J. BECK. *Florist, Fruitist and Garden Miscellany.*

23   J. C. LOUDON. *The Gardener's Magazine*, vii.

24, 25   J. C. LOUDON. *Encyclopaedia of Gardening*, 1827.

26   J. DOUGLAS. *National Auricula and Primula Society (Northern Section) Year Book*, 1954.

27   R. H. BRIGGS. *Ibid*, 1949–50.

28, 29   ANON. *Ibid*, 1957 (ii).

30   A. SIMMONDS. *Journal Royal Horticultural Society*, lxxix.

31   G. E. LODER, E. A. BUNYARD. *Ibid*, lvi.

32   A. SIMMONDS. *Ibid*, lxvii.

33   A. SIMMONDS. *Ibid*, lxvi.

34   E. H. M. COX. *Plant Hunting in China.*

35   A. SIMMONDS. *Journal Royal Horticultural Society*, lxix.

36   A. SIMMONDS. *Ibid*, lxviii.

37, 38   A. SIMMONDS. *Ibid*, lxxix.

39   *Selections from the . . . Papers of Thomas Andrew Knight* (1841).
        N. B. BAGENAL. *Journal Royal Horticultural Society*, lxiii.

40   C. S. ORWIN. *The Reclamation of Exmoor Forest.*

41   A. SIMMONDS. *Journal Royal Horticultural Society*, lxxix.

42   E. A. BOWLES. *Handbook of Crocus and Colchicum.*

43   J. C. LOUDON. *The Gardener's Magazine*, ix, and *Arboretum et Fruticetum Brittanicum.*

44   J. C. LOUDON. *The Gardener's Magazine*, i.

45   J. C. LOUDON. *Ibid*, xii.

46   ANON. *Transactions of the Horticultural Society*, vi.
        E. H. M. COX. *Journal Royal Horticultural Society*, lxxx.

47   *Journal Kept by David Douglas During His Travels in North America 1823–27.*
        F. R. S. BALFOUR. *Journal Royal Horticultural Society*, lxvii.
        A. G. HARVEY. *Douglas of the Firs.*

48   A. SIMMONDS. *Journal Royal Horticultural Society*, lxxix.

49   E. H. M. COX. *Plant Hunting in China.*

50   A. SIMMONDS. *Journal Royal Horticultural Society*, lxxix.

51 P. M. SYNGE. *Ibid*, lxxviii.

52 E. H. M. COX. *Ibid*, lxxx.

53 J. MIDDLETON. *A General View of the Agriculture of Middlesex.*

54 J. C. LOUDON. *Encyclopaedia of Gardening.*

55 J. SMITH. *Transactions Horticultural Society of London*, vi.

56 E. A. BUNYARD. *The Gardener's Chronicle*, 1939.

57 M. KEENS. *Transactions Horticultural Society of London*, ii.

58 ANON. *Ibid*, v.

59 W. ROBERTS. *Journal Royal Horticultural Society*, lxiii.

60 N. HOLMES. *The Gardener's Chronicle*, 1953.

61 J. C. LOUDON. *Encyclopaedia*, 1826.

62 J. C. LOUDON. *Arboretum et Fruticetum Britannicum.*

63 E. M. BETTS. *Thomas Jefferson's Garden Book.*

64 ANON. *Killerton and Its Gardens.*

65 H. M. COLVIN. *A Biographical Dictionary of English Architects.*

66 *Journal of Botany*, 1899 and 1905.

67, 68 J. C. LOUDON. *Arboretum et Fruticetum Britannicum.*

69 C. C. HURST in G. S. THOMAS. *The Old Shrub Roses.*

70 JAMES MAIN. *Journal. The Gardener's Magazine*, ii.

71 C. C. HURST in G. S. THOMAS. *The Old Shrub Roses.*

    A. P. WYLIE. *Journal Royal Horticultural Society*, lxxix and lxxx.

72 C. C. HURST in G. S. THOMAS. *The Old Shrub Roses.*

73 T. HAY. *The New Flora and Silva*, vii.

74 J. C. LOUDON. *The Gardener's Magazine*, vi.

75 J. C. LOUDON. *Arboretum et Fruticetum Britannicum.*

76 A. POPE. *The Gardener's Magazine*, vii.

77 A. POPE. *Ibid*, viii.

78 W. J. BEAN. *The Royal Botanic Gardens, Kew.*

79 J. M. COWAN. *Journal Royal Horticultural Society*, lxv.

80 J. W. BESANT. *Ibid*, lxv.

81 F. G. PRESTON. *Ibid*, lxv.

    J. S. L. GILMOUR. *Ibid*, lxxx.

82 J. C. LOUDON. *Encyclopaedia of Gardening* (1826).

83 J. D. HOOKER. *Sketch of the Life and Labours of Sir W. J. Hooker.*

84 W. BECKFORD. *Italy : with Sketches of Spain and Portugal.*

85 W. R. DAWSON (editor). *Smith Papers of the Linnaean Society.*

86 R.T.P. and J.D. *The Gardener's Magazine*, vi.

87 J. C. LOUDON. *Ibid*, xiii.

88 J. C. LOUDON. *Ibid*, xv.

89 *Wrightson's Triennial Directory of Birmingham*, 1825.

    W. WEST. *The History, Topography and Directory of Warwickshire*
       1830.

A Short History of Henry Hope & Son.

90 J. C. LOUDON. *Encyclopaedia of Gardening*, 1826.
91 T. A. KNIGHT. *Transactions Horticultural Society*, ii.
92 W. WHALE. *Ibid*, vii.
93 *Architectural Magazine*, i.
94 A. MERRICK. *The Gardener's Magazine*, vii.

General

F. C. CARRITT. *Calendar of British Taste 1600–1800.*

C. HUSSEY. *The Picturesque : Studies in a Point of View.*

D. LYSONS. *Environs of London.*

D. and S. LYSONS. *Magna Brittanica.*

J. STEEGMAN. *The Rule of Taste from George I to George IV.*

Chapter Seven: 1841—1882

1 V. MARKHAM. *Paxton and the Bachelor Duke.*
2 J. C. LOUDON. *The Gardener's Magazine*, vi.
3 W. BLUNT. *The Gardener's Album* (M. Hadfield, editor).
4 J. C. LOUDON. *The Gardener's Magazine*, xv.
5 J. C. LOUDON. *The Suburban Gardener.*
6 J. SMITH. *Historical Record of the Royal Botanic Gardens, Kew.*
   W. J. BEAN. *The Royal Botanic Gardens, Kew.*
7 A. MURRAY. *Book of the Royal Horticultural Society.*
8 *The Gardener's Chronicle*, 1873.
9 REV. A. BARRY. *The Life and Works of Sir Charles Barry.*
10 C. HUSSEY. *Country Life*, cxiv.
11 H. N. HUMPHREYS. *The Gardener's Magazine*, ix.
12 W. D. DALLIMORE. *Holly, Yew and Box.*
13 J. SMITH. *Historical Record of the Royal Botanic Gardens, Kew.*
   W. J. BEAN. *The Royal Botanic Gardens, Kew.*
14 SIR J. D. HOOKER. *Sketch of the Life and Labours of Sir W. J. Hooker.*
   SIR A. W. HILL. *Journal Royal Horticultural Society*, lxvi.
15 R. W. T. GUNTHER. *Oxford Gardens.*
16 F. G. PRESTON. *Journal Royal Horticultural Society*, lxv.
   J. S. L. GILMOUR. *Ibid*, lxxx.
17 G. W. ROBINSON. *Ibid*, lxv.
18 A. SIMMONDS. *Ibid*, lxxix.
19 E. A. BUNYARD. *The Gardener's Chronicle*, 1918.
20 J. C. LOUDON. *Arboretum et Fruticetum Britannicum.*

21   J. M. COWAN.   *Journal Royal Horticultural Society*, lxv.

22   J. T. JOHNSTONE.   *Notes From the Royal Botanic Garden, Edinburgh*, xx.

23   SIR F. MOORE.   *The Gardener's Chronicle*, 1937.

24   RT. REV. J. W. HUNKIN.   *Journal Royal Horticultural Society*, lxvii, lxxii.

25   J. H. VEITCH.   *Hortus Veitchii*.

26   E. H. M. COX.   *Journal Royal Horticultural Society*, lxviii.

27   E. H. M. COX.   *Ibid*, lxxx.

28   A. SIMMONDS.   *Ibid*, lxxix.

29   R. FORTUNE.   *Three Years' Wandering in the Northern Provinces of China.*
   A Residence Among the Chinese: Inland, on the Coast and at Sea.
   Yedo and Peking: A Narrative of a Journey to the Capitals of Japan and China.

30   W. J. BEAN.   *The Royal Botanic Gardens, Kew.*

31   J. D. HOOKER.   *Himalayan Journals*, and *Journal of a Tour in Morocco and The Great Atlas.*

32   SIR G. LODER.   *Rhododendron Year Book*, 1950.

33   J. P. C. RUSSELL.   *Ibid*, 1947.
   Journal Royal Horticultural Society, lxxxiii.

34   F. STREET.   *Hardy Rhododendrons.*

35   E. MARKHAM.   *Clematis.*

36   J. COUTTS.   *The Gardener's Chronicle*, 1930.

37   T. K. HODDER.   *Journal Royal Horticultural Society*, lxxxi.

38   E. MARKHAM.   *Clematis.*

39   R. H. JEFFERS.   *Journal Royal Horticultural Society*, lxxix.

40   J. C. LOUDON.   *Arboretum et Fruticetum Britannicum.*
   F. J. HANBURY.   *Journal of Botany*, xxviii.

41   R. H. JEFFERS.   *Journal Royal Horticultural Society*, lxxix.

42   C. C. HURST in G. S. THOMAS.   *The Old Shrub Roses.*

43   *Rose Annual*, 1907.

44   KNIGHT and PERRY.   *Synopsis of the Coniferous Plants Grown in Britain.*

45   *The Gardener's Chronicle*, 1886.

46   J. H. VEITCH.   *Hortus Veitchii.*

47   C. BLAIR.   *The Gardener's Chronicle*, 1937.

48, 49   A. SIMMONDS.   *A Horticultural Who Was Who.*

50   E. A. BUNYARD.   *Handbook of Hardy Fruits: Apples and Pears.*

51   A. SIMMONDS.   *A Horticultural Who Was Who.*

52   H. G. BULL (editor).   *The Herefordshire Pomona.*

53   REV. S. REYNOLDS HOLE.   *The Gardener's Chronicle*, 1877.

G. TAYLOR. *The Victorian Flower Garden.*

54   E. A. BUNYARD. *The Gardener's Chronicle,* 1930.

55   G. FOX WILSON. *Ibid,* 1927.

56   ANON. *Country Life,* xvii.

57   RT. REV. J. W. HUNKIN. *Journal Royal Horticultural Society,* lxxii.

58   O. H. MACKENZIE. *A Hundred Years in the Highlands.*

M. T. SAWYER. *Journal Royal Horticultural Society,* lxxv.

59   F. J. HOPE. *Notes and Thoughts on Gardens and Woodlands* (edited A. J. Hope).

General

J. STEEGMAN. *Consort of Taste 1830–1870.*

Chapter Eight: 1883—1939

1   G. TAYLOR. *Some Nineteenth Century Gardeners.*

2   F. JEKYLL. *Gertrude Jekyll: A Memoir.*

3   G. F. WILSON. *The Garden,* 1900.

4   SIR O. SITWELL. *Left Hand, Right Hand.*

5   THE EARL OF MORTON. *Journal Royal Horticultural Society,* lxxxii.

6   C. C. HURST in G. S. THOMAS. *The Old Shrub Roses.*

7   G. TAYLOR. *The Victorian Flower Garden.*

8   E. A. BOWLES. *Handbook of Narcissus.*

9   REV. J. JACOBS. *Hardy Bulbs for Amateurs.*

10   H. J. WRIGHT. *Sweet Peas.*

11   J. C. P. M. DAVIS. *Journal Royal Horticultural Society,* lxx.

12   L. F. RANDOLPH. *Iris Year Book,* 1950.

13   SIR F. C. STERN. *Journal Royal Horticultural Society,* lxv.

B. R. LONG. *Ibid,* lxxi.

14   *Iris Year Book,* 1938.

15   *Ibid,* 1931.

16   M. C. ALLWOOD. *Carnations and All Dianthus.*

17   C. KELWAY. *Bulletin, Hardy Plant Society,* i.

18   *Iris Year Book,* 1953.

19   R. PARRETT. *The Russell Lupin.*

20   W. T. STEARN. *Journal Royal Horticultural Society,* lxxx.

21   H. V. TAYLOR. *The Apples of England.*

22   G. FOX WILSON. *The Gardener's Chronicle,* 1927.

23   G. E. FUSSELL. *Journal Royal Horticultural Society,* lxii.

24   J. M. S. POTTER. *Ibid,* lxxvii.

25   J. H. VEITCH. *Hortus Veitchii.*

26   C. H. CURTIS. *Journal Royal Horticultural Society*, lxxiii.

27   ANON. *The Gardener's Chronicle*, 1937.

28   A. TROLLOPE. *The Last Chronicle of Barset.*

29, 30   A. SIMMONDS. *Journal Royal Horticultural Society*, lxxix.

31   *Journal Royal Horticultural Society*, xxvi.

32   R. HURST. *Journal Royal Horticultural Society*, lxxiv.

      M. J. SIRKS. *Ibid*, lxxx.

33   E. A. BOWLES. *Ibid*, lxxv.

34   J. M. COWAN. *Ibid*, lxv.

35   J. W. BESANT. *Ibid*, lxv.

      R. D. TROTTER. *Ibid*, lxxiv.

36   F. G. PRESTON. *Ibid*, lxv.

      J. S. L. GILMOUR. *Ibid*, lxxx.

37   H. V. TAYLOR. *Ibid*, lxvii.

38   J. NEWELL. *Ibid*, lxxxii.

39   .L. R. E. MARTIN. *Ibid*, lxxi.

40   E. H. M. COX. *Plant Hunting in China.*

41   SIR FREDERICK MOORE. *Journal Royal Horticultural Society*, lxviii.

42   E. H. WILSON. *A Naturalist in Western China.*

      E. H. M. COX. *Plant Hunting in China.*

      J. H. VEITCH. *Hortus Veitchii.*

43   ANON. *North Western Naturalist*, 1942.

44   J. M. COWAN (editor). *The Journeys and Plant Introductions of George Forrest.*

45   RT. REV. J. W. HUNKIN. *Journal Royal Horticultural Society*, lxvii.

46   LORD ABERCONWAY and SIR W. W. SMITH. *Ibid*, lxxiv.

47   E. H. M. COX. *Farrer's Last Journey.*

      E. H. M. COX (editor). *The Introductions to England of Reginald Farrer.*

48   LT.-COL. L. C. R. MESSEL. *Journal Royal Horticultural Society*, lxv.

49   ANON. *The Gardener's Chronicle*, 1931.

      H. F. COMBER. *Ibid*, 1931.

50   F. HANGER. *Rhododendron Year Book*, 1946.

51   W. J. BEAN. *The Royal Botanic Gardens, Kew.*

52   G. BONE and SIR F. KEEBLE. *Journal Royal Horticultural Society*, lxvi.

53   *The Gardener's Chronicle*, 1909.

54   H. DENHAM. *Journal Royal Horticultural Society*, lxvii.

55   E. H. M. COX. *Ibid*, lxvii.

56   A. STEWART. *Alicella.*

57   SIR W. LAWRENCE in C. SPRY. *Flower Decoration.*

58   S. Y. BARKLEY. *Trees of Westonbirt School.*

59   A. B. JACKSON. *Catalogue of Trees and Shrubs at Westonbirt.*

60   LORD ABERCONWAY. *Rhododendron Year Book*, 1947, and *Journal Royal Horticultural Society*, lxxv.

Index

The reader's attention is drawn to the following large sub-headings in this index: collectors (of plants), gardeners (British professional), gardens (botanic), gardens (split up under country), nurseries, nurserymen. A separate index for the Appendix will be found on p. 508.

Index to the Appendix

MORE ABOUT PENGUINS, PELICANS AND PUFFINS

For further information about books available from Penguins please write to Dept EP, Penguin Books Ltd, Harmondsworth, Middlesex UB7 ODA.

In the U.S.A.: For a complete list of books available from Penguins in the United States write to Dept DG, Penguin Books, 299 Murray Hill Parkway, East Rutherford, New Jersey 07073.

In Canada: For a complete list of books available from Penguins in Canada write to Penguin Books Canada Ltd, 2801 John Street, Markham, Ontario L3R 1B4.

In Australia: For a complete list of books available from Penguins in Australia write to the Marketing Department, Penguin Books Australia Ltd, P.O. Box 257, Ringwood, Victoria 3134.

In New Zealand: For a complete list of books available from Penguins in New Zealand write to the Marketing Department, Penguin Books (N.Z.) Ltd, P.O. Box 4019, Auckland 10.

In India: For a complete list of books available from Penguins in India write to Penguin Overseas Ltd, 706 Eros Apartments, 56 Nehru Place, New Delhi 110019.